THE MALAGASY REPUBLIC

N

MOZAMBIQUE CHANNEL

INDIAN OCEAN

Diégo-Suarez

Nossi-Bé
Ambanja
Vohémar

Analalava

Antalaha

Majunga
Port-Bergé
Marovoay
Mananara

Soalala
Ste.-Marie
Island

Maevatanana
Lake
Alaotra
Fénérive
Ambatondrazaka

Betsiboka River

Tamatave

Ivato
Tananarive
Brickaville
Arivonimamo
Moramanga
Vatomandry

Tsiribihina River
Betafo
Antsirabe

Morondava
Ambositra

Mangoky River
Mananjary

Morombe
Fianarantsoa
Manakara

Ihosy
Vohipeno
Farafangana

Onilahy River
Mananara River

Tuléar
Betroka

Sakoa

Ampanihy
Antanimora
Fort-Dauphin

MILES: 0   100   200

THE MALAGASY REPUBLIC

Madagascar Today

Virginia Thompson and Richard Adloff

1965

STANFORD UNIVERSITY PRESS

STANFORD CALIFORNIA

Other books by Virginia Thompson and Richard Adloff

The Left Wing in Southeast Asia
Minority Problems in Southeast Asia
French West Africa
The Emerging States of French Equatorial Africa

All photographs courtesy of the former Ministry
of Overseas France, except No. 7 courtesy of
the World Council of Churches and Nos. 5,
26, 28, and 29 by Richard Adloff.

Stanford University Press
Stanford, California
© 1965 by Virginia Thompson Adloff and Richard Adloff
Printed in the United States of America
L.C. 65-21495

To Emma McLaughlin

CONTENTS

ABBREVIATIONS

A.E.O.M.	Association des Etudiants d'Origine Malgache
A.J.D.M.	Association de la Jeunesse Démocratique Malgache
A.K.F.M.	Ankotonny Kongreiny Fahaleovantenan Madagasikara (Party of the Congress of Independence)
A.M.I.	Assistance Médicale Indigène
B.D.P.A.	Bureau pour le Développement de la Production Agricole
B.N.C.I.	Banque Nationale pour le Commerce et l'Industrie
C.A.I.M.	Compagnie Agricole et Industrielle de Madagascar
C.A.P.	*Certificat d'aptitude pédagogique*
C.A.P.S.I.M.	Comité d'Action Populaire et Socialiste pour l'Indépendance de Madagascar
C.A.R.	Collectivités Autochtones Rurales
C.C.C.A.M.	Caisse Centrale de Crédit Agricole de Madagascar
C.C.C.E.	Caisse Centrale de Coopération Economique (formerly C.C.O.M.)
C.C.O.M.	Caisse Centrale d'Outre-Mer
C.C.S.M.	Confédération Chrétienne des Syndicats Malgaches
C.E.A.	Commissariat d'Energie Atomique
C.E.A.M.P.	Caisse d'Equipement Agricole et de Modernisation du Paysannat
C.E.A.P.	Comité d'Entente et d'Action Politique
C.E.P.	*Certificat d'études primaires*
C.E.T.A.	Centre Economique et Technique de l'Artisanat
C.F.A.	Colonies Françaises d'Afrique (as applied to the monetary unit, the C.F.A. franc)
C.F.D.T.	Compagnie Française de Développement des Fibres Textiles
C.F.T.C.	Confédération Française des Travailleurs Chrétiens
C.G.O.T.	Compagnie Générale des Oléagineux Tropicaux
C.G.T.	Confédération Générale de Travail
C.H.E.A.M.	Centre des Hautes Etudes Administratives sur l'Afrique et l'Asie Modernes
CITAB	Compagnie Industrielle des Tabacs
C.M.	Crédit de Madagascar
COMEPLAST	Compagnie Malgache de Produits Métallurgiques et Plastiques
COSOMA	Comité de Solidarité de Madagascar
C.R.A.M.	Communes Rurales Autonomes Modernisées

C.T.M.C.	Confédération des Travailleurs de Madagascar et des Comores (see F.M.M. for Malagasy name)
E.D.F.A.	Electricité de France Australe
E.E.M.	Electricité et Eaux de Madagascar
E.N.F.O.M.	Ecole Nationale de la France d'Outre-Mer (now the Institut des Hautes Etudes d'Outre-Mer)
F.A.C.	Fonds d'Aide et de Coopération
FARMAD	Laboratoires Pharmaceutiques de Madagascar
F.C.E.	Fianarantsoa–Côte Est railroad
F.E.D.	Fonds Européen de Développement
F.E.R.D.E.S.	Fonds d'Equipement Rural et de Développement Economique et Social
F.I.D.E.S.	Fonds d'Investissement pour le Développement Economique et Social
FIPIMA	Fivondronam Pireneno Malagasy (Malagasy National Union)
FISEMA	Firaisana Sendikaly Malagasy (Malagasy Labor Union)
FITIM	Société de Filature et de Tissage de Madagascar
FIVAMA	Democratic Rally of the Malagasy People
FMG	Franc malgache
F.M.M.	Fivondronambenny Mpiasani Madagasikara (same as C.T.M.C.)
F.N.M.	Front National Malgache
G.N.A.C.	Groupement National d'Achat des Cafés
I.F.A.T.	Institut des Fruits et des Agrumes Tropicaux
I.F.C.C.	Institut Français du Café et du Cacao
I.L.O.	International Labor Organization
I.R.A.M.	Institut de Recherches Agronomiques de Madagascar
I.R.C.T.	Institut de Recherches du Coton et des Textiles Exotiques
I.R.H.O.	Institut de Recherches pour les Huiles et les Oléagineux
I.R.S.M.	Institut de Recherches Scientifiques de Madagascar
JINA	Jeunesse Nationaliste
L.M.S.	London Missionary Society
M.D.R.M.	Mouvement Démocratique de la Rénovation Malgache
MONIMA	Mouvement National pour l'Indépendance de Madagascar
M.R.P.	Mouvement Républicain Populaire
M.R.S.M.	Mouvement du Renouveau Social Malgache
M.S.M.	Mouvement Social Malgache
N.C.H.P.	Nouvelle Compagnie Havraise Péninsulaire
O.A.M.C.E.	Organisation Africaine et Malgache pour la Coopération Economique
O.A.U.	Organization of African Unity
O.C.A.M.	Organisation Commune Africaine et Malgache
O.H.E.	Office des Habitations Economiques
O.R.S.T.O.M.	Office de la Recherche Scientifique des Territoires d'Outre-Mer
PADESM	Parti des Déshérités Malgaches
PANAMA	Parti Nationaliste Malgache
P.C.M.	Parti Communiste Malgache
P.D.M.	Parti Démocratique Malgache
P.P.M.	Parti Populaire Malgache
P.S.D.	Parti Social Démocrate
P.U.P.M.	Parti de l'Union du Peuple Malgache
R.C.M.	Rassemblement Chrétien de Madagascar

R.D.A.	Rassemblement Démocratique Africain
R.N.M.	Renouveau National Malgache
R.P.F.	Rassemblement du Peuple Français
R.P.M.	Rassemblement du Peuple Malgache
SACIMEM	Société Anonyme des Cigarettes Melia de Madagascar
S.A.R.M.	Société pour l'Aménagement Rural de Madagascar
S.A.R.P.A.	Société Anonyme Rochefortaise des Produits Alimentaires
SATEC	Société d'Assistance Technique
S.C.A.M.A.	Société des Conserves Alimentaires de la Montagne d'Ambre
S.E.I.T.A.	Service d'Exploitation Industrielle des Tabacs et des Allumettes
S.E.M.	Société d'Energie de Madagascar
S.E.R.P.	Syndicat d'Etudes et Recherches des Pétroles
SEVIMA	Société d'Exploitation des Viandes de Madagascar
S.F.I.O.	Section Française de l'Internationale Ouvrière
S.I.C.E.	Société Industrielle et Commerciale de l'Emyrne
SIFOR	Société Industrielle de Fort-Dauphin
S.I.M.	Société Immobilière de Madagascar
S.M.D.R.	Sociétés Mutuelles de Développement Rural
S.M.I.C.	Société Malgache d'Investissements et de Crédit (formerly C.M.)
S.M.I.G.	*Salaire minimum interprofessionnel garanti*
S.M.O.T.I.G.	Service de la Main-d'Oeuvre des Travaux d'Intérêt Général
SOBAMAD	Société Bananière de Madagascar
SOCOFRAM	Société Cotonnière Franco-Malgache
SOMALAC	Société d'Aménagement du Lac Alaotra
SOMAPECHE	Société Malgache de Pêche
SOMASAK	Société Malgache de la Sakay
SORAFOM	Société de Radiodiffusion de la France d'Outre-Mer
SOSUMAV	Société Sucrière de Mahavavy
SOTRASSUM	Société de Traitement des Sables du Sud de Madagascar
S.P.M.	Société des Pétroles de Madagascar
S.T.A.R.	Société Tananarivienne de Refrigération et de Boissons Gazeuses
T.A.I.	Transports Aériens Internationaux
T.C.E.	Tananarive–Côte Est railroad
T.D.E.	*Taxe de développement économique*
U.A.M.	Union Africaine et Malgache
U.A.M.C.E.	Union Africaine et Malgache pour la Coopération Economique
U.D.M.	Union des Démocrates Malgaches
U.D.S.M.	Union Démocratique et Sociale de Madagascar
U.E.M.	Union des Etudiants Malgaches
U.I.	Union des Indépendants
UNAM	Union Nationale Malgache
UNIUM	Union des Intellectuels et Universitaires Malgaches
U.P.M.	Union du Peuple Malgache
U.S.D.M.	Union des Sociaux-Démocrates de Madagascar
V.V.S.	Vy Vato Sakelika ("Iron and Stone")
W.F.T.U.	World Federation of Trade Unions

INTRODUCTION

Contemporary Madagascar confronts an observer with several phenomena that for outsiders are difficult to understand, let alone explain. One of the most puzzling of these is that the Malagasys, after engaging in a widespread and bloody revolt against French rule in 1947, should have gained their independence peaceably 13 years later and now maintain exceptionally amicable relations with their former colonial masters. Another is the stagnation or even decline of the economy just at the time when the population, long stationary numerically, is expanding rapidly and suddenly.

Revolts by colonial peoples in Asia after World War II were not uncommon, but in Africa they were very rare, and the Malagasy revolt was especially remarkable because it involved a people renowned for their docility. Moreover, unlike the Asian rebellions, which dragged on inconclusively for years, the Madagascar outbreak was so quickly (and brutally) repressed that it left a political vacuum on the island which persisted for the next seven years. In certain respects the revolt and its repression were responsible for delaying development of the island's economy, but they were almost immediately followed by a striking increase in the population and a period of prosperity for Madagascar's export trade.

Neither of these phenomena can be easily explained. To some extent the failure of the economy to keep pace with the population's growth can be attributed to natural causes, such as the dispersal and small size of Madagascar's producing areas and economic resources, the difficulties of intercommunication, and the frequency of floods and cyclones. As for the revolt, it too was partly the outgrowth of such material factors as the privations endured by the Malagasys during World War II and the forced labor they performed during the war years.

Although Madagascar is less than 250 miles from the African mainland, its people are exceptionally insular in their viewpoint, besides being self-sufficient in foodstuffs and conspicuously ethnocentric. Their basic wants are few and easily satisfied—enough land to grow rice for the family's food and house the family tomb, and a herd of cattle just large enough to give their owner social status and provide sacrificial animals for the cult of the ancestral dead. A little extra work is justified by the desire to buy cotton cloth, alcoholic beverages, and perhaps a bicycle, but beyond this the average Malagasy peasant sees little reason to exert himself. Rural Malagasys have been aptly described as contemplative farmers or herders, addicted to burning over the forest and pasture to fertilize the land and sometimes practicing cattle theft as a congenial and lucrative sport. Many Malagasy country folk resist any attempt to alter such economically wasteful customs, on the ground that they are consecrated by tradition.

To invoke the sanctity of custom is not merely a Malagasy device to disguise indolence—respect for custom is felt to be an essential safeguard against evil and misfortune. And it is not solely the untutored Malagasy rustic who is beset by a thousand daily fears, for the most highly educated Merina aristocrat is also a prey to similar anxieties. Like his peasant compatriot, he is uneasy lest he may have failed to propitiate some of the innumerable spirits that surround him and that are capable of doing him infinite harm. For the many Malagasys who were converted to Christianity and also for those who were in constant contact with the colonial administration, new apprehensions were added to their preexisting and perennial ones.

Since the great majority of Malagasys feel that the only safe course is not to deviate from time-honored practices, any government or leader who tries to introduce profound changes encounters a resistance that is normally passive but occasionally active, as it was during the 1947 revolt. The horrors associated with that revolt and its repression seem to have turned the Malagasys even further away from the path of violence and to have strengthened a determination not to be drawn into a world conflict. Many Malagasys apparently believe that because their island is remote it can remain immune from international complications if they make no incautious moves, but the elite realize that Madagascar's remoteness is no guaranty that it will always be left alone. Actually the Malagasys' best protection today is that their island's location is not now regarded as very strategic and that it has no natural resources coveted by other countries.

Nature in general and geography in particular seem to be the forces that have shaped Madagascar's history and the psychology of its people. As an island at one time largely governed by an indigenous dynasty and whose inhabitants have since then spoken a single language, it might be thought that Madagascar would form a cohesive unit. But the country has so huge an area, its surface is cut into so many mutually isolated regions, and its population is so small compared with its size that Madagascar has never been fused into a cohesive nation. Geographically, economically, socially, and politically it is compartmentalized, each region living largely unto itself. Internal migrations have been going on for many years, to be sure, but Madagascar has not in consequence become a melting pot. The coastal peoples are separated by physical and psychological barriers from those on the high plateaus, and among the latter difference in social status and to some extent economic condition keep caste distinctions alive. To these causes of division must be added the political frustrations felt by the Merina, who had sought independence from France to reassert their hegemony over the island, only to have it slip through their fingers and into those of the *côtiers,* or coastal tribes, at the last minute. Typically Malagasy in nature has been the manifestation of this frustration by aloofness and withdrawal rather than by violent or even legally aggressive opposition. Eventually, however, the population's rapid growth and the increased means of communication will perforce lead to greater understanding and a more integrated society.

In the meantime, the Malagasys—mutually segregated and wanting mainly to be left alone—naturally have little interest in cultivating contacts with the strangers in their midst. More docile than disciplined, more practical than philosophical or intellectually curious, timidly reserved and not dynamic, affable rather than warmhearted, meticulously courteous to strangers but basically indifferent to them, the Malagasys are not easy to comprehend—in part because they set so little store by such comprehension. Except for the Tourist Department, the services of the Malagasy government—including that of "Information"—seem not to have grasped as yet the need and usefulness of facilitating the visits and inquiries of outsiders. Nevertheless, on a field trip to Madagascar in 1962, the writers found the island attractive in many places and its inhabitants charming and polite, if reserved. Many Malagasys as well as French residents were notably hospitable and were extremely generous in giving information and devoting time to persons whom they had never seen before and were unlikely to meet ever again. Indeed, the writers were the recipients of so much kindness in Madagascar that they are unable in the space available to acknowledge their gratitude individually, as that kindness merits.

The warm thanks of the authors are extended to two scholarly historians of Madagascar and four curators of libraries containing invaluable source materials on the island. Governor Hubert Deschamps, the outstanding authority on Madagascar's history, and Dr. Raymond Kent, author of the first scholarly study in English of contemporary Madagascar, *From Madagascar to the Malagasy Republic,* were most generous of their time and helpful in their criticisms of the chapters on political developments. The writers gained much useful information from the many relevant and unusual documentary sources placed at their disposal by Messrs. P. Duignan of the Hoover Institution, J. C. Froelich of the C.H.E.A.M., M. de Ferry of the Institut des Hautes Etudes d'Outre-Mer, and J. Valette, director of the National Archives at Tananarive.

V. T.
R. A.

San Francisco, California
April 1965

Part one

HISTORY AND POLITICS

Chapter one

THE HISTORICAL BACKGROUND

Anthropologists, linguists, and historians have long been stirred to study and speculation by the mystery surrounding the origins of the Malagasy peoples, the time of their arrival on the island, and the very name of Madagascar itself.[1]

Scholars now generally agree that the basis of Madagascar's population was constituted by successive waves of immigrants from the region of Indonesia, of which the earliest reached the shores of the great island some centuries before the Christian era and the most recent came in the fifteenth century. These immigrants, speaking a Malayo-Polynesian language, seem to have absorbed gradually the many other immigrants of diverse origin who found their way to Madagascar in the course of the centuries from Africa and the Arabian peninsula. From their home islands the immigrants brought with them their techniques of fishing and of cultivating rice and taro, and their languages and socioreligious customs, including the cult of the dead. To their new home they also brought a social organization (similar to that of sub-Saharan Africa) comprising the political unit of the clan, made up of descendants of a common ancestor, and its cultural group, the tribe.

Although in time the newcomers established their hegemony over most of the island's tribes, they themselves underwent a transformation as a result of contacts and fusion with other peoples, and Arab and African influences have survived in certain areas of Madagascar. Negroes from the east African coast are believed to have introduced some plants, animals, and implements into the island, and Arabs made other important contributions to the coastal zones. It may well have been the Arabs who introduced a written language, sorcery, slavery, the practice of circumcision, a patriarchal system, and a political organization which transcended that of the tribe. In any case,

---

[1] Numbered notes appear at the back of the book, pp. 467–81.

they founded kingdoms along the coasts, married into high-ranking Malagasy families, and left a strong imprint upon the tribes, especially the Antaimoro and the Sakalava. Furthermore, it is to the Arabs that the world is
indebted for the first written documents about Madagascar.

[Through internal migrations, tribal warfare, and intermarriage, Madagascar gradually reached some political and social cohesion. Except in the
extreme south, where there was a considerable dispersal of tribes, the island
was covered with a mosaic of kingdoms by the end of the eighteenth century.] Almost all of these kingdoms were loosely organized, each under its
own chief and feudal hierarchy, consisting of various strata of nobles, freemen, and slaves. With the exception of the Sakalava confederation and the
Betsimisaraka kingdom, which temporarily controlled large areas on the
west and east coasts respectively, all but one of the other "states" were
small, weak, insecure tribal units beset by internal and external conflicts.
This exceptional state, Imerina, which was situated on the so-called high
plateaus,* was founded by a people later called the Merina, who were of
predominantly Malayo-Indonesian origin. Favored by geographic and climatic conditions, the Merina succeeded in establishing their ascendancy
over neighboring tribes, but they themselves were not immune to internal
conflicts and divisions. It was not until the late eighteenth century that they
became united under the leadership of an able king.

In 1787 there came to the throne of Imerina a remarkable prince with the
unwieldy name of Andrianampoinimerina, who set up his capital at Tananarive and consolidated his rule over all the Merina tribes. By deflecting the
Merinas' warlike energies to external conquest, he brought all the central
region of the high plateaus under his sway. At the same time that he pushed
out the frontiers of his realm, Andrianampoinimerina strengthened its
foundations by a series of innovations which were carried out within the
context of Merina ancestral traditions. The outstanding administrative,
judicial, and fiscal reforms initiated by this illiterate monarch, who never
left the central plateaus, survived his reign and earned for him the titles of
"father of his country" and of "first Malagasy nationalist" from twentieth-
century Merina intellectuals.

Andrianampoinimerina welded the Merina into one people united on the
basis of his own undisputed but paternalistic authority, with an administration directly responsible to him. His vassal chiefs became merely the
administrators of their fiefs, but at the same time he left room for initiative

* The term "high plateaus" is commonly although incorrectly used both by French writers and
in Madagascar itself in referring to the mountainous region that forms the island's elevated
central plain. Because of its acceptance in current usage, it will be used in this book.

and responsibility at the base of the social structure. Tribal notables and village councils (*fokonolona*) were assigned the tasks of maintaining public order and providing mutual aid in the rural areas. Justice was rendered in the King's name, and he promulgated a penal code which not only reinforced the sacrosanct and absolute authority of the monarchy but also punished theft, the practice of sorcery, and the use of tobacco and alcohol.[2] Although the King claimed sole proprietorship of the land, those who cultivated it were for all practical purposes its owners, and forests were held to be communal property. Increased agricultural production was one of the King's major goals, and he repeatedly exhorted his subjects to work. In return for the security he provided, the King required his people to give their labor for the building of roads, bridges, and dikes, to perform military service, to pay rent for the land they farmed, and to pay tribute in proportion to their feudal obligations.

During the reign of King Andrianampoinimerina, Merina society became more rigidly stratified. At the top of the social hierarchy and immediately under the king were the nobles (*andriana*), who were themselves divided into two groups. Below the *andriana* came the freemen or *hova*—a name widely and erroneously applied by early Western writers to all the Merina—who formed a middle class of traders, craftsmen, and well-to-do farmers. The lowest group in the social system consisted of slaves (*andevo*), of whom there were four castes, but not all of them were of servile origin. Those who were enslaved temporarily because of unpaid debts were treated with more consideration than those who became slaves as the result of Merina military conquests.

Fortunately for his country, King Andrianampoinimerina, who died in 1810, was succeeded by an exceptionally able warrior and administrator—his son, who took the name of Radama I. It was he who modernized and reorganized the Merina army, extended his kingdom to the east coast at the expense of the Betsimisaraka, and installed military posts in the Sakalava country. Of more lasting significance was his friendly reception of Europeans who came to Madagascar, particularly the English and the French. Although he welcomed them primarily in the hope of enlisting their help in conquering the island, he also open-mindedly accepted some wholly alien aspects of Western civilization which they brought with them. Protestant missionaries were allowed to open schools and churches and to introduce the printing press, and despite the opposition of some of his most influential subjects the King was even persuaded to abolish the slave trade. In 1828, however, he died at the age of 36 before he had time to do more than open the way for Madagascar's entry into the modern world. His successor,

Queen Ranavalona I, vainly tried to continue his pattern of conquest and to turn back the clock by excluding disruptive European influences from her kingdom.

More than 300 years had passed since those European influences made their first appearance in Madagascar. In 1500 the Portuguese were the first Europeans to reach Madagascar, about whose existence they may have learned from the accounts of Arab traders. Since they first sighted its shores on the feast day of St. Lawrence, Captain Diego Diaz and his sailors named the island in the saint's honor.* During the ensuing decades, other Portuguese followed in their wake and set up a few trading posts along the coast, but these posts proved to be ephemeral. Unable to make converts to Christianity among the Malagasys, with whom their relations were anything but cordial, and finding no gold, slaves, or ivory on the island, the Portuguese abandoned Madagascar early in the seventeenth century. During the sixteenth century and the first half of the seventeenth, some French, English, and Dutch navigators and pirates touched at Madagascar, where they exchanged guns and ammunition for supplies of food and water. They were no more successful than the Portuguese, however, in establishing a secure base on the island until the first French chartered companies were formed in the early years of Louis XIV's reign. Even with such royal backing, the fate of the small French settlements installed on Madagascar (at Fort-Dauphin and Ste.-Marie) and in the Mascareignes Islands (later called Mauritius and Réunion) hung in the balance. Disease, internal dissension, and the hostility of some Malagasy tribes all but wiped out the early settlers, and only Ste.-Marie survived as a French possession. In the nineteenth century, still more formidable adversaries were to appear in the form of English competitors for the favor of the Merina monarchs, as well as Merina traditionalists determined to preserve their country and their own power intact from all alien innovations.

Because of the authoritarian and superstitious character of Queen Ranavalona I, the warnings of her tradition-bound sorcerers and reactionary courtiers, among whom was the prime minister, Rainiharo, found a ready response. Missionaries were forbidden to preach and to teach, and then Malagasy Christian converts were martyrized. In 1845 all Europeans were first deprived of the right to trade in the interior and then informed that they must either perform *corvée* labor or leave the island within a fortnight. The great majority of the Europeans were repatriated by an Anglo-French expeditionary force, but two—a Scotsman and a Frenchman—stayed on.

---

* Marco Polo is said to have been the first to use the name "Madagascar," in the thirteenth century. On the basis of hearsay, he had mistaken for a large island the coast of Somalia, farther to the north, where the Arab settlement of Makdachou (present-day Mogadishu) was situated.

Cameron, the Scot, enveloped the wooden royal palace in a stone structure, a curious ensemble which is one of the present-day tourist sights of Tananarive. The Frenchman, Jean Laborde, now seems an almost legendary individual, for his accomplishments—extraordinary as they were—did not survive him.

Laborde, a Gascon blacksmith in search of wealth and adventure, had been shipwrecked on the coast of Madagascar. Sometime later he found his way to the Merina court, and for many years he enjoyed the Queen's favor. Relying on his native talents and using conscript labor, he carried out a one-man industrial revolution, manufacturing an astonishing range of articles at Mantasoa that included cannon, textiles, paper, and sugar. On a small scale and under primitive conditions he managed to reproduce much of the merchandise then current in Europe, introduce new plants, and improve the breed of local animals. So long as Laborde did not try to import European ideas, the Queen was delighted by these Western innovations, and she even entrusted to him the education of her son and heir, Prince Rakoto. Laborde succeeded in awakening the young prince's interest in Europe generally and in France in particular.

Laborde's growing influence and the death in 1852 of Premier Rainiharo ushered in a brief period of liberalism at the Merina court. The most aggressive of the English Protestant missionaries was William Ellis, who lost no time after he came to Tananarive in promoting British interests there. Events seemed to play into his hands, for in 1857 a plot to depose the Queen was uncovered, in which Prince Rakoto was involved, allegedly as an indirect result of his asking for France's aid in developing the country. This confirmed all the Queen's latent suspicions and led to the expulsion from Madagascar of all Europeans, including Laborde. From that time until her death in 1861, the Queen ruled with an iron hand. Not only did she try by harsh methods to crush all internal opposition to her rule, but she aimed to extend Imerina's territories by military conquest. Her army succeeded in establishing a military post at Ihosy in the Bara country and founded the town of Fianarantsoa as a replica of Tananarive among the Betsileo, but her campaigns against the Sakalava were failures. Moreover, they impelled some Sakalava chiefs to ask for French aid and protection, which in turn led to France's occupation of Nossi-Bé, an island off the northwest coast. Although France did not possess a foothold on Madagascar itself and held only the two small islands of Nossi-Bé and Ste.-Marie, the Queen not only had failed to enlarge her territories appreciably but by her aggression had provoked the intervention of a foreign power, the very move she was most anxious to avoid.

With the reign of Queen Ranavalona I, the era of Merina conquests virtually ended, and subsequent monarchs never succeeded in imposing their rule over the entire island. Yet for nearly a century the Merina did administer two-thirds of Madagascar, although the degree to which they made their authority felt differed in the various regions. Imerina was directly ruled by the Queen with the aid of a council of nobles, and policy statements were read to her assembled subjects at gatherings called *kabary*. The Betsimisaraka and Betsileo areas were governed by the Queen's Merina administrators in collaboration with the local chiefs. In the remaining areas of her kingdom, the tribal chiefs retained more power, but they were subject to control emanating from the Merina military posts.

In 1861, Prince Rakoto's accession to the Merina throne as Radama II was hailed with great relief by all the Europeans, particularly the French. Idealistic and naïve, he immediately instituted far-reaching reforms such as freeing prisoners, abolishing the death penalty and ordeal by poison, and establishing freedom of trade and of religion. Laborde was welcomed back to the Merina court and granted a royal charter to establish a trading company with island-wide rights to the produce of lands and mines. In 1862 the King made a treaty of "perpetual friendship" with France and gave local French residents extraterritorial rights. Merina conservatives were shocked and angered by this sudden avalanche of reforms and of concessions to foreigners, and the English Protestants in Imerina were resentful of the special favors accorded to the French. The reactionaries stirred up widespread agitation and hatched a plot which culminated in the strangling of King Radama II in 1863.

His brief reign was followed by that of his wife, Queen Rasoherina (1863–68), who tempered the forces of reaction. She reinstated the death penalty and annulled the treaty with France and the charter of Laborde's company, but continued to permit freedom of religious worship. It was during her reign that there came to the fore the most remarkable Merina statesman since King Andrianampoinimerina. This was Rainilaiarivony, a member of the *hova* caste, husband successively of Queens Rasoherina and Ranavalona II and III, and Premier of his country from 1868 to 1895.

Through his own caste origin and his close relations with three queens, Rainilaiarivony had the support of influential elements among the Merina bourgeoisie and nobles. He made use of the authority thus derived and of his own marked talents to attain two main objectives. The first of these was to maintain himself in power against the intrigues of those who either disapproved of his policies or wanted to displace him, and in this he succeeded brilliantly. As to his second aim, however—that of preserving the independence of his country by playing off France against England—he ultimately failed, partly because of international developments beyond his control.

By temperament and by force of circumstances, Rainilaiarivony was a middle-of-the-road statesman. He distrusted all foreigners and Western sociopolitical concepts, but he also recognized their strength and the impossibility of keeping Madagascar isolated from the modern world. In making their choice between the two most threatening evils, he and Queen Ranavalona II clearly preferred the English to the French, but the Premier took care not to alienate France irreparably. He entered into treaties impartially with Britain, France, and the United States on the basis of equality. Rainilaiarivony realized that, to avoid any pretext for intervention by a Western imperialist power, he must modernize his country. Yet he knew that he must move cautiously so as to avoid stirring up the local forces of reaction that had been the undoing of Radama II. Consequently he refused to grant property rights to foreigners, although he permitted them freely to trade and to practice their religion. He deliberately neglected road-building so as to hamper any invading force that might attempt to reach Imerina from the seacoast.

It was in the field of internal administration that Rainilaiarivony proved himself to be a judicious and effective innovator, for here he could pursue his two chief objectives simultaneously. Reforms in the administrative and judicial systems would give the Merina realm the appearance of being a modern state in the eyes of the world, and at the same time would strengthen his own position. By appointing ministers of foreign affairs, finance, education, etc., and agents directly responsible to the central government, he strengthened the authority of the Merina monarchy at the expense of the recalcitrant nobles and vassal chiefs. The agents whom he posted in remote areas and the emissaries he dispatched throughout the realm gave him reports on the state of the country and enabled the Queen's subjects to bypass the feudal authorities by bringing their complaints directly to the attention of the central government. The two law codes promulgated in 1868 and 1881 further strengthened the powers of the monarchy by penalizing severely those who plotted against the Queen or her representatives or were guilty of embezzlement. By this legislation the Premier also tried to modify obsolete Malagasy customs without unduly offending the traditionalists, and to orient the country's social evolution in accordance with Western and particularly with Christian ideals. Although Rainilaiarivony feared to go so far as to abolish slavery, the new laws forbade slave-trading and the future enslavement of the Queen's subjects. Moreover, polygamy was thenceforth forbidden, as was the drinking of alcoholic beverages, school attendance became obligatory, and Sunday was made a day of rest—all measures that reflected the growing influence of the English Protestants at the Merina court.

In February 1869 the balance which Rainilaiarivony had been holding between France and England was definitely tipped in favor of the latter when the Queen and many members of the nobility were converted by English missionaries, and the Protestant Church became the official church of Imerina. Next, British officers were employed as military instructors and one of them was named commander in chief of the Merina army. The decline of France's influence was precipitated by her European defeat in 1870 and by Laborde's death eight years later. The need to economize induced the French government to cease subsidizing the French Catholic missions in Madagascar in 1871, and their operations were further restricted by Malagasy government regulations and some forms of persecution. At that time Rainilaiarivony was counting over-heavily on British support and was underestimating the strength of Premier Jules Ferry and the French deputies favorable to an aggressive colonial policy.

With the opening of the Suez Canal in 1869, England became eager to eliminate French influence in Egypt and consequently was willing to barter by giving France a free hand in Madagascar. France's interests in the great island at that time were represented by some dubious historical claims dating back to the days of the chartered companies and by the protectorate treaties with some Sakalava chiefs which had given the French control over Nossi-Bé. The validity of those treaties was denied by the Merina government, and in 1878 a specific dispute arose between the French and Rainilaiarivony when he refused to permit Laborde's heirs to inherit his property in Madagascar. France presented the Merina government with an ultimatum, which the Premier rejected, although he had failed in his efforts to enlist support in Europe against France. There followed the first Franco-Malagasy war of 1883–85, during which the French fleet successively occupied Majunga, Tamatave, Diégo-Suarez, and Vohémar. The English urged Rainilaiarivony to make peace, and in December 1885 he decided to negotiate.

In the meantime the political atmosphere had changed markedly in France, for the French military defeat in Tonkin had led to Ferry's downfall and the eclipse of the pro-empire forces. France wanted to liquidate the Madagascar venture, and the treaty with Rainilaiarivony was so hastily and ambiguously drafted that it did not clearly establish a French protectorate over Imerina. It did, however, require the Merina government to pay an indemnity of 10 million francs and lead to France's occupation of Diégo-Suarez and the installing of a French Resident-general at Tananarive, complete with military escort. The Resident-general was empowered to represent French trading interests and to control Malagasy foreign affairs, but was not authorized to intervene in internal Merina affairs.

Tensions inevitably developed between the aging and increasingly suspicious Rainilaiarivony and the aggressive French Resident, Le Myre de Vilers, and unpleasant incidents marred relations between the Malagasy population and the French military detachment and Catholic missionaries. Open warfare might have been avoided, however, had not an Anglo-French agreement in 1890 paved the way for France to exert more pressure on the Merina government. Reportedly in return for France's recognition of a British protectorate over Zanzibar, England was willing to agree to a French protectorate over Madagascar.

French deputies to the National Assembly from the neighboring island of Réunion, supported by some Metropolitan newspapers, were pressing the government to take over Madagascar. In France the pendulum had swung back in favor of imperial expansion, and more knowledge was available there about the Madagascar hinterland, thanks to the explorations in 1865–70 of the great French scientist Alfred Grandidier.[3] Gabriel Hanotaux, Minister of Foreign Affairs, appealed to the deputies in November 1894 to establish an effective "protectorate over Madagascar, with all its consequences," and to whet their appetites, stress was placed for the first time on the economic advantages offered by Madagascar's undeveloped land and mineral resources. In 1894 an ultimatum was sent to the Merina government, and when it was rejected, war broke out. An expeditionary force of 20,000 men, composed of professional colonial troops and some French and Senegalese conscripts, disembarked at Majunga in February 1895. Slightly more than seven months later, on September 30, a column of 4,000 men under General Duchesne, exhausted from hacking their way through mountains and jungle and almost without provisions, reached the outskirts of Tananarive. They bombarded the Queen's palace, where a white flag was promptly hoisted, and then entered the capital, whose population offered no resistance. Of the 5,592 casualties among the French forces, fewer than 50 died in battle; the rest were victims of fever and the lack of proper food and medical care.

The rapid collapse of the Merina government reflected the weaknesses in its structure and in the Premier's policies. Rainilaiarivony had counted too heavily on France's military depletion and political discord, and also on Anglo-French rivalry to checkmate France's aggressive designs on Madagascar. Furthermore, his modernization of the administration was superficial, for he feared the repercussions locally of making any thorough reforms. The few Western advisers whom he trusted were Englishmen mainly concerned with the Malagasys' moral welfare. Although under their guidance notable advances had been made in the fields of education, medicine, and Christian conversions and in a superficial Europeanization of living standards in Tananarive, vital aspects of the economy had been neglected. Such "modern" enterprises as existed were confined to essentially primitive trading operations, the economy remained based on slave labor and the *corvée*, and virtually no public works—especially communications —were undertaken. The isolated outlying areas of the kingdom were almost totally undeveloped, and their populations increasingly resented being governed by Merina officials. Because of this mutual distrust, men were recruited for the army only in Imerina. Even the conscientious English officers employed by the government to train them could not impose discipline on such conscripts or infuse them with patriotic ardor. It was in vain that Queen Ranavalona III—who had come to the throne in 1885 at the end of the first Franco-Malagasy war—announced that she would not cede to the invaders even so much land as could be covered by a grain of rice, for her soldiers put up virtually no resistance.

Given more time, more realistic foreign advisers, and more experience of world affairs, Madagascar might have been able to remain independent. But in 1895 the Merina government still retained side by side both traditional and modern elements, and even so exceptional a premier as Rainilaiarivony could not fuse them into an efficient and harmonious administration. By his caste and his education he was kept aloof from the traditionalist masses, and he was also too far in advance of his times for the society into which he was born. Because he could be wholeheartedly neither a traditionalist nor a modernist, Rainilaiarivony was unable to mold the Malagasy people into one nation.

Chapter two

FRENCH COLONIAL RULE

The French Protectorate and Revolt of the Fahavalo

General Duchesne brought with him to Tananarive a treaty providing for an effective French protectorate over Madagascar, which the Queen signed on October 1, 1895. By its terms the Resident-general was to control Malagasy internal as well as external affairs, and the Queen was pledged to carry out such reforms as the French government deemed essential. The protectorate formula was popular in France at that time because it was regarded as the least expensive device for administering a colonial territory and because minimal official controls promised a relatively free hand to French capitalists and traders in the island. Duchesne was instructed by the Paris government to make as few changes in Madagascar as possible, and he carried out his orders to the letter. Except for exiling Premier Rainilaiarivony in 1895 to Algiers, where he died the following year, and for the abolition of slavery at the very end of the protectorate period on September 27, 1896, the existing Merina administrative structure was left almost intact. Indeed, so calm did the situation appear to General Duchesne that he soon repatriated most of his troops, keeping only enough to garrison posts at Tananarive, Tamatave, Fianarantsoa, and Majunga.

Yet beneath this apparent calm great changes were taking place both among the Merina and in the outlying areas. Although the mass of the population in Imerina remained impoverished and downtrodden, a new oligarchy based on recently acquired wealth and on power derived from holding public office was swelling the Merina ruling classes, especially in Tananarive. Socially, however, the old interdictions on intermarriage and intermingling continued to be observed, and caste lines were only slightly blurred between the nobles and the top crust of the bourgeoisie. This process, however, was not so apparent or so immediately crucial as the veritable revolution that was taking place among some elements in the non-Merina populations. It soon became clear that the surrender of the Merina army marked the beginning, not the end, of indigenous resistance to the invaders and what they stood for.

In Imerina, the government's quick and complete collapse was interpreted as a proof that the gods were angry with the Queen and her court for becoming Christians and introducing foreign-inspired changes in the social order. In order for the ancestral deities to be appeased, the invaders and their innovations must be destroyed, so the first victims of the revolt were English missionaries and their Malagasy converts. (It was at this time that a new superstition gained credence, of which much was to be made during the 1947 revolt and later: that Europeans were heart-snatchers.) Among the populations of the outlying regions where the Merina administration had broken down the old tribal structures, the powerlessness of the central government also was an incitement to revolt. In this case, however, the uprisings were directed mainly against unpopular Merina officials and not Europeans. But everywhere the revolts bespoke a violent rejection of change and the wish to return to the security of traditional beliefs and authority. The transition from this pagan defensive reflex to xenophobia was easy, and as the uprisings spread they took on an increasingly nationalistic character.[1] This reorientation was encouraged by some feudal chiefs and even by Merina officials, who hoped to fish profitably in the troubled waters and so organized armed bands, which swarmed over the island. Inevitably, these bands attracted individuals motivated solely by their hope for personal gain, and their lawlessness and pillaging gave the whole movement unjustly the name of "revolt of the *fahavalo* (bandits)."

So massive and complex in their motivation did the uprisings become that it is not surprising that the new French authorities failed to grasp their significance, especially that of the anti-Merina grievances of the coastal populations. Because they had been ordered to establish a protectorate, the French officers felt they must not tolerate a revolt against the Merina administration; hence they suppressed it harshly. This inevitably deflected some of the popular resentment from the Merina to the new French masters. In Paris these uprisings were no better understood, but they served as ammunition for those who wanted the status of Madagascar to be transformed from that of a protectorate to that of a colony. These "annexationists" were spearheaded by spokesmen for the French inhabitants of Réunion Island, who saw in Madagascar a nearby, logical field for their expansion.[2] They were supported in their attacks on the protectorate system by French businessmen, settlers, and Catholic missionaries in Madagascar itself. Their goal of a monopolistic position in Madagascar could be reached only if it became a French colony and the treaties made by the Merina government with Britain and other powers were abrogated.

The issue was not settled by the compromise between the two systems contained in a treaty which a new Resident-general, Laroche, brought to the Queen for her signature on January 18, 1896. Two months later, after the rainy season ended, the revolts broke out anew and with increased xenophobic fervor. As one man, the annexationists blamed the treaty and especially Laroche, and eventually their pressure resulted in passage of the law of August 6, 1896, which declared Madagascar to be a French possession. Fortunately for the honor of the French Chamber, the deputies at the same time voted for the immediate freeing of all slaves in Madagascar. On September 27, 1896, Laroche read aloud the proclamation of emancipation—his last act of authority before turning over the civil and military command of the island to General Joseph Gallieni.

The Legacy of Gallieni

Gallieni's assumption of power in Madagascar marked the beginning of a new era, and there is almost no aspect of the island's development on which that famous soldier did not leave his mark. By good fortune, the instructions Gallieni received from the Minister of Colonies accorded with his own temperament and with the policies he had evolved as the result of his recent military campaigns and administration in Tonkin. The first of these was the *politique des races,* according to which all ethnic groups in a colony were to be governed by their own leaders and on the basis of equality. The second policy—that of the *tache d'huile*—proved to be of more practical and immediate use to Gallieni, for very soon after his arrival on the island almost the entire population was in revolt.

Although the situations in Tonkin and Madagascar were not analogous, Gallieni found that he could effectively apply in the latter, as he had in the former, what he called his oil-spot (*tache d'huile*) policy—the automatic radiation of influence from a given military and administrative center. To Gallieni, the military posts set up in the areas pacified by his army were only to supply a curtain of security behind which the countryside was to be reorganized and revitalized. Reassured by the presence of the military garrisons, the villagers were given arms to defend themselves, organized to build schools, roads, and dispensaries, and shown how to increase agricultural production. In each sector to which this policy was applied, there was to be but a single authority. This was the French officer in command, who was at one and the same time soldier, administrator, judge, and engineer, and who was responsible only to Gallieni himself. In Madagascar as in Tonkin, Gallieni found a very able collaborator in the officer who later became Marshal Lyautey, to whom he entrusted the administration of the southern region.

Largely owing to such men as Lyautey and to his own *tache d'huile* policy, Gallieni with fewer than 9,000 men (of whom more than half were Senegalese) subdued all Imerina, then in 1897 dealt with the Sakalava rebels, and next turned southward. By the end of the century it looked as if Madagascar had been almost wholly pacified, and troops were gradually withdrawn. In 1904, however, another revolt broke out, and it took one more year to subdue the southeast. The manner in which this revolt started, spread, and was ultimately checked bears a striking resemblance to the great rebellion of 1947. But if, in the 43 years between those two uprisings, Madagascar was singularly free from internal violence, this was in large part due to the solid foundations that Gallieni laid during the nine years he was in charge of the island.

The long-range objectives of Gallieni's *politique des races* coincided during the first few years of his governorship with the policy directives of Paris. Later Gallieni did not always see eye to eye with his superiors there, but for most of his incumbency he was given a remarkably free hand. Now that Madagascar had become legally a colony, he was instructed to put a stop firmly but not brutally to Merina hegemony over the island, and everywhere to exercise his power directly through the hereditary chiefs of each population group. Briefly he tried to utilize what was left of the Queen's prestige to restore order in Imerina. But soon he became convinced that she and her courtiers were either actively aiding the rebels or serving as the focus for their revolt. A few weeks after his arrival at Tananarive he took the drastic step, which he later regretted, of having the Queen's uncle and a *hova* minister executed for complicity in the uprisings. The Queen herself was placed under increasingly tight controls, then exiled in February 1897, first to Réunion and then to Algiers, where she died in 1917. (The return of her remains to Tananarive in 1939 sparked an outburst of nationalist feeling.) The day after her departure from her realm, Gallieni gave free rein to his republican instincts and abolished the institution of royalty and "other feudal survivals," as well as the office of premier. Clearly Gallieni had thereby exceeded his instructions, but his actions were later upheld by the French deputies, who also named him governor-general of Madagascar.

Gallieni has often been quoted as saying that his ambition was to make Madagascar French, sap English influence there, and diminish the powers and the pride of the Merina. He fulfilled these mutually complementary aspirations, but they were too negative or too nebulous to represent the totality of his accomplishments on the island. Undoubtedly they reflected the first orders that he received from Paris and perhaps his own earliest goals. In their pursuit, however, he encountered unsuspected complications and gained an experience that forced him to revise his value judgments and the order of his priorities. The basic conflict which he never totally resolved was that between his nationalistic ardor to further French economic interests and his humanitarian zeal to promote Malagasy welfare. Initially he seems not to have foreseen that these two goals might become incompatible, or that in pursuing them he might find himself involved in a maze of superficially unrelated ventures.

"To sap English influence" Gallieni had to make French interests preeminent in Madagascar's trade and culture. So far as trading was concerned, tariff walls were effective in curtailing the importation of British and American goods and protecting French merchandise in the Malagasy market, but it was not so easy to legislate changes in the cultural field. The Christian missions, both English Protestant and French Catholic, monopolized educational facilities at that time in Madagascar, the former being predominant in and around Tananarive and the latter mainly in the other regions. From the purely religious viewpoint Gallieni was an indifferent liberal and favored freedom of worship, but as an anticlerical product of his times and as a promoter of French culture he felt that he must undermine the educational role of the British missionaries. To force them to use French as the linguistic vehicle in their schools he forbade them to teach in English or in Malagasy, and to give the British missionaries some competition among the Malagasy Protestants, Gallieni invited representatives of the Paris evangelical mission to come and work in Madagascar. The latter move naturally displeased the French Catholic missionaries and did little to alter a political hostility that was hardening along religious lines. Anglo-French rivalry, which theoretically should have been settled by the annexation treaty of 1896, was perpetuated and was transposed to an internal Malagasy situation, in which the Merina upper classes became identified with aristocratic English Protestantism and the coastal tribes (*côtiers*) with French Catholicism or secular republicanism, or both.

By locating in the coastal regions most of the lay schools that he created, Gallieni intended not only to offer a counterattraction to English missionary education but to provide the non-Merina peoples with a training that eventually would enable them to become teachers and minor functionaries. To encourage local self-government, Gallieni organized the notables in a given area and revived the *fokonolona* (village councils), which he considered such an admirable institution that in 1903 he transplanted it to regions where it had never been indigenous. By such long-term measures Gallieni hoped to "diminish the power and the pride of the Merina" and to carry out his orders to destroy Merina feudalism. Toward these same objectives he found that he could get more immediate results by applying his *politique des races* to the economic domain. In taking away their land from

the outstanding Merina adversaries of the French and in distributing much
of it to their former slaves, Gallieni hoped to accomplish two things. These
were to undermine the source of Merina upper-class wealth and to enable
the freed slaves to earn a livelihood. In both respects he was doomed to disappointment.

The French emancipation proclamation of September 1896 effectively
freed many of the slaves whose condition of servitude had not been mate-
rially improved by previous mission-inspired royal edicts to the same effect.
This French gesture appeased public opinion in France and it also earned
some gratitude from former slaves in Madagascar, for very few of them
joined the rebel bands fighting the French and then only because they could
find no other means of support. Indeed, this lack of alternative sources of
livelihood was the crucial problem arising from the abolition of slavery, for
the ex-slaves were either unable or unwilling to farm the land of their
former masters. To solve this and some other pressing financial and economic problems, Gallieni revived forced labor, though for only a limited
period and for a specific purpose. Every able-bodied man between the ages
of 16 and 60 was required to give 50 days' free labor (later reduced by him
to 30) to executing public works, and if he so wished he could thereafter
continue to be employed as a wage earner. In this way the east-coast railroad from Tananarive to Tamatave was begun, and a road network began
to spread throughout the island—a marked departure from the past, because
the Merina government had deliberately neglected the means of communication. Nor would such a development have occurred at all had its financing
been left to the Paris government, for in 1900 a law had been passed requiring French colonies to be self-supporting except in periods of direst
distress. In a subsistence economy like that of Madagascar at the time, Gallieni could never have financed public works from local taxation, even
though he had revised the tax rolls, made their assessment more equitable,
and used native institutions for their collection. The efficacy of such methods
was reflected in the growth of Madagascar's budget from 5.5 million francs
in 1899 to 24.5 million in 1905, and the tripling of its foreign trade, in which
the French share rose sixfold.

Because Madagascar's trade with France fell off somewhat during the last
two years he was in office, Gallieni was then accused of failing to promote
French economic interests as he should have. Actually he was interested in
economic development and granted large concessions to French companies
and individuals, but as a means of promoting human welfare and not to enrich any given group. Initially he encouraged Réunionais immigrants and
some of his noncommissioned officers to settle in Madagascar, but when he
realized that a cause of the 1904 revolt was their excessive demands on the
Malagasys, he turned against what he came to call "premature coloniza-

tion." Similarly he became disillusioned with the French trading companies, which had abused the favored position he had created for them by eliminating foreign rivals. Thus some of Gallieni's basic objectives were radically altered in the light of his experience, while certain of the temporary solutions he worked out simply to cope with an immediate situation served as guidelines for Madagascar's administration for many years thereafter. A main reason for this was the sound basis on which Gallieni's policies rested. Convinced that solid knowledge was essential to win the population's cooperation, he required his administrators to learn the Malagasy language and to gather basic data about the resources, customs, laws, and natural phenomena of the regions in which they were posted. To ensure that research would be permanently carried on, he created the Malagasy Academy. And to increase the island's productivity and raise native living standards he formed the auxiliary corps of doctors and nurses (Assistance Médicale Indigène, or A.M.I.) and created a chain of hospitals and medical posts where the Malagasys received treatment free of charge.

During his nine-year proconsulship, Gallieni accomplished his self-imposed tasks and carried out his orders, but with some results that he did not foresee. He never succeeded in resolving the conflict between his nationalism and his humanitarian ideals, although increasingly he gave priority to the latter wherever possible. As to "sapping English influence," Gallieni succeeded in virtually eliminating the English language and British trade from Madagascar. But in a latent and more dangerous form, English influence survived in the tenacity with which the Merina *andriana* and *hova* used Protestantism to express their hostility to the French and their disdain for the Malagasy Catholics. This development was not apparent at the time Gallieni left Madagascar, but he remained there long enough to be dissatisfied with the misuse of the *chasse gardée* which he had created for the French traders, settlers, and cultural assimilationists.

As for Gallieni's third goal—to humble the power and the pride of the Merina—this was certainly accomplished insofar as the Queen, court, and army were immediately concerned. But the Merina upper classes never forgave the French for the ease and rapidity with which Gallieni conquered the whole island, which their monarchs had never been able to do, and the short shrift he gave to his Merina opponents. Years afterwards they sought consolation by picturing the revolt of the *fahavalo* as a rebellion of patriots, puffing up the accomplishments of the Merina monarchy out of all proportion to their reality, and making the Queen's palace the physical focus of Merina nationalism. In regard to the Merina, as in other matters, Gallieni was pragmatic and kept a singularly open mind. As time went on, he began to feel that he had overestimated the coastal population's capacities and underestimated those of the Merina. The rehabilitation of the Merina civil

servants, whom he had dismissed from their posts, especially in the peripheral regions, started in Gallieni's lifetime.

To most of the Malagasys, Gallieni seemed and still appears to be a great
king of their island, and even the Merina have had to admit that it was he
who first gave unity to Madagascar and to all its peoples.

Gallieni's Successors

Two civilian governors-general divided almost equally the nine-year interval between the departure of Gallieni and the outbreak of World War I.
The first of the two, Victor Augagneur (1905–10), showed more vigor and
initiative than did his successor, Albert Picquié (1910–14), who largely carried forward and completed the work his predecessor had begun.

Politically the two men were somewhat left of center, and they were both
strong republicans who feared and disliked the military as well as the
missionaries. They also shared a weakness for bureaucratic paperwork, tidy-
ing up the administration by meticulously regulating Franco-Malagasy relations in such matters as forced labor and the indigénat* and insisting on
shortsighted economies. By balancing Madagascar's budgets, they were able
to indulge their own anticlericalism and at the same time to please their superiors in Paris, but this was done in part by withdrawing official subsidies
from mission schools and closing the regional schools which Gallieni had
set up in the provinces. Because of these moves, for many years all Malagasy
civil servants (including teachers and doctors) were trained at the Ecole Le
Myre de Vilers at Tananarive, and the education of the coastal populations
and therefore job opportunities for them almost ceased to exist. Furthermore, the economies thus unfortunately accomplished were offset by the
increased cost of the administration as a whole. (To be sure, they were not
responsible for the fact that in 1912 the administration of the Comoro Islands was united with that of Madagascar.) In their obsession to replace
army officers by civilian administrators, however, these two governors-general saddled Madagascar with a machinery of government that was both
more centralized and more expensive than before. In justice to their accomplishments, it should be added that they continued Gallieni's policy of creating and expanding the means of communication. They extended the road
network through most of the central plateaus and completed the railroad
from Tananarive to Tamatave, but these roads were of little benefit to the
coastal inhabitants. By concentrating the government and public works in
the center of Madagascar, Gallieni's two immediate successors were reversing his politique des races. Either from inertia or from conviction, Augagneur and Picquié favored the better-educated and more politically ex-

* A native-status legal "code" that enabled administrators to impose arbitrarily certain penalties
on noncitizen Malagasys for offenses other than statutory ones.

perienced Merina above other tribal groups, and gradually the highest posts in the civil service open to Malagasys were again being filled with Merina.

World War I

Ironically enough, the last task assigned to Picquié, who had liquidated the remnants of Madagascar's military administration, was that of recruiting Malagasys for service in World War I. Very soon after the war broke out, however, Picquié was replaced by Hubert Garbit, on whom devolved the main task of mobilizing Madagascar to help in France's war effort. Garbit had been chief military officer under Augagneur, and was therefore an obvious choice as Madagascar's wartime governor-general. The first of his two tours of duty in that capacity covered most of the war period, during which he applied himself so vigorously to the task that he recruited 45,963 Malagasy "volunteers" for service in France. Of these, reportedly four-fifths came from the central plateaus and 41,355 were combat troops, who were commended on several occasions for bravery under fire. According to official figures, 4,000 Malagasy soldiers were killed in action, but an unknown number of thousands more died of wounds and illnesses suffered in France.* Those who survived the war made their contribution to the growth of Malagasy nationalism. The most influential of these World War I veterans was Jean Ralaimongo, a former Betsileo schoolteacher who organized a Malagasy movement in France during the early 1920s. To Madagascar itself the veterans brought back ideas detrimental to French prestige, which had been based on the Malagasys' belief that the French were superior and invincible beings. These veterans recounted how they had seen with their own eyes white men slaughter each other and even work with their hands.

The V.V.S.

Such revolutionary ideas were well suited to the psychological climate created by wartime conditions in Madagascar. The Malagasy people had been forced to send to a distant land a large number of their men and a larger proportion of their resources to help fight for a cause that was wholly alien to their interests and experience. It was above all the Malagasy people who "contributed" 5 million gold francs to the war loan fund and produced massive quantities of foodstuffs and graphite for shipment to France. Again it was they who mainly suffered from the shortage of consumer goods and from the black market and profiteers that were its inevitable consequence. The sufferings and privations of the coastal populations were on

* Dandouau and Chapus, p. 279. According to another authority, however, 6,000 Malagasys were recruited as laborers; 34,386 came to France, of whom 2,368 died there. Sarraut (p. 44) also described the great majority of Malagasys who went to France as "peasants from the coastal regions" who were both "docile and robust."

the physical plane: these *côtiers* were resigned to the exigencies of their masters, and in that role they had simply exchanged the Merina for the French. But the Merina of the central plateaus, who had never wholly accepted the French conquest and the resulting demotion in their status, experienced a reaction that was more psychological and emotional. To their pent-up sense of collective humiliation was now added a bitterness toward the French, born of the wartime sacrifices demanded of them. These feelings found expression in a movement that had been organized among Merina youths shortly before World War I and that later took the name of Vy Vato Sakelika (Iron and Stone), or V.V.S.

The origins of the V.V.S. go back to the last years of Picquié's governorship, and the movement showed from the outset a typically Merina combination of Asian and Malagasy characteristics. As in similar secret movements of about the same period in southeast Asia, the young students who formed the first group in 1912 had been excited by Japan's victory over Russia seven years before, wanted to preserve their own cultural heritage, and admired and at the same time resented Western technical superiority. Typically Merina were the symbolic initiation ceremonies, the pledge to fight for the fatherland, and the movement's leadership by Protestant ministers and teachers. With a membership not exceeding 300, secretly organized into small groups at Tananarive and among the Merina in the Betsileo region, the V.V.S. kept its objectives—though not its existence—unknown to the French authorities until December 1915. Then the government announced that it had uncovered a plot hatched by the V.V.S., which was to culminate the following month in the poisoning of all the Europeans living in Madagascar.

No caches of arms or hidden kegs of poison were ever produced in support of the fantastic charges. Only the wartime psychosis due to France's desperate plight in Europe at this time can explain the credence placed in them by the French residents of Tananarive and their demand for severe punishment of all the V.V.S. members. Wholesale arrests were made and nearly 200 students were sent to the concentration camp of Nosy-Lava on the west coast. Of the 41 tried under the Malagasy penal code for incitement to revolt, seven were acquitted and the rest were condemned to hard labor for periods varying from five years to life. In May 1916 the French Evangelical Missionary Society protested against the severity of these sentences, and gradually local public opinion and the French authorities showed better sense and a calmer judgment. In 1921 a general amnesty was declared, and among those who benefited from it were two young medical students, Joseph Raseta and Joseph Ravoahangy, and the founder of the V.V.S., a Merina Protestant minister named Ravelojoana. Later all three became very influential members of the Malagasy nationalist movement, of which the

Merina-dominated V.V.S. was the forerunner but not the sole source. A whole series of events—the postwar depression, the abuses by French settlers and companies in Madagascar, the serious omissions and commissions of the local French administration, and the leadership of the Betsileo war veteran Jean Ralaimongo—were required to give island-wide dimensions to what had begun as a Merina protest movement.

The role played in the early postwar years by Jean Ralaimongo was strikingly similar to that of his Negro African contemporary, André Matsoua of the Moyen-Congo. Both men were veterans of the French army who stayed on in Paris after the war and who became close associates of French left-wing intellectuals and other leaders from Asia and Africa seeking the independence of their countries from France. Like Matsoua, Ralaimongo protested against the use by France of colonial troops in the Rif and Syrian campaigns, denounced the abuses of the concessionary companies and white settlers in the colonies, and urged his compatriots to acquire French citizenship as the only effective way of defending their rights and of making any collective progress.* Again like Matsoua, Ralaimongo returned home to be prosecuted by the colonial administration and denounced by the local French conservatives—thus acquiring a popularity among his fellow countrymen that became particularly evident when he died during World War II. But significant differences in the careers of these two men should also be noted. Unlike Matsoua, Ralaimongo never became involved in dubious financial transactions, secret organizations, or religious protest movements, and it was his forthright and firm stand on political and economic issues and not the halo of martyrdom that attracted his popular following. Because of his journalistic campaigns against the *indigénat* and forced labor, his struggle to prevent a white settler from evicting Malagasy farmers from his concession, and above all his role in the antiadministration demonstrations at Tananarive in 1929, Ralaimongo was not allowed thereafter to leave Antalaha district. In 1942 he died there at the age of 58, and the thwarting of his lifelong ambition to make Madagascar a Department of France and the Malagasys French citizens was largely responsible for the nationalistic and insular orientation of later efforts by the Malagasys to improve their status.

The comparative indulgence with which Ralaimongo was treated seems to have been due to no official policy of liberalism but to the slight importance attributed to him and his followers by the local French government. Garbit doubtless thought that he had dealt effectively with the V.V.S. leaders and that he had checked a source of future trouble by eliminating from

---

* In 1920, Ralaimongo founded the Ligue Française pour l'Accession des Indigènes de Madagascar aux Droits de Citoyens Français, which received the support of such literary figures as Anatole France and André Gide.

the textbooks used in Malagasy schools all references to the French Revolution. Later he also established press censorship, forbade the holding of public meetings without official authorization, and by a decree repressing vagabondage empowered the government to imprison undesirable persons. In September 1917 Garbit left the colony for three years to take charge of the operations of the Malagasy troops and laborers in France.

The Settlers and Administrative Reforms

None of the three governors-general who followed in rapid succession—Martial Merlin (September 1917–January 1918), Abraham Schrameck (January 1918–July 1919), and M. Guyon (July 1919–May 1920)—remained in Madagascar long enough to effect drastic policy changes. Such of their energies as were not taken up in promoting the war effort were engaged in a power struggle with the local French community.

In 1915 Garbit had set up mixed commissions composed of officials and settlers to win the settlers' cooperation in increasing Madagascar's food and mineral production for export to France, and he proposed to the authorities in Paris that an assembly be created in Madagascar that would represent French economic interests there. Although Paris turned down this suggestion on the ground that it did not take Malagasy interests sufficiently into account, Garbit's recognition of the importance of the local French residents stirred them to aspire to play an effective role in the management of public affairs. On the ground that too many settlers were then mobilized and fighting in France, Garbit did not accede to all their proposals, but on November 16, 1916, he did form an advisory committee composed of prominent French citizens to study "all questions of general interest."[3] Although this committee had a technical rather than a representative character and was merely consultative, it nevertheless enabled spokesmen for the settlers to express their opinions on taxes, tariff rates, and the like. Governor Merlin, soon after his arrival at Tananarive, created another outlet for local French opinion at a higher level, when he began convening regular meetings of the presidents of the island's chambers of commerce.

All these evidences of the administration's good will toward the resident French community did not satisfy the settlers' demand that they no longer be treated as second-class citizens but be given the same permanent representative institutions that they would have if they were living in France. As soon as the war was over, the settlers began an intensive campaign in the local press and in France, demanding official recognition of their rights and complaining of the high and growing costs of the administration's operations in Madagascar. Their clamor became so insistent that Governor Schrameck on his own initiative held an economic conference at Tananarive, which met from January 15 to 31, 1919. Its purpose, he said, was "to associate, to the degree compatible with the personal responsibilities of the head of the colony, the settlers of Madagascar in the discussion of the big economic questions that have arisen in the postwar world." Far from appeasing the French residents, however, this gesture was interpreted by them as an oblique confirmation of their importance. They formulated a resolution, which they asked the governor-general to forward to Paris, asking that a "financial delegation of settlers" be set up in Madagascar with the same wide powers as their counterparts had in Algeria, and that a representative be sent to France to promote their interests there on a permanent basis. Schrameck lost no time in calling the conference delegates to order, describing them as a minority compared with the Malagasys and not even qualified to speak for a majority of the white settlers. At the closing session of the conference he said without equivocation:[4] "So long as I am governor-general of Madagascar I shall permit no interference with or any check on the administration's actions except such controls as are laid down by law."

Schrameck's successor, Guyon, was unable to find a compromise acceptable to both Paris and the settlers, so the latter demanded the reappointment of Garbit, who they believed was fundamentally more favorable to their cause. After his return to Madagascar Garbit tried to revive the proposal that he had vainly made in the first war years and also to give some Malagasys opportunities for regularly expressing their views on the conduct of public affairs, but once again the Paris government would have none of it. This was the period of the post–World War I depression, and the French authorities feared the financial repercussions of Garbit's program. Both out of concern for the Malagasys' welfare and because of its addiction to centralized government, Paris had no intention of granting the settlers in Madagascar any share in the executive power there. Garbit's second term as governor-general did not cover quite three years (May 1920–March 1923), and he left the island before this problem could be settled. The last proposals that he drafted, as well as many of the public works and administrative measures that he initiated, were taken over with some modifications by his successor, Marcel Olivier. The final project, as submitted by Olivier and accepted by Paris, called for the setting up of an assembly, to be called the Economic and Financial Delegations. By a decree of May 7, 1924, its competence was said to be purely advisory, and its resolutions would in no way bind either the local administration or the French government. Although these delegations never gave much satisfaction to any of the groups evolved, they served to familiarize some Malagasys with parliamentary procedures, and they continued to function until the outbreak of World War II.

Unlike his predecessors, Olivier brought to the governorship of Madagascar twenty years of experience in the colonial service, mainly in French West Africa. He had the good fortune to serve at Tananarive during a period of abundance (February 1924–February 1930), and to leave the island on the eve of the first major political manifestation and just prior to the world economic depression. Aside from the Economic and Financial Delegations, his innovations included creating a bank of note issue (Banque de Madagascar et des Comores), drafting land laws and instituting a land survey, and beginning the railroad from Fianarantsoa to Manakara, for the construction of which he set up a forced-labor corps called the S.M.O.T.I.G. (Service de la Main-d'Oeuvre des Travaux d'Intérêt Général).* Finally, Olivier tried to reorganize the administrative units and decentralize them so as to bring them into line with the new means of communication. Many of his innovations did not long survive his incumbency, the most permanent of them being the new credit facilities and the public works he initiated or completed. Oddly enough, the only major natural disaster during Olivier's governorship—the cyclone of March 3, 1927—led to the rebuilding on a vastly improved and apparently permanent basis of the town and port of Tamatave. The street riots described below, which occurred at the very end of Olivier's tenure of office, reflected the discontent that had been accumulating beneath the surface. They were a portent of the political troubles that were to plague Madagascar intermittently during the three decades that followed.

The Beginnings of the Malagasy Nationalist Movement and the Settlers' Grievances

Although the 1920s were a period of superficial tranquillity and relative prosperity, neither Malagasys nor French settlers were wholly at peace or content. The main grievances of the Malagasy masses were socioeconomic, whereas those of the elite were largely political and personal. In the eyes of the Malagasy peasantry, the changes that Olivier had made in the Merina land laws in 1926 (described in Chapter 16) jeopardized their rights to their ancestral lands, and the land survey that he instituted three years later heightened this feeling of insecurity as well as the fear of higher taxation. As to the Malagasy youths who were liable to service with the S.M.O.T.I.G., they intensely disliked the military-style regimentation of their lives and work and being forced to labor on projects that yielded no immediate benefits. Furthermore, the hinterland Malagasys resented being compelled to work far from home in the humid and hot coastal zone around Manakara. Nor was the institution of the S.M.O.T.I.G. any more popular with

* See p. 446.

the resident French community. In particular, the settlers resented the fact that the S.M.O.T.I.G. workers received three times the daily pay of their own laborers, and all the French residents complained that as taxpayers they would have to meet the interest payments on the loan that the government had contracted to carry out its public-works program. Official waste and extravagance and the neglect of settlers' interests were the leitmotif of their complaints during the post–World War I decade.

To substantiate their charges that the government's operating expenditures were unnecessarily high, they pointed to the new administrative units and councils that Olivier had created supposedly in the interests of a decentralization of power. If these bodies had proved to be useful as instruments for the wider diffusion of authority or as media for voicing the aspirations of either the settlers or the Malagasys, the financial burden they entailed might have been accepted with better grace. The Councils of Notables, however, which in theory if not in practice met once yearly in each district headquarters, served mainly as vehicles for transmitting the French administrator's orders to the rural populations. And the Malagasy members of the Economic and Financial Delegations, meeting separately from their European colleagues, simply registered acquiescence in the government's proposals. To be sure, the debates of the European section of the Delegations often contained spirited criticism of official acts, but even as a safety valve their institution had only limited utility. As the cleavage between the desiderata of the settlers and those of the Malagasy elite became more acute, both sides turned increasingly to the local press as a more satisfactory channel for expressing their grievances and proposing courses of action.

Frustrated in their attempts to win satisfaction of their demands from the French government, the extremist faction among the settlers organized a Ligue des Intérêts Economiques de Madagascar in March 1925.[5] Some of its members used such local newspapers as *La Feuille de France, L'Echo de Tananarive,* and *Le Colon de Tamatave* to express the wish that the "Anglo-Americans" would take over Madagascar so that its European population could "remain white and French." To understand this remarkable reasoning, one must reconstitute the political climate of the period. It was compounded of multiple fears, whose strongest undercurrent was that the Bolshevik Revolution was spreading to Madagascar. Proof of its contagion was seen in the island's first labor strikes and peasant demonstrations in 1925–26. The next year the settlers' fears were further confirmed when a Russian-born French citizen named Paul Dussac joined the staff of the newspaper *L'Opinion,* founded shortly before at Diégo-Suarez by the Malagasy nationalists Jean Ralaimongo and Joseph Ravoahangy. Dussac, after failing to make his living as a settler since his arrival at Diégo-Suarez in 1922, had turned to giving legal counsel for the defense on a semiprofessional basis to Malagasys standing trial in the law courts.

Dussac was not long content with a journalistic audience restricted to the isolated provincial town of Diégo-Suarez, and early in 1929 he moved to Tananarive. There he founded another newspaper, *L'Aurore Malgache,* with the help of some Malagasy nationalists and resident French sympathizers. Among his Malagasy collaborators were Abraham Razafy, secretary of the S.F.I.O. section at Tananarive and formerly a member of the V.V.S., and Jules Ranaivo, who soon gained renown as a nationalist politician and journalist. His French associates, Edouard Planque and François Vittori, occupied minor posts in the local administrations and were members of the French Communist Party. Considering the background and views of such recruits to the cause, it is not surprising that Ralaimongo's moderate campaign aimed at obtaining French citizenship and greater education opportunities for the Malagasys soon underwent a marked and radical change.

Early in 1929 the atmosphere in Tananarive had been made propitious for a reorientation of the nationalist movement as a result of a strike organized there by students of the Medical School. Although this strike had no political implications, the new nationalist leaders thought that they could profitably employ the tension it had created, and they chose May 19, a public holiday, to stage a demonstration. Accounts of what actually took place that day differ widely. According to some sources,[6] the incident was deliberately distorted by writers so as to make the French public believe that it had been communist-inspired. Certain historians claim that the administration first gave permission for the holding of a public meeting on May 19 and then withdrew it at the last minute, with the result that the streets of Tananarive were filled with angry demonstrators. Still another version, and one with an amusing aspect, is that given by the communist writer Pierre Boiteau.[7] He admits that the organizers of the demonstration chose to stage it in front of the centrally located Excelsior movie theater, where they knew that the police would refuse admission to any Malagasy. Planque appeared leading a dog, and as a European he was admitted to the theater. This was the cue for Vittori to shout to the crowd that discrimination was being practiced by the French in favor of dogs and against Malagasys, and to demand freedom and independence for Madagascar. Accounts differ as to exactly how the crowd reacted to Vittori's stage-managed slogans, but for some hours they milled through the streets and around the offices of the government-general. In any case, the nationalist response was sufficient to alarm the resident

French conservatives, who demanded stern reprisals. Some Malagasys well known for their nationalist sentiments were dismissed from their jobs or were placed under arrest either at home or in prison. Dussac, Planque, and Vittori were imprisoned and later brought to trial, during the course of which they were defended by lawyers sent to Tananarive by the French Communist Party.

The campaign of repression, however, did not get seriously under way until Léon Cayla, Olivier's energetic successor, arrived in Tananarive in February 1930. In short order he began efficiently rounding up suspects. His decree of December 4, 1930, gave the administration arbitrary powers to arrest and detain those it deemed guilty of acts likely to create hatred of the French government. The liberal use of this decree by the local authorities, not only in the early 1930s but even more in 1947–48, gave the Cayla regime an unenviable notoriety in liberal circles. Indeed, the numerous arrests, the suspensions or suppressions of local newspapers, and the iron grip exercised over labor and other Malagasy organizations all made Cayla's nine-year incumbency as governor-general seem a harsh and interminable period. Yet those who have condemned Cayla's shortsighted and unjust measures have usually overlooked his economic accomplishments and the comparative liberalism of his later years in Madagascar.

Cayla came to Tananarive at a time when Madagascar's foreign trade had declined disastrously, unsold goods were piled up in the ports, and unemployment was widespread. He incurred great unpopularity by retrenching government expenditures drastically, including suppressing posts for nearly 600 Europeans. With a loan he was able to raise, he pushed through a big program of public works. These included completion of the Fianarantsoa-Manakara railroad, the port of Tamatave, urbanization plans for four large towns, promotion of Madagascar's external and internal air services, and the construction at long last of an overland link between Diégo-Suarez and the rest of the island. By the mid-1930s he showed more liberalism to Malagasy nationalists and journalists, and even to French communists. The restrictions placed on the movements of Jules Ranaivo and Joseph Ravoahangy were lifted; Dussac, Planque, and Vittori were freed; and nationalist newspapers began to reappear, though sometimes under new names.* In 1936 the advent to power in France of the Popular Front government contributed to a further loosening of the official controls and even to some concessions to nationalistic demands for equal rights with Frenchmen. Cayla considerably eased the conditions under which Malagasys could obtain

* *L'Aurore,* for example, was first reborn as *La Patrie* and then became *La Nation Malgache.*

French citizenship,* and in 1939 elections were held for the first time in Madagascar to choose a Malagasy delegate to the Conseil Supérieur des Colonies in Paris. Significantly, it was Ravelojoana, founder of the V.V.S., who obtained 11,000 of the 14,000 Malagasy votes cast.[8]

Madagascar on the Eve of World War II

The last years before the outbreak of World War II brought a very few political concessions and some degree of political awakening to the urban elite, especially in Tananarive, but the mass of the Malagasys accepted the rule of the French *fanjakana* (administration) as docilely as they had that of the Merina monarchs. Indeed, the two governments shared certain characteristics—insistence on unquestioning obedience, lack of imagination, isolation from and irresponsibility to their subjects, and a degree of uniformity in their structure—and both were the object of quasi-religious veneration on the part of the rural Malagasys. Authoritarianism was the outstanding feature of the two administrations, but the Merina queens never had the means that the French had of exacting rapid compliance with their orders throughout the island.

Under French rule all the administrators in Madagascar, from the governor-general down to the Malagasy canton chief, were appointees. There were, to be sure, a few councils or assemblies to which a limited number of candidates were elected. But none of these councilors had more than advisory powers, and the electorate comprised only a small proportion of the European population and an even smaller percentage of the Malagasy. Since 1913 the French citizens living in five settlements could elect some of their municipal councilors, and beginning in 1924 somewhat under 7,000 of the 24,000 Frenchmen then resident in Madagascar were empowered to choose 36 of the 40 European members of the Economic and Financial Delegations.[9] In the eyes of the administration, the latter electorate represented the local French economic interests that were important enough to be worth consulting on specific financial and technical matters. During the first seven years of their existence the Delegations' European members petitioned the Paris government three times for voting powers, particularly in the political field. After 1931 they apparently became discouraged, perhaps because

* According to the decree of March 3, 1909, a Malagasy seeking naturalization as a French citizen must be 21 years of age, prove his knowledge of the French language, and have his candidacy approved by the French administrator of the region in which he lived. If this application was so approved, it was forwarded by the governor-general to the Minister of Colonies, who might or might not recommend that final action be taken by the President of the Republic. Cayla greatly simplified the procedure in April 1938 and made the acquisition of French citizenship easy for Malagasys who had certain educational qualifications or who had rendered recognized services to France.

Paris consistently refused to accede to their wishes or because the depression not only reduced the number of French settlers in Madagascar but also underscored their dependence on the local colonial administration for survival. In the late 1930s the European members of the Delegations continued to scold the administration for its "extravagant" expenditures and to seek more control over taxation, but the resident French community seemed to have finally concurred with the government's view that it would be inopportune, even dangerous, to transfer Metropolitan political institutions to the colonies.

If the French authorities were unwilling to share executive power with their compatriots, they were certainly not going to give any to the Malagasys. Since the mid-1920s, village chiefs elected directly the Councils of Notables and indirectly the 24 Malagasy members of the Economic and Financial Delegations. As no minutes were kept by either the Notables or the Malagasy Delegates, we have few clues to the political thinking of the rural leaders who formed the electorate for both groups. But we do know that the sessions of the Malagasy section of the Delegations were very short and that its members, in 1925, accepted without a murmur the administration's draft budget, which the European Delegates rejected. However, a French student of the Delegations reported in 1938[10] that with each passing year the Malagasy section became less of a rubber-stamp body and that its members had begun to debate the proposals submitted to them which they formerly had approved without any discussion.

Even though the bodies to which the rural Malagasy elite could elect representatives were only advisory, they provided more of a medium for the expression of indigenous opinion than was available to the Malagasy urban elite. To be sure, most of the Malagasys who had acquired French citizenship were town-dwellers and could vote for municipal councilors, but by the time World War II broke out only 8,000 of a total population of some 3 million had qualified for and sought naturalization. Political parties for the Malagasys were nonexistent, and because of tight official controls the press and labor organizations offered only the most limited opportunities for self-expression. As for political evolution, Madagascar was far behind not only an *ancienne colonie* like Senegal but also the other dependencies that had sizable settler communities, such as Indochina and North Africa. The most acceptable explanation for the backwardness of Madagascar's populations seems to be that they were isolated, both geographically and psychologically. Madagascar is separated from France by 10,000 kilometers, and the only nearby French territory is Réunion Island, populated entirely by French citizens and administratively a department of France. The physical isolation of Madagascar from the mainstream of world developments might not have hampered its development so seriously had the populations on the island itself not lived in mutual aloofness.

During the interwar period, French colonial society in Madagascar had the rigid form of a pyramid. At its apex was the governor-general, whose theoretically close dependence on the Minister of Colonies was so attenuated by the slow means of communication of those days that in practice he could act virtually as an independent agent. Under the governor-general, from whom all local honors and material benefits flowed, was the small group of his associates, who created an atmosphere described as resembling that of a nineteenth-century German princely court.[11] Below them in strictly hierarchical order were some high officials—civilian and military—who associated exclusively with each other and not with the mass of the functionaries, army officers, and settlers ranged beneath them in still another self-contained social unit. Some of the settlers were permanent members of the local French society, but most of the Frenchmen in Madagascar were transients from heterogeneous social backgrounds. All but the very top level had at least one thing in common—in Madagascar they occupied a social and economic position higher than that from which they came in France. Moreover, the functionary in this society—again excepting the highest echelon and contrary to the situation prevailing in French Black Africa—was almost certain to make his whole career in Madagascar. Thus the strata that composed this inbred and isolated little world which gravitated in its own orbit had little intercommunication except for transacting official business.

Malagasy society, with its own caste divisions based on birth and wealth, had relations of peaceful coexistence with French society but few close contacts. Only a few intellectuals and artists on both sides tried to close the social gap between them through professional organizations such as the Académie Malgache and the Association des Ecrivains et Journalistes de Madagascar and through individual friendships. It was in this small group of Frenchmen that Jean-Joseph Rabearivelo, the most famous of all Malagasy poets, found his few European friends. But Rabearivelo over the years became physically and spiritually exhausted by his inability to earn a living for himself and his family and also to find the time needed for self-education and writing. In 1937 he committed suicide, despairing of admittance as an equal to a society whose culture he had acquired solely through his own efforts and whose recognition he craved.

Rabearivelo's tragedy is especially poignant but not typical of Franco-Malagasy relationships of that period. On the French side, the prevalent attitude could be described as one of paternalistic benevolence combined with firmness, but the French generally kept to themselves; as for the Malagasys, their reactions normally ranged from awed obedience by the uneducated masses to aloofness or resentment on the part of the Merina elite. Even where a few direct contacts existed, the breakdown of traditional authority and the growth of individualism that were the sequels of the *présence française* and of French rule were effecting changes in Malagasy society that were not always apparent even to its own members. From the standpoint of future developments, the most significant of these changes were the continued rise of the Merina bourgeoisie (*hova*) as businessmen and functionaries, and the tacit alliance that had been formed between this class and the Merina aristocracy (*andriana*). The steady decline of the latter's fortunes since 1896 was making them more inclined to join forces with the *hova* against the dominance first of France and later of the coastal tribes.

Chapter three

WORLD WAR II AND THE POSTWAR REFORMS

On June 15, 1939, less than three months before the outbreak of World War II, the authoritarian Cayla was replaced by a governor-general of very different caliber. He was Marcel de Coppet, a member of the French Socialist Party, a Protestant, and an intellectual who frequented Paris literary circles.

With an eye on the gathering storm clouds, de Coppet lost no time in preparing to carry out a plan for mobilizing Madagascar's resources that had been drawn up in Paris some years before in anticipation of a wartime emergency. Under this plan, Madagascar was to increase the production of certain items that would be needed in France and also to send troops and laborers there. When war was declared, therefore, the Malagasys—who were rapidly mobilized—were brought to the ports of embarkation and dispersed among seven specially constructed camps. Between September 1939 and June 1940 some 15,000 Malagasy troops and laborers were sent to France, contributions to the French war effort amounting to 9 million francs were collected in Madagascar, and the nationalists even stopped their propaganda, probably because their antipathy to Hitler's racial doctrines exceeded their hostility to French rule. Either in gratitude for such reticence or, more probably, to increase the local population's cooperation, de Coppet made a graceful gesture that had the appearance but not the reality of a political concession. On October 17, 1939, he appreciably enlarged the electorate for the Malagasy section of the Economic and Financial Delegations, but the competence of that body remained purely advisory and within less than two years its meetings were suspended.

France's defeat in Europe in the late spring of 1940 came as a great shock to both the European and Malagasy populations. De Gaulle's famous appeal of June 18 aroused widespread response in Madagascar, and de Coppet and the general commanding the troops at Tananarive together cabled the French High Commissioner in Cameroun, who had come out for Free

France, that Madagascar would continue to fight on the side of the Allies. Within a few days, however, the British attack on the French fleet at Mers el Kebir caused the governor-general and high-ranking French officers to change their minds.[1] Nevertheless, the Vichy regime, irked by de Coppet's vacillations, ordered him to return to France under military escort, and Cayla was sent back to his old post. Nine months later, in April 1941, a new governor-general was sent out to replace Cayla, who had now reached the retirement age. This was Armand Annet, an ambitious civil servant who had previously served in French Somaliland.

In the narrative that Annet wrote later in self-justification,[2] it is made clear that he believed his highest duty to be obedience to the orders of his superiors, in this instance Marshal Pétain. On arrival in Madagascar he found the population calm and untroubled by political discord, he said, and suffering only minor hardships as a result of the British navy's blockade of the island.[3] According to other sources, Annet at once embarked on a campaign of repression, suspending the Economic and Financial Delegations, dissolving trade unions, and organizing an espionage network and a strong-arm Légion des Combattants.[4] Under his rule, racial discrimination appeared[5] in Madagascar, as was shown by the distribution of rationed drugs and food only to Europeans and the requirement that the Malagasys queue up separately to be waited on in stores. There is no doubt that some of the French conservatives in Madagascar approved of such measures and had strong fascist sympathies, as already evidenced by the cable that Gaston Pialat, director of the Compagnie Marseillaise, and other like-minded *colons* had allegedly sent to Mussolini in 1936 congratulating him on the conquest of Ethiopia. In 1940–41 the British blockade heightened their resentment against the Allies, for it hampered their foreign-trade operations.

The British Invasion

From Annet's reports, it is clear that the local partisans of de Gaulle organized some resistance units, but apparently those set up by the French were separate from the Malagasy units. By mid-1942 the former gave positive proof of their existence through clandestine broadcasts of "Free Tananarive" radio and the chalking up of the Cross of Lorraine, even on government buildings, but it is hard to gauge the effectiveness of the latter. Early in his administration Annet had interned Jules Ranaivo* and Dr. Raseta in a camp at Moramanga, and the outstanding Malagasy leader, Jean Ralaimongo, died in August 1942. In describing the nationalists' resistance effort to the French deputies some years later, Dr. Raseta mentioned no positive

---

* Ranaivo's daughter, the first Malagasy woman to join the Free French in 1942, was executed in the Moramanga prison as a spy by the authorities loyal to Vichy.

achievements and only used the conditional tense:[6] "We wanted to continue the war alongside Great Britain, we could have set up a government that cooperated with the Allies, and we would have renounced our goal of independence lest it be considered a stab in the back of our Allies-in-distress." All such declarations of intention and estimates of the strength of Annet's opponents must remain conjectural, for on May 5, 1942, the British navy in a surprise attack captured the French naval base at Diégo-Suarez. This move was prompted by the British fear that the Japanese, after their capture of Singapore on February 15, were themselves planning to take over that deep and well-protected harbor. At all costs, Churchill felt, the Japanese must be prevented from getting a base in the Indian Ocean, which they might use as a staging area to join forces with Germany and Italy somewhere in the Middle East.

The British attack was made without the participation of Free French troops and even without notification to General de Gaulle. The reason given for this slight was the desire to avoid a repetition of the fiasco at Dakar in September 1940, for which the presence of Free French forces was held partly responsible. De Gaulle was not mollified by the leaflets which the British distributed throughout Madagascar, stating that they were in the island only to forestall an Axis attack and that as soon as that danger was eliminated it would be handed over to Free French control. Initially, American troops had been scheduled to join in the Madagascar campaign, but at Durban the British commander learned that they were not coming, so that thousands of leaflets showing the Stars and Stripes entwined with the Union Jack had to be burned in the boilers of his ship.[7] The defense of South Africa certainly played a part in motivating British strategy, and Zulu troops were among those used in conquering the island.[8]

After Diégo-Suarez fell into their hands, the British hoped that Annet would accept the inevitable and that further military operations would be unnecessary. But the governor-general and some of his high-ranking collaborators carried out Vichy's orders to "defend French sovereignty against the enemy invaders"; hence the British had to capture one by one the strongholds of Mayotte (July 2), Nossi-Bé and Majunga (September 11), Tamatave (September 18), Tuléar (September 30), and Fort-Dauphin (October 1). Tananarive was declared an open city, and the British occupied it without firing a shot.

The British officers who wrote accounts of this campaign reported that they found sympathy for the Free French and their allies widespread among all but the top echelons of the local French community, but that the latter as a whole were so isolated that they knew little of the course the war was taking. In particular, they felt that Churchill had sought an easy victory in

Madagascar to offset British reverses in Southeast Asia, and they were frankly skeptical about the danger of an Axis attack on Madagascar until a small Japanese submarine one night stole into Diégo-Suarez harbor and damaged a British warship anchored there.[9] After that they placed more credence in British propaganda, and the latter made every effort to avoid offending French susceptibilities. Though much of the resistance which the British encountered was *pro forma,* it took the form of destroying bridges, tearing up rails, and blockading roads. The fact that Annet and his top echelons chose to surrender six months to the day after the British began their invasion suggests that a major consideration in prolonging their resistance may have been to qualify for the combatants' pension to which they would not otherwise have been entitled.*

The Free French Administration

True to their promises, the British kept most of the French civilian officials at their posts and on January 7, 1943, turned over the government of Madagascar to the Free French, retaining for the duration only the naval bases of Diégo-Suarez and Tuléar, as well as a liaison mission at Tananarive. General Paul Legentilhomme, the recently appointed Free French high commissioner for the Indian Ocean, and Pierre de Saint-Mart, a career official in the colonial service, took over from the British and began Madagascar's second mobilization for the Allied war effort. Some 2,000 Europeans and 28,000 Malagasys were then called up, and it was announced that Madagascar would become the military staging area for the recapture of French Indochina.[10] Forced labor was revived and used to repair the means of communication, pressure was exerted on the population to resume and increase agricultural and mineral production, and 150 million francs were collected as "contributions" to France's war effort.

Some Malagasy recruits distinguished themselves during General Leclerc's trans-Saharan march and attack on Bir Hakeim, but after the reassertion of French sovereignty over the island early in 1943 Madagascar's military importance went into eclipse. Thereafter Madagascar held interest for the Allies almost solely as a source of needed foodstuffs and minerals. Until that time the island's populations had suffered comparatively few privations as a result of the war. True, the British blockade had curtailed

---

* Soon after the liberation of France, Annet was tried by the Free French courts and condemned to "national degradation" for his actions in Madagascar. It was not until November 1949, however, that what came to be called the "trial of the generals of Madagascar" took place. By that time, passions had cooled and the generals were acquitted, even though in their defense they used the same arguments as did Annet. These were that they had simply done their duty by carrying out orders, and that in any case the British invasion of Madagascar had been totally unnecessary.

the import of such items as drugs, cloth, flour, and fuel, which were felt to be of prime necessity by the European component. But a few makeshift industries manufacturing soap, clothing, and the like were able to fill some of these needs for the duration, and the great mass of Malagasys, in whose lives imported goods had never played much part, simply reverted to a subsistence economy. Some shortages were acutely felt, but locally grown foodstuffs were plentiful and no one went hungry. Exporters inevitably suffered as a result of the stoppage of shipping, but the planters, both European and Malagasy, received help from the government. A law of August 20, 1940, provided them with loans amounting to over 8 million francs to keep their plantations in production, and a string of warehouses was built to stock the crops harvested until such time as they could be exported to France.

As in French West Africa, it was not until after the Free French assumed control of the government that the native populations began to feel intensely restrictions and regimentation. The Allies quickly absorbed the 100,000 or so tons of coffee, rice, tapioca, frozen meat, hides, and skins that had been stocked in Madagascar's ports and soon demanded additional supplies. More and more workers were requisitioned to labor ever longer hours on plantations, in mines, and on restoring roads, bridges, and railroads. Shortages became acute, especially in the extreme south; for the United States, Great Britain, India, and South Africa, even with the best will in the world, could supply only a small proportion of Madagascar's needs in consumer goods, fuel, and spare parts. What could have been avoided, however, was the grave error made by the local administration in setting up an Office du Riz in 1944. Malagasy farmers were forced to sell their entire crop to this organization at the very low price set by the government, and then had to buy back later what they needed for themselves at much higher cost. The lack of sufficient transportation, of distribution facilities, and, above all, of honest supervision meant that much of Madagascar's rice harvest found its way into the black market, to the sole profit of speculators. Of all the mistakes made by the French administration in Madagascar, the operations of the Office du Riz probably had the most grave repercussions, and they continued to be felt in the first postwar years. More than any other single cause, it seems to have been responsible for the explosion that occurred in 1947.

New Institutions

Governor de Saint-Mart succeeded General Legentilhomme in May 1943 as head of the Free French administration of Madagascar. For lack of alternative civil servants, Saint-Mart had to retain the French functionaries who had served under Cayla and Annet, and their continuance in posts of authority contributed toward perpetuating the abuses that had made the

Vichy regime unpopular with the Malagasys. In December 1943, however, the visit to Tananarive of René Pleven, then Minister of Colonies for the Provisional French government at Algiers, gave the Malagasys a preview of the reforms in colonial policy that were to be advocated the next month at the Free French conference in Brazzaville. Speaking to a crowd estimated at some 50,000 assembled in the stadium at Tananarive, Pleven pledged that "the administration at long last would give Malagasy problems the attention they merit and have never received."[11] Specifically he said that the Economic and Financial Delegations would be revived and that the electorate would be enlarged, the *fokonolona* (village councils) would be revitalized and reorganized, and two new organizations would be set up. The first of these, a Directorate of Malagasy Affairs, was to replace the old Directorate of Native Affairs, which over the years had come to devote itself wholly to administration and to neglect completely its policy-making functions. (On July 9, 1946, the name of the Directorate was changed to that of Political Affairs.) The second was to be a Mixed Franco-Malagasy Commission, in which European and Malagasy membership would be equal and whose function would be to study ways in which "improvements could be made in all aspects of Malagasy social life."

Both of these new organizations began meeting in January 1944, but it was not until the following November that the *fokonolona* were reorganized and the Economic and Financial Delegations were reconvened. Of these evidences of the Free French leaders' determination in 1944 to give the Malagasys a new deal, the most interesting was the Mixed Franco-Malagasy Commission. Not only were the numbers of its French and Malagasy delegates equal, but for the first time they met together. The Malagasy members were chosen with a view to their representing all the tribes and regions of Madagascar. Most of them had never before traveled any distance from their homes or been associated with public affairs. During the first two sessions all the talking was done by the French and Merina delegates, and the very silence of the coastal delegates pointed up the need for fundamental reforms in the educational system. (To fill this obvious gap between the evolved and underdeveloped Malagasy tribes, the Free French government in 1945 contributed nearly 20 million francs to increase the pay of Malagasy doctors and teachers.) The Mixed Commission did produce some reports and documents, but after a little over a year's existence it was superseded by a Representative Council.

The Economic and Financial Delegations were also rapidly eclipsed, meeting only once, in November 1944, before that body too was shelved to make way for the new representative organization. Before expiring, however, the Delegations' final session did afford Governor de Saint-Mart the

chance to make a speech in which he envisaged a speeding-up of the Malagasys' political development and a more cordial Franco-Malagasy entente.[12]
He also appealed to French civil servants and settlers "no longer to regard
each other as rival brothers, but to give mutual support in the general interest." For his own part, Saint-Mart promised to "put an end to administrative delays and red tape which discourage initiative and hamper production, and to the sterile quarrels [among functionaries] in regard to their
respective competences." Most important of all, Saint-Mart also took this
occasion to announce the government's decision to merge the Delegations
and the Mixed Commission into a single council, the majority of whose
members would be elected and which would have certain powers.

Regarding such powers, the Representative Council that was created on
March 23, 1945, marked an advance over the Delegations, which was only
an advisory group, but it was retrogressive compared with the Mixed Commission in that its electorate was separated sharply into European and
Malagasy colleges. Nevertheless, in having a majority of its members elected
at all, the Representative Council embodied the most progressive move thus
far made by the French government in Madagascar. Each of the two colleges elected 30 members to the new Council, and these elected members
constituted two-thirds of its total membership. The remaining one-third
were named by the governor-general on the recommendation of the chambers of commerce and the newborn labor unions. For the purposes of this
election, Madagascar was divided into nine circumscriptions that were
identical with its administrative regions. The electoral college composed of
French citizens numbered some 16,000. That of the Malagasys comprised
about 75,000, drawn from no fewer than 23 social categories described as
"representing all the vital forces in the country." An interesting innovation
applied to candidates in this election—as well as to those for the newly constituted corps of Notables and the District Councils—was the requirement
that they be members of the ethnic group that predominated in the circumscription in which they ran.

The composition of this council, and its inability to exercise any control
over the budget, were severely criticized by Joseph Girot, a left-wing European who was Madagascar's sole representative in the French provisional
constituent assembly that met at Paris in 1945 (sessions of May 15 and July
5). He criticized the Free French government for empowering the governor-general to dissolve or suspend the Representative Council, set up a separate administration for southern Madagascar (decree of February 4, 1945),
and name all the members to the newly created government council (decree
of May 4, 1945). He also called on the government to abrogate the Cayla
decree of 1930, which was still depriving the Malagasys of democratic free-

doms, and to offer adequate compensation to functionaries and others in Madagascar who had suffered from discrimination under the Vichy regime. In his replies to these charges on June 29 and July 5, 1945, the Minister of Colonies admitted that the new institutions he had set up in Madagascar hardly embodied the spirit of the Brazzaville reforms, but he defended them as temporary expedients and as a first step in the political education of the Malagasys. Madagascar, he said, would soon have democratic representation and wholly elective institutions. Indeed, when the Representative Council held its first meeting, on September 26, 1945, events had moved so fast that it already seemed to be an anachronistic body.

MADAGASCAR'S POLITICAL EVOLUTION, 1945–46

The end of World War II, far from easing Madagascar's economic situation, brought increased hardships to its populations. Because of its progressive reintegration into the French economy, Madagascar experienced the same shortages as were felt in France as a result of war damage to French industry. To the physical distress and suffering this entailed was added an intellectual and emotional malaise. This was the ferment among the Malagasy elite caused by the new ideas generated in 1944–45. They strongly believed that the reforms proposed by the Brazzaville Conference of 1944 and the principles embodied in the Atlantic Charter and the Charter of the United Nations should be applied to Madagascar. And this was the theme of the speeches made in the fall of 1945 by Raseta and Ravoahangy, candidates for election by the second college to the first Constituent Assembly of the Fourth French Republic. (The first college was also entitled to send two deputies to that assembly, and it elected Georges Boussenot and Roger Duveau.) A large proportion of the small Malagasy electorate stayed away from the polls, but Raseta and Ravoahangy were elected by very meager majorities on November 18, 1945.

Malagasy Nationalists in Paris

The two men set out at once for Paris, where they established close contacts with a group of Malagasy intellectuals, whose outstanding member was Jacques Rabemananjara.* A Betsimisaraka Catholic, Jacques Rabemananjara had received his higher education in France, where he had built up a considerable reputation as a writer and poet. From this meeting of militant nationalist and literary minds in Paris was born, on February 22, 1946, the Mouvement Démocratique de la Rénovation Malgache (M.D.R.M.), which soon created branches throughout most of Madagascar.

* Not to be confused with Raymond Rabemananjara, who was also a long-established resident of Paris, a writer, and a prominent Malagasy nationalist.

But in Paris the Malagasy deputies called themselves the Madagascar Delegation or Mission and as such entered into contact with all French groups and leaders that they thought might be useful to their cause.

Naturally they were most eager to establish close relations with the French provisional government, but it was not until February 1946 that they were able to talk with Marius Moutet, Minister for Overseas France, and to give him a memorandum containing three main points.[13] These points stressed that prior to the French occupation Madagascar's existence as an independent state had been recognized by the Great Powers, that the annexation law of 1896 had been imposed unilaterally and by force, and that France should now take the initiative in proposing a wholly new and friendly basis for the relationship of the two countries.

During the month of March 1946, the Malagasy deputies invited representatives of all French political parties, trade unions, religious groups, and economic and cultural associations to come to Neuilly, where they were living, and talk with them about Madagascar's future status. One result of these exchanges was the drafting of a proposal by the Malagasy Mission which was submitted to the Constituent Assembly on March 21. Briefly, it proposed abrogation of the annexation law of 1896 and the confirmation of Madagascar's status as a free nation, with its own government, army, parliament, and financial autonomy, within the French Union. The French reaction—even on the part of liberals—was so immediately unfavorable to this proposal that the Malagasys quickly drafted a second one, which they submitted to the Assembly on April 9. This called for the opening of Franco-Malagasy negotiations and the election of a Malagasy Constituent Assembly that would determine the exact form that the future free state of Madagascar would take as a member of the French Union.

As this was no more acceptable to the French government than the previous proposal, Moutet came up with a counterproject. But because it contained no reference to Franco-Malagasy negotiations and mentioned only a "local assembly to be chosen by the widest possible electorate for the purpose of enabling the Malagasys to show how they felt about the constitution of a nation freely united with the French Union," this counterproject was rejected by the Malagasy Mission. Finally, on April 13, the Malagasy deputies produced a third proposal, whose essential point was the organization under the auspices of a Franco-Malagasy parliamentary commission of a referendum in Madagascar in regard to its future status. No action was taken on this third attempt, for the first Constituent Assembly ended its work before examining the proposal. All that the Malagasy deputies could do in Paris, while awaiting the vote that ultimately rejected the May 1946 constitution, was to form a Franco-Malagasy committee and try to keep the question of Madagascar before the public.

On June 2, Raseta and Ravoahangy were reelected to the second Constituent Assembly in Paris, and three times during its sessions—on July 23, August 9, and September 17—one or the other of them revived the question of a referendum and reaffirmed Madagascar's wish to remain a member of the French Union. Nevertheless, neither then nor later did the French legislators define precisely what was meant by that Union, but it is clear from the assembly debates of the period that the French deputies did not share the expectation of their Malagasy colleagues that the French Union would shortly become a confederation of fully autonomous states.

The Political Evolution of Madagascar and of French Negro Africa

In early 1946 the Malagasy deputies were politically far in advance of their Negro African colleagues. The latter were resting on their laurels, proud of their accomplishments in getting the assembly to outlaw the *indigénat* and forced labor and to extend French citizenship to all the peoples of Overseas France. This was the period when the French West African and Equatorial African leaders were mainly absorbed by their vain effort to bring about abolition of the dual electoral college in their respective territories, and certainly they were not thinking in terms of autonomy, much less independence. The high hopes that they and the Malagasys initially held that, with the help of French liberals, more progressive laws would be passed by the Parliament gradually ebbed away. The only French political group that consistently showed an active interest in them was the Communist Party, which was already declining from the zenith of its postwar power. All the overseas deputies were conscious of and afraid of the revival of conservatism in France during the summer of 1946, and they all turned to their home countries to provide the pressure that would be required to preserve the progress they had made under the first Constituent Assembly and to make further advances. To promote these efforts the Negro Africans founded the interterritorial Rassemblement Démocratique Africain (R.D.A.), and the Malagasys the island-wide Mouvement Démocratique de la Rénovation Malgache (M.D.R.M.), but after the first series of local elections the paths followed by those two popular movements diverged. After going through a phase of extreme radicalism and an open trial of strength with the local colonial administration, the R.D.A. drastically changed its policy to one of collaboration with the French government and the pursuit of its objectives through the orderly processes of law. The M.D.R.M., on the other hand, had immediate recourse to violence, either deliberately or inadvertently, and in the ensuing holocaust was itself liquidated.

So similar were the situations in Madagascar and French West Africa during the critical months of 1946–47 that the causes of their later divergencies merit examination. In both regions the populations had suffered acutely during the war from the practice of racial discrimination, from forced production and privations, and from black market speculators. The Negro and Malagasy elites had been similarly stirred by the war-engendered ideas of national emancipation and democratic freedoms. Negro and Malagasy villagers had listened to the complaints and criticisms of soldiers demobilized from the French army and *maquis* and from Nazi prison camps. These soldiers were bitter at the delays in their repatriation long after the war ended and at being treated less favorably than French veterans. Thus the mood of deep discontent that prevailed during the first postwar years in Negro Africa and Madagascar had the same basic causes, but in Madagascar certain local factions made them more acutely felt and their consequences more dangerous.

In Madagascar, French prestige suffered more damage from such criticisms of their treatment because the demobilized Malagasy *tirailleurs* formed a larger proportion of the total population and were concentrated in a smaller area than in West Africa. Then, in the spring of 1946, reports of the abolition of forced labor and the *indigénat* led to a mass desertion by workers of public-works enterprises, mines, and plantations. As Madagascar's foreign trade was more dependent on plantation and mineral output than was West Africa's, the effects of their desertion on the Malagasy economy were more serious. Another consequence of this sudden and large-scale exodus of their laborers was that the European producers became embittered toward both the local population and the administration, far more than was the case in West Africa, where planters and miners formed a much smaller percentage of the white community.

In three important respects the situation in Madagascar was so essentially unlike that in West Africa that these differences were responsible in large measure for the disparity in the evolution of those two regions during the first postwar decade. First of all, the resident Europeans in Madagascar were more conservative, isolated, and antagonistic to the local administration and to the native population than were their West African counterparts. A large portion of the planter and small-merchant component in Madagascar was made up of poor and ignorant settlers from Réunion Island, who treated the Malagasys as their inferiors and were disliked in return. In Madagascar there was a long history of antagonism by both the planters and the French businessmen to the colonial administration, which for years they had accused of neglecting their interests, coddling the Malagasys, and mismanaging public affairs in a high-handed and extravagant manner. A second main difference lay in the role played by the Christian missions in Madagascar and West Africa. While the colonial administrators in both regions were generally secular-minded and anticlerical, the Protestant missionaries and their converts in Madagascar had acquired a position and posed a problem that had no analogy in French Negro Africa. The identification of the Merina upper classes with Protestantism and anti-French sentiments caused the missionaries and ministers of the Protestant churches in Madagascar to espouse the nationalist cause. In the concurrent contest for Malagasy converts, the French Catholic missionaries could not afford to be left behind, and to some extent they too jumped on the nationalist bandwagon.

The island's politico-religious situation pointed up what was probably the most crucial of all the elements that differentiated Madagascar at that time from French West Africa and Equatorial Africa. This was the role played and the uncompromising attitude adopted by the Merina—of all of Madagascar's tribes the most evolved politically and culturally and the strongest numerically. For nearly a century the Merina had ruled over almost all of Madagascar's other tribes and had been recognized internationally as the rulers of a sovereign state. This remembrance of things past indelibly colored the upper-class Merina outlook, and the Merina nationalists would settle for nothing short of the restoration of their country's independence. It was because of this that they parted company earlier than did the Africans with the French Communist Party, whose leaders were insisting that the proletarian revolution in Europe be given precedence over independence for any and all of the French colonies. The evolution of political parties in Madagascar was greatly influenced by the fact that no French political party at the time would give support to any colonial group or association that aimed to sever the ties between its country and France.

The First Political Parties in Madagascar

Before World War II, no political parties, properly speaking, existed in Madagascar. Only three of the French parties, the Socialists, the Radical Socialists, and the Communists, had representatives on the island—Frenchmen—with whom a handful of Malagasys were associated. After the Liberation, some of the new political groups that were formed in France established branches in Madagascar, notably the Mouvement Républicain Populaire (M.R.P.), but the Radical Socialists virtually disappeared as a political force both locally and in France. The Communists organized some Confédération Générale de Travail (C.G.T.) unions and a Communist Study Group, which reportedly had two Malagasy members.

Because of the aid given Malagasy nationalists during the interwar period by some French socialists and communists, the nationalist leaders in

1945–46 based their program on two assumptions that soon proved to be erroneous. The first was that only through the victory of left-wing parties in France could Madagascar achieve independence. The second miscalculation was that the French socialists and communists would actively work for the restoration of Madagascar's sovereignty, or at least for its autonomy. What the nationalists learned through their many talks with French liberals during the winter and spring of 1946 was that in the Parliament the Section Française de l'Internationale Ouvrière (S.F.I.O.), the M.R.P., and the Communist Party (C.P.) were willing to support only reforms of an egalitarian and democratic nature for the colonies, which they viewed not as individual countries, each having its own problems, but as an integral part of the French Republic. The French left-wing leaders sincerely believed that it was in the interests of the colonial peoples themselves to remain closely tied to France, and that if they were granted independence some other imperialist power would simply take them over and replace France. Inevitably, French right-wing parties could conceive of the colonies only as segments of the Fourth Republic, one and indivisible. They were concerned, however, solely for their own or for narrowly national interests, and they too were convinced that, should France turn its colonies loose, other powers, notably the communist ones, would quickly seize them.

Gradually the Malagasy nationalists came to realize that they could expect no decisive help from France and must rely on themselves, and this led them to organize their party—the M.D.R.M.—in depth on the island. The French political parties as well as the administration in Madagascar were disturbed first by the creation of the M.D.R.M. and then by the popularity that it quickly won among the Malagasys. The French parties realized that the success of this first all-Malagasy party would end the political tutelage in which they had held the nationalist leaders, and the administration foresaw that it would lead to disorders and trouble on the island.

Already, in November 1945, the election of Raseta and Ravoahangy had stirred unrest in Madagascar and caused the forming of new parties, both Malagasy and European. The Christian missions entered the political arena by sponsoring rival parties. The Mouvement Social Malgache (M.S.M.) was a Catholic movement, which never succeeded in playing a prominent role. More effective was the Protestant-backed Parti Démocratique Malgache (P.D.M.) led by the Reverend Ravelojoana and composed of members of the Merina nobility and bourgeoisie. The third and most important of the Malagasy parties was the Paris-born M.D.R.M., founded by Raseta, Ravoahangy, Ranaivo, Raherivelo, and the two Rabemananjaras. All these Malagasy parties wanted independence for Madagascar; they differed only in timing and method and as to whether it should be achieved within the framework of the French Union. Early in 1946 the resident French community, particularly its settler element, in a reflex of self-defense founded the Ligue de Défense des Intérêts Franco-Malgaches. One of the new League's main aims was to offset what its members regarded as the criminal weakness and vacillation of the local administration caused by the spread of Malagasy nationalism.

Labor unrest and the anti-French propaganda spread by demobilized war veterans were intensified by the sudden proliferation of a violent and ill-informed press at Tananarive. In the spring of 1946, some 34 such papers contributed to the ferment by printing garbled reports and rumors, particularly regarding the activities of the Malagasy deputies in Paris. These papers gave credit to those deputies for the abolition of the *indigénat* and of forced labor by the Paris assembly. The tabling on March 21 of the deputies' proposal in regard to Madagascar's future status was described in *La Nation Malgache* on April 16, 1946, as a "gesture of *rapprochement* and clemency, made in a sublime spirit of forgiveness and forgetting":

The Malagasy people, unjustly deprived of their independence, crushed by taxes, terrorized, trampled underfoot, enslaved in the twentieth century, have the right to break completely with the authors of their misfortunes. But once again ... they have not done so and have agreed to remain in the French Union. But this will be the last concession, the final attempt to conciliate the Malagasy nation with the French government. If France rejects this proposal ... she alone will be responsible for the Franco-Malagasy rupture, and our people will wash their hands of whatever may follow. ... We are more than ever determined to recover our independence and ... if necessary will plead our cause before the United Nations.

Such inflammatory articles found response in the confused and tense atmosphere that prevailed especially at Tananarive on the eve of the referendum on France's constitution of May 5, 1946. A false report that France had abrogated the annexation law and granted Madagascar independence spread rapidly through the capital, and some Europeans began to pack their belongings.[14] The French government failed to issue a denial, so that uncertainty regarding official intentions further contributed to heightening the nationalist fever and breaking down the authority of the administration throughout the island. The concurrent announcement that Saint-Mart would be replaced by a new governor-general gave France the opportunity to reassert its control over the island, but this chance was thrown away. The newly appointed governor-general was none other than Marcel de Coppet, whose easygoing liberalism had made him popular with the Malagasys but whose vacillations had permitted the Vichy regime to gain control of Madagascar in 1940. By some incredible blunder, his return to Madagascar coincided to the day with the seventeenth anniversary of the May 19, 1929, nationalist demonstrations at Tananarive. It was obvious that the nationalists would utilize this double celebration to stage another demonstration, especially in view of their disappointment over the recent defeat of the French constitution.

When de Coppet refused the police permission to disperse the crowd, some of whose members were carrying banners reading "Down with the Annexation Law" and "Long Live de Coppet," the nationalist firebrands interpreted this as an invitation to direct action. That evening, Europeans were stoned in the streets of Tananarive, and this impelled de Coppet to resort to strong measures. He doubled the number of *gendarmes* and police and placed them under the orders of his new security chief, M. Baron, whose brutal methods soon earned him a sinister renown. Fearing violence, de Coppet ordered numerous arrests, and he himself went nowhere without a police escort. He failed to call a meeting of the Representative Council and promised reforms which he never carried out. Some violent incidents in the Majunga region led de Coppet to expect an outbreak on Bastille Day (July 14), so he chose that time to return to Paris to report. During his absence and pursuant to his orders, a change was made in the Parti des Désherités Malgaches (PADESM) so as to transform it into an organized opposition to the M.D.R.M.

As is usual in such cases, the government's persecution of the M.D.R.M. served only to add to its popularity and growth. Its leaders shrewdly took over the committees that had been formed to ensure the election of Raseta and Ravoahangy in November 1945, and used them as the framework of a national organization. It was to circumvent the requirement by the administration in Madagascar that all associations obtain prior permission to organize that the M.D.R.M. leaders had their party registered officially in France. The M.D.R.M. immediately took root in the island, though the assertion that it had 300,000 Malagasy members within a few months of its birth seems hardly credible.[15] Its leaders' claims to the effect that the M.D.R.M. represented most of the tribes in Madagascar, however, seemed substantially justified by the results of the election of June 2, 1946. The clearcut victory of the M.D.R.M. candidates for reelection to the second French Constituent Assembly, in which Raseta and Ravoahangy won three-fourths of all the votes cast, indicated that they had won a greater share of the electorate's confidence than they had had six months earlier.

One important reason why the number of the M.D.R.M.'s followers grew so rapidly and also why it became increasingly involved in direct and violent action was the adherence to it in early 1946 of two clandestine extremist organizations. These were the PANAMA (Parti Nationaliste Malgache) and the JINA (Jeunesse Nationaliste), both born during World War II, modeled after the *maquis* cell organization, and to a large extent now staffed by Malagasy veterans of the Resistance.* Although the Merina continued to dominate the M.D.R.M., the inclusion of PANAMA and JINA members did enlarge representation of the coastal tribes, and thus substantiated to some extent the M.D.R.M.'s claim to being a democratic and all-Malagasy national movement. At the same time, however, the new members introduced elements of discord and conflicting views in regard to the means of achieving the M.D.R.M.'s objectives, and such disagreements were to show up as grave weaknesses in the months to come. However, in the summer of 1946 the advocates of direct action seemed to be in the ascendant, as shown by a series of incidents that occurred in different parts of the island, in which hostility to the administration was directly or indirectly displayed.

In June at Sabotsy, a suburb of Tananarive, two Malagasys were killed in a brawl with the police, and at their funeral new incidents occurred, during which stones were thrown at the United States consulate. The French Communist Party sent a lawyer to defend those arrested as the ringleaders, but all of the accused were given prison sentences of varying duration. In July, 50 recently demobilized Malagasy veterans killed five Comorians and wounded nine others in a mosque at Tamatave, probably because a majority of the policemen recently recruited by the administration were from the Comoro Islands. A similar manifestation of tribal prejudices which had anti-French overtones occurred at Tananarive in early October, when a fight broke out between Malagasy veterans and Senegalese *tirailleurs*. Less conspicuous than the foregoing outbreaks, but contributing perhaps even more to the general agitation characteristic of this period, was the series of strikes and work stoppages that provided a backdrop against which the main drama was beginning to take shape.

It was the economic situation even more than the political ferment that exacerbated the emotions of the French settlers and other conservatives in Madagascar. They blamed the government for enacting ill-advised reforms not desired by the mass of Malagasys and demanded a return to the coercive methods of the good old days. In the many cables sent to Paris officials, in the resolutions passed by the local chambers of commerce and employers' associations, and in the articles written for Tananarive's European press, the local administration in general and de Coppet in particular were charged—

* Because they were secret societies, no precise information is available on the size of their membership. P. Boiteau, the French communist writer, naturally played down their size so as to make the M.D.R.M. appear to be a nationalist and not an extremist movement. He stated (*Contribution*, p. 363) that the PANAMA and JINA together had no more than a thousand members in all Madagascar in 1946.

and justifiably so—with lacking a firm and consistent policy. De Coppet, as a socialist intellectual and a Protestant liberal, was especially vulnerable to such reproaches, for he alternately gave his support to the PADESM and to the M.D.R.M. Because the High Commissioner tended to make personal issues out of his political and religious convictions, de Coppet came to regard Ravoahangy, a Lutheran and a protégé of the S.F.I.O., with favor, and by extension to encourage the growth of the M.D.R.M. In July 1946 he loaned Ravoahangy his airplane and an administrator as escort for the avowed purpose of persuading the Malagasy laborers—demoralized by the abolition of forced labor—to return to work. Inevitably this gesture further antagonized the settlers, who claimed that Ravoahangy, far from preaching a back-to-work campaign, was using the facilities de Coppet had placed at his disposal to spread fiery nationalist doctrines.

Little notice was taken by the M.D.R.M.'s irreconcilable opponents of the fact that both in Paris and in Madagascar Ravoahangy reiterated his party's wish to remain a member of the French Union, and that such declarations caused consternation among the M.D.R.M. extremists who insisted on total and immediate independence for Madagascar. At this stage it might have been possible for the French liberals and the more flexible Malagasy nationalists to work out some compromise if real concessions had been made by both sides. But during the autumn months of 1946 the strong pressures exerted on the French government by conservatives in Paris and in Madagascar and France's acceptance of a constitution less favorable to colonial aspirations than that of the preceding May ruled out this possibility. The first indication of the intentions of the French government was the transfer to another post of Robert Boudry, secretary-general of Madagascar, whose sympathetic attitude toward Malagasy aspirations and recent conversion to Marxist doctrines had earned him the enmity of the colonialist diehards. It was Boudry who later asserted that on September 30 de Coppet was instructed by Minister Moutet to do everything possible to prevent the M.D.R.M. from succeeding in being accepted by the Malagasys as a national movement. If this was true, it must have appeared to the French authorities at the time that the best way to restrict the M.D.R.M. to Imerina was to transform the PADESM into an anti-Merina party promoted by the coastal tribes.

The M.D.R.M. leaders rightly interpreted this administration-sponsored reorientation of the PADESM as a strategy designed to undermine the nationalist movement. They placed the same interpretation on the measures of decentralization undertaken in conformity with the French constitution adopted in October, which also perpetuated the division of the electorate into first and second colleges. By the decrees of October 25 and November

9, 1946, Madagascar was divided into five provinces, each with its own administration, assembly, and financial autonomy, and each entitled to send five delegates to a representative assembly to be set up at Tananarive. The setting up of such institutions, and above all the grant of French citizenship to all peoples born in the overseas territories, would have satisfied Ralaimongo and his followers in the 1920s but not his heirs in the late 1940s. The extreme nationalists were so angered by these developments that through the newly constituted labor unions they organized a series of successful strikes, which were carried out by both white-collar and manual workers. (So effectively were the work stoppages enforced, particularly by the unions of transport workers and civil servants, that the government had to yield and improve wages and working conditions as well as try to check the steady rise in living costs.) The moderate nationalists, too, were disillusioned by the new constitution and seriously considered boycotting the elections to the National Assembly in Paris that were slated to be held on November 10, 1946.[16]

Under the new constitution, Madagascar was entitled to elect five deputies (three by the second and two by the first college), five senators to the Conseil de la République, and seven members to the French Union Assembly. After weighing the pros and cons, the M.D.R.M. leadership decided to take part in the elections and to honor its commitment to membership in the French Union—but now it sought the status of associated state for Madagascar, which meant that it would not form an integral part of the French Republic.* This decision reawakened the latent and widespread French fear that the Malagasy nationalists' strategy would simply result in France's being replaced by another imperial power in Madagascar. In an article in the Metropolitan press[17] written by a European in Madagascar, the M.D.R.M. leaders were accused openly of being "agents of the Anglo-Saxons." In partial explanation of such reactions, it should be recalled that the deterioration of the Indochina situation at that period was hardening extremist attitudes on both sides. From the outset the M.D.R.M. had affirmed its solidarity with the Viet Minh's struggle for independence (as well as that of the Indonesians), and during the abortive Fontainebleau conference in July 1946, Raseta had reportedly established contact with Ho Chi-Minh.[18] To understand the atmosphere in which the legislative elections in Madagascar took place, it is necessary to remember that the Haiphong incident, which made the war in Indochina inevitable, also occurred in November 1946.

* Of the four categories into which the October 1946 constitution divided the former French Empire, only the overseas departments and overseas territories were integrated into the one and indivisible French Republic.

According to the M.D.R.M. leaders' charges and complaints, the administration in Madagascar before, during, and after the elections of November 10 was guilty of several offenses—exerting undue pressure on the electorate by providing the PADESM candidates with facilities and by using strong-arm methods against the candidates of the M.D.R.M., deliberately manipulating the electoral rolls, stuffing the ballot boxes, and falsifying the results of the vote to ensure the nationalists' defeat.[19] Yet, despite these alleged official machinations, Raseta and Ravoahangy were reelected for the third time to the French assembly, and their M.D.R.M. running mate, Jacques Rabemananjara, was also victorious. The election of that Betsimisaraka Catholic was especially important to the M.D.R.M., since it served to disprove the contention of its opponents that the M.D.R.M. was simply the party of Protestant Merina. While none of the PADESM candidates was elected, and the M.D.R.M. took 71 per cent of the votes cast, its candidates did not enjoy a uniform degree of popularity. On the west coast Raseta had a close call (21,475 votes to 19,014 for the PADESM candidate, Totelehibe); Ravoahangy won by a landslide in the central circumscription (44,101 votes to 5,718 for Ralaimihotra); and for the newly created east-coast seat, Rabemananjara received more than twice as many votes as his rival (28,227 against 12,619 for Pascal Velonjara).

Decisive as these results seemed to be, the elections did not bring any easing of the tension in Madagascar. On the contrary, the Malagasy delegation in Paris cabled a protest to the governor-general on December 13 against the continuation of arbitrary actions on the part of his administrators under terms of the Cayla decree of 1930. Violence simmered throughout the island and even erupted in different places, so the government thought it prudent to postpone to January 1947 the elections that were to have taken place in December 1946.

Inevitably, the campaign leading to those elections greatly heightened the tension. When they did take place on January 12–19, the M.D.R.M. chalked up another triumph. It won all the seats reserved to the second college in the provincial assemblies of Tananarive and Tamatave, and a majority of those of Fianarantsoa and Tuléar, and only in the Majunga assembly was it reduced to a minority position. This success assured the M.D.R.M.'s control of the newly instituted representative assembly and, through it, assured the election of its candidates to the Conseil de la République and the French Union Assembly. It was at this juncture that the Paris government asked a favor of Ravoahangy and Rabemananjara: to put on the M.D.R.M.-sponsored list for election to the Conseil de la République a European socialist for whom the French cabinet was particularly eager to obtain such a post.[20] For reasons that were never publicized, the M.D.R.M. turned a deaf ear to this plea, showing an intransigence that it paid for later. Perhaps in reprisal for this refusal, the government decreed a change in the voting procedure on the eve of the senatorial elections. Under a new rule requiring the two colleges to vote as one body in the provincial assemblies, the PADESM candidates received the support of the conservative European members of the first college, so three of them were elected to the Conseil de la République.

Chapter four

THE REVOLT OF 1947

In mid-March 1947, Governor-general de Coppet, just after his return from Paris, set March 30 as the date for holding the frequently postponed elections to the Conseil de la République. Three days before those elections were to take place, 20 members of the M.D.R.M. politburo met on March 27 at noon in Tananarive to discuss the party's internal organization and the tension in Madagascar's troubled political relationships.[1] Raseta was still in Paris; hence the meeting was attended by only two of the three Malagasy deputies.

After an animated discussion the decision was reportedly reached to avoid open clashes with the administration. A telegram to this effect was drafted in French by Rabemananjara and translated into Malagasy by Ravoahangy. Bearing the signatures of all the politburo members, including that of the absent Raseta, it was sent to all M.D.R.M. branch leaders. It instructed members of the party to keep "calm and collected in the face of all maneuvers and provocations calculated to create trouble among the Malagasy people and to sabotage the peaceful policies of the M.D.R.M." Later, when the wording of this message was closely scrutinized, spokesmen for the government claimed that it had been written in code and was the signal for starting the revolt, whereas its signatories asserted that it meant simply what it said. The ambiguity in its phraseology may have been due either to a defect in Ravoahangy's translation or to the need then felt to gloss over a fundamental difference in viewpoint between him and Rabemananjara, which later came to light in their mutual recriminations. It is perhaps significant that this famous telegram is not mentioned in the account of the revolt written by Pierre Boiteau, the French Communist Party member most closely associated with the M.D.R.M.

At midnight on March 29, a little over 48 hours after the telegram was sent, surprise attacks were carried out in two widely separated parts of the island at almost the same time. An attack on the military camp at Moramanga was repelled with heavy losses; another, against the arsenal at Diégo-Suarez, failed in its objective of capturing the firearms stored there. Short-lived and equally abortive assaults were made on Tananarive, Fianarantsoa, and Fort-Dauphin. The fact that these widely separated attacks were simultaneous clearly indicated that they had been planned by some central organization. They were so badly prepared and so poorly executed, however, that even the few troops stationed on the island were able to hold the rebels in check. Nevertheless, the failure of these initial outbursts did not mean the end of the revolt, for they set in motion a spontaneous movement in which various malcontents participated.

The malcontents were inspired in part by the same pagan and xenophobic emotions as had dominated the *fahavalo* movement in 1896. Some of the rebel bands, particularly in the forest zone, were led by fanatical sorcerers, who convinced their ignorant followers that the ancestors wanted them to destroy all agents and purveyors of modern change, and gave them amulets guaranteed to turn bullets into harmless drops of water. To this unleashing of primitive violence can be attributed the wholesale murder of officials, doctors, teachers, and the like, regardless of color of skin. Insofar as the re-establishment of French control was concerned, the outbreak of such cruelty and superstition had the advantage of eliminating the Merina elite from the revolt. Some of their younger members, who favored independence for Madagascar at almost any price and who may have been the revolt's initial instigators, were soon shocked into dissociating themselves from it publicly. Yet they sympathized, as did many liberal Frenchmen, with the Malagasys who had legitimate grievances, which they expressed by joining the rebels. Not more than one-sixth of the island's total surface was involved in the revolt, but it is significant that the region most affected was the east coast, where almost all the export crops were produced and where the Malagasys had suffered most from spoliation of land and requisitioning of labor.

From the end of March to the following August the revolt spread through the east coast and forest zone and overflowed into the high plateaus, though it stopped 30 kilometers short of Tananarive. In the process, the rebels gained control of the two coastal railroads, destroyed many bridges, burned plantations, and killed and in some cases tortured white planters and other residents. Early in August, military reinforcements from France and Africa began to arrive in increasing numbers; they included additional North African and Senegalese troops as well as parachutists and Foreign Legion detachments. Slowly the rebel zone was circumscribed and its area reduced. The rebels, lacking food and ammunition, either surrendered or sought refuge in the forest, where the terrain made pursuit and capture difficult. By the end of 1948 the military aspect of the revolt was ended, but the real pacification of Madagascar had been set back by at least half a century, less as a result of the rebellion itself than of the repression that followed it.

The number of those who died as direct or indirect victims of the revolt has been the subject of widely different estimates offered at different times by very different sources. Not surprisingly, the largest figure—over 90,000— was given out by the French communists; the administration, naturally on the defensive, started with the large total of 80,000, but eventually whittled this down to 11,200. Supporters as well as adversaries of the government's post-revolt policy of repression, however, agreed that by far the largest number of victims were noncombatant villagers—men, women, and children who sought refuge from the fighting in the forest, where they died of hunger, exposure, and exhaustion by the thousands. As for the Europeans, at the most several hundred were murdered, mainly isolated planters, and about a thousand soldiers were killed in combat. Forty-three "official" executions of Malagasys were recorded.[2] Even if this number approximated reality, the summary procedure of the law courts that authorized them, the manner in which the sentences were carried out, and the fact that some of the executions took place as late as 1951 all gave the general impression that justice had been manipulated rather than rendered. This feeling was reinforced by the wholesale sentencing to varying periods of imprisonment or forced labor of 5,000 to 6,000 Malagasys, and above all by the trial of the three Malagasy deputies, which became a *cause célèbre*. This trial took place at Tananarive from July 22 to October 4, 1948, under physical and psychological conditions that were highly unfavorable to the accused, even though they were defended by lawyers sent from Paris for this purpose and though the forms prescribed by law were respected.

The whole truth about the revolt of 1947 has never been discovered and probably never will be. No Malagasy, curiously enough, has tried to write its complete history. The reasons for this abstention given to the writers by Malagasys in Madagascar were the lack of sufficient documentation, the impossibility for any Malagasy to view the rebellion as a whole, the tendency of each participant to dwell exclusively on his own role, and the reluctance of all the Malagasys questioned to recall a period that involved great physical and mental suffering for them. The data brought to light at the trial of the three deputies were fragmentary, but they were conclusive in regard to the cruelties of which both sides were guilty during the revolt, as were the police during the repression. Confessions allegedly forced from Malagasy prisoners under torture were retracted in the courtroom, so it became hard for the public to decide where the truth lay. Nevertheless, there was no denying certain facts: the head of the Security Services, Baron, was dismissed from his post because of the brutal methods used by his agents; two major witnesses whose testimony would probably have greatly helped the defense were summarily executed three days before the trial opened; and Maître Stibbe, the Parisian lawyer sent by French left-wing sympathizers for the defense of the M.D.R.M. deputies, was set upon by "unknown assailants" a few hours after his arrival in Tananarive.

The trial at Tananarive outraged many French humanitarians and led to genuine soul-searching on their part as to the causes of the revolt. They agreed that the loss of French prestige during World War II, the massive requisitions of Malagasy crops and labor, the blind aloofness of the administration and abusive harshness of the Réunionese settlers, the contagion of postwar ideas of emancipation, the fiery oratory of the M.D.R.M. leaders in favor of independence, the fanatical incitement by tribal sorcerers—all these had indubitably contributed to the outbreak. But to the Frenchmen well acquainted with the docile, tolerant, and generally apathetic Malagasys, no single agency or even the combination of all the causes cited could wholly account for the violence of either the revolt or its repression. Unhappily, the "problem of Madagascar" as seen in the light of the revolt and its aftermath became a political football used by politicians in the Paris Parliament from 1947 to 1956 to attack the members or policy of rival parties. To be sure, a handful of liberals imbued with a sense of abstract justice worked hard to help improve the situation of the Malagasy victims of the revolt, and to some extent they could take credit for the amnesty that at long last was granted to the Malagasy political prisoners. Nevertheless, for nearly a decade the fate of the Malagasy rebels was periodically used for purposes of purely political attack or defense. Pinpointing responsibility for the revolt became a form of parliamentary sport in Paris in which consecutively or simultaneously the blame was fastened on the M.D.R.M., the local French administration, the resident European community, the Communist or Socialist Party, and individual ministers or governors. The role played in the tragedy of Madagascar by each of the principal accused merits examination.

The Responsibility of the M.D.R.M.

At the trial of the three Malagasy deputies, the government's case rested on the contention that the revolt had been planned by the M.D.R.M. leaders from the time that they first organized their movement. This was also the belief held by the local French community, some of whose more extreme members regarded all Merina as accomplices of the M.D.R.M. and urged such reprisals as executing some thousands of Malagasy hostages.[3] De Coppet was barely able to forestall such excesses, but he did have to yield to the pressure to arrest Ravoahangy and Rabemananjara before their parliamentary immunity was lifted. The two deputies offered to make an appeal to

the people to remain calm, and each of them denied any responsibility for
the revolt, although Ravoahangy later laid some of the blame on Rabemananjara. If their denials are taken literally, Ravoahangy and Rabemananjara probably spoke the truth, but in view of their widespread sources of
information as to what was going on in Madagascar, it is difficult to believe
that they did not have foreknowledge of the revolt. Whether they could
have stopped it if they had tried is another question and one open to
conjecture.

Considering the M.D.R.M.'s triumphs at the polls in 1946–47, which had
given it three deputies in the French National Assembly, control of three
provincial assemblies and of the whole Representative Assembly, and probably at least three seats in the Conseil de la République, there was no reason
for it to have had recourse to violence. Such considerations, however, probably did not carry equal weight with the young firebrands of the PANAMA
and JINA, or with the left-wing members of the M.D.R.M. politburo itself,
such as Tata Max and J. B. Rabeatoandro. Such men wanted total and immediate independence for Madagascar and were too impatient to use the
slower legal processes of attaining sovereignty step by step.

Splits along ideological and methodological lines were not the only divisions that beset the M.D.R.M. leadership from the outset. R. W. Rabemananjara, a founder and historian of the movement, also writes of the conflict
along ethnic lines that sometimes made the Merina-dominated Tananarive
headquarters of the M.D.R.M. refuse to accept the directives of the politburo in Paris.[4] Inevitably there were also differences in viewpoint between
the Young Turk element, who urged that more opportunities be given to
women, laborers, and half-castes, and the "vieux Malgaches," who could
think in power terms only of the traditional social castes. Undoubtedly it
was to avoid irreparable divisions in its ranks that the M.D.R.M. never
formulated a precise doctrine that might have resolved the conflict between
its moderates and its left wing. The overriding concern of the moderates
was to make the M.D.R.M. a truly national movement, and to do so they
based its appeal largely on patriotism. At the M.D.R.M.'s inaugural ban-
quet at Paris, Raseta lifted a glass containing some of Madagascar's "consecrated soil." Candidates for membership in the movement were required
to "swear faithfully to serve with all my soul the sacred cause of the land of
our ancestors, devoting all my life to its well-being, power, freedom, and
independence."

The revolt of 1947 and its aftermath gave special cogency to the question
of how far the M.D.R.M. could justify its claim to being a national and not
just the ethnic or regional movement that its opponents asserted it to be.
Merina certainly predominated among its leaders, but other tribes were also

represented in its top ranks and were especially strong among the *militants de base*. Votes recorded in the four elections that took place between November 1945 and February 1947 showed that the M.D.R.M.'s largest following was in the high plateaus, but it was also strong enough in the west and east coast regions that its candidates were elected in those circumscriptions. To be sure, the Malagasy electorate was then very small—perhaps 260,000 registered voters out of a population of somewhat over 3.5 million—and abstentionism was a characteristic of all the elections of that period. Less than half of the electorate voted in November 1946, and under 25 per cent in January 1947; only 35 per cent of the registered voters cast their ballots in the constitutional referendum of October 13, 1946. Insofar as Malagasy public opinion existed at the time, the M.D.R.M. strove to express the popular will, for it was the first political movement in Madagascar which drew to it a following that cut across tribal and regional lines. Its only clearly formulated goal was self-government leading to national independence— though the means for achieving it were deliberately left vague, as was its economic program, which consisted solely of criticisms of the colonial domination of the economy.

Had the M.D.R.M. been allowed to evolve normally, it might in time have drawn up a socialistic platform and perhaps a neutralist doctrine, but it was dissolved on May 10, 1947, after a life-span of 15 months. Insofar as the M.D.R.M. had a "foreign policy," this consisted of sympathy with other colonial peoples striving for freedom and of proposing the organization of a regional community based on cooperation with its Indian Ocean "neighbors," India and Australia.[5] Curiously enough, some of the rebels in different parts of the island announced that they expected aid for their revolt from the strongest anticolonial power, the United States. Such a belief was perhaps inspired by the sympathy openly expressed for Malagasy nationalist aspirations by some American missionaries on the island. Naturally French communists as well as conservatives publicized such reports so as to prove that American agents had been encouraging the rebels for their own nefarious and imperialistic purpose.[6] No proof has ever been produced, however, to show that the Malagasy rebels received material help from any outside source whatsoever, and further confirmation of this was provided by their almost total lack of modern firearms and ammunition. In fact, the isolation of Madagascar largely accounts for the failure of the revolt and for the effectiveness of its repression. Had the Malagasys received material aid from a powerful neighbor as did the North Vietnamese, or international diplomatic support as in the case of the Indonesians, they might also have fought their way to freedom. Those who defended the harsh methods used during the repression pointed out how ideally Madagascar's terrain was suited to guerrilla operations. They stressed that even if the means used to end the revolt were brutal, they had the virtue of disposing quickly of the threat of a prolonged jungle war such as those that were beginning to devastate Malaya and Burma at that time.

The Role of the Administration and the Parliament

In 1947–48 the French right- and left-wing politicians, in a rare display of solidarity, held the French government in general and de Coppet in particular both directly and indirectly responsible for the revolt in Madagascar. Since Marius Moutet, Minister of Overseas France under four governments, and Marcel de Coppet, twice governor-general of Madagascar, were both socialists and were in office at the time of the revolt, the political enemies of the S.F.I.O. seized this golden opportunity to attack the party in Parliament. Yet it should be noted that the Madagascar revolt was never used as was the war in Indochina as an issue on which to overthrow the government, probably because it aroused so little interest in Paris. It was not until exactly one month after the revolt broke out that debate on Madagascar was placed on the National Assembly's agenda, and then it was postponed for another ten days because the deputies gave priority to a discussion of the shortage of bread in the Paris region.[7] When the debate on the Madagascar revolt finally opened, only 75 deputies were present. Later debates on Madagascar problems aroused greater interest, for they involved the controversial general question of lifting parliamentary immunity, a subject of concern to every member of the National Assembly. In June 1947 the Assembly dispatched a mission of inquiry headed by René Coty to Madagascar, but it remained there only three weeks.

The consensus of the few Frenchmen concerned or knowledgeable about the Madagascar revolt—excepting the communists—placed most of the blame for the uprising on the M.D.R.M. leaders, but some share of responsibility was also allotted to the policy of successive French governments, the personnel of the local administration, and the European community resident in the island.

In Parliament and in the press, French conservatives accused Moutet and de Coppet (and by extension the whole Socialist Party) of promoting legal and institutional reforms in Madagascar that were tantamount to a "policy of abandon." The settlers in Madagascar, the most articulate and reactionary element among such critics, had resented above all the abolition of forced labor. The president of the European planters' association even wrote Moutet in a vain attempt to get him to use force to stop Malagasy workers from deserting the plantations.[8] However, it was de Coppet who, being closer at hand, became the main target for the settlers' attacks. His "supine" reaction to the hostile demonstration that greeted his return to Tananarive on May 19, 1946, recalled to the minds of old-time European residents his wartime indecision between Pétain and de Gaulle. Furthermore, the mistrust which de Coppet inspired became mutual. The governor-general refused to take seriously the stream of dire warnings of trouble ahead sent him by the various settlers' organizations. He either ignored their authors or treated them like "colonialists or slavers." Worse still in the eyes of his settler critics, de Coppet not only tolerated but actually encouraged the seditious actions and speeches of the M.D.R.M. leaders, and after the revolt broke out they were not mollified by his public condemnation of the M.D.R.M. as the party responsible for the uprising. Almost as one man the settlers rose in their wrath to accuse de Coppet of criminal negligence and to demand his immediate recall.[9]

At the other end of the French political spectrum, the communists indicted de Coppet and Moutet as responsible for the revolt—but for very different and quite devious reasons. According to the thesis of the extreme left wing, the Socialist Party had tried vainly to undermine Malagasy support for the M.D.R.M. by dividing up the island into five provincial electoral circumscriptions and backing a rival organization, the PADESM. But because the M.D.R.M. was a widely based national movement, it continued to be victorious at the polls. This failure merely strengthened the government's determination to destroy the M.D.R.M., by force if necessary. Consequently de Coppet, the communists charged, encouraged abuses by the settlers and atrocities by the Senegalese troops stationed on the island so that the goaded Malagasys would revolt and the army thus be given the excuse needed to intervene and liquidate the M.D.R.M.

The exasperation of the Malagasy people, following the refusal of the French government to negotiate [with the M.D.R.M. representatives], as well as the exactions of all kinds through which they were victimized, the example of the Vietnamese people who took up arms in spontaneous reaction to the bombing of Haiphong ... all these explain how the revolt broke out.[10]

The French Communist Party's position in regard to the Madagascar revolt, however, was complicated by the ambiguity of its relations with the M.D.R.M. For years the communist spokesmen in the Parliament wholeheartedly maintained that the M.D.R.M. deputies were innocent and supported every proposal for amnesty of Malagasy political prisoners, thus fully exploiting the revolt and its aftermath for its nuisance value in attacking whatever French government was in power. Neither this support nor the revolt itself altered either the Communist Party's insistence that the M.D.R.M. give up its goal of independence for Madagascar or the latter's refusal to do so. A special appeal was made to the Malagasy nationalists at the Communist Party Congress held at Strasbourg on June 25–29, 1947, two months after the revolt broke out:[11]

In the present state of world affairs, the French Union remains the setting most favorable to the realization of your ambitions, with the aid of the French working class and people. The breakup of the French Union would bring you no more than superficial independence, so stay with us in the French Union.

Neither then nor later, because of that party's refusal to give priority to their number-one objective, did the Malagasy nationalists conform with the directives of the French Communist Party, but they did accept support from the communists on specific issues. The French conservatives never succeeded in proving that the M.D.R.M. was dependent on the Communist Party. De Coppet denied a charge that he had sent a cable in December 1946 claiming documentary evidence of the M.D.R.M. deputies' having accepted funds from the French Communist Party.[12] Among the documents captured during the revolt by the police was a list of victims marked for slaughter by the rebels, and this list included the name of the leading French communist in Madagascar, Pierre Boiteau.[13] This could be variously interpreted as disproving any link between the rebels and the M.D.R.M. or between the M.D.R.M. and the French Communist Party, but either way it undermined some of the conservatives' principal contentions.

The very violence of the attacks on the French government's policy in Madagascar by both the extreme right- and left-wing parties made a midway position seem the reasonable one to be taken by the French public and the parliamentary majority. The traditionally anticolonialist party of Jean Jaurès could not be seriously accused of deliberately planning the Madagascar revolt, but neither could it be wholly exonerated from responsibility. There could be no doubt that the administration in Madagascar had been amply and clearly warned that a revolt was brewing, and no satisfactory explanation was forthcoming as to why it had not taken adequate preventive measures. On March 27 de Coppet had wired his provincial chiefs discounting rumors of an imminent uprising but suggesting the advisability of vigilance. This warning was not transmitted to the isolated administrative posts, nor could it be described in any case as an alert. Rather, it appeared to be de Coppet's way of washing his hands of responsibility: if no revolt ensued, he could not be called an alarmist, but if there was an uprising he could prove he had issued a warning. The best that could be said for de Coppet was that he was honorable and honest but weak and overoptimistic. He had indeed asked for troop and police reinforcements as soon as he reached Tananarive. It was not his fault that because of the Indochina war they had not arrived by the time the revolt broke out, nor could he be held responsible for the atrocities committed by the Senegalese *tirailleurs*. Furthermore, he had stood up to the hysterical *colons'* demands for bloody reprisals against the Malagasys and also refused to place the whole island under a state of siege, though he had been empowered to take exceptional measures by a decree of September 26, 1947.

The Colonial Relationship

From the long debates on Madagascar in the French parliamentary bodies during 1947,[14] it became clear that responsibility for the revolt would have to be spread over time, space, governments, and individuals, and could not be placed on any one minister, governor, or group. Essentially the revolt may well have been the inevitable denouement of the colonial relationship as it had evolved in Madagascar. This is the conclusion reached by O. Mannoni, professor of philosophy and later head of the information service in Madagascar, who is the author of an original analysis of the revolt of 1947.[15] In collaboration with the well-known Parisian psychoanalyst Professor Lacan, Mannoni applied the methods of psychoanalysis to the reciprocal reactions of Malagasys and Europeans living in Madagascar. Mannoni concluded that the Malagasys' greatest psychological need was security. Consequently all the efforts of the Malagasy were directed to establishing ties of permanent dependency on those he believed to be capable of protecting him adequately—first his ancestral deities and then, after the French conquest, the white man. Reared in a feudal society that was both authoritative and paternalistic, the Malagasy transferred his feeling of dependency to the French administration, which he often called his "father and mother." Unlike the Africans also subject to French rule, whose goal at that time was total equality with the people of France, the Malagasys' ideal was a vertical relationship in which they would be assured protection by a solidly entrenched authority.

The European in Madagascar, on the other hand (still according to Mannoni's analysis), had gone there to escape from a European society which in one way or other had proved unsatisfactory to him. In the colonial life he wanted a more powerful position than he had enjoyed at home and in the Malagasy a docile servitor who would never compete with him as an equal. The relationship worked out between them had proved in general mutually satisfactory until it had been drastically altered by the war and by the postwar reforms. That the Malagasys should want to emancipate themselves, as the M.D.R.M. stridently proclaimed, aroused the European's resentment and latent racist fears. The average Malagasy, too, was frightened —but by the prospect of individual responsibility that was implied in the reforms of 1945–46. In a reflex of fear mingled with guilt, the Malagasys turned violently against the Europeans because the latter had abdicated their position as protectors. And to reestablish the patron-client relationship, they accepted the authority of the nationalist leaders of their own people, who asserted that the country must be independent and have its own government, which they would control.

The Search for Scapegoats

Certainly the subtleties and knowledge that went into Mannoni's analysis were beyond the competence and even probably the interest of most Frenchmen concerned with their country's colonial problems. Quite possibly, too, they might not have accepted Mannoni's premises. All were agreed on the prime necessity for restoring order and French authority in Madagascar. And almost everyone also admitted that the policy of favoring the Merina against the coastal tribes, practiced since the turn of the century, had been a grievous error on the part of all the French governments. Other French *mea culpas* acknowledged responsibility for oppressive wartime economic measures and the failure of postwar efforts to alleviate the Malagasys' misery. But something more tangible than past mistakes was needed, and scapegoats for the revolt of 1947 had to be found.

The only ones that seemed to meet most of the general requirements for that role were the Merina upper classes and, by extension, the leaders of the M.D.R.M. All but the communists assumed that the M.D.R.M. was the cover organization for a conspiracy to restore Merina hegemony over Madagascar. The fact that Ravoahangy was a nephew of Queen Ranavalona III and that Raseta was also a Merina, though of a much lower caste, as were Jules Ranaivo and Dr. Raherivelo, lent credence to this assumption. Only the communists had kind words to say about the old Merina monarchy, which they pictured as a progressive national state,[16] but even they did not advocate its integral restitution. That the M.D.R.M. deputies would be found guilty of instigating the revolt was virtually certain when the National Assembly, by a vote of 324 to 195 on June 6, 1947, decided to lift their parliamentary immunity to prosecution, and then refused to transfer the site of their trial from Tananarive to France.

When the prosecuting attorney at Tananarive, after placing Ravoahangy and Rabemananjara under "preventive arrest," asked the National Assembly to lift their parliamentary immunity and also that of Raseta, the deputies found themselves in a serious quandary. No doubt the great majority were convinced of the guilt of their Malagasy colleagues and they therefore complied with the request, but they attempted at the same time both to assure them a fair hearing and to safeguard the principle of parliamentary immunity. A public trial, it was argued, would give the accused the chance to prove the innocence they proclaimed, and the Assembly further specified that the M.D.R.M. deputies should be charged with "an attack on the internal security of the state," a political crime whose maximum penalty would be banishment. Although the Assembly permitted Raseta to be sent back to Madagascar for trial on July 19, 1947, it did give him a hearing on May 6. (This gave Raseta an opportunity to defend himself, which he did surprisingly poorly, and also provided the occasion in the corridors of the Palais Bourbon for an infuriated European colleague from Madagascar—Jules Castellani—to slap him.)

On August 7, 1947, the Conseil de la République lifted the parliamentary immunity for its Malagasy members with more reluctance than had the National Assembly, because their arrest in Madagascar had taken place under even more irregular circumstances. Jules Ranaivo, Justin Bezara, and Dr. Raherivelo had been elected M.D.R.M. candidates to the French Senate on March 30, the day after the revolt broke out. Yet the announcement of their election was delayed for several weeks so as to avoid the whole question of their parliamentary immunity and to give the police time to arrest them in the distant places in Madagascar where they lived. Then, after some hesitation, the Parliament refused a plea to have the trial of the M.D.R.M. leaders and others accused transferred away from Tananarive, where passions were running so high that it was feared the resident Europeans might take justice into their own hands. The National Assembly finally allowed itself to be convinced by the arguments that shifting the site of the trial to France would be an unjustified insult to the magistracy of Madagascar, give heart to the rebels, who would interpret the move as liberating the M.D.R.M. deputies, and risk a kidnaping by irate *colons* of the prisoners on their way from the jail to the airport. A more plausible explanation was the fear of the majority of deputies that the communists would profit unduly from the opportunity for propaganda that transfer of the trial to a court in France would afford them.

Each of the three parliamentary bodies did dispatch a mission of inquiry to Tananarive to question the prisoners and witnesses involved in the revolt, the French Conseil Supérieur de la Magistrature sent Maître Maurice Rolland to report on the judicial aspects of the trials, the Paris press assigned outstanding reporters to cover Tananarive's *cause célèbre,* competent lawyers came from France (including two well-known African barristers, Lamine Gueye and Maître Santos) to defend the accused, and the defense was given over a year to prepare its case. On the other hand, the dismissal of Baron and Vergoz, respectively head of the Security Services and examining magistrate, confirmed other evidence that torture had been used by the authorities to extract confessions. What was even more serious was that the prosecution in December 1947 had been permitted by the new M.R.P. Min-

ister of Overseas France, Paul Coste-Floret, to change the charges against
the principal Malagasy accused to *complicité d'assassinat,* a common-law
crime that could entail capital punishment.

Of the 32 outstanding Malagasys tried by the Criminal Court at Tananarive, six—including Ravoahangy and Raseta—were condemned to death
and Rabemananjara to forced labor for life, on October 4, 1948. Probably
because of his comparative youth and his literary reputation in France and
also because he was not a Merina and had not been involved in the V.V.S.,
as had Raseta and Ravoahangy, Rabemananjara was treated with more
leniency. No mention was made of the fact that he had made propaganda
broadcasts under the Vichy regime during World War II, while Raseta had
been interned at Moramanga for his pro-Allied sentiments and had not
been in Madagascar at the time of the revolt.

Such inconsistencies and irregularities, and even more the severity of the
sentences given out by the civil and military courts in Madagascar between
1947 and 1951, aroused strong suspicions among the French public and in
Parliament that justice had gravely miscarried in the island. In large part,
the failure to insure justice could be traced to the vacillations of the National Assembly. Its members registered only weak protests when they were
presented with irrefutable evidence of inhumane procedures and actual
violations of the law. Even in regard to the circumstances under which
parliamentary immunity could be lifted, the Parliament would take no decisive step to prevent a recurrence of what had happened to the charges
brought against the Malagasy deputies. In fact, it was not until July 31,
1953, two years after a new legislature had been elected, that a law was voted
whereby deputies whose immunity had been lifted could be prosecuted only
under charges specified by the Assembly. During the decade that followed
the revolt in Madagascar, the history of its handling by the French government and Parliament is a sorry one. The deputies usually waited to be faced
with *faits accomplis* either by the Paris government or by the administration
in Madagascar: after balking each time in a halfhearted way, they invariably yielded to politically inspired pressures. In so doing, they encountered
no lively opposition or sustained protests from the men who replaced the
M.D.R.M. deputies and senators as Madagascar's official representatives
in Paris.

Amnesty

It took France 13 years to deal with the problems posed by the 1947 revolt
in Madagascar. Of these the most thorny was that of amnesty for Malagasy
political prisoners, whose number, at its maximum in 1948, approximated
5,750, according to the report of Maître Rolland on April 16, 1948. In De-

cember 1947 the French government voted 500 million C.F.A. francs as a first gesture toward the "relief and rehabilitation of the victims of the revolt,"* but political prisoners and their families were not considered to be "victims." Actually, among the Malagasys most severely "victimized" at this time were the many civil servants who had been suspended or dismissed from their posts for alleged though not always proved involvement in the revolt. The plight of these unfortunates might have been forgotten or wholly ignored had it not been for the prodding of the government through oral and written questions submitted to the Minister of Overseas France by the communist parliamentarians.

Indeed it was largely because of the efforts of the French Communist Party and its sympathizers that the Malagasys most seriously in jeopardy as a result of the revolt—political prisoners and their families—were given material and legal aid. Leaving aside the question of motivation, it was the communist-sponsored Comité de Solidarité de Madagascar (COSOMA) that supplied them with food, clothing, and books, and in some cases with French lawyers for their defense. In the French Parliament, communist spokesmen used the annual budget debates as an opportunity to keep alive the question of amnesty and the whole *affaire de Madagascar*. Through the efforts of the C.G.T. labor unions and of liberal intellectuals, the communists gradually mobilized French public opinion in favor of the imprisoned M.D.R.M. deputies by organizing mass meetings and drawing up petitions in their behalf. In the mid-1950s French Catholic laymen and clergy added the weight of their influence to such appeals.

For several years after the revolt, the Communist Party seemed to be waging a hopeless battle in the face of public indifference or the widespread conviction that the M.D.R.M. deputies were indeed responsible for the horrors of the 1947 uprising. But time was performing its task of healing, and the sense of guilt left by the Tananarive trial was festering in the French liberal conscience. On July 15, 1949, one week after the Cour de Cassation rejected the appeal for clemency submitted by the six Malagasys sentenced to death by the Tananarive Criminal Court, President Vincent Auriol was induced to commute their punishment to life imprisonment in a fortified place. The communists and their front organizations continued to apply pressure, and in September 1950 these six Malagasys were transferred from Madagascar to a fortress in Corsica. In 1951 the French extreme left cited the death sentences, which continued to be passed by some military courts

---

* Disagreement over their respective shares of the financial responsibility for the damage incurred during the revolt and repression was not settled until 1954, when the Metropolitan government agreed to pay 80 per cent of the claims and the territorial budget was charged with the remaining 20 per cent.

in Madagascar, as evidence of the administration's continuing campaign of "staggered intimidation," and its spokesmen in the National Assembly pressed for an amnesty or a drastic revision of the court verdicts of 1947–48.[17] No further progress was made in this domain, however, until 1955—a long period of inaction for which the French deputies were for once not to blame.

In February 1953 a group of French socialists submitted a proposal to the National Assembly that would have extended to all overseas political prisoners the amnesty which it decreed for those imprisoned for wartime collaboration in France. Since 1950, political prisoners had been released from Madagascar's 98 jails at the rate of about 100 a month, with the result that by that time only some 1,600 were still incarcerated.[18] To the general surprise of the assembly and to the consternation of some of his African colleagues, the Malagasy M.R.P. deputy, Jonah Ranaivo, disapproved of the application of the socialists' draft law to his compatriots. He claimed that such a measure, though theoretically desirable, would in application take the Malagasys wholly by surprise, and he successfully torpedoed its application to Madagascar by getting the relevant clause referred back to committee. Although the next year Ranaivo came up with an amnesty measure of his own, this was not taken very seriously as reflecting a profound change in his views, but rather as being prompted by the imminence of elections in Madagascar. The principal relevant change that was taking place that year and the next, 1954–55, was the advent to power in France of more liberal governments led successively by Pierre Mendès-France and Edgar Faure.

In June 1955 the amnesty question for Madagascar was revived as the result of a conclusively favorable sampling of public opinion conducted on that island by a committee headed by Professor Massignon. However, the new proposal submitted to the National Assembly that month concerned only political prisoners who had been condemned to less than 15 years' imprisonment. The communists promptly protested that such a measure would do nothing to alleviate the fate of the three M.D.R.M. deputies and those Malagasys who had also been condemned to serve life terms in jail. While they failed to broaden the amnesty measure, the pressure exerted largely by the communists did result in September 1955 in the release of the three deputies from the Corsican fortress and their transfer to restricted residence in France. (Raseta remained in the Cannes region, Ravoahangy practiced medicine at Toulouse, and Rabemananjara rejoined his literary circle in the Présence Africaine group at Paris.)

A last-ditch stand against even this measure of clemency was made again by a Malagasy deputy—not Jonah Ranaivo this time, but Pascal Velonjara. Elected in June 1951 to the National Assembly on the PADESM ticket, Velonjara made his maiden speech to that body four years later on the amnesty issue. Claiming that such an amnesty was opposed by a majority of Malagasys, he strongly urged on July 13, 1955, that this draft law be defeated. The Guinean deputy, Barry Diawadou, and the French liberal Catholic, Dr. Louis Aujoulat, both expressed shocked surprise and in barely veiled terms accused Velonjara of anti-Merina racial discrimination.

The amnesty law passed its final reading on March 24, 1956, and by the end of that year the state of siege was lifted from the last areas of Madagascar to which it had been applied for the preceding nine years. Two months later the *loi-cadre** also was enacted by the French Parliament, and this heralded a period of greater autonomy in all the overseas countries. On May 18, 1957, all political prisoners were freed, but not all of the Malagasys were permitted to return to their homes or to run for elective office in the near future. For the most famous among them, the three M.D.R.M. deputies, the question of their return to Madagascar and political activity there had by that time become complicated by party developments on the island.† It was not until mid-1960, on the eve of the celebration of Madagascar's independence, that they set foot once again in their native land.

* See pp. 81 *et seq.*
† See pp. 116–19.

Chapter five

ELECTIONS AND THE LOI-CADRE

It was not until almost a year after the revolt broke out that the French government yielded to the clamor of the Madagascar *colons* and replaced Marcel de Coppet by a new governor-general. This was Pierre de Chévigné (February 1948–February 1950), a professional army officer without colonial experience but with a distinguished record in the Free French forces during World War II. De Chévigné was made of sterner stuff than his predecessor, and soon made it clear that in his person France intended to remain ruler of Madagascar. He also pleased his compatriots in the island by removing many of the official economic controls that still regulated prices, quotas, and rationing. In fairness to his policy it should also be noted that he considerably increased local government institutions as well as educational facilities for the Malagasys. De Chévigné's outstanding success lay in his reestablishment of law and order and in the revival of Madagascar's economy, but he failed signally to restore the "climate of confidence" between the Malagasy and European communities, which had been shattered by the revolt and the repression.

At the very outset of his administration, it looked briefly as if de Chévigné might establish an understanding with the moderate Malagasy nationalists, for in his first speech to the Representative Assembly on March 31, 1948, he said: "France knows and understands that the Malagasy people want to preserve their own soul and character, and also that they want to follow a peaceful and straight path by the side of France. It is France alone that can lead the Malagasy to the goal to which they quite legitimately aspire—that of a state freely associated with all other members of the great community of the French Union." When the governor-general realized that his words had been taken to mean that the French government now agreed in principle to Madagascar's autonomy in a federal French Union, he hastily called a press conference to refute such an interpretation. A year later, when he opened the ordinary session of the representative assembly for 1949, he spelled out clearly just how far the Malagasys could expect to go so long as he remained at the helm of the government:[1]

I promise the young men of this country that they will not be disappointed in the future if they adopt a realistic and not a visionary viewpoint. They will live better than their ancestors, they will see their country develop, and they will have an increased share of political responsibility. But they must beware of trying to go too fast and of ignoring social realities. Without the presence of France they would simply plunge their country into the anarchy and internal strife that ravaged it late in the nineteenth century.

Nine months before he uttered these words of cold comfort, de Chévigné had shown his true character. He had ordered the execution of "General" Samuel Rakotondrabe* and countenanced the strong-arm methods used not only against Malagasy prisoners accused of participating in the revolt but against some of the civilian population during the "pacification." In particular, he would tolerate no attempt to reconstitute the M.D.R.M. either by its local militants, who had gone underground, or by the communists, who he believed had been assigned to Madagascar for this purpose by the French Communist Party. To implement this policy, de Chévigné did not hesitate to use his authority to manipulate the elections of December 1948 and to expel from Madagascar four communist members of the French Union Assembly.

Although the French Union Assembly did not hold its first session until December 1947 or welcome its first members from Madagascar until April 1949, that parliamentary body from the outset became deeply involved in Malagasy problems. It frequently debated the causes of the revolt, the fate of the M.D.R.M. prisoners, and the course of Madagascar's elections; and the first mission it ever sent to any overseas territory went to Madagascar in November 1948. The French Union Assembly's composition and competence naturally predisposed it to be deeply concerned with this troubled dependency, but further impulse was provided by the turbulent activities of four of its members there, all Communist Party specialists on colonial questions. Raymond Barbé, the Party's spokesman in the Assembly, went only briefly to Madagascar in December 1949, but he remained there long enough to stir up trouble, as he had done in French Equatorial Africa and Réunion Island, by his incendiary speeches. His fellow assemblymen, however, refused the plea made by Tananarive's prosecuting attorney to lift Barbé's parliamentary immunity,[2] although they had done so in regard to two other communist members, Raymond Lombardo and Pierre Boiteau. Lombardo had been born in Madagascar in 1914 and had worked there

* See p. 57.

as an engineer in the meteorological service before being chosen in November 1947 by the Communist Party to sit in the French Union Assembly. As a side activity, Lombardo edited a bilingual newspaper in Tananarive called *Fraternité-Fihavanana,* in which he kept up a steady stream of attacks on the administration, army, and magistracy of Madagascar. Because he was a French citizen and a parliamentarian, Lombardo got away with his campaign of denigration throughout the trial of the M.D.R.M. deputies, but in November 1948 he went a step too far. In his newspaper's issue of November 25 he allegedly accused the French authorities of subjecting schoolchildren to harmful inoculations (instead of antimalarial ones), with the aim of destroying the younger generation of Malagasys. After a stormy debate on December 30, 1948, in which the assemblymen cast doubts on the legality of de Chévigné's expulsion of Lombardo and also on the accuracy of the official translation of the offending article, they agreed to lift Lombardo's parliamentary immunity on condition that he be prosecuted in France. By January 1949, Lombardo's place in Madagascar had been taken by Pierre Boiteau (who had been head of Tananarive's botanical garden since 1946), with the periodic assistance of another French communist assemblyman, Jacques Arnault. By invoking local quarantine regulations, de Chévigné effectively restricted Arnault's propaganda tours in Madagascar during the spring of 1949.[3] On November 1 of that year he arrested Pierre Boiteau, who had been so indiscreet as to get into a fistfight with a policeman at the Tananarive airport, and the French Union Assembly reluctantly agreed on October 26, 1950, to lift Boiteau's parliamentary immunity.

De Chévigné's high-handed actions—and the Parliament's toleration of them—stemmed from the widespread conviction that the communist French Union assemblymen were covertly using their position to revive the M.D.R.M. in Madagascar. Lombardo and Boiteau had organized the Groupe d'Etudes Communistes at Tananarive in February 1946 before becoming members of the French Union Assembly. Though that study group reportedly had only two Malagasy members, it had numerous contacts with the various nationalist organizations. Consequently, when the M.D.R.M. was dissolved and many of its members arrested in 1947–48, the Communist Party was in a good position to provide substitute leadership. In this way the program of the M.D.R.M.—which was the basis of its strength—survived that movement's dissolution, for all of the nationalist parties that proliferated in the mid-1950s owed their major inspiration to M.D.R.M. doctrines. Beginning in July 1947 a few by-elections had been held to replace some of the M.D.R.M. provincial assemblymen who had been imprisoned. But it was the election of Madagascar's first French Union assemblymen on December 20 and of new Councilors of the Republic on December 19 that would disclose, albeit indirectly and only partially, how much hold the M.D.R.M. still retained on the Malagasy population.

De Chévigné's first concern was to eliminate from the provincial assemblies—the basic electorate for the December 1948 elections—as many M.D.R.M. members as possible. So he applied pressure to cause them to resign, apparently of their own free will. In reaction to this move there first came to public view a young bank employee of Tananarive, a Merina with Chinese blood named Stanislas Rakotonirina, M.D.R.M. assemblyman in the provincial assembly of Tananarive and future stormy petrel of Malagasy politics. Rakotonirina, after being arrested and tortured by the police, was formally acquitted of participation in the revolt just in time to become a candidate for the elections in December 1948. According to the petition that he and other M.D.R.M. assemblymen of Tananarive submitted to the French Union Assembly mission of inquiry in November 1948, they had been summoned only a few days before to a meeting by Louis Labrousse, French chairman of the permanent commission of the Representative Assembly.[4] Rakotonirina maintained, and Labrousse later denied, that this meeting had been called on the initiative of de Chévigné for the purpose of persuading members of the second college not to run for election either to the French Union Assembly or to the Conseil de la République.* André Blanchet, the capable and experienced reporter of *Le Monde,* who was in Tananarive at the time, confirmed the general testimony if not the details given by Rakotonirina. Each of the M.D.R.M. councilors, he wrote on November 4, 1948, was called individually before the head of the Sûreté to answer to fabricated charges accusing them of trafficking in medicines, running black-market ventures, and the like. "So much pettiness sickens me," he added, "but I am even more alarmed by the stupidity of such a policy."

On the grounds that only 52 of the total of 92 provincial assemblymen of the second college could take part in the elections, as compared with all 48 members of the first college, the French Union Assembly mission urged the administration to postpone the elections, but de Chévigné ignored their advice.† Despite the powerlessness or unwillingness of a large proportion

* According to Rakotonirina, Labrousse said to him: "Be careful, for you are dealing with a very authoritarian man who won't hesitate to carry out his threats . . . and who is warning you [to desist] through me."
† The first college, composed of R.P.F. (Rassemblement du Peuple Français) members, elected to the Conseil de la République Daniel Serrure, a merchant, and A. Liotard, a local businessman. Three of the French Union assemblymen elected were Frenchmen—Paul Gentet, a planter; Paul Longuet, an agricultural engineer; and Maurice Charlier, a businessman—and four were Malagasys. The Malagasys were Voca, a Sakalava; Ramampy, a Betsileo; Randretsa, a Merina; and Rasafiala, who died very shortly after the election.

of the electorate to express its will, the results of the December 1948 elections
were cited by the conservatives as a victory for the PADESM and a defeat
for the M.D.R.M. in general and the Merina in particular.*

Time was to show that such a conclusion was little more than wishful
thinking, and to qualified observers it was already clear that the repression
and continued application of martial law to many parts of the island made
the resumption of any normal political life still impossible. Dissolution of
the M.D.R.M. was followed by disintegration of the PADESM, the P.D.M.,
and the M.S.M. (Mouvement Social Malgache), mainly because the cohesion prompted by the existence of a strong nationalist organization to
which they had all been opposed was now lacking. Moreover, the mass of
Malagasys now associated elections with dire consequences—the frequent
electoral consultations from November 1945 to February 1947 had led to
the revolt—and were in so numb an emotional state that they did not care
to exercise their franchise. Much the same attitude of indifference prevailed
among the European electorate, especially the transient element of civil
servants and army personnel who lived in Tananarive, but this was less
true of the Frenchmen who lived in the rural areas or provincial towns.

The administration's pressures and manipulations could determine who
would be the candidates for any given election, and its results, but the local
authorities could not create confidence in either the so-called victors or the
institutions to which they were pronounced elected. A major stumbling
block to any real improvement in the existing situation was the mutual
fear and distrust that continued to characterize Franco-Malagasy relations.
Many Europeans could find explanations if not excuses for the revolt, and
they were willing to forget if not to forgive provided the Malagasys would
"take the first step toward reestablishing a loyal collaboration."[5]

The Malagasys, for their part, particularly the Merina elite, were not concerned in reaching an "understanding" with the Europeans, and would
collaborate with them only insofar as circumstances compelled them to.
The failure of the revolt had taught the Malagasys the futility of an uprising and had also given many of them a repugnance to violence, but that
did not mean that they were permanently reconciled to the "French presence." In reading the nationalist Malagasy press of this period, one can see
plainly between the cautiously written lines the attraction that the *mystique*
of independence still held for both the writers and their clientele. The
fundamental divergence in their outlooks was shown clearly in July 1949
by the European and Malagasy reactions to the lightening of sentence
granted by the President of the French Republic to the six Malagasys con-

* Of the 140 assemblymen, 113 actually voted. See *Marchés Coloniaux,* Jan. 22, 1949.

demned to death by the Tananarive court. The conservative French-language newspaper *Tana-Journal* expressed shock at this "insult to the memory of the victims of the revolt," and the *Avenir de Madagascar* was sure that the President's ill-advised clemency would be interpreted by the Malagasys as a "sign of weakness that will alienate our loyal friends and increase the arrogance of our enemies."[6] Naturally the Malagasy-language press was filled with rejoicing, and it also contained long extracts from the Metropolitan extreme-left papers, which gave credit for this success to the "progressive popular forces" and their spokesmen. Thus the French Communist Party scored a notable success among the Malagasy nationalists.

Commutation of the three deputies' death sentences largely accounted for the atmosphere of instability and uncertainty that prevailed in Tananarive during the late summer and autumn of 1949. This climate gave rise to rumors to the effect that de Chévigné was about to resign, that all the verdicts of the Tananarive court concerning the revolt were going to be revised, and that elections would soon be held to choose successors to the three M.D.R.M. deputies in the National Assembly. None of those rumored events took place, although elections were held toward the end of the year in all the provinces except Fianarantsoa for the partial renewal of their assemblies. Such elections were of only secondary importance and abstentionism continued to be an outstanding characteristic. The provincial assemblies had few powers and their members did not fully exercise those they possessed, in some cases leaving major decisions to their permanent commissions. Nevertheless, their composition provided almost the only clue to the evolution of Malagasy public opinion during this period. As might be expected, virtually all the coastal populations that voted supported the pro-French candidates running on the PADESM ticket, whereas the situation in Tananarive was different and more complicated. In the capital city itself the two competitors were "autonomists" but neither one got widespread support, for the Parti Démocratique Malgache candidate, by 800 to 500 votes, nosed out his communist rival. In the rural areas and suburbs the electorate's apathy was even more pronounced, and nonnationalist candidates received such votes as were cast. It was not in such elections but through the medium of labor, youth, and church organizations that "political" activity was evident. The indirect approach and extremism generally characteristic of this phenomenon was well exemplified by the way in which the Comité de Solidarité de Madagascar (COSOMA) was founded and evolved.*

In February 1950 it was announced that de Chévigné would be replaced

---

* See p. 67. On August 31, 1950, this organization began publishing a journal called *Fifanampiana (Solidarity)*.

by Robert Bargues. The new governor-general was a colonial inspector
with long experience not only in French Negro Africa but in the Antilles
and Indochina. He remained in Madagascar until October 1954, a term of
duty more than twice as long as that of his two predecessors. If de Chévigné
should be credited with having restored order in the island and confidence
among its *colons*, Bargues could justly claim to have bound up the wounds
left by the revolt, markedly improved Madagascar's economy, and increased
somewhat the Malagasys' participation in the conduct of local government.
While it cannot be said that Madagascar made any great political strides
during Bargues's incumbency, there was evidence to show that its population had now reached the stage of political convalescence. A resolution
passed by the Representative Assembly expressed the wish of its members to
be consulted on the "main problems" of Madagascar, and it was decided in
its April 1950 session to give priority on its agenda to the subjects that its
members, and no longer the administration, deemed to be the most urgent.*
The much-publicized declaration by Madagascar's Catholic bishops on
December 23, 1953, regarding the legitimacy of the Malagasys' aspiration
to independence revived nationalist sentiment and greatly promoted its
growth.†

During Bargues's comparatively long tenure of office, two French cabi-
net ministers and the president of the French Union Assembly visited
Madagascar, and seven elections were held—in complete calm. A moderately
worded nationalist petition was handed to François Mitterand, Minister of
Overseas France, when he visited French outposts in the Indian Ocean in
December 1950–January 1951. Because this petition raised the question of
Madagascar's future status, Mitterand announced unequivocally to the
Tananarive Chamber of Commerce that his government felt it would be
premature to accede to the communist-sponsored proposal that Madagascar become an Associated State in the French Union.[7] In April 1951 the
Overseas Commission of the National Assembly voted to maintain the
dual college in Madagascar though it favored the single electoral college
for French West Africa. Although the size of Madagascar's electorate was
greatly enlarged, from about 256,930 to 885,000, for the legislative elections
of June 1951, the number of the island's parliamentarians and provincial
assemblymen was not increased.‡ Clearly the 1947 revolt had undermined

* On August 30, 1950, the assembly voted to raise the pay of Madagascar's parliamentarians in
Paris to 400,000 C.F.A. francs a year after they learned, to their surprise, that the African territories were paying their representatives salaries higher than those paid by Madagascar.
† See p. 201.
‡ Madagascar still had five deputies in the National Assembly, of whom three were elected by
the second college. All the provincial assemblies had 12 members of the first college and 18 of
the second college. Later, on March 30, 1952, Tuléar's assembly was enlarged, and thereafter it
had 14 members of the second and 21 members of the first college.

the confidence of French liberals and even the African deputies and made them hesitate to grant the Malagasys concessions they approved for Negro Africans.[8] In part, one should note, this reticence stemmed from the failure of Madagascar's parliamentarians to press their country's case. The deputies elected to the National Assembly on June 17, 1951, and the French Union assemblymen chosen on October 10, 1953, were—with few exceptions—nonentities. Among the exceptions should be mentioned Albert Sylla, a Betsimisaraka doctor from Tamatave, and Roger Duveau, a French lawyer who had begun his career in Madagascar as a planter and trader. Both men eventually became promoters of liberal and nationalistic legislation for Madagascar. In June 1954 Duveau was named Secretary for Overseas France in the Mendès-France government. This was the first time a representative from Madagascar entered the French cabinet, and Duveau used his post to put forward the amnesty proposal that became law on March 24, 1956. In 1951, however, Duveau strongly opposed the single electoral college for Madagascar, and as recently as 1955 Sylla came out against an amnesty for the three M.D.R.M. deputies despite the fact that he favored it for other Malagasy political prisoners.

Although the results of the June 1951 elections gave little apparent indication of the revival of nationalism, soon to come, they were in two respects significant straws in the wind. If no nationalist candidates were elected, at least an arch-conservative like Jules Castellani was not returned to the National Assembly, and if Stanislas Rakotonirina was defeated he at any rate had been permitted to run for election, and the following year he won a seat in the Tananarive provincial assembly. Most promising of all was the markedly larger Malagasy participation in the vote, apparently the result of the virtual tripling of the electorate, even though abstentionism continued to be the rule among electors of the first college.

In the March 30, 1952, elections for the provincial assemblies, both of the foregoing trends were carried over.[9] The indifference of the first college could still be attributed to the feelings of transiency and political impotency of almost all of the white population, but now also to Bargues's refusal to permit the development in Madagascar of French political parties. "We must avoid giving the Malagasys the spectacle of our political quarrels and a taste for them," he said.* The increased interest on the part of the Malagasys in exercising their franchise was shown by an 80 per cent participation of the registered voters for the second college. Late in 1951 a revision of the

---

* *Marchés Coloniaux*, April 19, 1952. So successful was this policy that the R.P.F. never succeeded in gaining more than a toehold in Madagascar. Indeed, when the representative assembly decided by the close vote of 12 to 11 in its meeting of March 30, 1953, to invite General de Gaulle to visit Madagascar, it was clearly specified that he was being invited as the Liberator of France and not as the head of a political party.

island's electoral circumscriptions to reflect changes in population distribution decreased the vote of the rural element and increased that of the town
dwellers. Furthermore, in creating six new mixed communes, Bargues had
already encouraged the urban populations to take greater interest in public
affairs as well as to form the habit of voting. Logically these developments
should have swelled the support given to nationalist candidates, whose main
following came from the urban elite, and in effect that is what happened in
the capital city, where former M.D.R.M. leaders were elected. But elsewhere,
moderate candidates carried the day, and though some election results were
questionably valid, a large proportion of former assemblymen were reelected. This apparent rejection of extremism and of any politicization of
Madagascar's elective bodies was regarded as vindicating Bargues's policies.

When Bargues left Madagascar in the fall of 1954, he could look back with
satisfaction on his tenure of office there. He had placed the main accent on
economic progress, and there was undeniably a close link between the Malagasys' greater prosperity and their political moderation and calm over the
past four years. Bargues also had given the population greater opportunities
for self-expression by judiciously enlarging municipal and rural councils
and by opening a few of the higher administrative posts to Malagasy civil
servants. Although Tananarive had its moments of agitation, they seemingly did not trouble the placidity of provincial life, and by no means all of
the institutional reforms promised by Bargues actually materialized.[10] Even
the French members of the Representative Assembly began to complain
about the government's ignoring of the resolutions it passed and about
Bargues's failure to keep assemblymen properly informed as to why without notification he withdrew items from the session's agenda or added
them.[11] Although the assembly elected in March 1952 was not quite so much
of a rubber-stamp body as its predecessor, largely because of the lively opposition provided by Stanislas Rakotonirina, it was certainly dominated by
its first-college members and continued to leave major decisions to the government and to its permanent commission.

In contrast to the African territorial assemblies of that period, Madagascar's assembly almost never heckled and rarely opposed the administration,
nor did it use the device of sending out "missions of inquiry," as the African
assemblies did, to thwart or embarrass government policies and officials. A
resolution passed on April 1, 1954, reflects the general modesty of the Madagascar assembly's aims: "Considering the need felt by assemblymen for
more detailed information on the problems of the island as a whole, the
Representative Assembly asks that a tour of its members be organized so
that they can acquire firsthand knowledge of the different economic zones
of Madagascar."

An analysis of the subjects debated by the assembly from 1952 to 1955 shows its preoccupation with socioeconomic matters and its shunning of political subjects. Very seldom did the assemblymen refer to the revolt of 1947, and then only to reiterate their opposition to Madagascar's paying for repair of the damage from its own resources. They evinced a marked interest in the status of civil servants, the development of educational facilities, the problems attendant on the growth of alcoholism and taxation, and projects for road building and the mining of Sakoa's coal*—in that order of importance. They seemed only slightly interested in land concessions, municipal organization, and hunting licenses—all subjects that were passionately debated in the African assemblies. Regionalism was conspicuous in many of the debates in the Madagascar assembly, especially during the budget sessions, when the coastal representatives often complained that the taxes paid by the peripheral populations benefited only those of Tananarive. In particular, the coastal assemblymen stressed the numerical predominance of Merina among the students of Tananarive's lycées and the patients treated in its hospitals. Virtually the only subject on which they displayed an island-wide outlook was that of Malagasy civil servants. In their eagerness to have them treated on a par with French functionaries, the Malagasy assemblymen displayed a solidarity conspicuously absent from their attitude toward other subjects that concerned only their fellow countrymen.

Regional and ethnic differences continued to color all the discussions of the burning question of the early and middle 1950s—that of an amnesty for the political prisoners of the 1947 revolt. The Frenchmen who joined the Malagasy nationalists in pressing for immediate and unlimited amnesty were impatient and annoyed with the *côtiers* who hesitated to advocate freedom for the top M.D.R.M. leaders. Obviously the *côtiers* did not want to hasten the end of the existing artificial political situation, in which they were the main beneficiaries of a calm that was maintained by the avoidance of divisive issues and the quarantining of aggressive Merina nationalists. That such a situation bred laziness and irresponsibility and perpetuated political immaturity was grasped by a few far-sighted leaders of the coastal populations such as Philibert Tsiranana.

Of Tsimihety peasant origin, Tsiranana was one of the very few non-Merina Malagasys who graduated from the Ecole Le Myre de Vilers at Tananarive.† During the revolt and repression, he had the good fortune to be studying at the University of Montpellier in France, and it was not until 1952—two years after he returned to teach in Madagascar—that he entered politics. In April 1952, a month after he had won a seat in the Majunga provincial assembly, Tsiranana was elected to the Representative Assembly,

---

* See pp. 410–11.
† This school played the same role in training leaders in Madagascar that the William Ponty School played in French West Africa.

where he was not long in making his mark. There he became the first Malagasy member to complain publicly of the administration's strategy in getting important questions referred to the permanent commission, whose small and predominantly European membership made it easier to exert pressure and virtually to assure acquiescence. There, too, he took issue with his fellow countrymen who through indolence or fear of making a decision excused themselves from attending most assembly sessions. "The assembly has been in session barely two weeks," he pointed out on one memorable occasion (October 28, 1954), "yet over half of its members have already left for home and the agenda is far from exhausted." Tsiranana's energy, high degree of education, and common-sense approach to politics made him stand out over other *côtier* candidates for election to the French National Assembly on January 2, 1956, when he received about two-thirds of the votes cast in the third circumscription. But to some extent he owed his rapid political success also to a concatenation of circumstances that had nothing to do with his personal qualifications for leadership.

Late in 1954, André Soucadaux, a career colonial administrator with a highly successful record as governor in French Negro Africa, succeeded Bargues as governor-general of Madagascar. He also happened to be a strongly secular-minded socialist who, soon after he arrived at Tananarive, became convinced that he must alter what he considered to be an undesirable political situation in the island. He became alarmed by the organizational strength of the Catholic Church in Madagascar when, a few days after he took office, some 20,000 Catholic Malagasys paraded in front of his residence in commemoration of a local church anniversary. Nor could he approve of the influence that the Protestant Church maintained over the Merina upper classes, although the nationalism it now engendered was less nostalgic than formerly for the past glories of the monarchy and was more concerned with present and future practical problems. The extreme form of nationalism was currently being cultivated by the communists, under cover of the COSOMA, the C.G.T. unions, and such student movements as the Parti de l'Union du Peuple Malgache (P.U.P.M.).* By that time, the old parties such as the PADESM and the P.D.M. were either dead or moribund, and obviously there could be no question of reviving the M.D.R.M., even under another name. The only party born in Madagascar since the revolt was the Union des Indépendants (U.I.), formed in 1953 by the troublesome Stanislas Rakotonirina with the help of the Catholic mission of Tananarive, making it thus doubly unpalatable to the new governor-general. The municipal-reorganization bill, which had finally passed the French Parliament on November 15, 1955, would introduce elections under the

* See pp. 222–23.

single college in Madagascar within the foreseeable future, but not in time to affect the legislative elections of January 2, 1956. In fact, the scheduling of elections to the National Assembly for that date followed so closely after the sudden fall of the Faure government on November 29, 1955, that there was little time for any electoral campaign, let alone for organizing a new party. So fluid was the political situation in Madagascar that inevitably the January 1956 elections produced some unexpected results.

Such surprises, however, were confined to the votes of the second college, for as usual the electorate of the first college largely abstained from voting and chose undistinguished Frenchmen to represent it in the National Assembly.* It was the second college, not the first college, of the third circumscription that reelected the French deputy Roger Duveau—an unmistakable evidence of the Malagasys' gratitude for his help in keeping alive the amnesty question in the National Assembly. Still another unexpected development was the 2-to-1 victory of a Betsileo, Rakotovelo, over the Merina Stanislas Rakotonirina, in the first circumscription, which occurred despite the support given the latter by Catholic nationalists and by the communists. The protests filed against the election of both Rakotovelo and Tsiranana were so similar in presentation and phraseology that they obviously emanated from the same sources—identified later in the National Assembly as the COSOMA, the C.G.T. trade unions, the P.U.P.M., and the manager of the newspaper *Imongo Vao Vao*.[12] No doubt this common (and communist) origin was a major reason for the assembly's decision to validate the elections of Rakotovelo and Tsiranana.

The installation of a socialist government in France as a result of the January 1956 elections decisively influenced the political evolution of Madagascar in two ways. In respect to one of these influences—that of the *loi-cadre* of June 23, 1956—all of the French dependencies were profoundly affected by its passage. But as applied to Madagascar this law had consequences very different from those resulting from its application to Negro Africa. This differentiation did not occur by chance, for in Madagascar its motivation was to undermine Merina domination of the island. This was also the main motive behind the second influence mentioned above—the setting up of a local socialist party, which was established under Soucadaux's auspices and under the leadership of Philibert Tsiranana.

The Loi-Cadre of June 23, 1956

The *loi-cadre* which the Mollet government succeeded in pushing through the Parliament had been long in the drafting, and it embodied a number of the concepts held by France's three liberal governments over the preceding

* These were Louis Bruelle and André Sanglier.

two years concerning the way in which the French dependencies should evolve politically. In its final form, as it left the hands of Ministers Gaston Defferre and Félix Houphouët-Boigny, the *loi-cadre* was tailored primarily for French Negro Africa. Even though it did not meet with wholehearted African approval, it did satisfy the Africans' aspirations insofar as it gave them their first share in the executive power and eliminated the two cumbersome and top-heavy governments-general. To the Africans, in early 1956, the institution of universal adult suffrage and a single electoral college and, above all, a government council that could become an embryo ministerial cabinet were the chief benefits they expected from the *loi-cadre,* and only a minority among them was concerned with the unfortunate effects of "balkanizing" Negro Africa. To the Malagasys, on the other hand, application of the relevant decentralizing provisions of the *loi-cadre* to Madagascar was the key issue. The elite, particularly in the high plateaus, rightly discerned behind the official stress placed on the virtues of decentralization the government's intention of demoting the Merina. Whereas in Negro Africa territorial autonomy was to be established at the expense of the federal government, the Parliament had no wish to weaken the administrative structure of each territory. Quite the contrary. In Madagascar, on the other hand, in order to deprive the central government at Tananarive of much of its authority, the Parliament strengthened the powers of the provinces.

In seeking the reasons why successive French governments and Parliaments continued to treat Madagascar differently from the African dependencies, the student must go back as far as the 1947 revolt and perhaps earlier. To the French this revolt seemed to confirm what had been indicated by the V.V.S. and by the riots of May 19, 1929: that the Merina would not rest until they had ousted France from Madagascar and reasserted their hegemony over the island. Since the suppression of the revolt, the Merina had effectively been barred from open political activities and the *côtiers* had been given more educational facilities and job opportunities. Now the *loi-cadre* provided the legal framework for institutionalizing and perpetuating this artificial bolstering of the *côtiers* and holding down of the Merina. Ironically enough, the new administrative structure set up under the *loi-cadre* proved in time to be no more satisfactory to the *côtiers* than it was to the Merina.

While the *loi-cadre* was still in the drafting stage and before its provisions were known, the rumor that France was going to give Madagascar a new statute raised high hopes among the Malagasys, as well as fears lest they be treated less liberally than the Africans. By mid-March 1956, it was clear that there was no question of abrogating the annexation law of 1896 or of granting an immediate and total amnesty to all political prisoners, which were the issues of major concern to the Merina elite. Soon they were further disillusioned to learn that the government intended not only to maintain Madagascar's division into five provinces—to which that of Diégo-Suarez was soon to be added—but also to deepen this division by creating executive councils at the provincial level. When the provincial structure had been created in 1946, the nationalists had opposed it as an artificial device designed to break up the M.D.R.M. movement, and after ten years they continued to oppose it as a divide-and-rule tactic. The coastal populations, for their part, wanted the provinces to be given the widest possible autonomy, and were against any measures that might strengthen the central administration.

When the National Assembly, on March 20–21, 1956, debated how the *loi-cadre* should be applied to Madagascar, it was obvious that, as always, the Malagasys would be treated differently from the Africans, although no one—including the government—knew just how the problem of Madagascar would be handled. The Overseas Commission and even Minister Defferre himself could not decide whether a government council for the whole island should be set up. Generally speaking, the *côtiers* seemed to be against creating any central executive or legislative body. Advocates of a territorial government council and assembly, on the other hand, urged that the historic, geographic, and linguistic unity of Madagascar should be recognized institutionally. They also stressed that the island's social and economic development would be retarded unless there were some coordinating machinery at the top level. The danger that decentralization might degenerate into fragmentation, cited by the nationalists and communists, was substantiated on December 11, 1956, when the spokesmen for the Fort-Dauphin region, heartened by the example of Diégo-Suarez, asked to be separated from Tuléar's administration and to form a separate province.

Although the "centralists" could be said to have won over the "federalists," the administrative structure worked out in 1956–57 for Madagascar seemed at the time an ingenious compromise likely to satisfy all but the most intransigent extremists. The total powers transferred from France to Madagascar were the same as for the Negro African federations, but the division of those powers inside the island territory was to be different. The Parliament noted the similarities between the countries of Negro Africa and the provinces of Madagascar, but did not push the analogy too far. The powers of the Malagasy provinces were expanded, but representatives of the country as a whole kept or were given powers of control over them. These far exceeded the simple ability to coordinate their common services, which was given to the "Groups of Territories" that now replaced the governments-general of French West Africa and Equatorial Africa.

Madagascar's representative assembly was not consulted about either the *loi-cadre* or the decrees of April 27, 1957, which regulated its application to the island, and the structure Madagascar was given represented a compromise worked out between the government and Parliament in Paris. At the highest level were placed the high commissioner, government council, and representative assembly; in parallel positions at the provincial level came the *chef de province*, executive council, and assembly. The new powers given to the provinces aimed at strengthening the "personality" of each of them. This "personality," which was based on genuine regional and ethnic differences, had been reinforced over the past decade, so it was not wholly the artificial creation that the "centralists" claimed it to be. The *chef de province* was to preside over the six-man executive council, which would be chosen by a 40-member assembly directly elected by universal suffrage voting as a single college. Each of the provincial assemblies, acting as an electoral college, was to choose nine members to sit in the territorial or general assembly. This 54-man assembly, in turn, elected a government council for all Madagascar: it was to be made up of eight members, including six chosen by the assembly to represent each of the provinces, and four or five French officials, normally heads of the public services and appointed by the high commissioner.

The highest-ranking French official, formerly called governor-general and now high commissioner, was to play a dual role under the new system. He was to represent the French Republic in Madagascar and was also to be head of the local government. In the former capacity he was responsible for the maintenance of law and order and could negotiate certain types of agreements with neighboring countries. As head of the local government he would preside over meetings of the government council, whose members would be called ministers; it would be invested by a simple majority of the territorial assembly. Under certain specified circumstances, the assembly could overthrow the government council and the high commissioner could dissolve the assembly.

Although the *loi-cadre* gave the central administration preeminence over the provincial ones and although representatives elected by the people voting as a single college would now share the executive powers with the highest French officials in Madagascar, no segment of Malagasy opinion found it wholly satisfactory. The "federalists" continued to fear Merina domination not only of the central government organs, which would be located in Tananarive, but also of provincial posts because of the lack of qualified cadres among the *côtiers*. The "centralists" for their part resented the allocation of any executive powers at all to the provinces, and begrudged the money that Madagascar would have to spend on top-heavy territorial and provincial services that would inevitably overlap in certain domains. The Merina nationalists had no use at all for a system that stopped short of total independence. The communists complained that the high commissioner was still the repository of too much power, and they wanted him to be made responsible to a territorial assembly that would be elected directly by the population and would fully control the provinces.

The elections of March 30, 1957—which were to determine indirectly the nature and temper of the territorial assembly and the new government council—took place in an atmosphere of general though not intense disillusionment and dissatisfaction. Except for a few incidents created by embittered Europeans,[13] the elections went off calmly, even in Tananarive, where only about half of the registered electorate voted. The provincial population showed less indifference, participation in the voting ranging between 65.6 per cent and 78.7 per cent of a total electorate numbering some 2.5 million. More interest might have been aroused by this election had it been centered on some major idea or concept. But the lists were made up mostly of local personalities, all of whom vaguely declared themselves in favor of peace and of economic and social progress.

In general, moderate candidates triumphed in the provinces of Majunga, Tuléar, and Fianarantsoa despite the existence of not-so-moderate groups in their capital cities. The more extreme elements won in Diégo-Suarez and Tamatave provinces, and also inevitably in Tananarive, where left-wing labor and Christian organizations joined forces. In Tananarive a list nominally made up of "independents" but in reality inspired by left-wing Catholics led by Stanislas Rakotonirina, who had become mayor of that city on November 18, 1956, won 27 out of the 40 seats at stake. Similarly minded candidates obtained 12 seats in the Diégo-Suarez provincial assembly, while even more extremely oriented nationalists won 13 other seats there and another 13 in the Tamatave provincial assembly. Candidates advocating Franco-Malagasy entente or supporting frankly provincial interests carried 13 seats in the Tananarive assembly, 17 in Tamatave, 32 in Tuléar, and all 40 seats in Fianarantsoa and Majunga. French nationals, including some from Réunion Island, won 35 of the 240 seats contested.[14]

All the provincial assemblies, between May 13 and 19, 1957, elected their executive councils and representatives to the territorial assembly. At the end of May all eight ministers of the new government council had been chosen, including three who were not members of the territorial assembly (Gervais Randrianasolo, a moderate provincial assemblyman of Fianarantsoa; Paul Longuet, French Senator from Tamatave; and Alfred Ramangasoavina, municipal councilor of Tananarive). The other ministers were Justin Bezara, a former leader of the M.D.R.M., who had been imprisoned for eight years following the revolt and was at the time a municipal councilor of Diégo-Suarez; Philibert Raondry, from Fianarantsoa; Alexis Bezaka, mayor of Tamatave; and Philibert Tsiranana, deputy from Madagascar to the National Assembly and assemblyman from Majunga, who was elected on May 27 vice-president of Madagascar's first government council. He was also the founder of the Parti Social Démocratique de Madagascar (P.S.D.M.), destined to become Madagascar's foremost political party.

Chapter six

POLITICAL PARTIES AND THE REFERENDUM
OF SEPTEMBER 1958

After the *loi-cadre* was passed in June 1956, there came a sudden proliferation of political parties in Madagascar. Between then and June 1960, when the country became independent, parties frequently formed alliances that were soon broken up, and new groups were set up and then dissolved. The confusion created by this amoeba-like process made it hard to see the basic pattern in the swiftly changing scene. Some alliances or mergers were based on a common ideology, which might be Christian (Rassemblement Chrétien de Madagascar, or R.C.M.) or socialist (Parti Social Démocrate, or P.S.D.) or Marxist (Ankotonny Kongreiny Fahaleovantenan Madagasikara, or A.K.F.M.), and some parties, despite claims to a nation-wide basis, might be purely regional or provincial (Renouveau National Malgache, or R.N.M., and Mouvement National pour l'Indépendance de Madagascar, or MONI-MA). Of these parties, some were wholly new formations, such as the P.S.D. and Union Démocratique et Sociale de Madagascar, or U.D.S.M., which owed their origin to events in the mid-1950s; others were the prolongation or expansion of committees formed to contest the legislative elections of June 1951 and January 1956; and still others had recognizable politically organized antecedents. Thus the R.C.M. could be traced back to the combined P.D.M.–M.S.M. and the U.I.; the A.K.F.M. to the Groupe d'Etudes Communistes, U.P.M. and C.E.A.P.; and the MONIMA and R.N.M. to the M.D.R.M.

The genesis of almost every one of these parties or groups could be found in the nationalist issues that had led to the formation of the first three post–World War II political movements. At that time all were agreed on the goal of independence, but the M.D.R.M. settled temporarily for autonomy in the French Union, the PADESM would accept sovereign status only by slow stages, and the P.D.M.–M.S.M.—who joined forces for electoral purposes—would be satisfied with nothing less than immediate and total independence. Their differences in the timing and method of attaining inde-

pendence overlay older and more fundamental differences, which still subsist—despite strong denials—between those who want to restore Merina
hegemony and those who fear its revival. Malagasy parties may have various names and slogans, Catholic or Protestant sponsors, Marxist or conservative platforms, or half a dozen other distinguishing marks without affecting or revealing the major cleavage between them. This is the basic ethnic
conflict between the Merina of the high central plateaus and the non-Merina
tribes of the peripheral regions. It is largely because the Malagasys are so
preoccupied with this purely local problem that all the attempts by French
political parties to take root in Madagascar have failed. This holds true for
the R.P.F. and M.R.P. as it did for the S.F.I.O. and the Communist Party.

The Communists

The communists were the first French party to send emissaries to Madagascar and to try to win converts among the Malagasys. After World War I,
Franco-Malagasy communist contacts were made both in Paris and in Tananarive—an association that first came to public attention in the incidents of
May 19, 1929. Four years later the Secours Rouge International founded a
branch in Madagascar, with which Jules and Paul Ranaivo were associated.
These two men eventually were involved in the 1947 revolt and in 1959 were
elected officers of the A.K.F.M. In the mid-1930s, the rise to power of the
Popular Front government in France encouraged left-wing organizations
in the colonies. In Madagascar the sudden increase of trade unions and
strikes aroused suspicions among French officials and settlers that communists were behind this labor agitation. Soon after World War II broke out,
the Communist Party was suppressed in both France and the colonies, and
the communist movement did not revive in Madagascar until after the
Liberation.

The M.D.R.M. deputies—especially Raseta—made profitable contacts
with the French Communist Party soon after they arrived in Paris at the
end of 1945, although it soon became apparent that they did not see eye to
eye in regard to Madagascar's future status.* In Tananarive, two French
Communist Party members, Lombardo and Boiteau, organized a small
Groupe d'Etudes Communistes. Although this group had more European
than Malagasy members and remained discreetly in the background during
the revolt, it fully exploited the Tananarive trial of the three M.D.R.M. deputies in 1948 for propaganda purposes. The initial refusal by French members of the Tananarive bar to defend the accused deputies provided an opening for the Communist Party to send lawyers from Paris to take charge of
their defense. Maître Pierre Stibbe, principal counsel for the defense, was

* See pp. 61–62.

not one to hide his own light or that of the Communist Party under a bushel, and he kept the arguments on behalf of the accused before the French public.* In 1949 the French Communist Party was urging a revision of the Tananarive trial as the best means of keeping antigovernmental action there alive, whereas the Malagasy nationalists wanted simply a general amnesty. This was the second important point within a short period on which the Party and the nationalists disagreed.

This disagreement with the Malagasys coincided with the communists' rebuff at the hands of the R.D.A. in Negro Africa. These phenomena, plus the growing conviction that the Communist Party would never take over the government in France, led to a drastic revision of the communists' policy in regard to Madagascar. Realizing that communism made progress in the French dependencies only when it appeared to be an ally of nationalism, the party leaders decided to take over and push the most extreme nationalist demands. In the Parliament they began urging dissolution of the French Union, independence for the overseas territories, and, for the Malagasy political prisoners, total and immediate amnesty. By late 1950 they had founded the COSOMA in Madagascar and promoted C.G.T. unions and a left-wing press there, and they began turning over leadership of the movement in the island from Frenchmen to the Malagasys whom they had trained. French Union assemblymen—Marcel Egretaud, Gaston Donnat, and M. Julien—made periodic visits to Madagascar in the early 1950s to encourage and advise, but more and more they left policy-making and operational programs in the hands of Gisèle Rabesahala, Raza Karivony, Zélé Rasoanoro, René and Henri Rakotobe, and other Malagasys.†

In April 1951 the new Malagasy leadership of the extreme left-wing movement gave proof of its effectiveness in the municipal elections at Tananarive, when a slate of communist candidates headed by Zélé Rasoanoro won 12 per cent of the votes cast. The next year, however, trouble broke out among the Malagasy leaders, who reportedly began accusing each other of misappropriating funds, being employed by the police, and the like.[1] Donnat, sent by the Party from France to straighten out the situation, soon restored order, and it was said that he urged indirect action through the discreet creation of more labor unions and COSOMA cells, and closer contacts with liberal religious and student groups.

Since Gisèle Rabesahala and the Rakotobe brothers belonged to promi-

* See p. 57.
† Gisèle Rabesahala, probably the most interesting member of this group, was born in 1930 and had been initiated into communism by Lombardo and Boiteau, whose secretary she had been, and later by trips to Moscow and Peking. Rémy Rakotobe had studied in Vienna under the auspices of the W.F.T.U., and later at the University of Prague. During the 1950s he was often abroad in Iron Curtain countries, and was said to be one of the few Malagasys who spoke Russian.

nent Catholic families, it was easy to establish contacts with left-wing Catholics, particularly after the bishops of Madagascar in 1953 endorsed Malagasy independence aspirations as legitimate. As to the student element, many of those who had returned to Madagascar after completing their studies in France had been well indoctrinated by the Communist Party there. In the early 1950s they formed the Parti de l'Union du Peuple Malgache to keep alive the issues of independence and amnesty. It was not difficult for the communists to take it over and slightly modify its name to the Union du Peuple Malgache (U.P.M.). They took care, however, to include noncommunist elements in its politburo, so that it would appear to be primarily a nationalist party when it participated in local elections. The U.P.M. provided the hard core for a short-lived Comité d'Entente et d'Action Politique (C.E.A.P.) made up of small left-wing organizations,* but the C.E.A.P. broke up soon after the legislative elections of January 2, 1956.

   In those elections the U.P.M. caused some surprise by supporting Stanislas Rakotonirina, head of the Union des Indépendants (U.I.) which was made up of Catholic socialists.† The U.I., along with a similar smaller organization of Catholic *côtiers* called the Union Nationale Malgache (UNAM) headed by Alexis Bezaka of Tamatave, marked the effective debut of Catholics as torchbearers of nationalism and a decline in the nationalist leadership among the Protestants. In the first years after World War II, the Protestants organized by Ravelojoana had been more intransigent than the Catholics or even the M.D.R.M. in demanding immediate independence for Madagascar, but they were not involved as a party in the 1947 revolt. Indeed, the P.D.M. showed remarkable flexibility, teaming up with the Catholic M.S.M. for electoral purposes and, after the revolt, continuing the struggle for independence with such diverse allies as the C.G.T., S.F.I.O., League for the Rights of Man, and Jeune République. Perhaps an overwillingness to compromise, shown by its acceptance of such partners, as well as its change of leadership, undermined the P.D.M.'s strength. Ravelojoana's successor, Gabriel Razafintsalama, was a devout Protestant and an able journalist but not dynamic, and under him the P.D.M. slid downhill, to become by 1956 a weak cryptocommunist organization called the Front National Malgache (F.N.M.). In the meantime, the Malagasy communists had found an eminently suitable candidate to support in elections at Tananarive. There they backed Stanislas Rakotonirina, who, as an ardent Merina nationalist and Catholic and as head of a small party ostensibly if not actually opposed to communism, would provide them with just the cover of aggressive nation-

---

* Front National Malgache, a reincarnation of the P.D.M.; Rassemblement du Peuple Malgache; and Union pour la Défense des Intérêts Malgaches.
† See pp. 88 and 200.

alism that they sought. Rakotonirina was duly elected mayor of Tananarive on November 18, 1956, and to a considerable—though unknown—extent, the U.P.M. was responsible for his victory. Similarly, in the elections
of March 31, 1957, for the provincial assemblies, the successes registered by
the extreme nationalists and left-wing elements in Tananarive, Tamatave,
and Diégo-Suarez could be traced in large part to U.P.M. support.

The Parti Social Démocrate

While communist strength in Madagascar grew steadily over two decades,
despite several setbacks, another party that started as the local annex to a
French party became the outstanding political organization in Madagascar
a little more than a year after its founding. This was the Parti Social Démocrate (P.S.D.), created in Majunga province by Philibert Tsiranana initially
as a branch of the S.F.I.O., which he joined soon after he was elected to the
National Assembly in January 1956. The P.S.D. was established with the encouragement of High Commissioner André Soucadaux, who was himself
not only a socialist but also representative in Madagascar of a French government now dominated by the S.F.I.O. Such patronage might have been
enough to damn the P.S.D. in the eyes of the nationalists had not the party
had the good fortune to be headed by an exceptionally able and educated
côtier, Philibert Tsiranana, who was helped in organizing the new party by
a competent group of French socialists, in particular Eugène Lechat. Because it was at the time the only coherent and well-organized political movement, the P.S.D. was able to spread into other provinces from its birthplace
in Majunga and to attain a majority position in the territorial assembly.

On May 28, 1957, Tsiranana was chosen to head a government council
composed of two leftist nationalists, one socialist, and five ministers who described themselves as moderates. On the basis of geographical distribution,
the government council included two representatives from Tamatave and
one from each of the other five provinces. Because of the composition of
the new Malagasy government, the central province of Tananarive and
consequently the Merina were relegated to a position hopelessly inferior
to that of the *côtiers.* The majority in the assembly (29 out of 54) were
clearly partisans of a sincere application of the *loi-cadre,* which meant
that they were *côtiers* and "federalists" who wanted the central government to be used largely for purposes of coordinating policy and services
for the provinces. The minority, composed principally of extreme nationalists and left-wingers from the towns of Tananarive, Tamatave, and Diégo-
Suarez, simply wanted a central unitary government for the whole island,
but they were primarily concerned with the issues of immediate independence and total amnesty, which would be settled in Paris and not in

Madagascar. The only unifying force in the minority group was its concerted antigovernment stand on every main issue. On the other hand, not
only did the P.S.D. have a superior organization but its leaders early
grasped the fact that the essential objective for any political party was to
gain control of the government. After they succeeded in doing this, it was
a comparatively easy task to make themselves into a mass party.

Regional and Sectarian Parties

Passage of the *loi-cadre* and lifting of the state of siege from all of Madagascar by the end of 1956 encouraged the formation of so many political
organizations that by mid-1957 they numbered 27.[2] The great majority were
not parties but political clubs, comprising no more than a few dozen members, who enjoyed discussing the main nationalist themes and criticizing
those in power without assuming any responsibility or contributing to the
solution of problems. Most of these formations disappeared after they failed
to win seats in the March 1957 elections. A few of them, however, which had
started as regional or sectarian movements acquired an interprovincial following, and new parties were formed as new and important issues arose.
Among these should be mentioned the Union Démocratique et Sociale de
Madagascar (U.D.S.M.), some of the Christian parties, the MONIMA or
Mouvement National pour l'Indépendance de Madagascar, and the Renouveau National Malgache (R.N.M.).

The U.D.S.M. was founded by two brothers, Norbert and Antoine Zafimahova, members of the Antaisaka tribe and natives of Farafangana, where
their party was launched in 1957. Owing to various agreements and mergers
with a succession of smaller parties of the south and of the Betsileo region,
the U.D.S.M. won top position in two provinces. Antoine Zafimahova became head of the provincial council of Fianarantsoa, and another prominent
U.D.S.M. leader, Charles-Emile, became head of Tuléar's council. On May
25, 1957, Norbert Zafimahova was elected president of the territorial assembly by 47 out of 54 votes, and he was reelected to that post the next year.
Since the U.D.S.M.'s platform with regard to cooperating with France in
carrying out the *loi-cadre* decrees was virtually the same as that of the P.S.D.,
the two parties had every reason to come to terms. Their leaders, nevertheless, failed to reach an agreement to demarcate the zones of political influence to be granted each party—in principle the P.S.D. was to operate unhindered in the north and the U.D.S.M. in the south of the island—and except for a brief period in mid-1958, when they got together, the two parties
drifted farther and farther apart.

Of the remaining parties, which occupied a vague no-man's land between
the P.S.D. and the extreme left-wing nationalist group, the R.N.M. and the

MONIMA, as well as the small Christian parties, born late in 1956 or early in 1957, were only embryonic formations until mid-1958. What caused them to coalesce and later to expand was an important move made by the extreme left-wing nationalist elements in reaction to the National Assembly's failure on March 18, 1958, to grant a full and immediate pardon to the last of the Malagasy political prisoners. A group of intellectuals and politicians proposed at a public meeting in Tananarive that all Malagasy political movements hold a round-table discussion to "study together problems relating to the country's independence" at Tamatave May 2–4. Ten parties accepted the invitation, but neither the P.S.D. nor the U.D.S.M. was officially represented at Tamatave. Nevertheless, three ministers of the government council and 19 elected members of municipal and provincial assemblies were among those present. Their appearance at a congress that had been organized by predominantly left-wing groups and that emphasized the theme of independence pointed up a serious schism in the government coalition and the failure of the assembly and the government party to agree on basic policy.

The P. S. D. Government and the Territorial Assembly

Between the spring of 1956, when the debate on the *loi-cadre* began, and May 1958, when the Tamatave Congress was held, there had been a significant evolution in the thinking of the P.S.D. leaders and of the assemblymen in regard to the four main issues of that period. These issues were Madagascar's future statutory relations with France, amnesty for the three M.D.R.M. deputies, the role of provincial governments in Madagascar, and the relationship between the government and the territorial assembly. Generally speaking, the P.S.D. government moved toward the position assumed by the extreme-nationalist assemblymen instead of imposing its more conservative views on the assembly. The course of this evolution, however, indicated a more widespread basic agreement in regard to Madagascar's autonomy and unity than in regard to amnesty and the government's authority vis-à-vis the assembly. Throughout this period the P.S.D. remained a party of only localized membership and influence, so it was Tsiranana's moves as vice-president of the government council rather than as head of his party that carried weight.

In his maiden speech to the National Assembly on March 20, 1956, Tsiranana spoke of the Malagasy people's fear lest the *loi-cadre* provide their country only with provincial councils and omit a central government that was necessary to reinforce their national unity. Yet far from wanting the provincial structure to be eliminated, he wanted the provincial assemblies to be more fully and equally represented in the central organs of government. It was Tsiranana who persuaded his fellow deputies to give all the provincial assemblies the same number of members and nine representatives each in the territorial assembly, "so that none of our provinces should feel like a poor relation." In his next speech, in the Palais Bourbon on January 29, 1957, Tsiranana took up the burning question of Madagascar's future status; he stressed his fellow countrymen's fear lest it be inferior to that given to the Africans and implied that he would settle for autonomy. "The extremists," he said, "want independence but we moderates favor the golden mean. We are eager to have provincial autonomy so that the *côtiers* can have their own schools, but we also want a central authority so as to avoid balkanizing Madagascar."

The elections of March 31, 1957, gave the numerically superior *côtiers* definite control of the provincial assemblies, and consequently of the territorial assembly and government council, and this in turn caused a marked diminution in their fears of Merina domination. They therefore were no longer afraid to voice the desire for greater freedom from France, which they shared with all other Malagasys. Only the lack of a quorum prevented passage by the assembly in July 1957 of a resolution drafted by six representatives from Diégo-Suarez and Tamatave, which described the *loi-cadre* as quite unsatisfactory and asked France to convene a round-table conference to discuss independence for Madagascar. By early December 1957, when the P.S.D. held its annual congress, the temper of the assembly was unmistakably in favor of some radical move. Tsiranana was not yet ready to adopt the most extreme nationalist view, but he did come out for abrogation of the annexation law of 1896, accepting the *loi-cadre* only as a step forward on the road to independence, and proposing a future relationship with France similar to that which bound together nations of the British Commonwealth.[3] As to the role of the provinces, Tsiranana was now on the fence. On December 22, 1957, he told the assembly that he had approved their existence for social and economic objectives, but that "personally I have never wanted the provinces from the political point of view. If it were decided today to suppress the provinces I would gladly accept that decision. I believe we are beginning to feel that the existence of provinces is not always good ... If we see that the provinces do not work out, let us see what can be done about it in the future."

The implications of Tsiranana's new stand were sufficiently clear for the French government to take alarm. At a conference in Paris attended by the new native executives of the overseas territories in February 1958, the Malagasys were convened separately from the Africans lest the latter become infected by the Malagasys' demand for independence.[4] It is noteworthy that at that conference it was a Frenchman, André Bessières, vice-president of the Tamatave provincial council, who voiced the audacious and far-reaching demands of his Malagasy colleagues. These were suppression of the provinces as political units, a corresponding strengthening of the central power, a government council wholly responsible to the territorial assembly, and total amnesty for all political prisoners. If there was still any uncertainty in the minds of French officialdom as to the political desires of Madagascar's elected representatives, it was dissipated by two resolutions passed almost unanimously and after a very animated debate by the territorial assembly on April 23, 1958. The less important of the two asked that the vice-president of the government council be named premier and made fully responsible to the assembly. The key resolution called on France to revise Article 8 of the constitution, to recognize Madagascar's right to independence, and to grant it the status of an autonomous republic in the framework of a federal French Union. The assemblymen turned down the proposal that Madagascar ask for the status of an Associated State freely associated with France and, in fact, did not even discuss the possibility of Madagascar's acquiring total independence without maintaining any ties at all with France.

If all politically conscious Malagasys were agreed on their wish to have more freedom from French controls, the same could not be said concerning their attitude toward provincial governments or the amnesty. A resolution proposed by Alexis Bezaka at the session of April 23, 1958, to suppress provincial councils fell short by six votes of the 36 needed for its passage. As to the amnesty, the same unanimity was not maintained that was displayed at the assembly's session of November 14, 1957, in which the government and the European and Malagasy assemblymen in a mood of forgive-and-forget asked the National Assembly to amnesty all political prisoners. After the National Assembly on March 18, 1958, had enlarged the scope of its amnesty law but excluded the three M.D.R.M. deputies from taking part in any political activities until 1963, the reaction in Madagascar was mixed. Conservative Europeans pointed out that the three M.D.R.M. deputies were freely enjoying life in France, did not regret their part in the 1947 revolt but only its failure, and if allowed to return to Madagascar would use the "halo of martyrdom" that now surrounded them to stir up trouble again.[5] The Malagasy press was bitter about the restrictive aspect of the National Assembly's vote, and the municipal council of Tananarive in protest refused to vote the town's budget. The territorial assembly had the most lively debate of its career on the issue, in the course of which it became obvious that the government did not relish the prospect of the M.D.R.M. deputies' return.[6] Tsiranana's newspaper, *La République,* was cited for a comment in its March 15 issue to the effect that Raseta, Rabemananjara, and Ravoahangy were "persons known for their dictatorial tendencies." Old wounds were reopened when the *côtier* assemblymen were accused by their central-plateau colleagues of having voted the November 14 resolution "out of fear." Only with the greatest difficulty was agreement reached on the wording of a cable to be sent to the Paris government reaffirming the assembly's stand in favor of amnesty and expressing disappointment at the restrictive aspects of the new amnesty law.

The discussion of this subject, like that of almost every question that arose in the assembly elected in 1957, degenerated into a confrontation between the Tananarive group and the *côtiers*.* For example, a seemingly irrelevant debate on rates at the hospital of Befelatanana was soon embittered by complaints that discrimination was practiced there against patients who were not residents of Tananarive. Sometimes this regional rivalry was overlaid or paralleled by a feeling of resentment common to all the assemblymen, including Europeans, against the "authoritarian" actions of the government. Although the government was now very largely in the hands of Malagasy ministers, the deep-rooted opposition to an arbitrary administration dating from the days of colonialism reasserted itself. Twice the assemblymen placed the government in a minority position—once (on July 1, 1957) over the amount of family allowances and later (on March 31, 1958) over the appointment of directors to the Crédit de Madagascar—but on both occasions Tsiranana was hastily assured that the majority did not want to overthrow him but merely to censure his government. It was almost in the nature of a reflex reaction that the Tananarive group denounced the high pay for cabinet ministers (1,800,000 C.F.A. francs a year) or the *côtier* assemblymen complained that the "dictatorial" government was usurping the powers of the provincial councils, but they suddenly and firmly closed ranks behind the Tsiranana government when any difference of opinion arose between it and the French administrators. This seldom happened, because High Commissioner Soucadaux was careful to keep such clashes to a minimum. But on the occasions when a conflict occurred between the assembly and the government, the habit of assembly opposition to the administration reasserted itself. More serious, inside the government itself some ministers on occasion refused to abide by the decisions taken by a majority of their colleagues, including the vice-president of the government council. Such an occasion occurred during the Congress of Independence held at Tamatave May 2–4, 1958.

The Congress of Independence at Tamatave

Two weeks before the Congress of Independence met at Tamatave, the P.S.D. held its third congress, and this offered an opportunity for comparisons. Judging by the origin of the P.S.D. delegates, the party's strongholds

---

* The Tananarive group included Maître Marcel Fournier, Stanislas Rakotonirina, Jean Goulesque, Albert Tostivint, Louis Ratsimba, Emile Rasakaisa, Alexandre Ranatanaela, Charles Ramarotafika, and René Rakotobe.

were in the coastal provinces of Majunga, Fianarantsoa, and Tuléar, and its membership—then estimated roughly at 15,000—was made up largely of minor officials and *petits bourgeois*. Although the delegates discussed the agenda in closed sessions, the stress on party discipline was apparent, for on every issue the minority yielded to the majority and all resolutions were adopted unanimously.[7] Neither the P.S.D. nor the U.D.S.M. accepted the invitation to attend the Tamatave Congress, but a number of P.S.D. assemblymen and three members of the government were present.

The Independence Congress at Tamatave was attended by delegates from ten political "parties," of which the only important ones were the U.P.M., R.N.M., and MONIMA, and 80 per cent of them came from Tananarive. If this congress could not be said to be widely representative, it was a psychological success, for it did bring together for the first time all open partisans of independence and all the discussions were conducted in the Malagasy language. Furthermore, they formulated precise steps by which independence was to be achieved and set up a permanent delegation to work out the methods by which unity of action could be assured and negotiations with France undertaken. While the Negro Africans were still only asking France to recognize their right to independence, the Malagasys at Tamatave insisted on independence itself, and they hoped to achieve it peacefully by invoking the French people's traditions of freedom. Specifically they envisaged an independent Madagascar as a unitary and democratic republic whose constitution would be drawn up by an assembly elected by universal suffrage.

The Tamatave Congress might have caused no more than a fluttering in the dovecotes had it not also denounced the territorial assembly's resolution of April 23, 1958, on Madagascar's future status as "tending to deflect Malagasy opinion from its legitimate aspiration for independence." This particularly infuriated Norbert Zafimahova, head of the U.D.S.M. and president of the assembly, who registered a formal protest. The Tamatave Congress, he said, represented only a minority of the population and included would-be leaders who had been rejected at the polls, whereas the assembly, whose members had all been democratically elected, alone was qualified to speak for the Malagasy people.[8] As head of the government, Tsiranana had to decide what to do about his three ministers who had gone to Tamatave without asking his leave and had presumably voted in favor of the controversial resolution. A compromise was finally worked out whereby the explanation that the ministers went to Tamatave only as private individuals was accepted by Tsiranana in return for their subscribing to a statement that confirmed their belief that the territorial assembly was the only valid spokesman for the country.

The Referendum of September 28, 1958

The decisions taken at Tamatave and their repercussions on the local political scene were soon given new significance and new dimension by the coup of May 13 at Algiers which brought General de Gaulle back to power in France. The new French government at once gratified one of the major Afro-Malagasy demands when it made the vice-presidents of the African and Malagasy government councils prime ministers in name as well as in fact. Then de Gaulle let it be known that he would draft a constitution for the Fifth French Republic that would establish a federal relationship between its component parts and would be submitted to a referendum both in France and in the overseas territories.

This development brought to Paris two Malagasy delegations, one headed by Tsiranana and composed of three assemblymen and three senators, and the other representing the Tamatave Congress. The latter, in a press conference held at Paris in mid-July, claimed to speak for majority Malagasy opinion, which—it was asserted—was thoroughly disillusioned with the *loi-cadre* and was convinced that only the return of the M.D.R.M. deputies to Madagascar and the bestowal of total independence on that island would restore mutual confidence and cordial relations with France.[9] Tsiranana, for his part, told the Parisian press that his country wanted only a status analogous to that of Togo, under which defense, diplomacy, and currency problems would be left to the French government, and independence would come in perhaps 20 to 30 years.[10] The great majority of Malagasys, he said, were satisfied with their present government, though they would like more flexibility in relations between the central administration and the provinces. "Our nation is too small to leave the French orbit, and as we don't want to become the prey of great powers we do not think that independence for Madagascar is viable at present." It was in this spirit that Tsiranana worked for a month on the constitutional advisory committee, and at least one of his suggestions—that of replacing the term "federation" by "community"—was incorporated in the final draft. In terms of Tsiranana's own political future, this summer sojourn in Paris had two important consequences: it cemented close relations between himself and General de Gaulle and it established him in the eyes of French and African politicians as an influential overseas leader.

The stand taken by Tsiranana, and consequently by the P.S.D., in favor of the new constitution and the Franco-African Community was in sharp opposition to that of the extreme nationalists and Marxists, who used the permanent delegation of the Tamatave Congress to spearhead their campaign for a "no" vote. As always in Madagascar, the main issue—in this case, immediate and total independence—became blurred by other considerations.

The P.S.D. and U.D.S.M., which joined forces in a Cartel des Républicains to promote an affirmative vote in the referendum, based their campaign mainly on the dangers of a communist take-over should Madagascar vote itself independent. Norbert Zafimahova in a broadcast asserted that a negative vote would be construed internationally as "Madagascar's wish to separate itself from the Western world and would invite the communists to try to get a foothold on the island on the pretext of bringing us aid."[11] This "threat of communism" was also decisive in inducing the influential Christian missions in Madagascar to throw their weight on the side of an affirmative vote, especially since those opposed to the new constitution included the hard-core Marxists of the U.P.M. Moreover, for internal reasons peculiar to Madagascar, the prospect of independence frightened some of the farseeing intellectuals. They feared that the withdrawal of France would lead to a Merina-imposed revival of feudalism, which in turn could be followed by a bloody *côtier* uprising.[12] To still others, and perhaps to the majority of politically conscious Malagasys, the question resolved itself into whether or not confidence should be placed in General de Gaulle himself, and his visit to Madagascar late in August did little to clarify the situation.

Tananarive was de Gaulle's first major stop on his fast-moving trip to French-speaking territories, which was prompted by the forthcoming constitutional referendum. His reception on August 22 by the Tananarive public was a mixed one, in part owing to extraneous circumstances such as a defective public-address system and a poor translation of his remarks into Malagasy.[13] His failure to pledge an amnesty for the three M.D.R.M. deputies and abrogation of the annexation law, or even to mention the word "independence," cost him considerable support, and his speech aroused enthusiasm only when he turned and pointed to the Queen's palace on the hill above him, saying that Madagascar under the new constitution would again become "a state just as it had been when the *rova* was inhabited." However, the lukewarm reception that he received at Tananarive may have had one important consequence: it was perhaps largely responsible for the big concession that de Gaulle announced at his next stop, Brazzaville. There he said that, although the overseas territories would have to choose on September 28 between the Community and independence without French aid, those who then voted for the Community could later have their independence if such proved to be their wish.

This major concession, along with the other considerations mentioned above, caused a shifting of alignments in the ranks of the constitution's opponents and supporters. An amusing incident occurred in Nossi-Bé, where the municipal council had asked in June that the island be transformed into a department of France and where, in late September, a crowd of 2,000 persons refused to permit the left-wing mayor of Diégo-Suarez, Francis Sautron, to make a speech against the constitution.[14] Tananarive's left-wing Catholic mayor, Stanislas Rakotonirina, also ran into trouble. In a swift turnabout from his previous position, he opted for a negative vote in the referendum, with results disastrous to himself and his party. The Union des Indépendants was hopelessly split, and Rakotonirina's own career was ruined because Tsiranana never forgave him, and his Catholicism prevented his joining the communists. Much the same could be said about Alexis Bezaka, mayor of Tamatave, but his opposition to the constitution came as no surprise and his political future was not so seriously blighted, though early in October 1958 he was forced to resign as Minister of Health.

On September 10, 1958, the government council came out in favor of an affirmative vote in the referendum. Although some of the ministers dissented, governmental solidarity prevailed: all the dissenters except Bezaka simply abstained from voting and did not go so far as to join the opposition.[15] On September 28, 1,767,475 of a registered electorate numbering 2,154,939 actually voted. What was significant on that occasion was the large number of negative votes cast, particularly in the towns of Tananarive, Tamatave, and Diégo-Suarez—392,557, against 1,363,059 affirmative votes. This vote showed the strength of the Malagasys' desire for independence, the slight importance many of them attached to continuing French aid, and the organizational ability of the numerically weak opposition forces. Curiously enough, neither the permanent delegation, which had chalked up so surprising a success, nor the Cartel des Républicains, which had campaigned effectively for an affirmative vote, long survived the referendum intact.

Chapter seven

THE AUTONOMOUS REPUBLIC

On October 14, 1958, at Tananarive 234 of Madagascar's 240 provincial assemblymen met under the chairmanship of Norbert Zafimahova and in the presence of High Commissioner Soucadaux and Premier Tsiranana. Except for 13 assemblymen from Diégo-Suarez and 12 from Tananarive who abstained, all voted in favor of the government's proposal that Madagascar proclaim itself an autonomous republic and member state of the Community. In a transport of enthusiasm, French and Malagasy assemblymen embraced each other, while nearby cannon fired a 101-gun salute to mark the historic occasion. The next day Soucadaux returned to the assembly to bring France's congratulations to the "first sister-republic of the Community" and to announce abrogation of the annexation law of 1896.

During the days that followed, the euphoric atmosphere gave way to dissension. Heated discussions, sometimes acrimonious, marked the debates on use of the Malagasy language as a linguistic vehicle for the assembly, limitation of the time allotted to individual speakers, and above all the design and colors for a national flag. (Finally the majority agreed to adopt the red-and-white flag of the Merina monarchy provided a green band was added to it to denote the coastal regions.) Naturally the most controversial of all the subjects debated had to do with the new governmental institutions and the timing and manner in which they would be formed. Ministerial portfolios had been quickly reshuffled on October 8, when Bezaka was dropped from the cabinet, and Tsiranana was fully prepared and able to railroad his program through the assembly. The latter quickly agreed to transform and compress itself into a provisional constituent and legislative body of 90 members. The government, for its part, pledged to draft a constitution within two weeks and submit it to an advisory constitutional committee. This committee, composed of five members for each province and seven named by the government for their special competence, was to report on it after 30 days of study. The provisional legislature would then vote on the amended or revised draft constitution within two weeks after it was submitted. Until the new constitution was adopted, the provincial councils and assemblies would continue to function. Furthermore, a high council of the Malagasy republic composed of the heads of the provincial councils was to be created, and under the chairmanship of the premier it would study various laws and economic projects that he submitted to it.

Needless to say, the tactics by which this program was rushed through the assembly, the tightness of the timetable laid down, and above all the authority it left in the hands of the Tsiranana government aroused lively resentment. The P.S.D. machine was able to quickly squelch proposals from the floor to submit the new constitution to a popular referendum, to hold new elections immediately for a constituent assembly, and to dissolve all provincial councils and assemblies. In a tempestuous session all amendments to Tsiranana's measures were rejected; Rakotonirina was shouted down every time he tried to speak, and finally subsided, and Bezaka, along with other members of the opposition, left the assembly hall in disgust before the final vote was taken.[1]

By mid-October the government had ready for publication a platform that was said to be that of the Cartel des Républicains (the P.S.D. and the U.D.S.M.). As might be expected, it stressed liberty, equality, and fraternity. Its only unusual feature was the inclusion of socioeconomic projects, which all parties up to that time had tended to overlook because of their general absorption in politics. Albeit vaguely defined, this platform did stress the goals of full employment, total literacy, and agrarian reform in the interests of peasants and herders, and it held out the prospect of fiscal concessions to both foreign capitalists and impoverished Malagasys.[2]

Inasmuch as almost all of these were objectives to which it would be hard to take exception and as the government clearly had the intention and power of compelling acceptance of its own brand of constitution, the opposition resorted to reviving the tried-and-true issues of independence and amnesty. The U.P.M. lost no time in trotting out those old war-horses, and on October 22 it published a communiqué asserting that the independence-*cum*-amnesty principles laid down by the Congress of Tamatave were "the sole valid expression of the will of the Malagasy people." The use of this strategy against Tsiranana proved highly effective and so embarrassed the government that it eventually had to reverse itself completely on both points. At the same time, however, the extreme left wing's tactics in regard to its partners in the Permanent Delegation were so authoritarian that that organization broke up by the end of 1958.

Even during the Congress session at Tamatave, it was clear that agreement among its ten party delegations was wholehearted only on the question of independence, and that profound differences separated the hard-core Marxists from the "pure" nationalists and the Christian organizations. The U.P.M. campaigned for united action to win independence through a merger of all the parties represented at Tamatave in one political organization. Resistance to such a merger became more apparent when de Gaulle announced the issues to be settled by the September 1958 referendum, and it further increased after the Malagasy Republic was proclaimed in October. The four parties that composed the R.N.M. under Bezaka, the MONIMA led by Monja Jaona, and the Christian parties all broke away from the left-wing Marxists, who thereupon united to organize the A.K.F.M., or Party of the Congress of Independence. Thereafter the A.K.F.M. held a clear-cut position as an intransigent opponent of the Tsiranana government in all domains, whereas the other breakaways occupied a fluctuating middle position between the two, casting their weight on one side or the other.

A Third Force?

The R.N.M. and the MONIMA had so many points in common—notably their leaders' former membership in the M.D.R.M., their strong advocacy of total independence for Madagascar, and their equally intense opposition to communism—that it seems surprising they never merged. Yet despite the claim to a national following suggested by the names they gave their parties, each was basically a regional movement held together by a feudal loyalty that bound its members to their leader. The R.N.M., composed of four small parties,* was grafted onto Bezaka's old Balance Party, on whose organizational framework it rested, and it also won popularity through Bezaka's close friendship with Jacques Rabemananjara. This intimate relationship with the M.D.R.M. enabled the R.N.M. at the outset to establish a beachhead in the central province, but eventually it was squeezed out there between the P.S.D. and the A.K.F.M. By the time municipal elections were held, in October 1959, it had become a Betsimisaraka party, whose strength was restricted to the main town and northern region of Tamatave province. A year later it was split by a decision taken by the majority of its members to join the P.S.D.

Like that of the R.N.M., the MONIMA's strength was regional, tribal, and personal, resting "ideologically" on both its nationalist and anticommunist orientation. Even more than the R.N.M., it was built around a single personality, that of Monja Jaona, an Antandroy who had become mayor of Tuléar. Late in 1959 it rallied to the P.S.D. when Tsiranana came out in favor of independence for Madagascar, but it proved to be an unstable ally.

---

* Union Nationale des Autochtones Madécasses, Comité d'Action Populaire et Sociale pour l'Indépendance de Madagascar, Parti Populaire Malgache, and Union Travailliste et Paysanne.

Once again the common bond of intense nationalism and anticommunism—in this case especially strengthened by devotion to Christian principles—led to the formation in December 1958 of the Rassemblement Chrétien de Madagascar. The R.C.M., however, was distinguished from the other groups that broke away from the Permanent Delegation in being a federation of Christian parties that had been formed in the center, east, and northeast of Madagascar about the time of the March 1957 elections. At the peak of its strength the R.C.M. had 11 member organizations and two coordinating organs—a National Council and a National Bureau—but it never developed outstanding leaders. This lack of glamorous personalities and of a close-knit organization accounted for the R.C.M.'s weakness at the national level, and perhaps also for its popularity with the Malagasy peasantry, who generally mistrusted national political parties and their high-powered leaders.[8] How successful the R.C.M. was at the local level came as a surprise to observers of the Malagasy political scene when it carried a number of rural communal councils and the mayoralty in four full communes in the elections of October 11, 1959. This success induced the R.C.M. to tighten its overall organization and to try to eliminate mutually hostile elements inside its ranks. One faction, headed by J. F. Jarison, was made up of coastal Christians who supported the P.S.D. government; the rival faction was led by Michel Randria, a Betsileo whose grievances against Tsiranana as a Tsimihety and an opponent of provincial autonomy cost him the mayoralty of Fianarantsoa and sent him into political eclipse. Jarison, on the other hand, was rewarded with high ministerial posts, and though the R.C.M. under his leadership never merged with the P.S.D., it usually supported Tsiranana's government in the assembly.

For some months late in 1959 it was expected that the three parties just mentioned would get together and form a "third force" that could hold the balance of power between the P.S.D. and A.K.F.M. Certainly this seemed to be the direction in which at least the R.N.M. and R.C.M. were moving, or being prodded to move by the Catholic missions. But the Jesuits, who were the most politically active Catholic element, never found in Randria, Bezaka, or even Jacques Rabemananjara the leader who could galvanize and guide a third force. Although the movement toward greater unity in 1958–59 brought about the reduction of the nearly 30 Malagasy political parties to six big ones—P.S.D., A.K.F.M., R.N.M., R.C.M., MONIMA, and U.D.S.M.—and although the government party generally succeeded in disposing of dangerous rivals, no further large regrouping has yet occurred.

The A.K.F.M.

If the hard Marxist core hopelessly alienated the strongly anticommunist nationalist parties that had originally joined the Permanent Delegation, the new extremist party, the A.K.F.M., which emerged from that Delegation in the fall of 1958, enjoyed some compensatory advantages. It inherited the prestigious name of the Tamatave Congress (this permitted it to slough off the communist U.P.M. label), and it also took over the network of local committees which the Permanent Delegation had created during the referendum campaign. The A.K.F.M. also picked up some outstanding nationalist members, notably the Reverend Richard Andrianamanjato and Henri Razanatseheno, who were neither Marxists nor frightened of Marxism and who could and did provide a nationalist leadership of value to the new party. Renamed, reinvigorated, and reorganized as the A.K.F.M. appeared to be and was, it was fundamentally the old U.P.M. in its doctrines and its cadres, and as such it found itself with the same supporters and detractors as its predecessor. The A.K.F.M.'s main assets were the simplicity and clarity of its stand in favor of total independence and amnesty, its unswerving opposition to the *côtier* government in power, and its solid organization and aggressively militant press organs.*

From the outset, the A.K.F.M. took pains to sidestep the organizational pitfalls that had led to the infiltration and downfall of the M.D.R.M., and also to avoid appearing to be a communist party, which would have made it isolated and vulnerable. Its leaders decided to make the A.K.F.M. a party of cadres, whose membership never exceeded 20,000, and to link its local sections directly to the national directorate.[4] The latter consists of a politburo of 11 members, which meets regularly at Tananarive; a national council composed of the politburo plus two members from each of Madagascar's six provinces; and finally a national congress composed of delegates from the party's 280 sections, which meets about once every two years. The pyramidal structure of party cells follows that of the administrative units, rising from the village base through the district, region, and province, and party dues have been set at 100 C.F.A. francs (about 45 cents) a year. Vertically, close contact is maintained by regular reports sent in from the local sections to the central organs and by visits at six-month intervals to the cell network by members of the politburo.

Party discipline, in which Malagasy parties are usually weak, reinforces this tight-knit structure. It was shown most conspicuously in July 1959 when three of its moderate leaders, including its secretary-general Henri Razanatseheno, were expelled from the A.K.F.M. because they persisted in opposing the majority decision to organize a demonstration in favor of independence during de Gaulle's visit to Tananarive for the Community's executive council meeting.[5] Consequently Gisèle Rabesahala became the party's new secretary-general, and under her guidance—although Andrianamanjato remained nominally president of the A.K.F.M.—the party veered to the

---

* *Imongo Vao Vao, Mandroso, Ny Rariny,* etc.

left. By the end of 1959, however, two other developments had induced the A.K.F.M. again to change course and to reappear in nationalist guise. The more important of the two was France's pledge in December 1959 to grant Madagascar independence. The other was the new twist given to the old amnesty issue by the abortive attempt of the communists to bring Raseta back to Madagascar.

On July 11, 1959, with the aid of French Communist Party members and fellow travelers in the French Ministry of Interior, Raseta was placed aboard an airplane in Paris bound for Tananarive. He traveled under a false name and without the knowledge either of top French officials or of the other two M.D.R.M. deputies. When his plane stopped to refuel at Djibouti, he was intercepted by agents of the Sûreté and sent back to France, to the accompaniment of loud protests from the extreme Marxists, both French and Malagasy, and to the general mystification of observers of the Malagasy scene. Tsiranana, in a speech to the assembly on October 6, 1959, claimed that the Raseta *coup de théâtre* was planned by the communists with a dual objective. This coup consisted, he said, of discrediting the amnesty pledges made by both the French and the P.S.D. governments, and of eliminating Raseta as a potential rival to the A.K.F.M. extremists for leadership of the Malagasy left-wing nationalists. The incident proved, he went on to say, that the communists were trying to foment antagonism among the three M.D.R.M. deputies and to prevent the return of any of them to Madagascar. The communists had moved when they did, he added, because the negotiations for a total amnesty which he had been conducting with General de Gaulle were on the verge of a successful conclusion.

Whether the failure of Raseta's clandestine return to Madagascar was a real or planned fiasco has naturally never been admitted by the A.K.F.M.'s left wing. The likelihood of its being a real setback was substantiated by the reported creation in the spring of a genuine Malagasy communist party.* Early in 1960 the A.K.F.M. certainly adopted a more cautious policy, and its noncommunist nationalist leaders, notably Andrianamanjato and Joseph Jaozandry, reappeared in the party's front ranks, but this turnabout probably was due mainly to France's pledge of independence in December 1959. In any case, from this time forward the A.K.F.M. placed its stress on a national Malagasy brand of socialism rather than a Marxist one.

The A.K.F.M. has always denied being a communist party, but it has not denied and cannot deny the presence of communist party members in its ranks. The stubbornness and violence of its opposition to the P.S.D. government has alarmed the rural elements and civil servants, and its barely disguised Marxism and materialism have frightened the Catholics. Its strongholds are in the towns of Tananarive, Diégo-Suarez, and to a limited extent

* See p. 132.

Tamatave, and despite the much-publicized presence of *côtiers* and Catholics in its leadership and ranks, the A.K.F.M. is unquestionably a predominantly Merina bourgeois and Protestant party. This means that nationalism must be emphasized by the A.K.F.M. and that its extreme Marxist economic doctrines have had to be watered down. These phenomena are evident in the evolution of the plan published in the spring of 1959 as one that emanated from the Malagasy communists.* Consequently the socioeconomic program that the A.K.F.M. National Council formulated in January 1960 stressed only the lay aspect of the future Malagasy Republic, socialization of the means of production and transport, restitution to Malagasy farmers and herders of the lands that had been taken away from them by force or by trickery, and the acceptance of aid from all foreign sources to carry out economic development schemes under a "scientifically" established plan.

For some years after its birth in 1958, the A.K.F.M. was the strongest if not the most powerful party in Madagascar, because of its structure, doctrine, and discipline. It was, and still is, the only Malagasy party that could possibly challenge the P.S.D., though it has not yet succeeded in doing so. Its main weaknesses—lack of widespread support from either the masses or the elite—cannot be overcome because they are inherent in its "Merina-mindedness" and consistent obstructionism. If the P.S.D. is patently weak where the A.K.F.M. is strong, and also strong where the A.K.F.M. is weak, this can be, and to some extent has been, remedied. Progressively the P.S.D. has been taking over the A.K.F.M.'s organization and program, but it remains vulnerable in doctrine and in quality of membership.

The Structure and Policy of the P. S. D.

In its rapid successive moves to attain dominance, the P.S.D. leaders came to realize that they must steal the thunder of their most uncompromising adversary, the A.K.F.M., and also undermine the only other movement capable of challenging their party's authority. This was the U.D.S.M., its major partner in the Cartel des Républicains during the referendum campaign. In respect to the U.D.S.M., the P.S.D. employed the time-honored tactics of dividing and ruling to get rid of its main leader, Norbert Zafimahova. When it came to the A.K.F.M., the P.S.D. adapted that party's organization to its own needs and then adopted the A.K.F.M.'s demands for total independence and amnesty as its own.

With a few modifications and additions, the P.S.D. copied the structure

* This plan called for the abolition of taxes for five years and their replacement by the compulsory sale of the possessions of certain persons, up to a total of one million C.F.A. francs in each case. The type of person liable to such "taxation" or compensation was described as the "man who owns a house with four rooms or 50 head of cattle"; after being shorn of his superfluous possessions, he would "become proletarian again like an ordinary person." See Hardyman, "Madagascar Faces the Future."

that the A.K.F.M. had inherited from the U.P.M. Its principal innovation was to create intermediate units, the 72 federations, between the 700-odd party sections and its 30-member executive committee. (As of early 1964, the P.S.D. had reduced the number of federations to 41 and expanded its sections to 1,200.) Since the P.S.D.'s organization developed almost wholly after it came to power, not only did it follow the administrative pattern in its structure, but its leaders and propagandists were identical with those who held political or bureaucratic posts. When Tsiranana was elected president of the republic on May 1, 1959, André Resampa, Minister of the Interior, became the party's secretary-general. Resampa's official position and forceful personality enabled him to exert pressure effectively on Malagasy civil servants, particularly the teachers, to join the P.S.D. Revival of the *fokonolona*,* and the creation of hundreds of rural communes and municipalities greatly enlarged the potential and actual ranks of the P.S.D., for people either climbed on the bandwagon of their own volition or were helped by party militants to see that it was to their advantage to do so.

In this way the P.S.D. very rapidly became a mass party, although its organization and the quality of its membership left much to be desired. By 1962 it had between 300,000 and 400,000 members, though some of its leaders made the fantastic claim of twice that figure.[6] The rank and file of Malagasys joined the P.S.D. because one of its local leaders inspired confidence or, more often, because it was in control of the government and therefore able to dispense protection and favors. In the place of a doctrine that might have inspired a valid loyalty, the party leaders simply tried to take over and politicize a wide range of organizations and then to establish some kind of controls over this vast and inchoate membership. It was Resampa's task to tighten the party structure, settle controversies between the P.S.D. militants and civil servants, especially in the provinces, and compress the party organs to a more manageable size—all of which he did effectively, but more by forceful methods than by persuasion.

Had Resampa been a Merina and not a member of the Bara tribe, he might conceivably have been as effective a militant for the A.K.F.M. as he was for the P.S.D. In his organizational reforms he borrowed heavily from the A.K.F.M., and in 1962 he reportedly tried to give the P.S.D. a similar Marxist orientation. But this ran counter to the view of Tsiranana, who realized that there existed inside the P.S.D. many divergent tendencies and who, like Houphouët-Boigny after 1950, preferred a pragmatic to a doctrinal approach. The president did not want to risk alienating any of his party's members by taking a rigid ideological stand. Cautious and flexible by temperament, Tsiranana espoused causes only after he became convinced

* See p. 139.

they had wide popular support, and on occasion he drafted a platform in such general terms that it was open to various interpretations.

Starting as a provincial coastal party under the auspices of the French S.F.I.O., the P.S.D. reversed the Malagasy tradition by which all political movements originated in and spread out from Tananarive and had strongly nationalistic platforms. By 1959 Tsiranana had quietly cut his ties with the S.F.I.O. and was working to give the P.S.D. a wide national base. However, the fact that his following came very largely from the rural masses gave it a "reactionary" character, in comparison with that of the other parties launched by the urban, usually the Merina, elite. Inasmuch as the foundations of the P.S.D. rested on the peasantry and minor civil servants, who characteristically feared any drastic changes in the status quo, Tsiranana long maintained that "only a minority of malcontents" wanted independence, and that the majority of Malagasys did not favor total amnesty for political prisoners.[7]

Tsiranana had other reasons, too, for championing so conservative a viewpoint. He was among the rare Malagasys who realized that Madagascar's isolation and underdevelopment constituted a danger, and he believed that the best way to counter this was to cling closely to France. On the other hand, it was politically hazardous for him to keep on denying the rising popular demand for independence, which the A.K.F.M. was assiduously cultivating. Fortunately for Tsiranana, developments in French-speaking Negro Africa opened a way out of this dilemma. In December 1959 General de Gaulle agreed not only to grant independence to the Mali Federation and permit it to remain in the Community, but also to continue giving it financial and technical aid. Tsiranana quickly opened negotiations with France and succeeded in obtaining equally advantageous terms for Madagascar. In this way he satisfied fundamental Malagasy nationalist aspirations and at the same time cut much of the ground from under the A.K.F.M. Total amnesty, the other popular A.K.F.M. slogan, posed political problems that were not so easily overcome. Using one excuse and then another, blaming the French Parliament for dilatory tactics and the A.K.F.M. for torpedoing his amnesty negotiations with de Gaulle, sometimes claiming that neither the M.D.R.M. deputies nor the Malagasy people really wanted them to return, Tsiranana kept postponing the moment when he would have to take decisive action on this issue. He managed to do so until after independence was formally ceded and then arranged for the return of the M.D.R.M. deputies on his own terms.

For the first 14 months of the autonomous republic's existence, however, it was far from clear how the independence and amnesty issues would be settled, and the future of the P.S.D. seemed to be precarious. Would inde-

pendence lead to a communist take-over of the island? If the M.D.R.M. deputies were permitted to return to Madagascar, might they not stir up violence
again, or at least offer competition dangerous to the P.S.D. leadership? In
brief, had they retained their vast popular following, and how really firm
were the P.S.D.'s foundations?

Between October 1958 and December 1959 Tsiranana devoted much of his
time to creating a legally unassailable position for himself and his government, while Resampa concentrated on consolidating the party structure. To
combat his party's most formidable enemy, the A.K.F.M., Tsiranana had
formed an alliance with the U.D.S.M., then a regional party in the southeast led by the Zafimahova brothers, whose outlook was about as conservative as his own. After their joint victory in the referendum, however, the
U.D.S.M. began to develop in a way displeasing to its partner. On a platform that skillfully blended Christian socialism with a mild dose of nationalism, the U.D.S.M launched an intensive and surprisingly successful campaign to win over and mobilize the rural masses. A party congress held early
in 1959 in the Tananarive suburb of Isotry brought together several hundred
delegates from all over Madagascar. It showed clearly that the U.D.S.M. had
now expanded far beyond its original starting point in Fianarantsoa province and was invading regions that the P.S.D. regarded as its own strongholds. Adroitly Tsiranana managed to win over two prominent Fianarantsoa politicians (Senator Robert Marson and Provincial Assemblyman Paul
Sileny), and their defection marked the outbreak of hostilities between the
two former partners.

Actually the main battle was fought in the assembly at Tananarive, where
a "doctrinal quarrel" over the draft constitution served as a cloak for party
rivalries, and above all for personality conflicts. In a presidential regime such
as that proposed by Tsiranana, he would put himself and his party firmly in
the saddle. By advocating a parliamentary regime, Norbert Zafimahova saw
a chance for himself as president of the assembly to play as influential a role
as the chief executive. In February 1959 he got a pledge from the 20 U.D.S.M.
assemblymen to resign their seats in the event that a majority of their colleagues voted in favor of a presidential-type constitution. But within a
month the P.S.D. had succeeded in undermining the loyalty of the U.D.S.M.
assemblymen and by a maneuver had also captured the presidency of Fianarantsoa's provincial council. Seeing that the fight was now hopeless, the
Zafimahova brothers preferred to withdraw rather than continue the struggle. Norbert went to Paris and Antoine pleaded ill health, so neither was
present on April 29, 1959, when the assembly—with only one adverse vote
—accepted a constitution of the presidential type. Two days later, Tsiranana
was elected president of the republic by exactly the same virtually unanimous vote. Thus the U.D.S.M. members not only failed to resign as they

had pledged but voted in favor of both the P.S.D.-tailored constitution and the P.S.D. presidential candidate.

Charging that Norbert Zafimahova's absence on the day the constitution was voted was "inadmissible," the P.S.D. assemblymen forced him to resign as president of the assembly on May 22, 1959. He was replaced by Jules Ravony, nominally also a member of the U.D.S.M. but already well on his way to joining the P.S.D. Confirmation of the U.D.S.M.'s decline came in the municipal elections of October 11, 1959, when it lost to the P.S.D. its two strongholds of Farafangana and Manakara. But by this time the U.D.S.M. was in any case hopelessly split. A small faction under Norbert Zafimahova now called itself the Union des Sociaux-Démocrates de Madagascar (U.S.D.M.) and joined the groups opposing the P.S.D. A majority of former U.D.S.M. members led by Ravony and Dr. Albert Sylla drifted into the P.S.D. camp and were rewarded with high government posts.

By the time Tsiranana was so overwhelmingly elected president of the Malagasy Republic, he had established himself as Madagascar's most skillful politician and as a "valid interlocutor" for negotiating with France. Except for the A.K.F.M., which maintained its strength in Tananarive and Diégo-Suarez, he had eliminated or neutralized all those who had voted "no" in the referendum, such as Stanislas Rakotonirina, or those who had come out against his draft constitution, as was the case of Norbert Zafimahova. Either because they had actively opposed his policies or seemed likely to do so, Tsiranana had dismissed the provincial or municipal councilors of Tananarive, Diégo-Suarez, and Majunga and replaced them by appointed "special delegations." He had virtually eliminated elective government at the provincial level and hastily instituted it at the lower rural communal level. He appealed for national unity but made it possible only under his leadership.

Tsiranana was most freely criticized by those Merina who could not forgive the rapid rise of this Tsimihety former cattle herder and primary school teacher to the eminence of president of the republic at the age of 47. He was also resented by those ultranationalists who looked with disfavor on his friendship with General de Gaulle, who called Tsiranana "my friend and my companion."[8] But even those who refused to regard Tsiranana as an ambitious parvenu or a traitor to his country could not deny his dictatorial tendencies. He had engineered the adoption of the first constitutional law by a congress of provincial assemblymen in which the territorial assembly did not participate as such. To assure approval of the second constitutional law, he had hastily set up a committee of 37 members, of whom the government named no fewer than 28. Then he had drafted a constitution for a bicameral Parliament, in which this committee would automatically become the senate, thus guaranteeing an easy passage through the legislature for the constitution itself. Finally he had maneuvered his own election as president only two days later.

To be sure, Tsiranana's rapid and comparatively easy successes would not have been possible had he not found capable collaborators, such as Resampa, and had not the party been made up largely of inexperienced and ignorant men willing to accept strong guidance. Probably his victories would have been impossible had not the opposition also been so divided and individualistic. The A.K.F.M. preserved a certain unity by means of party discipline, but its ideological division between extreme nationalists and Marxists prevented its charting and pursuing a consistent forward course. The other parties opposed to the P.S.D. were led by men intent on maintaining a firm control over their personal following and unwilling to work as a team with other leaders. The P.S.D. had no one who could compete in intellectual brilliance, oratory, and culture with Richard Andrianamanjato, nor any policy that was based on a doctrine like that of the A.K.F.M. Its press organ, *La République,* stressed "socialism" as the P.S.D.'s guiding principle but never went so far as to define it. Probably only the French S.F.I.O. advisers of the P.S.D. ever conceived of its socialism in abstract terms, and if there was any practical application of that political philosophy it was in the very visible growth of *étatisme*. Yet in extending the party's grip over all phases of national life, the P.S.D. needed above all more cadres, a sector in which it was exceptionally weak owing to the *côtiers'* lack of education. It had to scrape the bottom of the barrel merely to find enough qualified men to fill the main administrative posts. Even the members of the assembly had so little knowledge of the business of government that some of them failed to grasp the most rudimentary concepts. As Alexandre Ranatanaela, an exceptionally frank assemblyman, put it to his colleagues on August 27, 1959: "Before voting the constitution, when the question arose as to what governmental regime we should give Madagascar, we were greatly embarrassed. We did not know how to distinguish between a presidential and a parliamentary regime, for all such things are new to us."

Considering the P.S.D.'s lack of cadres and the self-interest and naïveté of the great majority of its amorphous membership, it is a wonder that it survived at all as a party, let alone that it established a clear-cut ascendancy over its rivals. Part of the answer lies in Tsiranana's skill as a political strategist and in the appeal of his jovial and commonsense personality for the masses. Furthermore, he and Resampa formed a purposeful and energetic team who knew what they wanted for their party and worked together to get it. In this way and by such means, they could without disaster to the P.S.D. assume responsibility for such unpopular actions as postponing national elections for a new assembly and also postponing the return of the exiled M.D.R.M. deputies.

Chapter eight

INDEPENDENCE AND AMNESTY

When Tsiranana went to Paris early in February 1960 to negotiate the transfer of powers, he astutely took with him delegates from a wide range of Malagasy parties.* Moreover, his mission was accorded the publicly expressed confidence of 84 of Madagascar's 90 assemblymen. Early in January, Raseta, still in France, had given his blessing to Tsiranana's negotiations, to the embarrassment of some A.K.F.M. extremists,[1] and the other two M.D.R.M. deputies followed suit at a press conference in Paris on February 17, 1960.[2] Their joint declaration indicated that by then a bargain had been struck, by which Tsiranana in return for their support had agreed to ask France to grant total amnesty to all Malagasy political prisoners after Madagascar's independence was declared. The three-month period between the acceptance by France of the principle of Madagascar's independence and the announcement on March 26, 1960, of the success of the Franco-Malagasy negotiations was marked by a political unity among the Malagasys such as they have never known before or since. It was in the glow of this unprecedented political harmony that Tsiranana requested and obtained special powers for his government during the period from mid-January to early October 1960, when a newly elected assembly would meet for its first budgetary session. In addition, because of the unusual affability of the Malagasy parliamentarians, he was able to prevail on them to accept austerity measures that adversely affected their living standards.

This idyllic period in Madagascar's political life could not long endure. It soon became evident that the slogan of "independence and amnesty," which for so many years had served virtually every Malagasy politician as an effective vote-catching device, had quite different meanings for those who used it as a rallying cry. When "independence and amnesty" materialized, the

---

* His delegation included such politicians as Emile Ramaroson, a former collaborator of Stanislas Rakotonirina on the Tananarive municipal council, and Rajaonson, president of the Senate and a former leader of the A.K.F.M.

established party alignments and in some cases party objectives underwent changes. Ironically enough, independence and amnesty grievously disappointed the groups that had been most vocal in advocating them, and benefited above all the P.S.D., which had been most reluctant to ask for them.

To the P.S.D. the winning of independence and amnesty brought an unexpected extension of its influence and a reorientation of its foreign policy. In particular, Tsiranana, who for years had refused to ask France for an "immediate independence that could only be fictitious," came to realize late in 1959 that Madagascar had everything to gain and nothing to lose by following the example of Guinea and the Mali Federation. While in New York attending the autumn session of the United Nations General Assembly, Tsiranana had been impressed by the official welcome given Sékou Touré by the Americans, and even more by the probability that the cautious and francophile Houphouët-Boigny would soon ask for independence for the Entente states.* De Gaulle's concessions to the Mali Federation† dispelled any lingering doubts that Tsiranana might have had on the advisability of his following a similar course, which had the additional advantage of enabling him to outflank his domestic opponents on the very issues that were the lifeblood of their political strength.

To make sure that Madagascar's independence would not mean isolation, which Tsiranana regarded as highly dangerous in view of the intensity of the cold war at the time, he linked his country firmly with the Western world, especially with France and the European Economic Community, and with the conservative French-speaking Negro African countries. This gave Madagascar's independence another dimension which inevitably brought the P.S.D. government into new areas of conflict with the extreme left-wing and nationalistic Malagasys, who had envisaged very different foreign alignments for a sovereign Madagascar. Before the negotiations on the transfer of powers had been completed, the A.K.F.M., in early March 1960,[3] had already shown its hand by insisting that Madagascar withdraw from the Community and the franc zone and demand that France give up its military and naval bases on the island. Even the economic program that the A.K.F.M. advocated at the same time had international implications contrary to those of Tsiranana's. The A.K.F.M. leader maintained that Madagascar could never be truly independent until it nationalized the island's natural resources, transport, trade, and industry, took back the land acquired by foreign *colons* and companies "by trickery or by force," and accepted aid from the Eastern as well as the Western bloc.

* These were the Ivory Coast, Niger, Dahomey, and Upper Volta.
† See p. 109.

This program had the double advantage of offering a positive alternative to that of the P.S.D. and of diminishing the credit that that party might gain from its successful negotiations with France by denigrating the value of the independence thus won. Although this program satisfied both the left-wing and nationalist elements of the A.K.F.M., it could not wholly gloss over the profound differences in regard to independence that differentiated the Marxists from the Merina nationalist members. To the handful of Malagasy Marxists and their French and Russian sponsors who were trying to use the A.K.F.M. as a Trojan horse for the communist take-over of Madagascar, the attitude of the Merina nationalists with whom they had joined forces proved to be deeply disappointing. From the outset the latter had refused to be guided by the French Communist Party,* and this continued to be true even after the Marxists had accepted the priority given by the Malagasy nationalists to independence and amnesty over more revolutionary concepts. Briefly—and erroneously—the extreme Marxists had been encouraged by the revolt of 1947 into believing that the time was ripe for more direct action. They mistook the violent defensive reflex of a profoundly frightened and exasperated segment of the population as indicating a genuinely revolutionary situation. The extreme nationalists, along with the rest of the Malagasys, recoiled in horror from the devastation and mutual recriminations associated with the revolt and its repression. This collective renunciation of further violence, together with the denunciation of communism and all its works by the influential Christian missions, made Madagascar an unpromising field for the sowing of extreme left-wing doctrines.

What the dedicated Marxists either did not grasp or refused to admit was that the Merina nationalists with whom they were closely associated wanted only an independence that would restore their own rule over Madagascar. The Merina simply assumed that this would automatically follow if the French could be persuaded to give up their rule of the island. Apparently they did not realize that the "popular democracy" which they had joined their Marxist comrades in advocating would inevitably mean government by the numerically strongest element—the *côtiers*. Nor did the Merina seem to have thought through how so socially divided a tribe as theirs, in the event that they actually managed to take over power, could remain sufficiently united to govern the island. Some were monarchists and some republicans, but all the Merina seemed to take for granted that the traditional feudal class divisions between aristocrats, bourgeois, and slaves were permanent.[4] In the noble caste alone there were seven subdivisions, not to mention the additional cleavages caused by family and personal feuds. And

* See pp. 61–62.

there was very little social contact between the individual *andriana* and *hova* Merina, although they might go to the same school, attend the same church, and belong to the same political party. Much less would a Merina of either the noble or bourgeois caste consider fraternizing with a *côtier*. Indeed, one of the chief obstacles to the spread of Merina influence had always been the reluctance of Merina civil servants to leave the high plateaus even for a tour of duty on the coast. Although many Merina claimed that their social aloofness would in no way hamper their leadership of a national state, it would certainly make it no easier. Nor did they have any plan for persuading the *côtiers* to accept a reassertion of Merina leadership, to which the latter would certainly object, for it would deprive them of the advantages they had gained as a result of French rule and two years of P.S.D. government under the *loi-cadre*.

In the same unrealistic way, the Merina nationalists persisted in demanding the return of the three M.D.R.M. deputies without weighing its far-reaching political implications. In their eyes, Raseta, Ravoahangy, and Rabemananjara were symbols of national aspirations that had been frustrated by alien conquerors and not three individuals who for many years had been away from Madagascar and might no longer be capable or desirous of leading a nationalist movement. The immediate advantage that both the Marxists and the Merina nationalists hoped to gain by the exiles' return was the trouble they anticipated it would cause for the P.S.D. government. In the late spring of 1960 the prospect of Madagascar's independence, to be followed by the return of the three M.D.R.M. deputies and by the election of a new legislature, seemed to the A.K.F.M. leaders most propitious for their hopes of a drastic change in the domestic political situation. This probably lay behind the surprising announcement made in early May by the A.K.F.M. politburo that it accepted the agreements that Tsiranana had negotiated with France for independence and future cooperation.[5] So convinced were the Merina of the *côtiers'* incompetence that they were sure Tsiranana's government would collapse without the backing of the French administration and that all they would then need to do would be to pick up the pieces. They seem not to have foreseen that the *présence française* might be maintained through the continued activity of French political advisers in the guise of technicians, or that Tsiranana would be clever enough to come to terms with the exiles before agreeing to their return.

As a vote-getting slogan, amnesty had been coupled with independence by the nationals and radicals ever since the Tananarive trial of 1948. And as was the case with the demand for independence, Tsiranana had long hesitated before committing his government to total amnesty. In 1958 the P.S.D. leaders had been alienated by the M.D.R.M. deputies' advocacy of a "no" vote in the September referendum, and in 1960 they feared lest the return of such glamorous national heroes would diminish their own following on the island. To a lesser extent the A.K.F.M. had by then also become somewhat worried about the effect on their own party's popularity of the exiles' return, but continued to believe that it would adversely affect the P.S.D.'s membership more than its own. If Madagascar's two major parties were growing more alarmed by the prospective repercussions of the exiles' return, it was also now becoming clear that the three M.D.R.M. deputies themselves were deeply concerned lest their long absence from Madagascar should result in a disastrous loss of popularity.

Raseta's communist affiliations made him the obvious candidate for the A.K.F.M.'s support, but because of his advanced age and ill health, he was a less formidable competitor for political leadership than Ravoahangy or Rabemananjara. Raseta himself must have expected more than the honorary position that the A.K.F.M. was willing to accord him, for he formed a splinter movement, the Malagasy National Union (FIPIMA), in February 1963 when he finally realized that he was not going to be given or was unable to capture the leadership of the left-wing movement. Ravoahangy, also aging, took a more realistic view of his own situation and of his popularity in Madagascar. During his exile in France, he had come to enjoy security and relative affluence as a physician in Toulouse, and he realized that his following in Madagascar was limited almost wholly to the Protestant Merina aristocracy, of which he was a member. Rabemananjara, who had a French wife and a coterie of admirers in Paris literary circles, could hardly expect to find such a congenial milieu in Tananarive. He was the only one of the three M.D.R.M. deputies, however, whose youth, trained intellect, and oratorical abilities matched his halo of heroic martyrdom and justified his hopes of playing a prominent role in the political future of his country.

In view of the disparity in their chances of future political success in Madagascar and the personal divergencies between them, Tsiranana in the spring of 1960 did not have to deal with the M.D.R.M. deputies as a united front. Ravoahangy and Rabemananjara had not been on good terms since their publicly expressed mutual recriminations for responsibility in the 1947 revolt,* and Raseta's ill-fated attempt in July 1959 to return to Madagascar with the connivance of the French communist Robert Ballanger and without the knowledge of his fellow exiles isolated him from the other two. By mid-1959 Tsiranana seems to have written off Raseta, whom he described as "no real patriot" because he was trying to revive "ancestral hatreds" between the Merina and coastal tribes.[6] Ravoahangy, it soon became evident, could be won over by the prospect of a cabinet post.

It was indispensable, however, for Tsiranana to come to terms with Rabe-

* See p. 54.

mananjara before the latter's return to Madagascar, for among the three exiles he was Tsiranana's only formidable rival. Already Rabemananjara was being courted by the A.K.F.M. as well as by the Catholic missionaries. Since he was a Betsimisaraka and a M.D.R.M. nationalist martyr, his membership in the A.K.F.M. would lend substance to that party's contention that it was not controlled by Merina and Marxist extremists. Then, too, as a Catholic intellectual imbued with French culture, Rabemananjara could provide the leadership needed to build up the third force which the Catholic missionaries were trying to create between the P.S.D. and A.K.F.M. In the immediate future Tsiranana could give Rabemananjara a ministerial portfolio, a more tangible temptation than either the A.K.F.M. or the Catholic mission could offer, as well as the eventual prospect of becoming Tsiranana's heir-apparent, for only Resampa among the P.S.D. talent could dispute Rabemananjara that likely eventuality. By the end of April 1960, Rabemananjara had evidently yielded to the P.S.D.'s siren call, for he made a public declaration to the effect that he had "always recognized President Tsiranana's eminent role in the great work of national liberation."[7]

June 1960 proved to be a busy month of preparation for the momentous events to come. The French Parliament ratified the agreements with Madagascar by a slightly larger vote than the one by which it approved the very similar agreements with the Mali Federation, debated at the same time.[8] A P.S.D. congress held at Tuléar decided that elections for Madagascar's new legislature should take place before the end of 1960, although the mandate of the incumbent legislators did not expire until the following year. Still later in the month, Tsiranana brought back from France the first group of amnestied Malagasy political exiles, including Joel Sylvain and Tata Max. But it was not until three weeks after the proclamation on June 26 of Madagascar's independence that the three most prominent Malagasy exiles were brought back to their native land by Tsiranana himself in his private plane.

On July 18, thousands of Malagasys from all over the island made their way to the airport 50 kilometers from Tananarive, hours before the president's plane was due to arrive. The delirious welcome that they gave the three M.D.R.M. deputies contrasted strikingly with the Malagasy people's habitual reserve and with the restrained manner in which they had greeted the preceding group of political returnees. Only two incidents of mob violence marred the ceremonies marking the deputies' return: one on July 20 in front of the Tananarive town hall and the other the next day at a Protestant church in that city which was holding a service of thanksgiving. In those two clashes between youthful demonstrators and the police some 30 persons were wounded and 20 automobiles damaged.[9] It was widely feared at the time that such violence might be the prelude to a well-organized campaign with xenophobic and communistic overtones, but there were no more incidents. The three M.D.R.M. deputies made a concerted appeal for national unity, and early in August they issued a common official declaration to the effect that they belonged to no political party, either Malagasy or foreign, and that their aim was to work solely for the "higher interests and unity" of their country.[10]

It seemed clear that the three former M.D.R.M. exiles had accepted the role of nationalist symbols rather than of individual political leaders, which had been implicitly assigned them upon their return by their compatriots. Such a symbolic role was consistent with the lack of bitterness and absence of xenophobia that characterized the Malagasys' comparatively sober celebration of their independence. The only visible signs of their country's new status were small changes in army uniforms and in some street names. When the ultranationalist press proposed removing Gallieni's statue from the main street of the capital, Tsiranana said he saw no reason to deny what Gallieni had done for Madagascar and that he would consider the proposal only if Gallieni's statue were replaced by one of General de Gaulle. The sweet reasonableness of Madagascar's internal and external relations astonished many members of the 72 delegations from foreign countries and organizations that came to celebrate Madagascar's transition to national sovereignty at Tananarive on July 29–31, 1960, and some of them said it was too good to be true or to last.

The Legislative and Provincial Elections

Immediately after the independence celebrations, Tsiranana announced that the long-awaited elections for the legislative assembly would be held on September 4, 1960, those for the provincial assemblies on September 11, and those for the Senate on October 2. By early August the electoral campaign was in full swing, with Tsiranana tirelessly stumping the island's seven electoral circumscriptions* and holding numerous conferences with delegations from all the parties except the A.K.F.M. To prevent a dispersal of the moderate vote, which could mainly benefit the A.K.F.M., he urged the other parties to get together and run their candidates on "lists of national union." To this all the delegates agreed in principle, but they found that in practice they could not carry it out. Personal and regional considerations proved to be more compelling than Tsiranana's appeal for national union, especially after it became apparent that the P.S.D. expected other parties to accept its leadership and that it would not treat them as genuine collaborators.

---

* The six provinces and Tananarive town.

Only in Majunga did a clear-cut contest develop between the P.S.D. and the A.K.F.M. There Jean-Jacques Natai was able to marshal virtually the whole province behind his *"fokonolona"*-sponsored slate of candidates, who were, however, loyal primarily to himself and only secondarily to the P.S.D. In Diégo-Suarez, Justin Bezara not only ignored Tsiranana's appeal but formed a new party, the FIVAMA (Democratic Rally of the Malagasy People) to contest the elections. He thus weakened the opposition to the A.K.F.M., which was powerful in that provincial capital, by refusing to join forces with the two local P.S.D. leaders, Céléstin Aridy and Victor Miadana, both of whom had been ministers in Tsiranana's government. Resampa headed the P.S.D. ticket in Tuléar province, where the A.K.F.M. was also opposed by different lists sponsored by the MONIMA and by the U.D.S.M. Fianarantsoa province, where the Christian parties and the U.D.S.M. were strongest, had no fewer than six lists of candidates, as did Tananarive town. There two of the three former M.D.R.M. deputies found themselves competing for the votes of the same electorate. Ravoahangy carried out Tsiranana's wishes by heading a list of national union, whereas Raseta not surprisingly assumed a more partisan position and accepted the A.K.F.M.'s sponsorship of his candidacy. As to solidarity inside the P.S.D. itself, the situation in Tamatave province was complicated. There Bezaka's R.N.M. supported a slate called the Miara Mirindra, headed by Rabemananjara, which included some breakaway P.S.D. members and known supporters of Tsiranana such as Albert Sylla and Jean-François Jarison. But this list was opposed not only by the A.K.F.M., as expected, but by a rival or orthodox P.S.D. ticket led by Arsène Rakotovahiny and five other locally prominent members of the government party. In all Madagascar there were 28 lists, which totaled 471 candidates for the 107 seats at stake in the legislative assembly. Most of Madagascar's small parties or political clubs were responsive to Tsiranana's astute appeal to pool their electoral resources, but the major parties opposed to the P.S.D. at this time—especially the A.K.F.M., U.D.S.M., and MONIMA—preferred to take their chances with the electorate as separate political entities.

The election of September 4 was a success for the government party, but it did not appreciably enhance the control it had had over the preceding assembly. Voter participation, including that of the European electorate for a change, was higher than ever before—75 per cent of the 2,400,000 registered electors, compared with 72 per cent for the 1958 referendum. In the outgoing 90-man assembly, the government had had 50 P.S.D. members, as well as 18 U.D.S.M. and ten R.C.M. members, on whose support it could usually count, and the extremist groups had no representatives. The new assembly included 81 P.S.D. members, the lists headed by Rabemananjara and Ravoahangy won 16 and seven seats respectively, and the A.K.F.M. placed three of its candidates running in Tananarive town (Raseta, Andrianamanjato, and Jaozandry). The P.S.D.'s strength was confirmed in its former bastions and beyond. In Majunga province it won 96 per cent of the votes, in Tuléar and Diégo-Suarez 80 per cent, and in Fianarantsoa 60 per cent. No exact appraisal of its strength in Tamatave was possible, for the party there was frankly split, and only in his capital city was Tsiranana certainly in a minority position. Outstanding individual casualties of this election were Stanislas Rakotonirina, Norbert Zafimahova, Justin Bezara, Francis Sautron, and Arsène Rakotovahiny. Two Frenchmen—Eugène Lechat and André Lemaire—were elected, a sharp decline compared with the 22 who had sat in the outgoing assembly.

Many of the defeated candidates—and this was especially true of the A.K.F.M.'s list (which had won 103,000 of the 364,000 votes cast in Tananarive province)—would have been elected had a proportional system of voting been adopted. But under the system by which a ticket that wins a majority of the votes in a given electoral circumscription takes all the seats at stake, the P.S.D.'s victory was larger in terms of assemblymen elected than was justified by the actual tally of votes it chalked up. Furthermore, neither the A.K.F.M. nor Ravoahangy's followers could be represented on key committees, for neither had the ten members required, under the assembly's rules, as a minimum to constitute a parliamentary group. This more or less forced Ravoahangy's supporters to vote with the P.S.D. majority and reduced the three A.K.F.M. deputies to a position of parliamentary impotency.

In the provincial-assembly elections of September 11, the P.S.D. repeated its victory on a smaller scale. Although this was the second electoral consultation of the population within a week and although the A.K.F.M. preached abstention in four of Madagascar's six provinces, 60 per cent of the registered electorate actually voted. In the provincial assemblies only those seats not already filled by the province's deputies and senators were open to election by direct universal adult suffrage for a five-year term. Here again the pattern established a week earlier was repeated: the P.S.D. took all the seats available in the four provinces of Majunga, Tuléar, Diégo-Suarez, and Fianarantsoa, shared in the victory of Rabemananjara in Tamatave, and won in Tananarive province, though it lost to the A.K.F.M. in the capital city. In the still less important senatorial elections of October 2, in which only 36 of the 54 seats were to be filled by an electoral college composed of 107 deputies, 93 provincial assemblymen, and 11,000 municipal and rural councilors, the P.S.D. and Christian Party candidates made a clean sweep. This time the A.K.F.M. called for total abstention, having withdrawn at the last minute the only slate of candidates it presented at all, in Diégo-Suarez province.

Inasmuch as the president of the republic was empowered to appoint the remaining 18 senators, it was no wonder that the opposition parties recognized the uselessness of competing.

October 3, the day after the senatorial elections, marked the end of the period for which the government had been granted special powers to negotiate the transfer of sovereignty from France and to install the administrative machinery of an independent Malagasy republic. It remained to be seen if the new assembly, which held its first meeting on that very day, would be able to effect any change in the situation.

Chapter nine

CONSOLIDATION OF TSIRANANA'S POWER

The consummate skill with which Tsiranana had stolen the opposition leaders' thunder, turning their slogan of independence and amnesty against them and utilizing it to further his own ends, continued to serve him well in his next self-assigned task of consolidating his own power. His basic strategy was to win over or neutralize the moderate elements among his opponents, and thus isolate his hopelessly intransigent enemies in the A.K.F.M. This strategy he used both inside and outside the Parliament, where it hinged on the issue of constitutional change, and with both individuals and parties, to whom his appeals were made in the name of national unity. Tsiranana's tactics to some extent brought him into conflict with the most partisan element in his own party, led by André Rasampa. Like his counterparts in the monolithic single-party states of French-speaking Africa, Resampa favored the elimination of all opposition to the P.S.D. and the adoption of a formal party doctrine—in this case "Malagasy socialism." Tsiranana, on the other hand, was at his best as a pragmatist, simply preempting whatever he found useful, regardless of its name, and being concerned only with its practical value. Thus far he has been remarkably successful in avoiding extremes and finding middle-of-the-road solutions.

The Government and the Parliament

After the elections of September 1960, Tsiranana's first move was to prevent the formation of a third force by his moderate opponents. He did this by the time-honored device of offering the men most likely to lead such a movement posts in his cabinet, and at the same time he tried to distribute other political plums as evenly as possible among the provinces. Resampa, on the other hand, firmly believed that to the victor belong the spoils, and he would have liked to place every post that carried responsibility in P.S.D. hands.[1] While Tsiranana naturally was not going to take into his government any politician likely to oppose P.S.D. policies, he wanted to use his patronage potential to win over as many as possible of the 25 deputies who owed allegiance to Rabemananjara and Ravoahangy, particularly the 16 Catholics who composed the Miara Mirindra party. As a confirmed socialist, Tsiranana favored a lay republic, and as head of a party that included non-Christians he was averse to Catholic mission influence on local politics. To check any attempt the Jesuits might make to constitute a political group midway between the P.S.D and A.K.F.M., Tsiranana took two seemingly irrelevant but fundamentally related steps. He expelled a politically overzealous French priest* and he made Rabemananjara a minister in his cabinet.

Because of what Tsiranana aptly called the "voracity of certain appetites," it took him until October 10, 1960, to form the first government set up after Madagascar became independent. He himself assumed the portfolio of defense as well as the premiership. He persuaded his old friend Calvin Tsiebo, a Bara schoolteacher and long-time member of the P.S.D., to give up the post of president of the assembly, to which he had just been elected, and accept the vice-premiership. The Labor portfolio went to the R.C.M., in the person of Jarison. Albert Sylla, who still had one foot in the U.D.S.M. camp, was named Minister of Foreign Affairs, Ravoahangy was given the Health portfolio, and Rabemananjara that of National Economy. Eugène Lechat and Paul Longuet, the two Frenchmen on whom Tsiranana most relied, were retained as Ministers of Public Works and Finance respectively. Most of the remaining cabinet positions went to P.S.D. members—that of Interior to André Resampa, Agriculture to René Rasidy, and Education to Laurent Botokeky—as did the nine secretaryships of state. With the exception of the A.K.F.M., Tsiranana could justifiably claim that his was a government of national unity and one as widely representative as possible of Madagascar's various interest groups, regions, and tribes. However, if the French were Madagascar's twentieth tribe, as Tsiranana fondly called them, they were its smallest one and yet they had two representatives in the cabinet, while the Merina, the largest and most evolved of all Malagasy tribes, had only two spokesmen. One of these was Dr. Joseph Ravoahangy, who retained a following among the Protestant aristocracy of Tananarive but who could no longer be regarded as an ultranationalist Merina.

Having distributed ministerial posts with an eye primarily to winning over party leaders, Tsiranana next turned his attention to such opposition forces as remained unappeased in the Parliament. Considering the overwhelming majority of P.S.D. deputies (81), the fact that the A.K.F.M. "intractables" numbered only three, and that in between came 26 men who

* Père de Puybaudet, who was charged with confusing freedom of religion with freedom to play politics.

more often than not voted with the government, it seems surprising that Tsiranana, who was operating under a semipresidential regime, should have concerned himself seriously with the parliamentary opposition. However, because self-government was so new to Madagascar and party discipline so lax, each Malagasy deputy and senator acted as a law unto himself. The fact that the so-called head of a party promised to support the government was no guaranty that his followers would do likewise. Even the P.S.D., which as the government party had more prizes to offer than the others, was not immune to rebellion within its ranks, and in the spring of 1961 it expelled for lack of discipline three prominent members, including Senator Robert Marson.[2] Madagascar's newly elected deputies and senators naturally wanted more powers for themselves and fewer for the government. This attitude played neatly into the hands of the A.K.F.M., which gave it the prestige of a "doctrine," using it as leverage and as ammunition in its propaganda for changing the constitution.

In its electoral campaigns of August and September 1960, the A.K.F.M. had stressed the theme that Madagascar must make *tabula rasa* of its April 1959 constitution if it were to be transformed into an independent popular democracy. Besides wanting a revision of Madagascar's relations with France so that they might be more in keeping with its new sovereign status, the A.K.F.M. propagandists insisted that the semipresidential regime be replaced by a parliamentary one. For exactly the opposite reason—the replacement of a semipresidential by a strongly presidential regime—the Resampa faction of the P.S.D. also favored making a clean sweep of the 1959 constitution. This element saw no reason why the P.S.D., victorious at the polls, should tolerate any opposition at all, listen to long-winded senators discuss minor points of procedure, or consult the population again except perhaps in terms of a simple referendum. Tsiranana did not adopt such an extreme attitude, claiming that it was unnecessary to do more than make minor changes in the constitution. He did, however, curb the deputies' attempts to widen their own powers, gradually undermined the senate's authority, and again sought to legislate for a time without parliamentary interference under another grant of special powers.

The legislative assembly which Madagascar elected on September 4, 1960, got off to a bad start. Its first sessions were taken up with an acrimonious examination of defeated candidates' accusations of fraud and coercion by the government during the electoral campaign. This was followed by wrangling over the composition of the assembly's eight committees. All but the P.S.D. deputies complained that the government party was monopolizing the key offices of committee president, vice-president, and *rapporteur*. They also charged that the government only exceptionally appointed members of the

Miara Mirindra and Ravoahangy groups to represent Madagascar at international meetings.

Twice during 1961 there were specific conflicts in authority between the government and the assembly. In June, 32 deputies including six members of the P.S.D. signed a request asking the government to allow it "to pass resolutions dealing with every phase of national life."[3] This was turned down on the grounds that it would "further encourage the deputies' already pronounced addiction to demagogy." The next month a spokesman for the Miara Mirindra group complained that high P.S.D. functionaries were using their authority to prevent deputies who belonged to other parties from holding public meetings in their constituencies. Resampa, not surprisingly, upheld his provincial prefects, though he did admit that some of them had acted tactlessly. In a spirited reply, Resampa countercharged that the members of the Madagascar Parliament were given to interfering in civil-service appointments, ordering such officials about, and even, on occasion, disturbing the public order.[4] There is little doubt that the actions of both parliamentarians and officials were open to criticism, but the government used every opportunity, whether wholly justifiable or not, to keep a whip hand over the Parliament.

The assembly reacted to displays of governmental authoritarianism in much the same way as its predecessors had reacted toward the colonial administration. Indirectly it criticized official policy when it repeatedly insisted that Malagasy be promoted as the national language, Malagasy traditions and customs be preserved against corrosive modernization, and the administrative cadres be more rapidly "Malagasized." The deputies attacked the government directly for its failure to explain official policies to them and to send ministers to answer their questions during debates, and for its repeated usurpations of the deputies' prerogatives. The P.S.D. leaders, for their part, criticized the deputies for the wordy repetitiousness of their debates, their absenteeism and—when present—their unruly and undisciplined behavior, and above all their provincial outlook, particularly evident during the budgetary sessions, when national interests were sacrificed to parochial ones.

If the government showed its lack of respect for the assembly by infringing the deputies' constitutional rights, it actively moved to eliminate some of the rights held by the senate. The two most original features of Madagascar's constitution were the bicameral Parliament and the broadly based electoral college, which chose the president of the republic. It was not until May 18, 1962, that Tsiranana obtained the assembly's approval of a direct consultation of the total electorate, although his election on May 1, 1959, was overhasty and somewhat irregular. At about the same time he moved to downgrade the powers of the senate. Madagascar's "Chamber of Reflection" from the outset took its role very seriously, used the Malagasy language in preference to French, and gave exhaustive readings to every draft law it examined. Its members, especially the one-third who were appointees, complained frequently that on official occasions they were treated like poor relations and were shown even less consideration by the government than were the deputies. The P.S.D. leaders, in turn, charged that the senate's procedural methods were too slow and pushed through a constitutional amendment on June 5, 1962, which emasculated the senators' powers to delay legislation that had already been passed by the assembly. A few days earlier the government had asked for special powers from the Parliament to govern by decree for a four-month period. This was reluctantly granted for the second time. It then issued 130 regulations, almost all of which laid the legal groundwork for implementing its new economic policies.

The practical steps by which Tsiranana gradually gained the essence of what he wanted without profoundly troubling the established order and tranquillity dear to the Malagasys displeased the extremists. Both the Resampa wing of his own party and the A.K.F.M. felt that he did not go far enough and, above all, that he was not operating according to a "doctrine." Richard Andrianamanjato, the A.K.F.M. president, stressed in the assembly the inadequacy of the government's "tinkering" with the constitution, and warned that if the existing trend went unchecked Madagascar would gradually and imperceptibly slide from a semipresidential to a wholly presidential regime.[5] It was pointless, he went on to say, for the A.K.F.M. to take part in the debates concerning slight constitutional alterations: only a complete revision of the constitution would enable the country to acquire the parliamentary regime that it should have. Resampa, on the other hand, wanted a constitutional change that would set up a strongly presidential regime, as "the only one capable of meeting the needs of the hour." A speech that Resampa made at the socialist congress in Milan late in the spring of 1961 had caused quite a stir in Tananarive, for it suggested a sharp divergence from Tsiranana also in regard to economic policy. Resampa may well have been called discreetly to order, for he soon issued a statement saying that he had been "misinterpreted and that my thinking is identical with that of President Tsiranana."[6] He spelled this out by saying that he advocated state intervention in the Malagasy economy only if and where private enterprise failed, and the acceptance of aid from the Eastern bloc countries only if aid from the West should prove clearly deficient.

Resampa's views were certainly nearer those of the majority of P.S.D. militants than were Tsiranana's. Clearly they wanted to hurry him along the path that he was determined to take at his own deliberate pace. Resolutions

passed at the P.S.D. congress in Majunga on July 21, 1961, asked for a revision of the clauses in the Franco-Malagasy agreement of June 27, 1960,
which "impinged on Madagascar's sovereignty," and the elimination of
French politicians and technicians from the local scene. The cabinet still
included two Frenchmen, and 1,800 French technicians were employed by
the Malagasy Republic—a larger number than that in any French-speaking
Negro African state at the time. Tsiranana, like President Senghor of Senegal, refused to deprive himself entirely and hastily of the services of foreigners whom he trusted and needed, but slowly yielded ground on this
point. The number of French technicians was progressively reduced, and
Longuet, after being replaced as Minister of Finance by a Malagasy whom
he had trained, resigned from the cabinet altogether on September 21, 1963.
In response to the plea for a doctrine or declaration of principles, Tsiranana
finally obliged by a campaign in his newspaper supporting "Malagasy socialism." He was careful, however, never to define that socialism beyond
stating that it was not of Marxist inspiration.[7] Typical of Tsiranana's predilection for half-measures was the choice of the site of his residence and
offices. He refused to alienate wholly the Merina aristocracy by taking over
the Queen's *rova* (palace), but as head of the Malagasy government he felt
entitled to make use of the palace of Premier Rainilaiarivony, which did no
more than irritate the Merina bourgeoisie.

If Tsiranana was himself generally impervious to the extremists' attacks,
he showed himself sensitive to criticisms of his government as a dictatorship.
Again and again he pointed out to foreigners that the opposition in Madagascar was free to organize and to have its own press. To be sure, the police
seized newspapers that published "too many stupid lies,"[8] but as of the
spring of 1961 there were at least 40 journals still being printed. Tsiranana
could not resist contrasting the proliferation of opposition movements and
the opposition press in Madagascar with the lack of both in French-speaking
African countries that he had visited. Our citizens are freer than elsewhere,
he told a French journalist in October 1961,[9] because Madagascar is a genuine democracy and anyone who wants to found a political party may do so.
This possibility indeed contrasted with the situation in French-speaking
African one-party nations, but Tsiranana had the same attitude as did the
leaders of those states in regard to a real opposition. Like them, he said he
"favored an opposition" in principle, "provided it was constructive and not
systematically obstructionist" as was the A.K.F.M. Tsiranana accurately ap-
praised the A.K.F.M. as neither a truly communist nor a truly revolutionary
party, but he deeply distrusted its "30 or so leaders who were trained in Moscow, Prague, or Peking" and who continued to receive orders from international communist centers.[10] For some time Tsiranana had hopes of detach-

ing the Merina nationalists from the hard communist core of the A.K.F.M., and it was in large part to provide a setting propitious for such an eventuality that in the autumn of 1961 he organized a series of meetings with party leaders for the avowed purpose of working out a generally acceptable minimal political program.

The Colloquia of Malagasy Parties

A significant clue to Tsiranana's thinking at the time he convened the first party colloquium at Antsirabe on October 21, 1961, was provided by an interview printed in *Le Monde* the next day. The multiplicity of parties in Madagascar, he said, does not stem from its tribal divisions, for there is only one genuine divisive element—that is, the separation of the high plateaus, specifically Tananarive, from the coast. The 33 or so "parties," some of which were no more than electoral committees or cliques, were almost all centered in the capital city. As head of the republic he felt it to be his duty to invite all the party leaders to Antsirabe in the hope that they could agree on a common program that would take into account all national interests. If this came to pass, it might lead to new political alignments and a diminution of the number of parties, "of which I feel a little ashamed, as there are far too many of them. If I want fewer parties it is not because Madagascar or my party is experiencing internal troubles . . . and I remain the enemy of a single party." As Tsiranana repeatedly said, he was working to eliminate political divisions so that the natural unity which the Bon Dieu had bestowed on Madagascar by making it an island and by giving its people a common language might be reinforced.

The Antsirabe meeting of late October was distinguished by the presence of not only all the moderate opposition members but those of the A.K.F.M. as well. This encouraged Tsiranana to exhort them to regroup into a national coalition of parties, but the only tangible result of this meeting was the formation of a permanent committee to prepare for future colloquia. The next meeting was held at Tananarive on November 6, when 28 politicians representing 11 parties got together to work out a common political program. This committee was presided over by Vice-Premier Calvin Tsiebo, who urged its members to reach some concrete understanding even if they could not agree on a single party organization. The permanent committee then chose a subcommittee of ten, which comprised representatives of the P.S.D., A.K.F.M., U.D.S.M., R.N.M., R.C.M., and four other less important political groups. But on November 22, before this committee had advanced far in its work, the government made a sensational announcement. In a radio broadcast Tsiranana said that the R.N.M. had decided to merge with the P.S.D. and that ten outstanding Malagasy politicians were also joining as

individual members. These included Jacques Rabemananjara, Joseph Ravoahangy, Justin Bezara, and Albert Sylla, but conspicuous by their absence
were any of the A.K.F.M. leaders and Alexis Bezaka, head of the R.N.M.,
who was attending the U.N. General Assembly meeting in New York. Two
days later, Norbert Zafimahova's U.S.D.M., Jarison's faction of the R.C.M.,
and a small Fianarantsoa party called Asavadodoabo (or Asavadidrano,
an offshoot of the U.D.S.M. founded by Rakotovelo) joined together. They
assumed a curious on-the-fence position, in which they drew a distinction
between Tsiranana, whom they would support as head of the state, and the
P.S.D., as the government party which they still refused to join. Bezaka
upon his return from New York repudiated the decision made by other
leaders of the R.N.M., formed a new splinter group under his own leadership, and attacked the P.S.D. government in a pamphlet so vitriolic that the
authorities seized all the copies on which they could lay their hands.

Although never officially published, the main points of the common political program adopted by the committee of ten were printed before Christmas 1961 in a Tananarive newspaper.[11] The program endorsed a semipresidential regime, but urged suppression of the senate and of the provincial assemblies. In foreign relations it advocated a more "positive neutralism,"
specifically the acceptance of aid from all foreign sources, an autonomous national defense, and omission of all reference to the Community in Madagascar's constitution. In the economic field, it urged agrarian reforms, some nationalization of natural resources, and creation of a Malagasy currency
without necessarily leaving the franc zone. Foreigners should no longer be
allowed to participate in local politics, it stated, and their immigration ought
to be more strictly regulated. While these proposals were moderate in comparison with some African programs of the period and represented a compromise between conservative and radical views, they diverged considerably
from Tsiranana's declared policies, being both more socialistic economically
and more narrowly nationalistic politically.

The next colloquium, which took place at Antsirabe on December 27,
studied the common program behind closed doors, and it broke up after discussing only the preamble. The imminence of the New Year holiday was
given as the official reason for its failure to make greater headway, but evidently the real cause was disagreement over the recommendation to suppress
the senate. To get over this hurdle still another colloquium was scheduled
at Tananarive on January 23, at which Richard Andrianamanjato was the
rapporteur. But by this time the political atmosphere, which had been no-
ticeably calm and relaxed during the preceding three months, had again
become tense. This was due mainly to the arrest at Tananarive late in January of the secretary-general of the Paris Association des Etudiants d'Ori-

gine Malgache. He had returned to Madagascar to attend the funeral of his father, an outstanding Protestant Merina, but had allegedly, prior to his departure from France, distributed pamphlets containing charges "highly injurious to the government."[12] The opposition press attacked the government for the arrest, the discussion of the common program became heated and recriminatory, and after meeting only two days the conference was adjourned *sine die* by Tsiebo. Reportedly it was the charge that the government was made up wholly of *côtiers* which proved to be the straw that broke the P.S.D. camel's back. More likely, it was the government's marked success in winning over so many leaders to the P.S.D. in November that made it now indifferent to the success or failure of its party unity drive. On February 28, 1962, Tsiranana said that he did not despair of making further progress toward union, and he especially praised Andrianamanjato for the objectivity and liberalism he had shown during the colloquia.[13] Some observers thought this unusual gesture heralded a rapprochement with the nationalists of the A.K.F.M.

The Evolution of the A. K. F. M.

As yet Tsiranana has not succeeded in detaching the nationalists from the Marxists of the A.K.F.M., although it is still possible that eventually he will be able to do so. Raseta's formation of a splinter group, the FIPIMA (Malagasy National Union), in February 1963, which reportedly was the result of personality conflicts rather than ideological differences,[14] undoubtedly weakened the party. The attainment of independence and amnesty in 1960 eliminated the A.K.F.M.'s principal appeal to the Malagasy, and forced its leaders to transfer their main propaganda effort to the fields of foreign relations and economic matters. Although the A.K.F.M. leaders offered ideological reasons for the position they took on such questions, their actions suggested that they were automatically opposing every P.S.D. policy simply because it was the *côtier* government of Tsiranana that proposed them. When the government assumed a strongly pro-Western line, the A.K.F.M. at once urged closer ties with the Eastern bloc countries. Largely because Tsiranana encouraged investments by foreign capitalists, the A.K.F.M. came out in favor of greater control of the economy by the state. To a surprising extent the A.K.F.M.'s stand was popular with the Malagasy masses, though for reasons that had nothing to do with ideology. Because nature had made Madagascar self-sufficient economically, even though at a subsistence level, the great majority of Malagasys—while not actively xenophobic—could get along without foreign intervention or even foreign aid and preferred to do so.

The insularity and passivity that pervade Malagasy nationalism, coupled with the exclusive character of the Merina component, have proved to be formidable handicaps to the A.K.F.M. (as well as to the P.S.D.) leaders in their efforts to induce the rank and file of the population to take more positive action. Periodically, the French Communist Party has sent its overseas experts, notably Robert Ballanger and Léon Feix, to help the A.K.F.M. Marxists prod their followers into activity. After each such visit there is a noticeable stepping up of international communist propaganda in the island, as occurred when A.K.F.M. members were mourning for Patrice Lumumba and when they denounced American imperialist maneuvers in Cuba. Flurries of this sort soon subside, however, and the Malagasys' complacency and calm are then restored. Even the 50-odd Malagasys who were left-wing firebrands while they were students in France, and on whom the communist party thought it could count for future leadership in Madagascar, have tended to become docile functionaries if taken into the civil service on their return to the island. Decolonization is taking its toll of French communist as well as other French controls in Madagascar, and the Malagasy Marxists now prefer to bypass the Paris party headquarters and to deal directly with the international communist centers in Moscow or Peking.

After the *loi-cadre* made it possible for Tsiranana to acquire and then consolidate his power, the A.K.F.M. and especially its Marxist wing—after a spurt late in 1959—not only failed to make further headway but actually began to lose ground. Its press and its labor and youth movements,* which in 1957 had been in the vanguard of their respective domains, began to lose this leadership position to rival organs set up by the P.S.D. The conviction that it was futile to work through such a hybrid movement as the A.K.F.M. seems to have prompted a group of hard-core Marxists to set up an authentic Malagasy communist party (Parti Communiste Malgache, or P.C.M.) in 1958. Tsiranana, among other authorities, has testified to the existence of such a party,† but because of its clandestine nature no reliable data about it are available. One of the few written accounts purporting to describe the activities of this party comes from the inevitably biased pen of a strongly anticommunist French writer, G. Albertini.[15]

According to this source, it was not until two years after its founding that the P.C.M. was able to hold its first congress, at Tananarive, on March 18–20, 1960. There it was decided to create a school for cadres, organize cells at Antsirabe, Lake Alaotra, and in the Comoro Islands, and print a newspaper, *Ady Farany* (The Final Struggle), on a press that the party had bought in

* For comments on the FISEMA, see p. 454.
† At a press conference on July 30, 1960, he said that a Malagasy communist party existed but it was too small to be of any significance.

1958 but never used. As party secretary-general, the congress elected Jean-Anselme Randrianja, who undertook two contact-making trips to Iron Curtain countries and to China in October 1960 and in June–July 1961. Since both trips were believed to have been financed by Moscow, their purpose presumably was either to train Randrianja in revolutionary methods or to appraise his credentials as the valid representative of Malagasy communism. Thus far Randrianja has not succeeded in getting his P.C.M. recognized as the official communist party in Madagascar, either because Moscow did not want to alienate its old friends among the communist leaders of the A.K.F.M. or because the newborn P.C.M. was having grave internal trouble. In his annual report to the party, Randrianja said that he had had to expel from the P.C.M. in July 1961 two men who had infiltrated it for the purpose of foiling the P.C.M.'s propaganda during the September 1960 electoral campaign and of replacing the existing politburo by one that they themselves could control.

Besides the difficulties caused by such subversive action, Randrianja had to contend with more basic and permanent weaknesses in the P.C.M., which he stressed in the traditional communist manner of the auto-critique. These were the lack of contacts between the members of the central committee and the politburo, and at the lower echelons between the party's predominantly intellectual membership and the toiling masses. The dispersal of the P.C.M.'s leadership over the whole island and the lack of a permanent and well-organized base to serve as a regular meeting place were given as causes of the first-mentioned lack of contact. The second grave weakness was attributed to the fact that 80 per cent of the P.C.M.'s members were under 30 years of age and a goodly proportion consisted of students still in secondary schools. The extreme youth of the P.C.M. may account for the fact that the timetable it adopted for the seizure of power is based on that of the Chinese Communist Party.

It is hard to believe that so raw, new, and semiorganized a party as the P.C.M. could seriously challenge the established and experienced communist leaders of the A.K.F.M., yet it has been more than a mere nuisance to them. So small numerically are the extreme left-wing forces in Madagascar that the organization of the P.C.M. or even of a splinter group like Raseta's FIPIMA can seriously jeopardize their solidarity. For this reason and because the A.K.F.M. is basically split between Marxists and extreme Merina nationalists, Tsiranana seems no longer to take the local communists, by themselves, very seriously, but he worries about them a good deal in the light of their possible alliance with Asian communists. The presence of a small but active Chinese minority in Madagascar, as well as the "Asia-mindedness" of the Merina—who like to think of themselves as more Javanese than African—has given him new cause for alarm since the communist threat in 1964 to the nearby island of Zanzibar.

National Unity

By strengthening the P.S.D.'s organization and stressing Madagascar's geographic and linguistic unity, Tsiranana hopes to weld the island's tribes into a single people. Having been almost too successful in expanding the P.S.D.'s membership, he is trying now to weed out the opportunists and the dead wood and to make the party less vulnerable to subversive infiltration. In late 1962 there was a redistribution of party membership cards, but if, as was rumored at the time, a purge of undesirables was begun, it was certainly a most discreet one. No sensational expulsions on a mass scale were reported, and the only indication of a marked change in party policy consisted of Tsiranana's and Resampa's efforts to curtail the power of certain regional leaders.

Bezaka, because of his negative vote in the 1958 referendum and his refusal in 1961 to accept the other R.N.M. leaders' decision to merge with the P.S.D., was and probably is lost as far as the government party is concerned. Although he cannot be wholly discounted as a political figure because of his considerable talents and personal following in parts of Tamatave province, his insistence on playing a lone hand has lessened his ability to cause the government trouble. Jarison, and with him most of the influential Catholic leaders of Fianarantsoa province, rallied to the P.S.D. early in 1962. In Diégo-Suarez province, Bezara also accepted Tsiranana's unity appeal, and in any case his political career appears to be almost over. Also in that province, the personal feuding between Aridy and Miadana reached such a point in 1962 that Tsiranana reportedly had to step in and settle the dispute, which threatened to break up the provincial P.S.D. party organization. Tampering with the iron grip that Natai kept on Majunga province also posed delicate problems, but Resampa has reportedly been successful in cutting him down to size. The fact that Natai is a French citizen from Ste.-Marie island and a Franco-Malagasy half-caste precludes his ever playing a prominent role on the Malagasy national scene, as does Aridy's admixture of Comorian blood. In the last few years Manja Jaona's political stature has shrunk, even as a provincial leader of Tuléar. On a very small scale he has been emulating Gandhi, by rejecting the products of a modern industrial society and advocating a sterile return to Antandroy customs and traditions. Resampa and Rabemananjara continue to be Tsiranana's outstanding collaborators, although there has been some faltering in that triumvirate's teamwork.

As to the individual opposition leaders, a few of them—such as Stanislas Rakotonirina and Norbert Zafimahova—have through their own errors in political judgment been self-liquidating. The fact that Francis Sautron is a Frenchman from Réunion Island as well as a member of the extreme left wing has militated against his playing any longer an important political role in the town of Diégo-Suarez. But without waiting for such adverse factors to be wholly operative, the government thoughtfully replaced the municipal council that Sautron headed by an appointive special delegation. It apparently did not dare to take such high-handed action in Tananarive town, where the A.K.F.M. had a majority of the municipal councilors. The government did take care, however, to see that Mayor Andrianamanjato's able Marxist wife—the only Malagasy woman engineer in the country—was eliminated from the council and that the mayor himself was checkmated by the appointment of a P.S.D. prefect, Germain Ralambo, as his superior in the official hierarchy. On April 27, 1964, Andrianamanjato was defeated by one vote when he ran for reelection as mayor of Tananarive, suggesting a new and perhaps serious schism in the A.K.F.M. ranks, which Tsiranana might utilize to win over the A.K.F.M. president.

Richard Andrianamanjato, because of his integrity, intellectual brilliance, wide culture, and oratorical ability, is the opposition leader who is by far the most formidable adversary of Tsiranana and the P.S.D. in Madagascar today. If his wife is the convinced Marxist she is rumored to be, the Reverend Andrianamanjato appeared to the writers when they talked with him late in 1962 to be above all a sincere and emotional patriot who simply confounded Merina with Malagasy nationalism. Were Tsiranana able to overcome Andrianamanjato's traditional Merina prejudices against the *côtiers* and persuade him to join forces with the P.S.D. in creating a united Malagasy nation, a great step would be taken in bridging the gulf that still divides the Merina from all the other Malagasy tribes. As recently as May 20, 1964, Philippe Decraene wrote in *Le Monde*:

Tsiranana's heading the government seems like the revenge of the *côtiers* on the Merina, of the republic over the monarchy, of African over Asian elements, of the conquered over the conquerors, of former slaves over former masters ... and it is also the triumph of Catholics over Protestants.

Since 1958 Tsiranana has been tirelessly preaching national unity, up, down, and across the island, and it is said that he has been making a little headway. In this task, Tsiranana's genial personality and explosive vitality are his greatest assets. Furthermore, he has been able generally to keep under control two such disparate characters as Rabemananjara and Resampa, whom he has made his closest collaborators without naming either his heir apparent. Tsiranana has been able to utilize Rabemananjara's many foreign contacts and prestige abroad to lessen Madagascar's international isolation, although Rabemananjara has no technical training that qualifies him for the post of Minister of National Economy. To strengthen the P.S.D. and the civil service, Tsiranana has also turned to good account the boundless energy and frank partisanship of the self-educated Resampa. In recent years Resampa has shown a new flexibility and a political maturity for which Tsiranana is in great part responsible, and he has done his chief the great service of keeping him in touch with the militant wing of the P.S.D. party.

There is little doubt that Tsiranana continues to lag behind the P.S.D. vanguard, which would like to see the government adopt an economic and foreign policy strikingly similar to that of the A.K.F.M.[16] The president, however, refuses to cut his ties with France, the Common Market countries, and the conservative African leaders, and he will not speed up appreciably the "Malagasization" of the administration, the nationalizing of the economy, or the execution of drastic agrarian reforms, though he has been moving slowly in some of those directions. For example, the French Ministers in Tsiranana's cabinet have either resigned or been given less important portfolios, while the number of French technicians employed has been gradually reduced.

If the success of his temperate methods is to be judged in electoral terms, he can point to the senatorial elections of August 4, 1963, when the P.S.D. took all the seats at stake, although the A.K.F.M. and MONIMA ran a joint list of candidates in Tananarive and Tuléar.[17] Similar victories have been won in the municipalities and rural communes, though some of these must be attributed to a gerrymandering of the electoral circumscriptions.[18] The National Assembly is not a rubber-stamp body like those that now exist in many African states. Madagascar's deputies continue to accuse the government of dragging its feet, especially in regard to agrarian reform, although Tsiranana has rendered their protests ineffective. He obtains from the assembly special grants of power when he chooses to ask for them, and since his reelection on March 30, 1965, as president of the republic—for the first time by direct universal suffrage—his authority has been enhanced. He has also been careful to transfer quietly to the domain of normal legislation the regulation of local administration which was formerly laid down in the constitution and was therefore much harder to alter. He remains concerned chiefly with the reality rather than with the appearance of power, and to him it is far more important to remain popular and in touch with his people than to acquire prestige abroad.

Tsiranana feels his way, using half-measures and never pushing a policy to its logical conclusion, and seems unworried by the absence of consistency or of clear-cut solutions. An opposition exists which can usually express itself freely, and the regime that Tsiranana heads is certainly not an oppressive one. Nevertheless, through his party Tsiranana means to control all essential activities in the country; hence the freedom which the Malagasy people enjoy is a relative one. The population is not acutely unhappy, and if the government has not been able to satisfy its longing for a higher living standard, neither has the opposition known how to exploit its discontent. It should not be concluded, however, that Tsiranana's present preeminence is largely the result of his opponents' mistakes. Applying the prudence of a peasant and using trial-and-error procedures, Tsiranana has constructed his own policy for attaining national unity. Typical of his personal philosophy was the comment Tsiranana made with a smile to a French journalist in May 1964:[19] "We permit the opposition to exist, but we are careful not to let it act."

What President Tsiranana currently fears more than the organized opposition parties is a split within the ranks of the P.S.D. itself. Reportedly, it is the growing antagonism between the followers of the moderate pro-Western Jacques Rabemananjara and those of the more radical and neutralist André Resampa that motivated the speeding up in 1964–65 of the elections scheduled for the urban and rural communes, the legislative assembly, and the presidency of the republic.

In June 1964 the surprise vote by the A.K.F.M. members of the assembly in favor of the government's development plan indicated that once again a rapprochement might be in the making between the nationalists of the A.K.F.M. and the Resampa wing of the P.S.D. During the communal elections of December 1964, Tsiranana is said to have had difficulty in preserving his party's united front, but he and the other P.S.D. leaders have emphatically denied that there is any danger of a secessionist move. Yet the sensitiveness of the P.S.D. leadership to any airing of this schism is evidenced by the fact that the government in June 1964 banned *Le Monde* in Madagascar for three months because it published a series of articles in which Philippe Decraene wrote of the struggle between Rabemananjara and Resampa to become Tsiranana's successor. A purge of dissident elements seemed then to be taking place in the P.S.D., for Resampa admitted in a letter to *Le Monde*, published on January 10, 1965, that his party was having disciplinary difficulties and was engaged in "pitilessly eliminating such of its members as were guilty of deviationism."

Late in February 1965 the government announced that presidential elections would be held the following March 30, about a year ahead of schedule. This came as a surprise, for the P.S.D. scarcely needed further confirmation of its popularity at the polls. In the local-government elections of December 13, 1964, it had won 598 of the 784 seats at stake in the municipal and communal councils, compared with 132 for the A.K.F.M. and 54 for all the other parties. Nor was the official explanation—that Tsiranana wanted the renewal of his mandate to coincide with execution of the national five-year plan—very convincing. A more plausible reason was the need that the president must then have felt to reassert his control over the extremists in his own party. To promote his moderate program and his own candidacy, Tsiranana tirelessly toured the provinces during the early months of 1965.

On March 30 Tsiranana won the most impressive triumph of his career in terms of voter participation and of massive support for reelection as president of the Malagasy Republic. Of the registered electorate, 97 per cent actually voted, and of the 2,208,275 votes cast, 2,153,236 went to Tsiranana, 53,231 to Raseta, and 807 to the only other candidate, a Malagasy businessman who ran as an independent. To be sure, two of Tsiranana's main opponents did not enter the race. Monja Jaona withdrew his candidacy on March 22 so that the opposition could concentrate its votes on Dr. Raseta. The A.K.F.M. did not support Raseta and ran no candidate of its own, largely because its dynamic president, Richard Andrianamanjato, was too young to be eligible for the presidency. Its half-hearted call for abstentionism in the election was little heeded. This party seems to be retreating from its previous position of systematic obstructionism to the P.S.D. government, either because its leaders are convinced of the futility of such a policy or because they believe that Tsiranana is slowly implementing an economic and international program that is increasingly in harmony with their own. The A.K.F.M. responded favorably to the appeal for cooperation renewed by Tsiranana on the day of his inauguration as president. Despite its failure to change the electoral system to one of proportional voting, the A.K.F.M. has agreed to participate in the legislative elections to be held later in 1965, after which its position should become clearer than it now is.

It is doubtful that a merger of the A.K.F.M. nationalists with the P.S.D. would serve Tsiranana's cause. Party unity has just been restored under his guidance and may last for some time to come; should A.K.F.M. radical militants join forces with the P.S.D. extremist wing, the party might be definitively split. In any case, all programs of national unity among Malagasy political parties that are based on abstract doctrines seem bound to fail, for the basic cleavage is not an ideological one but a power struggle between rival ethnic groups.

Chapter ten

LOCAL-GOVERNMENT INSTITUTIONS

King Andrianampoinimerina and later Premier Rainilaiarivony were the two Merina who created the central and local governments for most of Madagascar, which the French took over and progressively modified. That King established a strongly hierarchized administration for Imerina and transformed the peripheral areas he had conquered into vassal states. Imerina was divided into six districts and these into subdivisions based on the number of tribes in each district.[1] The outlying regions were also organized on a tribal basis, albeit more loosely, and each tribal chief was made responsible to the central government. The King, whose power was absolute, was assisted by a council composed of the great Merina chiefs. His decisions were transmitted throughout his realm by special officials (*vadintany*), who saw to it that laws were executed, taxes collected, and justice rendered in his name. At the base of the administration, the King retained the *fokonolona*, which was the clan or portion of a clan that lived together in a village. It was a cooperative communal group, held together by ties to a common ancestor and the need for mutual defense, and it also had a hierarchical structure. The *fokonolona's* executive officer was a headman (*mpiadidy*), who was assisted by a council of elders (*ray amandreny*) called by the villagers their "fathers and mothers."

This basic administrative structure was preserved almost intact by King Andrianampoinimerina's successors, and not until the late nineteenth century was it reorganized by Premier Rainilaiarivony, largely as a means of undermining the power of the Merina nobles. He divided the kingdom into six provinces and, influenced by Western European models, created a cabinet of eight ministers and a real bureaucracy. The corps of royal officials that he set up succeeded in weakening the aristocracy, but they themselves soon became rapacious intermediaries between the Queen at Tananarive and her people. For some years Premier Rainilaiarivony was so absorbed by Madagascar's foreign relations that he failed to notice how his newly installed

functionaries were getting out of hand and how the *fokonolona* were gradually extricating themselves from control by the central government. As
soon as the Premier recognized these dangers, he replaced the first batch of
officials by more amenable ones, entitled governors (*madinika*), to whom
he gave the means of asserting their authority over the *fokonolona*. To
strengthen the self-help and mutual-aid aspects of the *fokonolona* and to
make it a more useful tool for the central government, Premier Rainilaiarivony encouraged its members to draw up "charters" or mutual agreements
among its members. These charters bound the elders and the villagers together and defined their rights and obligations toward each other and the
central government in such matters as keeping order, maintaining public
works, and helping paupers.

In this way the *fokonolona* was prevented from evolving into an embryonic democracy (of which the germs existed in its initial form), for the
Premier's domestic policy was aimed above all at strengthening the powers
of the central government. Another ancient and potentially democratic
institution, the *kabary* (literally, discourse), was similarly transformed.
Originally the meeting of the *kabary* was an occasion on which the monarch's subjects could petition the throne with impunity, but Rainilaiarivony
made it into an empty ceremonial in which the Queen read to her assembled
people a speech that he himself had prepared. At various points in her discourse the Queen would ask the rhetorical question, "Is it not so, my people?" To this her listeners invariably and amiably replied, "It is so."[2]
Similarly, the Merina feudal lords became agents of the royal power in relation to their vassals, over whom, however, they were allowed to retain
some strictly delimited authority.

Outside Imerina, the degree to which the royal power was asserted depended on the distance from Tananarive and the personality of the Queen's
representative. Some of the governors of her 27 provinces became wealthy
and as powerful as viceroys, while others commanded no more than an isolated fort.[3] Under their orders were placed various local potentates, ranging
from tribal kings to heads of families or clans and to canton and village
chiefs. In brief, this was a flexible colonial system in which no attempt was
made to assimilate the populations or to associate them with the government,
but it met the Premier's main criterion: it was well enough adapted to their
needs for the coastal populations who had been conquered militarily by the
Merina to accept the Queen's authority. Although the Merina system encouraged neither nationhood nor popular democracy, it had the great virtue
of eliminating the powerful chieftaincies, thus freeing Madagascar from one
of the problems that has most troubled Negro Africa.

Under the protectorate that France thought it had established in 1885, there was, naturally, no question of wiping out the existing Merina system. The annexation law of 1896 gave Gallieni as governor-general a free hand in this respect, but for nearly a decade thereafter he was preoccupied with quelling island-wide revolts. One of his first acts was to replace the Merina governors by Europeans, at first army officers and then progressively civilians. By 1902 civilian administrators were in charge of Imerina, the Sakalava country, and the extreme south. Military *cercles* were being transformed into 20 provinces, which were then subdivided into districts. In principle, the new provinces were based on ethnic divisions, but a few very large tribes were spread over several provinces and some small ones were brought together in a single district. The European hierarchy stopped at the district level, where the officials were supposed to act as guides and supervisors for their Malagasy subordinates and where eventually they acquired almost unlimited authority. Under their rule came the Malagasy canton chiefs, who were the workhorses of the whole system and who were transferred frequently from one post to another to prevent them—if possible—from abusing the considerable powers that they might have acquired.

In pursuing his policy of humbling the Merina, Gallieni simply replaced the Merina functionaries at the top echelons by Europeans and—insofar as possible—in the lower posts by *côtiers.* At the village level the most drastic and least fortunate changes were made, although Gallieni with his usual thoroughness had set up a committee of eight to study the problem for nearly a year before he took action. On March 9, 1902, he produced what he called the charter of local collectivities, by which the *fokonolona* was recognized as the basic cell of the administration in Imerina, with a view to rooting official action in local traditions. The modifications this charter made in the existing system concerned the collective aspects of the *fokonolona,* which were strengthened, and the role of the *mpiadidy,* which was drastically altered by turning him into a minor functionary of the central government. Following much the same evolution as the Negro African village chief under French rule, the *mpiadidy* ceased to be primarily the spokesman for his fellow villagers and became a collector of taxes (from which he was paid a percentage), supervisor of *corvées,* and policeman for the central authorities. On July 5, 1903, Gallieni made the *fokonolona* the electorate for the Councils of Notables, which he created as advisory groups to the district chiefs.

Gallieni was so pleased with his version of the *fokonolona* that by a decree of September 30, 1904, he extended it to the rest of the island, where vaguely similar institutions existed but had never developed strongly as in Imerina. Thus the French administration, like the Merina monarchs, tried to utilize the *fokonolona* as a handy and inexpensive instrument of the central government. In so doing they made the grave mistake of trying to turn into an administrative unit what was essentially a community of human beings bound together by the mystic ties that resulted from their relationship to a common ancestor.[4] During the 20 years that followed, the centralized and bureaucratic character of the administration became increasingly pronounced, and at the same time the Merina once again came to predominate in the Malagasy civil service, not only in the high plateaus but also in the coastal regions.

At that period the governors-general were absorbed in their power struggle with the white settlers,* which culminated in the creation of the Economic and Financial Delegations. It was largely to counteract the aggressive Europeans in that body that a Malagasy section in it was created, but its functioning did not give the Malagasys any more real power than before. Much the same could be said of the Councils of Notables, although they were reorganized in 1926 and again in 1930, and of the fokonolona, which, albeit nominally revived, were ineffectual, for they continued to be ignored by European and Malagasy civil servants alike. The municipal councils, despite an enlargement of the electorate and of their powers, continued to be dominated by their mayors, who were civil servants appointed by the central government. Administrative changes made during the interwar period sounded drastic when announced, but in effect they did little to reverse or even deflect the established trends.

Owing to a marked increase in the means of communication in the mid-1920s, Governor Olivier felt it desirable to make some changes in the units of local administration. By replacing the 20 provinces and 75 districts inherited from the time of Gallieni by six regions and 44 provinces, he gave preeminence to the provincial heads in the bureaucratic hierarchy. Then Governor Cayla, in the name of the economies necessitated by the world depression in the 1930s, increased the number of regions to eight and gave them each a budget, reestablished the districts (to the number of 87) and cantons (706), and suppressed the provinces altogether, thus placing the district officer at the top of the district bureaucracy. Both of these series of contradictory changes resulted in greater uniformity and in more direct administration from Tananarive. On the eve of World War II there were more elective bodies (in the Western sense of the term) in Madagascar than in French Negro Africa, but the electorate was very restricted and elections were confined to wholly advisory bodies such as the chambers of commerce, the Malagasy section of the Delegations, a few municipal councils, and the Conseil Supérieur des Colonies.

The radical changes in colonial policy heralded by the Brazzaville conference of early 1944 brought some innovations and revivals to Madagascar.

* See p. 24.

Some of the innovations, such as the Representative Council, and some of the revivals, including the Economic and Financial Delegations and the special government for the south, did not long survive the end of World War II. But the attempts to revitalize the *fokonolona* (by the decree of November 9, 1944) and to give a new dimension to provincial administration (by the decrees of October 25 and November 4, 1946), as well as the creation of autonomous circumscriptions, proved to be more durable, though they were profoundly modified over the following years. Regardless of the forms they eventually assumed, their very existence in the early postwar years contrasted sharply with the lack of any similar institutions in French West Africa and Equatorial Africa. There the politically conscious elite were almost wholly concerned with increasing their representation and power in the French Parliament, the two Grand Councils, and the 12 territorial assemblies, and not until the mid-1950s did they show much interest in institutions of local government. In Madagascar, however, the existence of a sizable European settler element and of a remarkable indigenous institution, the *fokonolona,* prompted official concern for the development of media for local self-government. Until the end of World War II, the factors that very largely determined the government's attitude toward local administration were its own convenience or the benefits that might accrue to it therefrom, though lip service was paid to the civil educational value of municipal councils and *fokonolona* for the population. Beginning in 1944, political and to some extent economic considerations became the principal determinants in shaping the attitude of both the government and the elite toward local administration.

The Provinces

The decree of February 14, 1945, disappointed those who had hoped for a break with the past, since it merely revived the practice of renaming administrative units and drawing new boundaries for them. By that decree the number of regions was halved to four, a separate government for the southwest and south-central part of the island was reconstituted, and Tananarive and its suburbs were designated an autonomous circumscription, although this new unit was still headed by an administrator-mayor. Undoubtedly it was the alarm caused by the rapid development of Merina nationalism in the winter of 1945–46 that impelled the Paris government to propose for the first time a genuine decentralization of Madagascar's administration, the main purpose of which was to prevent Malagasy opinion from uniting behind the demand for independence. That such was its motivation was unequivocally asserted by the M.D.R.M. deputy, Raseta, when the Constituent Assembly on April 25, 1946, debated and accepted the proposal to divide

Madagascar into five "natural regions" or provinces and to give each of them an elected assembly with some voting powers. By a decree of November 9, 1946, the five newly created provinces were provided with their own budgets and assemblies. Not only did these assemblies comprise more elected Malagasy members (18) than Europeans (12), but they also served collectively as an electoral college for the new territorial representative assembly at Tananarive.

Under the last-mentioned decree, the local administration was appreciably enlarged, for new units were added to the old ones at many levels, and the province, the municipality, and the *fokonolona* underwent drastic changes. Six autonomous circumscriptions were carved out of some of the provinces, but the greater part of the area of each province was divided into districts, and their administrative organization reproduced the provincial organization on a smaller scale. The district officers were given advisory councils, to replace the outmoded Councils of Notables, and these new councils were composed of two Notables elected by universal suffrage for an indefinite period from each of the cantons that made up the district. Below the district came the *gouvernements* and cantons staffed by Malagasy functionaries drawn mainly from the Merina bourgeoisie; at still lower levels the *chefs de quartier* and *fokonolona mpiadidy* were drawn principally from the ranks of wealthy farmers and rural artisans. The canton chiefs, as members of the civil service, were not always native to the area, whereas the *chefs de quartier* and *fokonolona mpiadidy* were invariably local men. (Confusion sometimes arose when the appellation of *mpiadidy* was also accorded to the *chefs de quartier*.) The *quartier* embraced a group of villages whose *chef*, unlike the *fokonolona mpiadidy*, was not popularly elected but was chosen by the district officer from a list of three names prepared by the Notables of the *quartier*. The *chef de quartier* was paid a higher salary than was the *fokonolona mpiadidy* (though both received a percentage of the taxes they collected), and he wore an armband with the letter F, showing that he was a direct agent of the *fanjakana* or administration.[5]

Governor-general Bargues, soon after his arrival in Madagascar early in 1950, showed himself to be a strong believer in decentralization at all administrative levels. Not only did he create many new municipalities and spur development of the *fokonolona*, but he gave the provinces scope to show the "initiative and decisiveness" that, at least in theory, had also motivated the reform of 1946. In his first speech to the representative assembly, on April 1, 1950, he proposed to delegate some of his own powers to the *chefs de province*, give them advisory councils similar to his own privy council, and transfer from the representative assembly to the provincial assemblies the right to make decisions on matters of purely regional interest.* Above all, he wished to see the provincial assemblies empowered to contract and utilize loans under loose supervision by the central government. Bargues believed that such loans would virtually eliminate the subsidies granted by the representative assembly on an annual basis, which, because they varied from year to year, hampered the provinces in drawing up their long-term development plans.[6]

Other arguments advanced by Bargues on behalf of his decentralization projects included those used by many of his predecessors—the geographic and ethnic diversity of Madagascar and the concentration of services and facilities in the capital city, which had led to the neglect of peripheral areas. For various reasons the representative assembly was not enthusiastic about his proposals. Not unnaturally its members were averse to relinquishing some of their prerogatives, to increasing already heavy administrative expenditures by the formation of provincial services that might duplicate those of the central government, and to giving more authority to the corps of provincial officials, whom they already regarded as dictatorial.[7] Nearly three years passed before Bargues could persuade the assembly (as well as the Minister of Overseas France) to accept his decentralization measures, and this was done only after he had promised to hold expenditures to the minimum and to define precisely the limitations of the powers of provincial civil servants. In time these fears were justified: the government's operating expenses mounted rapidly, the trend toward centralization became evident at the provincial level, and the provincial and district officials, according to many testimonials, behaved like little Caesars toward their Malagasy subordinates.

After the passage of the *loi-cadre* on June 23, 1956, decentralization in Madagascar reached its extreme point.[8] In Negro Africa, for which the *loi-cadre* was primarily designed, the strongest trend favored territorial autonomy and the breakup of the governments-general. As to Madagascar, the legislators of 1956 recognized that the socioeconomic phenomena, which undeniably differentiated the various regions, had been accentuated by the quasi-provincial system introduced a decade before, and they felt that these justified setting up a more decentralized regime in the island. On the other hand, those who stressed Madagascar's unifying geographical and linguistic features firmly rejected the creating of provinces based on tribal divisions and had misgivings about any measures that might fragment the island. Nevertheless, the way in which Madagascar had been moving toward de-

---

* These were provincial primary education and scholarships, the expansion of agricultural production, child welfare, and the like.

centralization, particularly since 1953, seemed to offer a compromise solution. This was government at two levels, central and provincial, each with an executive council chosen by an elected assembly. The central government was given a slight ascendancy over the provincial, and the result was indeed original. Madagascar's government at that period could not be properly called federal, regional, or centralized.

Provided in some instances with the means of appealing directly to the Paris authorities, the provinces in action became surprisingly independent of the central government, although both the governor-general and the representative assembly found ways of indirectly exerting pressure on the provincial councils, assemblies, and civil servants. The fragmentation of authority and responsibility, however, was such that the division of powers between them posed delicate problems, and some juridical and even political conflicts soon arose. Furthermore, the split-level governmental system proved to be more ingenious than practical, for it was not only cumbersome but very expensive, especially as the numerous councilors and assemblymen that it entailed demanded the same living standards as their counterparts in France.

The Merina nationalists, who had strongly opposed provincialization from the beginning, lost no opportunity to make the new regime unpopular. They claimed that it had been intentionally contrived in France in line with the classic divide-and-rule colonial policy, and that it satisfied the aspirations of no segment of the Malagasy population. Even Tsiranana, who had initially favored considerable provincial autonomy, complained within a year after the *loi-cadre* became effective of a lack of coordination between the central and provincial authorities.[9] In Negro Africa, the *loi-cadre* had given rise to some friction between the new native executives and the old-line civil servants, but in Madagascar these same difficulties were aggravated by the antagonism shown toward such reforms by the white settlers and by what one writer called the "thousand conservative reflexes of the administration."[10] As to the Malagasys' reaction, the election of a government council controlled by *côtiers* in May 1957 caused the specter of Merina domination to recede, and with it the fear of a strong central government. After the referendum of September 1958, the provincial assemblies meeting in a congress at Tananarive chose for Madagascar the status of an autonomous republic, and this opened the way for still another revision in the island's administrative structure.

The constitution of April 29, 1959, strengthened the hand of the central government but at the same time permitted the provinces to retain a degree of autonomy and also to make their voices heard in the Tananarive Parliament. In creating a bicameral legislature, Madagascar was unique among the French-speaking states that voted to remain in the Community. Although the government appointed 18 of the 54 members of the newly created senate for their expertise or to represent special-interest groups, two-thirds of the senators were to be chosen by the provinces on an equal basis of six for each province. The electorate for the senate was to be composed of urban and rural councilors and of members of the provincial assemblies,* and in order to avoid a total turnover every six years, the mandates of half the elected senators were to expire every three years. Malagasy respect for age and experience was said to have motivated this institution, as well as the desire to give the rural populations a chance to make their voice heard by the government.[11] The authorities, however, have had second thoughts concerning its value, for since mid-1962 the senate's legislative powers have been largely whittled away, although its president, on occasion, still has an important role to play.†

As for the provincial administration, its powers were shorn even more severely than were those of the senate, and from the time the constitution was drafted, it was obvious that the central government intended to take over most of the provinces' prerogatives and revenues. The provincial councils, which had been embryonic local governments, were eliminated, as were the *chefs de province* who had been their chairmen. In place of the *chefs*, secretaries of state, delegates of the central government, were appointed. The secretary-delegate was responsible to the Minister of Interior, but he was also in his own right a junior member of the cabinet. He appointed his two main assistants *(controleurs généraux)*, gave orders to the technician who headed the provincial services, and prepared the agenda for the sessions of the provincial assembly, whose decisions he was required to carry out. In theory, his role as provincial executor was equal in importance to that of central government delegate, but in practice the latter far outweighed the former. Though the secretary was usually a man born in the province to which he was appointed, he was not a civil servant but a politician whose career depended upon the continuing favors of the party in power.

The most important role assigned to the provincial assemblies was that of electoral college for the national assembly. But on a day-to-day basis the provincial assembly was left with only such authority as was not assumed by the central government and its delegate. Moreover, its membership auto-

---

* In the constitution, the term "general council" is applied to the bodies that are the heirs of the old provincial assemblies. The writers, however, have preferred to continue using "provincial assembly" because of the confusion that might arise between "general council" and the former provincial and government councils.

† See p. 125.

matically included the deputies and senators elected from the province to the Parliament at Tananarive, who were also very susceptible to political pressures.* The assembly was competent to make decisions regarding provincial primary education, public works, and health and welfare work, but was left with little money to carry them out. In traveling throughout Madagascar late in 1962, the writers heard no expression of nostalgia for the two-year period when provincial government had functioned under the *loi-cadre*, but they listened to many complaints about straitened provincial finances. Only Tuléar and Majunga provinces have been consistently prosperous enough to be financially independent of the central government.

Since independence, the drive to eliminate the senate and the provinces as administrative units has been gathering momentum. Considering the little power they are allowed to wield, 54 senators and 240 provincial assemblymen are undeniably expensive luxuries. Characteristically, Tsiranana wants to take no drastic action and apparently prefers to let nature take its course. An indication of his policy of creeping centralization was the appointment in November 1963 of the first civil servant to replace the secretary-delegate of Tananarive province. The process of demoting the provinces still further in the administrative hierarchy is probably under way.

Fokonolona and Rural Communes†

At the same time that the government was rigorously curbing provincial autonomy, it was enlarging the powers of rural and urban communes. Apparently the P.S.D. regarded the exercise of power at the provincial level as likely to breed separatism, whereas it saw the lower-echelon councils as controllable instruments well suited to furthering the civic education of the masses. Under French rule the *fokonolona*, a traditional body, coexisted peaceably with the municipality, an alien institution imported from France, because the former operated only in rural regions whereas the latter was restricted to urban centers. This is still the case, but what is now uncertain is whether the *fokonolona* can survive in juxtaposition to more recently organized rural bodies.

Contrary to its authors' intentions, the decree of November 9, 1944, failed to arrest the decline of the *fokonolona*, largely because the latter had lost one of its two essential functions.‡ Except for the period of the 1947 revolt and the chronic cattle thefts in the south and west, the defense of rural settle-

* The balance of the 240 provincial assemblymen were to be elected by universal suffrage for a five-year term.
† The writers are greatly indebted for material in this section to an unpublished manuscript written by Jean Comte in 1962, entitled *Les Communes Malgaches*.
‡ See p. 139.

1 The last Queen of Madagascar, Ranavalona III, who reigned from
   1883 to 1895 and died in exile at Algiers in 1917.

2 One of the palace buildings of King
Andrianampoinimerina (1787–1810) at
Tananarive; in the foreground is his
filanzane, carried by bearers.

3 The palace (*rova*) of the Queen in Tananarive.

Cabinet of the interim government of Madagascar (1959). *Front row:* Rakotovelo,
G. Randrianasolo, E. Rakoto, A. Sylla, President P. Tsiranana, P. Raondry, A. Resampa, L. Rakotomalala.
Second row: C. Ramanantsoa, J.-J. Natai, V. Miadana, A. Ramangasoavina, M. Fournier, A. Andriamirado,
L. Botokeky. *Third row:* R. Rasidy, E. Charles, P. Longuet, J.-F. Jarison, C. Aridy.

Justin Bezara, one of the leading political
figures of Diégo-Suarez.

6 Monsignor Ramaro Sandratana, the first Malagasy
bishop, who was consecrated in 1948.

7 The Reverend Richard Andrianamanjato leader of the opposition party, A.K.F.M., and mayor of Tananarive.

8 President Philibert Tsiranana.

9 A helicopter given to Madagascar by France.
President Tsiranana is seated beside the pilot.

10 Enrollment of "volunteers" for
civic service (see Chapter 23).

11 A coffee bush.

12 Harvesting of cape peas.

28 The Canal des Pangalanes
on the east coast of Madagascar.

29 Avenue de l'Indépendance in Tananarive.

30 Modern buildings in Tananarive, with older brick structures in the background.

ments had been assured by the central government for many years. Consequently the members of the *fokonolona* tended to become more and more dispersed into hamlets of only 20 or so inhabitants. In return for maintaining security, however, the government allotted the *fokonolona* far more unpaid and disagreeable duties than privileges, and this discouraged the growth of any civic spirit. Its *mpiadidy* was saddled with responsibility for *corvées,* small public works, tax collections, etc., in return for a pittance amounting to no more than 5,000 C.F.A. francs a year. As Jean Comte aptly put it,[12] the *mpiadidy* was in a difficult position, for he had to have enough prestige and alertness to assure compliance with the government's orders but should not be so dynamic as to alienate the villagers by rousing them too often from their customary apathy. The mystique derived from relationship to a common ancestor, the second essential characteristic of the *fokonolona,* still provided some degree of social cohesion. This was evidenced in the respect that continued to be shown for ancestral customs and the heads of family and clan. Nevertheless, this too was declining, for Malagasy youth—like other young people in Africa and Asia—were increasingly rejecting the discipline imposed by traditional authorities. Despite the loss of much of its purpose, the *fokonolona* survived—although on a somewhat clandestine level—for its members wanted to prevent the administration from utilizing for alien purposes such moral authority as it continued to possess.

A gubernatorial circular of May 4, 1948, listed the reasons why the administration had become discouraged in its attempts to revitalize the *fokonolona* and announced plans for a new experiment. Collectivités Autochtones Rurales (C.A.R.) was the name given to the 103 rural settlements selected for experimentation by a special official committee. It was believed that Malagasy villagers would plan and carry out community development projects if their organization were given a firm legal base and more stable and permanent financial resources. These prerequisites were provided by successive regulations of December 27, 1949, June 7, 1950, and November 21, 1955. On December 20, 1956, the better-endowed C.A.R. were given a new name, Communes Rurales Autonomes Modernisées (C.R.A.M.). Confusingly enough, however, the distinction between them was not always strictly observed, and on February 7, 1958, more precise rules governing their elections, the number and duties of officeholders, and the use of their resources were laid down.

The persistence with which the government tinkered with the rural organizations it installed alongside the *fokonolona* displayed a rare continuity in official policy, but at the same time the many changes it made betrayed dissatisfaction with the results. If the government erred, it was not for lack of documentation, for the *fokonolona* as an institution had been often and thoroughly studied by French scholars.* Governor-general Soucadaux himself prompted one of the best analyses of the subject, that of Georges Condominas, whose mission in 1955 indicated why the C.A.R. and C.R.A.M. had failed to take root in Imerina. He also shed light on the sociology of the *fokonolona* and compared its evolution with that of the Annamite commune in Vietnam.†

Handicapped by the grave defect of being alien to Malagasy traditions, the C.A.R. and C.R.A.M. were also seriously inhibited by the attitude taken toward them by two different groups of French officials and some Malagasy extremists. The ultraconservative officials claimed that the C.A.R. and C.R.A.M. were expensive innovations not wanted by the rural Malagasys, who, moreover, would be incapable of running them efficiently. The other group of French officials, who opposed development of rural initiative through the C.A.R. and C.R.A.M., treated them with the same authority as they had the somnolent and acquiescent Councils of Notables. Seeing in them—particularly in their financial resources—simply another instrument for direct administration, these officials gave them an orientation that sapped their vitality. The extreme form that the C.R.A.M. took was that of the Groupement des Collectivités, started on November 21, 1955, which soon degenerated into a technical department of the administration. Because it came completely under the thumb of the district officer and his subordinates in the economic services, the Malagasys for whom in principle it was designed took no interest in or responsibility for its management. By early 1958 only 25 of the original 38 C.R.A.M. still existed, and of these not over half functioned even reasonably well.

Curiously enough, the other element most overtly hostile to the C.A.R. and C.R.A.M. was the left-wing and nationalist extremists of Tananarive. Not crediting the French with trying to develop rural government by and for the Malagasys, this element saw in the creation of the C.A.R. and C.R.A.M. only the official intention of setting up deceptively named bodies, the better to tighten the administration's controls. They claimed that the new organizations simply perpetuated forced labor and collective penalties for villagers who failed to carry out the district officer's orders. These aspects of the C.A.R. and C.R.A.M. were subsequently eliminated, and then the opposition took another line of attack. It denounced the election of their

---

* The *fokonolona* as a field of study has even attracted a Russian scholar, A. S. Orlova.

† Condominas, p. 74. The Annamite commune, which had many points in common with the *fokonolona* during much of the nineteenth century, managed to remain independent of the central government for a longer time. This may have been due to the fact that the Annamite emperors used the commune as a means of colonizing the underpopulated region of Cochin China and therefore permitted it to continue exercising greater autonomy and initiative.

officials as having been rigged so that the district officers could work through puppets of their choice.

Proponents and adversaries of the C.A.R. and C.R.A.M. shared the view that those organizations had become too much the appendages of the administration, but they differed on whether this had been the original intention. In any case, the C.A.R. and C.R.A.M. were so susceptible to manipulation by any central government that Tsiranana, not unnaturally, did not resist the temptation of utilizing them when he came to power in mid-1957. Like his predecessors, he tried to redeem them by improvements in their organization, and a number of them responded well to this treatment. So promising did they appear to him a year and a half later that he had them institutionalized in the constitution of April 29, 1959. The rural communes, along with the provincial assemblies, were made the electoral college for choosing two-thirds of Madagascar's senators. Then, a few months later, the cabinet—seeing in the election of officers for the rural communes an easy means of winning popular support for the government—decided to expand their number. This was done suddenly and drastically, against the advice of the district officers, who had proposed spreading such an expansion over a three-year period.[13]

A law of September 12, 1959, empowered the secretary-delegates, after agreement with the district officers-in-council, to set up rural communes in the provinces. Consequently, by January 1, 1960, when they started functioning, there were 739 rural communes in Madagascar, or nearly triple the number that had existed the previous year.* In great haste, elections for their officers were organized, and they took place on October 11, 1959; the results were not encouraging. The great majority of rural voters had no idea of what the new communes were for, and most of the officers elected not only were illiterate but lacked a sense of civic responsibility. Many of the new "rural mayors," as they were officially called, saw in their office only a golden opportunity to practice nepotism and embezzlement, and one of them reportedly was forced to resign because his wife complained that since he had become mayor he was neglecting the family rice field.[14]

Congresses of rural mayors held in each province during the winter of 1960–61 shed light on the difficulties that were besetting the new communes. Almost without exception the rural mayors and their councilors complained that they received too little pay for their services. Although the communes naturally differed in size and wealth, the mayor's salary ranged from 4,000 to 9,000 C.F.A. francs a month, and the average annual income of a rural commune amounted to about 1,735,000 C.F.A. francs. About two-thirds of

* Of these, 197 were in Fianarantsoa province, 135 in Tananarive, 117 in Tamatave, 114 in Majunga, 109 in Tuléar, and 67 in Diégo-Suarez.

this sum was derived from rebates on two taxes—the head tax collected by the province and the *centimes additionnels* by the canton—and they had not been paid on time or in full. Financial troubles, however, were not the only ones the communes were experiencing. Two kinds of difficulties were caused by the Malagasy civil servants. Either they were too few or too inexperienced to provide the proper guidance for the newborn communes or, like their French predecessors, they could not resist trying to run them, especially when their mayors were inept or inert. Party politics were still another curse with which the communes had to contend. The P.S.D. leaders were apt to overlook abuses by mayors who were party members, and deputies—for personal or political reasons—were prone to intervene in communal affairs for or against a rural mayor or a provincial functionary.

The airing given to the new communes' trials and tribulations brought about some improvements in 1961–62, and this was facilitated by removal from the constitution of all reference to the communes and by their transfer to the more flexible field of legislation. Steps were taken to stabilize and increase their resources (of which 60 per cent was to be supplied by subsidies and taxes and 40 per cent by raising loans) and to ensure that less of their revenues would be spent on salaries and more on economic development. In 1962 the communes that were financially weakest were brought together into *syndicats,* which pooled their resources to purchase equipment, and both their prestige and their duties were increased by making them responsible for carrying out a specific part of the national economic plan. Undoubtedly many of the defects arising out of the communes' overhasty installation are being or will soon be remedied, and probably a better balance between the central authority and local autonomy will be attained. What has not yet been dealt with is the danger arising from the coexistence of two rural organizations such as the commune and the *fokonolona,* for one may strangle or sap the vitality of the other. Since the commune is an alien modern institution and the *fokonolona* is an anachronism rooted in Malagasy traditions, some way will have to be found to preserve and combine the desirable features of each.

The Municipalities

If the modern civic education of the Malagasy peasants began only with the establishment of rural communes, that of Madagascar's town dwellers started much earlier. On January 28, 1896, ten days after France established a protectorate in Madagascar, the three towns of Nossi-Bé, Ste.-Marie, and Diégo-Suarez, which had the largest number of French residents, were removed from the authority of the Merina administration and organized into municipalities.[15] A year later, after a colonial regime had been installed, they were given some financial autonomy and placed under the close control of a mayor named by the administration, which also appointed a council to advise him. The mayor was a high-ranking French civil servant who was at the same time head of the province in which the town was located. On an experimental basis, in October 1897, this system was extended with satisfactory results to Tamatave and Majunga. In November 1898 the inland towns of Tananarive and Fianarantsoa were provided with their own budgets and given an administrator-mayor. But they did not receive the legal status of a commune or municipal council until 1908, nine years after Paris had authorized the governor-general-in-council to create more communes. Furthermore, Governor-general Augagneur, in his bureaucratic way, laid down more precise rules for the municipalities and made the regulations governing all of them uniform.

Under so highly centralized a municipal regime, the French population became restive, so the authorities worked out a compromise solution. By the decree of October 9, 1913, a new type of municipality was created, in which the council was given some voting powers and some elective French members, although the handful of Malagasy councilors continued to be appointed by the governor-general. World War I broke out before this new regime could be tested, and it was not revived until the 1920s. It was set up progressively in Fianarantsoa and Diégo-Suarez (July 1920), Antsirabe (November 1920), Tuléar (September 1921), Mananjary (October 1923), Morondava (July 1932), Antalaha (February 1939), and Fort-Dauphin (December 1943). Decrees of May 6, 1923, and May 7, 1939, enlarged the French electorate and reduced the residence requirements for French candidates on the municipal councils, and they also introduced the principle of electing a few Malagasy councilors by a very restricted electorate.

Thus the elective principle was accepted prior to World War II, but it was not until the 1950s that all newly created municipalities were given wholly elected councils. (Communes with an appointed mayor but with an elected council were called *communes de moyen exercice*.) The total number of *communes de moyen exercice* was brought up to 20 by raising to the status of municipalities Ambositra, Farafangana, and Manahara (December 1950), Arivonimamo and Ambatolampy (April 1951), and Ambatodrazaka (December 1951). Altogether some 500,000 persons, or about one-eighth of Madagascar's total population at the time, lived in urban communes, that of Tananarive accounting for nearly half that number (200,000). With regard to the creation of local-government institutions, Bargues was the most zealous governor-general Madagascar had ever known. In one year, 1951, he created seven municipalities (compared with the 13 that had been set up during the preceding 46 years), and he set the precedent of

holding annual conferences of mayors. Bargues also enlarged the municipalities' financial resources and the electoral college, and gave the Malagasys
numerical equality with Frenchmen on the municipal councils. The un-
deniable progress made by urban government under Bargues did not, however, alter the fact that the municipalities remained almost wholly under the
control of the administrator-mayors.[16] Certainly Bargues would have liked
to move faster toward a system of wholly elective urban government,[17] but
he was hindered by the requirements that Paris laid down for setting up full
communes. These were that a town must have sufficient financial and manpower resources to assure its solvency and competent management.

Since Madagascar, by the mid-1950s, had the surprisingly large number
of 20 urban communes in a country where 85 per cent of the population was
rural, the municipal-reorganization bill of November 18, 1955, was accepted
by the Malagasys with none of the enthusiasm it aroused among the French-
speaking Negro Africans. Probably because the representative assembly,
when consulted on the subject by the Mendès-France government, urged
retention of the dual-college system, the original draft of that bill excluded
Madagascar.[18] Since this seemed unfair to many French deputies of the
National Assembly, Madagascar was included on the bill's third reading
on the same basis as French West Africa and Equatorial Africa. It is noteworthy that no Malagasy deputy urged Madagascar's inclusion or even participated in this vital debate.[19] The 1955 bill raised the status of Madagascar's
five provincial capitals to that of full communes, and after Diégo-Suarez
became a province in November 1956 its capital city followed suit. Although
this bill introduced the important principle of a single electoral college for
six mayors and municipal councils, the only ripple it caused in Madagascar's
representative assembly concerned Tananarive's electoral *arrondissements*
(wards).*

The indifference with which the Malagasys received the gift of six full
communes was shattered during the campaign that preceded the election
of their mayors and councilors on November 18, 1956. Inasmuch as this was
the first time that Malagasys and Europeans had voted together and as the
political extremists were concentrated in the main towns, especially those of
Tananarive, Diégo-Suarez, and Tamatave, strong emotions were aroused.
Although left-wing and Catholic nationalists combined to elect Stanislas
Rakotonirina mayor of Tananarive and Justin Bezara mayor of Diégo-

---

* Some Tananarive assemblymen felt that so large a town should have more than 37 municipal
councilors. Under the old system, Tananarive had had only 28 councilors, chosen on a 50-50
basis by the two electoral colleges, and a budget of some 550 million C.F.A. francs, comparable
to that of a town of 35,000 inhabitants in France. See minutes of the representative assembly,
April 21, 1956.

Suarez,* extremists were not generally the victors in this election. Europeans were by no means eliminated from the municipal councils, winning nine of the 37 seats at stake in Tananarive and 13 of the 33 in Tamatave. Only about half of the registered electorate voted, and the abstentionism notably of Europeans was held mainly responsible for the extremists' victory in Diégo-Suarez.

Application of the *loi-cadre* led first to the creation of 15 new *communes de moyen exercice* and then, in 1959, to their promotion to the status of full communes. This development, along with the vast expansion that year of rural communes, required the holding of elections throughout Madagascar in both old and new urban and rural centers. An additional reason was furnished by the poor functioning of most existing communes. In January 1959 the municipal councils of Majunga and Diégo-Suarez were dissolved and replaced by "delegations" appointed by the government, because the councilors of those two towns refused to vote the budgets.† In Tananarive, streets were left unrepaired and hygiene was neglected, so that Rakotonirina lost much of his popularity as mayor, and in Fianarantsoa Mayor Marcel Randria lost support because of similar inaction. Among the full communes, only that of Tamatave functioned fairly well.[20] Poor city government provided ammunition for the government's opponents, who, in any case, were now much better organized than they had been in November 1956. In the elections of October 11, 1959, in the rural communes the P.S.D. won overwhelmingly, and in the coastal towns with small Merina populations‡ it was also victorious, but in the big centers—particularly those of the high plateaus—it was reduced to a minority position.§ Moreover, in Tananarive itself 26 out of 37 seats went to the A.K.F.M., whose president, Richard Andrianamanjato, was elected mayor. At Diégo-Suarez the A.K.F.M. won an absolute majority of the municipal councilors, and the communist Francis Sautron once again became its mayor.

On the whole, the elections of October 11, 1959, marked a distinct success for the P.S.D. government. Nearly 90 per cent of all the seats at stake went to the P.S.D. party or its allies, and the A.K.F.M. lost out in the towns of Antalaha, Moramanga, and Ambatolampy, where it had scored successes in the referendum vote of September 1958. Yet the A.K.F.M.'s victory in such important centers as the national capital and the island's foremost naval base was intolerable to the P.S.D. leaders. On August 27, 1960, under its special

---

* Bezara was soon replaced by the Réunion communist Francis Sautron.
† Some assemblymen protested against these dissolutions as "undemocratic." See minutes of the representative assembly, Feb. 21, 1959.
‡ Fort-Dauphin, Majunga, Mananjara, Manakara, Fénérive, Farafangana, and Ambohimahasoa.
§ The P.S.D. won only ten seats in Antsirabe, ten in Diégo-Suarez, and five in Tamatave.

grant of powers, the P.S.D. government promulgated a new ruling on municipal organization. By its terms any town whose management "threatens democratic principles" might exceptionally and for a limited period be placed under an appointive mayor and municipal council. This regulation neatly opened the way for the government to give Tananarive a special statute and thus undermine its control by the A.K.F.M. Later in 1960 a prefect-delegate of the government was given powers over town affairs which could checkmate those of the mayor and his council, and more *arrondissements* were created as municipal electoral units on the scale of one to each 5,000 inhabitants. In the elections held at Tananarive in February 1961 this maneuver did not prevent Andrianamanjato from being reelected mayor and an A.K.F.M. majority from being returned to the council. Moreover, the prefect-delegate, Germain Ralambo, proved to be no match for the brilliant mayor in the day-to-day handling of the town's business. There is little doubt that Andrianamanjato would once again have been reelected mayor in April 1964 had there not been a schism in the A.K.F.M.[21] In this case, as in earlier ones, Tsiranana's government profited by the division among its opponents.

In December 1964, elections took place in the 26 urban and 739 rural communes of Madagascar. As had been expected, the P.S.D. won overwhelmingly in the rural areas and the A.K.F.M. held its ground in the capital city (where Richard Andrianamanjato was reelected mayor), as well as in Antsirabe. Such progress as the P.S.D. made was not at the expense of its only serious opponent, the A.K.F.M., but of the small secondary parties. Throughout the election campaign it was evident that the P.S.D. leaders were having trouble in holding together the right and left wings of their party.*

As yet, few generalizations can be made about Madagascar's local-government institutions. The rural communes are too recent a creation either to merit the optimism of the official view or to justify the pessimism of their detractors. Much the same can be said about the municipalities, many of which are likewise newborn. Moreover, they vary so greatly in size and scope that any general comments about them are perforce inaccurate. (The budget of Tananarive municipality, for example, came to 1,113 million C.F.A. francs in 1962, but that of Ste.-Marie amounted to only 7.5 millions.) One characteristic, however, they do share: such development as has taken place in local government in Madagascar has been directly related to the degree of usefulness of its institutions to the rulers of the country.

Since 1959, centralization has been the trend in Madagascar, but the old

---

* *Le Monde,* Dec. 22, 1964. See p. 137.

structures—often under different names—have been allowed to subsist. The six provinces have been divided into 19 prefectures and 91 subprefectures, and the island has 45 administrative *arrondissements* (subdivisions or wards) and 691 cantons. The greatest expansion, obviously, has come in the number of full urban communes (26), and even more in that of rural communes (739). Virtually the only countermovement in this Topsy-like profusion of administrative units has been the elimination of *gouvernements,* briefly held over from the Merina monarchy, and the suppression of the autonomous circumscriptions. These circumscriptions were installed in November 1946 and reorganized in February 1957, but they failed in their purpose of facilitating the administration of overlarge provinces and widely dispersed ethnic groups.

Chapter eleven

THE CIVIL SERVICE AND THE JUDICIARY

One of the main reasons for the nonsuccess of the efforts that have been made by independent Madagascar to simplify a top-heavy and costly administration has been the role played by its civil servants. Politically and financially this has handicapped the government and its policies as gravely in Madagascar as in French-speaking Negro Africa, and for many of the same reasons.

Because of the French predilection for direct rule and belief in the universality of French policies, the civil service evolved similarly throughout France's colonial domain. Since there was not any question in French minds of independence for the overseas territories until the late 1950s, it was taken for granted that French officials would fill all the top administrative posts. However, the need for doctors and teachers was so acute that the local health and education services were made relatively accessible to native candidates. To be sure, in none of the government departments were any legal barriers erected against their admission and promotion, but in practice the lack of educational opportunities for schooling above the primary and secondary levels prevented all but a handful of native aspirants from acquiring the necessary diplomas. Furthermore, in Madagascar the local-born candidate for a post in the civil service labored under additional handicaps. These were the exceptionally restrictive policy concerning education for all the Malagasys and a chronic fear of the rebirth of Merina nationalism.

Under Gallieni, the island seemed to get off to an unusually favorable start. He was eager to help the *côtiers* overcome their cultural backwardness as compared with the Merina of the high plateaus. To train future functionaries, especially doctors, teachers, interpreters, and clerks, he founded the Tananarive Medical School and Ecole Le Myre de Vilers, and he also required French and Malagasy functionaries to learn each other's language. But Gallieni's successors neglected schools for the *côtiers*, with the result that Merina again came to be used as government officials in the coastal regions. Nevertheless, even though by the end of World War II four-fifths of all the Malagasy civil servants were Merina, they were sharply subordinated to the French officials. In part this was because of the prevailing educational policy at Tananarive, where all the island's secondary schools were located and where the Merina therefore had a geographical advantage over other tribes.

Theoretically, the lycées of Tananarive were open to any student who qualified academically for admission, but in practice even those Malagasys who managed to pass a difficult entrance examination were not sure of being admitted. The highest-ranking French official in the region where the candidate lived had to give his written approval, and this was determined by his view of the "moral value," living standards, and, above all, the political record of the candidate and his family. During the interwar period, access to the civil service (and to French citizenship) was made easier for Malagasys, especially after the world depression necessitated budgetary economies. Such economies were effected mainly at the expense of European functionaries, whose number had increased by over 40 per cent between 1924 and 1933[1] and who after 1933 were mostly replaced in the subaltern posts by Malagasys. On the eve of World War II there were 9,570 Malagasy and only 1,935 European civil servants; the former had developed some mutual-aid organizations, the oldest of which dated back to 1909. As of 1939, the Malagasy functionaries were organized into two main unions, one of these being affiliated with the French communist C.G.T. labor federation. Both unions, however, had the same objectives: the merging of all civil servants into a single cadre and identical terms of employment for Malagasys and Europeans.

Numerically and organizationally the Malagasy civil servants were strong enough to profit by the Free French government's encouragement of labor unions, beginning in 1944. That year the payment of functionaries' salaries absorbed half of Madagascar's revenues, and Governor-general de St. Mart announced frankly that he would have to reduce the number of Malagasy civil servants by weeding out the incompetent. In this way he hoped to make essential economies, deflect the Malagasy elite to employment in fields other than government service, and improve the status of a smaller and better-qualified corps of Malagasy functionaries.[2] Naturally such a policy aroused Malagasy opposition. Consequently, in November 1946, after the government had refused to increase the civil servants' pay to meet the fast-rising cost of living, many of the Malagasy unions joined the European functionaries in going on strike. This strike was partly successful, but it benefited mainly the Europeans, for four months later the outbreak of the revolt dealt a severe blow—although indirectly—to the Malagasy civil service.

The 1947 revolt led to much examination of past mistakes, which did not spare policy errors concerning the Malagasy civil servants. Depending upon the critic's political convictions, the administration of Madagascar was blamed for widening tribal divisions there by posting Merina officials among the coastal populations, or for failing to alleviate Merina frustrations by giving them positions commensurate with their talents. (French functionaries were also criticized for their failure to keep in touch with the Malagasy population and with the liberal trends in contemporary world opinion.) Of the 14,501 Malagasy civil servants employed in early 1947, all but about 2,000 were Merina and barely 20 occupied posts in the higher echelons.* The severity with which the revolt was put down evoked a new series of criticisms in regard to its effect on the Malagasy civil servants. Under a special regulation of June 18, 1947, issued by de Chévigné, Malagasy functionaries were demoted or dismissed for their alleged (but not necessarily proved) participation in the revolt. Of the 308 Malagasy civil servants dismissed for *inaptitude morale,* by mid-1951 only 104 had been taken back into government service, and many of those not reintegrated never had the chance to prove their innocence before a court of law.[3]

Despite this large-scale and arbitrary reduction in force, Madagascar continued to have a civil service far out of proportion to the size of its population. To some extent this was due to the policy of provincialization† applied in 1946, by which central and provincial public services coexisted and often overlapped. Then, beginning in 1950, the Paris authorities began sending to Madagascar many of the French officials for whom there was no longer any place in Indochina.[4] Some of them were needed and welcomed there, but many were overqualified for their new posts and were a heavy burden on the island's finances. Although the Paris treasury paid the salaries of high-ranking administrators, magistrates, and officers of the *gendarmerie* among the 4,000-odd Europeans employed by the Madagascar government in early 1953, the territory's budget had to meet the cost of their lodging, emoluments, and expatriation allowances. Again and again the European settlers and the representative assembly complained vainly[5] about this influx, which the local government was powerless to control and which had reached such proportions that the civil servants were absorbing three-fourths of the island's revenues.

* For details, see National Assembly debates, May 8–9, 1947; Conseil de la République debates, July 24, 1947; and French Union Assembly debates, May 24, 1949. The "special cadres" were staffed only with Malagasys, the "local cadres" by Frenchmen born in Madagascar or Réunion Island, and the "general cadres" by highly qualified French citizens, almost without exception natives of France. The distinction between the local and special cadres disappeared in 1950–51.
† See p. 144.

The Lamine Gueye law of June 30, 1950, which in principle established total equality between native and French civil servants (except in regard to expatriation benefits), added to the budgetary burden without offsetting the disproportionately large number and pay of the non-Malagasy functionaries serving in Madagascar. In that island, as in French Negro Africa, the decrees applying the Lamine Gueye law perpetuated rather than removed some of the inequalities in the pay, pensions, and family allowances accorded to Malagasy and European civil servants.[6] (The question of family allowances never became so vexatious in Madagascar as in Black Africa, because comparatively few of the Malagasy civil servants were polygamous. It did, however, cause the government increasing concern, for the payment of family allowances was encouraging among functionaries the Malagasy habit of adopting children.)

Governor-general Bargues made a genuine effort to help Malagasy functionaries ascend the rungs of the hierarchical ladder, and by mid-1951 he was able to announce that 160 Malagasys occupied administrative posts that previously had been held only by Europeans.[7] But the accession of a handful of Malagasys to the post of deputy-mayor or even district officer did not solve the basic problem of the civil service of Madagascar. This was the presence on the government's payroll of too many highly paid Europeans and too many insufficiently paid Malagasys. The injustice of discriminating against the Malagasy functionaries as well as the general overstaffing of the public services were the subjects of many resolutions by the relevant unions and of lengthy and heated debates in the representative assembly.[8] The fact that the assembly at that time (and later) was composed largely of functionaries assured a lively interest and sympathetic hearing for their colleagues' grievances.

Civil servants' unions struck in January 1952, June 1954, May 1955, and May and August 1956, but not very effectively, for they did not present a united front and the government was able to avoid dealing with the basic issue involved, either by referring the question to a series of special study committees or by granting small concessions first to one group of functionaries and then to another. A reform of 1955, however, deserves special mention. First, the age limit was raised for candidates applying for admission to the civil service. Then higher cadres were created in such services as the Treasury and the Post and Telegraph, which had not had them before, and posts in them were reserved for Malagasys.

By the time the *loi-cadre* was applied to Madagascar in 1957, the civil-service problem had acquired new dimensions and political overtones. The distinction that it drew between the State (Metropolitan French) and Territorial (Malagasy) cadres, the creation of more provincial public services, and the growing politicization of the bureaucracy finally forced the government in 1958 to set about drafting a fundamental code for Madagascar's civil service. As to qualifications for admission to this service, the task was not too difficult. The big advance in secondary and higher education for Malagasys since World War II was beginning to bear fruit, and with each succeeding year more and more Malagasys were qualified to hold high government posts. This phenomenon and the creation of a single territorial civil service that included all categories of the administration's employees caused the number of Malagasy functionaries to increase drastically, and even by the end of 1957 they were said to account for one-tenth of the total population.[9] What proved to be especially delicate was the drafting of rules by which an incumbent functionary who lacked the proper diplomas could be promoted to a higher post. Of necessity this would have to depend upon the recommendation of his current superior in the hierarchy, who was a Frenchman, and this offended the susceptibilities of the ultranationalists in the assembly.

In other ways, too, the old resentment of the Malagasy civil servant toward his more privileged French counterpart took on new political aspects.[10] To the former, the salary and emoluments earned by the state civil servant established the new living standard to which he felt he could legitimately aspire. But the Malagasy government council, whose members under the French administration individually had supported the Malagasy functionary vis-à-vis his French colleague, began to have second thoughts. Each time the French Parliament voted a pay raise for its own bureaucracy, Malagasy civil servants would expect an analogous increment. Since there were already some 12,000 Malagasy functionaries and the prospect was that their number would increase considerably, the government felt that it must draw the line, but hesitated as to just where this should be done. It wanted to make up for past injustices, and the assembly voted to increase the pay for Malagasy civil servants by 4 per cent in 1957 and by 10 per cent in 1958. At the same time, however, it did not want to mortgage the country's future, especially at the expense of the peasant taxpayer, whose annual earnings were already far below those of his compatriot civil servant. A strike for pay parity with Metropolitan officials in November 1957 by the Cartel des Fonctionnaires, FISEMA, and autonomous and Christian civil-servants' unions convinced the P.S.D. leaders and the assembly that the Malagasy civil service must be completely dissociated from that of France and that its members must agree to accept an austerity program.[11]

The most obvious way by which the cost of the bureaucracy could be brought down, and at the same time nationalist sentiments assuaged, was to replace the French officials serving in Madagascar by Malagasys.* A long step in this direction was taken early in 1959, when Tsiranana signed four agreements with the French government specifying how many and what category of Frenchmen his government wanted to employ. That same year the first group of 30 Malagasys was sent to the Ecole Nationale de la France d'Outre-Mer (E.N.F.O.M.) in Paris for training, and plans were laid to open an Ecole Nationale d'Administration Malgache at Tananarive.†

On the principle of "Malagasization" of the higher posts in the civil service all political factions in Madagascar were for once agreed, but not on the tempo at which this principle should be applied. Obviously it was most easily done in the general administrative cadres, and on October 6, 1959, Tsiranana was able to announce to the representative assembly that all provincial chiefs and half the district officers had been replaced by Malagasys. He insisted, however, that to maintain efficiency in the technical services his government must retain some French technicians, whom France would supply and pay. "In less than a year," he said, "I hope to have reconstructed the entire Malagasy civil service, and then we shall have a worthy instrument with which to administer the country."

Debates in the assembly and senate that concerned the civil service were always lively, and they became more and more heated as Madagascar neared and then won independence. Madagascar's legislators continued to show the same fears of Merina domination and of abuses of authority by high functionaries and the administration as they did under French rule. To these chronic fears, self-government now added the suspicion that party politics were demoralizing civil servants. Merina continued to predominate among Madagascar's functionaries but not to the same extent as before, and they were still reluctant to serve outside the high plateaus. As of 1962, Merina formed 23 per cent of the total population and accounted for 59 per cent of all Malagasy functionaries, and they had taken over virtual control of certain public services. Merina civil servants were required to do at least one tour of duty in coastal areas, but they were still so recalcitrant about this that in February 1964 the government took severe measures against those who refused to go to the post to which they had been assigned or who left it without official permission.[12] To offset Merina predominance, the government has been trying to give the needed training to non-Merina candidates for the civil service. In 1959, 21 of the 30 Malagasys sent to the E.N.F.O.M. were

* To what lengths such sentiments could carry some Malagasys was illustrated by a much-quoted statement that appeared in 1958 in a Tananarive newspaper. Its author wrote: "You Frenchmen in 60 years of colonization have never seriously trained Malagasy cadres. Give us our independence and you will see that in five years we will have Malagasy aviators and even the atomic bomb."

† This school in 1962 had 52 students.

côtiers, but because of the lack of proper preparatory schooling it has not yet been possible to include representatives of all 18 tribes.

In 1960, after Madagascar became independent, what was called a *crise d'autorité* occurred in the countryside despite the fact that by that time almost all the high civil-service posts were occupied by Malagasys. Disregarding the nationality of the incumbents and the new names given to their offices, the pent-up resentment against the *fanjakana*'s grip was expressed actively in the rural areas and verbally in the assembly. The peasantry, confusing independence with anarchy, refused to obey the district officers, and the assembly hesitated to give those officials control over the rural guards and *gendarmerie* needed to restore their authority.[13] One cause of the legislators' hesitation to reinforce the power of the central government was their conviction that the P.S.D. leaders were manipulating civil servants for party purposes. Already such deep-rooted suspicions had been shown during the debates on the government's draft code for functionaries.[14] The assembly readily accepted the government's proposals on the basic principles of such a code—the right of functionaries to organize and to enjoy equal and fair treatment in matters of pay, promotion, pensions, disciplinary measures, and the like—but it was openly skeptical of the government's impartiality in applying them. Specifically in such matters as the right to strike and to engage in side business and political activities, as well as the inclusion in the civil service of auxiliary agents and *cheminots* (railroad employees) and the recruitment of women as functionaries, many of the assemblymen and senators clashed sharply with the P.S.D. ministers.

The government, for its part, worried about many of the same things as did the assemblymen and senators, but for different reasons. The *crise d'autorité* made it difficult to collect taxes, and cases of embezzlement among the official tax collectors—the new name given to the old canton chiefs—were becoming alarmingly frequent. Another cause for concern was the instability of rural officials, and the government placed responsibility for this mainly on the legislators, who, it alleged, intervened in regard to transfers or postings so as to curry favor with the individual civil servant or with their constituents. Still another source of worry to the P.S.D. leaders was the hesitation, or refusal, of some highly trained Malagasys to enter government service. In 1961 about 100 Malagasys then serving in the better-paid French civil service were reportedly reluctant to give up the advantages they were enjoying for an austere life which only sheer patriotism could make acceptable.[15] Moreover, the same reluctance to place nation before self was displayed by certain Malagasy students who had completed their studies in France. In October 1959 Tsiranana made an urgent appeal to them to return and serve their country, and he added as an inducement, "We will pay their return fare even if they are not scholarship-holders."[16]

The principal bone of contention, however, between the P.S.D. leaders, on the one hand, and the legislators and civil-servants' unions, on the other, concerned the continued employment of foreign advisers and experts. Repeatedly but in vain the cabinet ministers assured the assemblymen and senators that France was not trying to foist off on Madagascar its unwanted and unqualified nationals but was sending only those specifically requested by the Malagasy government. Madagascar did not yet have enough qualified technicians of its own, and even if it had, they would cost more to the local taxpayer than did the foreigners, whose salaries France itself was paying. It was the official policy to employ as many Malagasys as compatible with maintaining administrative efficiency, but for the time being the 2,000 or so foreign employees were indispensable and far from being a useless expense.[17]

Independence brought louder and more numerous demands for a total and immediate "Malagasization" of the cadres, and matters came to a head during the legislature's budgetary session in November 1960. The storm broke when the government proposed reducing the 1961 budget deficit by a 10 per cent cut in all Malagasy functionaries' salaries. The government was attacked for attempting to reduce the already impoverished Malagasy civil servants to direst misery and for employing so-called foreign experts who were none other than unqualified and unpopular holdovers from the former French administration. Their salaries might well be paid by France but each of them cost the Malagasy taxpayers 40,000 or more C.F.A. francs a month for lodging and special emoluments. The government defended itself by stating that the pay of 25,150 Malagasy civil servants, who had just had a salary increase, amounted to the huge sum of 6,167,399,594 C.F.A. francs and accounted for almost all of the administration's very heavy operating expenditures.[18] Nevertheless, in order to have the government's proposal accepted, the ministers had to promise that the 10 per cent cut would be temporary and would not affect the lowest-paid category of functionaries. Later, when the government tried to carry over the cut into the 1962 budget, it could do so only by reducing the percentage to 7 per cent and promising to eliminate the reduction entirely in 1963.

Both the adamant attitude of the Parliament and the prevalence of corruption among Malagasy functionaries seem now to have convinced the government that it cannot tamper with that segment of the elite without running grave risks. It has speeded up the dismissal of European civil servants, whose number was reduced between June 1959 and June 1962 from 2,401 to 1,746.* Perhaps with the aim of making the P.S.D. government thoroughly

* The greatest reduction has been in the domain of general administration, from 293 to 122, and the largest number of Frenchmen still employed were in the teaching profession, where they still came to 767. For details, see minutes of the representative assembly, June 21, 1962.

unpopular, the A.K.F.M. opponents of the government have been asking for a total reorganization of the administrative structure that would automatically reduce the number of civil servants employed. Though such a course of action has everything reasonable to recommend it, no governing party would dare risk alienating such a powerful if small element of the population. Moreover, the great majority of the Malagasy elite are not in favor of such an extreme step. They are convinced—and no amount of presidential eloquence can dissuade them—that the Malagasys are naturally talented enough to run their country without the help of outsiders. A corollary to this is their conviction that the demands for better pay and more privileges on the part of the Malagasy civil servants should and could be met without inflicting any injustice on the peasantry, if only the expenses attributable to the employment of foreign technicians were eliminated.

The Judiciary

The judicial system that France installed in Madagascar resembled that set up in other French dependencies, but it evolved somewhat differently because of two factors. The more important of these was the existence of an indigenous written law code prior to the French conquest, and the second was a fairly strong nationalist movement which caused the administration to strengthen its grip on the whole judicial network.

As in so many other fields, it was Gallieni who inspired the dual jurisdictional system that survived with comparatively few modifications until after World War II. Under the wholly French system professional magistrates applied French law in all cases involving French citizens, including naturalized Malagasys, and also in those concerning members of the resident Chinese and Indian minorities. Under the second system, French administrators, advised by two Malagasy assessors, judged cases involving solely Malagasys. In so doing they applied customary local law, slightly modified by French penal law for certain severe penalties. The wholly French system comprised 35 courts—a court of appeal, four courts of first instance, 18 courts of justices of the peace of limited competence, four courts of justices of the peace of wide competence, and eight criminal courts. The Malagasy system consisted of a Chambre d'Annulation et d'Homologation for criminal cases, 35 second-degree courts, and 85 first-degree courts. In all Madagascar there were only a handful of magistrates, so that justice was almost entirely in the hands of administrators acting as judges, and this meant that the government was often judge as well as party in a legal dispute. This grip of the administration on the rendering of justice, far more than the code of law applied, aroused the resentment of the Malagasys, as it did of the Africans in French West Africa and Equatorial Africa.

The Merina monarchs promulgated six law codes, of which the most famous was that of Queen Ranavalona II in 1881, called the Code of 305 Articles. Missionary influence was obvious in its provisions regarding marriage, women's rights, slavery, and the manufacture and sale of alcoholic beverages. Its Malagasy character was shown in its dealing with such matters as sorcery, adoption, the practice of *tavy*,* and the violation of tombs. This code was intended only for application in Imerina—in 1873 the Queen had given the Betsileo a code of their own—and the less-evolved coastal tribes were still judged according to their own customs. But because the Merina ruled most of Madagascar and because only their laws were written down, the various Merina codes profoundly influenced tribal customary law everywhere.

Since the Merina code of 1881 reflected an indigenous attempt to move nearer to European legal concepts, the separation of the French from the Malagasy judicial systems under Gallieni seemed to some observers to be a retrogressive step.[19] Indeed, the main drawback to his judicial system as applied to the Malagasys was its failure to respect the principle of the separation of powers, and its major asset was the rapidity of its procedures. Yet this advantage was to some extent offset by the attempt embodied in a decree of May 9, 1909, to safeguard the Malagasys against certain hasty and arbitrary judgments. This decree made the administrator-judge's verdict in criminal cases subject to review by the Chambre d'Annulation, which was composed of three magistrates, two officials, and two Malagasy assessors.

By July 1926 the wheels of justice had slowed down to such a degree that Governor-general Olivier empowered qualified Malagasys to judge civil cases in courts of first instance.[20] Their knowledge of the language and of local customs speeded up the hearing of litigation and reduced the number of appeals. But true to the tradition of two-steps-backward-one-step-forward, the colonial administration during the interwar period enhanced the power of the administration at the expense of abstract justice, notably in 1930 with promulgation of the so-called Cayla decree. Under its provisions (and those of the *indigénat*) representatives of the government could punish Malagasys for a whole gamut of offenses ranging from neglecting their farms to failing to pay taxes to endangering the security of the state. Furthermore, each district officer had at his disposal a contingent of the *garde indigène*, a military form of rural police, who saw to it that his decisions were carried out.

Abolition of the *indigénat* and suppression of native justice in criminal litigation, where it was replaced in the spring of 1946 by courts applyng

* See pp. 325–27.

French penal law, seemed to presage a reversal of the established trend. As a result of the latter move, however, only 31 magistrates in Madagascar became theoretically responsible for judging all the criminal cases for a population of over 4 million. Madagascar being but one of the Overseas Territories, all of which were in the same judicial plight, it would obviously take years before it could get the 400 to 500 magistrates needed—not to mention the lodgings and courtrooms they would require to enforce the new law.* As a makeshift arrangement, justices of the peace were given limited competence in criminal cases—but time passed and the "temporary" was fast becoming a permanent situation. Moreover, the new justices of the peace were none other than French administrators, and since there were fewer courts than formerly and no longer any Malagasy assessors in criminal cases, the situation, in the eyes of the Malagasys, was even worse than before. In fact, one eminent French jurist, Maître Ravaillé, was quoted as saying that if there had been twice the number of magistrates in Madagascar in 1947, there would never have been any revolt.[21]

Such a statement certainly oversimplified a complex situation for which there were other causes, both old and new, but it did point up the dramatic void that had occurred in the rendering of justice in Madagascar. (In 1947 there were 32 fewer criminal courts than in 1946, and the number of cases they handled had declined by half.) Among such causes were the continuing abuses of the administration's authority in judicial matters, and, by extension, those abuses committed by the "forces of order," the backlog of cases due in part to the slowness and complexity of the new legal procedures, and the basic premises—as well as the omissions—of French penal law. Gaps in the French criminal code in such matters of Malagasy concern as cattle thefts and tomb violations could in time probably be filled in, but fundamental differences in outlook could not be remedied so easily. A main grievance of Malagasy plaintiffs, even when they won their case in a French court, was that almost never did they retrieve a stolen article or receive compensation for damage inflicted, and the imprisonment of the guilty party brought them no satisfaction. They were not concerned with repairing the damage done to society as a whole, and consequently preferred Malagasy law, which aimed at satisfying the aggrieved individual.[22]

Madagascar's situation of shortage of law courts and magistrates was reversed for law-enforcement personnel. The nationalist demonstration that greeted de Coppet on his arrival at Tananarive on May 19, 1946, caused him to send a hurry call to Paris for more and better-equipped policemen and

* In 1949 it was estimated that the proper juridical equipment of Madagascar would take ten years' time and cost 3,500 million C.F.A. francs. See French Union Assembly debates, Dec. 27, 1949.

*gendarmes.** Outbreak of the revolt in 1947 led to the hasty recruiting of Senegalese and Comorians for service in Madagascar. They were soon feared for their brutality† and resented as foreigners by the Malagasys, and these emotions still color their attitude toward all the "forces of order." The way in which the revolt was suppressed, the trial of the M.D.R.M. deputies at Tananarive, and the holding of thousands of suspects for long periods in prison without trial contributed further to the bad repute of justice in Madagascar. Although the French government refused to free the judiciary from the control of the executive branch by lifting the state of siege from all the island and by abrogating the Cayla decree, it did desire to improve the judicial network. Beginning in 1952 it increased the number of law courts and judges there, and although administrators still predominated as justices of the peace, they were being progressively replaced by magistrates, notably through transfers from Indochina.‡

Autonomy in 1957 and independence in 1960 brought profound though not rapid changes in Madagascar's laws and the personnel that enforced them, but fewer transformations of the judicial structure. Indeed, the slowness with which changes were and are being made has disappointed both the general Malagasy public and their representatives in parliament. In rural areas the majority of cases are said still to be settled almost clandestinely by *fokonolona* "courts." In defense of its *festina lente* policy the government has pled that the proper training of magistrates requires considerable time and that Madagascar must maintain high standards of justice. When charged with retaining the overlarge corps of police and *gendarmes* inherited from the period of repression that followed the revolt,§ it has pointed to the breakdown in rural law and order when the district officers were deprived of such means of enforcing their authority and also to the restraints in the 1959 constitution on the power of the executive branch.

* The Indochina crisis prevented his receiving total satisfaction in this respect, but 550 policemen were added to the 1,400 already stationed on the island, and the number of mobile detachments of *gendarmes* was raised from two to ten. See National Assembly debates, May 9, 1947.

† Stanislas Rakotonirina claimed that the reason he had been arrested and tortured at the time of the revolt was because he had protested in a speech in the representative assembly against Baron's recruiting of Senegalese and Comorians for the local police force. See Stibbe, p. 27.

‡ As of 1952, Madagascar had some 100 magistrates, or about one-fourth of the number it needed. Although the French treasury paid their salaries, as well as those of the *gendarmes,* the changes made in Madagascar's judicial system had already cost its own budget over 800 million C.F.A. francs. See National Assembly debates, March 21, 1952, and French Union Assembly debates, Feb. 17, 1953.

§ During budget debates in the 1950s, French deputies often objected to the expense of such a large force of *gendarmes* in Madagascar. On July 23, 1955, it was said that there was then one *gendarme* for every 4,300 Malagasys and 600 square kilometers. As to the *garde indigène,* its members were paid from Malagasy and not French revenues.

Article 18 of the constitution created a High Court, composed of three magistrates and eight parliamentarians, which was empowered to try the president of the republic as well as his ministers for treason or infractions of the penal code. The constitution also provided for setting up a Conseil Supérieur des Institutions, to pass on the constitutionality of laws and regulations, and a Supreme Court to fulfill the tasks currently performed by the French Conseil d'Etat and Cour de Cassation. Courts of first instance were maintained in the six provincial capitals, with branches in the smaller towns. Where none such existed, courts under district officers, aided by assessors, judged cases as before, except that they were renamed Courts of Traditional Law.[23] The existing Court of Appeals was empowered to hear appeals from the Traditional Law Courts and Labor Courts. Each criminal court was presided over by two magistrates and three assessors, and the criminal courts were augmented by special courts to handle cases of cattle thefts. Legal procedures were basically the same as before but were simplified owing to Madagascar's need for more speedy justice and its shortage of money and qualified personnel.

Among the Malagasys the lack of qualified magistrates was due largely to the low salaries they received, considering the long years of preparation, including study in France, that were required of them. Yet legal training had started earlier in Madagascar than in French Negro Africa, though for some years Tananarive's law school operated as an annex to that of St. Denis on Réunion Island.[24] After World War II it was taken in hand by the University of Aix, and its standards were gradually raised to those of a Law Faculty, but as of 1959 not one of the 119 magistrates then serving in Madagascar was a Malagasy. In February of that year, Maître Marcel Fournier, Madagascar's first Minister of Justice,* successfully negotiated an increase in the facilities for training Malagasy judicial personnel at the E.N.F.O.M. in Paris. When the Ecole Nationale d'Administration Malgache opened its doors in 1961, it had a special section for training the island's future magistrates. It will, however, take some time before Madagascar can produce enough indigenous magistrates to fill its needs, and the government has been frequently criticized because the magistracy is the branch of government service in which "Malagasization" is proceeding most slowly.[25] Thus far the P.S.D. leaders have turned a deaf ear to pleas that the government lower its educational standards for the magistracy so as to admit the less well-educated côtier candidates.

If the "Malagasization" of the judicial cadres was the nationalists' first

* On the eve of independence Maître Fournier voluntarily resigned his post so that a Malagasy —René Rakotobe—could become Minister of Justice. This "graceful gesture" was much applauded in Madagascar.

goal, that of replacing French law by Malagasy law was the second. In both matters the government agreed in principle but disagreed on the time required to make the change smoothly and effectively. In 1957 the representative assembly passed a resolution asking for the codification of Malagasy juridical customs, but it was not until 1960 that a specially appointed committee got to work on the project. The groundwork had been well laid by two eminent French scholars, E.-P. Thebault and G. J. H. Julien, but a great deal more had to be done to gather together all the written Merina documents and the relevant oral traditions from the 17 other tribes. The parliamentarians finally agreed that this task should be done by stages and the draft codes written first in French and then translated into Malagasy. Similarly, they were willing for French law to serve wherever Malagasy law was deficient or vague, and, though eager to preserve Malagasy customs, they were also anxious to have them evolve according to modern jurisprudence.[26] Already, since independence, some profound revisions have been made in the island's criminal law, which has taken on a more authoritarian and punitive character. Penalties for such offenses as cattle theft, acts of sorcery, and traffic in Indian hemp have been made considerably more severe, though no changes have been made in those for usury.[27] The general trend, however, is to harmonize Malagasy law with French law.

Inevitably some disputes have arisen between the government and the most ardent nationalists regarding the imposition of such penalties, how far to streamline the *gendarmerie* and *garde indigène,* whether the provincial or central government should pay for their services, and the like. In the assembly discussions,[28] old grievances dating from French rule came to light, for example, the holding of villagers collectively responsible for setting bush fires and the use by administrators of rural police as orderlies or messenger boys; and new ones were aired, such as the P.S.D.'s use of the judicial services for party ends.*

Despite such denials, Tsiranana's government—or any Malagasy regime, for that matter—would certainly not fail to utilize any of the readymade instruments it has inherited from the French to reinforce the authority of the party in power. *Le Monde's* able reporter Philippe Decraene noted in the spring of 1964 (issue of May 20) that since independence Tsiranana has created and placed directly under his authority a *gendarmerie* composed almost wholly of *côtiers,* whose numbers were three times larger than those of the national army commanded by a general of Merina origin.

---

* Minister of Interior Resampa denied this vigorously. In the assembly on February 21, 1959, he said: "The government has never, and I repeat never, displaced a magistrate for political motives."

Chapter twelve

FOREIGN RELATIONS

During 64 years of colonial rule, the Malagasys never forgot that under the Merina dynasty their country had exchanged envoys with some of the great Western powers. It was in large part a yearning to restore Madagascar's "diplomatic personality" that made the Merina in particular press so vigorously for national independence. Tsiranana himself, though more prudent and despite his misgivings as to the consequences of such independence, was nevertheless also seduced by the prospect of his country's taking its place in the comity of nations and achieving international recognition through membership in the United Nations. When Madagascar was admitted to that body on September 20, 1960, there was profound and widespread gratification among the Malagasys, but it soon became evident that independence did not mean the same thing to all of them.

To the average Malagasy and to some of the elite, independence meant freedom to return to their ancestral customs without foreign interference, to left-wingers it meant that Madagascar could now develop ties with the Eastern bloc, and to the president of the republic it meant no change in his commitment to keep Madagascar in the Western camp. In fact, since independence, Tsiranana has reinforced his ties with France, the European Economic Community, and the United States, from which he expected and has received both military support and financial and technical aid. Beginning early in 1964 he apparently became obsessed by the fear that Madagascar might not remain immune from the troubles plaguing East Africa, and in particular he was alarmed at the prospect of infiltration by Asians. Some observers feel that he is too sophisticated to believe in the dangers to his country that he has so luridly portrayed, but others think that he is genuinely and deeply apprehensive about Indian and Chinese immigration and communist subversion. At all events, during 1964 he devoted much of his effort to strengthening Madagascar's military defenses.

Madagascar's Military Situation

World War II and the revolt of 1947 completely reversed the military view of Madagascar and the Malagasys that France had held for nearly half a century. Between the annexation in 1896 and the British invasion in 1942, Madagascar had military value in French eyes as a reservoir of manpower and foodstuffs needed for the defense of France in time of war and for the policing of the empire during peacetime. Britain's conquest of the island for the purpose of forestalling a Japanese attack, defending South Africa, and protecting the Allies' sources of petroleum in the Middle East gave back to Madagascar some of the importance it had lost in the mid-nineteenth century. (The opening of the Suez Canal in 1869 deflected maritime traffic between Europe and the East, and Madagascar, which had been a point for refueling and provisioning ships on the Cape route to India, was thereafter bypassed.) Yet this new perspective on Madagascar did not give rise to any changes in the island's military organization until the 1947 revolt showed up some of its weaknesses and dangers. Its major weakness was the lack of coordination between the civilian and military authorities, especially in the provinces affected by the revolt,[1] and the gravest danger lay in the impetus given to rebellion by the disgruntled and recently demobilized Malagasy veterans of World War II.

On October 1, 1947, a reorganization was undertaken and the island was divided into six military subdivisions, corresponding to its five provinces and the autonomous circumscription of Diégo-Suarez. The fortification of the great deep-water natural harbor of Diégo-Suarez—classed as a strategic base of the French Union in 1946—was undertaken as complementary to that of Djibouti, which commanded the south end of the Suez Canal. Yet the expense of building and maintaining the arsenal, drydock, and repair shops was such, and the laborers working there so demanding, that Diégo-Suarez barely escaped being shut down as a naval base in the early 1950s. Eventually it was saved after the French government had stressed to the National Assembly that it had economic as well as strategic importance. The French navy gave employment and training to 570 Malagasys (of a total of 1,700 men stationed there), and the base did odd jobs for local civilian enterprises that brought in an annual income of several hundred million C.F.A. francs.[2] In view of the existence of the Diégo naval base and the big military aviation base at Ivato, near Tananarive, the whole island, it was claimed, could become "one huge aircraft carrier" or staging area for the defense of the Indian Ocean. A decree of June 14, 1949, had already organized the collective defense of the French possessions in that ocean under the commander stationed in Madagascar, and in August 1951 contacts were made with the British in Nairobi concerning joint defense of the Mozambique Canal.[3] The closing of the Suez Canal after the Anglo-French-Israeli invasion of November 1956 brought into clearer perspective Madagascar's potential in commanding the sea-lanes from Capetown to India and farther east. In the early 1960s, Madagascar's newly sovereign status brought ever stronger demands from the A.K.F.M. and extreme nationalists that France evacuate Diégo-Suarez and its other bases on the island. On the other hand, the troubles in East Africa and especially in nearby Zanzibar made the P.S.D. government eager not only to keep French troops in Madagascar but to have them reinforced and more strongly equipped.

The number of European French troops of all categories stationed throughout Madagascar at the time it became independent did not exceed 7,000.[4] The small size of the French garrisons in the island, the useful work of the French army in road and bridge building and in making topographical surveys, and the benefits to local trade because of its presence made its retention there a poor target for attack by either Malagasy nationalists or economy-minded Frenchmen. Moreover, the agreements of defense and cooperation signed early in 1960 provided for the transfer of the 4,482 Malagasys then serving in the French armed forces to Madagascar's new national army, and the training and equipping of that army by France. Like the newly independent French-speaking African states, the Malagasys' pride dictated the creation of their own army, navy, and air force, but they could not afford to make these military arms more than symbolic units. In fact, the Tsiranana government in imposing military conscription on September 30, 1960, for all citizens between the ages of 20 and 50 hoped to accomplish two very practical supplementary purposes. These were to drain dangerously idle youths from the towns and to utilize them to carry out socially useful public works, euphemistically called civic service. Unlike their African colleagues, however (with some of whom they were closely associated in the organization later called the Union Africaine et Malgache), the Malagasys did not count primarily on diplomacy or regional defense pacts but on French troops to assure their external defense.

Actually, in the past decade neither the French nor the Malagasy government has relied heavily on the loyalty of troops recruited from among the Malagasys. The Malagasy veterans of World Wars I and II never gave France their loyalty in the way the Negro Africans did, and in fact they were an element actively hostile to French rule during the revolt of 1947. Consequently France made less of an effort to secure for the Malagasys the same treatment as French veterans received in regard to pensions and liability compensation. The concession that pleased the Malagasy veterans most of all was the pledge of the French government in 1958 to repatriate the bodies of their comrades who had died abroad so that they could be laid to rest in their family tombs.[5] Probably this general attitude—lukewarm at best and antagonistic at worst—was responsible for the fact that only a small proportion of the Malagasys liable to military conscription were actually called to the colors during the 1950s, so that independent Madagascar had relatively few men trained to carry arms.

This lack of military training was displeasing neither to the average Malagasy nor to his government. By and large, the Malagasys were a people opposed to violence and not attracted to the profession of soldiering. Only in Imerina did there exist a strong military tradition, and even there it was confined to the *hova* caste, for under Merina rule the nobles and slaves had been exempted from military service. When Madagascar became independent, there existed only one Malagasy colonel (a Merina named Gabriel Ramanantsoa, who was promoted to the rank of general in July 1961) and 27 officers of lower rank, seven of whom were graduates of St. Cyr. A national army without rigid educational requirements did offer the *côtiers* a chance to rise fast from the ranks and at Fianarantsoa a military preparatory school was opened in October 1961. Because of the cleavage between Merina and *côtiers,* however, the government has qualms about building up an officer corps that might throw its weight on one side or the other and seize control of the government, and feels it safer to create a much larger *gendarmerie* and police force composed mainly of *côtiers*. Thus, for reasons of thrift, political caution, and efficacy in external defense, Tsiranana prefers to depend mainly on French military support. Malagasy troops number only 2,600, compared with 7,800 policemen and 3,000 *gendarmes*—whose pay makes a very large dent in the country's budget. Some military equipment is supplied to Madagascar by the United States and West Germany, but the great bulk is given by France, which continues to regard Madagascar as a bastion in the Indian Ocean worth guarding at considerable expense.* In fact, military assistance in one form or another has accounted for 40 per cent of the total aid given by France to Madagascar.[6]

Relations with France

Of all the countries that voted to join the Franco-African Community, Madagascar has remained most consistently attached to France and seems to be the least apprehensive about French neocolonialism. It is also the least decolonized overseas territory, judging by such superficial evidence as the number of resident French and their clinging to colonial ways of life. As of January 1, 1964, there were still 1,736 Frenchmen serving in the gov-

---

* Madagascar, the Comoro Islands, Réunion, and French Somaliland make up what France calls its Third Overseas Zone, which is under the command of a rear admiral. A wholly Malagasy Conseil Supérieur de Défense has been constituted, but the principal organization is the Franco-Malagasy Defense Committee, whose members are the president of the republic, the French ambassador, and the officer commanding Zone 3.

ernment of Madagascar,* and a considerable proportion of the 52,000 Frenchmen still living on the island continued to use the familiar form of "tu" in addressing Malagasys—a habit that by then had almost completely died out in French-speaking Africa. In foreign affairs, Tsiranana has staunchly defended French policy in Algeria, nuclear testing in the Sahara, and the restoration by French troops of Léon Mba as president of Gabon, but not the French recognition of communist China.

Inevitably this pro-French policy of Tsiranana's has displeased the A.K.F.M. and the extreme-nationalist press, and amid the usual encomiums of General de Gaulle and the expressions of gratitude for French generosity to Madagascar an occasional sour note is struck.† Malagasy assemblymen have been especially critical of the number, quality, and cost to Madagascar of the French technical assistants. The Merina nationalists in particular have wanted to get rid of the white settlers, especially those from Réunion Island, and to loosen the grip of French monopolies on the island's export-import business and shipping. There is a widespread desire, even on the part of some P.S.D. leaders, to reduce Madagascar's present dependence on France, but no effective steps have been taken in that direction. While the average Malagasy might notice little difference in his own life if French aid were withdrawn, the elite would certainly have to lower their living standards. And even the most ardent Malagasy nationalists have not rebelled against French culture—on the contrary, they have absorbed it remarkably well. It has been said that Richard Andrianamanjato, president of the A.K.F.M., who is an ardent advocate of the Malagasy language and a defender of Malagasy culture, uses Cartesian logic and the purest French to enhance his arguments.

The cordiality that has pervaded Franco-Malagasy relations since Madagascar's independence is the more surprising in view of the longevity and strength of the local nationalist movement, the horrifying memories of the 1947 revolt and its repression, the chronic resentment against France's economic grip on the country, and the high percentage—about one-fourth of the votes cast—against joining the Franco-African Community. The present happy state of affairs can be attributed in part to the enlightened governorships of Bargues and Soucadaux and even more to the statesmanship of President Tsiranana and General de Gaulle. The close friendship that has developed between these two leaders has unquestionably contributed to the

---

* Of these, 105 were in general administration, 159 in "special" administration, 61 in justice, 956 in education, 101 in health, 86 in post and telegraph, and 268 in the technical services. There were also 54 French military officers.

† Alexandre Ranatanaela, the aggressive deputy from Antsirabe, told the assembly on January 18, 1960, that Madagascar owed no gratitude to France for its aid, because France was only beginning to pay back the "blood debt" it owed to the Malagasys who had fought for France during two world wars.

special warmth with which France's policy of cooperation with all its former dependencies has been applied to Madagascar. When Tsiranana made a state visit to France in October 1960, General de Gaulle went to the airport to meet him, and the Malagasy president has reciprocated by naming the new university at Tananarive for *l'homme du 18 juin*. In Madagascar towns there has been no wholesale renaming of streets for Malagasy heroes, and Gallieni's statue was removed from its prominent position in Tananarive at the request of the French Embassy and not at the demand of the Malagasys.

During 1963–64 Franco-Malagasy relations became, if anything, even closer than before, and the politico-economic disengagement that took place in those two years in French-speaking Africa did not occur in Madagascar. Tsiranana has shown growing concern over the danger of invasion by Asians and communists, and he believes that France is the only bulwark that can be depended upon to protect his country against this menace. Early in 1964 Tsiranana was said to have brought to de Gaulle a huge dossier filled with reports of communist plots in Madagascar, written by his "overzealous and credulous agents."[7] Whether or not the General was convinced of the reality or imminence of this peril is not known, but he was apparently responsive to Tsiranana's urgent appeals for strengthening Madagascar's military equipment. In November 1964, Tsiranana again went to Paris especially to ask the French government to slow down its withdrawal of troops from Madagascar and its demobilization of Malagasy soldiers from the French army. He told Premier Pompidou that Madagascar's armed forces alone could not defend the island without at least the logistical support of the French army. He added that although France had agreed to maintain a force of 2,000 men at three points on the island, this would not offset the loss of over 3 billion C.F.A. francs which the French army and navy had been spending each year in Madagascar. Resampa has concurred in this request, but he would like to see the French garrisons maintained on the island largely for financial reasons.

France's monetary aid has been running at the annual rate of some 10 billion C.F.A. francs, of which 1 to 1.5 billion a year have been going to the Malagasy army. French aid far outweighs that from all other sources combined, and the "communist menace" has proved to be a good means of leverage with certain other Western-bloc countries. Tsiranana certainly made good use of it when he went to London and Washington during the summer of 1964.

Relations with Western Bloc Countries

In Madagascar's relations with Western powers other than France, Great Britain heads the list chronologically. Its active role in Imerina in the mid-nineteenth century made it then the most influential foreign nation on the island. As competition between the British and French for control of Madagascar became acute—partly as the result of the anti-French activities of some English missionaries—the familiar accusations against Perfidious Albion appeared in the French accounts of that period. The British occupation of Madagascar in 1942 reawakened such old fears. In the early postwar years, however, some of the most conservative French residents there, far from being alarmed by the prospect of British domination, were said to be actively seeking an "Anglo-American" protectorate in the belief that it would ensure the white man's supremacy in Madagascar. French parliamentary debates in the late 1940s contained veiled references by Communist Party spokesmen to mysterious intrigues between French settlers and businessmen in Madagascar and the governments of South Africa and Mauritius through Indian and Greek agents, who were rumored to be landing arms and setting up clandestine radio posts on the island.[8] Soon, however, Britain began liquidating its own empire, and the liberation of India made allegations of its designs on Madagascar seem absurd. Thereafter the Communist Party reassigned the role of whipping boy in the Indian Ocean to the United States.

Even at the time of the Merina monarchs, the United States had diplomatic relations with Madagascar, and after the French conquest it maintained a consulate at Tananarive, which, however, was closed several times either because of world crises or simply for lack of business. During the 1947 revolt, rumors circulated to the effect that the United States was aiding the rebels, and one French officer in southern Madagascar was astonished to be greeted warmly by some insurgents in the belief that he was an American envoy.[9] After the revolt the French communists charged that American blueprints for war against the Soviet Union in the Indian Ocean called for utilizing Madagascar's resources. This they claimed was responsible for the French government's project of strengthening the fortification of Diégo-Suarez, for deliveries of graphite to the United States, and for plans to develop Sakoa's coal deposits and Mahavavy's sugar mill.[10]

Since most Malagasys were credulous, wary of foreigners, and inexperienced in international affairs, such charges did not fall on wholly barren ground. Charles-Emile, French Union assemblyman from Tuléar, repeated them to the representative assembly at Tananarive on October 27, 1954, during discussion of an offer of American aid under the Point Four program. This offer concerned an economic survey of the Lake Alaotra region and involved the modest sum of 567 million Metro. francs, but Charles-Emile feared that it might lead to Madagascar's "subjection" to the United States. In later years, especially after independence, various Malagasy politicians and officials were invited to visit the United States or went there in search of private capital investments, but some of the island's deputies were not wholly reassured of the purity of American motives.

During the assembly's debate on a standard-type aid agreement which the United States proposed to Madagascar in 1961, it was clear that some Malagasys were pleased to find a source of assistance other than France, while others were disappointed that the country was being offered only American merchandise and not dollars. Some feared that the United States was aiming to harm Madagascar's rice by dumping wheat on the island or were trying to "soften up" the Malagasys by sending them cheap luxury goods. An Independent deputy, Louis Ratsimba, described some of the conditions attached to the American offer as embarrassing and shocking, not to say humiliating, but Arthur Besy, president of the P.S.D. group in the assembly, urged grateful acceptance, adding that in his personal view American prestige might suffer unless the Malagasys expressed their thanks to the United States.[11] Some American scientific and trade missions have visited Madagascar without as yet noteworthy results, although in July 1963 Washington agreed to guaranty American private investments in the island. Also in that year, 13 Malagasys were studying in the United States on scholarships offered by the American government. Early in 1964, when Zanzibar's new government requested the United States to remove its satellite-tracking station from that island, Madagascar acquired a new importance in the eyes of American strategists as an alternative location for such operations.

By the time President Tsiranana paid his state visit to Washington in July 1964, American aid to his country totaled about $3.5 million in value. It had been used to promote rural-welfare programs, to aid in secondary-road building, and to equip the *gendarmerie*. On this occasion President Johnson promised to increase American financial assistance to Madagascar, but apparently the Malagasy president has been disappointed that this pledge has not yielded more substantial results. At a press interview in Paris early in 1965,[12] Tsiranana complained somewhat bitterly about the insufficiency of United States aid to underdeveloped countries, noting that the new nations that expressed the most radical views were the very ones that received the largest amounts of American aid. He held the American government, in its failure to provide aid on a massive scale, partly responsible for the expansion of communist China's influence throughout sub-Saharan Africa.

As to the aid provided by other Western-bloc countries, Italy sent two trade missions to Madagascar in 1962–63, and the Italian petroleum company Agip has been active there. But of France's five Common Market partners, only West Germany has shown marked interest in the island. For some years the P.S.D. has maintained contacts with the German socialists, and in 1962 Tsiranana went to Bonn on an official visit. While there he agreed to establish diplomatic relations with West Germany and negotiated a loan of 1.5 billion C.F.A. francs for road building. As of 1965, West Germany was training 55 Malagasy air-force pilots and was arranging to supply Madagascar with six coastal patrol boats. More recently Spain and Sweden have each shown a flicker of interest in Madagascar.

Among the non-European nations aligned with the Western bloc, the Malagasys have established their main contacts with Israel and the noncommunist countries of the Far East. The Israelis have cultivated the Malagasys for the same reasons as they have the Negro Africans (and with equal success). In 1961 Tsiranana was the official guest of Ben-Gurion, and his daughter remained for five months in Israel with the Young Pioneers. Israel has also trained other Malagasys and has invited P.S.D. leaders to visit it. Its Foreign Minister, Mrs. Golda Meir, went to Tananarive in January 1963. Aside from the Malagasys' spontaneous admiration for Israel's accomplishments, Tsiranana has another reason for cultivating its friendship: he has come to fear Arab penetration of Madagascar by way of the Comoro Islands and the Comorian minority around Majunga.[13] Tsiranana's continuing preoccupation with subversion was betrayed by the signing of a trade agreement with Japan on May 9, 1963, and by the cordial reception in the winter of 1963–64 given to President Macapagal of the Philippines and President Lee Kuan Yew of Singapore, as well as by his visit to Taipeh in April 1962 and his decision, announced early in 1964, to exchange diplomatic missions with Nationalist China. While the Macapagal visit served to remind the Merina of their ancestral home in the Far Eastern islands, the ties established with Singapore and Taiwan underscored Tsiranana's solidarity with anticommunist Chinese leaders.

Communist Countries

Madagascar's celebration of independence in July 1960 brought to Tananarive a Soviet delegation and a message of good wishes from the president of the U.S.S.R. In the same year a few publications in Russia gave evidence that some scholars there had begun to study Malagasy history, customs, and political parties.* Three Soviet scholars who have recently been specializing in Madagascar are L. A. Korneyev, A. S. Orlova, and S. Datlin.[14] Not surprisingly, they are critical of the P.S.D., especially for maintaining close relations with France; they approve of the A.K.F.M., but do not refer to any communists in its ranks. According to a Trotskyite view, there is little to choose between the P.S.D. and the A.K.F.M., since they are equally disappointing to the true communist believer.[15] Although several A.K.F.M. leaders had gone frequently to Iron Curtain countries and Gisèle Rabesahala had founded a cultural Madagascar–U.S.S.R. Association, the Soviet Union's direct influence on the Malagasys remained slight.[16]

---

* Up to that time the news agency Tass had usually taken its occasional bulletins on Madagascar from dispatches in *L'Humanité*, thus forgoing the propaganda mileage it could have obtained from a thorough treatment of the 1947 revolt.

In 1961, when the Russians sent a trade mission to Tananarive and proposed opening an embassy there, nothing came of their initiative. Tsiranana told the French journalist André Blanchet,[17] "We are not opposed in principle to the presence here of a Soviet ambassador, but in practice we are being prudent." The Soviet trade mission was equally noncommittal after its members learned that the Malagasys wanted to sell their products but would not promise to buy Russian goods in return, and nothing further was heard of their offers. Then in January 1963 a report reached Tananarive that Soviet warships had appeared off the extreme southern coast of Madagascar. The flurry this caused provided the opportunity for Tsiranana to make an urgent appeal in Paris for reinforcement of Madagascar's defense of its long and vulnerable coastline. Immediately the Soviet government apologized for the incident and calm was restored, especially after it was learned that the "warships" were fishing vessels and that the Russian sailors had only given cigarettes to local fishermen.[18]

The happy ending to this episode, which was soon followed by a general *détente* in Soviet-American relations and increased tension between Khrushchev and Mao Tse-tung, led to an era of better feeling between Tananarive and Moscow. In April 1963, ten Soviet tourists visited Madagascar; they were followed by Professor Tretiakov of the U.S.S.R.'s African Institute, who came for several months to study the island's economic situation. Tsiranana received his Russian visitors cordially, and in a jovial mood he warned them that the Malagasys who called themselves communists were in reality only bourgeois. "We other socialists," he added, "are much nearer to you than they are, for we truly come from the people."[19] In 1964 a delegation of eight Malagasy students attended a youth forum in Moscow. The same year, Madagascar negotiated trade agreements with the U.S.S.R., Poland, and Hungary and began negotiating for a similar agreement with Czechoslovakia.[20]

Just as Tsiranana's anxiety about Soviet aggression was beginning to recede, however, a series of events early in 1964 reawakened all his fears about communist penetration. France's recognition of the Peking regime, Chou En-lai's tour of sub-Saharan Africa, and the revolutionary outbreaks and mutinies in nearby Zanzibar and East Africa deeply troubled the Malagasy president and also gave him further grounds to press his demands for more aid from the Western nations. He credited the French government with having "good reasons" for its decision to recognize Red China, but said that "for once I shall not follow General de Gaulle ... The Russians and Chinese are rivals only in appearance, but in fact their actions complement each other perfectly. Already one can see the results of their cooperation in Zanzibar and East Africa, and in Somalia the Soviet government is spending millions to build military bases."[21] Madagascar, he went on to say, had excellent relations with Nationalist China, and it was not in its interest in any case to recognize the Peking government. "China is too big a country and we are too small a country [to do so safely] ... There are about 13,000 Chinese in Madagascar and the danger of a massive infiltration is great."*

That Tsiranana should so obviously regard communist penetration of Madagascar as a graver danger to his country than neocolonialism put him into the camp opposing "revolutionary" Africa and even set him apart from most of the moderate African leaders.

African Countries

In dealing with the newly independent states of Africa, Tsiranana's main difficulty is that he seems to their leaders to be motivated by contradictory impulses. At times the Malagasy president appears to be one of them, but at others he seems aloof and even in opposition to the strongest currents in contemporary African feeling. Nevertheless, Tsiranana has brought his countrymen and the Africans closer together, for without his prodding the average Malagasy and even members of the elite would remain complacently isolated. Insularity characterizes even leaders of the P.S.D.'s political opposition, who theoretically believe in cooperation with like-minded ex-colonial peoples and who have sometimes attended Afro-Asian and revolutionary inter-African conferences.

Tsiranana's support of General de Gaulle and of his Community was so unequivocal that many observers prophesied that Madagascar's independence and the Community's disintegration would aggravate the Malagasys' inclination to isolation. Yet just the contrary has occurred, largely because the trio who run the P.S.D. are aware of the dangers to which a policy of isolation from Africa would expose Madagascar. It took some time, however, before Tsiranana could bring himself to participate in the conference called at Abidjan in October 1960 to hammer out a joint stand in the United Nations by French-speaking Negro African states on the question of Algeria. At first Tsiranana declined to attend on the grounds that "Algeria is an internal French affair and we Malagasys and Africans should not interfere in that domain."[22] However, at the last moment he changed his mind, presumably because he had confidence in the conference's two main sponsors, Houphouët-Boigny and Senghor, who were his close personal friends and whose thinking was the nearest to his in all French-speaking Africa. Once he had taken the plunge, Tsiranana became one of the most ardent members of the Brazzaville bloc and—as its name unmistakably showed—of the Union Africaine et Malgache (U.A.M.), to which it gave birth. The

* See pp. 271–74.

U.A.M.'s charter was signed at Tananarive in September 1961, and a Malagasy, Jules Razafimbahiny, was chosen secretary-general of its economic branch, the Organisation Africaine et Malgache pour la Coopération Economique (O.A.M.C.E.).

In March 1961 Tsiranana's newfound "African vocation" showed itself in an ill-fated attempt to reconcile the warring factions in the ex-Belgian Congo by convening a round-table conference of their leaders at Tananarive. Not only did this conference fail in its primary objective, but it almost soured the local Malagasys on any further association with African affairs. They particularly resented the physical inconveniences caused by the presence of over 100 Negro visitors, as well as the government's muzzling of the press and radio lest sentiments offensive to their guests be expressed. This experience confirmed the deep-rooted sense of superiority to the African Negroes of the Malagasys, and especially of the Merina, who are still conscious of their Asian past, although they have little knowledge of or interest in contemporary developments in the Far East. The *côtiers* share this sentiment, perhaps because some of them are the descendants of African slaves and do not care to be reminded of their servile background. Although some aspects of Malagasy culture are of Arabic origin (as is the case with their neighbors, the Comorians), neither the *côtiers* nor the Merina seem to recognize any relationship with the African Arabs. Indeed, some Malagasys have regarded the Franco-Algerian conflict as a quarrel between white men.[23]

In view of this Malagasy heritage of emotional aloofness tinged with sentiments of superiority, it has been hard for Tsiranana to find many areas of agreement with the newly sovereign African states. He has succeeded with the moderate African leaders, both French- and English-speaking, but not at all with the revolutionaries. Official visits have been exchanged with the presidents of the Ivory Coast, Liberia, and Senegal, and Tsiranana has especially strong ties with Houphouët-Boigny, who contributed generously to the relief of Madagascar's cyclone victims in 1959. Tsiranana also entertains friendly feelings for President Tubman of Liberia, but he has openly regretted that other English-speaking Negro leaders do not always understand the position of French-speaking Africans and regard them with a "certain mistrust."[24]

Along with Africans of all political persuasions, he condemns Portuguese colonization on the Dark Continent and racialism and *apartheid* (despite Madagascar's long-standing trade relations with South Africa). He also is a proponent of African unity. Tsiranana, however, is no Pan-Africanist, and he has come out strongly against the type of supranational organization advocated by Nkrumah. His advocacy of an *Afrique des patries* modeled after General de Gaulle's ideal for Europe, and, above all, his consistent support for the French president, whether in Algeria, Gabon, or Madagascar, have angered his colleagues in what was formerly the Casablanca bloc. Adding injury to insult, Tsiranana stood up for Nicolas Grunitsky after President Sylvanus Olympio of Togo was assassinated in January 1963 and for Moise Tshombe as premier of the Congo in June 1964. If it had not been for Tsiranana's genial and attractive personality and for his remarkable ability to present a highly unpopular cause in an amusing and down-to-earth fashion, he might well have been read out of recent all-African meetings. At the O.A.U. conference at Cairo in July 1964, Tsiranana was the only head of state to support Tshombe's admission on the grounds that he was the legal representative of the Congolese government. The Malagasy president was forthright in his remark to the assembled company: "Tshombe won't go to hell, but if he should, there will be many of you there to welcome him."[25]

In March 1964, Tsiranana had been reluctant to see the U.A.M. transformed into a purely economic association, and in February 1965 he was among the strongest advocates of reconstituting the U.A.M. as a politically oriented grouping under a new name—the Organisation Commune Africaine et Malgache (O.C.A.M.). He believed that such an organization was necessary as a bulwark against subversion by revolutionary African states and by communist China. He also favored admission to it of Tshombe's Congo government.

In his fears of communist penetration and his general conservatism, Tsiranana makes Houphouët-Boigny seem almost radical, and he has certainly been odd-man-out in gatherings dominated by such firebrands as Sékou Touré, Nkrumah, and Nasser. Tsiranana's anticommunist views, as well as his pro-French attitude and his support for the United Nations in the Congo and Cyprus, might be forgiven him if he and his compatriots were more willing to identify themselves as Africans. The Africans' resentment of his unwillingness to do so was shown clearly at the Addis Ababa conference in May 1963, when he made a vain plea that the word "Malagasy" be added to whatever title was to be given to the association formed there. He was told flatly that if the Malagasys did not consider their state African, then Madagascar had no place in the newborn Organization of African Unity.[26] Tsiranana accepted this ultimatum because he felt that his country could not afford to be left out of such an organization, but there is no evidence that he and his fellow Malagasys have undergone any genuine change of heart. They do not feel themselves, or want to be considered, Africans, but current events seem to be drawing them ever closer into the African orbit. In a press interview at London in July 1964, Tsiranana was quoted as saying: "If the Bon Dieu proposed to me that Madagascar should be rejoined to the African continent, I would ask him to let it remain an island."[27]

Part two

THE SOCIAL AND CULTURAL FIELDS

Chapter thirteen

RELIGION

Malagasy Customs and Beliefs

Reinforcing the unity created by Madagascar's insular situation and its language, traditional Malagasy religious beliefs and customs reflect a strong homogeneity. Although divergencies exist, these can be traced mainly to markedly dissimilar physical environments and, above all, to the impact of foreign religions—Christianity and Islam—which have influenced the island's many tribes in varying degrees.[1] The Malagasys' customary religion makes no attempt to explain the universe or the problem of good and evil, but creates a mystic social bond between descendants of a common ancestor. Its chief function is to prescribe highly practical ways of avoiding giving offense to the omnipresent ancestral spirits.

Malagasy individuals do little to help outsiders understand their beliefs, for they are inarticulate and vague when they can be persuaded to talk about their religion at all. Broadly speaking, there seems to be a widespread belief in the immortality of the soul and in the existence of a superior creator-deity. He is thought to be all-seeing, omnipotent, and absentmindedly benevolent, but too remote to take any direct interest in human welfare. In the Malagasy pantheon he heads a hierarchy of secondary deities, former kings, and distant ancestors, and a multitude of less powerful but more active spirits. The spirits may be mobile or live in such natural haunts as rocks, rivers, and mountains, and they are believed to be usually malevolent. For the individual Malagasy, the most potent of these spirits are those of his immediate forebears, who concern themselves constantly and intimately with family affairs. As a rule, they reveal their wishes to their descendants through dreams, which are interpreted by the head of the family.

Although traditional Malagasy religion has neither priests nor temples, the family tomb is the most sacred of all hallowed places (in the Merina code, the execution of a criminal was considered a less severe penalty than to be denied burial in the family tomb), and the head of the family or clan has special powers that derive from his role as intermediary between the living and the dead. Respect for the wishes of the ancestors is enforced by means of taboos (*fady*), some of which are collective and some individual. In the case of the latter, some *fady*—such as those that result from being born on an unpropitious day—can never be conjured away, but for the great majority one form or other of offsetting protection can be found.[2] Hence the importance attributed by the Malagasys to divination, and in this procedure one category of sorcerers—those who are healers as well as fortune-tellers— can be most helpful. (A Malagasy must avoid at all costs falling into the hands of the other type of sorcerer, who is wholly nefarious and the personification of evil.) Collective taboos embody general precepts, such as those that forbid marriage between members of certain castes or the eating of certain foods. The Malagasy is supposed to shun innovations and, as nearly as possible, to live as his forebears have done.* Transgressing these taboos exposes him to the spirits' vengeance, which he believes can take the form of the loss of crops and cattle, grave illness, and even death.

The surest method of appeasing the ancestral spirits is to perform ceremonies in which they are offered gifts. The spirits are pleased by offerings of rice, honey, and alcoholic beverages, and above all by the sacrifice of cattle. This cult of the dead involves the Malagasy in a lifetime of what some observers describe as a "cascade of macabre rites,"[3] An occasion for joy and feasting to the Malagasy is the ceremony called *famadihana,* or washing a corpse and reclothing it in a fresh shroud. (Relatives take pieces of the old shroud, which are thought to bring luck.) This ceremony is accompanied by speech-making, dancing, and singing, and food and drink are plentiful. In fact, Malagasys would have *famadihana* as often as their finances permit, but the French administration, after struggling vainly to abolish the custom, finally succeeded in restricting it to the dry-season months.

Madagascar's constitution pledges the freedom of religious practices and the respect for custom. This constitutional guaranty and, even more, the profound veneration in which customary practices are held have prevented the Malagasy government from tampering with the cult of the dead, even though it has every reason to want to do so. From the practical standpoint, the country's productivity is diminished, since the many ceremonies related to the cult of the dead draw relatives from far and near to the family tomb, and for more or less extended periods take them away from their work on plantations or in mines. Another undesirable consequence has been a veritable holocaust of the island's cattle, for the finest specimens of the herds are sacrificed.

---

* For political consequences of this belief, see pp. 134–38.

In a less tangible domain, that of Malagasy psychology, the cult of the dead has had even more stultifying effects. Although it has made for social stability and tranquillity, these benefits are more than offset by its unfortunate consequences. The price of an orderly society based on fear of the ancestors has been the prevalence of superstition, a general reluctance to take any initiative, and a chronic sense of guilt and dependence. Even the elite are not immune to superstitious practices, and it is said that on the night before elections, Western-educated politicians in Tananarive seek the aid of royal spirits by making a pilgrimage to the tombs of the Merina monarchs in the *rova*. Malagasy parliamentarians tend to turn down any proposals that would institute changes, on the ground that they are "against custom." In recent years, however, the parliamentarians have tended to condemn "customary practices which are harmful to individuals and property."*

A study by Richard Andrianamanjato[4] casts considerable light on two aspects of Malagasy psychology that are among the most puzzling to outsiders. The many rules and regulations governing all aspects of Malagasy life have made for a pervading sense of guilt (*tsiny*). Because he cannot manage to conform to them all—for they apply to his relations with his fellow man as well as with the spirits—his only hope of warding off the unhappy consequences of oversight or negligence is by constantly excusing himself. (Andrianamanjato notes that Europeans listening to a Malagasy orator are often astonished that he spends three-fourths of his allotted time in apologies and only a fourth on the substance of his speech.) Inasmuch as "love and understanding give absolution," the Malagasy hopes that by such precautions he can achieve *tody*—a term with many meanings, of which the most current is a sense of security resulting from the overcoming of many difficulties. The net result of observance of Malagasy beliefs is an impersonal and nonindividualistic life. A man cannot, or should not, live for himself but for his children, to whom he is expected to leave his worldly goods intact. To fulfill his innumerable obligations and to escape harm, the Malagasy must avoid the new and the unknown, for in this negative way he is least likely to offend a spirit or violate a taboo.

Because of their profound sense of guilt and apprehensiveness, the Malagasys are far from being a nation of dynamic individuals, and this is one of the most formidable handicaps that an enterprising government of the island must face. From the standpoint of Christian and Islamic proselytizers, however, certain Malagasy beliefs—or in some cases the very omissions in these beliefs—provide avenues of approach to the people. The Malagasy con-

* At the assembly session of Jan. 5, 1960, the majority of deputies denounced such an instance at Vohemar, in which it was said that an evil sorcerer had entered the body of an innocent young girl and forced her to commit suicide.

viction that the universe is ordered and that the individual must bear the consequences of his acts is basic also to other religions. Moreover, because Malagasy traditional beliefs have never produced an ecclesiastical structure and are without mystic appeal, the Christian missions especially have found Madagascar a favorable field of activity.

The Islamic Element

At the turn of the century, French scholars showed a marked interest in Islamic and Arabic influences in Madagascar.[5] For some years thereafter, however, Islam seemed so marginal and lacking in prestige among the populations of France's Indian Ocean possessions that there was little incentive for further research. Muslim converts in Madagascar, by remaining on the coast—where they were small-scale merchants and sailors—failed to spread the faith among the influential Merina and Betsileo tribes of the high plateaus. Even on the coast, Malagasy and foreign Muslims were and still are too few in number, too scattered, and too heterogeneous to carry much political or cultural weight.

Madagascar possesses four distinct groups of Muslims, of which two are indigenous and two are foreign. The longest-established group is to be found on the southeast coast and consists mainly of the Antaimoro, whose ancestors were converted to Islam in the seventh century. Although their religion was strengthened by a new wave of Muslim immigrants in the fifteenth century, the Antaimoro practice a superficial form of Islam, as do the more numerous and more recently converted Sakalava. The Sakalava Muslims are spread over a wider area, from Cap d'Ambre to Morondava, but their religious zeal apparently has not been intensified by the presence in their midst of a large, profoundly Islamized colony of Comorians. Of the foreign Muslims, the Comorians—45,000 strong—are far more numerous than the Indians, who number 13,000 and are not all Muslims. More than half of the Comorians live in the town and environs of Majunga, and they are thought to be responsible for such conversions of Malagasys to Islam as have been made in recent times. Like the Comorians, the Muslim Indians live mainly in the west-coast towns, but they belong mostly to the Ismaeli sect.

Within the past few years the sudden growth in the number of Comorians living in Madagascar, the uneasiness caused by Pan-Arab and Pan-Islamic propaganda in nearby countries, and the fears of an influx of Indian immigrants have reawakened interest in Madagascar's Muslim population, but it is political in nature rather than scholarly or religious. Two studies[6] stress how little is known about Madagascar's Muslims, and only informed guesses place their total at 80,000 to 100,000. Under the French administration, fewer than a dozen Malagasys were invited each year by the government to make the pilgrimage to Mecca. Most observers of the Malagasy scene note that the local Muslims live peaceably if somewhat apart from other religious communities, and that they seem wholly untouched by the new trends stirring the Muslim world.

As to religions, Madagascar is unique among the French-speaking territories in or near Africa. It has only a small Muslim population, whose members are psychologically as well as geographically remote from the main centers of Islam. Moreover, the Malagasys have been Christianized to a remarkable extent, for only some tribes in the extreme south apparently remain impervious to Christian influences. Not only are at least half of the Malagasys Catholic or Protestant, but this Christianized portion of the population includes virtually all the members of its most evolved tribes.

The Christian Missions

All of the newly independent French-speaking states that were formerly French colonies are deeply indebted to Christian missionaries, especially for their pioneer work in the fields of education and health. Madagascar, like Vietnam, owes a particular debt of gratitude to missionaries, for it was they who devised a written form for the principal native language, using the Latin alphabet, and who introduced the printing press into both countries. In other respects, however, the history of missions in the two areas is dissimilar. In Indochina, only a brief contest for influence took place between two nationalities of Catholic missionaries, and until World War II the main struggle of the French Catholic mission was with a local French administration that was mainly anticlerical and influenced by Freemasonry. In Madagascar, on the other hand, during the late nineteenth century non-French—mostly British—Protestant missionaries were pitted against French Catholic missionaries, and each group actively supported its government's claims to control of the island.

After this contest had been settled in France's favor, the tension in Madagascar between British and French missionaries as such gradually subsided, but to some extent it was revived after World War II in the political rivalry between their respective converts. Although the antagonism in this field was never clear-cut, the Merina Protestant nationalists advocated independence and regarded the Catholic *côtiers* as unpatriotic and pro-French. By the mid-1950s, however, the religious aspect of the conflict between them had become blurred by the transformation of many Malagasy Catholics into ardent nationalists and by the politically neutral attitude assumed by the Malagasy Protestants after the revolt of 1947. At present the identification of Catholicism with the pro-French, socially inferior *côtiers,* and of Protestantism with the aloof Merina upper classes tends to be obscured by the more direct struggle for political power.

Missions before the French Conquest

The earliest attempt to evangelize the Malagasys dates from the latter half of the seventeenth century, when some Lazarist priests accompanied the first French settlers, who established themselves in the extreme south of the island. On Christmas Day 1672, they were massacred by local tribes, as were most of the settlers, in the chapel they had built there, and it was not until early in the nineteenth century that a second and more successful move was made to introduce Christianity into Madagascar. In 1819 an English minister, sent by the London Missionary Society (L.M.S.), succeeded in making his way from Tamatave to the high plateaus, where he was warmly welcomed by King Radama I. During the 1820s he was joined by other English missionaries, and together they worked out a written form of Malagasy using the Latin alphabet, began a Malagasy-English dictionary, and started teaching the three R's, the Bible, and useful crafts to several thousand Merina children.

The death of King Radama I in 1828 brought to the throne Queen Ranavalona I, who personified the hostile pagan reaction to such alien innovations as Christianity. In 1836 she not only drove out of Madagascar all the Western missionaries but began persecuting their Malagasy converts as well.[7] After her death in 1861, Christianity underwent a brief revival under King Radama II, who, however, introduced a divisive element by favoring —over their English Protestant counterparts—some French Jesuit missionaries who had recently come to Madagascar from Réunion Island. The reign of Radama II lasted only two years, and under his two successors, Queens Rasoherina and Ranavalona II, the pendulum swung back again in favor of the English Protestant missionaries.

Although the English missionaries sought to improve the lot of slaves in Imerina, they did not endeavor to make converts among them, for they realized that such converts would harm the prestige of the religion they were trying to introduce. Instead, they concentrated their proselytizing efforts on the most influential elements in Merina society, the *andriana* and *hova* castes.* They scored a sensational success and a triumph over the Jesuits in 1869 when they converted the Queen, premier, and courtiers; and Protestant Christianity was made the state religion. Subsequently the English missionaries persuaded the Queen to force her subjects to burn "heathen talismans" and manuscripts in Arabic, and their intolerance was un-

---

* Slaves of upper-class Merina were allowed to carry their master's Bible to the church door, but had to remain outside during the services.

doubtedly responsible in large part for the emphatic rejection of all alien novelties and insistence on the return to ancestral customs which has characterized Malagasy nationalism since that time.

France's defeat by Prussia the year after the Queen's conversion was followed by an injudicious economy move on the part of the French government in withdrawing subsidies for the Catholic mission in Madagascar. These two related events dealt an almost fatal blow to the prestige and activity of both France and Catholicism there. For the next 15 years, Protestant—mainly English—influence increased, the L.M.S. missionaries having been reinforced by other Protestants sent by the Anglican Church (the Society for the Propagation of the Gospel) in 1864, the Norwegian and American Lutheran missions in 1866, and the Quakers in 1867. As of 1885 about 132,000 of the 146,500 children of school age—including some girls—in Imerina were being taught in Malagasy at Protestant primary schools, and for more advanced studies the Protestants had founded one college, three normal schools, and two industrial schools. They had also built hospitals at Tananarive, Antsirabe, and Fianarantsoa, and in 1886 they opened a medical school in the capital. In Tananarive, too, they launched some publications, to which Malagasy writers contributed. Thus in certain vital ways the Protestant missions, especially the L.M.S., left a lasting impression on the country. On the eve of the French conquest, 33 missionaries of the L.M.S. were working in Madagascar, and the society could boast 280,000 Malagasy members in its 1,000 or so churches. All the other Protestant denominations combined had only about 150,000 members and 600 churches.

Although there was a resurgence of paganism at the time of the *fahavelo* revolt, the French annexation of Madagascar inevitably gave the Catholic mission there a much-needed boost. A considerable number of Malagasys turned from Protestantism to Catholicism simply because it was the religion of most of their new rulers. From the religious angle the French administration that was installed at Tananarive in 1896 was faced with a situation unique in France's colonial history: it had to establish its authority over a country where in many places the masses were fiercely rejecting Christianity as an alien innovation and where the indigenous elite was almost solidly Protestant and pro-British. To Madagascar's new governing group, the English and American missionaries were doubly suspect, as foreigners and as Protestants,[8] but the Jesuits' proselytizing zeal was also clearly troubling the public order. The Jesuit missionaries were trying to better their position at Protestant expense, for Protestant successes in high Merina society had until then forced the Jesuits to seek converts among the slaves and coastal populations. Not only was the number of Malagasy Catholic converts vastly smaller than that of the Protestants (136,000 compared with some 430,000), but because they came from such humble strata of society the prestige of Catholicism suffered.*

Gallieni personally held no brief for the Catholic missionaries but made use of them in eliminating English influence in Madagascar. Inasmuch as the Anglo-French agreement of August 5, 1890, guaranteed religious freedom to the English missionaries and since Gallieni did not want to alienate gratuitously the Merina Protestants, he invited the Paris Société des Missions Evangeliques to come and work in Madagascar. In 1899 he began to develop secular education and to require mission schools soliciting official subsidies to adapt their curricula to that of the state schools and to teach in the French language. Naturally this cut deeply into the Protestant missions' virtual monopoly of education, but it was in the field of public health that he almost eliminated their role. Despite the protests of the L.M.S. and the Quakers, Gallieni took over their hospitals and the medical school and required that all doctors practicing in Madagascar should have a French medical certificate. At the same time, however, Gallieni guaranteed freedom of religious practices and clamped down on the Jesuits for their aggressive tactics, and he welcomed to Madagascar other Catholic orders, such as the Lazarists and the Fathers of the Holy Spirit. In time Gallieni came to appreciate the good work being done by the Protestant missionaries, and they, in turn, became reconciled to their less influential position. The Lutherans managed to hold their own in the south, but many of the English missionaries in Imerina either accepted the cooperation of French Protestant clergymen and teachers or were replaced by them. From the standpoint of education, Protestants remained definitely in the lead, for when Gallieni left Madagascar they were giving instruction to 145,000 children, compared with the 65,000 who were in Catholic mission schools.

Unfortunately the modus vivendi reached under Gallieni between the two major Christian missions in Madagascar was abruptly broken by his successor. Augagneur, a strongly anticlerical socialist, on his own authority closed down the Protestant-sponsored Y.M.C.A. and took the even more serious step, on Nevember 23, 1906, of forbidding teaching to be done in churches. Considering that in Madagascar's rural areas almost all Protestant churches were used as schoolrooms, this move was tantamount to closing 90 per cent of the Protestant primary schools.[9] Nor was Augagneur more indulgent to the Catholics, for he put an end to all official subsidies to their schools. As a result of these various measures, many Malagasy children were deprived of their chance for an education, since the state was unable at the time to replace the mission schools with state-run institutions. The

* Of the 47 high Merina officials and 95 gouverneurs in the last years of the monarchy, only four were Catholics. See Deschamps, Histoire de Madagascar, p. 218.

next governor-general, Picquié, proved to be much less militantly anticlerical than his predecessor. In 1913 he reaffirmed the freedom of religious worship, stressed the separation of church and state, and also tried to revive the
impartial policy of Gallieni's regime. He limited the number of churches
that could be built in a given area, and made the authorization to construct
new ones subject to official inquiry and approval.[10]

With the outbreak of World War I, the Malagasy Christians lost many of
their missionaries, but as a result they grew more self-reliant. The same
period also saw the revival on a small scale of the old quarrel between Catholics and Protestants. When G. Mondain, a prominent French Protestant,
gave testimony in 1917 that led to an amnesty for some Malagasy members
of the V.V.S., the Jesuits accused the Malagasy Protestants of having been
implicated in that so-called plot.[11] Nevertheless, the Malagasy Catholics and
Protestants showed little antagonism toward each other. The bitter rivalry
between their respective missionaries was also by that time definitely a phenomenon of the past, and the administration itself became more flexible in
dealing with both. The interwar period brought a sharp expansion of both
Protestantism and Catholicism in the coastal region, and Imerina and the
Betsileo country became almost solidly Christian territory.

The Protestant Churches

The influx of missionaries from new denominations and the rapid rise
in the number of Malagasy Protestants, especially during the interwar decades, led to several reorganizations of the Protestant churches in Madagascar. The oldest and largest missionary society of them all, the L.M.S., remained firmly entrenched in Imerina and drew other British Protestant
missionaries there. Literal evangelization was stressed by the L.M.S., along
with ardent individual piety and spectacular displays of religious faith.[12]
Because each L.M.S. parish stubbornly maintained its own autonomy, other
churches encountered difficulty in working with its members, and the Anglicans found themselves unable to collaborate with the L.M.S. In any case,
the ritual of the Anglican Church did not appeal to the Malagasy temperament, and the membership of that Church was largely confined to its base
in Tananarive. Similarly the Quakers, who had pledged that they would
conform to the practices of the L.M.S. when they came to Imerina, gave up
almost all mission activity there except teaching, and gradually withdrew
from the west coast as well. Their work among the Sakalava was gradually
taken over by the French Protestants and the Lutherans.

From a small beginning in 1896, the French Protestant mission grew
steadily in importance until it came to rank second to the L.M.S. in the
number of its members. It took the lead in persuading other Protestant de-

nominations to reduce their activities in the high plateaus and to concentrate more upon educating the coastal populations. Its initiative was also responsible for creating some organizational unity among the various Protestant missions. The area in which the Lutherans worked covered two-fifths of the island, but despite close cooperation between their Norwegian and American missionaries the number of converts was not commensurate with the geographic area of their endeavor. The smallest of all the Protestant missionary groups in Madagascar was that of the Seventh-Day Adventists, who were also the last to arrive, in the early 1920s. Most of the members they acquired were Malagasy dissidents from the older-established Protestant sects.

As the number of denominations represented in Madagascar grew, various attempts were made to check the dispersal and duplication of Protestant missionary efforts. At the same time, an effort was put forth to unite Malagasy Protestants in an autonomous Malagasy church (Isan-Enim-Bolana), give it jurisdiction over member churches, and turn over evangelical work in pagan areas to Malagasy missionaries. None of these moves proved to be wholly successful. A Federation of Malagasy Protestant Churches, more commonly called the Inter-Missionary Council, was formed as early as 1913, and it did succeed in dividing the island into zones of mission influence. The majority of its members, however, refused to accede to its Malagasy members' expressed wish to exclude missionaries from specified areas of the island and to reserve those areas solely for evangelization by Malagasys. Moreover, the Anglicans withdrew from the Council in 1927, the Seventh-Day Adventists never joined it, and the two Lutheran missions preferred to merge in an organization of their own. In fact, the Malagasy Protestants have been reluctant to give even their own autonomous church the authority to impose arbitration in disputes between member churches.

Typical of the individualistic and emotional tendencies in Malagasy Protestantism has been the spontaneous creation of at least three syncretic sects, which developed independently of Western missionary efforts and outside the orthodox Protestant parishes. Two of them were initiated in the high-plateau region by Betsileos reputed to be healers, and both were characterized by a mixture of pagan and Christian beliefs and by a fundamentalist interpretation of the Bible. Although they never developed into political protest movements as did similar sects in French Equatorial Africa, the "ecstatic excesses" of the more important of the two—the Disciples of the Lord—led the French administration to intervene on the grounds that its members were disturbing the peace. Gradually the Disciples took over the other movement, and in time both were absorbed by the orthodox churches, to which they brought considerable revivalist fervor. More undesirable from the viewpoint of the public authorities was still another independent religious sect founded late in World War II. This sect was called Tranozozoro (House of Reeds), and its xenophobic as well as nationalist tendencies were just beginning to alarm the European Protestant missionaries when the 1947 revolt broke out.

Although the Protestant missionaries have been unable as yet to unite their Malagasy churches in a single ecclesiastical organization, they have been more successful in founding interchurch youth movements. From the outset, the youths in the various Protestant parishes were grouped into Kristiana Tanora, but without common ties between them. In the 1870s, Y.M.C.A.s were founded at Tananarive and Fianarantsoa; their members wanted to develop along Christian lines of their own choosing and to break away from missionary guidance. In 1898 the Y.M.C.A. was reorganized, and six years later it sent Ravelojoana, then a young minister, to France for special training. On his return to Madagascar, however, the new governor-general, Augagneur, not only refused him permission to found a youth movement but arbitrarily put an end to all Y.M.C.A. work.

In 1924 another attempt was made to create a Protestant Malagasy youth movement, and again a young minister, Jean Bergbeder, was sent to France for training. Two years later he returned to Madagascar and formed the Foyer Chrétien des Jeunes, an organization similar to the American Christian Endeavor Societies, in Tananarive. From there it spread to provincial towns through the agency of its young civil-servant members, but its membership never reached a thousand. The Foyer aimed to cultivate a taste for good reading and sports among a select group of young men, whose main purpose, however, was to form and guide other more widely based youth groups. Among these were Scout movements for boys and girls and a Foyer for girls, all of which were slow to develop because they were so alien to Malagasy traditions. In 1949 some of the distinctively Western features of the Scout movement were eliminated or adapted to local customs, and after Malagasy scoutmasters were named, the number of Malagasy Boy Scouts tripled in the span of a decade. By 1957 the organization had over 3,000 Malagasy members, was training provincial Scout leaders in eight camps, and was meeting three-fourths of its expenses from membership dues.[18]

Credit for most of the financial and moral support that enabled the Foyers and Scout movements to develop must be given to the individual church parishes, but for many years they were reluctant to accord the same approval to the Foyer and other organizations for girls, because the older generation of Malagasy Protestants was conservative in regard to the social emancipation of women. At present, however, girls' organizations are firmly established and are even evolving in some centers into movements that include both boys and girls as members.

Today Western Protestant missionaries act as advisers to the Malagasy churches and operate under Malagasy orders. In proportion as the foreign missionaries' authority has been curtailed, Malagasy Protestantism has apparently taken on a less rigidly orthodox outlook, and its church leaders seem more inclined than before to unite closely. In part this may also reflect the slight numerical inferiority of Madagascar's Protestants to its Catholics. When Madagascar became independent in 1960, about half of its population was Christian, with 1,031,000 of these Catholic and 929,000 Protestant. Of the latter group, 320,000 belonged to the L.M.S., 264,000 to the Société des Missions Evangéliques, 232,000 to the Lutheran missions, 65,000 to the Quakers, 35,000 to the Anglicans, and 13,000 to the Seventh-Day Adventists.[14]

The Catholic Mission and Church

The early advantage gained by the Protestant missionaries in Madagascar enabled them to set the pace and determine the fields of activity for the French Catholic mission there. A great increase in the number of Malagasy Catholics during the interwar period narrowed the gap between the two, but the Protestants still had the edge over the Catholics in number and quality of converts and educational facilities; they were also ahead in training a Malagasy clergy and organizing Malagasy youth movements. During the 1930s, the administration eased the regulations for all the missions; after that, religious instruction in lay schools was permitted and property owned by a mission could be registered in its name.

To cope with its rapidly increasing membership, the Catholic mission created eleven dioceses in the interwar period. The most important of the older ones, those of Tananarive and Fianarantsoa, remained in the hands of the Jesuits; the Fathers of the Holy Spirit were in charge of the vicariates of Majunga and Diégo-Suarez, the Lazarists of Fort-Dauphin, the Salettins of Antsirabe, and the Capucins of Ambanja. Dissimilarities existed between these various orders in methods and outlook, but, unlike the Protestants, all of them were placed under one ecclesiastical hierarchy and were subject to the same general directives. This uniformity, as well as the fact that the Catholic mission worked mainly in rural areas and with the humbler social classes, inevitably differentiated its operations from those of the Protestant missions. Although the Catholics followed closely behind the Protestants in school- and church-building and in setting up a religious press,* they diverged when it came to developing their own clergy and youth movement. This was partly because the groups with which the Catholics mainly worked were more dispersed and less well educated, and partly because of the em-

---

* The Catholic mission published three weeklies, two of them in Malagasy (*Lakroa* and *Isanandro*) and one in French (*Lumière*).

phasis placed by the Catholic mission on obedience and conformity with the established ecclesiastical system. The Protestants did not lack leadership material; the Catholics were handicapped by it. This Catholic situation accounted to some extent for the continued predominance of European missionaries, who—even at the time Madagascar became independent—totaled 600 compared with only 150 Malagasy priests.[15] But the imbalance was also traceable to the celibacy required of the priesthood, which conflicted with the ingrained Malagasy tradition and "social duty" of producing as many progeny as possible.

In the early 1920s the Catholics started a Scout movement, at about the same time as the Protestants, which spread from Tamatave to Tananarive but went no farther. The Catholic Scout movement was slower to recognize the need to adapt what was an essentially Western institution to the Malagasy environment, so it was not until July 1957 that its techniques and cadres were "Malagasized." From then on it began to grow, but separate troops were maintained for French and Malagasy Catholic Scouts. Many other Catholic youth organizations were founded in the interwar and post–World War II years, and by the time Madagascar became autonomous in 1958 they totaled at least 38, of which 20 were for boys and 18 for girls. There was at least one movement for each age and social group, for manual and white-collar workers, for *côtiers* and Merina, and for every echelon of the ecclesiastical hierarchy.[16] The attempts made to merge them into larger units were not generally as successful as were those of the Protestants, and the organizations were also more dependent on outside subsidies.

The Christian Missions and Nationalism

If the nationalism of Madagascar as a whole has been strongly marked by the rejection of alien concepts and an intense desire to return to ancestral customs, that of the Merina has been as strongly conditioned by an imported religion—Protestant Christianity. Inevitably this latter identification was accentuated after the French conquest, and through the Y.M.C.A. and the V.V.S., the clergyman Ravelojoana provided a link between Merina nationalism and Protestantism which endured into the interwar period. In the early years after World War II, when the first nationalist party, the M.D.R.M., was launched, the Reverend Tata Max was a member of its politburo. During the 1947 revolt, the freedom that had been accorded the autonomous Malagasy Church by European Protestant missionaries and extended to the individual conscience by Protestant doctrine was liberally interpreted by some Malagasy pastors, who either actively sided with the rebels or let them use their churches as meeting places. Most of the Protestant church leaders denounced the atrocities committed during the revolt and initiated a policy of strict neutralism in the conflict. However, when the Inter-Missionary Council tried to persuade the Protestant clergymen in Madagascar to choose between a political career and their religious vocation,[17] it had little success, for the clergymen saw and still see no incompatibility between the two. This was exemplified by a French Protestant minister, André Lew, who became a leftist nationalist candidate in the municipal elections of November 18, 1956. And when the A.K.F.M. elected a president in 1958, it chose the Merina clergyman and nationalist Richard Andrianamanjato.

Like their Protestant counterparts, the Catholic missionaries tried to maintain a neutral attitude in the revolt, largely because they were still to some extent identified with the French colonial administration and because comparatively few Malagasy Catholics had committed themselves actively to the rebel cause. The rebels themselves, at least during the xenophobic phase of the revolt, drew no distinction between the two Christian sects. They inflicted physical damage on both Protestant and Catholic churches and mission schools for hundreds of miles along the east coast. Both Christian communities suffered from the dispersal of congregations, and many of the clergy and their flocks lost their earthly possessions and in some cases their lives. Yet in the years that followed the revolt there came a curious reversal of the political positions that had been assumed by Malagasy Catholics and Protestants. The Protestant churches as such adopted a more neutral attitude, although certain individual members and ministers continued to be active politically. Many of the Catholic Malagasy, on the other hand, became militant nationalists, particularly those in Tananarive, who were encouraged in this activity by the Jesuit mission of that province.* In cooperation with the extreme left wing they succeeded in electing Stanislas Rakotonirina mayor of Tananarive, but this victory was short-lived.† Such initiative was too inconsistent to have been taken at the direct instigation of their ecclesiastical superiors, but it was certainly the consequence of a far-reaching change in Vatican policy.

In the interwar period the Vatican had seemed to discourage native nationalism in the French colonies, although upon occasion its stand was ambivalent. In the mid-1930s, when Jacques Rabemananjara and some of his Catholic Malagasy friends founded a literary monthly, *Revue des Jeunes,* he was at first reprimanded by the Bishop of Tananarive for his temerity and then, a few days later, was congratulated by the same prelate for his spirit of

---

* The Jesuits of Tananarive came from Lille and were more radical in their views than their colleagues at Fianarantsoa, whose mother-house was in Toulouse.
† See p. 106.

enterprise.[18] The revolt of 1947 and the mission's role in it—active or passive —attracted the attention of Rome. The revolt and its repercussions were largely responsible for a change in Catholic policy in Madagascar that was later extended to other European dependencies. This change was first noted at the eucharistic congress held at Tananarive in 1951, when a message from the Pope, broadcast over the local radio, contained praise for Malagasy culture and the Malagasy fatherland but was devoid of any reference to French accomplishments on the island.[19] The message was interpreted as an encouragement of local nationalism; two years later, in November 1953, there was no room for further doubt of the Vatican's intentions, when all the bishops of Madagascar signed a letter that made history.

The signatories of this episcopal letter, while excluding recourse to violence, recognized the "legitimacy of the [Malagasys'] aspiration to independence, as of all other constructive efforts to attain that goal." This letter was sharply criticized by Governor-general Bargues,[20] and it shocked the French residents of Madagascar. Some of them asserted that the letter must have been drafted by the bishops on their own initiative, but the Holy See never disavowed the bishops' declaration. In fact, its message was confirmed and even amplified in a pastoral letter written in Jauary 1957 by Mgr. Claude Rolland, Bishop of Antsirabe. In it he told his 175,000 parishioners that "you have the right and duty to love your country and to promote its independence," even though at the same time he warned them that national sovereignty would not automatically solve their social problems.*

The Vatican's decision to dissociate the Catholic Church in Madagascar from the French administration there preceded by some years its active espousal of the cause of Malagasy independence. When Mgr. Victor Sartre became the first archbishop of Madagascar early in 1956, that island ceased to be mission territory and the Malagasy Catholic Church became autonomous. Since that time, several Malagasy bishops have been named, and two months before independence, Jerome Rakotomalala was consecrated as the first Malagasy archbishop. The progressive "Malagasization" of the ecclesiastical hierarchy, however, does not mean the end of European missionary guidance and control of the local Catholic Church, as it did of the local Protestant one. For the past few years the majority of European Catholic missionaries serving in Madagascar have been not French but Belgian, Canadian, Swiss, and Italian.[21] Their total number has not appreciably declined, so this appears to be largely a concession to the Malagasys' wish for more independence from France. The Vatican has promoted nationalism in

---

* *Le Monde*, Jan. 18, 1957. The Malagasy version of the bishops' letter was said to have contained a strong denunciation of the *loi-cadre*, not included in the French translation; see Méjan, p. 164.

Madagascar—as elsewhere—to win popular support and as a most effective means of combating communism, but it continues to stress discipline and conformity to its directives.

Today the Protestant-Catholic rivalry has been reduced mainly to a healthy competition in the matter of education and charitable works. Official subsidies, however, are far larger for the Catholic than for the Protestant organizations, partly as a result of the former's numerical preponderance but more because of the government's policy—despite a certain ambivalence in its attitude. The P.S.D. is led by Catholics, most of the cabinet ministers are also of that faith, and in April 1960 President Tsiranana visited the Pope. Nevertheless, the government is headed by secular-minded socialists, whereas a majority of the Malagasy deputies, who were Christians, refused to include the term "lay" in the constitution's description of the republic lest it suggest that the Malagasys were anticlerical.[22] Repeatedly the government has affirmed the separation of church and state and the latter's neutrality toward all of the religions practiced on the island. This attitude has prevented the Catholic mission from giving its wholehearted support to the present government, but it retains a strong if indirect influence on its policies.

Chapter fourteen

EDUCATION AND SCHOLARLY RESEARCH

Under the sponsorship of the Merina monarchy, English Protestant mission-aries initiated formal education in Imerina, where their schools had an im-mediate and remarkable success. They concentrated their educational ef-forts on upper-class children in Tananarive and elsewhere in the high pla-teaus, leaving to the Catholic missionaries who arrived later the task of teaching the children mainly of slaves and of the coastal populations. Al-though the Protestants also launched secondary and medical education in Tananarive, most of their schools, as well as those of the Catholics, were at the primary level.

In almost all the mission schools, instruction was rudimentary and prac-tical, with a strong religious tinge. Among the Merina, the zeal for learning was so great that some villagers, from their own meager resources, built schoolrooms and even paid the salaries of such teachers as they could get. In 1880 the Merina government made primary education compulsory, at least in theory, for all children between the ages of 8 and 16. It also forbade children to transfer from one school to another, hoping by this step to hamper the development of the more recently installed Catholic mission schools. As a result, on the eve of the French conquest there were 137,000 children—mostly Merina—in Protestant primary schools, compared with only 27,000 in the Catholic schools.[1] The early start given to education, and the monopoly exercised over it by the Christian and especially the Protestant missionaries, left an indelible imprint on Madagascar. As regards literacy, it put that island in the vanguard of the French colonies in Africa; it helped develop the written as well as the spoken form of the Malagasy language; it stimulated Protestant-Catholic rivalry; and by promoting the evolution of the Merina it widened the cultural gap between them and the coastal popu-lations.

Gallieni's contribution to the development of education in Madagascar was of far-reaching importance in many respects. He utilized rather than undermined the existing mission schools, but in addition he created state schools with Malagasy laymen and French noncommissioned officers as teachers. Without attempting to eliminate the competition between the English Protestant and French Catholic missionaries, he indirectly favored the latter by subsidizing only those mission schools that promoted the French language and culture and that conformed to the curriculum established for the state schools. Gallieni's most direct contributions were in the field of secondary education. Even though the great majority of Madagascar's present leaders owe their early training to mission schools, almost all the outstanding men attended one of the *écoles supérieures* which Gallieni founded in Tananarive.

The lay schools established by Gallieni on April 16, 1899, were grouped in two systems, each being subdivided into three degrees. The system designed for French children duplicated that of the Metropole and culminated in the baccalaureate granted at Tananarive by the two colleges, later called the Lycée Gallieni (for boys) and the Lycée Jules Ferry (for girls). The other system, exclusively for Malagasys, was given a practical and utilitarian bias. At the primary level Malagasy was the language of instruction, although a very large place was allotted to the teaching of French, and the stress was upon training pupils to develop their abilities in the traditional milieu. Primary-school children who were successful in a competitive examination could enter a regional, or second-degree, school, of which the outstanding one was situated at Mantasoa. There pupils were boarders and for three years were taught exclusively in French, and they were given some general education along with practical training. At this level, also, Gallieni created vocational classes in which were taught the basic principles and practice of agriculture, animal husbandry, and handicrafts. Girls' education had a special place in the Malagasy system, and at the regional school of Avaradrova young women were trained to become primary-school teachers or prepared for admission to the school for nurses and midwives at Tananarive. At the highest or third-degree level of the Malagasy system came the professional and medical schools and the Ecole Le Myre de Vilers, all located in Tananarive. The last-mentioned of these *écoles supérieures,* which constituted the apex of the Malagasy system, offered two-year courses for the training of minor civil servants, primary-school teachers, and candidates for the medical school.

Today the leaders of independent Madagascar regard Gallieni's influence on their country's educational system with mixed emotions. Although he made lay education competitive with that provided by the missions—in 1905, when he left Madagascar, 23,000 of the 40,000 primary-school children were attending public schools—he undeniably increased the island's school facilities. Gallieni also promoted use of a world language (French) while at the same time assigning to Malagasy an honorable place in the school curricula, and he instituted a type of training useful to Malagasy children in later life. In brief, he organized a public-school system that subsisted for the next 40 years virtually as he had established it. On the other hand, Gallieni was responsible for furthering the concentration of Malagasy schooling in Imerina, thus widening the cultural gap between the neglected *côtiers* and the Merina, who were already favored by their easier access to mission schools. Furthermore, the only diplomas and certificates that could be earned in the Malagasy school system had no validity outside of Madagascar, and even there they did not entitle their holders to enter the higher ranks of the administration or of the liberal professions.

On the whole, Gallieni's role in regard to education in Madagascar was far more beneficial than it was harmful. Exactly the opposite must be said of his anticlerical successor, Victor Augagneur, who ended all subsidies to mission schools. Augagneur's educational policy—or lack of one—served to embitter relations between the administration and the missions, heighten inter-mission rivalry, reduce the Malagasys' opportunities for any formal education at all, and still further concentrate in Imerina such school facilities as survived his withdrawal of subsidies. Some mission schools that were able to avoid closing for lack of funds were transformed into *garderies* (day nurseries), and instruction was provided by underpaid and unqualified teachers.

Under Hubert Garbit, who governed Madagascar during most of World War I, the financial position of the mission schools was somewhat eased by grants given to those that conformed to official standards, and an effort was made in the pedagogical field by publishing special textbooks for Malagasy pupils and a magazine, *Ecole Franco-Malgache,* designed to help Malagasy primary teachers. Wartime conditions, which reduced the number of French teachers serving in Madagascar and stressed economic production, inevitably accentuated the practical bias already given to Malagasy schooling, and this led to an increase in vocational instruction. In 1916 a step was taken whose significance escaped almost unnoticed at the time, when it was decided that in first-degree public schools all subjects except the French language should be taught in Malagasy. This decision ran counter to the assimilationist educational policy applied at that period in the great majority of French colonies, where a prime objective of the government was to create as thoroughly Gallicized an elite as possible.

Marcel Olivier, who succeeded Garbit in 1924 after the latter's second governorship, also believed that it was wiser to instruct Malagasy primary-school children in their mother tongue rather than in French. In this policy the government was supported by most of the conservative French residents of Madagascar. Their view was that the Malagasys needed only such schooling as would qualify them for subordinate posts in the administration or in the private sector, and they feared lest a thorough knowledge of the French language might arouse dangerous ambitions in them. A regulation of January 17, 1929, echoed this highly practical concept of education by limiting language teaching to only basic and rudimentary French, even though by that time it should have been apparent that the official linguistic policy had two serious drawbacks. One was that products of the Malagasy school system had such a poor knowledge of French that their usefulness to foreign employers was limited. The other was that zeal for schooling among the Malagasys was flagging because the existing system did not prepare them to fill high and remunerative posts. These handicaps were least evident among the Merina, because in Imerina the Catholic-mission and Metropolitan-type schools gave their pupils a thorough grounding in French, but in peripheral areas the government had to begin imposing penalties in 1929 for parents who refused to send their children to school.*

In 1933–34 a new curriculum was inaugurated for Malagasy second- and third-degree schools which allotted more time to the study of French, and concurrently a year of study was added to the course of instruction given in the regional schools. But the economies necessitated by the world economic depression of those years, together with Governor-general Cayla's authoritarian tendencies, brought school expansion almost to a halt. Madagascar, however, still held a very high place among French colonies in its literacy rate. On the eve of World War II, perhaps one-third of the children of school age were attending primary schools, and there had been a marked increase in the number of pupils receiving secondary education. Nevertheless, in 1938 only 250 of the 676 students attending the Lycée Gallieni were Malagasys, compared with 392 French boys and 34 Chinese, Indians, and Greeks.[2]

World War II further retarded the development of education in Madagascar because the colony was deprived of a number of qualified teachers and suffered a marked deterioration in school buildings, supplies, and equipment. On the other hand, official policy came to reflect the reforms intended to promote native welfare which were recommended by the Brazzaville conference of early 1944. In Madagascar, these reforms rejected the strictly utilitarian character that had been given to Malagasy schooling and aimed to replace that aspect of education by truly technical studies. More impor-

* In the assembly, on June 20, 1961, a deputy who had formerly taught school in the Antandroy region recalled how parents of school-age children, during the interwar period, had offered him gifts if he would send their children home from school.

tant, the Brazzaville reforms envisaged the giving of a Metropolitan-type schooling in all overseas territories. The question of what linguistic vehicle should be used in Madagascar's schools, which had plagued the country for nearly a half-century, was debated at length by the Mixed Franco-Malagasy Commission in 1945, but no generally acceptable solution could be found. On one point, however, there was wide agreement—the school system should be decentralized so that the coastal populations would have the opportunities for education that might enable them to catch up with the people of the high plateaus. As for the other educational recommendations made at Brazzaville—the expansion of primary and secondary education, and increased schooling for girls—Madagascar at that time was still ahead of all the French Negro African territories except possibly Senegal, but its main problems were the same as theirs: how to obtain more and better teachers and school buildings.

As of 1946, Madagascar had 1,104 state primary schools with more than 120,000 pupils. Enrollment in mission primary schools totaled 93,000, but of these, 22,000 boys and girls attended *garderies* still supervised by professionally unqualified teachers.[3] At the third-degree level, little change had been made in the three *écoles supérieures* since Gallieni founded them at Tananarive. The medical school continued to attract to its four-year course well-prepared and often dedicated students, who later rendered vital services to their country as doctors of the Assistance Médicale Indigène (A.M.I.). The Ecole Le Myre de Vilers also still played an important role in the professional training of the Malagasy elite, but its pedagogical methods had become obsolete. Moreover, the manner in which its students chose their future occupations was open to criticism, for the custom was that students with the highest grades in the administrative section of the school had first choice among the various government departments. Naturally they selected one in which the pay and other material advantages were the best. Teaching being in those respects the least-favored category of the civil service, the poorest students of the school and not those with the best marks or aptitude for teaching were the ones who entered that profession. Considerations of prestige, as well as of pay, adversely affected the number and quality of the students who enrolled in the highest agricultural, industrial, veterinary, and craft schools, for especially among the Merina, manual labor was still closely associated with a servile status.

With respect to secondary education of the Metropolitan type, the postwar picture was definitely brighter than it had been before. By 1947 the Malagasy students attending the Lycée Gallieni outnumbered those of any other nationality,* and total attendance there had risen to 884. In fact, there were

* There were 438 Malagasys, 392 Metropolitan French, and 54 other foreigners.

at that time so many applicants for admission to Tananarive's two *lycées* and one *collège moderne* that many qualified students had to be turned away. This prompted the government to create an *école primaire supérieure* to siphon off at an earlier stage in their schooling some of the promising students who would not be able to continue their studies as far as the baccalaureate. It also induced the Christian missions to enter the domain of secondary education on a much larger scale than before. The resulting sharp rise in the number of Malagasy bachelors of arts naturally increased the number of candidates qualified to apply for official grants to attend universities in France.

All the foregoing developments spelled considerable academic progress for Madagascar, but there were still gray if not black spots in its educational ensemble. Two-thirds of Madagascar's children, Governor-general Bargues told the representative assembly on April 1, 1950, were then receiving no education at all, and for lack of schools and teachers the largest percentage of illiterates continued to be among the coastal populations. Through the Fonds d'Investissement pour le Développement Economique et Social (F.I.D.E.S.) France was providing large sums to promote the building of schools in Madagascar, but only 8 per cent of the island's own revenues were allotted to its education budget. Many more trained Malagasy teachers were needed, yet of all the provincial capitals only Tuléar had acquired a normal school by the end of 1949. As of 1950, there were 2,137 monitors and 1,457 instructors teaching 72,000 boys and 45,000 girls in public primary schools, and 1,590 monitors and 1,516 instructors for 39,000 boys and 30,000 girls in mission educational institutions.*

The solution proposed by the French government and Senator Totolehibe, supported by the Malagasy elite and embodied in the decree of November 12, 1951, was to merge the two types of education then being given in Madagascar above the second-degree schools, and to raise the level of instruction throughout the unified school system to that existing in France. This reform provided a new perspective and a reorientation of the development of education in Madagascar as a whole, for until that time there had been very little chance for a Malagasy to earn a diploma recognized as valid in France.†

* These figures were cited in a debate on Madagascar education in the Conseil de la République, March 16, 1950.
† A local regulation of Sept. 8, 1921, had created two *brevets* in Madagascar, which—theoretically—could be exchanged for the French *brevet élémentaire* and *brevet supérieur,* but this was never honored by the Metropolitan academic authorities, on the grounds that they were not bound by a simple ruling of the Madagascar administration. Not even such theoretical equivalence was claimed for Madagascar's *certificat d'études primaires* (C.E.P.) or *certificat d'aptitude pédagogique* (C.A.P.).

Mission Schools

When the project of merging Madagascar's two educational systems was being debated early in 1951, a Malagasy bishop—Mgr. Ignace Ramaro-sandratana—expressed the fear that this reform would harm mission schools. Dr. Louis Aujoulat, the strongly Catholic Secretary of State for Overseas France at the time, took great pains to reassure the mission authorities on this point,[4] and eventually he was proved to be right. As of January 1, 1962, about 17 per cent of all Malagasy schoolchildren were attending mission schools, and their total number had grown by at least 50 per cent during the preceding decade.[5] It is difficult to gauge this growth accurately: the wide variations in the statistics of pupil attendance in mission schools are probably due to the inclusion in the largest figures of schools that are not officially recognized. Thus for 1950–51, some sources list 69,000, others 78,000, and for 1961–62 one can find figures ranging from 150,000 to 160,000. In any case, however, there is no question that the number of mission schoolchildren has grown appreciably since the reform of 1951. The concurrent growth in attendance at state schools, however, has been much greater, with the result that there are now probably twice as many pupils in state as in mission schools. There are various reasons for this phenomenon, which reverses the situation that existed prior to World War I, but the main cause is money.

With the reestablishment of official subsidies to mission schools in 1948, it seemed for a time that the competition between them and state schools had come to an end. Certainly the rivalry between the two became less acute, but it did not disappear altogether. State subsidies, including sizable gifts from F.I.D.E.S., were allotted to the missions, but solely for school construction and equipment, and they could not be used to pay teachers' salaries. Although low salaries did not affect the Catholic European missionary teachers, who had taken a vow of poverty, nor those Protestant teachers who were financed by affluent missionary societies, they did hamper the missions when it came to recruiting trained Malagasy lay instructors. In order both to qualify for official subsidies and to attract qualified Malagasy pupils, the mission schools had to follow the curriculum established for the state schools, but they simply could not afford to hire enough competent and accredited teachers.

The French administration in Madagascar, and later the Malagasy government, were determined to prevent competition between the mission and state schools by designating different areas of operation for them. In most of Madagascar the need and desire for schooling had become so great that there was room for all educational efforts, but chiefly because of financial considerations the role of the mission had become complementary to that of the state—a subsidiary position that the missionaries found difficult to accept. The public authorities, for example, wanted the missions to pioneer in virgin territory, especially among the primitive southern tribes. Starting schools there would in any case have been uphill work, and besides, they did not have sufficient funds to do so and also maintain their existing schools elsewhere. Understandably, the missionaries were reluctant to leave Tananarive and Fianarantsoa provinces, where 45 per cent of the schoolchildren were attending mission schools and where the literacy rate and the zeal for schooling were the most developed in all Madagascar, largely because of their own early efforts.[6]

The withholding or the granting of subsidies was obviously the government's strongest weapon in dealing with the missions, particularly after 1958, when it gained control of the distribution of funds assigned by F.I.D.E.S. for the development of education in Madagascar. Yet when the administration has tried to economize by cutting down mission subsidies, it has met with strong opposition to this policy from a majority of the members of the assembly, most of whom were educated in mission schools and have remained grateful to the missionaries who operated them. A conflict of this sort first occurred in 1953, when the French authorities began to apply a regulation issued on November 8, 1943, under which *garderies* not headed by teachers holding a *certificat d'études primaires* would be required to close within ten years. Another crisis arose in 1956 when the government wanted to make the *brevet élémentaire* the prerequisite for teachers in rural schools.[7] Whenever the authorities have criticized the missions for sumptuary expenditures, or for their failure to present requests for subsidies on time or with the proper documentation, the assemblymen spring to the missions' rescue and usually vote the subsidies asked for. But in regard to allotting time in the curriculum for religious instruction in all state schools the government has held firm. It has maintained its stand that pastors and priests may give religious education in some schools where students ask for it, but in others—such as the normal schools—the students must go to the nearest church for such instruction outside of school hours.

Certainly mission schools in Madagascar now labor under such heavy handicaps that it is surprising not only that they have kept their pupils but that enrollment has increased. With the exception of two preparatory schools—St. Michel operated by the Catholic mission and Paul-Minault by the Protestants—the quality of mission secondary schools is generally inferior to that of comparable public schools. Furthermore, the cost to Malagasy parents is higher, and in some mission schools it is said to absorb 30 per cent of a family's budget.[8] One reason for their success is that the demand for schooling, especially on the high plateaus, far exceeds the facilities available. In Tananarive, in fact, the authorities have had difficulty in protecting parents from unscrupulous self-styled schoolmasters, who, without the proper credentials or qualifications, open "schools" simply to make a profit. Another reason for the success of mission schools is the wish of pious Christian Malagasy parents to keep their children in a religious environment. Still another is the greater stress placed on the Malagasy language and literature in mission than in state primary schools and, conversely, on a more thorough training in the French language in mission secondary schools. Because French is taught in state schools mainly by Malagasys and in mission schools by French nationals, pupils in the latter institutions acquire a better command of a world language.

The Language of Instruction

Formal education has value in Malagasy eyes to the extent that it entitles the holder of a school diploma to remunerative employment. With the growth of the French community in Madagascar and of the number of posts open to Malagasys, especially since independence, fluency in the French language has taken on ever-increasing importance. On the other hand, national sovereignty has intensified the Malagasys' pride in their own language, and Malagasy has been rapidly supplanting French as the linguistic vehicle used in the Parliament at Tananarive and in the drafting of public documents. Yet French occupies an increasingly important place in the local educational system, both because the Malagasy language lacks precision and modern technical terms and because it cannot serve as a means of communication with the outside world.[9] Madagascar's constitution stipulates that French and Malagasy are the country's official languages, and the Franco-Malagasy cooperation agreement of April 2, 1960, provided that both languages were to be used in Madagascar with the aim of promoting the culture of the population.

It is ironic that a main cause of the present popularity of the mission schools, which initially stressed and developed the Malagasy language, should be the superior instruction given by them in French. The reform of 1951, which aimed at bringing an integrated educational system in Madagascar as close as possible to the Metropolitan model, provided the first strong impetus to the study of French, although this reform was itself a compromise. Under the reform curriculum, Malagasy pupils learned to read in their mother tongue during their first year at school, and in the second year studied French, both written and spoken. Gradually French took over as the linguistic vehicle, although the Malagasy student continued to read and write in his native language and candidates for the baccalaureate could offer Malagasy as a second language. The general purpose of this reorientation was to avoid removing the Malagasy child too abruptly from his milieu and at the same time to give him access to a world language. In practice the system did not work very well, and early in 1958 the government asked the provinces to alter the curriculum of the existing Malagasy primary schools so as to make it conform with that of the European schools and thus give Malagasy children an earlier start at learning French.

The chief difficulties in carrying out such a change have been the excessive size of school classes and, even more, the rural Malagasy teacher's defective knowledge of French. He has little opportunity to keep up what knowledge he has, much less perfect it, and too often both he and his pupils end up by speaking an almost incomprehensible jargon.[10] That the increased emphasis placed on the study of French after the reform of 1951 has not been markedly successful was indicated by the fact that seven years later it was said in the representative assembly that Malagasy students still regarded French at their *bête noire* and as their greatest handicap to promotion in jobs and to pursuing higher studies.[11] The question of which linguistic vehicle should be used in educating Malagasys has not yet found an answer. The present Minister of Education, Laurent Botokeky, believes that there is no incompatibility in having both French and Malagasy as official languages and that Malagasy children should learn both. As of April 1964, a committee composed of Malagasy educators was still studying the problem and trying to devise a curriculum that would give Malagasy its "due place" and at the same time not sacrifice the study of French. The basic dilemma is how to relate the school curriculum to what are called "Malagasy realities" and yet have it lead to diplomas recognized by France as the equivalent of Metropolitan ones.

School Facilities and Attendance

For many years Madagascar has been understandably proud of its high literacy rate and of the fact that so large a proportion of Malagasy girls attend school. In the latter respect it surpasses all the French-speaking African territories; in literacy it is outranked only by Congo-Brazzaville and Gabon.* Moreover, that nearly half of Madagascar's school-age children attend school is no recent phenomenon. For two reasons, this percentage has remained almost stationary over the past decade on the island. One is that the very rapid rate of the population's growth has outpaced the increase that has been made in providing the country with more schools. The second is

---

* As of 1960, 72.1 per cent of the children of school age were attending school in the former French Congo, compared with 66.8 per cent in Gabon and 46.5 per cent in Madagascar. In absolute terms, however, Madagascar led the others with 344,885 children (of whom more than 41 per cent were girls) in school, whereas there were only 82,221 in the Congo. See *Marchés Tropicaux,* July 30, 1960, and Kent, "The Malagasy Republic," p. 261.

that Madagascar has been devoting only about a tenth of its revenues in recent years to education, whereas a number of African countries have been allotting about a fourth of their income for that purpose.

One persistent handicap from which Madagascar suffers, as do the new French-speaking African nations, is the uneven distribution of its school facilities, but in the former it is the coastal regions and not the hinterland, as in Africa, that have always been disfavored. The concentration of schools on the high plateaus—a precedent set by the Christian missions—was perpetuated by Gallieni and his successors. Although this imbalance was long recognized to be a prime cause of the *côtiers'* cultural and economic backwardness, it was not until the *loi-cadre* gave the provinces control over primary education and enabled a *côtier* government to come to power that this faulty educational situation began to be corrected.

From the time when the representative assembly first met in 1947, no year passed without the voicing of complaints by its coastal members about the government's negligence in the matter of providing schools for *côtier* children. When the provinces had been set up in 1946, it had been hoped that this administrative decentralization would be followed by decentralization in the field of education. Indeed, each of the provincial capitals was promised at the time a pedagogical center of its own, but by the end of 1949 only one had materialized, at Tuléar. The next year Tamatave managed to get such a center, but this was because it provided most of the needed funds, which unfortunately were not sufficient to cover the building of lodgings for its teachers. Furthermore, the Tamatavians were disillusioned to find that because so few local pupils had been able to qualify for admission, half of the center's first class consisted of students from other provinces, mainly from the high plateaus.[12] When the 1951 reform was being debated in Paris and Madagascar, it became apparent that the only additional secondary-school facilities that the *côtiers* could expect to be given in the foreseeable future would come into being through a transformation of the regional schools into *cours complémentaires*.[13] Whenever the government was reproached for its neglect of provincial secondary education, the stock reply was that funds were lacking and that there were not enough adequately prepared students. Later, in 1956, when Fort-Dauphin finally got its own *lycée,* this argument seemed justified, for only 30 local students qualified for enrollment although the school was equipped to take 400.

In his farewell speech to the representative assembly in October 1954, Governor-general Bargues asserted that Madagascar then had enough secondary schools to meet the numerical demand, but he also admitted that they were too concentrated in Tananarive province, both in number and in quality. Such secondary education as was available in the coastal provinces at that time was so inferior to that of the capital that *côtier* parents begged their representatives in the assembly to insist on reserving more places for their children in Tananarive's *lycées*.[14] They protested that the Merina had taken over all the places available and urged the government to reserve openings for *côtier* candidates in the Lycée Gallieni and Lycée Jules Ferry on a quota basis for each province. The government refused to do so, on the practical grounds that the variations from province to province in the number of candidates qualified for admission were too great.

Obviously the only way to break out of the vicious circle was to make a vast improvement at the provincial primary level. In turn this depended on increasing the number of qualified teachers and also on the zeal of some of the primitive coastal tribes for education. Still another obstacle that would have to be overcome if rural schools were to be expanded was the dispersal of the population, except on the high plateaus, into small hamlets of only about 20 families. An inquiry conducted in 1953 in regard to comparative tribal literacy confirmed the cultural backwardness of the extreme south and the advanced position of the Merina of Imerina.[15] Among the latter, 65 per cent could read and write Malagasy and 25 per cent understood French. Corresponding percentages among the Betsimisaraka were respectively 22 per cent and 6 per cent, among the Sakalava 19 per cent and 5 per cent, and among the Antandroy 11 per cent and 1 per cent.

With the implementation of the *loi-cadre* in 1957 the situation was somewhat improved, both through decentralization of the primary-school system and through the installation of a government dominated by *côtiers*, who had every reason to help their fellow tribesmen improve their cultural status. Under the new law's provisions, the provinces were given control of and responsibility for their own primary schools and for the allocation of scholarships locally. After independence, the granting of scholarships took on more importance that it had had under the colonial regime. This became even more evident after the Malagasy government began charging fees to students in all the public secondary schools except those training teachers, claiming that the country would go bankrupt if it continued to provide schooling free of charge above the primary level to the rapidly increasing number of pupils seeking it. In 1960, when the provincial committees were authorized to grant scholarships, the formalities involved became more complicated than before, but it was still the central budget that provided the needed credits. Increasingly the provincial committees, as well as the committees that awarded grants for study abroad, were charged with practicing favoritism and with yielding to unfair political pressures in the allocation and withdrawal of scholarships.[16]

If the manner of awarding secondary-school scholarships, as well as the total sum available for such grants (only 40 million C.F.A. francs in 1961), has been unsatisfactory, it should also be noted that some progress has been made in giving more Malagasy children in outlying parts of the island the opportunity for formal education. In 1958 the grovernment drew up an educational program for each province that was to be carried out within the next four to five years, and for 1972 it set as its ambitious goal a literacy rate of 70 per cent, even taking into account the rapid population increase.[17] In 1959, the age limit for children finishing primary and secondary schools was advanced so as to make it possible for a larger percentage to complete their education, and a start was made in transforming the provincial colleges of Tananarive and Tamatave into *lycées.* As of 1962–63 it was estimated that 51 per cent (561,000) of all the children of school age were attending public or mission primary schools, and that 13,750 pupils were in state secondary schools and 8,956 in comparable mission institutions.[18] A comparison of the number of pupils from one year to the next gives a better idea of the effort that has been made in regard to schooling than do literacy percentages, which necessarily relate to a total population that is growing at a dizzying rate. The percentage yardstick, however, does provide a clue to the relative progress being made by the different provinces. In 1962, it was believed that of the school-age population in Tananarive province 63.4 per cent attended school, in Fianarantsoa 42.3 per cent, in Diégo-Suarez 35.6 per cent, in Tamatave 32.5 per cent, and in Tuléar 26.8 per cent.* On a wide geographic basis, only 10 per cent of the children in the extreme south attended school, whereas the percentage for the western part of the high plateaus ranged between 35 and 50 per cent. Thus the educational disparity between the different parts of Madagascar, though lessening, is still appreciable, and reducing it still further depends very largely on the progress made in teacher-training.

Teacher-Training

Madagascar's high literacy rate is all the more remarkable in view of the shortage of trained teachers, and would have been impossible to attain had it not been for the Christian mission schools. Not only did these schools give Madagascar a head start in formal education, but since World War II they have supplemented the public-school system to a very marked extent. This situation, however, has had one undesirable consequence. For so many years the government persisted in letting the missions carry a large share of the

---

* Within each province there were wide variations between districts. The lowest school attendance rate, 6.2 per cent, was to be found in Bekily in the extreme south, and the highest, 92 per cent, at Manjakandriano on the high plateaus. See Malagasy Republic, *Economie Malgache: Evolution 1950–1960,* p. 42.

educational burden that a long time passed before it took steps to train and pay adequately the lay instructors that it needed. After many delays it began adding normal classes to the *cours complémentaires* that were slowly formed in provincial capitals; only in the past few years did it raise those classes to the status of normal schools. Even the Ecole Le Myre de Vilers, which offered the most advanced pedagogic training in Madagascar, could not bestow on the profession of teaching the essential element of prestige. In 1957, the year before it was reorganized and designated a normal college, only four of the 200 students attending that school chose its teacher-training section.[19]

Throughout most of the 1950s, Madagascar had fewer than 2,000 certified instructors, and most teaching at the primary level was left to monitors and assistant teachers. At the interprovincial conference held at Tananarive on January 31, 1958, the Minister of Education said that he should recruit at least 12,000 instructors if the country's primary-school requirements were to be met. The greatest need existed in rural areas, and the representative assembly—many of whose members had themselves formerly taught school—showed itself exceptionally concerned for the country schoolteacher.[20] Some teachers profited by this solicitude to such effect that the Minister of Education complained on November 5, 1959, to the assembly that 75 instructors had refused to go to new posts because assemblymen had promised them they would not be transferred. At session after session, the country schoolteacher's hard lot was described and deplored by a succession of assemblymen. It was said that classes of over 100 were not uncommon, that the only lodging a rural teacher could find was a miserable straw hut, and that his salary was so low that he usually had to grow his own food and sometimes eke out a living by trading. Material hardships were accompanied by other disadvantages. Because he occupied the lowest rung of the civil-service ladder, the country teacher had little prestige among the villagers, and his pupils were quick to ape their parents' lack of respect. A teacher who refused a parent's request to let his child leave school and work for a time in the family rice field risked being the subject of a complaint to the local administrator. Such complaints could cause real hardship, for the teacher's promotion depended upon a favorable recommendation from the administrator. That official more often than not reported on the teacher's political views and his willingness to do odd clerical jobs and other such chores rather than on his teaching abilities. Poorly paid, overworked, and without honor in his village, he was left to vegetate for years in the bush without either supervision or intellectual stimulus. It was no wonder that many country teachers became apathetic and sank almost to the level of their pupils' ignorance, and that it was difficult to find talented Malagasys willing to take on that unrewarding task.

In 1959, the government began to try to make the teaching profession more attractive. Such moves had to come from official sources, for the existing teachers' unions had done little to improve the working and living conditions of their Malagasy members, and had even failed to carry through the one strike that they had called, in April 1956. Gradually the P.S.D. government, after it came to power, instituted paid vacations for teachers at regular intervals, gave them free housing or a housing bonus, raised their pay, and slightly decreased the number of pupils per class.* To raise the profession's prestige, the Minister of Education sent a circular early in 1959 to all administrators reminding them of the respect that they owed to teachers. By a move of greater practical importance, he made a teacher's promotion dependent thenceforth upon the recommendation of his superiors in the education service instead of that of the local administrator.

Such improvements as those just described, as well as the added training facilities and the higher professional standards required of teachers, have been bearing fruit. As of January 1962, Madagascar had seven normal schools (of which the one for girls at Avaradrova had 430 pupils), and their graduates received a certificate that entitled them to enter the Malagasy civil service as instructors. A center for training rural instructors was inaugurated in May 1962 at Mantasoa, with a curriculum directly related to the problems of country schools. For the higher teaching cadre, training continued to be given at the Normal College of Tananarive at the level of the baccalaureate, and its diplomas were recognized as equivalent to those granted by similar institutions in France. Although many of the Normal College's graduates continue to enter other professions, it is now turning out about 50 teachers a year. Similarly, a larger proportion of normal-school graduates than in the past become teachers: 275 out of 1,500 pupils in those schools during 1960 were undergoing teacher-training.

Thus the Malagasys are overcoming, albeit slowly, their distaste for the teaching profession, but for some time to come Madagascar must continue to make heavy demands on France for teachers. This is also true of other former French colonies, but in Madagascar's case an unusually large number must be recruited for the primary level. Under the cooperation agreement of April 2, 1960, France has been paying the salaries of the teachers it supplies at the request of the Madagascar government, and has been sending to the island a greater number than are sent to Senegal, the African state that still employs the largest number of French teachers. Of the more than 800 French teachers serving in Madagascar as of December 31, 1962, 416 were

* As of 1961, a beginning instructor was paid 34,000 C.F.A. francs a month. The average pupil attendance in state-school classes was 84—still far too high, and larger than the average of 59 in mission schools.

in primary schools, 248 in secondary schools, 131 in technical schools, and 38 in the services related to youth movements and sports. Such a large-scale dependence on France, especially at the level of primary instruction, is unfortunate in several respects. It makes undue demands upon Metropolitan France's resources in teachers and funds, and for the Malagasy government it is expensive in terms of the lodgings and various other benefits it must supply to European teachers, which could be considerably reduced if they were replaced by Malagasys.

Technical Instruction

Gallieni and the Christian missionaries were in accord that schooling for Malagasy children should have a practical bent that would help them lead more productive lives in their traditional surroundings. Consequently, pupils in both mission and state primary schools were taught the basic principles of farming, animal husbandry, and handicrafts, and in the gardens and workshops attached to the regional schools they were able to put into practice what they had learned in theory. At a higher level, more advanced instruction in agriculture, trade, industrial processes, and the like was offered in Tananarive's *écoles supérieures,* and at Diégo-Suarez the French navy gave local Malagasys both technical training and practical experience in its arsenal.

The study of Madagascar's educational system that preceded drafting of the reform of 1951 provided an opportunity for criticism of the existing facilities for technical as well as other branches of instruction. Members of the French Union Assembly mission which visited Madagascar late in 1948 declared them obsolete and deficient in both quantity and quality.[21] When he toured the island in April 1950, Dr. Aujoulat, Secretary of State for Overseas France, concurred in that judgment. The decree embodying the 1951 reform therefore included the creating of more and better technical-training facilities and of an apprenticeship system modeled on that existing in France. Early in 1951 F.I.D.E.S. agreed to finance the building of a technical college at Tananarive, which had been proposed long before by the representative assembly, and also the forming of five specialized *ateliers,* as well as apprenticeship centers and home-economics classes. In some places the new courses were given new installations, but in most instances they simply represented improvements in and additions to the existing regional schools. Thanks to this impetus, Malagasys were given modern technical training in wood carving at Betioky, marquetry work at Antsirabe, and rug-weaving at Tuléar, and were also helped to sell their output. In this field, as in that of general education, the goal was to raise technical training to the standard of that given in France, as well as to spread it more evenly over the whole island.

Because the upper-class Malagasys felt that manual labor was socially demeaning and financially unrewarding—as well as physically dangerous because tampering with the forces of nature was likely to unleash the spirits' hostility[22]—official attempts to encourage technical training did not meet with an enthusiastic response. Nevertheless, the large amounts of money and energy expended on promoting such training were reflected in an appreciable increase in the number of students attending Madagascar's technical schools, both old and new. As of January 1, 1954, the apprenticeship centers and technical college of Tananarive had a total of 1,460 students compared with 735 two years earlier, and in 1954 also, 46 million of the total education budget amounting to 335 million C.F.A. francs was allotted to technical instruction.[23] In 1956, however, there was a slowing down in the development of technical schools, whereas the number of students in other branches of education forged ahead. Nevertheless, in 1957 the technical college had 276 students in attendance, the trade school 145, and the more recently founded civil-engineering school 186, and all three institutions were awarding diplomas equivalent to those of French schools of the same academic standing. In 1960, for the first time, the Industrial School at Tananarive—which that year had 402 students—was authorized to award a technical baccalaureate.[24] As of 1962–63, the total number of students in state technical schools (one technical *lycée,* 447; one trade school, 306; and one civil engineering school, 218), as well as 16 technical colleges and numerous apprenticeship centers, came to 7,200. In addition, 1,361 young men and women were studying at 46 mission technical institutions, a considerable number of which were training girls in domestic science.[25]

So far as quantitative results are concerned, the promotion of technical education in Madagascar has been an outstanding success, but on closer examination some flaws become apparent. For one thing, a large percentage of the students at the Technical College are foreigners—there were 161 in 1959, as against 241 Malagasys. Another undesirable feature has been the entry into the civil service of almost every Malagasy graduate of the technical institutions, so that few of them have applied their theoretical knowledge directly to the country's practical problems. A more serious difficulty has been the inability of Madagascar's economy at its present stage of development to absorb anything like the number of Malagasy technicians that have already been trained, not to speak of those now pursuing such studies. In 1950 Madagascar was suffering from a lack of technicians, but a decade later it had an unemployable excess of them. Already by 1958 some mission technical schools had had to close or to be transformed into regular schools because of the lack of job outlets for their graduates.*

* This was the case of the Norwegian mission's home-economics school at Morondava and the Catholic apprenticeship center at Farafangana.

Certain attitudes among both Europeans and Malagasys played a part in further restricting the already limited number of positions in local trade and industry that were open to Malagasy technical-school graduates. The government's technical services as well as private employers frankly preferred to hire unskilled workers for low wages and then train them to fit their own particular needs. The Chamber of Commerce and some of the banks of Tananarive offered training courses open to other individuals besides those they planned to employ themselves, but this of course served to swell the number of trained local youths seeking jobs.[26] Still another difficulty arose from the freedom allowed students in technical schools to choose courses according to their personal inclinations and without relation to the prospective openings in the labor market. To correct this defect, Minister of Education Resampa, in 1959, ordered an island-wide survey of the exact needs of the six provinces for technicians, and this was to serve as the basis for a reorientation of the whole technical-school system. For some years the principals of Tananarive's technical schools and heads of the government's technical services have been canvassing potential employers for the most promising Malagasy students upon graduation, but with little success. One reason often given by European employers for their failure to take on more men who have been trained locally is that even those who hold a C.A.P. are reluctant to take jobs that require them to work with their hands or to live outside the main towns.[27]

Higher Education

It was not until the mid-1950s that Madagascar began to have higher-education facilities of its own. Before World War II only a few Malagasys had been able to receive at Tananarive's two *lycées* the academic preparation required of candidates for admission to universities in France, and almost all of the favored few able to go to France went there to study medicine. The post–World War II reforms made possible advanced studies for more Malagasys in France, but as of 1949 there were only 74 Malagasy scholarship holders studying there.* As many, if not more, self-financed Malagasys were attending schools in France. But aside from the very high cost to parents of the long trip and the living costs, there were only a few places available to overseas students in France's crowded educational institutions during the early postwar years.

Still another limiting factor was the fear aroused by the 1947 revolt in the

* See French Union Assembly debates, May 24, 1949. In 1949 those state scholars were given only 8,500 Metro. francs a month, and that year the French Minister of Finance cut out of the budget of the Ministry of Overseas France 100 million francs that had been earmarked for additional scholarships to overseas students. In 1951, however, the scholarship stipend was raised to nearly 20,000 francs monthly.

Madagascar authorities of exposing Malagasy students to the subversive political influences that were rampant in French universities. Already Malagasy students had shown themselves warmly responsive to the overtures made to them by the French Communist Party and to the radical student movements in the universities of Paris and Montpellier, to which the majority of them had gone. In fact, the Madagascar administration in 1949 abruptly suppressed the scholarships of 21 Malagasy students in France and ordered them to return home. Only the intervention of some parliamentarians and the Minister of Overseas France compelled the authorities in Madagascar to reverse their decision in the case of 17 of those students.[28]

These many drawbacks to encouraging study in France for larger numbers of Malagasy students induced the French government in 1950 to envisage the formation at Tananarive of an Institute of University Studies, similar to the one founded at Dakar, as a first step toward creating a University of Madagascar. In 1948–49, a center for holding Metropolitan examinations for law and the natural sciences had been established at Tananarive under the academic supervision of the University of Aix-Marseille. Furthermore, the nucleus for such an institute already existed there in the form of the long-established medical and law schools and of the Académie Malgache and the Institut de Recherches Scientifiques.* The government refused, however, to go forward with this project until there should be enough secondary-school graduates to provide an adequate number of students qualified to enter the institute. Some years had to pass before that reason for delay became invalid as a result of the postwar spurt in primary education and, even more important, the alignment of Madagascar's educational system with that of France as a result of the reform of 1951. On December 16, 1955, the institute finally and formally materialized, although in embryonic form.

For some years after the institute was officially launched, no further steps were taken to add to it the faculties that would warrant transforming it into the long-promised University of Madagascar. During the interval, the number of students at the institute rose to 312 in 1957 and 453 in 1959, and in the latter year a higher school of letters was created and attached to it. Inevitably the formation of a Malagasy government, and especially the assignment in May 1957 of the education portfolio to the energetic André Resampa, speeded up the process. On April 9, 1958, Resampa was able to report to the impatient members of the representative assembly that he had reached an agreement in principle with the French government about the future university, but he also told them that some delay must still be expected owing to the difficulty of recruiting enough qualified professors. There was therefore another pause until further progress was made possible by the Franco-Mala-

* See p. 226.

gasy cooperation agreements of April 2, 1960. The day after independence was proclaimed, a Fondation Nationale de l'Enseignement Supérieur was created, which comprised the university—named for General de Gaulle— and its annexed research institutes as well as the national school of administration. By designating the president of the republic as president ex officio of the university, the Malagasy government testified to the importance it attached to this new institution of higher learning. France had agreed to pay the salaries of faculty members it provided, as well as almost all the university's operating expenses. In 1964, however, Madagascar's own contribution to the university was greatly increased, to 30 million Malagasy francs, a sum ten times larger than it had granted the previous year.[29]

On October 1, 1961, the university opened its doors to 1,130 students, and it is expected that by 1970 the institution will be equipped to receive 4,700. Its most unusual feature is an Institut de Promotion Sociale, whose objective is to train an elite from among the coastal populations. For students who do not have the two baccalaureates, the university offers courses of training in rural-community work, as well as in medicine, pharmacy, nursing, and midwifery to a limited extent. Within a few years, it is hoped, more advanced education leading to recognized degrees in the last-mentioned subjects will be available. At present, the university can grant advanced degrees in law, letters, and the natural sciences equivalent to those given by the most respected Metropolitan universities. As of 1962, Madagascar's university had such an exceptionally large and well-qualified teaching staff that the percentage of its students who succeeded in their examination was markedly higher than in France. Of the students who entered the university in 1962, 30 per cent enrolled for medicine, 29 per cent for law and economics, 28 per cent for science, and only 6 per cent for agronomy.[30] At least one-fourth of its undergraduates that year were non-Malagasys, mainly French nationals, and a majority of the Malagasys were from the high plateaus. In November 1963, its liberal-arts department was raised to the status of a Faculty of Letters. At that time the number of students enrolled in the university had risen to some 1,750.

Malagasy Students in France

In 1934, Dr. Rakoto Ratsimananga—later renowned as a writer, scholar, and diplomat—founded at Paris an Association des Etudiants d'Origine Malgache (A.E.O.M.). It resembled a small, exclusive club, for at that time there were very few Malagasy students in France and the great majority of them belonged to the well-to-do Merina bourgeoisie. Three years later, a few leaders of the A.E.O.M. started the project of writing an encyclopedia in the Malagasy language,[31] but they made little progress before World War II began. In any case, the war caused the A.E.O.M. to suspend all of its activities, and when it was revived after the war it assumed a very different form. The 1947 revolt having eliminated the M.D.R.M. deputies from the political scene, the A.E.O.M. transformed itself from a cultural and social club into a political organization that was to be the self-appointed spokesman in France of Malagasy nationalism. At the same time its membership was enlarged by the greatly increased number of Malagasys studying in France, but in 1949 only nine of them—including Philibert Tsiranana—were *côtiers*. This small minority believed that promoting the cultural evolution of their fellow tribesmen should be given priority over independence for Madagascar, and it formed a group called the Amicale des Etudiants Malgaches Côtiers. This was the beginning of a schism that led the *côtiers* to form a separate Union des Etudiants Malgaches (U.E.M.), which became increasingly identified with P.S.D. policy and whose membership included only a small percentage of the Malagasy students in France.

The A.E.O.M., on the other hand, particularly after 1955, rapidly increased its membership and developed close relations with the French Communist Party and the International Students Union, both of which have aided its members with scholarship and travel grants to the Soviet Union and satellite countries.[32] Unofficial estimates put the number of Malagasys studying in such communist countries in 1960–61 at between 100 and 200.[33] In November 1962, Minister Resampa told the writers that his government opposed Malagasys' going to study in the iron-curtain countries and that whenever possible it had prevented them from doing so. Until 1960, the A.E.O.M. regularly presented demands to the French government for the island's immediate independence and for total amnesty of Malagasy political prisoners, along with denunciations of colonialism and capitalism. Madagascar's attainment of independence that year, and the amnestying of the M.D.R.M. deputies, deprived the A.E.O.M. of its nationalist political goals but did not alter its extreme left-wing tendencies.

A main reason for the P.S.D.'s eagerness to create a university in Madagascar has been its desire to keep Malagasy students at home, in the hope of shielding them from the radicalism that flourishes among them in France. As in French-speaking Black Africa, however, there have been other cogent and practical reasons for founding locally an institution of higher learning. The number of Malagasys studying abroad had doubled in the five years preceding independence, and their cost to the government and to their families had also risen sharply. A decree of October 28, 1959, divided Malagasy scholarship holders into three categories, of which the most privileged group received 522,000 francs a year. Among other motives for founding the Tananarive university was the desire to give more educational opportunities to the *côtiers* and thus help redress the cultural imbalance between them and the peoples of the high plateaus.

There are probably still three times as many Malagasys studying abroad at their own expense as those supported by government grants. The new policy has already reduced the number supported by grants from 458 in 1960–61 to 335 in 1962–63. It is planned that official grants should be given in the future only for higher studies not available locally, and that scholarships of all types will be awarded almost exclusively in fields directly related to the official development plan. In this way, it is expected, the government will have less difficulty than is now the case in persuading young men and women educated at government expense to put their talents and training to use in serving their country.

The refusal of many Malagasys educated abroad to return to Madagascar cannot be ascribed wholly to their irresponsibility. As long ago as 1950, Dr. Aujoulat admitted that foreign-trained Malagasys were justified in complaining about the local administration's inability or negligence in finding posts for them on the island.[34] The passage of time saw little change in this situation, although a provincial committee of inquiry in Tananarive in 1956 did canvass local business firms—to no avail—in regard to possible job openings for the 134 Malagasy students about to complete their training in France. The next year, when the representative assembly debated whether Malagasy students in France should be repatriated against their will for service in their home country, the government conceded the error of its ways in having failed to relate scholarship grants closely to the employment possibilities then existing in Madagascar.[35] There were only two fields, teaching and civil engineering, in which Malagasys reportedly had no difficulty in finding employment.[36] In 1959, Tsiranana ordered each government department to reserve ten posts for Malagasy scholarship holders due to return soon from abroad, and he also obtained France's pledge not to employ in the French civil service any Malagasy university graduates whose services were needed by their home government.[37]

Such steps, however, are only stopgap measures which offer no fundamental solution to a problem that can only become more acute, for the number of Malagasys receiving higher education is increasing by leaps and bounds whereas the country's economy has not improved at a similar pace.

Adult Education

On August 29, 1950, the representative assembly debated a proposal made by the government to introduce into Madagascar on an experimental basis the *education de base* which had been successfully tried out in some French West African countries. In addition to teaching illiterate adults how to read and write, this project involved using the most modern audiovisual media to teach rural Malagasys how to attain better living standards for themselves and their communities. The assembly approved this proposal in principle, but its heavy cost, together with Madagascar's already high literacy rate, caused the project to be shelved and preference given to the formation of night classes for illiterate adults.[38]

When night classes did not produce the desired results, especially in rural areas, the *education de base* scheme was revived. In 1959–60, 150 centers for *education de base* were opened in the six provinces, and these were attended by some 3,500 adults, of whom 75 per cent learned to read Malagasy with ease.[39] At Tsiranana's instigation, further steps in the same direction were taken by "volunteer" student-teachers, who spent their school vacations during late August and early September 1962 in teaching the "three R's" to illiterate adults. A year later the experiment was repeated on a larger scale, with 1,800 volunteer students teaching illiterates at 500 rural centers.[40] This was part of a wider cultural campaign organized by friends of the country's president as the Fondation Philibert Tsiranana, to which has been given the catchy description of "impôt du savoir."

Scholarly Research

Ever since Madagascar's existence became known to the Western world, its geographical isolation and the mystery surrounding the origin of its human and animal inhabitants have been the object of scientific study by Europeans. Unfortunately, the results of early work in these fields have largely been dispersed and are therefore almost unavailable today.

Over a 90-year period, beginning in 1864, the Grandidiers—father and son—produced their monumental works on the geography and bibliography of Madagascar. Under the Merina monarchy, the Jesuits installed an observatory near Tananarive, which is still contributing useful data on astronomy and meteorology. Another similar and contemporaneous effort was that of the English missionary and naturalist James Sibree, who in 1875 began publishing the *Antananarivo Annual*. This was the first periodical devoted to the scientific study of Madagascar, and it contained articles still highly valued by scholars. By the time the *Annual* expired in 1900, the torch had been taken up by Gallieni, who greatly encouraged the study of anything and everything that would add to the knowledge of Madagascar's past and present. He not only provided official support for scientific research but also gave it an organization and the means of publishing its findings. Reports of much of the work undertaken at his instigation came out in the *Notes, Reconnaissances et Explorations* that were issued in quarterly installments from 1897 to 1900.

Gallieni also encouraged the activities of the Comité de Madagascar, founded at the time of the French conquest. It published a magazine that later became the *Revue de Madagascar* (1899–1911), as well as a *Bulletin Economique de Madagascar* (1901–39), which dealt with subjects far wider in range than its title suggests. Scholarly missionaries, settlers, and civil servants wrote articles for those publications. Some of them also contributed pieces to the bulletins and memoranda of the Académie Malgache, a semi-official body created in 1902 by Gallieni. Since its founding the Académie has published more than 150 volumes dealing with the natural and social sciences. Among its more conspicuous accomplishments was the transformation of the *rova* of Tananarive into a museum housing its collections and various objects related to the Merina monarchy. At present, the Académie has 30 regular and 30 associate members, about equally divided between Europeans and Malagasys, as well as correspondents all over the world. Since Professor J. Millot retired in 1958, its president has been a Malagasy, Dr. Radoady Ralarosy.

The publications launched in Gallieni's time have continued to serve students and scholars as media for communicating the results of scientific work on Madagascar. After World War I came a period of assembling documents and organizing research, in contrast to the outpouring of original work which had occurred during the first years of the French occupation. Thus a collection of over 3,350 volumes, most of which dated from Gallieni's day but which have been augmented by later purchases, formed the basis of the government-general's library, officially founded in September 1920. Since independence it has been called the national library, and it is now used by 200 Europeans and Malagasys a day. As of 1961, this library comprised more than 80,000 volumes and 25,000 photographs and documents, and all of its staff except one were Malagasys.[41]

The sporadic and unsystematic nature of the scientific research carried on during the interwar period impelled the French government after World War II to try to coordinate such activities and also to relate them more closely to the island's practical needs. A Comité d'Etudes Scientifiques et Economiques formed in 1937 under the auspices of the Museum of Natural History at Paris produced a plan for economic and social development, but it was soon superseded by a Service de Recherche Scientifique, which did not survive World War II.[42] The continuing need for such an organization led to the founding in December 1946 of an Institut de Recherches Scientifiques de Madagascar (I.R.S.M.), which devoted itself to both pure research and analyses for practical purposes of the island's soils, flora, and fauna. It also maintained an oceanographic station at Nossi-Bé.

In regard to the considerable body of scientific work on Madagascar produced by scholars, two aspects deserve mention. One is the slight place given to the social sciences, and the other, the small number of contributions made by Malagasys. In the interwar period only a handful of ethnographic studies appeared, and they did little to update the far more extensive tribal studies that had been made at the turn of the century or before. The I.R.S.M. has issued numerous monographs on the natural sciences but only two major population studies, both produced by Louis Molet in the mid-1950s.[43] In July 1957 the I.R.S.M. was integrated into the Office de la Recherche Scientifique des Territoires d'Outre-Mer (O.R.S.T.O.M.), which created a territorial committee for Madagascar. The subsequent appointment of the outstanding French historian of Madagascar, Governor Hubert Deschamps, as head of O.R.S.T.O.M.'s department of the social sciences helped greatly to promote work in that field. Governor Deschamps inaugurated and himself contributed to a series of tribal studies under the general title of *Le Peuple Malgache,* of which several have already been published.

Only a few contributions have been made by Malagasys to the serious study of Madagascar and Malagasy life, and there is little indication of any appreciable increase in the near future. It may take years for current nationalist sentiments to give way to a more objective view among Malagasys of their country and its peoples. Popular interest in such subjects is indicated by the number of Malagasys frequenting the national library, zoo, and botanical gardens. The government is concerned about conserving evidences of the Malagasys' cultural past and has employed an able French archivist, Jean Valette, to head the Service of Archives founded in 1958. With the same aim, two laws were passed in 1961–62 which provide for safeguarding the island's historic sites and monuments. This pride in Madagascar's past, however, has not yet taken the more positive form of scientific research and scholarship. In the Académie Malgache, it has been and still is the European members who make virtually all of the scientific contributions, while literature remains the province and the center of interest of the Malagasy academicians.

Chapter fifteen

MALAGASY LITERATURE AND
INFORMATION MEDIA

Madagascar's rich oral traditions were committed to written form in the nineteenth century thanks to an enlightened Merina king and zealous English missionaries. Radama I is distinguished for, among other things, having introduced a written language for his people, an undertaking in which he was helped by foreign Christians who taught him Latin letters and introduced the printing press into the country. (The missionaries' contribution, however, had the unfortunate feature of reducing the Malagasy language to a spelling that bore little relation to its pronunciation.) In addition, Christian missionaries, both English and French, composed grammars and dictionaries. The Malagasy version of the Bible, translated by the Protestants, deeply influenced the style of many of Madagascar's writers. A single language for the whole island, based on the Merina dialect, has been one of the greatest unifying forces among the island's numerous tribes. In written form it has provided a lasting form of self-expression for a people naturally given to eloquence and rhythm.

Despite the periodic opposition of traditionalist Merina monarchs, the Protestant and Catholic missions' printing presses produced both sacred and profane literature in the form of periodicals, newspapers, and books. In 1875 there began to appear a veritable encyclopedia of information about Madagascar called the *Antananarivo Annual*. Its independent expression of views would never have been tolerated by the Merina authorities had the *Annual* been read by more than a handful of the native elite.[1] At about the same time the island's first newspaper, *Gazety Malagasy (Madagascar Gazette)* began publication. The government of that time, wanting to be independent of the mission facilities, bought its own printing press,[2] and in the 1880s proudly printed a new law code and a weekly newspaper. The mission and government presses issued publications by European and Malagasy authors, according to their respective needs; among them they covered a wide range of subjects, thus building up an invaluable source of written information about Madagascar. The output of the printing presses helped the Malagasys to learn French and English and to express themselves in those languages. The Malagasys' most original cultural contributions are not in the field of fine arts but in that of literature. Their writings have taken the form of proverbs, songs, novels, journalism, and, above all, poetry, to which the language lends itself and in which Malagasy authors have excelled.[3]

The rapid growth of nationalism after World War II sharpened the interest of the Malagasy elite in the preservation of their country's culture, and especially in the development of its language and literature. On May 8, 1958, the assembly enthusiastically approved a government proposal for the scientific study and the codification of Malagasy, to be carried out by the new Institute of University Studies. Although the deputies were lyrical in their praise of the beauties and subtleties of the language, they acknowledged that for it to become more useful as the national linguistic vehicle it must be enriched with foreign words, especially in technical fields. As a result of increasing nationalist pressure to use Malagasy rather than the other official language, French, for laws and government documents, the cabinet on November 16, 1960, appointed a committee to study the adaptations that such a step would require, especially the changes in spelling that would be necessary to make Malagasy conform more closely with current pronunciation. At its seventh congress in August 1962, the P.S.D. asked the government to print an official journal in Malagasy and to create a national academy similar to the Académie Française so as to purify and safeguard the language.[4]

The Press

Visitors to Madagascar are often astonished by the large number of newspapers and periodicals—18 dailies, 48 weeklies, 60 monthlies, 10 bimonthlies, and 19 quarterlies—published in a country where only half of a population totaling some 5.5 million are literate. The small circulation of these publications also occasions surprise, as do their concentration in Tananarive and the strongly political orientation of the press as a whole. As of 1961, all the dailies together sold no more than 44,000 copies and the weeklies 200,000.[5] All of the dailies and most of the other publications are printed in the capital. Fianarantsoa has two weeklies (*Lumière* and *Fanilo*), Majunga one weekly (*L'Aurore*), and Tamatave one monthly (*Ny Mizana*). Diégo-Suarez and Tuléar have no publication of their own, and their inhabitants perforce rely for news on radiobroadcasts or on the fitful arrival of the newspapers from Paris or Tananarive to which they subscribe. (See the Résumé of Newspapers and Periodicals in this section.)

Because of difficulties and delays in distribution (except that of the party organs), the relatively high price of each issue (5 to 15 C.F.A. francs), and the poor quality of local journalism, circulation of Malagasy periodicals has developed very slowly. Moreover, it is a moot question whether the sensationalism and vehemently partisan political tone of the daily papers have served to enlarge the number of their readers. Certainly, however, the close relationship between the Malagasy-language publications and political developments in Madagascar accounts for the official attitude, past and present, toward the press. In the case of both the French and the Malagasy administrations, the influence that the government has exerted has been repressive rather than educative, and it has had unfortunate if not seriously harmful effects on the evolution of Madagascar's journalism.

Except during the interwar period, when some French-language literary monthlies flourished briefly, the press in Madagascar has always been politically minded. The English-language press, which existed at Tananarive between 1875 and 1896, when the *Madagascar Times,* the *Madagascar News,* and the *Madagascar World* were published, was given an anti-French as well as a religious coloration by the Protestant missionaries who launched the island's first newspapers. France was out of favor in the capital during the last years of the Merina monarchy, so the French press—such as it was— of that period was mainly provincial, reflecting principally the views of French planters and traders. At Tamatave six or seven French-language papers were published between 1875 and 1902, and Diégo-Suarez had four, Majunga two, and Tuléar one.[6]

Inevitably the French conquest fostered the growth of a French-language press in Tananarive, and 1900 saw the birth of an official newspaper, *Vaovao,* and a privately owned one, *L'Echo de Madagascar.* These were followed by other French-language publications such as *L'Echo de Tananarive, L'Echo du Sud, Madécasse,* and *Le Colon.* Inasmuch as French newspapers in Madagascar were far freer than Malagasy ones to express their views, French writers and to a lesser extent Malagasys contributed mainly to the French-language press. When Ralaimongo started his newspaper, *Le Libéré,* he had it printed in France, but when he returned to Madagascar and tried to publish a newspaper there, he found his way blocked by a decree of December 15, 1927, that required the managing editor of a local newspaper to be a Frenchman. This decree accounted for the fact that the first newspapers in Madagascar to express strongly nationalist views were started by Paul Dussac.* Because both *L'Aurore* and *L'Opinion* were as much the product of the thinking and writing of his Malagasy collaborators as of himself, Dussac's French citizenship did not prevent the periodic seizure of his pub-

* See p. 27.

lications by the authorities under the powers given them by decrees of 1927 and 1930. The advent to power of the Popular Front government in France eased the application of Madagascar's press-control regulations, so that the prewar decade saw the appearance of a sizable Malagasy-language press, of which a few papers—*Takariva, Firenena Malagasy, Ny Rariny, Ny Gazetintsika,* and *Mongo*—survived World War II.

The elections of 1945–46 and the much greater freedom of expression permitted in the early postwar years caused a rapid development of Malagasy-language nationalist publications. In turn this provoked a strong reaction on the part of the local conservative French-language press, particularly after the 1947 revolt frightened the settlers and the business community. Newspapers expressing anti-French and pro-rebel sentiments were suspended. In some instances their editors and even their printers were prosecuted and imprisoned on charges of inciting hatred of the French authorities and endangering the public order. This repression was so severe that few local papers dared to report fully on the trial of the three M.D.R.M. deputies. The best coverage of the trial appeared in the Metropolitan press, especially in *Le Monde,* but the French papers did not reach Madagascar until weeks after they were published. The reticence of local reporters led the French authorities to conclude erroneously that public opinion in Madagascar was indifferent to the trial and its outcome.[7] Only *Fraternité,* owned by the French communist R. Lombardo, expressed the sense of outraged justice that the trial engendered among the Malagasy elite, and this paper was suspended several times and its owner finally deported.*

As the emotions aroused by the revolt and its aftermath gradually died down, a calmer view of the press and its legitimate functions was taken by local journalists as well as by the administration. This change was traceable largely to the attitude of the new governor-general, Robert Bargues, who—unlike his predecessor, de Chévigné—had a respect for information media and a desire to use them. Bargues was the first official of his rank to hold press conferences regularly in order to keep local journalists informed of government policies and to forestall the printing of false and sensational news stories. Furthermore, to help newspapermen learn more about Madagascar and to make Madagascar better and more accurately known abroad, he developed an official information service. It was Bargues who set up the first of 45 so-called Information Halls, which were equipped with radios, newspapers, and film projectors, and who either started new official publications or revived old ones (such as the *Bulletin de Madagascar* and *Revue*

---

* See p. 72. According to another communist writer, P. Boiteau (*Contribution,* p. 293 *et seq.*), 28 Tananarive papers were forbidden to print, either temporarily or permanently, between May 1, 1948, and May 1, 1949.

de Madagascar). He also sponsored the production of documentary films about the island. Bargues's tenure of office coincided with the political vacuum that followed repression of the revolt, and when political parties were revived under his successor, André Soucadaux, the local press likewise burgeoned again. The election campaigns held as a result of the *loi-cadre,* the referendum, and independence created a political ferment that was both promoted by and reflected in a sudden increase in the number of local publications in the late 1950s and early 1960s.

Today almost all the Malagasy-language dailies and a majority of the weeklies are organs of political propaganda, promoting the views either of a party or of their owners. Consequently, accurate and temperate reporting is sacrificed in favor of catchy slogans, libelous innuendoes, and slanted interpretation of the news. Malagasy periodicals are almost all ephemeral, with the exception of the party organs of the A.K.F.M. (*Imongo Vaovao* and *Fahaleovantenan I Madagasikara*) and of the P.S.D. (*La République* and *Madagasikara Mahaleotena*), the mouthpieces of the Catholic missions and community (*Fanilo, Lakroa,* and *Lumière*) and of the Protestant Malagasy churches (*Fanasina*), the official press (*Vaovao, Bulletin de Madagascar,* and *Revue de Madagascar*), and the humoristic weekly, *Hehy.* Rarely does a paper such as *Madagasikara Rahampitso,* which is apolitical and without support from or appeal to a special-interest group, attract a paying clientele. In some cases, a newspaper—for example, *Takariva*—survives because it is produced as a sideline by a remunerative printing press. The shoddy appearance, unreliable contents, and limited scope of most publications in Madagascar usually result in bankruptcy for their owners, whose only satisfaction must come from having controlled, for a time at least, a medium for expressing their views and making them known.

Because of lack of professionalism and of funds, the press in Madagascar is mediocre and at times absurd. The most improbable rumors are printed, no attempt having been made to verify or disprove them, as are some patently ludicrous statements that reflect Malagasy journalists' naïveté as well as inflated national pride. When a Malagasy rode his bicycle from Tananarive to Paris in May 1960, some Malagasy reporters asserted that his performance was more glorious than the much-touted discovery of nuclear energy by the great powers.[8] Only a few Malagasy journalists have either the means or the interest to go out and hunt down news, and they rely for their reporting on news agencies, official communiqués, and foreign-embassy releases. As the result of a contract concluded in January 1962 between the government and the Agence France Presse, an Agence National de Presse de Madagascar was created and given a monopoly of the dissemination of news in and about Madagascar, which was formerly shared by three agencies. Other news sources drawn upon by local reporters are monitored radiobroadcasts, both foreign and local, and even articles that have appeared in European and African papers. Almost none of the Tananarive publications has a network of correspondents throughout the island, although some have letterboxes to which provincial readers are encouraged to contribute.

The amateurish nature of Malagasy journalism reflects the fact that professional standards have not been formulated and maintained either by the three existing organizations in which the journalists are grouped or by the government. Membership qualifications and objectives are not clear-cut in any of the newsmen's organizations; hence they have not been very successful in promoting the interests of their members as a professional group. Some Malagasy journalists have been sent abroad for training on official scholarships, but to raise standards to any appreciable extent would require the founding of a school of journalism in the university at Tananarive. In 1962 the Malagasys saw for the first time a daily produced in Madagascar which exemplified Western standards of journalism in its format, advertising, news coverage, and editorial comment. This was *Le Courier de Madagascar,* which within a year of its founding had acquired a circulation of 16,000 and had readers throughout the French-speaking communities in the Indian Ocean. The most remarkable feature of that paper, however, was its sponsorship. In 1961 President Tsiranana became concerned that the French-language press in Madagascar had been reduced since independence to five weeklies and only a slightly larger number of monthlies. He took up the matter with two press federations and four regional dailies in France, and together they formed a company with headquarters at Tananarive to finance and launch a French-language daily paper. No similar step has been taken by the president of any other newly independent nation created from a former French colony.

Tsiranana is very proud of the fact that an opposition press exists in his country, and he often stresses to foreign visitors the contrast in this respect with the states of former French Black Africa. Although press laws are more severe than in France, they are not, from the government's viewpoint, free from loopholes. The law of February 27, 1959, which replaced the Metropolitan legislation of July 19, 1881, granted the press complete freedom to write and print without prior censorship, and official controls could be brought to bear only at the stage of distribution. At that point, newspapers whose contents were considered by the government to incite readers to disturb the public order or to disobey the laws of the land might be seized and their authors and publishers subjected to heavy fines. Because the great majority of Malagasy-language publications operated on a shoestring, this

Résumé of Newspapers and Periodicals*

Name and Place of Publication†	Language and Frequency	Estimated Circulation	Comment
Areno	Malagasy; weekly	3,000	Former name, *Fanazava*; owned by Dr. Ravelonanosy, prominent member of the R.C.M.; supports no party, is notably objective, and reflects independent views of managing editor Ramasindraibe.
L'Aurore, Majunga	Malagasy & French; weekly	1,000	Only newspaper distributed throughout Majunga province and the Comores; gives local news; takes no political stand.
L'Avenir Malgache	French; weekly	3,000	Former organ of Rassemblement des Français de Madagascar; expresses views of and is read by French of private-business sector.
Basy Vava	Malagasy; daily	2,500	Expounds extreme-left views in violent terms; one of the papers most often suspended by the government, its editor is frequently prosecuted for violating press laws.
Besinimaro	Malagasy; weekly	—	One of the few papers managed by a university graduate, J. B. Rajaona; attractive appearance, thoughtful, covers wide range of interests, has outstanding page on literature.
Le Courier de Madagascar	French; daily	16,000 (1962)	Began publication in May 1962 on initiative of Tsiranana, with collaboration of six Metropolitan press federations and newspapers; 6 to 8 pp., Western-style news coverage and format.
Fahaleovantenan I Madagasikara	Malagasy; weekly	3,000	Official organ of A.K.F.M.; sets political line for better-known *Imongo Vaovao,* but is less propagandist and less obviously communist.
Fanasina	Malagasy; weekly	8,500 (1959) 7,500 (1961)	Organ of Union of Protestant Churches of Madagascar; pro-A.K.F.M. and anti-Catholic; educational articles, church and social news of Protestant community.

* For most of the information in this résumé, the writers are indebted to L. X. Andrianarahinjaka's articles in *Lumière*, Feb. 10, 17, and 24, and March 3, 1961. Circulation figures relate to 1961 unless otherwise noted; they are probably overestimates based mainly on claims by newspaper owners.
† Published in Tananarive unless otherwise specified.

Résumé of Newspapers and Periodicals (*continued*)

Name and Place of Publication	Language and Frequency	Estimated Circulation	Comment
Fanilo, Fianarantsoa	Malagasy; weekly	4,500	Published by the Catholic mission of Fianarantsoa.
Fandrosoana	Malagasy & French; weekly	—	Mouthpiece of P.S.D. Minister E. Lechat; tries to define P.S.D. doctrine of socialism in abstract terms; sometimes used for government-policy trial balloons.
Feon Ny Mpiasa	Malagasy; weekly	3,000	Organ of FISEMA unions; strongly supports A.K.F.M.; readers mostly literate members of working class.
Feon Ny Tambanivohitra	Malagasy; weekly	—	Organ of rural labor unions of the C.T.M.C.; supports P.S.D.
Fiainam-Bahoaka	Malagasy; weekly	—	Organ of the autonomous unions of Madagascar; strongly supports A.K.F.M.
Fifanampiana	Malagasy; bimonthly	1,000	Organ of COSOMA; small tabloid format; supports A.K.F.M.
Fivoarana, Antsirabe	Malagasy; irregular	—	Organ of P.S.D. Federation of Vakinankaratra; strongly anti-R.C.M.; specializes in local political news.
France-Madagascar	French; weekly	—	Formerly voiced strong views of conservative French residents; now concentrates on news and advertisements of interest to foreign business community.
Hehy	Malagasy; weekly	10,000 (1959) 15,000 (1961) 7,000 (1962)	Very popular; humoristic, with good cartoons, illustrations; run by the two brothers Randriamanantena; formerly very pro-A.K.F.M., but has now become more moderate and serious-minded.
Hita Sy Re Vaovao	Malagasy; daily	1,800	Reincarnation of *Hita Sy Re,* suppressed in Nov. 1960; chief editor A. Ratsimbazafy, member of International Journalists Organization centered at Prague; virulent denunciations of imperialism, colonialism, and P.S.D. government; said to be used by local communists for trial balloons.

Résumé of Newspapers and Periodicals (*continued*)

Name and Place of Publication	Language and Frequency	Estimated Circulation	Comment
Imongo Vaovao	Malagasy; daily	6,000	Launched in 1952 by U.P.S.; now mouthpiece of A.K.F.M. with same editors as before—G. Rabesahala and R. and H. Rakotobe; most professionally produced Malagasy-language paper, widely read in Tananarive; in foreign news, attacks U.S.A. and defends communist states; anti-government.
Isika Vahivavy	Malagasy; weekly	—	For women readers.
Lakroa	Malagasy; weekly	8,000 (1959) 5,000 (1961) 8,000 (1962)	Founded 1927; describes itself as spokesman of Malagasy Catholics, not of the Catholic mission; strongly anti-communist.
Lumière, Fianarantsoa	French; weekly	—	Managing editor Père Gérard; ably presents views of Jesuit mission of Fianarantsoa; thoughtful editorials and analytical articles; moderate politically, favors a "third force."
Madagasikara Mahaleotena	Malagasy; daily	5,000	Only P.S.D. daily in Tananarive; constantly attacks and is attacked by A.K.F.M. papers; after legislative elections of Sept. 1960, changed from weekly to daily.
Madagasikara Rahampitso	Malagasy; weekly	10,000 (1959) 6,000 (1961)	Entirely apolitical; style is very popular in tone; publishes serialized novels.
Madagasikara Sambatra	Malagasy; weekly	5,000	Founded by Dr. Raseta, whose views it reflects closely; unusually wide coverage of world news in 4 pages attractively presented; supports A.K.F.M. except in advocacy of "positive neutralism" vis-à-vis world power blocs.

Résumé of Newspapers and Periodicals (*continued*)

Name and Place of Publication	Language and Frequency	Estimated Circulation	Comment
Malagasy Vaovao	Malagasy; daily	—	Founded by late A. Ramahazomanana, a militant nationalist; strongly anti-French and anti-P.S.D. until Tsiranana sought and gained independence, then supported government until owner's death; now less pro-P.S.D.; special weekly edition includes literary supplement.
Mandroso	Malagasy; daily	5,000	Managing editor S. Rasoamahenina; strongly nationalistic and pro-A.K.F.M. until 1960; more moderate in tone since independence.
Maresaka	Malagasy; daily	5,000	Owner, Ralaiarijaona, but reflects views of chief editor S. Rakotoarimah, who is proud of frequency with which his paper has been suspended and he has been prosecuted by government; formerly supported S. Rakotonirina, now more pro-R.N.M.
Matsilo	Malagasy; daily	2,500	Advocates same views as *Hita Sy Re Vaovao*; said to have been formerly pro-P.S.D.
Miasa	Malagasy; bimonthly	—	Organ of the C.C.S.M. labor unions.
Mita-Bé	Malagasy; irregular	—	Formerly organ of R.N.M.; now superseded as such by *Ny Mizana*.
Mitrongy Vao Homana	Malagasy; daily	1,000	Published by group of young left-wing militant Catholics, who support no political party, are strongly anti-communist.
Ny Feon I Madagasikara	Malagasy; weekly	—	No marked political tendency; publishes a wide variety of documents, old and new, public and private, with comments.
Ny Gazetintsika	Malagasy; daily	—	One of oldest surviving papers, founded in 1927 as a weekly, printing straight news; managing editor R. Rapiera, president of Syndicat de la Presse de Madagascar; nationalist, but objective in political reporting.

Résumé of Newspapers and Periodicals (*continued*)

Name and Place of Publication	Language and Frequency	Estimated Circu- lation	Comment
Ny Marina	Malagasy; weekly	—	Originally independent politically but increasingly pro-P.S.D.; fights anti-government opposition with sensational "revelations," unfair partisan accusations.
Ny Mizana, Tamatave	Malagasy; monthly	—	Currently the official organ of R.N.M. Federation of Tamatave.
Ny Ranovelona	Malagasy; weekly	—	Published by graduates of the Protestant school of Ambohijatovo; strongly pro-A.K.F.M.
Ny Rariny	Malagasy; weekly	300 (1962)	Published irregularly since 1938; reflects nationalist and anti-clerical views of managing editor J. Ranaivo; proud of its record of suspensions, lawsuits; supports A.K.F.M. but lauds socialism more than communism.
La République	Malagasy & French; weekly	5,300 (1959) 7,000 (1961)	Founded by Tsiranana, edited by Resampa; reflects government policy; tone is polemical.
Sahy	Malagasy; daily	—	Independent, objective reporting of news, especially of law cases, which it analyzes at length; no political alignment.
Sariaka	Malagasy; weekly	6,000	Reports news factually but with clear pro-government slant.
Takariva	Malagasy & French; weekly	—	Daily for many years, now weekly and bilingual; closely dependent for survival financially on Takariva printing press; popular style, runs contests, no political trend; former managing editor P. Rapatsalahy, now press attaché with UNESCO.
Telonohorefy	Malagasy; daily	1,500	Vehemently expresses pro-communist sentiments; resembles *Basy Vava*.
Tolona, Tuléar	Malagasy; irregular (mimeo.)	—	Organ of MONIMA; is little known outside Tuléar province.
Vaovao	Malagasy; weekly	23,500 (1961) 20,250 (1962)	Organ of government information service; heavily subsidized; well written, authoritative; supports whatever government is in power.

form of economic pressure had the effect of putting a large number of them out of business. Not only did such pressure evoke widespread criticism, but it proved unsatisfactory to the government for other reasons as well. Application of the 1959 law resulted in long-drawn-out lawsuits in many instances, and these further cluttered up the courts, which already had a heavy backlog of pending cases. Furthermore, if the verdict eventually went against the defendant newspaper, there was nothing to prevent its owner—if he had sufficient funds—from reviving it within a few days under a new name and with a body of readers enlarged by the publicity that its suppression had given it. Consequently the government sought to obtain for the Minister of the Interior greater authority to prevent this practice, and after a heated debate on December 14, 1960, the assembly reluctantly granted its request. During the discussion of this proposal the deputies repeatedly criticized the government for its failure to educate and inform the press. Above all, they censured the ministers directly concerned for playing what was simply a repressive role and one based on political-party considerations.

As if to justify this criticism, the P.S.D. at its ninth congress in the summer of 1964 approved a temporary suspension of any newspaper that published defamatory articles about the government. It also proposed that the government should exercise closer control over the foreign press in Madagascar.[9]

Radiobroadcasting

On April 2, 1931, a small station called Radio Tananarive was inaugurated in that city, and for some years thereafter it broadcast for two hours daily as the "voice" of the government of Madagascar. Since it was impossible to hear these broadcasts beyond the suburbs of the capital, a somewhat more powerful transmitter was built in 1938 at Alarobia, and the wavelength on which Radio Tananarive operated was changed. Even so, it did not reach listeners in the extreme north and south of the island, although it was audible at some points as far away as Elisabethville in the Belgian Congo. Despite their restricted range, radiobroadcasts quickly became popular in Madagascar, partly because of the delays in receiving newspapers in the provinces. On the eve of World War II, there were some 2,000 receiving sets on the island, about half of which were in areas that lacked electric power.[10] During World War II, Madagascar's isolation and the difficulties of internal communication, particularly after the British occupation, enhanced the importance of radiobroadcasting. For the first time, in 1943, the local station was used to transmit, at dictation speed, government orders and news to district chiefs and populations located in remote areas. The only other innovation of this period was a program of broadcasts from phonograph records chosen at the request of listeners.

After the war ended, Radio Tananarive extended its operating hours, and France resumed broadcasting to Madagascar for one and a half hours a day. But these programs, according to a report made by the French Union Assembly mission that visited Madagascar late in 1948, were not popular. In large part this was due to the choice of such subjects as rice cultivation and Malagasy folklore, about which the islanders felt they already knew more than anyone else.[11] It was not until the incumbency of Robert Bargues, who encouraged information media of all kinds, that any marked improvement of local broadcasting took place. It was Bargues who built and equipped with receiving sets the first Information Halls throughout the island. In March 1950 he added to the ten hours of daily broadcasts in French a new Malagasy-language program for eight hours a day, so as to "bring more news about Madagascar to the world and about the world to Madagascar." Bargues followed this up with an island-wide inquiry into listener reactions, and he learned that Madagascar's topography and climate made reception even worse than had been suspected. Steps were taken to improve the quality as well as to increase the duration of local broadcasts, and when Bargues left the island in 1954, Radio Tananarive was on the air with French- and Malagasy-language programs for 63 hours a week.

Despite the advances just described, technical difficulties continued to hamper broadcasting in Madagascar to such a degree that in 1956 some assemblymen refused to vote the budget allocation for the local radio service.[12] To deal with its deficiencies, the Madagascar authorities sought financial and technical aid from France, and in August 1957 SORAFOM (Société de Radiodiffusion de la France d'Outre-Mer) took over Radio Tananarive, which it renamed Radiodiffusion de Madagascar. With an initial grant of 52 million C.F.A. francs, SORAFOM's technicians installed new and more powerful transmitters on the island, and the number of broadcasting hours was augmented. By 1961, programs totaling 145 hours weekly were being broadcast from Madagascar, and on Sundays Paris relayed there three hours of taped recordings and news of current sports events.

The Malagasy government council, installed in 1957, soon showed its awareness of the radio's potential as a vehicle for both political propaganda and education. Because of the small number of receiving sets—perhaps 10,000 in all at that time—and their concentration in towns, the rural masses remained virtually untouched by developments outside their immediate environment. The number of Information Halls had grown steadily since 1950 and there were some 160 throughout the island, but many of them were not fulfilling the hopes placed in them by their founder. Their radio sets in some cases fell into disrepair, their reading matter was neglected because it had little or no interest for isolated villagers, and in certain places the Halls came to be used solely for storing rice or other perishable commodities.[13] In 1960 the government reequipped 96 of the Halls with receiving sets, and launched what it called Opération Transistor to encourage radio listening among the masses. Through the granting of loans and easy-payment terms over a two-year period, the Madagascar market for transistor radios was rapidly expanded, and sales rose from 5,439 sets in 1957 to 42,980 in 1962. There are now perhaps as many as 70,000 receiving sets in the island, and it is believed that 400,000 to 500,000 persons listen daily to local broadcasts.[14]

On January 1, 1962, the Société Malgache de Radiodiffusion, a state company headed by a Malagasy, Roger Rabesahala, assumed control of all broadcasting in Madagascar. Such a monopoly in the hands of the P.S.D. government naturally aroused criticism. Anti-government journalists had already complained that Opération Transistor was aimed directly at undercutting the opposition press, and in the assembly the anti-P.S.D. deputies asserted that local radiobroadcasts were invariably biased in favor of all the government's policies and activities.[15] Although the government was indeed culpable on the score of partisan news reporting, it did have to its credit an original and effective experiment in educational broadcasting. On May 15, 1961, a series of evening programs covering 20 hours weekly was begun under the joint sponsorship of the local radio service and the Fondation de l'Enseignement Supérieur. The series was entitled Radio-Université, and the level of the instruction it offered was sufficiently high to attract and benefit comparatively advanced students.

Remarkable as has been the growth of broadcasting in Madagascar over the past few years, the government considers that it still falls far short of its maximum development. Thus far Madagascar has resisted the temptation to install television, and has concentrated its efforts on developing radiobroadcasting and the radio audience. Much attention has been devoted—and with considerable success—to overcoming the technical difficulties of reception traceable to adverse natural conditions and also the problems caused by the almost equal use of two linguistic vehicles for broadcasting. When it is considered advisable to broadcast a program in both French and Malagasy, delays and duplication are inevitable. The language employed does not necessarily correspond with the ethnic origin of the listeners for whom a program is intended, but rather with their degree of formal education. Cultural improvement is the keynote of a large part of the French-language series, which employs more than 50 reporters, announcers, and technicians. The Malagasy-language chain has an even more numerous personnel, and the result is a broadcasting service that is considered to be more enterprising and dynamic than that of any of the French-speaking African nations south of the Sahara.[16] In March 1963 a Maison de la Radio was in-

augurated at Tananarive by the French Minister of Cooperation, its cost of
125 million C.F.A. francs having been financed through F.A.C. (Fonds
d'Aide et de Coopération). As of early 1964, Madagascar had two transmitters, one of 100 and one of 25 kilowatts, which had begun operating at the
Fenoarivo station a few months before. There were also eight less powerful
ones—three using medium-wave and five using short-wave transmission.

Part three

THE ECONOMY

Chapter sixteen

ECONOMIC POLICY AND PLANNING

In the time of the French Union, as in that of the French Empire, France's policy in both the economic sphere and the political one was based on certain broad principles that were believed to have universal value. It was assumed that what was a good general policy for a Far Eastern people such as the Vietnamese was equally valid for an African tribe. This assumption derived from the strongly humanistic trend in French thinking and also from practical considerations—particularly in the economic domain. A Senegalese deputy might sit in the French National Assembly and a cultured Cambodian be received as a social equal in Paris literary circles, but in economic matters the French were virtually unanimous in believing that the interests of their overseas territories should be subordinated to those of France.

Before World War II the colonies supplied French industry insofar as they could with the raw materials and markets it needed. This *économie de traite,* as it was called, was all but monopolized by French wholesale traders and navigation companies, whereas retail commerce was taken over by Asians alien to the country in which they traded. Generally speaking, Madagascar's indigenous population was made up of farmers, fishermen, and herders, and the Malagasy elite occupied minor posts in the civil service. During the wars in which France was involved, the colonies were expected to contribute unreservedly their manpower, resources, and money. In time of world depression or for outstanding public works France would grant the colonies loans or make fiscal concessions to their exports, but otherwise they were expected to pay their own way even though their economy was left almost entirely undeveloped.

After World War II a new principle was introduced into the economic relationship between France and its overseas dependencies. Their economy was to be developed along the lines of a plan drawn up in Paris and with funds supplied almost wholly by French taxpayers. Native welfare was in principle given priority, but this became far more of a reality in political and social respects than in economic ones, in which French monopolistic practices progressively reasserted themselves.

As a consequence, the chief beneficiaries of the plan's concentration on developing the means of communication and export crops were a minority of native farmers and the foreign traders, while the great mass of the population continued to live by subsistence agriculture. More closely than ever before, the economy of Madagascar and the African territories became integrated with that of France. The possibility that they might some day break away from France was not seriously considered until 1958. Thus the political sovereignty which came to those countries two years later (in the case of Guinea, in 1958) found them totally unprepared for independence from France in the economic domain. As for Madagascar, since 1960 the P.S.D. leaders have been trying to lay the bases for a genuinely national economy without, however, destroying the existing economic structure or abruptly ending Madagascar's financial and commercial dependence on France. However, Madagascar has become so accustomed to protection and privileges for its exports in the franc market that even with the help of the European Economic Community it will have great difficulty in adjusting to meet competitive world conditions.

French policies in pre-independence days, as described above, were inevitably modified in their application to Madagascar. That island's distance from France, its geographic formation, and the nature of its human and natural resources proved to be active or passive agencies for transformation. Earlier than in other French colonies economic planning was introduced into Madagascar, and it was there that military conscripts were first used as labor for public works. The presence of certain human elements not found elsewhere, as well as their interaction, was mainly responsible for the island's distinctive evolution. These were the "poor white" settlers from Réunion Island, the resident French businessmen and missionaries, successive governors-general (of whom the most influential was Gallieni), and, above all, the Malagasys, who passively resisted economic progress in the Western sense of the term.

All the above-mentioned European elements were eager to develop the island's economy and to promote French economic interests there, but basic differences arose between them in regard to the role that the Malagasys were to play in this process. Obviously Madagascar's development depended upon Malagasy labor, which was not voluntarily forthcoming; so all but the Malagasys agreed in principle that they should be compelled to work. Despite considerable pressure from the planters—to which it occasionally yielded—the administration took the stand that it would force the Malagasys to work only in their own or the public interest. The economic history of Madagascar between the French conquest and the outbreak of World War II was dominated by a struggle for power between the administration and the resident French planters and businessmen. By and large, that struggle centered mainly on Malagasy labor and who should have the authority to dispose of it.

Since World War II the problems posed by Malagasy labor, although somewhat different than before, have continued to cast a long shadow over the economic scene. After the use of forced labor was abolished in 1946, the profit motive proved to be ineffective in inducing the Malagasys to work. Since independence, the struggle to dispose of the Malagasys' labor has continued, but with different protagonists. These are no longer a French administration and French planters but a sovereign Malagasy government and its peasant compatriots, and the latter are no more responsive than before to appeals to their patriotism to work harder and to produce more for export and domestic consumption. The problem no longer has nationalistic overtones, as it had under French rule, nor is it linked to abstract ethical virtues, as it was in the time of Gallieni and Olivier. Producing more has become a matter of life or death, because a population that is growing at the rate of nearly 3 per cent a year can no longer afford the luxury of economic stagnation.

Under the Merina monarchs, the Malagasys lived in a virtually closed economy, and only a handful of privileged individuals bought any foreign merchandise at all—a little cotton cloth and a few firearms. Gallieni, as a fervent believer in economic and social development, pioneered "planning" in Madagascar, though in his day that term was not used. His policy was based on two principles which, he realized too late, were incompatible. These were to make the island a *chasse gardée* for French traders and settlers and to promote the Malagasys' well-being by inducing them to develop the economy. In his memoirs Gallieni wrote:[1]

There is no doubt that the Malagasy in all parts of the island can almost always procure without appreciable effort what he wants to nourish, clothe, and house himself. To leave the native in this condition is to renounce for him all progress, all improvement in his social and economic position. Using force in such circumstances is immoral, impolitic, and futile. So we must find not a material means of coercion but a stimulus that pushes the natives to work and gradually leads them to understand its advantages.

To this end, Gallieni linked taxation with education, so as to give the Malagasys both the necessity and the technical means of increasing production for export. With the money thus earned, they could buy imported

goods and also pay taxes that would be used to develop the island's infrastructure and improve its inhabitants' material and social welfare. But as
time went on, he realized that his compatriots, for whom he had created an
unassailably privileged position, did not share his concern for promoting
the Malagasys' evolution. On the contrary, they wanted to use the element
of coercion that Gallieni had introduced in the form of taxation as a means
of forcing the Malagasys to work for them, and the concessions that he had
granted them as devices to free themselves from official controls and to
build up monopolies in their own interest.

World War I accentuated the trends in this policy that were unfavorable
to the progress of the Malagasys. The practices of forced labor and the
économie de traite became more deeply entrenched because of the wartime
obligation to export the foodstuffs and ores required by the French army.
The economic conference called by Governor Schrameck in January 1919,
with a view to associating the local French businessmen and settlers more
closely with economic policy-making, showed clearly the intention of those
elements of orienting the economy in such a way as to promote their own
profits. To further foreign trade, of which they would be the prime beneficiaries, they urged the government to undertake a program of public
works costing 400 million francs, to be financed by a loan, and to requisition
Malagasys for work on their plantations. In both cases the Malagasys, as
laborers and as taxpayers, would bear the brunt of this burden, France
would advance the money, and the local administration's role was to be that
of providing the leverage. In brief, the resident French community wanted
to reap the maximum advantages from the public authorities with a minimum of official interference.

The Paris government approved of the purely economic aspects of their
proposals but refused to surrender control over policy-making or to give the
local French businessmen and settlers a free hand in dealing with the Malagasys. It so happened that the resolutions passed by the 1919 conference were
sent to Paris just at the time when Albert Sarraut, former governor-general
of Indochina, was formulating the first economic plan yet devised for the
French Empire as a whole. In its scope this proposal was imaginative, and
in its financing by France it represented a daring departure from the laissez-
faire tradition, but there was nothing novel about its main objective—that
of promoting the economic interests of France. The experts who helped
Sarraut draw up his plan, which was presented to the Chamber of Deputies
on April 12, 1921, adopted some of the Madagascar conference's proposals,
notably in regard to building a railroad from Fianarantsoa to Manakara
and improving the island's main ports.

In launching the Sarraut plan in Madagascar, a second attempt was made by the local administration to associate local economic interests closely with its execution, and it was largely for this purpose that Governor Olivier created the Economic and Financial Delegations in 1924. But by making the Delegations a purely advisory body he was able to keep a tight rein on their activities, and by adding a second chamber composed of Malagasys he sought to give native economic interests the first opportunity to express their views. The prosperity of the 1920s in Madagascar seemed to testify to the success of this formula of cooperation. Then came the world depression of the early 1930s, which caused a tightening of official controls and at the same time increased the resident Europeans' willingness to accept them. It was very largely because of the program of government-financed public works and loans to planters that Madagascar survived the depression as well as it did, but it was not until the eve of World War II that its economy began to return to the 1924 level.

In 1937 Governor Cayla asked Henri Guineaudeau, a pioneer French settler in Madagascar, to draw up a new plan as a sequel to that of Sarraut. Guineaudeau's project marked a notable advance over its predecessor, for it contained social as well as economic objectives and was better adapted to Madagascar's finances and needs.[2] World War II, however, began before it could be implemented. By the end of the interwar period, the local administration had clearly won its struggle vis-à-vis the resident Europeans, but the character of Madagascar's economy had not changed in the process. Fundamentally it was still an *économie de traite* with a favorable trade balance and profits for Frenchmen as its principal goals. The World War II years were difficult for the resident Europeans and very hard for the Malagasys: they reinforced the authoritarianism of the local administration and reawakened the French settlers' and businessmen's resistance to it.

So far as Madagascar was concerned, the economic and social resolutions passed by the Brazzaville conference early in 1944 had only one virtue: they restated the principle of native welfare, which had been disregarded since Gallieni's day. Conditions on the island and the climate of opinion there, however, were not propitious for the implementation of those resolutions. This also held true in regard to the Fonds d'Investissement pour le Développement Economique et Social (F.I.D.E.S.) for execution of the Monnet Plan in the overseas territories. During the early postwar years the steps taken by the administration to deal with the situation caused by shortages of equipment and consumer goods encountered resistance from the local French community. Then Malagasy nationalist agitation and the abandonment of enterprises by Malagasy workers after the abolition of forced labor undermined the structure of the economy. These various developments made the goals set by the Paris planners seem unattainable.

On October 18, 1946, Governor de Coppet announced that Madagascar was to receive under the Monnet Plan some 20 billion C.F.A. francs over the next decade for the purpose of doubling its production. This was to be accomplished by carrying out public works that would develop its most promising regions, link them together, and connect them with four or five well-equipped ports by the building of several thousand kilometers of permanent roads. The funds, equipment, and technicians needed to carry out this ambitious program were slow in reaching the island, and, in any case, the revolt that broke out six months later caused further postponement of the plan's application.

In 1948 a reexamination of the plan for Madagascar disclosed that it had serious weaknesses. In the winter of 1946–47 it had been hastily drawn up without adequate preliminary studies, and it comprised simply an un-coordinated list of the projects that each government department would like to see carried out. Furthermore, prices had risen sharply since then, and its cost was reestimated at 57 billion C.F.A. francs instead of 20. Subsequently the initial ten-year plan was divided into a series of four-year plans, for which France agreed to pay half the cost of the major investments, two-thirds the cost of social equipment, and the entire expenditure required for scientific research. Inasmuch as Madagascar was unable to finance its share of the plan, mainly the operating expenses of the projects constructed by F.I.D.E.S., it was authorized to raise long-term (20-year), low-interest (2 per cent) loans from the Caisse Centrale d'Outre-Mer (C.C.O.M.). Under the first four-year plan, the infrastructure was to absorb 67.5 per cent of the total expenditures, social projects 18.9 per cent, and production 13.6 per cent.

Governor Bargues, soon after his arrival at Tananarive in 1950, observed that the first plan was not stimulating production appreciably, and he attributed this failure mainly to a dissipation of the available funds among too many unrelated projects. In order to adapt the second plan (1953–57) better to Madagascar's needs and resources, he called on the services of a French planning expert, Maurice Rotival. Unfortunately, Rotival had no previous knowledge of the island, and his experience in the United States and New Zealand proved largely irrelevant to Madagascar.[3] In contrast to the first plan, the Rotival plan allotted smaller sums to the infrastructure, although the railroads and Tamatave port were to be modernized. Its main stress was placed on increasing the production of export crops, but rice as a food crop was also to be encouraged. The Communes Rurales Autonomes Moder-nisées (C.R.A.M)* were the agencies chosen to modernize Malagasy agriculture, and F.I.D.E.S. credits were to be concentrated in the seven regions

* See p. 149.

most suited to the development of agriculture for export. These were the Mahavavy–Sambirano–Nossi-Bé triangle (mainly for paddy and sugarcane), the valleys of the Betsiboka and Mahajama (rice, tobacco, and cattle), the hinterland of Morondava (tobacco and peanuts), the banks of the Mandrare (sisal), the basin of Lake Alaotra (paddy), the coastal districts of Tamatave and Fianarantsoa provinces (coffee, vanilla, cloves), and the delta of the Mangoky (cotton).

In common with planning operations in other French dependencies at that time, Madagascar's second plan suffered from a general paring down of F.I.D.E.S. credits, but for various reasons France was less generous to the island than to its African territories. The 1947 revolt had left an unhappy impression on the Paris authorities; Madagascar's distance from France and its economic self-sufficiency made its development seem less urgently needed; it had no spectacular resources that promised to yield large and immediate profits; and it was less demanding of funds than were the African countries closer to France. This comparative negligence on the part of France was attributed by Governor Bargues to Madagascar's moderation and prudence in carrying out the plan, and indeed the island for several successive years failed to utilize all the funds annually granted to it.[4] Bargues subsequently made a special trip to Paris, and he succeeded in persuading the government there to increase its proportion of outright gifts to 75 per cent and to reduce loans to 25 per cent of the credits allotted to Madagascar by F.I.D.E.S. Between 1947 and 1958 France's total aid to Madagascar under the plan amounted to some 44 billion C.F.A. francs.

Madagascar's third plan (1958–62) enlarged the proportion of investments devoted to increasing production (43 per cent of the total) and reduced those allotted to the infrastructure (39 per cent), but it retained the most original feature of the preceding plans—that of developing each region as an entity. In regard to production, the investments of F.I.D.E.S. had led to appreciable increases in Madagascar's export crops but had failed to improve its livestock output. Under the third plan, the political decentralization envisaged by the *loi-cadre* was to be matched in the economic domain. Smaller funds than before were allotted to Tananarive province, and more were placed at the disposal of the coastal provincial administrations. The rural commune now supplanted the C.R.A.M. and the C.A.R. as the organization favored to modernize the peasantry, and new crops and ores were selected for intensive development.

The changes initiated by the third plan merely made more glaring the lack of overall planning and the tendency to promote one product in the expectation that it would give rise to immediate prosperity and prove to be the panacea for curing all of Madagascar's economic weaknesses. Successive formulas for organizing the peasantry had not transformed agricultural techniques from primitive to modern. The same enthusiasm that had been displayed over the years to develop first rice, then coffee, and finally sugarcane was now focused on cotton, and the hopes formerly placed in gold mining were now transferred to prospecting for uranium and petroleum. In the judgment of René Dumont, an agricultural expert who came to study Madagascar's rural economy in 1959, the funds that had been wasted on the search for a "miracle" export crop or ore might far better have been spent on developing Madagascar's resources to meet the needs of its fast-growing population.[5]

In justice to the French authorities, however, it should be remarked that France supplied from its public funds almost all the money invested in Madagascar's development and that very little came from private sources. As for the Malagasys themselves, not only did they make no more than a slight financial contribution but in some ways they actually impeded economic progress. The elite were preoccupied with the questions of independence and amnesty, and the masses seemed unaware that economic problems even existed. Absorbed by the cult of their ancestors, obstinately given to such harmful practices as *tavy,* cattle thefts, and chronic nomadism, they were content to leave development projects to the government and trade in the hands of foreigners.

With the achievement of independence in 1960, the elite had less occasion to be concerned with Madagascar's relations with France if not with party politics, and they also turned their attention to the island's economic problems. The P.S.D. government, faced with a stagnant economy and rising living costs, was forced to cope with the problems created by the rapid growth in population. President Tsiranana increasingly stressed Madagascar's needs to match political sovereignty with economic independence, and his speeches were marked by a refreshing realism that contrasted with the tone of bland optimism that had characterized many official French utterances. Madagascar, he recognized freely, was essentially a poor country, ill-equipped as to infrastructure and industry. Its soil was of mediocre fertility, its mineral resources small and of little value, and it was periodically prey to natural disasters, particularly cyclones, but he believed that some of the handicaps could be overcome. One of these was the underutilization of such industrial capacity as it possessed; another was a top-heavy administration that required French subsidies and heavy taxation to support it; yet another was the importation of costly goods that could be manufactured locally; and finally there was the Malagasys' apathetic attitude toward economic progress.

To deal with these problems Tsiranana's A.K.F.M. opponents proposed nationalizing the foreign private enterprises that were monopolizing Madagascar's trade and transportation, radically reforming the land-tenure system, creating a wholly national currency, and dismissing alien technicians. Tsiranana, however, advocated raising Malagasy living standards through an increase and diversification of foreign investments and commerce, better organization of the local market, and far greater participation by the Malagasys in economic production. He rejected the A.K.F.M.'s dogmatic and doctrinaire approach, claiming that his socialism *à la malgache* was a more practical means of developing the economy. Nevertheless, he warned that if private investors and the Malagasys did not cooperate wholeheartedly with his moderate program, his government might be compelled to resort to more extreme measures. During the three years that followed independence, the evolution of Tsiranana's thinking on economic questions could be traced in his public speeches, but it was not until publication of the five-year plan in 1964 that the goals set by the P.S.D. government were clearly defined.

In July 1960, Tsiranana had appointed a Commissariat Général du Plan, and then, to advise its technicians, he also named a Conseil Supérieur composed of officials and representatives of the private sector. The Commissariat and Council were assigned the tasks of taking an inventory of Madagascar's resources, laying down the general principles that should govern the plan, and proposing the practical means by which they should be applied in yearly installments. To guide the planners, the government issued a few specific directives. They were expected to discover ways in which Madagascar could produce and export at competitive prices commodities for which market prospects were good, and also to devise a policy on imports so as to favor equipment goods and discourage the importing of articles that could be locally produced for domestic consumers. The first visible fruit of the Commissariat's labor was an analytical survey of Madagascar's economic and social development in the decade prior to independence, which was published in June 1962 under the title *Economie Malgache: Evolution 1950–1960*. The plan itself was not made public until it was submitted to Parliament in early 1964.

It contained no surprises in its general orientation and its stress on agricultural production. This also was true of its emphasis on small-scale industry through the processing of local raw materials and development of hydroelectric power. In confirmation of Tsiranana's reiterated pledges, it contained no provision for nationalizing existing private enterprises and called for close cooperation between the public and private sectors of the economy. Nevertheless, Tsiranana's diluted form of socialism was reflected in the plan's anticipated promotion of cooperative societies and its proclaimed objective of controlling the orientation of private investments and of internal trade generally. Yet the state was to intervene directly only in the domains considered essential for the development of the national economy and where the private sector had failed to invest. Malagasys were called upon to participate actively in the formation of companies of mixed economy (combining public and private funds), especially those handling internal transport and maritime shipping. Great opportunities were thus left open to free enterprise if it was disposed to take advantage of them.

Madagascar's Parliament was reassured by the fact that each year it would have an opportunity to approve or modify the annual program of the plan, but its members almost to a man disapproved of the government's proposal to finance the plan through a substantial increase in taxation. Over a five-year period, the plan's total cost was estimated in 1964 to come to 165 billion Malagasy francs. Of these it was hoped that 96 billion would be supplied from private sources, 31 billion from foreign governments (mainly France and its Common Market partners), 13 billion from national loans, and 10 billion annually from budgetary resources. The balance was to be provided from miscellaneous sources, especially from higher fiscal revenues. Because the Parliament considered that this placed too great a burden on the present generation of Malagasy taxpayers, the government agreed to study further the possibility of increasing the proportions to be provided by other sources.

The P.S.D. leaders were heartened by the general approval given to their plan by the National Assembly, where there were only three votes against it and one abstention.[6] Not unexpectedly, the plan failed to win the support of that dedicated dissenter, Alexis Bezaka, but surprisingly two of the three A.K.F.M. deputies, including Richard Andrianamanjato, voted in favor of it. Patriotism and the desire to avoid being charged once more with "systematic obstructionism" were the explanations given by the A.K.F.M. leader, but probably he was influenced also by the fact that the plan embodied projects that conformed with his own program. There is no doubt that Tsiranana has been moving gradually and unostentatiously toward the "peaceful revolution" long advocated by the A.K.F.M.

Probably Tsiranana will soon find himself in much the same position as some of the conservative French-speaking African leaders, such as Diori Hamani. Like the president of Niger, Tsiranana has been notably reluctant to adopt radical economic policies, and his government's trend toward *étatisme* has been due very largely to the sheer lack of alternatives. Although Tsiranana has succeeded in luring new capital to Madagascar, and a few of the established firms have been earnestly trying to adapt themselves to his new program, the amount and scope of private investments fall far short of achieving the proportions needed to carry out the plan. For political rather than economic reasons, foreign governments, especially that of France, will probably continue to be the only dependable large-scale source of the monetary and technical aid that Madagascar requires.

The greatest danger to execution of the plan lies in the probable failure of the P.S.D. government to enlist the active support of the Malagasy population. The peasants' increasing recalcitrance in paying their taxes is symptomatic of the distrust they feel toward the government, which is not very different from their suspicious attitude toward the French administration. They will no doubt offer passive resistance to the P.S.D.'s attempts to get them to perform forced labor, even if it goes by the more palatable name of civic service. As yet, the hard-core political opponents to Tsiranana's government have not succeeded in exploiting this rural opposition for their own ends, and it is quite possible that they could not do so if they made the attempt. In this instance the basic ethnic conflict between the Merina and the *côtiers,* which is harmful to the cause of national unity in other respects, may work in favor of execution of the P.S.D.'s national economic plan. The great majority of the Malagasys will give their loyalty and their labor to the government only if the plan succeeds in appreciably raising their living standards.

Chapter seventeen

LAND AND PEOPLE

Madagascar is like a world apart, whose outstanding characteristics are its vast size, its isolation, the variety of its soils and climates, and its under-population. The fourth largest island in the world after Greenland, New Guinea, and Borneo, it has an area of 590,000 square kilometers—somewhat less than that of Texas but greater than that of France. At its nearest point only 392 kilometers from the southeast coast of Africa, and not much farther from the clusters of volcanic islands called the Comoros, Seychelles, and Mascareignes, Madagascar is nevertheless very different from its neighbors in flora, fauna, and human inhabitants.

In outline an irregular lozenge, the island is oriented northeast-southwest, and it lies wholly within the tropical zone of the Indian Ocean. Throughout almost all of its length of 1,600 kilometers run the central or high plateaus (as this region is commonly referred to in Madagascar), which fall off abruptly to the eastern coast and more gradually to the west. The term "plateau" in this case is inexact, for central Madagascar is punctuated with mountains which have an average height of 1,000 meters, and its only flat areas are those formed by lakes and rice fields. Eroded and largely unfertile, the central plateaus are nevertheless the most important region of the island from the standpoint of political history and population concentration.

There are three main regions aside from the extreme north, which is fertile but so cut off from adjoining areas as to form an island-within-an-island. The west differs from the rest of Madagascar in having extensive rolling plains, some fertile river valleys, and a relatively sheltered coast. Prolonged droughts in the extreme south have resulted in periodic famines there for man and beast. The narrow east-coast region has soil and climatic conditions that make it suitable for the production of valuable export crops, but offshore reefs and frequent typhoons make it difficult of access and dangerous for shipping. To only a small extent has this inaccessibility been offset by a series of lagoons over which coastal traffic is possible for a short distance. Madagascar has many rivers, but none is navigable for long stretches. Climatic conditions, like the island's topography, are widely varied, and rainfall distribution is very uneven. In general the climates correspond to the geographic zones, being chilly in the island's center, warm and humid on the east coast, hot and very dry in the south, and alternately dry and rainy in distinct seasons in the west. Vegetation zones follow longitudinal lines, and are highly diverse. Dunes and lagoons which border the Indian Ocean give way to forested slopes that lead to the high cliffs marking the beginning of the central plateaus. These "plateaus" are in reality deforested mountainous areas and prairies, which spread out to become rolling pasturelands of the savannah type along the west coast. Numerous cactuses and other drought-resistant plants give an exotic appearance to the landscape of the extreme south, often referred to as the *pays des épineux* (country of thorny plants).

Madagascar's topography and climates are so diversified that many regions are isolated and intercommunication is difficult, particularly during the rains. Distant 10,000 kilometers from France, 6,000 from the Malay archipelago, and 3,500 from India, Madagascar is also isolated from other countries, including those of Africa, although in the case of the latter the isolation is more psychological and political than geographical.

Colonization and Internal Migration[1]

A striking characteristic of the Malagasys is the mobility of most of their tribes, which is responsible to a large extent for the way in which they have evolved socially and economically. Nothing is accurately known about the island's earliest migrants, and it can only be surmised that after wandering along the coastal lands some of them reached the high plateaus, where they cut down the forest and began to grow rice. The stronger groups absorbed or conquered weaker nearby peoples, and by the fourteenth century they were largely stabilized in specific regions, where they crystallized into tribes and formed kingdoms. This lessened but did not check migrations, and the population continued to be mobile, shifting about within the different kingdoms or from one to another, depending on the fortunes of war. With the founding of the Merina kingdom, though it did not cover all Madagascar, migrations were facilitated. The Merina government encouraged the colonization of empty lands and to a large degree assured the protection of life and property. Furthermore, the Merina conquests caused the migration— usually southward—of tribes unwilling to lose their independence and accept Merina rule.

During the middle and late nineteenth century, a number of French-speaking settlers came to Madagascar, where they installed themselves as planters or traders. These settlers, many of whom were from Réunion Island and some from Mauritius, developed export crops and a money economy which further stimulated Malagasy migrations. Then the French conquest also indirectly promoted migratory movements, because order was imposed throughout the island under a single administration and roads and railroads were built. Moreover, with the instituting of forced labor and the payment of taxes in money, Malagasys were compelled either to grow cash crops or to earn wages as laborers. To escape these servitudes, some of them took refuge in remote places, thus adding another element of mobility to the population. In time the medical care provided by the French and the enforcement of sanitary regulations led to population increases, and in impoverished regions this forced the younger and more enterprising members of tribes to emigrate.

Two main currents of population movements resulted from these developments. One, emanating from the plateaus of the center and north, was a movement of expansion on the part of the rapidly increasing Betsileo, Bara, and Tsimihety, who gradually colonized the vast, underpopulated plains of the west and northwest coastal regions. The other was more in the nature of temporary and seasonal migrations, which concerned chiefly the Antaisaka, Antandroy, Antanosy, and Antaimoro from the impoverished and arid south, who went north and east to work on the plantations or mines as laborers. Reportedly, about 40 per cent of the Antaisaka and 30 per cent of the Antandroy—totaling perhaps 2,000 a year—migrated permanently, but almost all of them sent back cash remittances, which helped to sustain their families at home. Thousands of Merina also fell into the category of migrants, but they left the high plateaus only with the greatest reluctance and usually went as civil servants to provincial towns. Over the past 50 years internal migrations have profoundly altered the ethnic map of Madagascar. By 1957 some 12 per cent of the Malagasys lived outside the areas in which they were born, and only the high plateaus and Tamatave province had populations that were predominantly indigenous. In some places the indigenous and immigrant peoples merged, but more often they lived juxtaposed as separate ethnic groups.

A marked taste for travel, the desire to escape from traditional authority, and the need to earn money have made the Malagasys in general a nation of nomads, but there are also counteracting forces which have kept them at home or have caused them to return there as often as possible. The family tomb and rice field, as well as the cohesiveness and conformism of Malagasy society, are magnets which irresistibly draw migrants back, and these same forces tend to make permanent emigration acceptable only in terms of a tribal expansion that involves the displacement of whole family units.

Mobility as a way of life has had both advantages and disadvantages for the island. On the credit side it has helped to develop many neglected or uninhabited regions to such effect that, according to Deschamps, "three-fourths of Madagascar owes its economic life to internal migration." It has swelled the tonnage of export commodities and introduced new agricultural techniques which have augmented the island's productivity, and has also brought modern concepts and ways of life to tribes never before in touch with the outside world. Furthermore, it has helped to solve the problem of overpopulation in famine areas. Because most of the migrants go to rural regions, they have not appreciably contributed to the growth of an urban proletariat, except perhaps in Tananarive. On the debit side, this nomadic trend has made for an unstable labor force. The frequency with which migrants leave their jobs without notice to return home, as a rule simply to attend a family celebration and sometimes for considerable periods of time, is disconcerting to employers and harmful to production. It is believed that some 2 million Malagasys each year travel on the railroad and 100,000 more by road or track, and that the result of these intensive population movements is the loss of several million workdays annually.[2]

The Demographic Situation

When attempts were made during the early years of French rule to estimate Madagascar's population, the pendulum swung back and forth between an optimism and a pessimism that were equally unjustified by facts. European observers at that period, assuming that the whole island was as densely populated as Imerina, believed that it was the home of teeming millions. After longer acquaintance, however, it was learned that large areas of the north and south were underpopulated and that the west was almost uninhabited. This caused the French to revise their earlier ideas and to jump to the conclusion that the Malagasys were a dying race, afflicted by a sense of drift and despair that was annihilating their will to live.[3] At the time of the conquest, some French officers estimated the population of Imerina at 782,000, and for the rest of the island their guesses ranged all the way from 2 million to 7 million. The first census based on the number of taxpayers, taken in 1900, gave a figure of 2.5 million, but the large-scale displacements resulting from the liberation of slaves and the revolt of the *fahavalo* necessarily made this an approximation, especially in regard to regional variations. More factual information was available about the non-Malagasy population, which grew considerably under Gallieni's governorship. As of 1905 it was estimated to total about 16,000, of whom 7,800 were French (slightly more than half of whom came from Réunion Island), 1,000 Mauritians, 2,800 Indians, 450 Chinese, 67 Arabs, and 3,500 Africans.

Not until after World War I were the census figures reliable, and those of 1921 gave a total population for Madagascar of 3,363,700 persons. This total was indeed very small for an island the size of Madagascar, but it was proportionately no smaller than the population totals of the French West African countries at that time. Internal migrations and some natural growth had brought about changes since the turn of the century, but the pattern of population concentration on the high plateaus and to a lesser extent on the east coast, with voids in the west, south, and north, remained essentially the same. Towns were either administrative centers or markets, and the urban component was still slight. Clearly the great majority of Malagasys lived as farmers and herders, as their ancestors had done, in scattered villages situated mostly in the fertile, well-watered lowlands and valleys. The non-Malagasy element was becoming larger with the development of a modern economy and administration: Europeans occupied the top posts in the government and in business, whereas the Asians had captured much of the retail trade and in some places were landowners as well.

During the interwar period the total population—according to censuses that were then being taken every five years—was growing at the rate of only 1 per cent, and some tribes were actually declining in size. An epidemic of plague in the mid-1920s caused ravages, especially on the relatively populous high plateaus, but Madagascar's retarded population growth was chiefly traceable to the heavy mortality rate, especially in young children, and that due to the prevalence of malaria, tuberculosis, and venereal diseases. The authorities began to despair of ever developing the island through the natural growth of its indigenous population, and toyed with the idea of bringing in more settlers from Réunion Island and laborers from the Comoro Islands. There was no question then of increasing the number of resident Asians, for the dangers or inconveniences of unrestricted Indian immigration were clear for all to see in nearby Mauritius. The solution envisaged was a wholly French administrative one, and consisted of encouraging an influx that already was spontaneous and increasing. The fact that neither the Comorians nor the Réunionese were liked by the Malagasys seems not to have been considered seriously, and two missions—in 1946 and 1950—were sent from France to study the details involved in possible mass transfers. From the pen of Louis Chevalier, a member of the Delavignette mission in 1950, came the best postwar study of Madagascar's populations;[4] it pointed out the risks of mass immigration to Madagascar in its existing state of underdevelopment.

Chevalier's warnings coincided with the early stages of a sudden spectacular increase of the indigenous population in Madagascar. During the decade from January 1, 1950, to January 1, 1960, the island's population increased at the rate of 2.3 per cent a year, the total rising from 4,207,000 to 5,298,000. Since then it has been growing at the same pace or even faster. An estimate made in 1962[5] gave a total of 5,536,243 Malagasys and 121,358 aliens on the island. Of the foreign residents, the Asians had become more numerous and the Europeans had declined slightly in number since independence. Inevitably the overall population growth has not been spread evenly throughout Madagascar with respect to either tribes or regions, some of which are now overpopulated to the extent that their inhabitants are reduced to very low living standards. The average density for all Madagascar is 9.5 persons per square kilometer; some areas are still uninhabited, whereas others—such as the islands of Nossi-Bé and Ste.-Marie—have a density of 50 per square kilometer. According to provinces, the density ranges from 4 per square kilometer in Majunga to 22 in Tananarive; on the island as a whole, 60 per cent of its inhabitants are concentrated in 20 per cent of the total area.

The sudden spurt in Madagascar's population from about 1949 on can be ascribed, in part, to a rise in local living standards but primarily to the larger funds allocated to the public-health service. It was due more to a decline in the death rate than to a rise in the birthrate, although this too had occurred. Endemic diseases, formerly devastating in effect, had been largely eliminated. Malaria, for example, which previously had caused 30 per cent of all deaths in Madagascar, by 1957 was the cause of only 16 per cent. Much more could be done to reduce infant mortality, but that also had declined. In 1962 it was calculated that more than 42 per cent of the population were then under 15 years of age and that only 3.2 per cent were over 65. Thus the nonactive element is not greatly outnumbered by the active population, which means that the latter must bear a considerable burden of support. A sharp drop in the 15–19 age group is explained by the high death rate resulting from shortages in medicine and clothing during World War II. For a few years this may hamper growth of the population, but by 1975 it is expected to total about 8 million.

Tribal Groups

Waves of immigration, continuous internal migrations, and domination of most of the island's population by the Merina have eventuated in the Malagasys' sharing of a common culture but not in the complete obliteration of tribal distinctions between peoples of diverse origins and multiple crossbreedings. Nowhere in Madagascar does there exist a pure racial type, and even the broad classification of the coastal peoples as Negroid and of the inhabitants of the high plateaus as Asian is misleading. Intermingling has taken place to such an extent that authorities differ as to how many distinct tribes actually exist among the Malagasys, the smallest number cited being 13 and the largest 20. Since the French conquest, profound changes have occurred in the size, locale, and way of life of the 17 tribes described below, in order of numerical importance. The population figures indicated are estimates made early in 1959, and should by now be appreciably larger.

Merina (1,248,531). This is the largest and most evolved of all the Malagasy tribes. Most of the Merina live in Tananarive province, but nearly 200,000 are now permanent or transient residents of other parts of the island. Rural Merina are competent rice farmers, and the elite supply the majority of the island's administrators and intellectuals. The latter group has assimilated French culture without losing its cultural identity, which seems to be of predominantly Indonesian origin. Memories of past glories under the Merina monarchs have been both an inspiration and a handicap to the present generation of this tribe. On the whole, remarkable individual achievements have been more than offset by a collective sense of frustration, first under the rule of the French and then under that of the coastal peoples. Aloofness characterizes the relationships not only between Merina and other tribes but also between the different castes into which Merina society remains divided.

Betsimisaraka (773,104). Spread out along the east coast from the Bemarivo River in the north to Mananjary in the south, the Betsimisaraka are the dominant tribe in the port city of Tamatave. Members of this tribe formerly ventured as far afield as the Comoro Islands. Although they seemed to have accepted alien rule, they did participate in the 1947 revolt. Nevertheless, because of their long contact with Europeans and their integration into a modern economy based on the cultivation of industrial crops, their outlook and social habits have changed. Betsimisaraka men work in Tamatave province's graphite mines and plantations, and some of them have grown wealthy as a result of the profitable sale of coffee, vanilla, and cloves.

Betsileo (637,611). Like the Merina, to whom they are culturally akin, the Betsileo probably are mainly of Indonesian descent, and they are even more skilled and industrious as rice farmers and craftsmen. Less able as warriors and administrators, they perforce accepted rule by the Merina monarchs, who treated them with more favor, however, than other subject tribes. In recent years some 130,000 Betsileo have emigrated from their native lands in Fianarantsoa province to colonize the valleys of the west coast and, to a lesser extent, the south coast.

Tsimehety (363,897). The 40 clans that make up the Tsimehety tribe are not ethnically homogeneous, but they have developed a strong family organization. Among the most robust and prolific elements of the Malagasy population, Tsimehety rice farmers and cattle herders are spreading out from their home north of the high plateaus throughout much of Majunga and Diégo-Suarez provinces. The Tsimehety, who are proud of their tribal record of having successfully resisted conquest by the Merina, continue to be independent-minded. They are hard-working but, except as sharecroppers, resist being tied down by contracts. Mobile, industrious, and adaptable, they are in the process of colonizing much of the northwest.

Sakalava (316,212). Inhabiting the west coast from Nossi-Bé to Tuléar, the predominantly rural Sakalava form a confederation of semi-independent clans which comprise some converts to Islam. Among the best-known Sakalava clans are the Masikoro, in the hinterland, and the Vezo, who fish along the coast near Tuléar. From the strong Sakalava kingdoms that flourished on the west coast before the Merina conquest derives the reverence for authority and custom that characterize present-day Sakalava, who are of a somewhat melancholy mien. Decimated by disease and addicted to intoxicating drinks, the Sakalava were long regarded as a race doomed to extinction, but in recent years this trend has been reversed. They are as yet unable, however, to resist being somewhat submerged by more enterprising immigrants who are taking over the fertile valleys in the west and leaving to the Sakalava only the pasturelands.

Antaisaka (302,354). Of diverse origins, this tribe has a rigidly cohesive organization which enforces conformity to custom, and particularly to a fanatical and economically ruinous cult of the dead. Partly to escape from oppressive authority and partly because of the tribe's very rapid population growth, many of its young men leave their homeland, whose center is Vangaindrano, to become either permanent expatriates or seasonal laborers on the plantations of the north and west. The cohesion of the patriarchal family among the Antaisaka is so strong, however, that its emigrants send back money to their relatives, whose other source of cash income is the sale of coffee.

Antandroy (277,144). For many years the authorities have been trying with little success to combat the prolonged droughts and the locust invasions that have caused periodic famines in the home territory of the Antandroy, which is the thornbush country between the Mandrare and Menarandra rivers. It is understandable, therefore, that this tribe is the chief source of migrant seasonal labor in Madagascar, despite the passionate attachment of the Antandroy to their cattle and to the arid land of the extreme south, which they defended successfully against Merina domination. Industrious but intractable, the Antandroy were long regarded as the most backward of all the Malagasy tribes, but in recent years better educational facilities and the new ideas brought back by seasonal emigrants have begun to change their way of life.

Tanala (215,639). The home of this highly mobile tribe is in the forest that lies between the zone of the Betsileo to the north and that of the Betsimisaraka to the southeast. Lacking a strong tribal structure, the Tanala were helpless to resist either the Merina or the French conquerors, but rebelled periodically against both. More than any other single tribe they participated in the 1947 revolt and were victims of it, and only now are they beginning to recover from the devastation it caused. The Tanala are skilled hunters and woodsmen. To some degree they engage in a shifting type of agriculture so destructive of the forest that the administration has tried, forcefully but ineffectually, to teach them better agricultural methods and the cultivation of export crops.

Bara (215,026). These seminomadic herders, whose habitat is on the low plateaus of south-central Madagascar, are perhaps of Melanesian origin. Their warlike tendencies find an outlet in cattle thefts, and only with the greatest reluctance do some of them take up farming. Emigration to the western plateaus has been necessitated by the high birthrate, and it is eroding their traditionally rigid social structure.

Antaimoro (178,215). Centered around Vohipeno, the Antaimoro are set apart from their neighbors by their descent from early Arab settlers and their Islamic customs and beliefs. They write the Malagasy language in Arabic script, using paper and ink made from local materials. Throughout Madagascar, Antaimoro sorcerers are renowned for the amulets they sell, which are an appreciable source of income for the tribe. Coffee-growing, too, has made some members of this tribe wealthy. The poorer Antaimoro, however, emigrate to the west and northwest of the island.

Antanosy (148,132). Islamic influences have been felt less strongly by this predominantly Negro tribe than by the Antaimoro. To escape Merina domination in the nineteenth century, the Antanosy moved south, and now inhabit mainly the districts of Betioky and Fort-Dauphin. Some members of this tribe work as laborers on European plantations.

Sihanaka (107,133). A hybrid tribe of rice farmers, cattle herders, and fishermen, the Sihanaka resisted but finally bowed to Merina and later French rule. They now occupy the basin of Lake Alaotra, which they are in part responsible for making one of the most productive regions of Madagascar.

Mahafaly (78,398). This pastoral tribe is related to the Antandroy. Like them, its members live in the far south, where they herd goats and cattle between the Onilahy and Menarandra rivers. Until they were conquered by the French, they were ruled by their own kings. Their distinctive type of family tomb (adorned with unique carved-wood posts called *aloalo*) constitutes an interesting element of the folk art of Madagascar. The mohair rugs which they have learned to weave and the wages they earn by working on nearby sisal plantations are providing new sources of income in addition to that represented by their traditional occupation of cattle herding. The Mahafaly live in one of the regions of the island least favored by nature.

Makoa (58,934). A Negroid tribe, the Makoa are descendants of African slaves, most of whom were brought to Madagascar from Mozambique in the nineteenth century. Although a few Makoa have intermarried with Tsimehety who have wandered far south of their usual home, the majority tend to remain aloof from other tribes and to live in a fairly compact group in the neighborhood of the Onilahy River.

Antankarana (35,556). This tribe is a mixture of Sakalava, Betsimisaraka, and Arab. Some of its members managed to escape Merina domination and emigrated to the west among the Sakalava, where they became Muslims. Those who stayed in the northeast accepted Merina rule and were not converted to Islam. The Antankarana engage in various occupations—in cattle herding and plantation farming and as factory workers in Diégo-Suarez and Vohémar.

Bezanozano (32,540). Related to the Sihanaka and Betsimisaraka, the Bezanozano live on the edge of the forest zone in the Mangoro River valley. Because they lacked a strong tribal organization they were easily conquered by the Merina, but their individualism makes them prone to revolt against authority. Members of this tribe do a little rice farming, but most of them are herders and woodsmen.

Antaifasy (28,453). The home area of this tribe is the vicinity of Farafangana, but many of its members emigrate as laborers to the north and northeast parts of the island. Their ancestors are believed to have come to southeastern Madagascar from Africa by way of the west coast, and they kept their independence until the French conquest.

Alien Minorities*

As of January 1, 1962, Madagascar's foreign residents included 51,865 French nationals. Of these, the Frenchmen born in France were the most numerous, prosperous, and transient, whereas those who came from Réunion were more permanent settlers, poorer, and more disliked by the Malagasys. The rest of the Occidental community was made up of small numbers of British, Swiss, Americans, Norwegians, Belgians, Portuguese, and some 400 Greeks. Among the nonwhites, the 40,377 Comorians were the largest group; then came 13,233 Indians, 8,901 Chinese, and 6,000-odd Arabs, Asians, and Africans. All of the Afro-Asians performed functions useful in

* With regard to Metropolitan French residents in Madagascar, see pp. 63–64.

the economic activity of Madagascar, and most of them were in fields in which the Malagasys were unable or unwilling to compete. None of that group, however, was or is truly welcome in Madagascar, for they are widely believed to have prospered at the expense of the native population and to be the forerunners of invading hordes of their compatriots.

Today in Madagascar the nonwhite alien elements form only a very small minority, both collectively and as individual ethnic groups, although they are very prolific and their numbers are mounting also because of clandestine immigration. It is extremely easy for small boats to land immigrants at many places along Madagascar's long and unguarded coastline,[6] but as yet no evidence has come to light that such landings have reached large proportions. What worries the Malagasy government considerably is its inability to control a situation that could easily get out of hand should the governments of India and China decide that Madagascar's uninhabited regions could serve as a suitable outlet for their ever-larger surplus populations. Already the Indians, the Chinese, and, to a lesser extent, the Comorians—relatively small as these minorities are—have created economic, social, and to some extent political problems with which independent Madagascar has not been able to cope. Its leaders feel that their hope lies in a policy of severely restricting immigration and the bestowal of Malagasy citizenship, and of expelling those foreigners who refuse to adapt themselves to Malagasy laws and the Malagasy way of life.

By strict application of appropriate legislation, the Malagasy government might conceivably be able to impose its will on aliens in the economic domain, where thus far they have often been able to avoid control; but to compel them to adopt wholeheartedly the Malagasy viewpoint and culture would be far more difficult, if not impossible. Almost all of Madagascar's aliens, particularly the Asians, are culturally unassimilated, albeit to varying degrees. The existence of 300,000 half-castes in Madagascar indicates the extent of cohabiting of Europeans, Indians, and Chinese with Malagasy women.[7] Since alien women immigrants began coming in, however, the minority groups have been living to an increasing extent culturally and socially apart. All of them have imported their own priests and teachers, and they cling to their traditional dress, language, and religion. Such acculturation as has occurred in the younger generation of Asians is in the direction of greater occidentalization, not of "Malagasization."

Since independence, more Europeans have left Madagascar than have come to it, but the number of Asian aliens has increased, as have their requests for Malagasy citizenship. A large proportion of the latter are the same individuals who previously sought and obtained French citizenship—and apparently for the same self-interested motives. Malagasy resentment of such moves was brought out in an impassioned debate on the country's nationality code, which took place in the assembly on June 21 and 29, 1961. All speakers at those sessions insisted that the privilege of Malagasy nationality should not be debased by being made too easy and accessible to aliens and half-castes whose loyalty to sovereign Madagascar was known to be dubious. Many deputies argued that Malagasy women should be forbidden by law to marry foreigners, and one went so far as to say that "we must eliminate everything that is non-Malagasy, for the political independence that we have acquired is but the means for 're-Malagasizing' our people." The government, for its part, has not gone further than to discreetly ask a few dozen "undesirable" foreigners to leave the island. That the Malagasy leaders may not always show such restraint, however, was indicated in a warning to alien residents by Tsiranana during a press conference on July 30, 1960: "Foreigners who are law-abiding will always be well treated by us, but do not be surprised if tomorrow we expel [other types of] foreigners. We want them to be assimilated and to speak our language, and only if they do so will we grant them Malagasy nationality."

The Réunionese. Immigrants from Réunion Island began coming to Madagascar long before the French conquest, and in the 1890s their spokesmen were among the most ardent advocates of France's annexation of the great island. At that time they regarded Madagascar as a potential dependency of Réunion and a logical field for their enterprise and expansion. After the conquest, many Réunionese soldiers demobilized from the French army settled in Madagascar, and more were attracted there when Diégo-Suarez became a French naval base. When the railroad from Tamatave to Tananarive was completed, the Réunionese began to infiltrate the high plateaus. Madagascar seemed a land of opportunity, and the number of Réunionese immigrants grew at a particularly rapid pace after World War II. In 1921 they numbered 5,420, and by 1954, 23,960.

During the first years of French rule in Madagascar, the Réunionese as French citizens were able to play an important role; and although most of them had never set foot in France, they claimed to speak in the name of the mother country. They soon became unpopular with the Metropolitan French residents in Madagascar and with the Malagasys, and the Réunionese heartily disliked both groups in return. Many of the Réunionese were of mixed blood, spoke French badly, and had almost no education. Lacking skills and capital, they became—with a few brilliant exceptions—small-scale planters on the east coast or occupied subordinate positions in the administration or in private enterprises. As planters they were dependent on Malagasy labor, but they generally abused the requisition system, underpaid their workers, and treated the Malagasys as an inferior and primitive people.

Indeed, the hostility that the Réunionese inspired in the Malagasys was shown clearly in 1947, when the former became both a major cause of the revolt and its main European victims.

Despite the unpopularity of the Réunionese in Madagascar, the Paris government persisted in linking its Indian Ocean dependencies together in various projects. A Comité de Collaboration was formed for the purpose of studying problems common to Madagascar and Réunion, and it even included Mauritius because the Mauritians were French-speaking, although their government was British. By the time World War II ended, Réunion's increasing overpopulation had made it economically dependent on Madagascar, and to a much lesser degree this was also true of Mauritius. Not only was Madagascar no longer an annex of Réunion, but the latter depended for its food on Malagasy rice and meat and was also meeting with serious competition from Madagascar's growing sugar production. It was to help solve Réunion's overpopulation problem that an experiment was undertaken in the 1950s at Sakay, where some hundreds of Réunionese farmers were installed, with their families, as colonists.* Although the undertaking was a technical success, it also proved to be far too expensive for the French government to finance on a larger scale. Moreover, it coincided with an upsurge of both the Malagasy population and Malagasy nationalism, and because of the persistent antagonism between Malagasys and Réunionese this experiment might easily have entailed political risks.

When Madagascar gained its independence in 1960, the more farsighted Réunionese settlers on the island realized that they must either adapt themselves to a government run by and for the Malagasys or leave. Many of them have stayed on, but a surprisingly large number availed themselves of the offer made by the French government to repatriate its nationals to France. Since Réunion was an overseas department of France, the Réunionese were entitled to free passage to the "mother country," and they hoped that the opportunities for a fresh start in life there would more than offset the difficulties they would encounter in adjusting to a very different way of living and climate.

The Greeks. Of the non-French European groups living in Madagascar, the Greeks are numerically the most important, even though they totaled only slightly more than 400 in 1962. In the manner and timing of their immigration to Madagascar and in their occupations—but not in the areas where they live—the Greeks resemble the Chinese more than any other alien resident group.

During the Merina monarchy a few Greek sailors visited the shores of

* See p. 334.

Madagascar, but it was not until after the French conquest that Greeks arrived in any number. The first wave of immigrants, which was of short duration, took place after the gold deposits of Andavakoera were discovered, and the second occurred when the railroad from Tananarive to Antsirabe was built.[8] Some 250 to 300 Greeks who had helped build the French railway from Djibouti to Addis Ababa came to Madagascar for a similar purpose. Many left the island after the work was completed, but perhaps half of them remained in Madagascar, settling either on the west coast or on the high plateaus. The Greek colonies at Majunga, Tananarive, and Itasy are close-knit communities, with their orthodox churches, mutual-aid societies, and observation of Greek customs. Although they do not marry outside their own community, they are not clannish like the Indians but so sociable that they serve as a kind of bridge between the European and Malagasy groups. Like the Chinese, the Greeks engage in a wide range of occupations. They start modestly as planters, restaurant-keepers, grocers, and, above all, traders, and some have acquired fortunes and prestige.*

The Yemenese. As long ago as 1904, shipping companies brought Yemenese Arabs to Madagascar as dock workers because they found the Malagasys unsuited to such labor. Capable and industrious, the Yemenese were considered well worth the expense of transporting them to and from Arabia, and they were sufficiently well paid so that they developed a tradition of going to work in Madagascar. Reportedly, nearly three-fourths of those who had served one contract term there renewed their contracts after a trip home.[9] While in Madagascar they keep in close touch with their families in Yemen and send home a large part of their wages. Their employers have built special camps and even mosques for them, and in the mid-1950s there were about 200 Yemenese contract workers stationed at Diégo-Suarez, 200 at Majunga, 120 at Nossi-Bé, and 160 at Tamatave. These workers do not meddle in local politics, or join local labor unions, or mingle with the Malagasys.

Aside from the workers under contract, about 1,000 Yemenese have settled in Madagascar, mainly at Majunga and Diégo-Suarez, where some of them are market-gardeners or merchants. Small as is the whole Yemenese community, the authorities have no wish to see the number of permanent settlers from Yemen increase. As transient dock workers the Yemenese have been very satisfactory, but as permanent residents they have often abandoned manual labor in favor of trading, smuggling, or idling. Left to themselves, the Yemenese have tended to live on the fringe of lawlessness, drifting from

---

* Senator Emile Mitsakis is a son of the founder of the firm Mitsakis Frères, and among Tananarive's outstanding businessmen are the Greeks Zelon, Athanase, and André Mellis and the four Cotsoyannis brothers.

one job to another and sometimes quarreling violently among themselves.

The Comorians. Because the Comoro Islands were administratively attached to Madagascar for 34 years (1912–46), the French came to think of the Comorians as indigenous to Madagascar, and on occasion even referred to them as one of that island's tribes. But from every other standpoint— ethnic, linguistic, and religious—the Comorians differ radically from the Malagasys. They are mainly of Arab descent, speak Swahili, and are strict Muslims. All are Sunni Muslims and adhere to the Sufi doctrine, and as of 1953 more than half of those living in Madagascar belonged to Muslim brotherhoods, of which the most important were the Chaduha, Qadriya, Riffay, and El Allaoui.[10] Each year the French government financed a trip to Mecca for one Comorian, who was chosen either for his outstanding piety or for the services that he had rendered to the administration.

In Madagascar the Comorian minority for many years presented no special problem, for it was of small proportions and its members seemed indifferent to Pan-Arabic and Pan-Islamic movements. In 1905 there were not more than 1,000 Comorians in all Madagascar, but by 1921 they numbered 6,300, and by 1934, 14,000. Their immigration increased greatly after a series of severe cyclones, from 1949 to 1951, had destroyed food crops on the Comoro Islands. Furthermore, improvements in the health service of those islands were so effective in reducing the mortality rate that the Comorians began to suffer from overpopulation, particularly on the islands of Grande Comore and Anjouan, where the population density was 130 per square kilometer. Some went to Zanzibar, others to Tanganyika, but the majority of the emigrants preferred Madagascar's west coast, with which communication by sea was easy and rapid. Throughout the 1950s, Comorian migration to Madagascar went on at the rate of 1,000 to 1,500 a year and was determined largely by economic conditions in the home islands.[11] Many of the Comorians in Madagascar are there as temporary laborers, but the immigration of their women in increasing numbers has added considerably to the permanently installed element. As of 1959 about 16 per cent of the Comorians living in Madagascar had been born there. By 1962 the Comorian population totaled 40,377, and was spreading from the west and north over the entire island.

Majunga and Diégo-Suarez provinces have long been the main centers of Comorian concentration, for they have vast empty spaces and the local population has been receptive to Islamic immigrants to the point of some intermarriage.[12] More than 18,000 Comorian immigrants live in Majunga province and nearly 14,000 in Diégo-Suarez province. They are predominantly town dwellers; more Comorians reside in the capital city of Majunga than in any town on the Comoro Islands, and in Diégo-Suarez province they also are to be found mainly in the principal city, although quite a number work for SOSUMAV.* Lacking special skills, the immigrant Comorians are employed as servants, retail traders, fishermen, and agricultural laborers, and they form an unstable proletariat of small-scale wage earners. As colonists and workmen in the underpopulated west-coast regions they were not unwelcome under French rule, and such disturbances as they occasionally were involved in were confined to their own community and usually occurred during sports events.

The burgeoning of Malagasy nationalism in the post–World War II period injected a new element into the picture, and one that is of increasing importance. In 1946 a fight broke out in Tamatave between recently demobilized Malagasy soldiers who had just returned from France and some Comorian residents, during which 14 Comorians were massacred while at prayer in the local mosque.[13] The recruitment of Comorians as policemen in Madagascar before and especially during the 1947 revolt exacerbated the feelings of Malagasy nationalists, who accused the Comorians of brutality. During the 1950s the overall increase in Comorian immigration and the marked growth in the number of Comorians living in Tananarive, Tuléar, and Tamatave further contributed to the deterioration of relations between the two communities, although they did not become dangerously tense. Indeed, in 1957 Madagascar's assemblymen gallantly agreed to continue paying the pension of the former Queen of Mohéli (the smallest island of the Comoro group), even though some of them expressed the opinion that it was high time for the Comoro Islands to assume that burden.[14]

Since independence and the adoption of a nationality code, the Malagasy government is showing its determination to restrict the immigration of all foreigners, and, as the largest and fastest-growing immigrant community, the Comorians are bound to be more affected by this policy than any other alien group. Moreover, the Comorians in Madagascar, as is the case with their compatriots in Zanzibar and Dar-es-Salaam, have yielded to the temptation to dabble in local politics. Although some have joined the P.S.D., others have been less perspicacious; late in 1961 about 20 Comorians were expelled from the island for having participated in opposition movements.[15] The rapid population growth in both the Comoro Islands and Madagascar, as well as the intensification of nationalist susceptibilities, will doubtless lead the Malagasy government to curtail the influx of Comorian immigrants and perhaps also the activities of the resident Comorian community.

The Chinese. In 1862 the first Chinese shop in Madagascar was opened at Tamatave by a Cantonese, who later married a Malagasy woman and

* See pp. 360–61.

fathered the first Sino-Malagasy half-castes on the island. It was not until 1897, however, that Chinese began to appear in Madagascar in large numbers. That year Gallieni brought in some 3,000 Chinese from North Vietnam to work on the Tananarive–Tamatave railroad. During its construction many of these coolies died, most of them from malaria, but some stayed on in Madagascar as small-scale merchants on the east coast. A larger number returned to the Far East with their savings, and the one Malagasy woman whom they took back with them is said to have been the object of such ridicule in China that she was repatriated to Madagascar at the expense of the French government.[16]

By the time Gallieni left Madagascar, in 1905, there were slightly more than 400 Chinese living on the island. Their number grew slowly by natural increase and more rapidly by successive waves of immigrants who arrived after each upheaval in China. Thus the local Chinese colony was enlarged after the split in the Kuomintang in the late 1920s, the Sino-Japanese war in the 1930s, and the communist take-over of mainland China in 1949, especially the last mentioned, which resulted also in the closing of the consulate of the Republic of China that had been installed at Tananarive in 1946. Since 1949 the ties between the Chinese in Madagascar and their home country have weakened. Although there is at least one school at Tamatave—the Ecole Chinoise Mixte—that is sponsored by pro-Peking Chinese, the majority of the Chinese residents in Madagascar appear to be anti-communist, even if not wholeheartedly devoted to the Nationalist Chinese cause. Chiang's picture hangs in many Chinese homes on the island, a handful of Chinese from Madagascar have gone to study in Taiwan—perhaps 30 altogether in the years 1956 to 1959—and at the time of the "Double Ten" celebration the flag of Nationalist China is usually flown by the local Chinese. Nevertheless, the enthusiasm they feel for the Taipeh regime seems to be only lukewarm. As time goes on, external evidences of their distinctively Chinese traditions become progressively fewer—no Chinese pagodas exist on the island, and even the Chinese women are increasingly adopting Western-style clothing. Chinese culture is kept alive, however, in the Chinese communal schools, the first of which was built in 1938 by adherents of the Kuomintang. Today there are a dozen or more such schools, the most modern and best-equipped of them being in Tamatave and Tananarive.

Under the French administration, Chinese immigration was restricted and the Chinese minority was closely controlled. Each Chinese was required to belong to what was called a congregation, the same type of organization as was imposed on the Indians and one that had first been developed for the Chinese community in Indochina. Membership in a congregation was theoretically based on the individual's province of origin in China, but in practice this was modified by family and clan connections, business friend-ships, and various rivalries. The members of a congregation annually elected their chief, who became the intermediary between the administration and the congregation as a unit, and he was made responsible for the collection of taxes and fines, the maintenance of order, and the management of the collectively owned property of its members. From the French viewpoint the congregation was a simple, inexpensive, and effective form of administra-tion, and it pleased the Chinese too because they always preferred to manage their own affairs with a minimum of official interference. On the whole, the Chinese in Madagascar were an orderly community, generous in supporting charitable works and always ready to oblige the administration by display-ing French flags on holidays and ordering their children to line the streets to welcome distinguished official guests. An unknown number of Chinese became French citizens, some embraced Catholicism, and some took French names to which they gave a Chinese pronunciation. (Thus Hélène became Hi-Lene, and Michel, Mi-Seng.) They adapted to French rule without losing their cultural identity, which they maintained through observing tra-ditional customs and sending their children to Chinese schools.

From the outset the Chinese were on friendly terms with the Malagasys, and intermarriage was fairly frequent. Most of the nearly 9,000 Chinese have settled on the east coast, in both urban and rural areas. By 1955 six towns had 200 or more Chinese residents each—Tamatave, Fénérive, Vato-mandry, Sambava, Diégo-Suarez, and Tananarive. In those centers they monopolize the retail trade in food to such an extent that when housewives say they are going "chez le Chinois" it means that they are going to the grocery store. In the most remote villages it is a Chinese who has opened a shop and has gone about collecting local produce for export, either on his own account or for one of the big export-import firms, and he is almost the only source of loans for hard-pressed farmers. These Chinese exact a high price for their services, but they are an important element in the local economy. Industrious, frugal, adaptable, and obliging, they perform tasks that the Malagasys do not or will not undertake, and they do not isolate themselves from their Malagasy neighbors either by their attitude or by appreciably higher living standards.

Since independence the Malagasy government—particularly President Tsiranana—has become somewhat suspicious of the political activities of the local Chinese, and Tsiranana has also been cultivating close relations with the Taiwan regime. At a press conference at Tananarive on July 30, 1960, he warned members of the Chinese community against secretly subsidizing certain extremist movements, but he offered no evidence that they had already done so. Apparently it is Tsiranana's obsession with the threat of communism in general and the Yellow Peril in particular that lies behind such fears, rather than specific instances of subversion on the part of the Chinese in Madagascar. It is virtually impossible for outsiders to know what is actually going on inside a Chinese community, but on the surface at least there seems to be little change in the traditional Chinese preoccupation with making money. The local Chinese who are under 50 years of age, and especially the ever-larger percentage of them who were born in Madagascar—of whom about half are now children—give every sign of regarding the island as their home. More and more Chinese are attending Madagascar's French schools and acquiring an education that enables them to take up professional careers rather than go into trade. In this respect they are not yet competitive with the educated Malagasys, and on the whole the Chinese are the aliens least unpopular with the indigenous population.

The Indians.[17] Indians began coming to Madagascar early in the nineteenth century, most of them indirectly by way of the east coast of Africa. For many years they were concentrated on the island's west coast, especially in and around Majunga, but like the Chinese they also settled as traders, moneylenders, and collectors of agricultural produce in the small hinterland villages. As they acquired financial security they brought their families and friends to Madagascar and began to spread northward and onto the high plateaus. As of 1905 there were fewer than 3,000 Indians in all the island, and between 1910 and 1935, Indian immigrants averaged about 200 a year. By early 1962 they totaled 13,233, the considerable growth this represented being due mainly to natural increase, for their immigration was subject to strict controls. Fewer than 1,000 of the Madagascar Indians are Hindus, and they are not only far less numerous but much less wealthy than the majority, who are Shiite Muslims from Bombay province or Pakistan. Another Indian group, which is neither Hindu nor Muslim, consists of the Ismaeli, who owe allegiance to the Aga Khan and pay heavy tribute to him.[18]

On an economic basis the Indian Muslims in Madagascar can be divided into four main groups, of which the largest (about 4,300) and the most prosperous is made up of the Bohora. Predominantly traders, the Bohora are also industrialists and plantation owners, and they are to be found throughout the island. They are strict Muslims, and many of them have been able to make the pilgrimage to Mecca. Their contributions have made possible the building of some 20 mosques in Madagascar. The mosque in Majunga also houses a Koranic school, in which Arabic and Gujerati are taught.

Almost as powerful economically as the Bohora, but fewer in number and less ardent Muslims, are the Khodja. They came to Madagascar from East Africa after the French occupation, and live mainly in Majunga, Marovoay,

Morondava, Morombe, and Tuléar. Most of them have become wealthy traders, competing successfully with the biggest French export-import firms on the west coast. About one-fifth of the Khodja have acquired French nationality, allegedly for the purpose of defending their economic interests as a group. Culturally, too, they are the most occidentalized Indians in Madagascar, and have retained the fewest ties with India. Although they continue to speak Gujerati among themselves, the younger generation attend Western-type schools, speak good French, and some—even a few women—wear European dress.

The Ismaeli, about 2,500 in all, scattered throughout the island, are wholesale and retail traders. About the same proportion of the Ismaeli as of the Khodja have become French citizens, partly as a result of urging by Aly Khan, when he visited Madagascar in 1951, to be loyal to the country of their adoption.

Of all the Indian groups in Madagascar, the Sunni are the poorest, numerically the weakest, and the most caste-ridden. They first appeared in Majunga in the 1870s and live mainly in that province's capital city, in Tamatave, and in Tananarive, where they work as artisans and small-scale traders.

The Indians in Madagascar are economically though not numerically the most important minority, especially on the west coast, where they control much of the industry and trade, notably that in textiles. Some years ago, like the Chinese, they were useful as intermediaries to the administration and the Malagasys, but during World War II they became wealthy and branched out into new fields of activity. By devious means they brought into Madagascar large quantities of rationed goods, from the clandestine sale of which they made huge profits.[19] Later the Office des Changes was able to restrict their operations, notably in limiting the amount of remittances to India, but this had the undesirable result that they began investing heavily in local urban properties. By foreclosing mortgages of deeply indebted rural Malagasys, the Indians also acquired sizable plantations and managed to get a grip on the trade in Cape peas.* To protect Malagasy landowners from eviction by their alien creditors, the French government tried to restrict the acquisition of real property by Asians, but the Indians succeeded in getting around this law. The usual practice was for a member of an Indian family—the one least fitted physically for military service—to become a French citizen and thus to be eligible legally to own land.[20]

Aside from the fact that the methods by which the Indians acquired their substantial holdings in Madagascar have been viewed as shady by the Mala-

* See p. 357.

gasys, there are two other characteristics that have made them equally unpopular. One is their social aloofness and the other their proneness to dabble in local politics. The French had organized the Indians into congregations and generally took their social and cultural apartness for granted, and there was no desire on either side to mix socially. Moreover, the younger generation of local Indians was showing a gratifying tendency to learn the French language and adopt a more Western way of life.[21] To the sensitive Malagasys, however, the Indians' aloofness, family solidarity, and attitude of cultural superiority were, and are, unforgivable. In the assembly the Malagasys complain that the local Indians have contributed heavily to the half-caste population but that they marry only the Indian girls who are brought to Madagascar from the east coast of Africa or from India itself. By the mid-1950s the number of Indian women living in Madagascar roughly equaled that of the men, and families of eight to ten children were not uncommon. From the economic viewpoint the Chinese are quite as acquisitive and unscrupulous as the Indians, but socially they are more affable and tactful, so there is no other group of foreigners in Madagascar so heartily disliked by the Malagasys as the Indians.

After World War II, and even more after India became independent in 1947, the Madagascar Indians were more aggressive politically and flouted local regulations more openly. During the 1947 revolt some of the Indians, including their consul, were believed to be backing the rebels financially, but later evidence indicated that only a few individuals had been so involved, largely for motives of personal gain.[22] Nevertheless, the attitude of the Indians who were active in local politics was clearly anti-French. In fact, in the January 26, 1955, issue of the Malagasy-language bulletin published by the Indian consulate at Tananarive there appeared an article which, in effect, urged the Indian community to support the Malagasy nationalists. The offending sentence, which was the object of a protest from the Quai d'Orsay to the Indian ambassador in Paris, stated that "it is the duty of Indians living abroad to act in such a way as to help dependent territories obtain their autonomy."[23]

Logically such sentiments should have made the Indians popular with Malagasy nationalists, but this has not proved to be the case. The attitude of the independent Malagasy government toward the resident Indians has been one of distrust, on both political and economic grounds. Most Malagasys appear to feel that the Indians are more against Western imperialism than specifically for Malagasy nationalism. Aside from their resentment of the Indians' clannishness and refusal to be assimilated, they fear India's imperialism in the islands of the western Indian Ocean. Soon after independence the P.S.D. government reportedly asked for the recall of the Indian ambassador, who was believed to be meddling in internal Malagasy politics. Undoubtedly some local Indians have given their support to one Malagasy political party or another, but probably more with the aim of promoting their own interests than in the hope of influencing national policy. Actually, most of the few Indians who have been expelled from the island, either by the French or by the Malagasy government, have been accused not of nefarious political activities but of sharp business practices, principally in circumventing the currency regulations.

The Provinces

The division of Madagascar into five provinces in 1946 did not take into consideration the island's geographic, ethnic, or economic differences. However, the various adjustments made thereafter, notably the creation of Diégo-Suarez province ten years later, were based to some extent on such factors, and province boundaries now better reflect Madagascar's natural regions. Because of internal migrations, only three of the six provinces have populations that are predominantly indigenous. In Fianarantsoa province 99 per cent of the inhabitants were locally born, in Tananarive 98 per cent, and in Tamatave 94 per cent, whereas immigrants account for 20 per cent of the population in Tuléar, 40 per cent in Majunga, and 75 per cent in Diégo-Suarez.

Tananarive (population 1,360,000 as of January 1, 1963). This is the fastest-growing province in Madagascar, its population having risen from 822,000 in 1947 to 1,093,000 a decade later. This rapid increase has been due to the ever-greater attraction exerted on the whole country by the metropolis of Tananarive, an attraction that has intensified since Madagascar became independent. Ever since the Merina monarchs made Tananarive city their capital, it has been the chief administrative, commercial, artistic, and intellectual center of the country, as well as the hub of its communications system, and now it is also the site of the university and foreign embassies. The only other important population concentration is at Antsirabe, an attractive spa linked with Tananarive by rail and road. Merina constitute virtually all of the indigenous population of this province, and in the rural areas they specialize in rice farming. The Betsileo account for over half of the province's nonindigenous Malagasys, who number some 50,000. Also in Tananarive province live the majority of Madagascar's foreign residents, including 32,000 Frenchmen and some 6,000 Greeks, Indians, and Chinese. In 1962 nearly 19 per cent of the province's total population were urban, and the technical services of the government are making a special effort to provide enough food for the still rapidly growing population.

Fianarantsoa (1,507,000). As of 1963, Fianarantsoa was the most populous of all of Madagascar's provinces. However, its population density—13.4 per square kilometer—is less than that of Tananarive, and only 2.7 per cent of its inhabitants are town dwellers. Fianarantsoa's largest single tribe is the Betsileo (500,000), who, like the Merina, are probably of predominantly Indonesian origin. Skilled and industrious rice farmers and craftsmen, they predominate in the provincial capital and in Ambositra. To the south live the seminomadic Bara; in the regions of Vohipeno and Manakara are found the Antaimoro; the Tanala roam the forest region between the Nosivolo and Matitanana rivers; and at Manakara reside some Antandroy. The Antaisaka live in a compact group between the Mananara and Itonampy rivers, and in the region of Mananjary and Nosy-Varika there are some thousands of Antandroy, Antambahoaka, and Betsimisaraka. Immigrant Merina form the largest nonindigenous Malagasy element in the province, and are concentrated on its most fertile plains and in the towns.

Mining and industry play only a small part in the developing economy of Fianarantsoa, which is based on the cultivation of rice and coffee and on cattle husbandry. Fianarantsoa has a great diversity of soil and climatic conditions and one of the best communications networks on the island. The provincial capital is linked to the coast by a railroad, and most of its main centers are connected by roads that are fairly good, except for those between its three coastal ports. As for those ports, Farafangana was recently closed to traffic for economic reasons, and Manakara has now become more active as a coffee-shipping port than Mananjary; none of them is easily accessible to ocean shipping. Nevertheless, these ports are adjacent to the richest of the province's three natural zones—the one that produces coffee, cloves, pepper, vanilla, and mica for export. Its second most productive zone is that of the plateaus, on which are grown large tonnages of paddy, some arabica coffee, and temperate-zone vegetables and fruits, including wine grapes. The only unproductive part of the province is its cliff region, where the forest—its sole potential economic resource—is too inaccessible for commercial exploitation.

Diégo-Suarez (439,000). Justice was done belatedly to the far north of Madagascar when this neglected area was given the status of a province in 1956. Although its appreciable contributions to the island's exports and the strategic value of its great harbor had long been recognized, almost no effort had been made before that year to remedy the mutual isolation of its most productive districts or to cut a road through the mountains which separated all the northern tip of the island from the remainder of the country. In this small but rich province live nearly half a million persons, making a density of 8.7 per square kilometer. Its largest and most dynamic tribe is that of the Tsimehety, who are now overflowing their traditional habitat of Vohémar,

Sambava, and Antalaha. In the mountain range of Ankara live the Antan-akarana, the Betsimisaraka are spread all along the littoral, and the Sakalava are to be found in Ambanja district and on the island of Nossi-Bé.

Certain areas that have been described as Diégo-Suarez's "pockets of pros-perity" account for 6.4 per cent of all the peanuts sold in Madagascar, 97.4 per cent of the cocoa, 23.4 per cent of the coffee, 48.7 per cent of the manioc, 96.5 per cent of the pepper, and 98.5 per cent of the vanilla. This province, moreover, has the largest sugar mill in Madagascar and produces almost all of the salt consumed by the island's residents. Because of the sparsity of its population, and especially its urban component (10 per cent), Diégo-Suarez has been able to produce chiefly export crops rather than foodstuffs, and it could grow even greater quantities if its communications system were adequate. The port of its capital city is essentially a naval base and is not equipped to handle merchandise shipments. The small ports of Antalaha and Sambava, on the east coast, are dangerous for shipping, and road con-nections between the ports and the hinterland are deficient and in the north-eastern region almost nonexistent. On the west coast, the island of Nossi-Bé forms a little world apart, and is itself composed of three districts having very different economies. Ambanja and Ambilobe districts, on the main-land, are formed by the two vast alluvial plains created by the deltas of the Sambirano River in the south and the Mahavavy in the north. Through the fairly well-equipped port of Hell-ville (named for Admiral de Hell, early nineteenth-century governor of Réunion), on Nossi-Bé, are exported an-nually over 50,000 tons of goods, mainly sugar, and nearly 200 oceangoing ships call there during the course of a year.

Majunga (708,000). Although Majunga has the second-best port in Mada-gascar, this province presents a discouraging picture, both ethnically and industrially, and has a population density of only 4.2 per square kilometer. It is the cradle of the Sakalava tribe, which is virtually stagnant numerically; about 100,000 Sakalava live in the regions of Besalampy, Mitsinjo, Soalala, Analalava, and Antsalova. The only other indigenous tribe, the Tsimehety, contrasts strikingly with the Sakalava, for it is growing as rapidly in Ma-junga as in adjacent Diégo-Suarez. The Tsimehety now account for one-third of the total provincial population, occupying all of the districts of Mandritsara, Bealanana, Befandriana-Nord, Antsohihy, and Port-Bergé. Many of the immigrants now living in Majunga are southerners—Antan-droy, Antaisaka, and Antaimoro—who are scattered throughout the prov-ince and cultivate rice and tobacco. Merina and Betsileo expatriates total some 100,000, and most of them live in the Betsiboka valley. Notable in Majunga's population picture is the concentration of almost all of Mada-gascar's Comorian minority, which constitutes nearly half of the residents of its capital city. The town of Majunga also has a sizable Indian colony, mostly merchants who have been hard hit by the trade slump that followed the evacuation in 1961 of its French garrison.

Majunga's economy is dominated by agriculture and stock-raising. The province produces over 200,000 tons of paddy a year, and more could be grown if the water supply were more abundant. A project for harnessing the falls of the Betsiboka River for irrigation and hydroelectric purposes has long been under consideration, and if carried out it would add 30,000 hectares to the area suited for rice cultivation. The output of tobacco (2,000 tons a year) and peanuts (10,000 tons) could likewise be increased, but in view of the uncertain market for both commodities this is unlikely to come about. The province also produces small amounts of tapioca (1,200 tons), arabica coffee (500 tons), and kapok (300 tons), all of which could be increased by the use of better farm equipment and the improvement of means of communication. Majunga's industry is in a sorry plight, for its once-flourishing production of tinned meat has declined sharply, its paka-weaving plant has survived only as a result of official subsidies, and the future of its cement plant is most uncertain because of high production costs and transport difficulties.

Tuléar (875,000). In contrast to Majunga, Tuléar has been contending successfully with severe natural handicaps, and its economic future looks comparatively bright. Its 168,000 square kilometers make it the largest of Madagascar's provinces, but the southern region is so arid as to be precariously habitable and it has a population density of 4.9 per square kilometer. The province's largest ethnic group is the Antandroy, who make up about one-third of its total population and whose numbers are growing rapidly. They provide laborers for the whole island; were it not for the large-scale emigration of Antandroy, the rate of Tuléar's population increase would be much higher. In the southeast live about 140,000 Antanosy, and on the plateaus a much smaller number of Bara; between the Onilahy and Manarandra rivers are found the Mahafaly. The rest of the population consists of some thousands of Vezo, Antaisaka, Betsileo, and Merina.

Although only 4.7 per cent of the population is urban, Tuléar has three attractive port towns. Of these, the provincial capital and Fort-Dauphin could attract far more residents if their present handicaps—notably shortages of water and housing—were eliminated. The capital's port now handles more than 50,000 tons of cargo a year and that of Fort-Dauphin some 30,000 tons, and improvements being made in the equipment of both should permit them to export and import greater amounts in the near future. The prospects of Tuléar's third port, Morondava, are not so bright because it suffers from almost irremediable physical drawbacks. Its situation at sea level on a low and sandy coast causes it to be regularly threatened with inundation, and during the rainy season it is cut off from the rest of the island except for weekly plane service.

Tuléar's economic wealth is made up of diverse products. Among its agricultural exports are sisal, tobacco, peanuts, corn, and especially Cape peas, the sale of many of these products being conditioned by market fluctuations. The most promising new crop is cotton, whose development depends upon the irrigation improvements now under way in the Mangoky and Morondava deltas. Tuléar's known mineral deposits are impressive, but for various reasons they have not been fully exploited. No firm decision has yet been reached in regard to extracting coal at Sakoa,* and prospectors have so far been disappointed in their search for petroleum deposits. Some mica, monazite, ilmenite, and industrial garnets, however, have been and still are being extracted. Fishing is a considerable resource for the Vezo tribe in the Morondava region. Animal husbandry is of great importance to the province, which has herds totaling nearly 2.5 million cattle, 230,000 sheep, 345,000 goats, and 50,000 pigs. The extension of stock raising, and even its survival, depends upon large-scale improvement of the water supply, which indeed is a *sine qua non* for the prosperity of the whole province.

Tamatave (914,500). This province has an area of 68,000 square kilometers and a relatively high population density of nearly 12 per square kilometer. Its largest tribe is that of the Betsimisaraka, who are to be found all along the littoral. Smaller groups of Bezanozano, Tanala, Antaisaka, Antaifasy, and Merina immigrants live farther inland. Foreign minorities consist of some 12,000 Europeans, of whom many are planters, and about 1,000 Indians and 2,800 Chinese, who are small-scale merchants both along the coast and in small hinterland settlements. Only 6 per cent of the population are town dwellers.

The creation of Diégo-Suarez province in 1956 deprived Tamatave of three districts that contained 15 per cent of its population, about one-fourth of its coffee plantations, and almost all of its vanilla production. Yet Tamatave province still possesses one of the most highly developed regions in all Madagascar, that of Lake Alaotra, which is also the largest such body of water on the island. It has, moreover, the best port in Madagascar and a good communications network that includes a railroad and a highway to Tananarive and a chain of partially navigable lagoons called the Canal des Pangalanes. This province comprises the richest region of export crops—coffee, perfume plants, cloves, and a little vanilla—as well as some graphite deposits. Unfortunately, its concentration on commercial crops, especially

* See pp. 410–11.

coffee, has led the inhabitants to neglect food crops and stock raising, and all of its agricultural output is highly vulnerable to the cyclones that periodically ravage the east coast.

Urban Centers

Madagascar's main towns have doubled and in some cases even trebled in population since the end of World War II, yet the Malagasys as a whole are still only slightly urbanized. Seventeen towns have populations of 5,000 to 20,000, and 29 of 2,000 to 5,000, and there is but one city with more than 100,000 residents. Tananarive has grown phenomenally, for it offers unique opportunities for government employment, wage-earning, education, and diversion. In 1913, 5 per cent of the island's population lived in towns, and by 1958 this percentage had only slightly more than doubled. The table in this section indicates in round figures the growth of Madagascar's six provincial capitals. Its other main urban centers are Antsirabe (18,500), Mananjary (13,600), Manakara (13,300), Fort-Dauphin (11,800), Ambositra (11,000), and Morondava (10,300).

City	Population			
	1914	*1941*	*1950*	*1961*
Tananarive	65,000	109,700	180,000	248,000
Majunga	7,500	23,700	32,200	52,000
Tamatave	9,000	24,800	28,700	48,000
Tuléar	1,500	17,000	18,500	40,000
Diégo-Suarez	12,000	17,600	23,900	39,000
Fianarantsoa	8,000	21,000	18,200	35,000

Unlike the situation in French-speaking Negro Africa, most of Madagascar's towns do not owe their existence to Europeans, although they did mainly create the conditions for expansion. Manakara is almost unique in that it came into being as a result of the building of the railroad and port in the twentieth century. Tananarive, the pre-French capital, remains an almost solidly Merina city, although its recent striking growth can be ascribed in part to the arrival of newcomers as well as to the absorption of adjacent Merina villages. Non-Merina Malagasys account for only 2 per cent of its population and non-Malagasys for 10 per cent, whereas the majority of the inhabitants of Diégo-Suarez and Majunga, and a large proportion of those of Tamatave and Fianarantsoa, are nonindigenous.

During the interwar period, urban planning was begun in Madagascar. An Office des Habitations Economiques (O.H.E.) was created in 1927, and that same year the port and town of Tamatave were almost wholly rebuilt after having been devastated by an especially violent cyclone. Governor Cayla made an effort to modernize and beautify Tananarive, Fianarantsoa, Majunga, and Tuléar, and years earlier Governor Garbit had developed Antsirabe as a spa. It was not until the sharp population rise after World War II that urbanization projects were taken seriously. Urban centers grew much more rapidly than in the past, and the towns and the labor market were not prepared to cope with the influx. Shortages in housing and water supply became acute in Tananarive and all the provincial capitals, and a rapidly increasing urban proletariat lived crowded together in unsafe and insanitary quarters.[24] Although, as part of the ten-year plan, urbanization projects were to be carried out in Madagascar's main towns, not only were they slow in getting under way, but the mere announcement that they would be undertaken caused a spate of speculation in land and a rise in already high rents.

Since the O.H.E. was obviously incapable of meeting the postwar challenge, a new "company of mixed economy," the Société Immobilière de Madagascar (S.I.M.), was formed on July 10, 1951. Most of its capital of 200 million C.F.A. francs was supplied by the Caisse Centrale d'Outre-Mer, but the government of Madagascar bought shares worth 60 million francs, and individual towns another 15 million. Two functions were assigned to the S.I.M. One was the purchase of suitable urban and suburban land on which to build as quickly as possible large-scale housing for low-cost rental or sale. The other was to loan money to individuals who wanted to build their own dwellings. Although during its first three years of existence the S.I.M. had granted 253 loans for building 523 lodgings and was lending money increasingly to Malagasys—40 per cent of the total in 1954, compared with 16 per cent in 1952—its record was considered unsatisfactory; moreover, it was in financial difficulties. An official inquiry in 1954[25] disclosed that housing conditions for laborers in Tananarive were appalling, as were slums in other towns, particularly in the coastal regions. For better promotion of housing activities, a Fonds de l'Habitat was created in 1955 with funds supplied from F.I.D.E.S. and the general budget; its objectives as well as its methods of filling the housing needs of the lowest-income group were precisely defined.

Establishment of the Fonds de l'Habitat brought to four the number of institutions granting loans for housing in Madagascar, which already included the O.H.E., the Crédit de Madagascar (C.M.), and the S.I.M. Judging by debates in the assembly, neither individually nor in the aggregate have they met what the country's elected representatives consider to be the towns' most urgent needs.[26] Repeated complaints against all of these organizations are to the effect that their operations are too small in scale, are too slow, and benefit most those who need them least—that is, the rich, who can offer guaranties for the loans they request. Another long-standing grievance is that Tananarive always receives the lion's share of the housing loans granted. To this charge the capital's elected representatives reply with some justification that Tananarive's rate of growth is unprecedented and that the widespread inundations of 1959 greatly aggravated an already acute housing shortage there. They also point to the fact that other towns have been dilatory about drawing up urbanization plans and that virtually none of their inhabitants has submitted a well-substantiated request for a housing loan. Gradually the coastal provincial capitals are being provided with more low-cost housing, electrical current, and water supply, and Fianarantsoa's problems in these respects are not great. Tananarive, in effect, is in a class by itself, and more drastic measures than those thus far tried will be necessary if decent living conditions are to be made available to most of its residents.

Chapter eighteen

TRANSPORTATION

Madagascar's underdevelopment is to a large extent traceable to the inadequacy of the island's means of communication. This, of course, is true of many other former colonies in the tropics. In Madagascar's case, however, the situation is especially crucial because there are virtually no navigable inland waterways and because the most populous and developed areas are in the center of the island, which is linked to the coastal regions by few and poor roads, two small and obsolete railroads, and very expensive albeit frequent air service. Although improvements have been made in the communications network of the high plateaus and the east coast, the rest of the island has been neglected, with the result that many regions are isolated from each other and from the main centers. The dispersal of a small population and of the producing zones over a vast area, as well as adverse topographic and climatic conditions, have been among the chief obstacles to the building and maintenance of means of communication.

Roads

Under the Merina monarchy, economic life was centered in the high plateaus and was in fact almost wholly confined to that region. This was the result not only of the many natural hindrances to intercommunication on the island but also of official policy. The Merina queens were beset by fears of an invasion by the European powers, and they deliberately neglected road building so as to make Imerina as inaccessible as possible. Only trails used by human porters connected the villages of the high plateaus and linked Imerina with settlements on the east and west coasts.

The French conquest demonstrated the futility of this policy, for the invaders were slowed down but not stopped by the absence of roads. The painful and long struggle of the French troops up from the west coast to Tananarive had at least the merit of convincing Gallieni of the urgent need to create means of communication, and he provided the impetus to both road and railroad construction. During the nine years of his governorship, he spent 29 per cent of the local revenues on the building of roads, under the direction of army engineers, from Tananarive to the ports of Majunga and Tamatave. His successors carried on this work until World War I began, and they joined Tananarive by road with Fianarantsoa and also Mananjary with Farafangana. Poor and dangerous as were the roads and tracks built or improved during that early period, they did reduce the number of porters plying between Tananarive and Tamatave from 63,000 in 1898 to 3,500 by 1902,[1] and cut down the cost per ton of merchandise transported from 1,300 francs to 700.[2]

Extension of the road network was resumed in 1925 under Governor Olivier, who conceived the idea of using prestation (forced) labor for that purpose at no cost to the island's budget. Roads or tracks were begun or completed to open up communications out of four main centers—Tuléar, Majunga, Ihosy, and Diégo-Suarez. Olivier's main purpose in undertaking this work was to facilitate the movements of the island's administrators, and to the district officers was left the task of creating dry-weather tracks in their respective areas for the convenience of planters and traders. The world depression of the early 1930s considerably reduced road-building activity, but when World War II broke out, Madagascar had 25,000 kilometers of more or less passable tracks or roads.[3] Even during the war, when shipping and motor-vehicle circulation were almost wholly suspended, some work was done to improve tracks for the evacuation of minerals needed by the Allies. By and large, however, the war left Madagascar in an even worse plight regarding communications than before, for the strategy used by the government to hamper the British occupation forces involved creating roadblocks and destroying bridges.

Madagascar's first postwar plan stressed improvement of the road network and gave it a new orientation. Priority thenceforth was to be given to tracks or roads that would promote development of the economy by serving the most productive and also the most isolated areas, as well as to widening and hard-surfacing those most used by motor traffic and building permanent bridges that could sustain trucks. Application of this policy did not lead to any marked increase in the whole road network, but did result in some improvements, particularly in the great artery that runs from Majunga to Ihosy via Tananarive, with its two branches to Tuléar and Fort-Dauphin and its links with the east-coast ports of Fénérive and Mananjary. New construction was limited to secondary and usually short sectors serving areas of special economic interest, such as the Lake Alaotra, Marovoay, and Ambato-Boeni regions.

By the mid-1950s it had become apparent that the increase in Madagascar's motor-vehicle circulation far exceeded the expectations of the first post-war planners and that the road network not only was too small but was deteriorating rapidly. On the coastal roads the many ferries slowed down driving and made it unsafe, and every year a large number of wooden bridges were carried away during the rainy season or collapsed under the weight of overloaded trucks. Even the few kilometers of hard-surfaced roads had been built with such economy that they had come to need resurfacing because of the unexpectedly heavy use made of them by motor traffic.

In 1956 a new five-year road plan was drafted, and the cost of 5.5 billion C.F.A. francs—a sum far exceeding the investments made by F.I.D.E.S. up to that time in road building in Madagascar—was to be met in large part by a new Fonds d'Investissements Routiers (Road Fund). After long and heated debates, the representative assembly reluctantly agreed that it should be financed by a tax on imported gasoline, and the fund was duly set up in November 1956. Almost at once, however, further difficulties arose, partly as a result of the financial decentralization effected by the *loi-cadre* and partly because the deputies disagreed on how the proceeds from the new fund (which amounted to 800 million C.F.A. francs in 1957) should be divided among the provinces. The next year a much more serious problem arose—an unexpected shrinkage in the fund's total resources because of the rapid and widespread substitution of diesel- for gasoline-powered engines. When the government asked the assembly to make up for this loss to the fund's revenues by voting a tax on fuel oil, the deputies again balked, but eventually did so. Some blamed the government for encouraging the change-over for reasons of economy, others claimed that the tax on fuel oil would be a burden to many Malagasy truckers who were operating on a shoe-string, while still others complained about the government's failure to have devised an overall road policy with special reference to the growing competition between truck and rail transport.[4]

On one point at least the government and the deputies were in agreement—the need to extend and improve Madagascar's road network, which was in extremely bad condition. The government therefore proceeded to create a Comité de Transports to study the "delicate" question of rail and road competition, suggest the principles under which the rates charged by truckers should be standardized, and reclassify all the island's roads. Under the program drawn up in 1960–61, the provinces were to select, resurface with crushed stone, and then maintain the roads considered to be vital to their economy, and the communes were to assure the upkeep of dirt tracks of purely local importance. Inasmuch as the central government had acquired, under the *loi-cadre,* some of the revenues formerly allotted to the provinces, it was to take over as "national roads" some of the highways hitherto maintained by the provinces, as well as the roads theretofore described as ones of "general interest." This reclassification would make the state responsible for maintaining some 8,000 kilometers of roads, at an annual cost of 58,000 C.F.A. francs per kilometer, and under the committee's program approximately 3,000 kilometers of provincial roads were to be taken over eventually as national roads.

In the 1961 program, priority was given to the north-south artery and to the roads leading from it to the main port towns. The plan called for building or improving 12,300 kilometers of asphalted roads at a cost then estimated at 80 billion C.F.A. francs. It allowed for a 25-year period in which to accumulate this huge sum; in addition to revenues provided by the Road Fund, financial assistance from the Fonds d'Aide et de Coopération (F.A.C.) and the Fonds Européen de Développement (F.E.D.) was anticipated. In 1962 it received from those sources 10 billion C.F.A. francs with which to make a start. As of 1963, Madagascar had a total road network of 40,000 kilometers, of which 2,000 were hard-surfaced and over 7,000 were passable throughout the year. The only province that had a good road network was Tananarive, and nearly half of all the island's motor vehicles were based there. Three-fourths of these vehicles, in fact, were registered in the national capital itself, where the per capita purchasing power was highest and where in 1962 the French firms of Citroën and Renault had opened automobile-assembly plants. Between 1950 and 1960 the number of motor vehicles imported into Madagascar had quintupled, and by 1963 there were 53,827, of which nearly half were privately owned cars. If and when Madagascar's ambitious road program is completed, the island will have an adequate system of main highways eight meters wide, with bridges capable of sustaining loads of 25 tons.

Railroads

Madagascar's 858 kilometers of railway line were built on the installment plan between 1910 and 1936. The older and more important of the two main lines is the so-called Tananarive–Côte Est (T.C.E.), 369 kilometers in length, which links the capital with the main east-coast port of Tamatave and has two branches on the high plateaus. It was initiated by Gallieni, financed by loans from France, built by paid Asian and local labor, and completed a year before the outbreak of World War I. During Governor Garbit's tenure the two branch lines were constructed, one from Moramanga to Lake Alaotra (168 kilometers) in 1922 and the other from Tananarive to Antsirabe (158 kilometers) in 1923. The volume of passenger and freight traffic carried by the T.C.E. is twice that of the more or less parallel line, the Fianarantsoa–Côte Est (F.C.E.), which was built between 1927 and 1936 and connects Fianarantsoa with Manakara. Although considerably shorter than the T.C.E. (163 kilometers), the F.C.E. was, from the technical standpoint, almost as difficult to build, but the loan needed from France for its construction was smaller, partly because the labor used was largely requisitioned.

All of Madagascar's railroads are single-track and have a meter gauge, and they serve only a comparatively small part of the island. Their carrying capacity is quite limited, and the imbalance between the freight transported from the coast to the high plateaus and that carried to the east-coast ports is marked in the case of both lines, though less so in regard to the F.C.E.

From the outset the construction of Madagascar's railroads and their improvement have been almost entirely financed by France, unlike the island's roads, which were paid for by local funds until after World War II. To replace the engines and rolling stock that had broken down or become obsolete during the war, new locomotives and cars were ordered in 1946, funds for their purchase being obtained from F.I.D.E.S. Fortunately for Madagascar, the delivery of this matériel was so delayed that it did not arrive before the rebels in 1947 attacked the T.C.E. line near the coast and greatly damaged its equipment and tracks. Moreover, two years later another disaster struck the same region when a cyclone destroyed the big railroad bridge at Brickaville. After these misfortunes, however, work went ahead steadily, and by July 1954 some of the worst curves had been eliminated and in some places the track had been relaid with heavier rails. In addition, many new cars had been put into use, and, most important of all, wood-burning locomotives had been replaced by diesel engines.

Although F.I.D.E.S. re-equipped Madagascar's railroads, calamities caused by nature and man resulted in their operating at a deficit during the early postwar years. Rates were raised in 1949, but this angered the public and did very little to reduce the deficit. The government therefore proposed, and the representative assembly agreed without debate, that the management of the rail network should be entrusted to a *régie,* which was to give it a businesslike administration although ownership was to remain in the hands of the state. The *régie* was headed by a board of directors which kept in close touch with the French Overseas Railroad Office in Paris and which included representatives of the local government, railroad employees, the representative assembly, and the general public. It was decided that the railroads' budget must be balanced each year, and this necessitated another, and substantial, increase in rates as of January 1, 1951. Later the *régie* lowered its tariffs for the transport of such food products as rice and manioc, but it offset this concession by charging more for other merchandise and for passengers. This high-rate policy made rail transportation in Madagascar so expensive that it cost more to send a ton of freight by train from Tamatave to Antsirabe than by ship from Marseille to Tamatave.[5]

At the same time as the *régie* increased most of its charges, it accomplished economies in operating costs by dieselizing the whole network, which resulted in an important saving of fuel and personnel. When the *régie* took over in 1951, the railroads employed 5,705 persons, and by 1955 their number had been reduced to 3,533, the reductions in force affecting all echelons of employees in about equal proportions.[6] By its liberality in supplying housing, medical care, and other amenities, the *régie* built up good relations with its employees and has been little troubled by labor disputes. After Madagascar became independent, however, the *cheminots* (railroad-workers) unions began pressing the government to take them into the civil service so that they could benefit by the material advantages of civil-service status. Because of the extra expense that this would involve, both the government and the *régie* resisted it despite the fact that it was supported by a number of assemblymen. Some of the deputies championed the *cheminots'* cause on principle, but the majority who did so were more politically motivated. They resented the fact that the *régie,* after it had been somewhat reorganized in 1959, excluded representatives of the assembly from its board of directors. This issue was part of a larger struggle going on at the time between the legislative and executive branches of the government, and it gave a focus to the deputies' displeasure over their growing inability to control such branches of the public services as the railroads and the post-telephone-telegraph department.

The government's stand against increasing the *régie's* expenditures at that time was given special relevance by the competition that was rapidly developing between rail, air, and road transport. From 1956 on, improvements in the island's road system and air services caused an alarming decline in the railroads' revenues. First-class passengers preferred the speed and greater comfort of air travel, and its cost was not appreciably higher than that of comparable accommodations on the trains. Second-class passengers were increasingly using *taxis-brousse* (small rural buses), which though crowded, uncomfortable, and unpunctual charged a great deal less than the cheapest fare on the railroads. More important still, trucks were carrying an ever-larger percentage of the valuable freight and thus the railroads were left to transport mainly "poor" products on which rate concessions had been made. At the same time, there was a rise in wages and family allowances, with the result that in 1957–58 the railroads incurred a large deficit. This forced the *régie* to dig deeply into its reserve fund and to borrow from the government. As the money it obtained from both these sources covered less than half of its deficit of 152 million C.F.A. francs, more stringent measures were necessary. The government set up a Transport Committee to study ways and means of coordinating rail and road travel, and in 1961 it periodically restricted road traffic on the sectors most competitive with the railroad between Tananarive and Tamatave.

Despite their high cost to the government and the public and the limited scope of their operations, Madagascar's railroads were and still are vitally important to the island's economy. In 1962 they set a record by carrying more than 2 million passengers and over 555,000 tons of merchandise. Periodically the assembly discusses the question of whether the two main lines should be connected by building 240 kilometers of track between Antsirabe and Fianarantsoa. It has been calculated, however, that an annual freight traffic of 80,000 to 100,000 tons of merchandise would be required to make this a paying proposition, and at present the freight moving between those two points does not exceed 30,000 tons a year. Only if substantial mineral deposits were discovered along this route could the needed tonnage be supplied; hence a decision has been indefinitely postponed.[7]

Air Transportation

Commercial aviation has developed spectacularly in Madagascar, and will no doubt continue to do so. It provides a means of communication eminently suited to an island situated far from France and notable for its vast dimensions, its mountainous terrain, the isolation of many areas during the rainy season, and the inadequate surface transportation.

Enterprising Frenchmen began to pioneer individually in this field in 1911, but it was not until the 1930s that the development of aviation was given its first strong impetus by Governor Cayla, who was himself a pilot. Owing to his encouragement, the first regular service for passengers and mail was started in 1934 between Tananarive and Broken Hill in Rhodesia, where connections could be made with the Europe-bound planes of Imperial Airways. It was Cayla also who initiated two internal air services in 1936, linking the capital with Diégo-Suarez in the north and with Tuléar and Fort-Dauphin in the south. By the time World War II began, airfields built by military engineers dotted the island and Madagascar had the best-developed air network of any part of the overseas French Empire except the North African countries.

World War II interrupted this expansion, and it was not resumed until about 1950. In that year, Air France landed its first Constellation on Madagascar, marking the beginning of regular service between Paris and Tananarive, and three years later Transports Aériens Internationaux (T.A.I.) opened a second service between those two cities. In 1952, a local commercial airline began regular flights covering 11,000 kilometers a week and serving

12 towns on the island. In the early 1950s, too, some planters as individuals
or in groups began using planes to move their produce to shipping ports,
fight locust invasions, and experiment with cloud-seeding. Perhaps the most
publicized of these operations was the transportation of vanilla by air from
Andapa, a rich producing region only 80 kilometers from the coast but so
inaccessibly located that theretofore its output had had to be carried by
porters to Antalaha. Flights to France and the Mascareignes increased in
number and popularity, but it was above all the internal air services that
expanded rapidly in the transport of passengers and merchandise. The
planes serving Madagascar became more numerous, larger, and faster, and
during the years from 1950 to 1960 F.I.D.E.S. invested a total of 3.2 billion
C.F.A. francs in the improvement of Madagascar's airfields, meteorological
services, and related facilities. In the course of that decade, the volume of internal air transport—passenger and freight—increased by 84 per cent, whereas the island's railroads experienced only a 53 per cent growth in such traffic.[8]

When the country's independence was attained, the Malagasys began
wanting to have their own aviation company, and in 1962 they took over the
existing internal air services. To the national company then formed they
first gave the unpropitious name of "Madair," which they later changed to
Air Madagascar. Of its shares, the Malagasy government holds 20 per cent,
with the option of increasing its participation to as much as 65 per cent.
Air France and T.A.I. supplied 44 per cent and 36 per cent, respectively,
of the company's initial capital of 400 million C.F.A. francs and also gave
it technical advice and loaned it personnel. (T.A.I. bowed out of the Madagascar aviation scene in 1963, but Air France continued its twice-weekly
service between Paris and Tananarive.) A Malagasy, Daniel Andriantsitohaina, heads Air Madagascar, which employs some 500 persons. Almost all
of the technicians and pilots are French, but they are to be gradually replaced by Malagasys. In its first operating year, 1962, Air Madagascar carried 103,000 passengers, 7,500 tons of freight, and 375 tons of mail over a
total distance of 2,400,000 kilometers.

Madagascar boasts that its new company provides the "most frequent air
service in the world," but the parties opposing the P.S.D. government have
denounced as extravagant many of the expenditures involved in promoting
that service.[9] To be sure, the airfields on the island have been reduced from
over 100 to 65. Those that were little more than emergency landing strips
have been abandoned and improvements have been made in the others. In
October 1963, France agreed to finance the construction of a new airport, capable of receiving the largest jet planes now in use, at Ivato, which is less
distant from Tananarive than the country's present international airport
at Arivonimamo. To many this seems an unnecessary extravagance, con-

sidering that Madagascar's second jet airfield, built at Majunga as an alternative to that of Arivonimamo, has remained virtually unused. Another target of criticism is the very high rates charged passengers by Air Madagascar, which preclude travel on its planes for all but government officials and rich individuals. Inasmuch as the peasant masses cannot afford to use planes for the transport of themselves or their produce, it is argued, the government should employ such funds as it can spend on transportation in building or improving roads in and for the rural areas.

Shipping: Navigable Waterways

Except in the southwest, Madagascar is well provided with surface water, and the island abounds in marshes, rivers, and lakes. The rivers of the west coast are longer and have more tributaries and gentler gradients than those of the east coast, but they are not much more navigable. All of the island's rivers are encumbered by rocks, rapids, and sandbars and are strewn with floating debris of all kinds, and the volume of their flow varies markedly with the season. None is navigable for more than short distances and by shallow-draft boats. The only body of water usable by boats for a considerable length is the Canal des Pangalanes along the east coast.

Three rivers on the west coast, navigable by small boats for short distances, serve to a limited extent for the transportation of produce from the hinterland to the ports. By far the most important of these is the Betsiboka, whose main tributary is the Ikopa (on which Tananarive is located). It brings down masses of sand, stones, and tree trunks to the Mozambique Channel, into which it empties near Majunga. The Betsiboka is used by barges between Marovoay and Majunga, but its upper reaches are not navigable even by dugouts, and the section between Marovoay and Maevatanana has become similarly unnavigable in recent years. Before World War II, the Compagnie Occidentale de Madagascar operated a boat service on the lower Betsiboka, but it ceased functioning after a road was built between Majunga and Maevatanana. Nevertheless, the Betsiboka still serves to carry some merchandise for export, notably rice. The second most navigable river on the west coast is the Tsiribihina, of which a portion over 70 kilometers in length is still used in shipping tobacco to the small port of Belo. The other main rivers of this coast—the Mangoky (which upstream is called the Matsiatra) and the Onilahy—are so shallow during the dry season and so torrential and encumbered with tree trunks when in flood that they are inadequate or too dangerous for navigation except by a few barges carrying Cape peas.

On the east coast, three rivers can be navigated for short distances throughout most of the year. These are the Ivondro, which debouches 13 kilometers south of Tamatave; the Iaroka, which empties near Andevoranto; and the Mangoro, whose lower course can carry barges of ten-ton capacity for a distance of more than 17 kilometers. These rivers, like a number of others of the east coast, contribute water to the so-called Canal des Pangalanes, a chain of lagoons extending from a point south of Fénérive to Farafangana. The eastern slope of that part of the island is traversed by numerous rivers, which flow steeply down from the central mountain massif to form lagoons averaging 40 kilometers in width where they enter the coastal plain. These lagoons, which extend over a total distance of 652 kilometers, are separated from each other by rocky outcrops called *pangalanes,* and since time immemorial they seem to have been used for the transportation of persons and produce between villages located on the same lagoon. The project of cutting through the outcrops and utilizing this internal waterway as an alternative and safer means of communication than the sea along this rugged and inaccessible part of the coast dates back to the Merina monarchy. For lack of the necessary funds and equipment, however, little was done until Gallieni revived the project with the aim of promoting trade in the area and of quickly provisioning his troops stationed inland. Work was begun as early as 1896, and by 1901 a continuous channel existed for 95 kilometers between Tamatave and Andevoranto.[10]

Despite the seemingly obvious economic interest of continuing this work toward the south, nothing further was done for the next 22 years. Cutting through the *pangalanes* proved to be difficult and expensive, as was dredging the area that had been opened to traffic, for some of the lagoons were too shallow for use in transporting much merchandise. In 1923 forced labor was used in resuming work at several points along the canal, and in 1931, France granted Madagascar a loan that enabled the local public-works department to speed up operations. On the eve of World War II, the canal was open to boat traffic at a number of places, but only between Vatomandry and the Ivondro was the water deep enough to take barges of 50 tons.

After the war a new study of the project was made, and its findings were published in 1948 as the Minot Report. On the basis of its conclusions F.I.D.E.S. granted several million C.F.A. francs to build a river port at Tamatave and improve the canal from that city to a point 30 kilometers south of the Ivondro. This work was completed in 1953 at a cost of 570 million C.F.A. francs. Then a study of the sector between the Ivondro and Manakara was undertaken, and the estimate for cutting through the remaining 30 kilometers of *pangalanes* indicated that very heavy expenditures would be required. In the years from 1949 to 1957, over 800 million C.F.A. francs were spent on the project. Extending the canal as far as Manakara not only would be technically difficult but would cost at least 1,400 more million. Consequently, by 1958 enthusiasm for the Canal des

Pangalanes had all but evaporated, and only the government and the residents of Tamatave urged continuation of the project. The work done on the canal up to that time had led to the closing down of the ports of Vatomandry and Mahanoro, and this had embittered the population of those towns. The businessmen of Manakara and Mananjary were also opposed to any prolongation of the canal because this would mean losing their shipping trade to Tamatave's port.[11] The big navigation companies joined them in opposing the project, inasmuch as the completion of the canal would automatically put an end to the high charges they were currently able to impose for loading and unloading cargo at the secondary east-coast ports. In the representative assembly, all the spokesmen for the lagoon area claimed that their constituents preferred that the government spend on road building such money as was available for transport in the region.

On February 14, 1959, the assembly turned down the government's proposal to make still another study of the project, on the ground that this would simply mean throwing good money after bad. A majority of the deputies were tired of the whole question, which had caused discussion for more than half a century. They argued cogently that neither the population nor the amount of exportable merchandise had grown in the proportions anticipated during the first postwar years, and that therefore the expenditure involved in completing the canal would be unjustified. Finally, the government agreed to postpone the decision in regard to extending the canal to Manakara until such time as the produce of the lagoon region reached an annual total of 1 million tons.[12] It is possible though not probable that this goal may be reached in the near future, for the region is suited to growing valuable export crops and has some mineral deposits. Although the Canal des Pangalanes has certainly not come up to the expectations of its early proponents, it has played a useful if limited part in the economy, and maintenance work is continuing on the sectors opened to traffic.

Shipping: Ports

Although Madagascar has a coastline totaling 5,600 kilometers, the island has very few natural harbors. Conditions are fairly favorable to shipping on the west coast, where some deep bays and the river estuaries offer adequate shelter. That coast, however, has neither the population nor the export produce that exist on the less favored east coast, which is exposed to trade winds and cyclones and where the sea is usually rough. Furthermore, south of Andevoranto the east coast is bordered by a sandbar and coral reef, and only at Tamatave and Manakara—the terminals of the island's two railroads—can ships find safe harbor. North of Andevoranto there is no bar, but the only natural maritime shelter that exists in this area is at Diégo-Suarez in the extreme north and at Tintingue on the west side of Ste.-

Marie Island. Neither of those two settlements is connected with a productive hinterland. Elsewhere along the east coast, ships must anchor in the
open sea, and loading and unloading operations are both time-consuming
and precarious. The island's topography, its inadequate means of surface
transport, and the dispersal of its population and producing areas are the
reasons for the existence of its many uneconomic and dangerous small
ports.

In view of the adverse natural conditions for shipping that prevail along
the east coast, it seems surprising that Madagascar's only well-equipped
deep-water port is to be found there. Gallieni elected to develop Tamatave
in preference to Majunga for both political and practical reasons. Foremost
among these was Tamatave's greater proximity to Réunion Island and to
Tananarive. Provisions could be more easily brought from Tamatave to the
high plateaus, where most of his troops were garrisoned, and it was from
Réunion that most of Madagascar's white settlers came, as well as the political pressure to annex the great island. Subsequently the rapid development of population and exports on the east coast confirmed the choice of
Tamatave as the major port destined for expansion, and with this in view
no fewer than 17 projects were drawn up in the course of a 30-year period. It
was not until the town had been almost wiped out in 1927 by a cyclone,
however, that the task of rebuilding the port on a large scale was begun.
Even when that had been accomplished, there was little improvement in
the port's operations, for they were controlled by four long-established
companies which represented only the interests of a small coterie of local enterprises and which clung obstinately to old-fashioned methods of handling
cargo.* The administration, which was eager to develop Tamatave as the
island's chief port, tried for years to persuade the companies to merge and
to modernize their methods, but in vain. They resisted until a wartime
emergency decree on July 15, 1940, put an end to their reign and the government took over operation of the port.[13]

The resumption of foreign trading after Madagascar's long isolation during World War II led to a paralyzing glut of freight at Tamatave in the
late 1940s. This bottleneck convinced the authorities that Tamatave port
must be improved to the point where it could handle at least twice the
amount of existing traffic. At that time it was expected that, after the anticipated completion of the Canal des Pangalanes, all the secondary ports as far
south as Farafangana would be abandoned, with the result that the shipping
they had handled would be concentrated at Tamatave. F.I.D.E.S. financed
the building of warehouses, derricks, and docks there, and by 1951 the port

* These companies were the Société du Wharf de Tamatave, Manutention Maritime, Batelage
de Tamatave, and Batelage des Chomeurs.

was receiving more than 57 per cent of all imports into Madagascar and shipping out over 47 per cent of its exports—a total of 328,000 tons, or nearly twice its prewar record of 183,000 tons in 1938.[14] In October 1952, Tamatave's port was given a new legal status and new management, modeled after those of France's major ports. Thereafter the port had its own budget and a board of directors that included, in addition to six civil servants, representatives of the chambers of commerce, shipping companies, the T.C.E. railroad, traders, the Tamatave municipal council, and the representative assembly.

Such an overwhelming proportion of the funds allocated by F.I.D.E.S. to improving Madagascar's shipping facilities went to Tamatave that all the other ports of the island were largely neglected, though to varying degrees. The government planned to close down those ports having open roadsteads so as to concentrate all ocean-going shipping at four main ports, but even some of these received a disproportionately small share of the F.I.D.E.S. bounty. Majunga, which ranks as Madagascar's second commercial port, still handles only 16 to 20 per cent of the island's total foreign trade. This is the more surprising because it is the outlet for a rich producing region and is nearer to Europe than Tamatave, which moreover has a more exposed port. Majunga's neglect can be explained by its proximity to the mouth of the Betsiboka River* and also to the fairly well-equipped port of Hell-ville, on Nossi-Bé island, which handles about 50,000 tons a year. In the 1930s a large sum was earmarked to improve Majunga's port, but after the first jetty was built, the harbor silted up so rapidly that work was abandoned on the eve of World War II. Since then the project has not been seriously revived, partly because the authorities cannot agree on whether it is better to continue dredging the existing harbor or to build a wholly new port. Some improvements have been made since the war, however, and in 1962 Majunga handled over 197,000 tons of freight, compared with 106,000 in 1938.

Diégo-Suarez, a major base for the French navy, is also Madagascar's third-ranking commercial port, although it handles less than 100,000 tons of cargo a year, or only 8 per cent of the island's total imports and exports. No port of Madagascar can rival Diégo-Suarez in size and security for ships; it also has a drydock and good repair facilities. Its growth as a trading port is so badly handicapped, however, by a mountain range that isolates it from the rest of the island that little effort has been made to develop it as such, and not until comparatively recently was a dock built there.

Tuléar is the fourth port which it is planned to retain for ocean-going shipping, largely because it has the most sheltered roadstead in the south

* See p. 293.

and not because of the tonnage of cargo it now handles, which amounts to only about 33,000 tons a year. Should it be decided to mine the coal deposits at Sakoa, the volume of exports through Tuléar would increase considerably.

Port facilities at Manakara, Morondava, Mananjary, Fort-Dauphin, and Vohémar, like those of Tuléar, have been improved since the war, but according to the official program these are to be only centers at which produce from inland areas will be collected by coastal vessels for shipment to one of the ocean-going ports. Beginning in 1957 with application of the *loi-cadre,* these ports were made the responsibility of the provinces in which they were located, and the type of management they have been given is analogous to that of Tamatave port. The remaining open roadsteads on the east coast either will be abandoned entirely or will serve purely as lagoon ports on the Canal des Pangalanes. Already three of them (Fénérive, Mahanoro, and Farafangana) have ceased to function as ports, leaving 17 still open to maritime shipping on the two coasts. Of these, seven are on the west and ten on the east coast. In 1960 the total freight tonnage handled by Madagascar's ports came to 1,031,000, Tamatave being responsible for nearly half (about 400,000 tons) and Tintingue for the smallest amount (some 1,300 tons).

Implementation of the policy of port concentration depends on completion of the road network leading to the ports from the producing regions and between the island's ports, and also on the attitude of the three shipping companies which have long almost monopolized the flow of Madagascar's foreign trade. Tramp ships flying many flags touch irregularly at Malagasy ports, but practically all the cargo that moves between Madagascar and Europe is carried by vessels of the Nouvelle Compagnie Havraise Péninsulaire (N.C.H.P.), the Messageries Maritimes, and the Scandinavia East Africa Line. Established in Madagascar before the French conquest, those companies long ago formed themselves into a Shipping Conference of the Indian Ocean for the purpose of coordinating freight rates and the schedule of ship movements. After World War II, they were so slow to restore adequate and regular services for Madagascar that the situation was the subject of a complaint in the Constituent Assembly by Madagascar's European deputy.* By 1950, however, they had renovated their fleets to the point where they met Madagascar's needs for the transport of passengers and cargo, but the ever-higher rates they charged were bitterly criticized by Madagascar businessmen throughout the 1950s.

Two explanations were offered by the shipping conference in extenua-

* In 1946 sanitary conditions were so bad on the *Ile d'Oléron,* a ship of one of these lines, that eight passengers died during a voyage back to France. See Constituent Assembly debates, Oct. 3, 1946.

tion of its high-price policy. The more valid of the two concerned the dispersal of Madagascar's ports and the deficiency of their facilities for loading and unloading, which meant that freighters were often immobilized for days awaiting favorable weather conditions to take aboard cargo of little value and small quantity. A specious argument advanced by the conference was based on the imbalance between Madagascar's import and export trade. It was indeed true that, in all but six of Madagascar's ports, imports far exceeded exports both in volume and in monetary value. Not mentioned, however, was the fact that this imbalance was corrected by the more than 150,000 tons of sugar exported annually by Réunion, which was included in the area served by the shipping conference.[15] To placate its critics, the conference made a few concessions in the mid-1950s. It gave a 10 per cent discount in freight rates to its regular clients, lowered its charges in ports where the facilities had been improved, and reduced the tariff for transporting Madagascar's bulkiest and "poorest" exports as well as imports of consumer goods most widely used by the Malagasys—but then it offset these concessions by raising rates for high-priced goods.

Malagasy nationalists, who vituperate against the "monopoly" allegedly held by the shipping conference,* seem not to realize that it could easily be broken if Madagascar developed its foreign trade enough to make it worth while for more ships outside the conference to serve Malagasy ports regularly. The Malagasy government is aware of this and is doing its best to increase the island's exports. At the same time it has been trying to create a national merchant marine, and the members of the shipping conference have been shrewd enough to help in its formation. The N.C.H.P. in particular aided in setting up the Compagnie Malgache de Navigation in 1960 (its capital was subsequently increased from 25 to 75 million C.F.A. francs) and the Société Malgache de Transports Maritimes in 1962 (to whose initial capital of 50 million C.F.A. francs all members of the shipping conference contributed). This cooperation is noteworthy in that the government in promoting a national merchant marine was not simply gratifying Malagasy pride and creating new jobs for Malagasys but was aiming frankly at lowering ocean freight rates. It is starting with the coastal trade and with that to the Mascareignes, and eventually hopes to have its ships ply between Madagascar and Europe. But the members of the shipping conference realize quite well that this will take a long time, and in the meanwhile the N.C.H.P. and the Messagéries Maritimes still carry 57 per cent of the traffic and the Scandinavian line 18 per cent.

---

* In 1960 the Hansa shipping company became a member of the conference.

Chapter nineteen

FINANCES

Currency

Before the Comptoir National d'Escompte was established in 1885, the currency used in Madagascar consisted of various coins, the most important of which was the silver piaster called *ariary*. The Banque de France notes introduced by the Comptoir circulated simultaneously with the *ariary* until World War I, when the Malagasys began hoarding *ariary* and paper money came into wider use. The banknotes, however, never wholly displaced *ariary,* and those coins continued to be used as the main currency in isolated regions.[1]

The dissimilar economic paths that had been taken by the various overseas territories when they became isolated from France during World War II caused concern to the Free French government in 1945 on two grounds. Its leaders were anxious that the inflation in postwar France should not spread to the French dependencies and also that the latter should not develop economic divergencies that might lead to political separatism. With the aim of counteracting those trends it created the Colonies Françaises d'Afrique (C.F.A.) franc for French Black Africa and Madagascar on December 25, 1945, and gave it the value of 1.70 Metropolitan francs. The overseas parliamentarians deeply resented this move, not only because it had been carried out suddenly and without consulting them but also because they feared its effects on the economies of their respective countries.

Their misgivings that it would increase the cost of living there proved justified, especially after three successive devaluations of the Metro. franc* inevitably affected the C.F.A. franc, which was pegged to it. Moreover, uncertainty persisted throughout the first postwar decade about the stability of the C.F.A. franc, for it was under incessant attack by elements in France that had an interest in re-establishing its parity with the Metro. franc. In October 1948 the government increased the value of the C.F.A. franc from

* On Jan. 26, 1948, April 27, 1949, and Sept. 19, 1949.

1.70 to 2 Metro. francs, but did not succeed in restoring public confidence in it. Actually, the latter was never devalued, but the uncertainty of its future had an adverse influence on investments in Madagascar, caused speculation and periodic flights of capital from the island to France, and led to at least one sensational currency scandal (in 1948) involving the loss to Madagascar of nearly 100 million C.F.A. francs.[2] It was not until three years after Madagascar became independent that it acquired a currency of its own.

Banking and Credit

Until independence, Madagascar had four deposit banks and four public institutions that granted special kinds of credit. The first of the deposit banks, the Comptoir National d'Escompte de Paris, as mentioned above, established itself in Madagascar in 1885, 11 years before the French conquest. (Thereafter it was closely associated with the administration and its operations were widened.) To enable the Merina government to pay France the war damages it owed under the treaty of December 17, 1885, the Comptoir loaned it 15 million francs. As guaranty for the repayment of this loan, the Comptoir was given control of revenues from customs duties. Until 1919 the Comptoir was the sole bank functioning in Madagascar, and it survived two world wars and one world depression in sound condition. Although in 1963 it closed two of its 12 agencies on the island, at Farafangana and Mananjary, it rebuilt its Madagascar headquarters at Tananarive and announced that it would continue to operate in the country in close cooperation with the independent government of Madagascar.

The economic expansion brought about by World War I led to the appearance in 1919 of two more French banks in Madagascar. One of these, the Banque de l'Océan Indien, backed mainly by the shipping firm Compagnie Havraise Péninsulaire, was a victim of the depression of the early 1930s. The second banking institution which had been founded in Madagascar at the same time, the Crédit Foncier, benefited by the disappearance of the Banque de l'Océan Indien and underwent some important changes. This bank's operations were mainly commercial despite the implications of its name, and its initial capital of 26 million francs was in large part provided by the Messageries Maritimes and the Crédit Foncier de Tunisie et d'Algérie. In 1952 the capital was increased to 100 million francs, when it became the Indian Ocean branch of the Banque Nationale pour le Commerce et l'Industrie (B.N.C.I.). At that time it ceased dealing in mortgages, in favor of short-term loans. The only other noteworthy banking development during the first post–World War II decade was the founding of another deposit bank, the Banque Franco-Chinoise; in 1951 it began operating in Madagascar with a capital of 106 million Metro. francs. Although at the time it attained independence in 1960, Madagascar had a fairly dense network of banking institutions, comprising 30 branches and four permanent bureaus, they were concentrated in only 18 towns; hence, not only was there sharp competition between them, but banking facilities were entirely lacking in some important centers.

Of all the banks set up in Madagascar, the most important and controversial has been the Banque de Madagascar et des Comores. During the early 1920s, the instability of the French franc led to a growing demand in Madagascar for locally issued banknotes. In 1925, therefore, private interests launched the Banque de Madagascar, with the participation of the governments of France and Madagascar, and it was given the exclusive privilege of issuing banknotes for a 20-year period. When the time came to renew this privilege after World War II, strong feelings were aroused and many impassioned debates on the subject took place in the three French parliamentary bodies.[3] The overseas parliamentarians and French liberals claimed that the Banque de Madagascar was too closely associated with big business in France and Madagascar, that it had done little to promote development of the island, and that the privilege of issuing notes should not be left in private hands. Among the bank's defenders was Roger Duveau, Madagascar's French deputy, who stressed that it had paid to the state 170 million of the 200-million-franc profits it had made since 1925. Moreover, he asserted, its abolishment would harm the economy of a country just recovering from a major revolt, and in any case its replacement by a national institution would be unjustifiably expensive. Eventually the parliament accepted the compromise proposed by the government, which left to the Banque de Madagascar the privilege of issuing notes for another 20 years but radically revised its management and policy. Under the provisions of a law of March 30, 1950, which embodied this compromise, the bank became a company of mixed economy. It was to open four new branches in Madagascar within three years and to start granting medium-term loans in addition to short-term ones. Its initial capital of 111 million Metro. francs was to be trebled, and the public powers—including the government of Madagascar—were to hold 56 per cent of its stock and to name eight of its 14 directors.

With the end of World War II there began a period in which the need for credit became acute in Madagascar. The rise in prices of Malagasy produce and of the island's imports, together with the scarcity of consumer goods and shipping, caused a marked increase in note circulation. Whereas in 1938 it had totaled 400 million francs, in August 1946 it exceeded 2 billion.[4] A considerable proportion of these notes, estimated at the time to total 800 million to 1 billion, was being hoarded by Malagasys because they found little to buy and did not grasp the utility of savings banks. Madagascar's existing banks were faced with heavy demands for loans, which they could not meet because their deposits had not increased proportionately.

This situation was not peculiar to Madagascar, and to remedy the lack of investment banks throughout its overseas territories France created the Caisse Centrale de la France d'Outre-Mer (C.C.O.M.) and the Fonds d'Investissement pour le Développement Economique et Social (F.I.D.E.S.). Two functions were assigned to the C.C.O.M., the first of which was to grant, from funds supplied by the French government, long-term low-interest loans to enterprises or for specific projects designed to modernize the economies of the overseas territories. Its second assignment was to handle the accounts of F.I.D.E.S., which was set up with the same general purpose and also financed by the French treasury. F.I.D.E.S. granted money to the extent of 90 to 100 per cent of the value of operations that were accepted as part of successive plans for the modernization and equipment of the overseas territories. The balance of such costs and the upkeep of projects launched by F.I.D.E.S. were to be financed by the territory concerned. Inasmuch as none of the territories was in a financial position to meet all of such costs, they borrowed from C.C.O.M. the funds required, at an interest rate of 1.5 per cent for a 25-year period.

Since the end of World War II, C.C.O.M.—whose name was changed in 1959 to Caisse Centrale de Coopération Economique (C.C.C.E.)—has been the predominant source of credit in Madagascar. From 1948 through 1960 it loaned to the public sector there a total of 18,231 million C.F.A. francs, of which about half was channeled through F.I.D.E.S., to finance the island's development plan. Thirteen loans amounting to 2,535 million C.F.A. francs were made to the private sector, and 600 million was loaned as capital to state companies and to companies of mixed economy,[5] at rates of interest ranging from 2.2 to 3 per cent. To such public or semipublic bodies as the territorial government, provinces, communes, and chambers of commerce, it loaned money for many different projects, such as paving streets, improving systems of water and electricity distribution, and building warehouses. It also helped to found and develop the various specialized credit institutions that were created in Madagascar during the first postwar decade to promote social and economic welfare.

The three most important of the institutions just mentioned were the Caisse Centrale de Crédit Agricole de Madagascar (C.C.C.A.M.), the Société Immobilière de Madagascar (S.I.M.), and the Crédit de Madagascar (C.M.). The C.C.C.A.M., successor to various prewar credit organizations for the peasantry, was provided with a capital of 293 million C.F.A. francs

to enable it to grant short-, medium-, and long-term loans to farmers, herders, and fishermen.* The S.I.M. was a mixed-economy company, capitalized
at 300 million C.F.A. francs, whose function was the granting of medium-
term loans to help individuals who wanted to build their own dwellings.†
The C.M. was entirely a state organization, founded in 1950 with a capital
of 223 million C.F.A. francs to lend money to various small- and medium-
scale industrial, commercial, and mining enterprises, as well as to individual
craftsmen and private builders.

By the time Madagascar's first government council was installed in 1957,
the island's credit facilities had become much more extensive than those
that had existed before World War II. Thanks to the C.C.O.M.–C.C.C.E,
long-term credit became available for the first time not only to public bodies
but to private enterprises that promoted the island's production. Another
helpful postwar innovation was the introduction of medium-term credit,
which was channeled through the C.M. also for production, and through
both it and the S.I.M. for building, especially for private housing. Short-
term credit continued to be provided, as it had been before the war, by the
deposit banks. The number of such banks and their resources had increased
since the war, but this expansion was accompanied by closer control over
credit operations. Beginning in 1948, the managers of the deposit banks
studied together the needs of local traders and decided to whom loans
should be made. By refusing credit to importers when the market was
glutted with goods and to merchants of questionable integrity, the bank
managers rendered a service to the public as well as to the banks themselves,
but the general effect was to tighten credit.[6] Furthermore, the postwar
credit institutions were not conspicuously generous about granting long-
and medium-term loans to the average Malagasy, who could not offer the
guaranties required and therefore continued to be the prey of usurers. The
C.M., the least specialized of the credit institutions, had granted in the
course of seven years (1950–57) loans totaling only 468 million C.F.A.
francs, of which over half had gone to housing projects and less than one-
fourth to activities designed to aid the rural economy.[7]

In the late 1950s the representative assembly frequently expressed dissatisfaction with the way in which the C.M. operated. It had four sources
of income, by far the most important of these being the C.C.O.M–C.C.C.E.,
which between 1950 and 1960 granted it a total of 700 million C.F.A. francs.
During that decade it had made 9,433 loans aggregating 4,436 million
C.F.A. francs, of which nearly half had been of the medium-term type and

* See pp. 337–39.
† See p. 283.

of which the largest shares had gone to aid agricultural production (39 per cent) and housing (31 per cent). Despite such sizable percentages for the promotion of economic and social welfare and the generally sound financial position of the C.M., it came under heavy fire from the Malagasy deputies. They claimed that it had failed to help the social categories that most needed money, as a result of its formalities and guaranty requirements, and also that it was too much under the thumb of civil servants and of the P.S.D. in rural areas.[8] In August 1960, immediately after independence, the C.M. was transformed into the Société Malgache d'Investissements et de Crédit (S.M.I.C.), which, unlike its predecessor, was not a state company but one of mixed economy financed in equal parts by the C.C.C.E. and the government of Madagascar. Apparently the new institution proved no more satisfactory than the former one, for three years later it was absorbed by the newly created Banque Nationale Malgache.

The Franco-Malagasy agreements of 1960 paved the way for the launching of an array of new financial organizations and of a national currency. On December 31, 1961, the privilege of issuing bank notes for the island was transferred from the Banque de Madagascar to an Institut d'Emission Malgache, half of whose capital of 500 million C.F.A. francs was supplied by the government of France and half by that of Madagascar. On July 1, 1963, the Malagasy franc (FMG) replaced the C.F.A. franc. It was pegged to the French franc, with a value of 1 FMG to 0.02 Metro. franc, and was guaranteed by the French treasury. More than a year before, on January 1, 1962, an Office des Changes had been created, with a Malagasy manager, and in March 1963 the legal groundwork was laid for the long-awaited Banque Nationale Malgache, wherein the Madagascar government was the major shareholder and several foreign banking organizations also participated. At about the same time, negotiations were successfully carried on with the Comptoir National for creation of a Banque Malgache d'Escompte et de Crédit, which began business on January 1, 1964. Almost all of its capital of 500 million FMG was furnished by the Comptoir, which also provided the new institution with technical advice and entrusted to it the management of its various branches throughout the island. The Comptoir, as well as the other prewar banks, plan to continue their commercial operations at Tananarive.

Investments

The Merina monarchs had neither the capital nor the technicians needed to develop their realm; moreover, they did not encourage foreigners to do so lest they end by taking over the island. Nor did the French, in the early years of their occupation, do as much in Madagascar as they did in North

Africa and Indochina. Madagascar's resources did not not lend themselves especially to development projects, and the island was geographically so isolated from other European colonies that France had little incentive to make it a showpiece. Because of repeated devaluations of the franc, it is difficult to estimate how much money, public and private, was invested in Madagascar before World War II, but authorities agree that it did not exceed 15 billion prewar francs. Of the public-fund investments, comparatively little was spent on increasing production, which at the time was considered to be the sphere of private enterprise. Private investments in Madagascar were much larger than public ones, totaling perhaps as much as 11.5 billion francs, and they were proportionately greater than in French Black Africa before World War II. Unfortunately such investments benefited the Malagasys only indirectly, and the profits they earned were almost entirely repatriated to France. A breakdown of private investments, as of 1946, allotted 21 per cent of the total to each of the three categories of trade, plantations, and industry, 17 per cent to shipping companies, 1.5 per cent to mining, and 4 per cent to banking.[9]

The profound change that took place after World War II in France's attitude toward investments in its dependencies naturally included Madagascar, into which for the first time the French government poured massive amounts of capital. Its financial aid to Madagascar took many forms, such as loans, outright gifts and subsidies, the payment of personnel, and military expenditures. Most of this money was of direct or indirect benefit to the country, but some of it primarily profited French businessmen. French public investments, channeled mainly through F.I.D.E.S., greatly exceeded those from private French sources, but both types are hard to evaluate because they have been so dispersed and also because the franc has been devalued several times.

According to a recent estimate,[10] F.I.D.E.S.—from 1947 through 1959—allocated to Madagascar sums equivalent to 800 million new French francs. Its successor organization, the Fonds d'Aide et de Coopération (F.A.C.), added 297.1 million to that total during a period running from January 1960 through September 1963. After Madagascar became independent, the forms taken by French official aid and the controls to which its use was subject were determined by bilateral agreements between France and the Malagasy government. At present F.A.C. finances from French public funds five categories of operations in Madagascar: specific investments made directly by the Malagasy government or jointly by it and France; expenditures for French technicians supplied by France to Madagascar; subsidies to balance the Malagasy budget; all or part of the capital for enterprises whose objective is the economic and social development of the island; and the expenses incurred by the permanent French aid mission whose headquarters are at Tananarive.

At least two-thirds of the French public funds invested in Madagascar have gone into improving its infrastructure, particularly the means of communication. In orienting the bulk of its investments to such long-term equipment projects, which helped to modernize the economy but held no promise of immediate monetary returns, the French government hoped to encourage French private capital to invest more heavily than in the past in the less risky and more remunerative enterprises. This hope, however, has been largely frustrated. Although postwar improvements in transportation have lessened Madagascar's isolation, no new resources have been discovered on the island that seriously tempt capitalists to invest there. The expectation of finding petroleum has proved unfounded, trading firms are already too numerous, and only relatively safe enterprises, such as the Société Sucrière de Mahavavy (SOSUMAV),* which are geared to the export market, have attracted private capital on a large scale.

Because so many companies are formed or go out of business each year, it is exceptionally difficult to gauge the amount of private capital invested in Madagascar since World War II. Some authorities, including Malagasy cabinet ministers, claim that such investments shrank steadily throughout the 1950s,[11] whereas others believe that they increased until 1958 and then began to decline. In 1957 a well-informed guess gave the figure of 14,600 million C.F.A. francs as the total of private investments during the 1946–56 decade.[12] A later study, in 1961,[13] broke down that total into 6,020 million C.F.A. francs invested between 1949 and 1953, and 8,580 million between 1954 and 1958. The growth apparent in the latter period was attributed both to transfers of capital from Indochina to Madagascar and to the fiscal concessions made by the Tananarive administration, beginning in 1951, to companies that reinvested a certain proportion of their profits in the country. Reinvestment of profits was probably the more important of the two, for it was thought to have accounted for at least 6 billion C.F.A. francs of the new investments made between 1951 and 1956.

Individuals or firms of Metropolitan French origin were believed to be almost wholly responsible for new investments during the 1950s totaling 11 billion C.F.A. francs, only a very small part of that total having been derived from purely local capital resources. The island's budget never contributed heavily to the development program, and in 1956 such budget allocations ceased altogether. Before Madagascar became independent, very little non-French foreign capital was invested in the country. Marshall Plan

* See pp. 360–61.

funds aggregating 1.3 billion C.F.A. francs were used to improve Madagascar's railroads, and small amounts of Swiss, British, Canadian, Greek, and Indian capital were invested in various enterprises. Such investments were of modest proportions not only because of the factors which inhibited all private investments but also because foreign capitalists were not welcomed in Madagascar by the French government, which regarded them as potentially dangerous interlopers. An American observer who visited Madagascar late in 1952 said that "Americans and British who try to do business in the island do so under petty and major difficulties which are not designed to encourage investment from their countries."[14]

The investment picture in Madagascar began to change with application of the *loi-cadre* in the late 1950s, and the change took another and sharper turn after independence in 1960. Uncertainty about the island's political future and especially about the Malagasy government's economic policy caused French private—though not public—investments to taper off and intensified the repatriation of the profits and savings of French firms and individuals on the island. Thus the loss of funds through such repatriations rose from 5 billion C.F.A. francs in 1956 to nearly 9 billion in 1958. This situation naturally alarmed the Malagasy government, and Tsiranana made many appeals to French private capital to show faith in his country by investing there.[15] He stressed the prevailing political calm, the improvement in the island's economy, and the freedom to transfer funds which was guarantied by the Franco-Malagasy agreements, and he also pledged that "Malagasy socialism" did not mean nationalization of existing enterprises or resources. Passing from words to deeds, the Malagasy government drew up an investment code in October 1961 which added appreciably to the advantages already conceded to foreign private capital invested in the country. Enterprises willing to make such investments were accorded fiscal and tariff concessions commensurate with the contribution made by their activities to the Malagasys' economic well-being.

Since Tsiranana became head of the Malagasy government, its receptiveness to private capital investment has succeeded in arousing interest in Madagascar among some new foreign investors. Nor has Tsiranana overlooked his own compatriots in this respect, and to a slight extent he has managed to tap this source of capital for the first time. The poverty of the great mass of Malagasys is all too evident, but there exists among them a small privileged class. These comparatively well-to-do individuals tend to hoard their money, spend it on imported luxury goods, or invest it in real property. Savings banks, introduced on the island in the 1920s, had little patronage until after World War II. Between 1950 and 1956 the number of depositors increased from 39,000 to more than 46,000, and the total amount of their deposits rose from 197 million C.F.A. francs to 573 million,[16] but such results are not impressive either in absolute or in relative terms. In August 1960 the government created the S.M.I.C.* to "mobilize Malagasy savings"—a task that was taken over in 1962 by its successor, the Société Nationale d'Investissements.

In 1962 Tsiranana launched a small national loan which was remarkably successful, partly as the result of political pressures, but its total was only 300 million C.F.A. francs. Perhaps it contributed to the development of a national consciousness, as its sponsors claimed, but some of those who subscribed generously to the loan did so under the misapprehension that this excused them from having to pay their taxes.[17] Under Madagascar's current development plan, a considerable part of the small-industries sector—oil mills, rice-husking plants, and the like—has been designated for Malagasy investment, but results have been meager. As recently as February 1964,[18] the Minister of National Economy complained that the Malagasy bourgeoisie who criticized the place reserved for foreign capital under the plan themselves refused to invest in enterprises that would help to develop the country and continued to place their money in land and buildings.

Tsiranana, as mentioned above, has been more successful in increasing the influx of foreign capital and in obtaining it from diversified sources than in promoting indigenous capital investment. Both the United States and the United Nations have small aid programs in Madagascar, but it is above all the European Economic Community, especially West Germany and Italy, which has provided the island with its largest new amounts of foreign capital. By the end of December 1963 the Common Market's Fonds Européen de Développement had allocated to Madagascar nearly $51 million, a sum larger than that provided any other former French dependency. French private capital has also financed new industries since Madagascar became independent—two automobile-assembly plants (Citröen and Renault, mentioned above), and factories to turn out plastics, blankets, and furniture. Nevertheless, the volume of such aid has been disappointing to the P.S.D. leaders. Many study missions from foreign countries have visited Madagascar since 1960. Their members say pleasant things about the island and sometimes make promises, but thus far most such promises have failed to materialize. Madagascar's plan calls for annual investments far exceeding those being made at present from local or foreign sources, and its success depends largely on inspiring greater confidence in the island's future on the part of both Malagasy and foreign capitalists.

Madagascar has an apparently stable government whose leaders are friendly to the West in general and to foreign capitalists in particular, and its local variety of socialism is neither doctrinaire nor militant. On the other

* See p. 305.

hand, the island's remoteness and the time and money required to develop its resources to the point where they will pay off militate against any sizable increase in the present slow rate of investments there. A vast expansion of the island's productivity and a change of heart among the Malagasy bourgeoisie will be required if investments from local resources are to increase appreciably. For some time to come, large-scale investments from foreign sources will probably continue to be motivated more by political than by economic considerations.

Budgets and Taxes

The Merina government derived its income from a complex array of taxes, some of which were paid in money and some in kind. They were not uniformly assessed, and they varied with the province and with the social status of the taxpayer, but in all cases government officials and feudal overlords pocketed a larger share of the amount collected than was legitimately their due. The state's largest single fiscal resource consisted of the 10 per cent ad valorem duties charged on the country's exports and imports, which were collected at six ports. But here again the cuts taken by officials (and by traders) siphoned off a considerable portion of the income which the government should have gained from the island's foreign trade, and apparently in no year did it ever receive more than the equivalent of 800,000 gold francs.[19] When the customs revenues had to be used to meet the debt to France contracted under the protectorate treaty of 1885, the government was gravely weakened financially. To be sure, it did not pay its officials regular salaries, and public works used unpaid *corvée* labor. Nevertheless, the revenues that remained after the debt payment amounted to only 400,000 gold francs, barely enough to pay for the upkeep of the court and for the purchase of firearms. As to the population as a whole, it was crushed under the weight of its obligations in money, kind, and services to the state and to the aristocracy.

During Gallieni's governorship, two laws were passed by the French parliament that both directly and indirectly affected the island's revenues. A law of 1898 made Madagascar an "assimilated" colony in regard to its tariff regime, which meant that French goods could enter the island free of duty. Gallieni thus lost a source of revenue that would have gone far to pay the salaries of the bureaucracy which he had installed. The second was the finance law of 1900, which obliged all French colonies to pay their own way except for military defense. This law had the virtue of giving Madagascar considerable financial autonomy, but, with the exception of loans raised in France for railroad construction, it deprived the island of the investment funds needed to develop the new colony.

Both the above-mentioned laws necessitated making changes in the fiscal system that Gallieni had taken over, with a few modifications, from the Merina regime. By 1901, taxes in kind had been replaced by direct taxes payable in money, but their assessment continued to vary from one region to another. The head tax became the mainstay of Madagascar's revenues, and it ranged from 10 francs in the poorest coastal areas to 30 francs in the neighborhood of Tananarive.[20] It yielded the government more income than did the taxes on rice fields, cattle, and marketplaces, combined with customs duties and other indirect taxes. To meet his growing operating expenses, Gallieni was forced to increase the rate of direct taxes several times, with the result that all Malagasy males between the ages of 16 and 60 came to pay an average of 25 francs a year in taxes.[21] Although paupers and the fathers of seven or more children were exempted, this tax burden was heavy for a population that had little money or salable produce. Well aware of this, Gallieni tried to console himself with the hope that his taxes would induce the Malagasys to work harder and grow more export crops. This hope was translated into a policy, which he enunciated to his subordinates at the same time that he codified rules for assessing and collecting taxes. In a circular issued on October 30, 1904, he described the head tax as the "indispensable stimulant" for teaching the Malagasys the value of "the law of work, without which there can be no moral or material progress."[22] It is unlikely that the Malagasys then appreciated the virtues of paying heavy taxes in money, but the proceeds therefrom permitted Gallieni to accomplish his remarkable work in many productive fields. Moreover, when he left Madagascar in 1905 the colony's deficit had become a surplus balance of some 700,000 francs.

Under Gallieni's successors the financial situation continued to be satisfactory. Although the replacement of army officers by civilian officials during Augagneur's tenure considerably increased the cost of administration, he offset this by trimming expenditures in other fields—unfortunately including that of education—and by instituting a small tax that enabled the health services to give medical care to Malagasys free of charge. The depression after World War I caused such a fall in the revenues derived by Madagascar from foreign trade that taxation was increased. Beginning in 1919 the head tax was raised and new taxes were imposed on land and on all unemployed males whether native or European. On the other hand, an effort was made to assess taxes more equitably. The exemptions theretofore granted to Europeans were eliminated and the principle of equality in taxation, regardless of nationality and status, was established.

The year 1924 marked a turning point in Madagascar's fiscal history. The island had recovered from four years of postwar depression and even had a favorable trade balance. The government began to place more reliance on indirect taxation, and business firms that had long enjoyed what was almost fiscal immunity were now called upon to bear a larger share of the tax burden. At the same time, the age at which men became subject to the head tax was raised from 16 to 19, and exemptions were granted to students, soldiers, the indigent, and invalids. The form in which the budget was presented was reorganized and made more efficient. A distinction was drawn between ordinary and extraordinary income and expenditures, and a separate budget was created for the railroads and ports.

It was also in 1924 that the consultative body called the Délégations Economiques et Financières was created by Governor Olivier, and this body provided European residents and Malagasys with their first chance to voice opinions on the budget and tax laws, about which the Délégations had to be consulted. The European delegates had strong opinions on such subjects, and they were largely responsible for some important fiscal changes that were made in the late 1920s and the 1930s. They were particularly alarmed by the steady rise in the volume of the budgets, which more than doubled between 1925 and 1929, and they urged the government to reduce its expenditures, especially for personnel. Although they did not succeed in getting the government to retrench—it did not do so until the world depression of the early 1930s compelled it to take such action—the European delegates did pressure the administration during the late 1920s into introducing a general income tax and reducing the percentage of direct taxes in total revenues from 62 per cent in 1927 to 52 per cent by 1930. Budget surpluses each year from 1925 through 1929, however, enabled the administration to ignore its critics and go its own way. In fact, Governor Olivier's incumbency coincided with a period of such prosperity for Madagascar's foreign trade that the island's economy was not greatly affected by the devaluation of the franc that took place at that time. In 1925, revenues amounted to 127,879,000 francs and expenditures to 100,275,000 francs, and the surplus enabled the government to launch a public-works program from its own resources. Even in 1929, when expenditures had soared to 267,530,000 francs, the island had a surplus of 14,300,000. It was not until the next year that expenditures began to exceed revenues, forcing the government not only to take drastic retrenchment steps but to dip deeply into its reserve fund.

The sharp reversal of Madagascar's financial situation beginning in 1930 compelled the local administration to ask the French government for a loan of 735 million francs to "finance public works of general interest," and it was granted the following year. Even so, in 1932 Madagascar's plight worsened, and the delegates reluctantly agreed to an increase in taxes. The head tax was raised to 150 francs, but they did succeed in reducing taxation on cattle and livestock products, for which the market had sagged badly. These fiscal measures, plus economies amounting to 58 million francs, brought some improvement in 1934, so that the government was able to reduce a few tax rates slightly. By that time, however, Madagascar had to meet heavy interest payments on its large loan, and by the late 1930s public-debt payments accounted for 20 per cent of total expenditures. Throughout the last years before World War II the island's revenues increased as a result of better trading conditions. Although it could not count on surpluses as it had done a decade before, Madagascar nevertheless managed to balance a budget that in 1938 exceeded the 1929 level by 30 million francs without incurring more debts.

The World War II period saw changes in Madagascar's public finances that were due to no voluntary alteration in policy but to circumstances beyond its government's control. After Madagascar was cut off from France because of the British occupation, its foreign trade was confined to non-French countries, and this led to the elimination of existing customs duties but not that of fiscal taxes on imports and exports. Then a devaluation of the franc reduced Madagascar's annual payments on its public debt to only 8 per cent of total expenditures and enormously expanded the volume of its budgets in terms of postwar francs. Thus the island's budget, which had totaled 297,690,000 francs in 1938, rose to 596,567,000 in 1945 and to 1,122,-099,900 in 1946. A more meaningful change was represented by the much larger percentage—28 per cent of total expenditures—allotted in 1946 to the economic and social services, especially the health service. In other respects, however, the trends established during the interwar period were not only perpetuated but intensified in the late 1940s. In the realm of expenditures this meant sharp increases in the amounts absorbed by the payment of official personnel, and in that of revenues a growing reliance on income derived from indirect taxation without, however, any corresponding diminution in the rates of direct taxes. A more fortunate "constant" held over from the late 1920s was the persistence of budgetary surpluses, which went to swell a reserve fund that grew steadily until 1952. These annual surpluses were the result of the government's consistently underestimating income and overestimating expenditures, and, even more, of unusually favorable postwar conditions for the sale of Madagascar's produce.

During the first postwar decade a great deal of Metropolitan legislation was enacted which had profound repercussions on Madagascar's budgets—some of it beneficial and some detrimental to the island's economy. In the former category were the massive investments made by F.I.D.E.S., which provided the island for the first time with some of the social and economic equipment of a modern state. Among the undesirable effects was the conspicuous increase in the number and salaries of civil servants in Madagascar. In 1947, for example, 883 functionaries were sent from France to Madagascar, and in the years that followed, their ranks were further swelled by civil servants transferred to the island from Indochina. Some of this numerical increase was justified by the new services set up under F.I.D.E.S., but a large number of officials were posted to Madagascar without relation to its needs in personnel and without consultation of its wishes in the matter. Then the Lamine Gueye law in 1950* added 500 million C.F.A. francs at one blow to the local administration's operating expenditures, and it was followed by successive rises in the pay and perquisites of both European and Malagasy civil servants. Not only was the size of the territorial budget growing rapidly—it quadrupled between 1946 and 1951—but the proportion of its revenues allotted to paying personnel rose from about 50 per cent of the total to 60 per cent. Members of the representative assembly, heirs to the prewar Délégations in this respect, took over and amplified their complaints about the overstaffing of the administrative services, but like their predecessors they could not effect any reform so long as the budget continued to produce sizable surpluses at the end of every fiscal year.

To some extent, the civil-servant problem was the result of France's postwar policy of decentralization in Madagascar, which had resulted not in any lightening of the overheavy administrative establishment but in a duplication of many services at the central and provincial levels. The creation of provinces in 1946 necessitated a division of the island's revenues between the central and provincial administrations. Generally speaking, the central government received the income from indirect taxes—on exports, imports, and sales, as well as registration fees—which fluctuated with the fortunes of the island's foreign trade but which were invariably larger than those granted to the provinces. Direct taxes, mainly on cattle, land, and merchants' licenses, and the head tax provided each of the provinces with a stable though very small income. While the revenues from indirect taxation were steadily augmented by enlarging the number and rates of such taxes, those deriving from direct taxation could not be similarly increased, and moreover, especially during the revolt and its repression, they became very hard to collect. It was not until 1953 that the provinces were authorized to raise their own loans from the C.C.O.M. to carry out development programs, and in the meantime they were dependent to varying degrees on subsidies granted by the central government to meet their operating expenses, mainly those of personnel. In 1948 all the provinces had to be allotted subsidies that ranged from 16 million C.F.A. francs for Tananarive to 10 million for Tuléar. By

* See p. 161.

1949 three of the provinces had surpluses, but two—Tananarive and Tamatave—continued to have deficits, and total subsidies and other contributions to the provinces that year aggregated about 1 billion C.F.A. francs. Madagascar's assemblymen protested against these subsidies because they created a sense of irresponsibility among the provincial administrations and because they varied from year to year with the central government's income and thus prevented the provinces from undertaking long-term planning operations.

After long debates in 1949 and 1950, the assembly accepted two official proposals to remedy the situation. One was to turn over to the provinces the proceeds from the general income tax, whose rates, however, were to be reduced for the heads of large families. The second was the creation on behalf of the provinces of a *taxe de développement économique* (T.D.E.). Because it was imposed at the rate of 2 per cent on all business transactions except the sale of such consumer goods as foodstuffs, the T.D.E. was harshly criticized by the assemblymen. To persuade them to accept it, the government promised to study ways and means of reorganizing the government-general with a view to reducing personnel expenditures. At about the same time the assembly agreed to encourage foreign capital investments by making fiscal concessions to companies that reinvested a specified percentage of their profits in local enterprises.

The reforms just described helped to stabilize provincial finances for the next few years, and the loans that the provinces began to contract with the C.C.O.M. in 1954 enabled them to draw up both operating and investment budgets. Because of continuing favorable trade balances until 1955, the central government could cope with its rapidly growing expenditures and even budget for limited annual investment programs. Moreover, Madagascar acquired such a large reserve fund—by the end of 1952 it amounted to over 4 billion C.F.A. francs—that the assembly decided that year to utilize reserves generously to supplement the activities of F.I.D.E.S. in economic and social development. In 1953 the budget rose to nearly 10 billion francs for the whole island; 85 per cent of revenues came from indirect taxes, and nearly 7.5 billion went to pay for the government's operating expenses, leaving about 2.5 billion for investment programs.

In a study of Madagascar's financial situation published in the spring of 1954,[23] the local authorities were praised for the "comparative lightness" of the island's tax scale, the "genuine and generally successful effort made to adapt its fiscal system to the economic and social conditions of the country," and the liberality of its policy toward foreign capital investments and the transfer of profits. Nevertheless, despite the fact that the condition of Madagascar's public finances was, on the whole, sound, some serious weaknesses were discernible. A few critics censured the government for its failure to assess taxes, especially direct taxes, on an equitable basis. In 1952, for example, the head tax amounted to the equivalent of 18 days' manual labor in Tananarive province, as against 32 days in Tuléar. The peasantry, obviously the poorest segment of the population, was saddled with too large a share of the tax burden, whereas wealthy individuals and especially companies got off lightly. Governor Bargues, in a speech to the assembly on September 18, 1952, also expressed concern over the central government's revenues. Madagascar's exports, he said, might not indefinitely provide the island with budgetary surpluses, and although its revenues were growing, expenditures—particularly nonproductive ones—were increasing even faster. Indeed, Bargues was especially fortunate in being in office at a time when Madagascar enjoyed its most prosperous years. Early in 1955 his successor, Governor Soucadaux, had to cope with a fast-deteriorating financial situation.

The first years of Soucadaux's governorship were marked by a sharp increase in administrative expenditures and an equally abrupt decline in revenues. Inasmuch as a large proportion of Madagascar's growing expenses was attributable to recent legislation passed by the French parliament—the overseas labor code, the municipal-reorganization law, and the loi-cadre— France agreed to pay an ever-larger share of Madagascar's running expenditures and to supply virtually all of its capital investments. The island's government, for its part, began to practice greater austerity and to take steps to increase local revenues—but not very effectively. Under the existing fiscal system the ceiling had been about reached for both indirect and direct taxation. Thus Madagascar, as it moved nearer to political independence, became ever more dependent financially on France.

In 1955 a severe decline in the prices received for Madagascar's main exports unhappily coincided with an equally sudden rise of nearly 2 billion C.F.A. francs in the island's expenditures. This rise was due mainly to application of the overseas labor code, to the indemnities that Madagascar had become obligated to pay to victims of the 1947 revolt, and to successive pay raises for a steadily increasing number of civil servants. The deficit that year amounted to 440 million C.F.A. francs, and in order to balance the island's budget the government was forced to draw heavily on the central and provincial reserve funds, which by the end of the year were reduced almost to their legal minimum. Despite this, the authorities were so accustomed to prosperity that they believed they were dealing only with a passing recession. They therefore optimistically drew up a budget for 1956 which totaled 11,872 million C.F.A. francs—larger by 1,119 million than that for 1955— and which included 1,553 million for investment. Although they took some steps in the direction of austerity, no basic changes were made in the fiscal system. Moreover, the assembly, while it voted some increases in the income-tax scale, also granted tax reductions to those enterprises whose activities were likely to promote the island's economic development.

The year 1956, however, proved no better than 1955 insofar as revenue from foreign trading was concerned; furthermore, Madagascar suffered damage that year from cyclones, floods, and drought. Income of the central government not only was smaller (by 78 million C.F.A. francs) than in 1955, but was 501 million less than estimated. The deficit could still be covered from the reserve fund, but new expenses amounting to some 300 million C.F.A. francs were in prospect as a result of application of the municipal-reorganization law of 1955. The provincial budgets were in even worse straits than was that of the central government. Only Tananarive province's budget could be balanced, and the deficits of the others totaled 165 million C.F.A. francs. While the last-mentioned deficits could be met from the provinces' reserve funds, they were alarming because they presaged further trouble ahead. Direct taxes, the mainstay of the provincial budgets, were becoming increasingly difficult to collect. By the end of 1956 such un-collected taxes aggregated nearly 2 billion C.F.A. francs, about half of them being at least two years in arrears.

In 1957 Madagascar's foreign trade took a turn for the better, with corresponding improvement in the central government's revenues, but this proved to be only a reprieve and one confined to the territorial budget. As for the provinces, the volume of their budgets continued to grow, and, with few exceptions, their revenues went on shrinking, mainly because of their administrations' decreasing ability to collect the taxes due them. Then in 1958 Madagascar's financial position began again to deteriorate, with a renewal of the budgetary deficits and inflationary trends that had been in evidence since 1955. A budget totaling 17 billion C.F.A. francs included only 279 million earmarked for investment, and in a few years such funds ceased altogether to figure in the budget. The cost of official personnel, which had been rising throughout the 1950s, shot upward sharply after application of the *loi-cadre*. The creation of provincial public services added to this cate-gory of expenditures 300 million C.F.A. francs in 1957 and 435 million in 1958. France, to be sure, was now paying all Metropolitan functionaries serving as state officials in Madagascar, but this did not by any means offset the overall growth in administrative expenditures attributable to the policy of "enhanced provincialization."

In a speech to the representative assembly on June 23, 1957, Governor Soucadaux stressed that Madagascar could not expect France to continue paying its ever-mounting debts unless the Malagasys themselves made a greater fiscal effort, and this view was endorsed by the newly installed vice-president of the government council, Philibert Tsiranana. However, local merchants bitterly opposed such a policy, claiming that the massive increases in taxation since 1954 were largely responsible for the current economic stagnation and the flight of capital from the island. The assemblymen, too, were reluctant to authorize fresh taxation, and in support of their stand they cited the conclusions reached by a special committee that Soucadaux had formed in October 1956 to study possible fiscal reforms. That committee had proposed the classical solutions of greater austerity on the part of the government, more effective tax collection, and, above all, fairer distribution of the tax burden. "Our real taxpayers," it concluded, "number only about 20,000 out of a total of over 4 million."[24] A proposal by one assemblyman that a two-year tax moratorium be declared for Malagasys whose income was less than 6,000 C.F.A. francs monthly between 1954 and 1956 was enthusiastically acclaimed by his colleagues, as was a suggestion that tax payments be staggered throughout the year instead of falling due in a lump sum prior to the harvest.[25] Such measures, however, obviously would not help to provide the government with the greater revenues it needed. The collection of back taxes, on the other hand, would certainly contribute to that end, especially since provincial budgets had risen to a total of 8.5 billion C.F.A. francs in 1957 and over 11 billion in 1958.

Both the administration and the assembly agreed that of all the causes of Madagascar's financial instability—the fluctuating prices received for its exports, the ever-heavier administrative structures, the rising cost of living, and the flight of larger amounts of capital each year from the island—the most serious was the population's mounting resistance to paying taxes. The worst offenders in this respect were the inhabitants of the capital cities—the rich residents as well as the floating population—whereas the population of Tuléar province, poorer and almost wholly rural, had the best record as conscientious taxpayers. The government was partly responsible for this state of affairs, for it had raised tax rates rapidly within a short span of time without attempting to reform the basis of taxation, to whose inequities its attention had been repeatedly called. Then, too, the increasing evasion of tax payment could be traced to some extent to the lack of public spirit on the part of all residents of the island, regardless of nationality. This attitude had been encouraged during the election campaign of 1957 by some candidates who promised to abolish all taxation if elected. The assembly felt, as did the government, that those responsible for such deceptions and provocations should be punished, along with chronic tax defaulters, but agreement could not be reached on the means.[26] The debates on this crucial question ended inconclusively, especially since the new constitution voted in

April 1959 was due to bring about still another drastic change in the island's whole fiscal system.

Under that constitution, which in effect rejected the "provincialization" that had been initiated in 1946 and strengthened by the *loi-cadre,* the central government (and no longer the provinces) again became the recipient of almost all the island's revenues. Thus there was a return to the system under which Tananarive doled out subsidies to the provinces, which were left with the right to collect for their own use only a few minor taxes. Moreover, the imminent institution of hundreds of rural communes, which would need resources of their own on which to operate, meant still another reduction in provincial revenues. At the central-government level, the policy of "Malagasization" of the cadres, to which the country was now committed, also would lead to heavier expenditures. Funds must be found to pay the Malagasy civil servants who were progressively replacing the European functionaries theretofore paid by the French government. In consequence, it was becoming ever more expensive to keep the administrative machine running, and to add to Madagascar's woes came the need to repair the extensive damage done to many parts of the island by the catastrophic cyclone of March 1959. The 1960 budget fortunately did not include heavier taxation, and the government, in presenting it, promised to pare its own expenditures to the bone, revise the fiscal system once the new rural communes had been set up, and seek larger amounts of foreign aid from more diversified sources. The new Malagasy leaders begged their compatriots in return to produce more and better goods for domestic consumption and for export. Madagascar's budget for 1960 reflected a period of transition, and it was not until the budget for 1961 was drawn up that it was possible to begin discerning the outlines of independent Madagascar's fiscal policies.

The 1961 budget totaled 19,568 million C.F.A. francs, slightly less than the record 1959 budget, which had come to nearly 22 billion. A salary cut of 10 per cent accepted by all the cabinet ministers showed, to some extent, that the government was trying to fulfill its pledge of retrenchment. Because of this and a paring of some "less essential sectors," administrative expenditures came to only 34.5 per cent of the total. The share allotted to the social services—16.3 per cent—seemed to have been excessively reduced, but actually those services received about 20 per cent of all expenditures, because the cost of primary education and of sanitary units (except hospitals in the provincial capitals) was being borne by the provinces. The most startling innovation was the cost of Madagascar's "expenditures of sovereignty," especially the new military establishment, which received over 2 billion C.F.A. francs, or nearly 11 per cent of total expenditures. In relation to Madagascar's revenues this budget meant a deficit of nearly 4 billion, more than half of which would be met by a French subsidy of 2,300 million. To make up the balance, the government proposed various fiscal changes, such as raising some import taxes by 10 per cent and making the income tax uniform throughout the island.* The two changes just described were accepted by the parliament, but its members balked at two other government proposals —a reduction of 10 per cent in the salaries of all civil servants and the imposition of a new "civic tax" on all adults that amounted to 150 C.F.A. francs for males and 100 for females. Malagasy deputies have consistently supported pay increases for functionaries and also have opposed creating new direct taxes that do not take into account the individual's ability to pay. Moreover, the civic-tax proposal was particularly distasteful to them because for the first time it would subject women to such taxation. After heated discussions, the government finally agreed to substitute—in place of the disputed tax measures and cut in civil servants' pay—a national loan to be raised by voluntary subscription for the purpose of defraying the cost of Madagascar's diplomatic misssions and defense organization.†

To many Malagasys the 1961 budget was a disappointment. Although for the first time in some years it contained an allocation for investment (1,100 million C.F.A. francs), it remained, as before, essentially an operating budget and one that perpetuated many of the undesirable features of the pre-independence budgets. Among these were continued dependence for its main revenues on the same indirect taxes, notably export and import duties, which fluctuated from year to year; measures to encourage the investment of private capital which had not yet proved conspicuously successful; the absence of proposals for making defaulters pay their back taxes; and the lack of any provision for bolstering the reserve fund, whose liquid assets at the end of 1960 came to only 215 million C.F.A. francs. However, the 1961 budget did contain some generally acceptable innovations. The assumption of revenues and expenditures of the provinces by the central government's budget confirmed and strengthened Madagascar's accession to sovereignty, and that budget stressed national rather than regional interests —despite the concurrent existence of 934 other minor budgets, most of which came into being after the rural communes were formed.

In drafting the 1962 budget, the government showed a stronger inclination to strike out along new lines, although that budget also exhibited many familiar characteristics. Its volume grew slightly, to 20,436 million C.F.A. francs, but so did its investment allocation (1,824 million). All operating

---

* In 1961 it was stated in the parliament that there were at most 67,000 persons in Madagascar whose annual income (150,000 C.F.A. francs or more) made them liable to payment of income tax. See minutes of the national assembly for Oct. 28, 1961.
† See p. 309.

expenditures were reduced by 2 per cent except for the services of education and health, and the government promised that it would reinstitute a customs tariff for the island, which had been in abeyance since 1942, so as to provide the treasury with another source of revenue. Encouraged by these developments, the members of the parliament went along with some of the government's proposals which they had rejected in 1961, and also approved some new taxes. They were amenable to a 10 per cent cut, for a specified number of years, in civil servants' salaries. With only slightly less reluctance they also adopted the proposals to increase the gasoline tax and the tax on profits (raised from 12 per cent to 14 per cent for individuals, and from 20 per cent to 24 per cent for companies), and to introduce a transactions tax that ranged from 1 to 3 per cent. The opposition criticized the last-mentioned tax as being simply a disguised revival of the unpopular *taxe de développement économique,* and it demanded that instead of raising taxes the government accomplish genuine economies by abolishing the provincial administrations and the Senate and by dismissing all foreign technicians. Ultimately, however, the parliament accepted all the proposed new taxes, which were expected to bring in about 1 billion C.F.A. francs. Nevertheless, Madagascar was still unable to meet from revenue more than about 85 per cent of operating expenses, and to balance its budget it had to obtain from France a subsidy of about the same amount as in 1961.

The 1963 budget was larger than the preceding one by 1,196 million C.F.A. francs, mainly because of increased expenditures for services related to economic development, especially cooperative societies, and for launching a literacy campaign and the "civic service."* This budget, the government hoped, would be brought into balance through a substantial rise in exports, which had already appreciably increased during the latter half of 1962, and no increases in duties or taxation rates were proposed. The only new source of anticipated revenue was a tax on uninvested profits, which had been imposed during the summer of 1962 under the regime of special powers granted by parliament to the government. This budget seemed less dependent on French generosity than its predecessors, for France's subsidy was scaled down to 1,700 million C.F.A. francs. In addition, however, France in November 1962 reduced the debt owed to it by Madagascar from 9 to 7 billion C.F.A. francs, to be paid over a 40-year period at an interest rate of 1 per cent. Although this budget elicited the usual criticisms from the opposition, it was approved by the parliament as a whole after comparatively short and good-tempered debates.[27]

Perhaps because the deputies seemed amenable, the government dared to

* See p. 464.

propose for 1964 a budget whose volume reached the record total of 23,725 million Malagasy francs—an increase of 8.4 per cent over that of 1963. A small reduction brought administrative expenditures down to 33.1 per cent of the total, larger allocations than before were made to the economic and social services (31.1 and 17.5 per cent, respectively), and about the same share as in 1963 was earmarked for the military establishment (10.7 per cent), whereas the operating expenses of other government departments were trimmed by 10 per cent. Several features of this budget deserve attention, for they reflect significant aspects of the government's new economic policy. As an associate member of the European Economic Community, Madagascar was beginning to receive funds from that source to enable it to align its exports gradually with world prices and no longer have to count on higher-than-world prices for some of its products in the French market. As to imports, the higher duties to be charged on products competing with Malagasy manufactures, as well as the fiscal exemptions to be granted companies starting new enterprises on the island, showed the government's determination to industrialize the economy to some extent. As compensation for the losses in revenue that the foregoing policies would entail, the government proposed raising registration fees, stamp duties, and the rate of the transaction tax.

The most noteworthy aspect of the 1964 budget, however, was its allocation for investments. Not only did it set a record—10 per cent of total revenues, that is, 2,336 million—but such investments were to be integrated with Madagascar's new plan. To finance the plan, the government proposed to carry out the long-promised fundamental fiscal reform, whose basic principle would be a fairer division of the tax burden between the urban and rural populations. In regard to lightening taxes for the peasantry and compelling town dwellers to pay regularly higher taxes, all were in agreement. But there developed a general feeling among the Malagasy parliamentarians that the government was asking the present generation of their compatriots to assume too large a share of financing the plan, and that it would be advisable to seek larger amounts of foreign capital for that purpose.[28] As of the present writing, this question has not yet been settled, but it seems likely that the project of fiscal reform will be largely dissociated from projects to finance the national plan.

Madagascar's 1965 budget largely confirmed existing trends. It came to 25.8 billion FMG, and was therefore larger by 2,075 million than its immediate predecessor. Operating expenditures rose by 1,330 million and capital expenditures by 492 million, and the budget could be balanced only by increasing the rates of customs duties on luxury imports and by insuring a more effective collection of direct taxes.

Chapter twenty

THE RURAL ECONOMY

AGRICULTURE

Madagascar is to a striking extent an agricultural country. Seven-eighths of its exports, in terms of value, are agricultural products. Four-fifths of its population are engaged in farming and herding, 87 per cent of all Malagasys live in rural areas or in settlements of fewer than 2,000 inhabitants, and even many of those who reside in the large towns pursue occupations related to agriculture. Yet, taking Madagascar's agricultural output as a whole, the unfavorable aspects appear at present to outweigh the favorable ones—although in part this situation is due to elements that are not necessarily permanent features of the island's economy.

Despite an old saying that Madagascar has the color and fertility of a brick, nature has not been unkind to the country. Except in the extreme south, the island has ample surface water and in some places fertile soil. Its great diversity of climates and soils enables its people to grow a wide variety of crops, of both tropical-zone and temperate-zone types. This means that Madagascar does not suffer, as do so many underdeveloped countries, from monoculture, and it is self-sufficient in food. There is also a reasonably good balance between the crops grown for domestic consumption and those for export. The climate, on the whole, is a healthful one, and Malagasys take readily to farming. Agricultural production has been rising since World War II, and it made particularly steady progress between 1950 and 1958. To be sure, the cyclone of 1959 caused a sudden 10 per cent drop in output and a loss to the island's revenues of some 3 billion C.F.A. francs, but production revived in 1960, when it reached a level 40 per cent higher than that of 1950.[1] The average annual growth during the 1950–60 decade was 3.6 per cent, or slightly more than the population increase during that period (2.3 per cent), thus providing an important stabilizing element for the economy.

Geographical and other physical factors dominate the long list of elements unfavorable to agricultural production in Madagascar, but there are man-made ones as well. Because of the island's topography, there are no vast stretches of arable land but only "pockets of prosperity," mutually isolated and often distant from the coast and the main consuming centers. Consequently, internal communications are difficult and costly to build and maintain, and production is limited. Exports are small in quantity, and most of them do not justify the cost of transportation to distant ports. Furthermore, the regions producing the "rich" crops for export, such as coffee, vanilla, and cloves, are the very ones that are most vulnerable to damage by cyclones and wind.

Even the small minority of Malagasy farmers who produce for the export market have a low cash income. Their poverty precludes purchasing the modern implements and fertilizers that would increase crop production, and the governments' efforts to help them break out of this vicious circle have had only limited success. This failure can be traced in part to the lack of contacts between officials and peasants and in part to mistakes in the government's projects. Madagascar's rural economy is so diverse that it does not lend itself to overall planning, but requires a specially tailored plan for each of its different producing zones. To some extent, however, the official attempts to organize and modernize the Malagasy peasantry have foundered because of psychological factors. In a certain measure, the apathy of the Malagasy peasant is traceable to physical causes, such as a poorly balanced diet and the many diseases which for years were largely responsible for the lack of growth of the population. But an even greater impediment to the expansion of production has been the individualism and conservatism that derive from certain social and religious customs.

Many of these economically detrimental customs are associated with the widespread cult of the dead. The Malagasy family must, at all costs, retain ownership of the land on which the ancestral tomb is located. This is the chief cause of the uneconomic fragmentation of real property in heavily populated regions such as the high plateaus, where the average family owns only one hectare of land, and many an even smaller area. Everywhere in Madagascar, however, the frequent ceremonies pertaining to the cult of the ancestors, which are both acts of piety and pleasant social gatherings, periodically draw relatives from far and near back to the family tomb. This is reflected in widespread absenteeism from work,* and it is also detrimental to animal husbandry because such large numbers of cattle are sacrificed at these ceremonies. Although the younger generation is attracted to luxury imports now more than in the past, the great majority of rural Malagasys

* See p. 455.

have few wants, and such as they have are directly related to the bare necessities for survival and to the ancestral cult.

If the average Malagasy peasant has enough rice land and cattle to feed and clothe his family, perform the proper ceremonies, and pay his taxes, he feels no further incentive to produce. Furthermore, his constant fear of offending the omnipresent and omnipotent spirits by departing from the way in which his ancestors lived has intensified his traditional peasant conservatism. As a result, he resists changing customs that in themselves have no religious connotations but are simply consecrated by time and habit. Some Malagasy traditions are socially useful—for example, the custom of mutual aid and collective responsibility that is exemplified by the *fokonolona* organization. Others, however, are distinctly harmful both to the individual farmer and to the country, such as the practice of burning over fields and forests to fertilize the soil (*tavy*), the debonair attitude toward contracting debts, and a preference for sharecropping under disadvantageous conditions to being employed under fixed terms of time and pay.

Because of the Malagasy's resistance to change, as well as his lack of formal education, he is unresponsive to the administration's efforts to improve his agricultural techniques and equipment, to pressure him into growing new crops, to provide him with credit and selected seed, to persuade him to register his ownership of land, and generally to integrate him into a group. Although the French showed a rare perseverance in such activities and spent very large sums in pursuing them, the government's agricultural policy was not a success. For one thing, there was little sense of urgency about such efforts: for many years the population was virtually static and land was plentiful, and except for a few regions that were highly developed, the rural economy remained much as it had been before the French came. Then, too, they found the Malagasy peasants disappointingly indifferent and even hostile to attempts to change their way of life and work. Furthermore, the government altered its course repeatedly and there were frequent shifts not only in its agricultural programs but in the personnel applying them, and at no time did it ever succeed in fully winning the cooperation of the peasantry. Indeed, the proliferation of programs and organizations served to heighten the Malagasy peasant's distrust of the *fanjakana* (government), as well as his tendency to expect salvation to come to him from some external and higher source and not as the result of his own efforts.

Put in simple terms, the agricultural problem which the government of independent Madagascar has inherited is that of persuading the Malagasy farmers to grow more and better crops, and of giving them the means to do so. Of the two aspects of this problem, the former—which is psychological

326 THE ECONOMY

—is more difficult to deal with than the latter, although a Malagasy government, in contrast to a foreign one, is certainly in a better position to influence its people. Among the many obstacles to the improvement of Madagascar's agricultural production, three deserve special attention: farming techniques, sharecropping, and the system of land tenure.

Farming Techniques and Income

Madagascar's area totals some 592,000 square kilometers, but less than 3 per cent is cultivated—and very largely by archaic methods and equipment —although probably 8 per cent of the island's surface is arable. This under-utilization of the land can be ascribed, in most places, to the small size, dispersal, poverty, and ignorance of the population, and to their exclusive use of such primitive farming implements as the *angady* (long-handled spade) and *antsy* (knife). Most of the plows and draft animals used in cultivation are owned by Merina and Betsileo farmers of the high plateaus. Indeed, nine-tenths of all the modern agricultural equipment is concentrated in that region and on the west coast, where the big companies and large concessionaires own most of the tractors and other agricultural machinery. Such equipment is almost unknown on the east coast, where crops do not lend themselves to mechanized cultivation.

The existence of huge tracts of uninhabited land, together with the migratory habits of Malagasy tribes, has favored the practice of shifting agriculture. Herders as well as farmers burn over vast areas of woodlands and grasslands every year to fertilize the soil. After a few seasons, the soil is exhausted and they move on to other regions, where they repeat the process, which locally is called *tavy*. The resulting destruction of trees and vegetation cover has led to widespread erosion and to the prevalence of a hard

Provincial and Individual Incomes, 1960

Province	Annual Provincial Income (*million C.F.A. francs*)	Rural Population	Income per Head (*C.F.A. francs*)
Diégo-Suarez	5,643	341,900	16,500
Majunga	6,555	597,700	10,900
Tamatave	7,996	786,600	10,200
Tuléar	6,909	770,700	8,900
Tananarive	8,434	964,200	8,700
Fianarantsoa	11,043	1,313,700	8,400
Total	46,580	4,774,800	
Average			9,800

Source: Malagasy Republic, *Economie Malgache: Evolution 1950–1960*, p. 70.

lateritic clay surface that has earned Madagascar the name of "the great red island."

Tavy has been particularly damaging to the high plateaus, which now have more people than the land can sustain and where landholdings have become uneconomically fragmented. The attention of the French National Assembly was drawn for the first time to this economic aspect of the "problem of Madagascar" by the Malagasy deputy Rakotovelo during the debate on the *loi-cadre* on January 30, 1957. He offered data drawn from a study[2] made by the local authorities of the Betsileo region, where an average farm family of four persons had an annual cash income reported to be only 12,315 C.F.A. francs, 1,415 of which went to pay taxes. A similar analysis of the earnings of farmers in Imerina[3] disclosed an even more precarious situation. Twenty per cent of these peasants were described as "rich" because they owned two hectares of rice land, five hectares planted to dry crops, a plow and a harrow, a few head of cattle, and some poultry. These "rich" families earned as much as 100,000 C.F.A. francs a year, and therefore were able to hire agricultural labor. A middle-income group, comprising about 60 per cent of the total peasant population of Tananarive province, was just able to meet expenses from the produce of 75 *ares* to two hectares of rice land, one hectare of dry-crop land, and one cow, with the use of a few modern implements. One-fifth of the farmers of that region were described as "poor," and for lack of sufficient land they had to hire out their services part-time. Either as day laborers or sharecroppers they earned somewhat less than 24,000 C.F.A. francs for 250 working days.

No comparable study of the income of east-coast Malagasy planters has been published, but it is known that a considerable part of the proceeds from the sale of their rich export crops is spent in purchasing rice, which is not grown there in sufficient quantity to feed the population. In 1960, for the island as a whole, landholdings per family ranged from one to six hectares, and the average annual cash income came to about 30,000 C.F.A. francs.[4] Yearly earnings of the individual farmer averaged 9,800 C.F.A. francs, but he cultivated his land for not more than 150 days and could supplement his income by doing wage labor or practicing crafts. Moreover, revenues cannot be considered solely in money terms, for Malagasy peasants consume from 50 to 80 per cent of their own produce. Then, too, certain crops bring in more cash income than others, so earnings vary with the region, the kind of crop, and the cost of moving it to market.

Sharecropping

Everywhere in Madagascar except on the east coast, in the extreme south, and in the Betsileo region, sharecropping (*métayage*) is practiced. It flour-

ishes particularly in the west-coast river deltas, around Lake Alaotra, on the
high plateaus of Tananarive province, and in Diégo-Suarez province. The
crops cultivated by sharecropping are cape peas, corn, manioc, *paka* (*Urena
lobata*), peanuts, and, above all, rice and tobacco. As of 1960, 15 per cent of
all the rice fields in Madagascar were worked by sharecroppers, as compared
with 2 per cent for dry crops, and there were 17,000 sharecroppers engaged
in growing tobacco.[5] Of a total area of some 150,000 hectares farmed by
sharecroppers, only 30,000 were owned by big concessionaires, either as individuals or companies. On the remaining 120,000 hectares, owned by small
Malagasy landowners, 125,000 sharecroppers were employed. The great
majority of sharecroppers are Malagasys, as are the landowners for whom
they work on small family farms.

The prevalence of this system seems due to the Malagasys' marked preference for sharecropping rather than working for wages on European-
owned plantations. Between Malagasy landowners and sharecroppers the
arrangements are almost always verbal, and for periods of time ranging
widely from one to 16 years. Companies and individuals holding large concessions normally employ sharecroppers for only short periods, and the
arrangements are specified in written contracts signed by both parties. The
considerable array of French legislation designed to regulate sharecropping
in Madagascar can be disregarded, for it was enacted exclusively with the
west-coast region in mind and was never enforced even there. The relations
as well as the agreements between landowner and sharecropper differ widely
with the region, crop, and ethnic group, but usually the sharecropper everywhere is allotted land on which to raise food crops and given building materials for a dwelling. In some cases the landowner supplies only land and
water, in others half or all the seed as well, and in still others also irrigation
facilities, plowing equipment, and even money loans. The sharecropper,
for his part, usually provides some of the seed, tills the soil, and cares for and
harvests all the crop. The respective contributions of owner and sharecropper naturally determine the division between them of the proceeds
from the harvest, but certain traditions have grown up in relation to specific
crops. For example, for *paka* and peanuts the proceeds are halved, whereas
for cape peas and sugarcane, one-quarter of their sales value goes to the
owner and the balance to the sharecropper.

Some French students of Madagascar's agriculture are inclined to find
sharecropping praiseworthy, on the whole, as a simple system congenial to
the Malagasy temperament and one that gives fair returns.[6] In recent years,
however, it has been increasingly deprecated as an impediment to agricultural progress if not a downright economic scourge. Its main drawbacks
are certainly that it encourages the practice of usury,[7] with which its evolution has been closely linked, and discourages initiative. An enterprising

sharecropper is not rewarded by greater returns for his efforts, as would be the case if he paid a fixed rent for the land he farms; hence he lacks any incentive to work harder and to use improved agricultural techniques.

Land Tenure and European Colonization

Individual and even collective property rights were unknown in Madagascar until the reign of King Andrianampoinimerina in the eighteenth century. He divided most of Imerina among the Merina tribes, and ordered their chiefs to subdivide the land among the various *fokonolona*. The *mpiadidy* (headman), in turn, was required to allot his *fokonolona*'s land among its member-families, so that they could grow foodstuffs—especially rice—and build houses and family tombs. Such property is still called "the land of the ancestors" in Imerina, and because it is usually rice land and associated with the ancestral cult it is regarded as a sacred trust and is almost never sold.

The land not allotted to the various tribes constituted a kind of public domain, and consisted mainly of forests and other areas difficult to cultivate. The Merina code of 1881 forbade the sale or rental of public land without specific authorization from the government. Although this code also laid down the principle that foreigners might not own any land in Imerina, the government actually did make some 30 sizable land grants to aliens after long-drawn-out negotiations and large gifts to the appropriate officials concerned.[8] Neither individual nor collective property rights, however, were ever secure under the Merina monarchs, for they were in reality only usufruct rights which could be rescinded at any time by the sovereign as ultimate owner of all the land in his domain. In practice, however, this rarely happened, and usufruct rights could even be bequeathed. In all but three Malagasy tribes, the legacy of parents was divided equally among all the children. Among the Antandroy, however, only sons could inherit, and among the Bara and Tanala daughters' rights were restricted to movable property.[9]

The first Franco-Malagasy conflict broke out over—at least ostensibly—a question of property rights related to the distribution of Jean Laborde's estate. This war ended with a treaty in 1885, which did not, however, alter the Merina government's refusal to permit foreigners to own land on the island, though from that time on they were allowed to rent it under long-term and renewable leases. After the Malagasys' defeat in 1895, the Queen finally yielded to French pressure and granted Frenchmen full ownership rights to land. A French law of March 9, 1896, confirmed the Malagasys' traditional usufruct enjoyment of property on which they had built or which they habitually cultivated, but unfortunately no record of such rights existing at the time was kept. This proved later to be a grave omission, especially after a decree of February 4, 1911, embodied the principles of the Torrens system of land registration used in Australia. Thenceforth, Malagasy land held under the traditional ownership system could not be mortgaged, and for a land title to be valid it must be registered with the legal authorities. Malagasys were given the option of registering their ownership rights according to this law, but French companies and concessionaires were obliged to register. After Madagascar was annexed under the law of 1896, France assumed the Merina Queen's rights and thus claimed to be ultimate owner of all the island and as such to be in a position to grant land concessions.

Creole settlers from the Mascareignes were already established on the east coast at the time of the French conquest. It was they who introduced the "rich" crops of vanilla, coffee, cloves, and sugarcane, which they grew on small plantations that nominally "belonged" to the Malagasy woman with whom a Creole planter was living.[10] Early in his Madagascar career, Gallieni strongly encouraged European colonization, both by his demobilized soldiers and by Réunionais immigrants, whom he aided with land grants and equipment. A French national with a capital of only 5,000 francs might obtain 50 hectares of state land without payment, and such grants were later increased to 100 hectares on condition that the concessionaires put them under cultivation. Even on such easy terms, however, there was little demand for concessions, and when Gallieni left Madagascar in 1905, there were only 630 European settlers who were actually cultivating 18,000 of the 400,000 hectares that had been granted.[11] Discouraged by this indifference and also by abuses committed by some of the settlers, Gallieni changed his mind and reluctantly concluded that Madagascar was not a *colonie de peuplement.*

Nor was Madagascar destined to become a colony for big concessionaires. To be sure, some companies and individuals had received vast land grants, but the great majority never got from them the huge profits that had been anticipated. Of the 900,000 hectares of land grants, 550,000 had gone to five large French companies* and the remainder to 2,000 individuals or smaller firms. Although many recipients of these concessions worked hard to improve their properties according to the terms of their grant, large areas were left untouched and some were simply held for speculation.

A small influx of settlers from France after World War I and a revival of interest by some important firms which were potential investors in Madagascar induced Governor Olivier to modify the provisions of the law of March 9, 1896. By a decree of September 28, 1926, the French state was de-

* These companies were the Suberbie, Grande Ile, Franco-Malgache de la Culture, Sambirano, and Delhorbe.

clared to be owner of all land that had not been fenced in or conceded, and this land was classified as being in the public or the private domain. Declared to be public lands were canals, railroads, riverbanks, etc., which were of general utility to the total population and were therefore made inalienable. The private domain was divided into rural and urban lands, and the rural was subdivided into two categories. One of these, comprising 750,000 hectares (with an additional 300,000 hectares earmarked for future expansion), was called "native reservations." Such reservations, except for pasturelands, which were kept for communal use, were to be allotted by the *fokonolona* to member families. Malagasys were also to be permitted to gather firewood and sow rice in swamps and waterways of the other category of rural lands, of which the balance would be conceded to settlers.[12] Concessions from this portion of rural lands were restricted to 100 hectares in each case, and they might be given free to veterans, heads of large families, and the like. Permanent title to them, however, depended upon fulfillment of specified development terms. To prevent speculation, more stringent conditions of development were imposed upon concessionaires of urban lands.

In 1929 the government began making a survey of the island with a view to fixing precise limits to all property rights; at the same time it made credit terms particularly attractive to settlers and companies holding concessions. That same year, administrators in rural areas were given a freer hand to simplify the complex and costly procedures required for registering title to landed property and for granting small concessions. They were empowered to preside over *tribunaux terriers,* or small courts especially constituted to go to the scene of a prospective grant, survey it, hear claims on ownership, and decide whether or not the grant should be made. By such measures the government was trying to prevent abuses by some Malagasys who produced false testimonials as to their ancestral usufruct rights over a property, and also by settlers who tended to ride roughshod over authentic Malagasy claims.

Although Governor Olivier's policy was in many ways well conceived, it failed to lure prosperous settlers and companies to Madagascar as he had hoped. Few of the concessionaires already installed there had made fortunes, and in fact some of them had grown so discouraged with farming that they had turned to mining. Then, about 1925, labor became increasingly scarce for all white planters. Many of the Malagasys who had originally worked as laborers on European-owned plantations had by then learned enough to start growing export crops on their own lands. Faced with a shortage of labor, especially acute at harvest time, the settlers called on the government to requisition workers for them. At first the government acceded, but this practice led to such abuses that the authorities became increasingly reluctant to continue it. Furthermore, the world depression, which hit Madagascar's exports severely in the early 1930s, forced some of the poorest settlers out of business. A few small planters managed to weather the storm, but in general only the most heavily capitalized and best-run plantations on the east coast survived. By 1935 virtually all of Madagascar's food crops were being grown by Malagasys, and of the 230,000 hectares devoted to rich crops Malagasy planters farmed 162,000.[13]

World War II dealt another blow to Madagascar's French agricultural companies and planters producing for export, and still more of them went to the wall. Some, however, were saved by the administration's purchasing and storing their crops for sale after the Free French government took over the island.* After the war came the 1947 revolt and its repression, which most adversely affected the areas of European colonization. The *petit colon* of the east coast virtually disappeared from the scene, and by 1957 Malagasys were producing 90 per cent of the island's export crops. Yet, in the postwar decade, the settlers and companies still operating received more encouragement and funds from official sources than ever before, and in large part this was responsible for far-reaching changes in their activities.

Although Europeans continued to operate the largest and most profitable coffee plantations, most of them turned their attention to new crops in new regions and to the development of mechanized farming. It was the European companies, and to a lesser extent individual French settlers, that promoted sugarcane cultivation in the northwest, sisal in the south, peanuts and other oleaginous crops (mainly *aleurites*) in Itasy, and rice and peanuts in the Lake Alaotra basin, using the most modern equipment and benefiting most from the government's technical and monetary aid.[14]

In general, Malagasy farmers filled the high plateaus, but in three regions there was room for European colonization. Antsirabe district acquired the largest number of French settlers, with 455 concessions covering 11,792 hectares, compared with 130 concessions totaling 6,410 hectares in Imerina. Two districts of the Itasy region together had during the first postwar decade 34 concessions comprising more than 13,000 hectares. But it was in the rice fields around Lake Alaotra that there developed the outstanding instance of what European colonization could accomplish by mechanized cultivation. In the northwest, on Nossi-Bé and in the Mahavavy delta, big companies and prosperous *colons* were growing sugarcane on huge, well-managed concessions. On a smaller scale, several other companies were producing sisal on sizable areas near Fort-Dauphin, tobacco was being culti-

* See pp. 37–38.

vated on concessions in the west-coast deltas held by individual settlers using sharecropper labor, and promising experiments with cotton-growing were being carried on in the Mangoky basin. At the same time, almost all of these companies and settlers were devoting their energies increasingly to the development of related processing industries. As such industries expanded more rapidly than did the production of the plantations which had given birth to them, the owners bought raw materials to an ever-greater extent from nearby Malagasy farmers.

To some degree, the Europeans of the post–World War II years in Madagascar were serving as pioneers of new export crops and agricultural techniques for the whole island, as their predecessors had done on the east coast. But the Malagasys' lack of capital, of technical skills, and of enterprise prevented their profiting fully from such examples, and overall agricultural production was lagging behind the country's obvious potential. Madagascar still had large empty spaces that seemed to cry out for development, and the Malagasy people seemed to be too few and dispersed and above all too apathetic to undertake the task effectively. An obvious answer was to bring in more industrious and skilled colonists from outside the island.

The idea of encouraging foreign colonists and laborers to come to Madagascar was not new. Coolie labor had been brought in from the Far East to work on railroad-building, but the few Chinese who stayed in Madagascar became traders, not farmers. Some Boer families, after the British victory in the South African war, settled on the high plateaus, but not in any great number. During the upsurge of fascism in the 1930s, Minister of Colonies Georges Mandel toyed with the possibility of bringing Jews from Central Europe to Madagascar, where climatic conditions on the high plateaus permitted white men to do manual labor. None of these schemes, however, actually materialized. After World War II they were revived with greater cogency, this time in relation to the problems posed by the vast increase in the number of displaced persons. France was subjected to considerable international pressure to open up Madagascar to white immigration on a large scale. In the late 1940s, the French government was far from desirous of introducing unknown foreign elements among the Malagasys, who had just been severely shaken by a revolt, but realized that it could not indefinitely maintain what seemed a dog-in-the-manger attitude.

After the Liberation, the authorities considered enticing peasant families to Madagascar from France, but they became discouraged by the lack of response from that milieu to the prospect of going 10,000 kilometers from home just to farm. Another possibility was to bring in white farmer-settlers from Réunion Island, which was beginning to suffer severely from overpopulation, but this scheme encountered some Malagasy opposition. For many years the Réunionais settlers in Madagascar had been unpopular with all elements of the resident population;* hence there could be no question of encouraging Réunionais immigration on a scale that would appreciably relieve that island's surplus-population problem. Obviously the project would—initially at least—have to be very limited in scope, and would require careful preliminary study. To survey the question of white immigration for all of France's dependencies (among other tasks), a Bureau pour le Développement de la Production Agricole (B.D.P.A.) was created on April 29, 1950, and Madagascar was given top place on its agenda. A group of experts, under the guidance of Governor R. Delavignette, was sent to Madagascar that year to select a site for the first experimental settlement and to study the conditions under which it should be set up.[15]

As the locale for the B.D.P.A.'s first experiment, the mission chose Sakay in the Ankaizina region, about 100 kilometers west of Tananarive, where the climate and soil seemed suitable for the cultivation of temperate-zone crops by white farmers and where there was almost no indigenous population. Members of the mission took note of the fact that to build roads, houses, and drainage canals would require considerable expenditures by the B.D.P.A., but that this was an indispensable first step. They also stressed the need for careful screening of the first settler families selected to launch the experiment, their close supervision by qualified technicians, and their winning of the cooperation of neighboring Malagasys. The Sakay Malagasys were not farmers but herders, who were afraid that their cattle might no longer be able to roam freely after the settlers started growing crops. To calm the opposition of Malagasy nationalists to the scheme, the experiment was to be confined at the start to nine Réunionais families and 1,200 hectares of land.

Although later the number of Réunionais immigrants was increased, as was the area of their operations, the B.D.P.A. has succeeded in two important respects. It has grown new crops by modern methods at Sakay and also has convinced the Malagasy government of the value of its work to Malagasy agriculture. The Malagasy authorities now recognize that in view of the very rapid growth in the local population it is of vital importance that Malagasy farmers should increase food production for domestic consumption and for export by making use of Western techniques. The B.D.P.A. has also allayed their fear lest the Sakay settlement become the forerunner of a large-scale Réunionais immigration bent on taking over much of the island's arable land. The Sakay experiment has demonstrated what can be done to increase the productivity of the whole high-plateau region, and as such it has been a remarkable technical success.[16]

---

* See pp. 44 and 268.

Nevertheless, the new orientation and extension of European colonization in general and the Sakay experiment in particular alarmed the Malagasy elite and revived its demand for reform of the land-tenure system. Increasingly resentment was expressed that public funds had been lavished upon hydraulic and other land improvements which benefited European concessionaires rather than Malagasy peasants. Jules Ranaivo, in a speech to the French National Assembly on December 17, 1954, asked the government to resume work on surveying the whole island—a project which had been in abeyance since before World War II—and to allow Malagasy landowners whose titles to their land had not been registered to use them as guaranty for mortgages.

To some extent the government responded favorably to these pleas. In 1955 it persuaded the F.I.D.E.S. directorate to reverse its decision against allotting funds for a land survey, and in 1956 it further eased the formalities for registering ownership of land for Malagasys who could offer proof that they had effectively occupied the area they claimed during the preceding ten years. But such measures did not wholly satisfy Malagasy critics. The survey financed by F.I.D.E.S. was confined to the Ambositra district of Tananarive province and to the area there slated for hydraulic improvements, and the titles granted to Malagasys under the new ten-year rule did not permit them to raise mortgages on such property. In justifying the latter restriction, the French authorities claimed that they were protecting from spoliation the easily indebted Malagasy peasant, who would otherwise lose his land to a foreign moneylender. It was also pointed out that although Malagasy nationalists bitterly objected to the injustices perpetrated by French concessionaires, they did not censure members of the Merina bourgeoisie, who often lived in towns and did nothing to improve the rural land they had inherited.

Perhaps the most constructive steps taken by the French administration in this sphere during its last years in Madagascar were the decree of February 24, 1957, which established the procedures by which the government could expropriate concessions that had never been developed, and a province-by-province study of the status of existing concessions, which was begun in March 1956. From this study it was learned that ownership titles had been registered for a total of 2,500,000 hectares, of which 1,900,000 had been surveyed. Concessions to which permanent title had been issued covered 600,000 hectares, and those with temporary titles 1,400,000, and less than half of all the area conceded had been developed.[17] These data impelled the P.S.D. government, after it came to power in 1957, to revive dead-letter decrees dating back to 1927 and 1946, which enabled it to tax undeveloped conceded areas at the rate of 700 C.F.A. francs per hectare and by this device to recuperate for the state more than 250,000 hectares. This action, however, did not satisfy all the Malagasy assemblymen, as was shown during the debates on the government's proposal to give fiscal encouragement to companies that reinvested their profits in Madagascar.[18] Some members of the assembly harped on the theme that Europeans had monopolized all the best land on the island, leaving to the Malagasys only the areas hardest to cultivate. They were especially incensed at the French settlers and companies in the Lake Alaotra region for gaining control of all the land improved by the technical services, and at those on the west coast for reducing the Sakalava there to the status of sharecroppers. Wherever land had been conceded to foreigners, they said, whole villages had been engulfed and prevented from expanding cultivation according to their needs.

To these critics the government replied that the republic's constitution confirmed respect for private property, that foreign capitalists must not be discouraged from investing and reinvesting in Madagascar, and that steps were being taken to safeguard legitimate Malagasy interests. On November 5, 1959, Tsiranana presented to the assembly a new land law, which he described as "revolutionary" and which had three main objectives. The first of these was to guaranty ownership of land to those who actively developed it; the second was to simplify, accelerate, and decentralize the procedure for granting concessions;* and the third was to replace the "obsolete native reservations" by land grants to rural communes for use by their members. Thenceforth the government would cede free of charge plots of ten hectares to "meet the needs of a growing population," but areas of 50 hectares or more would be granted only to those whose activities fitted in with the official plan for developing the island's economy as a whole. The administration also promised to hire 30 more technicians so as to complete the land survey of Madagascar.

In 1960 the government went further and set up two companies of mixed economy, which were charged with distributing some of the land in the public domain that the republic had inherited from the French administration. The first of these companies was the Société Malgache de la Sakay (SOMASAK), which was to apply the mixed-farming techniques developed by the B.D.P.A. for the greater economic and social well-being of 64 Malagasy families living near the Réunionais settlement. The second such company was the Société pour l'Aménagement du Lac Alaotra (SOMA-LAC), which was to improve the public domain in the Lake Alaotra basin, divide it into small plots, and sell these to Malagasy peasants.

Curiously enough, the Malagasy assemblymen were as suspicious of these proposals of the P.S.D. government as they had been of the French adminis-

---

* At that time 38,000 requests for concessions were pending.

tration's successive schemes for the organization of the peasantry.[19] They found the cost of launching SOMASAK—48 million C.F.A. francs—far too high, although the F.A.C. was footing the bill. Then they found fault with SOMALAC for selling improved land too dear to Malagasy peasants who, they feared, would never be granted full title to the property but would find themselves sharecroppers or "serfs." The most radical of the government's critics demanded the expropriation of all land held by foreign concessionaires and its distribution without charge among the Malagasy peasantry.

The P.S.D. government, for its part, has insisted that, as the majority shareholder in the new companies, it can control and orient their activities, and that such profits as they make from land sales will be reinvested to improve other areas of the public domain. It has consistently maintained that its policy is one of reform of the existing land-tenure system and that the drastic measures demanded by its critics—the nationalization of foreign-owned concessions and the elimination of usury and sharecropping—are not urgently needed. Official spokesmen reiterate that Madagascar still has vast areas of unutilized arable land, and that it is up to the Malagasy peasants themselves to make more productive the holdings already in their hands.

Agricultural Credit

The Malagasy peasant, whether the descendant of slaves or of free men, has never raised himself from a condition of chronic indebtedness and very low living standards. In the time of the Merina monarchs, even the farmers who were free men were the prey of moneylenders. Queen Ranavalona II's code of 1881 prescribed severe penalties for those who loaned or borrowed money at interest rates exceeding 120 per cent a year, but even moneylenders who remained within that usuriously high legal rate could sell the goods of a defaulting debtor and in some cases also enslave him and his family. As for the slaves who were suddenly liberated in 1896, they were totally unprepared to benefit by their freedom. Those who struck out on their own and tried to become farmers needed money immediately to pay for seed and for tools to prepare the ground for cultivation. Even before their first harvest, therefore, they found themselves heavily indebted. This was especially true in rural areas where the moneylender was also a shopkeeper, who easily tempted farmers to borrow money at usurious rates to buy goods in excess of those they strictly needed.

After the conquest, the French administration issued a series of regulations that progressively reduced the legal rate of interest on loans from 24 per cent a year in 1898 to 5 per cent in 1935. Only exceptionally, however, could such regulations be enforced, particularly in isolated regions where farmers who formerly had been slaves simply acquired new masters—the Indian and Chinese shopkeepers.[20] Since any additional effort on the part of such a debtor merely enriched the moneylender, and because the Malagasy peasant felt few needs, he lacked incentive to work harder and change his way of life.

For some of the same material and psychological reasons, the small-scale European planter likewise incurred heavy debts. This group consisted mostly of poor and unskilled immigrants from Réunion Island, who brought with them a Creole disdain for manual labor and unrealistic ambitions for grandiose accomplishments. Neither they nor the French soldiers demobilized from Gallieni's army, whom he encouraged to settle in Madagascar, had the money or patience required to create and maintain plantations in virgin land. Most of them settled on the east coast, where soil conditions and the abundance of rain were propitious for growing "rich" crops for export, but there they also suffered from cyclones and the dearth of labor. Even under optimum conditions they had to wait five years for their crops to come into bearing, and in the interval they became heavily indebted—in most cases to the big European import-export firms. The Comptoir National d'Escompte, the only bank operating in Madagascar until 1919, loaned money only to such companies and individuals as could offer reliable guaranties of repayment, and not to the Malagasy peasant or the impecunious French settler who needed it most.

A move to remedy this situation was made in 1912, but it had no practical effect before the outbreak of World War I. In 1916 the government made an effort to aid small planters, but the sum available for loans to them was so ridiculously small (600,000 francs) and the conditions laid down for repayment so stringent that it failed to meet their needs. Nor did the advent of the Crédit Foncier in 1919 do much to improve the situation, for, despite its name, it loaned money almost exclusively to commercial firms. Not until the decree of April 23, 1920, were the foundations laid in Madagascar for a credit-*cum*-cooperative system, which was expanded and somewhat modified by the decrees of April 19, 1930, and May 25, 1939. These regulations established on the island fundamentally the same system as was then operating in France, but with a local variation. At its base was a network of agricultural associations and cooperatives dependent on local *caisses,* and at the top of the pyramid a *caisse centrale,* which served as banker and supervisor for the whole system. Under the control of the *caisse centrale* there existed two separate groups of local *caisses*—one for Europeans and one for Malagasys—and they evolved along different lines. The former were organized on the basis of one per district and were managed by directors elected from and by the members of the cooperatives. The Malagasy *caisses* were everywhere in the charge of district officers, and they were more tightly organized on the basis of one per canton.

On the whole, the European network proved to be the more satisfactory of the two, although it was repeatedly attacked by the colony's merchants and there was difficulty in finding honest and competent managers. In the dark years of World War II it certainly helped many French coffee and tobacco planters to remain in business, and after the war it emerged with enhanced prestige and a sound financial position.* The Malagasy network suffered from several disabilities. These included its domination by district officers, as well as such complicated procedures and limited resources that it touched only a handful of planters and farmers, leaving the bulk of Madagascar's rural population still the prey of usurers. A main handicap under which both European and Malagasy credit-cooperative organizations labored was that they were all financed by the government and not from contributions by members. This continued to be true during the early postwar years, when the agricultural-credit institutions received additional funds from the Banque de Madagascar, the C.C.O.M., and the territorial budget.

Throughout the early 1950s the prewar credit institutions and cooperatives declined in number and lost ground and influence. Alongside of them there sprang up a series of organizations which took over or duplicated, rather than complemented, many of their activities. Such was the case of the Crédit de Madagascar, in particular, which became banker for the Collectivités Autochtones Rurales (C.A.R.) and the forerunner of the Caisse d'Equipement Agricole et de Modernisation du Paysannat (C.E.A.M.P.).† It was also true of the Communes Rurales Autonomes Modernisées (C.R.A.M.), the Groupements de Collectivités, and the various price-support funds. The situation became especially confused during the governorship of Soucadaux, who added new institutions without eliminating those already in existence. Among the present-day survivors of the earlier period is the Caisse Centrale de Crédit Agricole, which continues to grant short-, medium-, and long-term loans to individual farmers and planters.

Organization of the Peasantry

The launching of the C.A.R. in 1950 was related to the revival of the *fokonolona,* and was thus indirectly a reaction to the revolt of 1947.‡ Their

---

* In 1944 the island's credit institutions had 2,985 borrowers, almost all of whom were indebted for short-term loans of less than 3,000 francs. There were then altogether 35 agricultural cooperatives, of which 13 were European, with 308 members, and 22 were Malagasy, with 12,556 members.

† See p. 340.
‡ See pp. 144 and 149.

founding was motivated by the belief that theretofore the administration's actions in the rural milieu had failed because they had been at worst authoritarian and at best paternalistic. Consequently, official activity had destroyed local initiative and any prospect for establishing fruitful two-way contacts between the people and the government. To offset the predominantly political character of the C.A.R., a Conseil Supérieur du Paysannat was formed in May 1952 for the purpose of selecting two in each province and transforming them into organizations mainly economic in orientation. These new organizations, the C.R.A.M., were provided with supplementary funds by still another new institution, the Caisse d'Equipement Agricole et de Modernisation du Paysannat (C.E.A.M.P.), established in 1951. The C.R.A.M. were modeled after similarly named institutions that had been successful in Morocco, and were placed in the charge of French administrators. The first of them were created to experiment with developing new land by modern methods of cultivation, notably by associating rice with dry-crop farming, but it was planned that they should later branch out into forestry, fisheries, and animal husbandry.[21] The C.R.A.M. received ample funds from F.I.D.E.S. and from local budgets to buy modern equipment, including machinery. By late 1953 there were 17 C.R.A.M. already operating, and they had received a total of some 70 million C.F.A. francs.

Despite the ample funds placed at their disposal and the apparent enthusiasm with which the Malagasy peasantry accepted them, the C.R.A.M. soon ran into trouble, and only a few of them were successful. One prime difficulty they encountered was the administration's insistence that the C.R.A.M. select only enterprises that would give quick monetary returns, and that they use machinery for cultivating crops when in many cases mechanized cultivation was unsuitable. Overambitious projects were undertaken without sufficient preliminary study, and their execution was entrusted to civil servants who were not qualified technicians. Not only did the administration's strong grip on the C.R.A.M. antagonize the Agricultural Service's technicians, whose cooperation might have been enlisted, but the government did not succeed in establishing through the C.R.A.M. any closer contacts with the rural masses than in the past. Furthermore, the C.A.R., C.R.A.M., and C.E.A.M.P. functioned without relation to the agricultural credit and cooperative associations that had been longer in existence.

In 1955, the new Governor-general, André Soucadaux, tried to remedy this lack of coordination and contacts by creating still another type of rural organization—the *secteurs de paysannat*. This time, however, the *secteurs* were entrusted to technicians of the Agricultural Service, who in only a few cases utilized the framework provided by the earlier organizations. The operations of each technician of the new *secteurs* were on a small scale, for he was responsible for equipping and teaching modern methods to only 1,400 farmers cultivating altogether not more than 2,000 hectares. An important innovation was that he was instructed to show farmers by direct example how to use the seed, tools, and techniques that had been developed at the island's agricultural stations.

Under Soucadaux's plan, the *secteurs* were to be transformed eventually into cooperative societies, or Sociétés Mutuelles de Développement Rural (S.M.D.R.). As an intermediate step, however, the new *secteurs* were brought together in 1957 into Groupements de Collectivités. These Groupements included all existing rural institutions in a district, the traditional as well as the more recently constituted ones, and each was placed under the management of a council elected by all the Groupement's members but still headed by the district officer. The role of the chairman was restricted to financial supervision, and even this control was to wither away after the Groupements had developed the ability to manage and finance their organizations as true cooperative societies. The government's ultimate aim was to group all of Madagascar's farmers, herders, and fishermen into S.M.D.R. according to their occupations.

Another of Soucadaux's innovations, which he proposed to the territorial assembly in November 1956, was the transformation of the C.E.A.M.P. into a state organization to be called the Société pour l'Aménagement Rural de Madagascar (S.A.R.M.), which would serve as both banker and policy coordinator for the Groupements. It was to take over the liquid assets of the C.E.A.M.P., which then amounted to about 150 million C.F.A. francs. It received 80 million more from the C.C.O.M., the Crédit de Madagascar, and the territorial budget, for the utilization of which it would be responsible to the government. On its board of directors all the organizations from which it had received funds were to be represented, including the territorial assembly and the Ministry of Overseas France.

The reaction of Madagascar's assemblymen to Soucadaux's successive proposals was a mixture of approval, resignation, and skepticism.[22] They realized that since the end of World War II France had spent over 1,800 million C.F.A. francs in its efforts to modernize Madagascar's rural economy, and that if many of these had failed it was not the Malagasys who had paid the bill, except perhaps in terms of disillusionment. The new formula embodied in the S.A.R.M. pleased them to the extent that it was to be a state company on whose board of directors the assembly would be represented, and that it promised to bring some order out of the confused mass of overlapping agricultural organizations and to relate them more directly to the peasants' needs. At the same time that they gave their approval to the

S.A.R.M., however, they warned the administration that if the new orga
nization failed they would accept no further official attempts to organiz
or reorganize the peasantry.

In general, the government of independent Madagascar has taken ove
and developed the peasant organizations bequeathed to it by the last Frenc
governor-general. In particular, it has accepted the cooperative society a
the formula best able to improve the living standards of the peasants an
increase food production to supply the island's rapidly growing populatior
In 1963 alone, 300 new S.M.D.R. were formed, of which 250 were exclu
sively agricultural. It will take many more years, however, to train th
cadres needed by the S.M.D.R. and especially to instill the principles o
cooperation in Madagascar's individualistic, ignorant, and isolated peasant
The national assembly has on several occasions expressed concern over th
slowness of the peasantry's evolution and the meagerness of the result
achieved through the multiple rural organizations. But the assembly's im
patience is aroused less by the snail's progress of the cooperative movemen
than by the government's reluctance to deal with related questions, such a
the land-tenure system and the prevalence of usury.

The Technical Services and Organizations

Under the Merina monarchy, the presence of Réunionais planters o
Madagascar's east coast aroused the interest of the French government i
the island's agriculture, and as early as 1885 it appointed an agricultura
official to the office of the French Resident at Tananarive. In 1896, the sam
year in which the French conquered Madagascar, Gallieni formed an agr
cultural service, which promptly began to organize experimental station
Of these early stations, only that of Ivoloina, near Tamatave town, could b
called a success, but even there it was not wholly satisfactory. In 1902 th
Madagascar Chamber of Commerce urged the government to create
special service to study the diseases and pests that were afflicting expor
crops on the east coast.[23] This was not done, however, until the 1920s, an
meanwhile the agricultural service created more experimental stations a
well as numerous plant and seed nurseries throughout the island. Some c
these stations contributed to the improvement of agriculture in their imme
diate vicinity and gave some practical training to local farmers, but on th
whole they were regarded as unsatisfactory. The results of their experimen
were not coordinated or applied directly to Malagasy farming; they seeme
to operate in a vacuum and on too small and local a scale to warrant thei
continuance.

Between 1928 and 1932 the agricultural service was reorganized on a
island-wide basis, with headquarters at Tananarive. It was given respons

bility for the various specialized branches that then existed, and it is now also responsible for those that developed after World War II. Through one of them, the Service de Recherche Agronomique, established in 1950, it continues to be nominally in charge of the experimental stations, which have grown in number and changed their orientation over the years. In fact, however, these stations are being taken over to an increasing extent by highly specialized Metropolitan organizations, as described in the table on agricultural stations. In most instances they were founded to specialize in one or two regional crops, but, except for the station at Antalaha, they have all widened the scope of their interests, and many also now give practical training to local Malagasy farmers. Because of the diversity of Madagascar's climates and soils, each producing zone has been provided with its own station, but they differ widely in scope, resources, and equipment. The research done by these stations on coffee, vanilla, cloves, fibers, and oleaginous plants is financed in part by the proceeds from the price-support funds initiated by the government during the 1950s.

Since the end of World War II, agricultural research in Madagascar, as in Africa, has tended to become increasingly specialized, and large amounts of money have been poured into such projects in Madagascar not only by F.I.D.E.S. but also by half a dozen other Metropolitan French organizations. Of these, O.R.S.T.O.M. has the largest funds and widest range of activities. In 1948 it established an Institut de Recherches Scientifiques de Madagascar (I.R.S.M.), which fathered branches at Tananarive (for pedology, entomology, sociology, and botany), at Vendrove (hydrology), and at Nossi-Bé (oceanography and marine biology). Since 1959 the I.R.S.M. has increasingly devoted itself to problems of soil conservation, but it has also been conducting social studies on the growth of juvenile delinquency and the incidence of malaria in Madagascar. At present I.R.S.M. receives an annual subsidy from the central government's budget amounting to around 200 million FMG, but its expenses continue to be paid, to a great extent, from French public funds.

The other Metropolitan institutions that have been operating in Madagascar since World War II are not so diversified in their interests and tend to specialize in one or two crops. The Institut de Recherches du Coton et des Textiles Exotiques (I.R.C.T.) has been conducting research on sisal since 1948 and on cotton since 1955 at centers situated in Mangoky, Tuléar, Ankazoabo, and Kamoro. The Institut Français du Café et du Cacao (I.F.C.C.) has taken charge of coffee-growing at Ivoloina, Ilaka (Vatomandry), and Kianjavato, and has begun experimenting with cocoa cultivation at Ambanja. The Service d'Exploitation Industrielle des Tabacs et des Allumettes (S.E.I.T.A.) has long kept a permanent mission on the

Agricultural Stations in Madagascar

Locality	Climate	Specialty	Comments
Nanisana	Temperate	Fruit trees	Founded in 1896 to acclimatize temperate-zone fruit trees and to grow silkworms. Silkworm-breeding has been largely abandoned, but this station grows and distributes hundreds of fruit trees each year and experiments with a few food crops. It is now best known as a center for teaching agronomy.
Ivoloina	Humid tropical	Vanilla, pepper, robusta coffee, perfume plants	Created in 1898 to improve the main east-west crops, this station came to specialize in developing robusta coffee. Since independence (1960) it receives fewer funds, and has had to neglect research in favor of operations that most rapidly produce practical results.
Ambahiva-hibe	Tropical (altitude 400 meters)	Rice, peanuts, corn	Partly because of its remote situation in Diégo-Suarez province, this station—founded during World War I—has never attained more than local importance.
Marovoay	Dry tropical	Sugarcane, rice, tropical fruits, forage, peanuts	When the station was inaugurated in 1921, its purpose was to train cattle for plowing, but this soon became a secondary aim. In 1931 it began developing selected rice seed (*vary lava* variety), and after World War II, peanuts and sugarcane. Since 1949 it has offered practical training to west-coast farmers.
Alaotra	Tropical, high-altitude (750–800 meters)	Rice, manioc, peanuts	Founded in 1926, Alaotra has become Madagascar's premier station for basic research, notably in rice and manioc, and the center for experimentation in mechanized farming. Has the best-equipped laboratories and buildings on Madagascar, and since 1951 has been entrusted with technical guidance of the provincial stations of Ivoloina, Antalaha, Ankaizina, and Marovoay.

Agricultural Stations in Madagascar (*continued*)

Locality	Climate	Specialty	Comments
Ankaizina-Bealanana	Tropical, high-altitude (1,000 meters)	Arabica coffee, forage crops, beans, potatoes	Established in 1941 to develop arabica coffee, this station found local Malagasys so unresponsive to its efforts that it had to branch out to include fodder crops, flax, and tobacco. Its usefulness has increased since the B.D.P.A. started a farming settlement at Sakay.
Tuléar-Betanimena	Dry tropical	Fruit trees, cotton, corn, cape peas	This is a minor provincial station but is important for the arid southwest, to which it supplies fruit trees that can withstand prolonged droughts.
Antalaha	Humid tropical	Vanilla	Antalaha, as the center of Malagasy vanilla culture, has largely taken over research on this plant from Ivoloina.
Mangoky	Dry tropical	Cotton, sisal, fodder crops, castor beans	The success of the experiments in cotton-growing carried out by this station since its founding in 1952 led the authorities to launch a large-scale project for improving 100,000 hectares of the Mangoky River basin by irrigation works.

island, with headquarters at Lake Alaotra and Miandrivazo. In 1953 the Compagnie Générale des Oléagineux Tropicaux (C.G.O.T.) came to the island to encourage the cultivation of oleaginous crops, particularly peanuts, in the regions of Mandabe, Mahabo, and Kamoro. The most recent to come to Madagascar is the Institut des Fruits et Agrumes Tropicaux, which only in 1960 began small-scale experiments in banana-growing in the Ivoloina gardens. Since almost all the foregoing institutes and organizations cost the Malagasy taxpayer virtually nothing, the Malagasys are glad to have them continue working on the island. The C.G.O.T., however, has been sharply criticized in the assembly for operating on a needlessly lavish scale.[24]

A prerequisite to the success of the crop-specialization activities of the above-mentioned institutes is the work being done by the technical services connected with soil conservation, hydrology, antilocust operations, and agricultural education. French administrators and technicians from the time of the conquest to that of independence issued warnings about the dangers of Madagascar's widespread soil erosion, and inveighed particularly against the Malagasy practice of *tavy*.* For years the French authorities strove unsuccessfully to stop *tavy* by stern repressive measures, notably by holding entire villages responsible for the fires set in their environs and making them liable to heavy fines. Only after World War II, in January 1948, did it take the more constructive step of creating a Soil Conservation Bureau. In cooperation with the I.R.S.M., this bureau has prepared an island-wide map of eroded regions and has been seeding areas by plane and developing anti-erosion farming techniques.

As in many similar cases, the French were highly successful from the technical standpoint, but failed to enlist the Malagasys' cooperation, either in executing the project or in perpetuating it. An anti-erosion experiment conducted with success in two valleys near Lake Alaotra cost the French taxpayer millions of francs, and this land, after improvement, was restored to the peasants who had previously farmed it. These farmers, however, had not been properly taught or had failed to grasp the new techniques, for within a short time the area was reportedly as eroded as it had been before. As for the Malagasy elite, those in the government fortunately are convinced of the need to conserve soil and to end the practice of *tavy*—but this view is not shared by all the island's assemblymen, especially deputies from the east coast, where erosion is far advanced. They claim that *tavy* is indispensable for the production of food crops needed there, and they oppose reforestation as unduly restricting the area required for farming.[25] Resistance to the government is an automatic reaction on the part of former colonial peoples and one which, among the Malagasys, is reinforced by their innate opposition to changes in traditional practices. Probably large-scale distribution of fertilizers and better education of farmers will be required if the necessary change in attitude is to be accomplished.

A corollary to the Soil Conservation Bureau is the rural-engineering service. At first it was attached to the general agricultural service and concentrated on maintaining and extending dykes and canals built by the Merina monarchs on the high plateaus. Before World War I, however, it began branching out to undertake similar but larger-scale work on the west coast, where it initiated drainage and irrigation operations. In 1951 it was separated from the agricultural service, and its activities were widened to include improvements in rural housing. With the cooperation of related official services, it carried out large-scale drainage and irrigation work, especially in the regions of Lake Alaotra, Marovoay, Mahavavy, and Ambila. During the 1950–60 decade its improvements covered 80,000 hectares in the main producing areas.[26] Least successful were its operations in the extreme

* See pp. 325–27.

south, where many of its well-drilling operations failed for lack of proper equipment and adequate geological data on the water table. The Malagasy government is extremely eager to expand the scope of this service but is hampered by the shortage of funds and, even more, of qualified technicians.

In view of the fact that the work performed by the rural-engineering service called for large funds and trained engineers and was therefore confined to the main producing areas, the government conceived the idea of extending such operations throughout the island by a "big program of small projects." In so doing, it was inspired by the success of the Fonds d'Equipement Rural et de Développement Economique et Social (F.E.R.D.E.S.) in French West Africa, where the active cooperation of the peasantry had been enlisted. The government proposed, therefore, in 1957 to set up a F.E.R.D.E.S. in Madagascar, to which the central government, the province, and the community would contribute equally, the community's share being payable in cash, material, or services. A community needing a dam or a canal, for example, was expected to draw up a project and send it to the local administrator. If he deemed the project valid, he would send it to the provincial technical services for approval, for rejection, or for modifications on which all three parties would then have to reach agreement. In the proposal submitted to the assembly, the government envisaged a contribution by each province amounting to 21 million C.F.A. francs.

The attitude of the Malagasy assemblymen toward the project was far from enthusiastic. As usual, they were suspicious of the government's motives, reluctant to give local administrators more power, and apprehensive that F.E.R.D.E.S. would bring about a revival of forced labor.[27] Although the proposal was finally accepted by the assembly, F.E.R.D.E.S. soon ran into difficulties, created in part by the very people it was supposed to benefit. Rural communities either failed to submit any projects at all or submitted ones judged by the administrator or the technical services to be impractical, so that by the end of 1959 almost none of the funds earmarked by the central government for launching F.E.R.D.E.S. had been utilized. Up to the present, that organization has made no appreciable contribution to the small-scale public works that Tsiranana refers to as those of *ras de sol*.

Another government service concerned with improving the island's agricultural production which has not elicited the Madagascar assembly's wholehearted support is that of combating locust invasions. It is probable that the locust has always been one of the chief scourges of Malagasy agriculture; as early as 1617 a locust invasion of the island was recorded by a European observer. The Merina government seems to have made no attempt to deal with this pest, and the first locust invasion that occurred after the French occupation found the island defenseless.[28] Locusts have breeding grounds on the island and they also come from the east African mainland. If the season is exceptionally rainy, the insects must leave their breeding grounds to seek food. Conditions for such locust migrations were particularly favorable during the years 1898–1903, 1912–16, 1935–38, and 1944–49.

Gallieni organized the first antilocust operations on the island, but after the infestation tapered off in 1903, the organization, personnel, and interest that he had built up were allowed to disintegrate. For many years it was thought that all the locusts that plagued Madagascar came from Africa, and it was not until the 1920s that their breeding grounds on the island were discovered. On March 24, 1928, an antilocust organization was formed on a permanent basis, centered at Tananarive and headed by an official who controlled the observation posts and mobile teams scattered throughout the most vulnerable areas. In addition to the specialized agents permanently under his orders, this official could, in times of crisis, call on administrators for help and mobilize all the villagers in the locust-infested zone. In the period 1927–32 the first detailed scientific study was made of the "Malagasy locust" (*Locusta migratoria*), and much valuable information concerning its breeding cycle and migrations was gathered. Then in 1933 it was realized that a second type of locust (*Nomadacris septemfasciata*), of South African origin, had settled in the southern part of the island and also called for close observation. By the eve of World War II the antilocust service had the knowledge, organization, and equipment to fight locust invasions fairly effectively.

Unfortunately the war caused such heavy inroads on the matériel and personnel of the service that locusts began to swarm virtually unchallenged over four-fifths of the island in 1944–45 and again in 1947–49. Only the forest zone of the east coast escaped their attacks. By 1950, however, the authorities had acquired more effective means of combating these invasions through the use of military planes, radio bulletins, and chemicals, and they were able to increase their preventive operations as well. In December of that year, the antilocust service was reorganized, the number of observation posts and mobile teams was increased, and their material equipment was built up. But by then the area that had to be kept under surveillance was also much larger than before, covering a total of 300,000 square kilometers and including parts of Majunga and the high plateaus that before the war had been spared locust depredations.[29]

Locust invasions can now be said to be fairly well under control, but the threat is far from being eliminated. Each time the question of voting funds for the antilocust service is brought up in the assembly, some of its members always protest that the money so allocated is wasted. The great majority, however, continue to vote support for that organization, although they all express the wish that locust control could be made totally and permanently effective.

Agricultural Education

In the field of agricultural education, as in others, Gallieni was a pioneer. He ordered that gardens were to be cultivated by the pupils of the state primary schools, which he founded, and in 1903 he initiated a more advanced school of agriculture at the Nanisana agricultural station, which he had also established. By 1916 that school had trained some 200 Malagasys, but they became teachers and did not themselves do any farming. This miscarriage of Gallieni's plans, as well as the conservatism of the Malagasy peasants, made Governor Olivier skeptical about the value of formal agricultural education. Nevertheless, he launched two more agricultural schools, at Antsirabe and Tamatave, in which students were trained in a two-year course to become foremen on plantations. In the late 1930s these schools were giving instruction to more than 60 students a year.[30]

Among the ambitious projects embarked upon by the French government after World War II was that of transforming the Nanisana school into one that would train agricultural engineers. The prospect of obtaining an engineer's diploma attracted a considerable number of students to Nanisana —almost as many French as Malagasy—after it was officially opened on December 1, 1950, with a capacity of 80 boarders. But the administration soon found that it had failed to take into consideration two important factors. One was that the representative assembly had agreed to the rise in status of the Nanisana school only on condition that it turn out practical farmers and not functionaries,[31] and the other was that the French government proved unwilling to recognize Nanisana graduates as agricultural engineers.[32] In the early 1950s a mission headed by an official of the Ministry of Overseas France visited Madagascar, and urged that priority be accorded the practical training that was then being given at the stations of Ivoloina, Alaotra, and Marovoay. Consequently, in 1954 the Nanisana school was demoted and renamed the Agricultural College of Madagascar. Its students were bitterly disillusioned to learn that they would not become engineers but would only be certified as qualified foremen and agricultural monitors, and as such they found difficulty in getting jobs. To compensate to some extent for this disappointment, the government started a course at the Lycée Gallieni which would prepare a small number of specially qualified students for admission to the higher agricultural schools of France.

Until 1957 agricultural education in Madagascar was offered solely at the practical level, in three-year courses at the schools of Nanisana, Marovoay, Alaotra, and Ivoloina. Candidates for admission had to be holders of primary-school certificates, and graduates who entered the agricultural service as monitors were required to serve the government for ten years. To raise the academic standards of these schools, which were poor, better-qualified instructors were assigned to them beginning in 1955. They continued, however, to have difficulty in attracting good students, and together never produced more than 110 graduates in any one year, almost all of whom became low-ranking functionaries. Very different results were obtained at the farm-school run by the Syndicat Chrétien des Agriculteurs et Eleveurs, founded in 1950 near Fianarantsoa, which trained local farmers to use modern methods in working their own land.[33] Nevertheless, this farm-school was a very small affair, in which only 11 youths at a time were trained in courses lasting two months. To many observers it seemed incomprehensible that in a country so overwhelmingly agricultural as Madagascar, formal instruction in agriculture should be vastly inferior to the education given in other local schools and highly unpopular with the Malagasys. One plausible explanation was that schooling was associated in Malagasy minds with liberation from manual labor, and another was the undeniably poor monetary return of farmers in general and of graduates of the agricultural schools in particular.

Implementation of the *loi-cadre* in 1957 led to a "provincialization" of the island's agricultural schools, but brought no fundamental change in their curricula or student body. It simply transferred financial responsibility for their upkeep from the central government's budget to that of the province in which each school was located. The P.S.D. government, after it came to power, recognized the need for a radical reorganization of agricultural education, but took no practical steps in that direction for several years. In April 1961 it initiated a reform program by creating a rural college at Ambatobe, and this was followed by the transformation of the existing agricultural schools into Ecoles Pratiques Rurales. As the name of these schools indicates, no change was made in their practical orientation, but students were to be graduated at three levels, those at the highest level eventually receiving diplomas as agricultural engineers. Whether this will prove sufficient bait to attract more and better-qualified students, time alone will tell. As of 1961 fewer than 1 per cent of the holders of the *brevet élémentaire* in Madagascar were going to agricultural schools. Only 6 per cent of the students attending local technical schools and 2.5 per cent of the Malagasy students in institutions of higher learning in France had opted for an agricultural career.[34]

Food Crops

Madagascar's agricultural output cannot be clearly separated into food crops and export crops, for almost all are cultivated both for domestic consumption and for foreign sale. However, the crops described in this section are those grown principally as food for the island's population, and the following section deals with those that are marketed mainly abroad.

Rice. Food crops occupy about two-thirds of Madagascar's cultivated surface, and paddy is by far the most important of them. Rice, besides being the basic food of all Malagasys, has now become a major export. Both production and exports have fluctuated widely, for a number of reasons—varying climatic conditions, locust damage, marketing and transport difficulties, high production costs, competition from cheaper imported rice, and shifting official policies.

Paddy is probably Madagascar's oldest crop, and its existence and exportation were noted by early European navigators.[35] The technique of irrigated paddy cultivation may have been brought to the island by the ancestors of the Merina and Betsileo, who to this day are the best Malagasy rice farmers. During the last years of the Merina monarchy, many rice fields on the high plateaus were abandoned because of excessive taxation, although the growing of mountain rice on burned-over uplands (by *tavy*) increased. In the last years of the nineteenth century, the French military conquest and then the *fahavalo* insurrection, along with ravages by locusts, caused such a drop in rice production that in 1901 it was necessary to import 30,000 tons of the cereal into Madagascar. Gradually, however, rice-growing was resumed and increased so that on the eve of World War II Madagascar was harvesting 800,000 tons of paddy from 540,000 hectares of land.

Rice, either of the irrigated or mountain type, can be grown on the island in all but the coldest and most arid regions. Because of Madagascar's great diversity of climates and varieties of paddy, it is harvested throughout the year, the largest production occurring from April through June. In most places only enough paddy is grown to supply strictly local needs, either because suitable land or transportation facilities (or both) are lacking, or because farmers have turned to more remunerative crops. The most productive regions are in the provinces of Tananarive and Fianarantsoa and the area around Majunga, whereas the east coast and the extreme north and south of the island are deficient in rice. Yields usually are low, averaging 1.4 tons per hectare.[36]

All of the ordinary rice is grown by Malagasy farmers, usually on very small plots of ground. It was not until the mid-1930s that a few European *colons* began to cultivate paddy in the great valley of the Betsiboka River, their laborers being sharecroppers to whom they supplied land and water in exchange for part of the harvest. There and in the Lake Alaotra region they began to develop a high-quality type of rice called *vary lava* for export to France. The total area planted to paddy by Europeans, however, did not exceed 14,000 hectares, and during World War II they had to sell their output on the domestic market for a price that did not even cover production costs. Even with this rice available to local consumers in addition to the ordinary variety, Madagascar underwent acute shortages during the war years, owing to locust depredations, and the authorities took the step of creating an Office du Riz to protect consumers.*

After the war, the cultivated area as well as the yields of both ordinary and "luxury" rice increased. The surface planted to paddy expanded from 562,000 hectares in 1949 to 750,000 in 1957, and in the latter year 1,150,000 tons were harvested.[37] This rise was prompted in part by the greater demand from a growing and more prosperous population. In fact, per capita consumption of rice by the Malagasys is said to be the largest in the world today, averaging 150 kilograms a year; only in Burma is this figure possibly exceeded. Partly, too, the increase in rice culture—particularly that of *vary lava*—was the result of official encouragement. Hydraulic works have enlarged the irrigated areas, improved communications have facilitated shipments, and the experimental stations at Lake Alaotra and Marovoay have developed and distributed selected varieties of high-yielding paddy seed. The number of rice mills rose from 32 in 1947 to 74 by 1960, when their combined annual capacity for husking amounted to 450,000 tons of paddy and 2,400 persons[38] were employed by them. Nevertheless, the mills husk only 240,000 tons a year, and almost four times that amount is threshed by hand.

Exports have fluctuated widely, not only because of variations in local production and the steady rise in domestic demand but also because of competition that they have encountered for *vary lava* in the French market and for ordinary rice in the Mascareignes. From 1910 to 1924 the island's exports of ordinary rice steadily increased, but they declined with equal regularity from 1925 to 1936, first as a result of heavier local consumption and then because of a reduction in the supply owing to locust depredations. The mid-1930s saw Madagascar's first shipment of *vary lava* to France (316 tons in 1936), but also the failure of its ordinary rice to reconquer the Réunion market, where it was displaced by cheaper rice from Indochina. Then exports were suspended entirely between 1939 and 1949 because locusts had again reduced rice crops to dangerously low levels. Although the ban on exports was lifted in 1950, the Réunion market for Madagascar's ordinary rice had dwindled by that time almost to the vanishing point, and the French market had been invaded by less expensive imports of superior-quality rice from Italy, Southeast Asia, and Brazil. Moreover, France itself had become a rice producer during the war, and the output of its Camargues region offered ever-keener competition to *vary lava* imports. Through the

* See p. 38.

efforts of the government and exporters, new markets for some 35,000 tons a year of the island's ordinary rice were developed during the middle and late 1950s in West Africa and the Antilles, and France agreed to take about 15,000 tons of *vary lava* annually. The marked rise in Madagascar's paddy production during this period, however, was prompted chiefly by a sharp increase in domestic demand.[39]

In the late 1940s and early 1950s, the French administration was accused by some Malagasys of having no rice policy at all or of having one that encouraged only *vary lava* exports.[40] *Vary lava* constituted only a small fraction of Madagascar's total paddy production, and although a few Malagasys grew that variety of rice, its cultivation was virtually a European monopoly because of the amount of capital and care that it required. As for the ordinary varieties, the administration did intervene to check *tavy* cultivation of mountain rice and to control the stocking of rice and its shipment from one province to another. (More than 150,000 tons of rice are shipped each year from regions with a surplus to those with a deficit.) Thus it was almost exclusively the consumer who benefited from the authorities' solicitude. The Malagasy farmer who grew ordinary rice was left largely to his own devices, and he received a price for his output which was low and was determined simply by the law of supply and demand.

This *laissez-faire* attitude of the administration was altered by Governor Soucadaux, who became concerned, soon after his arrival in Madagascar, about the stagnation of rice exports and the spurt in domestic demand. In 1953 he lowered the export duties and internal-transport rates for rice shipments. Then he sought new markets for both types of rice and experimented with allowing the commodity to circulate freely throughout the island. He took steps also to increase and improve the output of ordinary rice, and considered establishing a price-support fund to make paddy cultivation more remunerative to Malagasy farmers. By the time Soucadaux left Madagascar, rice had become, in most years, the country's second-ranking export, valued at 14.5 billion C.F.A. francs annually.[41]

Naturally the P.S.D. government has been as eager as was Soucadaux to maintain and expand Madagascar's rice production and exports. Its concern has been prompted not merely by the continuing rapid growth of the population but even more by the disastrous floods of March 1959, which caused a panic among consumers, forced up the price of rice sharply, and gave rise to black-market speculation. After a conference that brought together representatives of rice growers, exporters, and technicians, the government issued a decree, on June 13, 1959, setting official prices for paddy and rice. To enlighten and placate the Malagasy deputies who had criticized the government's attempts to regulate the rice trade, the Minister of Finance told the assembly on November 9, 1959, that the P.S.D. rice policy was based on three main principles. These were to assure growers of a "just remuneration," to protect the consumer from speculative price fluctuations, and to safeguard the future of the island's rice exports.

To implement this policy the government took several steps in 1960, which had remarkably good results during the next two years. A Comité Supérieur du Paddy et du Riz and a Price Stabilization Fund were created to ensure larger and more stable returns to the farmers than ever before and to prevent a price rise in the domestic market for rice. In 1962 a record 50,000 tons from a total production of ordinary rice amounting to 1,300,000 tons were shipped out of the country, and France was persuaded to allot a quota of 14,000 tons to Madagascar's *vary lava* exports. Now the government is trying to find new markets for *vary lava* outside the franc zone, to make its ordinary-rice exports competitive with those from the Far East by bringing down production costs,* and to assure the population's access to rice supplies throughout the island by providing more facilities for transporting and storing paddy in the chief producing zones. It hopes to increase Madagascar's rice exports by 1972 to 100,000 to 150,000 tons a year, and at the same time to make sure that domestic rice supplies are adequate.

Tubers. Manioc, like rice, has been grown almost everywhere in Madagascar as a food crop for several hundred years, but only in the twentieth century did it also become an export commodity. It is the island's second-most-important food crop, mainly in the provinces of Fianarantsoa, Tananarive, and Tuléar, as well as the plains of the northwest. In the mid-1930s, yields declined because the mosaic disease attacked manioc plantations, but the Agriculture Service developed and distributed disease-resistant varieties; since World War II production has remained fairly stable. In 1961, 800,000 tons of manioc were harvested from 202,600 hectares.[42] Of that total area, all but 20,000 hectares—which are in the hands of European *colons*—are cultivated by Malagasys on plots of ground usually not larger than one hectare. Malagasys prefer rice to manioc as their basic food, but they esteem manioc as a supplementary crop which can be left in the ground and harvested whenever a rice shortage occurs. Five-eighths of the total crop is consumed in the areas where it is grown, in the form of fresh manioc.

Manioc has a brighter future as a food crop than when exported in the form of dried manioc, starch flour, and tapioca. Exports, which began in 1909, have gone almost entirely to France. The volume of such shipments has depended to a large extent on the policy of the French government,

---

* In 1962, estimated production costs on one hectare of rice field amounted to 18,500 C.F.A. francs. See assembly minutes for June 5, 1962.

which sometimes—but not consistently—has accorded premiums to Malagasy manioc growers and has protected Madagascar's exports of manioc and its derivatives from domestic and foreign competition in franc-zone markets. In 1938, shipments of those commodities represented nearly 6 per cent of Madagascar's total exports, by value, but by 1956 this percentage had dropped to 2.4, and only tapioca exports were holding their own.[43] Despite encouragement from the local administration in the form of tax concessions, low-interest loans to farmers, a Price Stabilization Fund created on April 28, 1958, and a search for new markets, the exportation of manioc and its derivatives has not regained prewar levels, and is even declining. In 1960, between 40,000 and 50,000 tons of manioc were processed in the island's eight plants—only one of which has modern equipment—for exportation and domestic consumption. That same year, tapioca exports amounted to 5,773 tons, those of flour to 926 tons, and those of dried manioc to 12,856 tons. Altogether they brought to their growers and exporters a total of 383 million C.F.A. francs.[44]

Taros and potatoes are the only other tubers grown widely in Madagascar, with a total production of 44,000 tons, almost all of which is used as food and animal fodder. Exports come to some 740 tons, of which 43 per cent is grown on the high plateaus. In 1960, 86 tons of potatoes were shipped to Réunion and 600 to Mauritius.[45]

Corn. Another long-established and widely grown crop is corn (maize), which continues to be important as a supplementary food but which has sharply declined as an export. The area planted to corn totaled 126,000 hectares in 1938, but by 1946 it had been reduced to 80,000 hectares. Exports, which began only in 1922, reached a peak of 54,000 tons (from a total production of some 90,000 tons) on the eve of World War II. For more than a decade thereafter, the exportation of corn was suspended, and by 1962 shipments—almost all of which went to Réunion—had fallen to 1,318 tons.[46] This decline was attributable both to the small monetary returns and to the policy of the Agricultural Service, which attempted first to reduce the varieties of corn grown and then to discourage production altogether, on the ground that corn was unduly exhausting the soil.[47] Production, however, has not dwindled as much as exports. It is now localized chiefly in the west of the island, particularly in Tuléar province, where corn is still a vitally important crop for both man and beast.

Wheat. Because of Madagascar's increasing difficulties in marketing its rice and manioc, as well as the concurrent rise in flour imports, the government has decided to encourage local wheat production. Wheat-flour imports increased from 3,671 tons in 1938 to 16,012 in 1961, and although this reflected a reassuring improvement in local living standards, it also cost Madagascar 695 million C.F.A. francs and accounted for 14.5 per cent of its trade deficit in 1961.[48] Formerly wheat was grown successfully on the high plateaus, but yields were so small and the crop so unremunerative that many wheat fields were abandoned by their cultivators and a flour mill that had operated at Antsirabe closed for lack of supplies. In the late 1950s, wheat production totaled only 60 to 80 tons a year. Experiments by the Agriculture Service have proved that wheat can be grown throughout most of Tananarive province and that yields can be vastly improved by the use of fertilizers. To bring about an appreciable increase in production, the government will have to expend a great deal of time, energy, and money in training farmers, organizing cooperative societies, and building flour mills. The authorities believe, however, that this effort will be more than repaid if they can reduce wheat imports appreciably and utilize local wheat and its by-products.

Fruit. Temperate-zone fruit trees thrive on Madagascar's high plateaus and tropical-zone ones on the east coast. Over the years, the Agriculture Service and enterprising individuals have done much to improve local fruit production and to introduce and acclimatize new species. Large quantities of fresh fruit are consumed by Malagasys and Europeans alike, and the main towns, especially Tananarive, are amply provisioned with a wide variety of fruit throughout the year. Perhaps 10,000 hectares in all are planted to fruit trees on the island, and their annual yield amounts to about 81,000 tons.[49] During World War II a preserved-fruit industry which operated on the high plateaus produced altogether some 150 tons, but its expansion was hindered by the high cost of sugar.

The only local fruit that might be exported on a large scale is the banana, which is indigenous to the east coast. The Tamatave Chamber of Commerce has been actively promoting the production of bananas for export to France, and special efforts were made to this end after 1958, when Guinea's banana shipments to the Metropole virtually ceased. In 1960 a newly formed cooperative society at Tamatave, COFRUMAD (Coopérative Fruitière de Madagascar) which grouped all the banana planters of that region, exported a few tons of the poyo variety to France, where it was well received. The next year, the Institut des Fruits et des Agrumes Tropicaux (I.F.A.T.) installed a branch at the Ivoloina station, where it has been working to improve the output of bananas and other tropical fruits. In September 1962, an agreement was reached between the government, COFRUMAD, and the shipping companies serving Madagascar. Those companies were given a three-year monopoly on the transportation of the island's banana exports on condition that they provide specially equipped banana boats and grant COFRUMAD's exports advantageous freight rates.[50] To develop banana exports, the government on February 19, 1963, sponsored a Société Bananière de Madagascar (SOBAMAD), in which it holds 10 per cent of the stock and COFRUMAD 30 per cent, the balance being controlled by Marseille importers. Madagascar is making a strenuous effort to increase banana exports to 100,000 tons by 1969, but their future in the French market—which has been paying higher than world prices for Madagascar bananas—is dubious. Although Madagascar exported only 11,000 tons of bananas in 1963, it was already encountering stiff competition in the French market, notably from Antilles and African exporters, who opposed France's allotting Madagascar the annual quota of 18,000 tons which it was asking.

Special mention should be made of an original, albeit very small, industry related to fruit-growing that has been developed in Fianarantsoa province. On some 130 hectares near Antsirabe, a few French planters have cultivated vineyards from which they now derive annually between 4,000 and 6,000 hectoliters of fair-quality wine, which is sold under the trade name of Lairavo. Because Madagascar is a good market for wine—in 1961 about 200,000 hectoliters were imported, at a cost of nearly 2 billion C.F.A. francs[51] —the government is helping to promote this industry. At Tsiranana's request a *section viticole* has been added to the Institut de Recherches Agronomiques de Madagascar (I.R.A.M.), its function being to prepare an inventory of areas suitable for growing wine-grapes in Majunga and Diégo-Suarez provinces.

Export Crops

Cape peas. At least as early as the seventeenth century, cape peas (*Phaseolus inamoenus*)—which resemble the American lima bean—were introduced into Madagascar from South Africa. They have become the main crop of the southwestern region, where they are grown in the inundated river valleys on a coastal band 400 kilometers long by 75 wide. The agricultural station at Tuléar has successfully fought an insect pest that was destroying stocks of the peas in silos, and has also improved the quality of the output. Very little of this crop is consumed locally, and exports attained a record total of 27,000 tons in 1919. Since then they have tended to decline, but they have now become stabilized at about 10,000 tons a year. Because cape peas require little care, they are a popular crop with Tuléar farmers. They could probably be cultivated on a much larger scale were it not for sharp price fluctuations resulting mainly from the almost total dependence of exports on a few British purchasers.

Oleaginous commodities. The dearth of vegetable-oil production in Madagascar accounts for the low consumption of fats by Malagasys, which averages only 2 kilograms per inhabitant a year.[52] Despite this obvious shortage, little has been done to promote the cultivation of oleaginous crops on the island, other than to encourage peanut-growing since World War II.

Peanuts can be grown everywhere in Madagascar except on land lying more than 1,000 meters in altitude. The main producing regions are the high plateaus, the west coast, and the southwest. Before World War II, exports dwindled irregularly from a maximum of 1,241 tons in 1923 to 306 tons in 1938, because most of the peanuts harvested during the 1930s were crushed in the island's 19 oil mills. In the early 1950s, Madagascar's shortage of fats impelled the French administration to encourage peanut culture on the island. The C.G.O.T. created two types of plantations: one at Kamoro was a pilot farm, where *colons* were trained to grow so-called eating peanuts by mechanical means; the other, near Morondava, distributed selected seed to Malagasy farmers, collected and standardized their output, and sold it to exporting firms.[53]

Owing to C.G.O.T.'s activities, peanut culture advanced rapidly. Between 1938 and 1956, the area planted to this crop increased from 5,200 to 35,000 hectares, and exports expanded thirty-fold. The producing zone spread along the whole west coast, and would have been extended still farther had not the authorities checked it for fear of soil erosion. In 1960, Diégo-Suarez province exported 2,700 tons of eating peanuts, Majunga 5,100, and Tuléar 7,000 (of a total production of 23,800 tons). In most years, domestic consumption in the form of eating peanuts accounted for only about 5,000 tons, and oil extraction for 40 per cent of the total output. The increase in peanut exports has given rise to a marketing problem. The Algerian market for peanuts has been decreasing since that country became independent, and in 1960 French buyers served notice that by 1963 they would cease purchasing any Madagascar peanuts except the best-quality eating variety.[54] The P.S.D. government is anxious to encourage production, especially for the domestic market, and on July 17, 1962, it placed restrictions on the importation of all vegetable oils. On April 17, 1963, it set up a Bureau de Commercialisation et de Stabilisation de l'Arachide, whose aim is to control the sale of the entire crop for eating and for crushing.

Coconut palms grow, but not in abundance, along both the east and west coasts of the island north of the latitude of Majunga and Tamatave.[55] The Malagasys use the milk of the coconut as food and drink and as a cosmetic, but they make little use of the shells for fiber or as fuel. The European coconut plantations, which cover only some 21,000 hectares (mainly in the northwest), are now obsolescent and their trees are afflicted with parasitic growths. At present they produce less than half the copra used in Madagascar's soap and oil industries. Total production, as nearly as it can be estimated, comes to about 14 million nuts a year.[56] I.R.H.O. (Institut de Recherches pour les Huiles et les Oléagineux) is now investigating the potential of the west coast as a coconut-palm-growing area.

Castor-bean plants are indigenous to many parts of the island, notably the extreme south, where they also have been planted by Antandroy tribesmen. To help meet the French army's requirements for plane-engine lubricants during World War I, castor-bean cultivation was made obligatory, but there were no exports from Madagascar to France until 1925, when 1,330 tons were sent to the Metropole. A peak was reached in 1936, when 3,270 tons of oil were exported, but such shipments ceased entirely during World War II, and the beans were then used on the island as fuel for the railroads. An oil mill for castor beans was built at Fort-Dauphin in 1950, but it ceased operating in 1954 after exporting 598 tons of oil in 1953. Production of beans now ranges between 500 and 2,500 tons a year, depending on the rainfall. Much larger quantities could be produced if Madagascar's output were assured a regular and remunerative market.

To meet France's needs for a quick-drying industrial oil in the years immediately after World War II, Madagascar's *colons* were encouraged to start plantations of *aleurite* or tung trees (*Aleurites fordii*), particularly in the Itasy district of Tananarive province. The great hopes placed in this commodity, however, were soon disappointed. Beginning in 1952, large amounts of Chinese tung oil were dumped on European markets, and as a result the price paid by French buyers for Madagascar's product fell sharply.[57] Many *colons* abandoned plantations that were just coming into bearing, but the few who hung on received aid from the government. Madagascar's assembly voted in 1953 and 1954 to grant them premiums and interest-free loans, and also reduced the export duty on their shipments from 2 per cent to 0.5 per cent.[58] Three years later the Ministry of Overseas France proposed creating a price-support fund for Madagascar's growers. Mainly because of the large number of Malagasys employed on the *aleurite* plantations, the assembly gave its assent in August 1957. These measures have not been very effective, however, and production has stagnated. In 1960 it amounted to only 3,300 tons.[59]

Sugar. It is believed that sugarcane was introduced into Madagascar from the Mascareignes about the year 1800. Cane grows readily throughout the island except at altitudes of 1,300 meters and more. Until the interwar period it was cultivated almost solely by Malagasy farmers on small plots of ground, mostly for family consumption, as sugar and a fermented beverage called *betsabetsa*. A few rudimentary mills to crush cane were built to ease Madagascar's sugar shortage during World War I, but thereafter Madagascar resumed importing almost all its sugar from Réunion until

1921, when the first modern sugar mill was built at Nossi-Bé by the Compagnie Agricole et Sucrière. In 1930 the Société Marseillaise de Namakia installed a mill in Majunga province, and shortly afterward the Société des Sucreries de la Côte Est built one near Brickaville. Before World War II the area planted to cane totaled some 14,500 hectares, of which 4,000—owned by *colons,* and mostly on Nossi-Bé—supplied Madagascar's sugar mills, which by that time numbered six, and its 11 distilleries.[60] Production in 1938 came to 18,270 tons of sugar (of which 12,101 were exported) and 19,666 hectoliters of rum (including 1,397 exported). When exports ceased during World War II, the internal market absorbed the entire output of both sugar and rum, which remained fairly stable.

In 1949 the Raffineries St. Louis, Compagnie Sucrière Marocaine, and Banque de Paris et des Pays-Bas joined together to finance a company called the Société Sucrière de Mahavavy (SOSUMAV), which shortly gave an impetus to sugar production in Madagascar. The territorial assembly granted SOSUMAV a concession of 10,000 hectares—about half of which was suited to cane-growing—in the Mahavavy delta, and also accorded its shipments exemption from export duties until 1958. In return, SOSUMAV promised to develop the entire delta by building irrigation canals and roads, and also to buy some of its cane supplies from nearby *colons* and Malagasy planters. Most important of all, it pledged to build on its concession the island's first refinery and equip it with the most modern machinery available. Grants from F.I.D.E.S. enabled SOSUMAV to construct a hospital, a school, and housing for the 3,000 workers it expected to employ, and the French government allotted its sugar exports a generous quota and higher-than-world prices in the French market. The fiscal and other favors extended to SOSUMAV aroused much opposition at the time they were made, and attacks upon them were renewed in 1957, when the company applied for long-term tax concessions. A French Communist Party spokesman asserted that American capital would control the company so as to implement the United States policy of stockpiling strategic commodities.[61] Other opponents insisted that the company would surely operate at a loss and could never produce sugar at competitive world prices. Actually the two most serious problems that have beset SOSUMAV have been a shortage of labor, which it solved by importing workers from the Comoro Islands, and the Fiji disease, which began to damage its plantations in 1954.

Despite these handicaps, SOSUMAV has been an undoubted success, and its production has virtually obviated Madagascar's need to import sugar. In 1960 it turned out 42,000 tons of high-quality sugar (most of it refined), compared with the 18,000 tons of unrefined sugar produced by the Compagnie Agricole et Sucrière of Nossi-Bé, the 15,000 tons of the Société

Marseillaise de Namakia, and the 9,000 tons of the Sucreries de la Côte Est at Brickaville. As of 1963, 28,500 hectares in Madagascar—of which 14,500 were in Diégo-Suarez province and 4,500 in Majunga province—were planted to sugarcane. Output totaled 1,426,220 tons of raw cane, of which 936,922 tons were processed industrially and the balance was used mainly to produce rum.[62] Approximately 150,000 tons of cane are consumed locally as food in one form or other, and 50,000 tons are used to brew *betsabetsa*. Since SOSUMAV began production in 1954, there has been a marked increase in Malagasy sugar consumption. It now amounts to between 30,000 and 35,000 tons a year, of which only 2,500 tons are refined. The per capita intake of somewhat less than 10 kilograms annually would almost certainly increase if the present price of 60 C.F.A. francs per kilogram could be brought down.

A larger internal market for Madagascar's sugarcane products is now of growing interest to the authorities. In 1963 Madagascar's exports of sugar attained a record total of 65,776 tons and those of rum more than 4,000 hectoliters, their total value being 2,179 million FMG. This placed sugar and rum second among Madagascar's exports, accounting for 10.8 per cent of the island's foreign sales by value. In 1962, however, France stopped paying higher-than-world prices for Madagascar's sugar, so that the future of such exports now largely depends on the agricultural policy of the European Common Market and on finding new markets outside as well as inside the franc zone.

Tobacco. The Malagasys of the high plateaus have long grown a chewing tobacco with a high content of nicotine, which is still sold in small quantities in nearby markets. In 1920, S.E.I.T.A., France's tobacco *régie*, sent a mission to Madagascar to study that island's possibilities as a source of tobacco to be used in cigarette manufacture in France. As the indigenous tobacco was unsuitable for this purpose, the mission, after experimentation, introduced successfully the Maryland variety of tobacco, then popular in Europe. Its production was encouraged by premiums to growers and the free distribution of seed and fertilizers, along with advice by members of the mission. In return for a monopoly of its sale and export, S.E.I.T.A. committed itself to purchase the entire tobacco crop at fixed prices.

Under this stimulus, production increased rapidly throughout the alluvion valleys of the west coast, and exports, which in 1922 came to only 56 tons, amounted to nearly 1,400 on the eve of World War II. The quality and curing of the output, however, were generally so poor as to make most of it unusable. In 1936, therefore, S.E.I.T.A. ceased giving premiums, forbade the cultivation of Maryland tobacco in two districts, and built warehouses and curing sheds in the producing zones.[63] This resulted in a temporary decline in production but also brought about an improvement in quality. Moreover, the move had a side effect that later, in the postwar years, accounted for the attitude of Malagasy nationalists toward the culture of tobacco. This was the concentration of Maryland-tobacco production in the hands of French *colons,* for whom Malagasys worked as sharecroppers, and the orientation of Malagasy farmers toward cultivating the indigenous types of tobacco used for local consumption and for the manufacture of cigarettes in Madagascar.

In 1947 the agreement between the local administration and S.E.I.T.A. was renewed along the same general lines as before, but during the middle and late 1950s both the monopoly held by S.E.I.T.A. and its policy came under increasingly bitter attack in the territorial assembly. No complaint was voiced about the prices S.E.I.T.A. paid for tobacco—on the contrary, the fact that they were high was a cause of Malagasy discontent inasmuch as it was the European *colons* (who produced almost all the tobacco exported) who benefited most from them. The Malagasy farmers, who were unable or unwilling to give as much care to the cultivation and preparation of their tobacco, resented S.E.I.T.A.'s regulations, which they considered unnecessarily fussy, as well as its refusal to allow them to grow as much tobacco as they pleased wherever they desired. Their complaints were backed by Malagasy nationalists, who seemingly were convinced that Madagascar could sell all the tobacco it cared to produce at prices as favorable as those paid by S.E.I.T.A.[64]

Matters came to a head in the late 1950s, when S.E.I.T.A. announced that from 1959 to 1963 it would progressively reduce its purchases of Maryland tobacco—which had lost favor in the French market—from 3,800 tons to 3,400. It also asked the government and planters to help finance the reconversion of Madagascar's plantations from the Maryland to the Virginia variety of tobacco. The European planters agreed to a tax for that purpose, as did the government. The latter, its spokesman said, had no organization comparable to that of S.E.I.T.A. for the purchasing, stocking, and shipping of local tobacco for export, and it was reluctant to tamper with a crop that ranked second or third in some years among the island's exports and brought in revenues of 1,200 million C.F.A. francs annually. Although in 1959 the Malagasy assemblymen reluctantly approved the tax for the reconversion of plantations over a five-year period, they held firmly to the opinion that— despite official denials—both the European planters and S.E.I.T.A. were making huge profits at the expense of Malagasy farmers. They urged that the S.E.I.T.A. contract not be renewed and that its monopoly be transferred to a national *régie.*[65] The government finally acceded to their wishes, and a state monopoly for tobacco was created on July 1, 1964.

Vegetable fibers. Madagascar is fortunate in possessing many spontaneous growths of fiber-yielding plants and trees, such as kapok and raffia palms. Their fibers are widely used in making cords, nets, and clothing, but fiber exports are subject to considerable variation and are generally unimportant. The one wild-fiber export of any significance is raffia, obtained from a palm that grows abundantly in Majunga province and on the east coast. Raffia exports in the form of mats (*rabanes*) came to 6,412 tons, worth 780 million C.F.A. francs, in 1960. The main obstacle to increasing such exports and improving their quality is the Malagasys' reluctance to give fiber plants and trees the care and hard work required. Only fiber plants developed by Europeans, such as sisal and cotton, play an important role in Madagascar's economy.

One fiber plant, *paka* (*Urena lobata*), grows wild throughout Madagascar, but only in the northwest, particularly in the Ambanja district of Majunga province, is it regularly harvested and also cultivated on plantations. Because it exhausted the soil and because only small amounts of *paka* fiber could be marketed abroad, the government in 1926 restricted the number of months during the year when the wild growths could be picked for export. That year *paka*-fiber shipments amounted to 2.5 tons. In 1950, such exports began to lessen and later they ceased entirely.

It was the establishing of a factory at Majunga in 1930 by the Société de Filature et de Tissage de Madagascar (FITIM) that caused fiber exports to decline and at the same time resulted in the cultivation of *paka* on plantations in the northwest. The demand of FITIM for this fiber in making sacks, nets, and cord caused production to rise from 450 tons in 1931 to 3,060 in 1939, at which time FITIM turned out 2,586 tons of products, mostly sacks, and Madagascar ceased to import jute from the Indian subcontinent.[66]

After World War II, FITIM modernized its plant, but almost at once it was faced with the problem of a shrinkage of local supplies. The Malagasy farmers of Majunga province found that they could cultivate the more remunerative crops of sugarcane, tobacco, and cotton on land where they had been growing *paka*. In 1953, FITIM also had to contend with the dumping on the Madagascar market of cheaper jute sacks made by foreign competitors, and if the government had not gone to its rescue it would have had to close its factory. That year a tax of 20 C.F.A. francs per sack was imposed on imports, and the proceeds were turned over to FITIM to use as subsidies for *paka* growers. In return, FITIM was required to accept official controls over its sales operations. Nevertheless, the area planted to *paka* continued to shrink, and by 1958 the company was again in difficulties. The tax revenues from imported sacks no longer sufficed to meet operating costs and to pay subsidies to *paka* farmers and gatherers. That year local *paka* production amounted to only about 800 tons, and Madagascar was forced to import some 2,000 tons of jute valued at 85 million C.F.A. francs, which, moreover, had to be paid for in sterling.

When in 1959 the government proposed new fiscal-relief measures for FITIM, the Malagasy assemblymen aired their usual suspicions of foreign companies operating in Madagascar. They wanted the government to encourage *paka*-growing in provinces other than Majunga, promote the exportation of FITIM's sacks to France, and distribute subsidies directly to Malagasy *paka*-growers.[67] The government's spokesman pointed out that it was to the country's interest to support an industry that made Madagascar relatively self-sufficient in sacks and that it was more practical to let FITIM, which had long experience and a ready-made organization, continue subsidizing the *paka*-growers. What finally induced the assembly to agree to the government proposal was the fact that FITIM employed a labor force of 2,000 Malagasys and that all the cultivators and collectors of *paka* were likewise Malagasy nationals. In 1960, FITIM produced 2,500 tons of sacks (of which about two-thirds of the raw materials used were locally grown) at prices that had become competitive with those of imported jute bags.[68]

Sisal-planting was begun in Madagascar in the interwar period. Because of the considerable capital and technical skill required, this field of enterprise has always been wholly European. Madagascar's first sisal exports date from 1922, when 42 tons of fiber were shipped to France, and by 1938 they had risen to 2,537 tons. On the eve of World War II, 3,500 hectares were planted to sisal in Tuléar province (of which 880 were in the Fort-Dauphin region) and 2,320 hectares in Diégo-Suarez province. The island's production fell off somewhat during the war, partly because of a decline in output of the Diégo-Suarez plantations, but all exports that were available were taken by Great Britain and the United States.

Encouraged by the high price paid for sisal in France in the late 1940s, most of the island's eight decorticating factories modernized their equipment. Moreover, new French companies sought large concessions in the extreme south, where an abundant labor supply existed and where the C.F.D.T. and the I.R.C.T. were carrying on research which indicated that that area was well suited to growing sisal. Production mounted rapidly from 3,080 tons of fiber in 1950 to 5,920 in 1951, for most of which two companies—the Société Malgache de Culture and the Société Foncière du Sud —were responsible. In 1952, however, there came a drop in sisal prices, partly because of saturation of the market and partly as a sequel to the American discovery of a synthetic substitute. In 1953 the government-general made its first move to counteract the drop by lowering the export duty on sisal fibers progressively from 5 per cent to 0.5 per cent. In December of that year a group of cord manufacturers in France signed an agreement with Madagascar's sisal-growers to buy 10,000 tons of fiber at higher-than-current prices. Then, from 1953 to 1958 the French Fonds pour l'Encouragement Textile paid a subsidy of nearly 10,000 C.F.A. francs per ton on sisal exports from Madagascar. Nevertheless, such measures of support were not enough to save two of the sisal companies in Tuléar province, which ceased operation. By 1959 only six companies* were growing sisal on the island, all of them concentrated in the Mandrare valley near Fort-Dauphin, and each asked the government for a loan of 12 million C.F.A. francs.

Because these six companies were wholly European enterprises and exported virtually all of their output, the Malagasy assemblymen were reluctant to grant the loans, especially since the requests came just at the time when hundreds of Malagasys were suffering from the aftermath of an especially severe cyclone.[69] However, a prolonged drought at that period in the south, where all the sisal plantations were situated, and the fear lest the 5,000 Antandroy workers employed on those plantations might have to emigrate if the companies ceased operation, induced the parliament to grant the loans, but only on condition that the companies pay interest on them.

As of 1960, the areas conceded to Madagascar's sisal companies covered a total of 25,000 hectares, of which 16,000 were planted to sisal. It is hoped that production costs (which are high) will decrease when all of that area is cultivated and comes into bearing. In 1960 the total production of sisal was 13,150 tons, of which 11,286 were exported, the balance being used by a modern rug and cord factory at Fort-Dauphin owned by the Société de Heaulme.[70]

Cotton, it is now generally believed, has the most promising future of all Madagascar's export crops. If the island does indeed become an important cotton-producing country, this will be attributable to the outstanding perseverance and cooperation of French officials, *colons,* and technicians, as well as to the generosity of the European Economic Community.

Attempts to grow cotton in different parts of Madagascar were made in 1900, 1904, 1926, and during World War II, but in each case they were abandoned either because of the ravages of insects or because rainfall was too irregular. After the war, the newly organized I.R.C.T. and C.F.D.T. sent experts to Madagascar to help technicians of the agricultural stations in Majunga and Tuléar provinces to continue experimenting with cotton culture and to make known their findings. The work was greatly aided by the

* Société de Heaulme, Compagnie Agricole et Industrielle de Madagascar, Société du Domaine de Pechpeyrou, Etablissements, Gallois, Société Foncière du Sud de Madagascar, and Société Malgache de Culture.

success of a French planter named Raccaud who, in 1951–52, grew cotton of remarkably good quality on his concession near Tuléar. With his aid an agricultural station was installed at Tanandara in the lower Mangoky valley to experiment with irrigated cotton culture. The I.R.C.T. was put in charge of the research, and the C.F.D.T. was given the task of applying the results and also of buying and exporting the output. At the same time both organizations worked to develop dry cotton culture on the much smaller area of *baiboho** in Majunga province. In the mid-1950s they built cotton gins at Tuléar and Majunga, and in 1961 these gins produced for export 950 tons of fiber from cotton grown on an area of 1,392 hectares.[71]

Of the five main problems posed by cotton culture, especially in the Mangoky valley, only two seem to have been solved. After years of experimentation, a variety called *akala* has been developed which gives high yields of long-fiber cotton of fair quality. Insecticides sprayed from airplanes have conquered the insects that were mainly responsible for the failure of early attempts at cotton-growing. A French company, the Société Neyrpic, is working on plans to irrigate an initial 5,000 hectares—a project complicated from the technical standpoint by the violent floods of the Mangoky River. It is estimated that to irrigate all of the 100,000 hectares of the Mangoky valley would cost at least 10 billion C.F.A. francs. In late 1962 the F.E.D. allotted 1,600 million to build irrigation canals on 10,000 hectares. If this proves successful, it is hoped that the rest of the money needed may be obtained.

The most difficult problem associated with cotton-growing in the valley is labor, which is scarce. The indigenous population are reluctant to grow cotton, so sharecroppers have been brought in to make up the labor force for the existing plantations and the agricultural station. However, many of them have become homesick and left the region, and in any case Madagascar's assemblymen are opposed to the use of sharecroppers.[72] In an effort to solve this problem, O.R.S.T.O.M. sent an anthropologist, Georges Condominas, to Madagascar in 1959 to make a sociological study of the probable relations between the indigenous tribes and the 2,500 immigrant families needed for the Mangoky project.[73] Condominas found that such a study must take into consideration the local land-tenure system and the established trek routes for animals, so as not to violate local custom. Furthermore, he reported, there already existed the difficulty of persuading the local population to turn to cotton cultivation instead of growing cape peas, which were easy to cultivate and left the farmers considerable leisure. Although

* Riverbanks on which floods had deposited alluvion soil.

cotton brought in revenues four times greater than those from cape peas, many of the Tanandara farmers had already given up growing cotton because of the hard work and persistence it required.

The government, in seeking a solution to the labor problem, set up a Société d'Aménagement du Bas-Mangoky in 1961 at the suggestion of the C.G.O.T., which, jointly with the Malagasy government, supplied most of the new company's capital of 130 million C.F.A. francs. This company's chief function is to control cotton production and to popularize the crop among the Malagasy peasantry. It is hoped that by 1970 cotton will be cultivated on 5,000 irrigated hectares in the Mangoky valley and that dry cotton culture will be undertaken on Majunga's *baiboho*. Fortunately there is one hurdle the authorities do not have to confront—that of finding markets for Madagascar's cotton output. The weaving factory at Antsirabe will gladly buy from local sources the raw cotton it now must import, and France stands ready to absorb any surplus production. As a further encouragement to cotton-growing, a Price Support Fund for cotton farmers was created in 1964, to be financed partly by France and partly by a local tax on cotton exports.

Vanilla. Vanilla culture was introduced into Madagascar in the mid-nineteenth century by planters from Réunion, to which it had been brought originally from Mexico and where the technique of pollination of the vines by hand had been discovered. In Madagascar the crop developed rapidly along the northeast and northwest coasts, and its cultivation then spread to the Comoro Islands. At present Diégo-Suarez is the greatest vanilla-producing area, accounting for 4,700 of Madagascar's total of 5,000 hectares planted to vanilla, and the little town of Antalaha has become the world's largest vanilla-shipping port.[74]

At first vanilla was a wholly European crop, but now 85 per cent of the 3,000-odd vanilla planters are Malagasys.[75] Preparing the beans for export, which demands skill, patience, and care, and collecting the harvest for export are in the hand of Asians or Réunionais. Altogether some 17,000 persons are thought to be engaged in the production and sale of Madagascar's vanilla. To many Indian Ocean farmers and traders vanilla has brought large fortunes, but to many others it has meant ruin. Production has fluctuated tremendously, sometimes from one year to the next, because it depends on two unstable factors—climatic conditions and price. In some years violent cyclones have wiped out entire plantations on the east coast, reducing exports and raising prices. Another aspect of the price factor is the control of the vanilla market by a few well-organized American buyers. Madagascar has been for the past 40 years the world's largest vanilla producer, usually accounting for about two-thirds of the supply, and the United States has been the largest single market, absorbing in recent years 600 to 650 tons of a world output estimated at 850 to 950 tons annually.[76]

During the early part of the interwar period, Madagascar's exports increased substantially, reaching a record total of 1,092 tons in 1929, as compared with 300 tons only five years before. By 1930, however, production had fallen to 875 tons, and for the rest of that decade it averaged 640 tons a year. In the early 1930s Madagascar's production alone exceeded world consumption, hence stocks accumulated and the price fell disastrously. Moreover, overproduction was accompanied by a deterioration in quality, the result of careless preparation and premature harvesting of beans to forestall theft. The government stepped in and, despite the protests of planters, exporters, and the local Chambers of Commerce, imposed rigorous standards for exports, which were enforced at the ports of Tamatave, Nossi-Bé, and (for Comoro Islands exports) Majunga. In 1948 the government intervened still more drastically because the situation had become even more critical than during the world depression. It ordered the destruction—with compensation—of 632 tons of inferior-quality beans stockpiled during the war, and it raised the export duty on vanilla from 21 per cent ad valorem to 40 per cent.

Since World War II, fluctuations in price and output have continued, with official controls remaining as spasmodic and generally ineffective as before. A Price Support Fund was indeed set up in 1953 but had to be basically reorganized eight years later. Between 1952 and 1956 the island's annual vanilla production did not exceed 400 tons, and in the latter year the price fell to $13 a kilogram. Output revived from 1958 to 1960, when the price rose spectacularly, first to $28 and then to $31 a kilogram, but in 1962 it plummeted again, to $13, and in 1964 to $10.20. These fluctuations naturally affected the position of vanilla among the island's exports; in 1959, for example, it attained second rank in terms of value, whereas in 1956 it had been only sixth.

During 1958, considered a good but not superlative year for vanilla prices, the United States bought $7,176,000 worth of vanilla from Madagascar.[77] The perennial importance of the American market has led Madagascar's vanilla planters and exporters to hold it responsible for alternating good and bad periods. They are unwilling to accept the discipline required to maintain the stability and quality of exports, and whenever the price of vanilla rises, production increases excessively and the quality of the beans deteriorates. By 1951 the increasing production of synthetic vanilla in the United States made that country the chief target of complaints by Madagascar's vanilla interests. American consumption of vanilla-flavored products was obviously growing, but there was no corresponding increase in American purchases of Madagascar's vanilla. Part of the Price Support Fund created in 1953 was allotted to advertising the merits of natural vanilla in the American market. When the government proposed a 2 per cent increase in export duties on vanilla to pay for advertising, the territorial assembly agreed only on condition that the island's vanilla producers and exporters form a single organization. This led to the establishing on August 31, 1953, of the Union Intersyndicale de la Vanille de Madagascar, to which the French government the next year contributed $20,000, also earmarked for publicity purposes in the United States.

Perhaps the most incomprehensible aspect of the whole vanilla question in Madagascar is the seeming inability of the island's producers and exporters to grasp the fact that their high-price policy has contributed to the stagnation of vanilla exports and the growing use of the synthetic product. Their hopes have been placed in a regulation issued on October 29, 1960, by the U.S. Food and Drugs Administration to the effect that only products entirely flavored with natural vanilla may bear labels saying they contain "vanilla." Inevitably those American manufacturers who have been using only 15 per cent of natural vanilla in their products are displeased by this ruling, and they have contested it.

Since Madagascar became independent, there has been an encouraging tendency on the part of both the authorities and the vanilla interests to improve the island's output and not to blame their misfortunes on the consumer. The P.S.D. government has intervened more frequently and effectively than its predecessor to restrain speculation by traders, standardize quality, insist on the liquidation of stocks before new export permits are authorized, and maintain a lower price for Madagascar's vanilla exports. Yet in 1963 those exports fell to the lowest level recorded in the past 15 years, amounting to only 292 tons valued at 1,049 million FMG, compared with 640 tons valued at 2,161 million the year before.

This sensational decline seems to have had some salutary effects. A conference held at St. Denis, Réunion, early in February 1964 led to the formation of a united front among all Indian Ocean vanilla growers vis-à-vis their competitors in Mexico and Tahiti. Even more promising was the conference convened by the Malagasy government at Tananarive on May 8, 1964, which brought together for the first time representatives of vanilla planters, traders, and consumers.[78] Although production will continue to be influenced by climatic conditions in Madagascar, such meetings and contacts may help to eliminate some of the most harmful factors affecting vanilla production and sales which are subject to human control.

Spices. Many kinds of spice-producing bushes, vines, and trees are grown in Madagascar, including cinnamon, nutmeg, saffron, and ginger. As yet, however, only two of them—cloves and, to a lesser degree, pepper—are important to the island's economy.

Clove culture began on Ste.-Marie Island early in the nineteenth century, and from there it spread to the hot, humid lowlands of the east coast. Plantations are concentrated on Ste.-Marie and in the Fénérive and Mananara regions of Tananarive province, which together account for about 80 per cent of Madagascar's total output of cloves. There are now close to 9 million clove trees growing on some 35,000 hectares. Yields vary widely, one good year alternating as a rule with two poor ones, depending mainly on climatic conditions. The clove tree grows readily on mediocre soils not suited to vanilla or coffee culture, but it is very easily damaged by wind. Whole plantations were wiped out by the cyclones of 1927, 1945, and 1959.

During the interwar period cloves were popular as a crop with the Malagasys, to whom they brought a cash income for comparatively little effort. Clove plantations spread, to the detriment of food crops, and the food situation became particularly crucial on Ste.-Marie. The periodic declines in output can be ascribed in part to the large amount of labor needed to harvest the crop, together with the instability of prices and production. Because the time for pollinating vanilla vines coincides with that of the clove harvest, not all the clove crop is picked if the price for cloves is low. For many years Ste.-Marie solved the problem by using prison labor, but the damage done to branches by careless picking made this practice uneconomic. Another cause of small production was the depredations in the early 1930s of caterpillars and insects, against which no effective steps were taken. Moreover, Malagasy clove-planters have resisted the government's proposals to replace obsolescent trees, because clove trees do not come into full bearing until 15 years after they are planted (although they produce for 200 to 300 years).[79]

Clove exports, in the form of dried cloves and oil, increased rapidly from 30 tons in 1901 to 6,500 tons in 1939. Since the war, shipments of dried cloves have fluctuated from 6,092 tons in 1958 to 1,331 in 1960, but oil shipments have been more stable, averaging 600 to 700 tons a year. For many years Madagascar's main customers for dried cloves were Far Eastern countries, especially Indonesia, which took nearly half of such exports for flavoring cigarettes, and India, which mixed them with betel nuts for chewing. Clove oil, of which Madagascar enjoys a virtual monopoly among world producers, has gone in about equal proportions to Europe and the United States, where it serves in the manufacture of perfumes and pharmaceuticals. The annual income derived by Madagascar from its clove-oil exports has amounted in recent years to between 250 and 350 million C.F.A. francs. It is impossible to gauge the average annual return realized by the island from dried-clove exports, for they have varied widely and the price has ranged between 80 C.F.A. francs per kilogram (1953) and 146 C.F.A. francs (1957).

Considering the importance of cloves to Madagascar's economy, it is astonishing that so little official effort has been made to promote their export. None of the island's agricultural stations makes a specialty of cloves, although the I.R.A.M. has studied some diseases of clove trees and has tried to improve the preparation of clove oil.[80] In December 1957 a Price Support Fund for cloves was set up, to be financed by an increase in the export duty on clove shipments from 6 per cent to 10 per cent,[81] which helped subsequently to stabilize production. In recent years a deterrent to increasing output has been the overproduction of cloves in East Africa as well as in Madagascar. Zanzibar's output alone, which amounts to some 15,000 tons a year, comes close to meeting the world's annual average demand of 20,000 tons.

The crucial state of the clove market induced Zanzibar and Madagascar, the two largest clove producers, to come to an agreement in July 1961.[82] By its terms, Zanzibar was authorized to export that year 12,000 tons and Madagascar 3,750. A particularly abundant crop on both islands in 1962 led to a renewal of the agreement on an annual basis. In 1964 Madagascar was allotted an export quota of 3,700 tons, but it still had 3,000 tons of unsold stocks.[83] Present hopes for a revival of the clove market hinge largely on a renewal of buying by Indonesia. That country's shaky economic situation in recent years has resulted in a sharp curtailment of its clove purchases and has caused it to try to produce enough cloves to meet its own needs.

Pepper has been grown in Madagascar for many years, but it was of very minor importance until after World War II. At first pepper was simply interplanted with coffee bushes and it gave very poor yields, mainly because of a root disease and destruction by birds.[84] In the mid-1930s new varieties of pepper vines were brought from Java, and pepper plantations were started by European *colons* on Nossi-Bé and at Sambirano and Mahavavy, where they thrived. Exports rose from less than 100 tons in 1934 to 252 tons in 1939. They ceased during World War II, but a new outlet for the crop was found through its use in the processing of locally preserved meat.

The generally high prices that prevailed during the postwar years caused a proliferation of pepper plantations, not only in the northwest but also along the east coast in the region of Mananjary. The area planted to pepper increased rapidly from less than 2,000 hectares in 1950 to nearly 8,000 in 1961, and the largest producers now are the provinces of Diégo-Suarez (4,120 hectares) and Fianarantsoa (2,400 hectares). Output tripled during the 1950–60 decade, and in 1960 Madagascar exported over 1,000 tons, valued at 458 million C.F.A. francs, of which 847 tons were shipped to France and

177 to Algeria.[85] Pepper production on the island has benefited by the research done at the I.R.A.M. station in Ambanja, and there is little doubt that Madagascar could produce twice the amount of pepper that it now does.

Perfume plants. Madagascar has a wide variety of perfume plants, both indigenous and imported, and for many years the distilling and exportation of their oils brought appreciable cash returns to a few European *colons* and Malagasy planters. All such exports went to France, where these essential oils were used in the manufacture of perfumes, drugs, foodstuffs, and even insecticides. However, the only perfume plants that became commercially important were ylang-ylang, vetiver, and lemon-grass. Lemon-grass oil, of which 55 to 60 tons were shipped out of the country annually before World War II, disappeared as an export in the mid-1950s, and today no more than 50 kilograms of vetiver essence are produced each year. Only ylang-ylang has survived as a fairly important export.

Ylang-ylang culture was introduced into Madagascar and the Comoro Islands from the Mascareignes. By the mid-1930s, exports of ylang-ylang essence from Madagascar reached 37 tons a year, outdistancing competitive shipments from Réunion, the Philippines, and Java. Like so many of Madagascar's coastal cultures, ylang-ylang is subject to severe wind damage and price variations, and thus fluctuates widely in both productivity and exports. From 1949 to 1951, annual shipments fell to a low point of 8 tons, but they rose in the late 1950s to 28 tons a year, worth some 90 million C.F.A. francs. The chief producing centers are Nossi-Bé and Ambanja, where European *colons* and Malagasy planters cultivate altogether about 14,000 hectares.[86]

Coffee. In the mid-nineteenth century some Réunionais *colons* planted arabica coffee on the east coast of Madagascar and later on the high plateaus, where the existence of indigenous coffee bushes showed that the soil and climate were suited to that crop. Some years later, however, the arabica bushes were destroyed by a pest and the planters turned to the Liberia variety.[87] The low prices paid for Liberia-type coffee in France, however, caused them to abandon it about 1910. They then turned to two varieties of canephora coffee—kouilou and robusta—which had been grown successfully at the Ivoloina station and were later planted along the east coast between Vohémar and Vangaindrano. Arabica continued to be cultivated on a small scale as a Malagasy family crop on a few thousand hectares in the uplands of Fianarantsoa province, for its growers were paid prices 15 to 30 per cent higher than those received for the canephora varieties.

Coffee production and exports increased slowly from 1910 to 1929. In the latter year, output totaled only about 5,000 tons, but progress was more rapid between 1930 and 1938, when it came to more than 41,000 tons. This rise was due largely to the enthusiasm with which the small-scale Malagasy farmers, under official encouragement, began to take up coffee-growing. Shortly before World War II began, Malagasy planters were producing about twice as much coffee as was being grown by European *colons,* from Madagascar's total planted area of 115,000 hectares.

In 1941, because foreign markets were cut off, exports fell sharply to 1,139 tons, and they did not return to the prewar level until some years after the Liberation. In 1946, with the abolition of forced labor, the *colons'* perennial shortage of plantation workers became still more acute. During the revolt, which broke out the next year, many of the east-coast plantations were destroyed. Some years passed before the French government paid the compensation that would enable the plantation owners to rebuild houses, replant land, and replace equipment. Furthermore, between 1943 and 1950, coffee-growers were compelled to sell their entire crop to the French Groupement National d'Achat des Cafés (G.N.A.C.), which paid a pittance of 2 to 3 C.F.A. francs a kilogram. Through its monopoly the G.N.A.C. amassed enormous revenues, and sizable profits were also made in Madagascar by the Chinese middlemen who collected and processed the crop and by the traders who shipped it to France. The growers, however, were so miserably paid that they could not meet operating expenses. Many European *colons* grew so discouraged that they either abandoned coffee cultivation in favor of trade or transport or left the island altogether. By 1949, 85 per cent of Madagascar's coffee production came from Malagasy farmers, but they gave almost no care to their plantations and merely harvested the crop when it was ripe. Exports fell to 30,740 tons in 1950 and to 27,000 tons in 1951, and only the remarkable freedom from pests and plant diseases enjoyed by the east-coast plantations prevented an even more drastic decline in shipments.

During the early postwar years, the Madagascar Chamber of Commerce and the administration began to be alarmed by the drop in productivity of the bushes, which had already become evident during World War II. In 1949 the head of the island's agricultural service was instructed to inspect the east-coast plantations;[88] he reported that over the next ten years Madagascar's coffee production would fall by two-thirds unless planters followed a program of replacing heterogeneous and over-age bushes, most of which were between 25 and 30 years old. To replant in the course of a three-year period with selected and homogeneous varieties over a discontinuous area of 60,000 to 70,000 hectares would, he estimated, cost 40 million C.F.A. francs a year. On the other hand, failure to do so would result in the loss of billions of francs to the government and coffee planters and traders. He also warned that it was not enough simply to replant and to care for the bushes—the farmers must receive expert guidance from a better-staffed and better-equipped agricultural service. Another step that he strongly recommended was the creating of a new research station that would specialize in coffee production.[89]

This report provided the basis for a long-range official program aimed at reviving coffee production and exports. On July 27, 1953, a special fund was created to finance it; to this fund the territorial budget contributed 100 million C.F.A. francs and the French government a subsidy. An intensive replanting program carried out between 1954 and 1956 resulted in the replacement of 22 million coffee bushes by selected and homogeneous plants and in a rapid increase of production. Exports rose to 52,000 tons in 1956; of the total output, good-quality beans rose from 48 per cent in 1953 to over 60 per cent three years later.[90] By 1956, coffee was cultivated on only about 195,000 hectares, but they supplied 43 per cent of the island's revenues, as compared with 33 per cent in 1938. This spurt in production and exports coincided with a fall of more than 29 per cent in world prices for coffee, which, fortunately for Madagascar, was offset by the higher-than-world prices paid for a quota of around 35,000 tons a year allotted to the island's coffee in the French market. In the mid-1950s, too, Madagascar began to ship coffee for the first time to the United States, and by 1957 sales to that country amounted to 13,621 tons. Additional aid to Madagascar's coffee planters was provided by a price-stabilization fund created August 7, 1956.

These various support measures have resulted in a small but irregular growth in the island's robusta-coffee production and exports, and in 1962 Madagascar exported over 50,000 tons of coffee, valued at 7.4 billion C.F.A. francs. Coffee remains Madagascar's single most valuable export, but since 1960 its primacy has been disputed by rice, and there are strong indications that it will continue to decrease in importance. Officials incline to believe that Malagasy farmers are losing interest in coffee cultivation because of world overproduction and the imminent loss of Madagascar's privileged position in the French market when the Common Market agreement comes fully into force. Realizing the uncertainty of the commodity's future, the authorities are now discouraging any extension of the area planted to coffee and are concentrating on improving yields and quality.

Cocoa. Madagascar's first cocoa plantations on the east coast, which dated from the mid-nineteenth century, were soon decimated by disease. This crop, however, gained a new lease on life after the Compagnie Agricole de Nossi-Bé introduced new bushes from South America, which began to flourish in the northwest about 1898. That area provided all the cocoa bushes later planted at Sambirano, for more than half a century the sole cocoa-producing region on the island. Its production was never large, ranging from 200 to 460 tons a year, but the beans were superior in quality to those produced in French Negro Africa and found a ready market in France.

About 80 tons were used each year in the local manufacture of chocolate candy and pastry, and the rest were exported to Europe.

The relatively high prices paid for Madagascar's cocoa in the late 1950s induced some Malagasy farmers to turn from coffee to cocoa cultivation, and between 1957 and 1960 they planted some 500 hectares to cocoa. Madagascar's cocoa comes entirely from Diégo-Suarez province except for that produced on 200 hectares in Tamatave province. The P.S.D. government is encouraging wider cultivation of this crop because it continues to be easily salable abroad, and it is hoped that by 1970 close to 6,000 tons a year will be available for export.

ANIMAL HUSBANDRY

Herds and Flocks

Cattle. No reliable data exist on the number of cattle in Madagascar, either in times past or in the present. They are found everywhere on the island, but the largest herds today are in the south and west. Cattle "census" figures are issued periodically, being compiled from reports by canton chiefs on the number of taxable animals. Because only about 15 per cent of the herds are subject to taxation and cattle owners have every reason to disguise the size of their herds, the real number is undoubtedly much larger than the published figures.

In the early 1920s Madagascar was thought to have 8 million head of cattle; in 1940, 4,500,000; and in 1960, 7,600,000. These figures, even if rough, do reflect a sharp diminution during the interwar period and a slow growth in the course of the 15 years that followed World War II. Although the total number of cattle now seems to be about what it was 40 years ago, and Madagascar's human population has increased rapidly since that time, there are still more cattle than human beings on the island. The present ratio of 1.43 head of cattle to one person is probably higher than is to be found anywhere else in the world except Australia.[91]

Excessive slaughtering by Malagasys for religious ceremonies and for sale to the meat companies and to traders in hides was mainly responsible for the great decline in the size of herds during the interwar period. The increase in the course of the 1950–60 decade is thought to reflect a decline in slaughtering rather than a natural increase. Official statistics indicate that before World War I about 250,000 head of cattle were slaughtered each year. Between 1920 and 1925 the annual slaughter rate rose to 520,000, and from 1950 on it fell to 300,000.

Principally through the Animal Husbandry Service, the French administration tried to enlarge the Malagasy herds and to improve their quality by crossbreeding with imported stock, arresting the deterioration of pastureland, digging wells and providing watering points, preventing cattle thefts, promoting better utilization of animal products, and training Malagasys as veterinarians. Mainly responsible for the relative ineffectiveness of the program was a basic divergence in the attitudes of French officials and Malagasy peasants toward cattle husbandry, the French view being dominated by economic considerations and the Malagasy by religious ones.

The Malagasys cherish their zebu cattle not as sacred animals but for sacrificial purposes. Like the Peuls of West Africa, the Malagasys regard cattle as living capital and as a status symbol. They love their animals almost as much as their children, and owners have even been known to commit suicide when a favorite bull died.[92] In Madagascar, cattle are a perennial subject of conversation, and there are 80 words in the Malagasy language to describe their physical attributes, particularly the horns and hump.[93] Malagasys want to own as many cattle as possible, regardless of age, size, and condition, and sacrifice them only with the greatest reluctance because the cult of the dead requires it. The worldly status of a Malagasy can be judged by the number of cattle sacrificed at his funeral, and the skulls and horns placed on his tomb are a permanent and visible indication of his wealth. Because the best specimens—preferably young bulls—are slain at religious and family ceremonies, the herd consists mainly of cows and over-age bulls.

In the light of this religious role of cattle, the Malagasy peasant is an owner rather than a breeder of animals, and until very recently he has shown little or no interest in the economic utilization of cattle and their by-products. There is an old Malagasy saying, "cattle grow like rice"—in other words, they receive no care or feeding. Bulls are not castrated until they are three to four years old, and therefore interbreeding is frequent and haphazard. Cattle are turned out to graze on pastures where mediocre grass grows only during the rains and after the land is burned over. No effort is made to avoid overgrazing or to cultivate fodder crops which might tide the animals over the long dry season. In regions where cattle theft is prevalent, the animals are driven into corrals at night. These overcrowded enclosures are never cleaned, for the Malagasys do not utilize manure, and contagious diseases spread rapidly. Thus far rinderpest has not infected Malagasy herds, but in some provinces—especially Tananarive—perhaps one-fifth of the cattle are tubercular. As a result of exposure to the extremes of heat and cold, the undernourished cattle have little resistance to disease, and it is believed that 70 to 80 per cent of the calves die during the first year.[94] Only once in three or four years does a cow produce a calf that lives to maturity. Death from natural causes or from slaughtering depletes the herds by some 14 per cent each year.

Depletion of herds is also caused by cattle theft, a Malagasy custom that was originally only a dangerous sport with social implications. Among certain tribes, notably the Bara, a youth could not hope to make a good marriage unless he proved his manhood by stealing cattle. Formerly, particularly on the high plateaus, only one or two animals were stolen at a time, and they served simply to provide the thief's family with sacrificial animals or meat.[95] With the establishing of meat-packing plants throughout the island, however, especially during the interwar period, cattle-stealing spread to new areas, in particular the west and south, where it developed into an organized occupation. Bands of as many as 80 armed men descended at night on villages and drove off whole herds, sometimes killing the owners who tried to defend their animals. The animals were seldom recovered, for they either were immediately slaughtered by the thieves for the meat or hide or, more often, were sold through agents to the packing plants.

The French law code specified penalties for cattle thieves, but they were rarely caught because they operated over vast areas and frequently with the collusion of relatives and fellow tribesmen. Moreover, after 1946 the suppression of native penal courts and of the *fokonolona*'s collective responsibility for the crimes committed by one of its members caused a renewed outbreak of cattle thefts, which in recent years have caused increasing concern to the Malagasy authorities. Two laws—passed on February 17, 1959, and June 9, 1960—increased the penalties for this offense, which was made punishable by execution or by forced labor for life. These laws also reinstated the principle of collective responsibility in such cases, and simplified the court procedure for dealing with them. Because the laws referred to are now being applied by Malagasy magistrates, they may be more effective than previous legislation in reducing cattle thefts. The most significant aspect of this development, however, is that it is one of the rare instances when Malagasy parliamentarians have not supported an ancestral custom simply because it was consecrated by tradition. They now recognize that it is a national menace and one that must be punished accordingly.

Under ordinary circumstances the development of a meat industry* in Madagascar should have provided an economic incentive for Malagasy herders to give more care to their cattle and to make better use of their animal resources. But the contrary occurred, because it revitalized the deep-rooted tribal custom of cattle-stealing. Owners were deprived of their animals without recompense and in many cases also lost the desire for herding, and even the thieves received little money for the purloined animals. Herds diminished and some packing plants had to close, mainly for lack of supplies.

* See pp. 413–14.

In somewhat similar fashion the tax imposed on animals by the French government had results that ran counter to the authorities' intention. In taxing all but the very youngest calves, the administration aimed primarily at forcing Malagasy owners to sell their surplus and unproductive cattle, thus adding to the local supply of fresh meat, and secondarily at increasing the state's revenues. The results, in both cases, were disappointing. Naturally, the animal tax was highly unpopular, and it was also felt to be unjust. Many of the animals taxed died from natural causes, or were slaughtered for family use, or were stolen, in which cases they were a total monetary loss to their owners. Moreover, there was often abuse in the arbitrary imposing and collecting of the tax by canton chiefs. As a fiscal measure, the tax produced insignificant revenues. It was so unpopular that some candidates for election in 1959 campaigned on this issue, using an argument that appealed especially to Malagasy voters: cows, they asserted, should not be taxed, because Malagasy women had always been exempted from taxation.[96] Yet those who were elected voted to perpetuate the tax, because it provided the provinces with needed revenues for which no alternative sources could be found.

If the meat industry and the animal tax have inadvertently and indirectly furthered the shrinkage of Madagascar's herds and done little to increase the country's revenues, it might be thought that in other ways the Malagasys could derive tangible benefits from their cattle. Under the Merina monarchs there was an export trade in livestock, and after the French conquest cowhides began to be shipped out of the country. From 1896 on, livestock exports to the Mascareignes increased, and during the Boer War more than 20,000 head of cattle were sent to South Africa. During the early twentieth century a few thousand head a year were shipped to Mozambique and Port Said. Since World War II, exports of cattle on the hoof have consistently totaled 10,000 to 11,000 head a year. In 1960 these exports brought in 1,700 million C.F.A. francs (but in value represented only 5 per cent of Madagascar's total animal production).[97] Shipments of cowhides reached their peak in the mid-1920s, following a veritable massacre of cattle. Hide exports ceased entirely during World War II, causing such losses as to discourage permanently some producers and merchants. Since that time this trade has never regained prewar levels, partly because of the cutback in slaughtering but even more because of the low prices paid for Madagascar's poorly tanned products. At present, probably only one-third of the potential supply of skins is prepared for sale. In 1962 Madagascar exported 2,449 tons of hides, valued at 208,700,000 C.F.A. francs.[98]

With respect to meat and milk, the Malagasys derive little profit from their animals' production. Malagasys are so avid for beef that the ceremonies involving animal sacrifices culminate in orgies of meat-eating. Although living standards, generally speaking, have risen since World War II, the average Malagasy eats less meat today than he did 15 years ago because the supply has not kept pace with the population growth. In 1950, local consumption of beef was estimated at 63,000 tons a year, and in 1960 at 66,000 tons for an appreciably larger number of consumers. Even taking into account clandestine and family slaughtering, the per capita consumption probably does not exceed 15 kilograms a year. To some extent, however, the decline in beef consumption has been offset by a slightly larger intake of mutton and goat meat. A major difficulty is that Malagasy cattle are undersized and also over-age when they are sold, so that they give less meat than might be expected, considering the number slaughtered each year.

Milk consumption also is limited, to some extent because of the small output of the indigenous cow (1.5 to 3 liters a day), but even more as a result of the Malagasy's general distaste for that beverage. The total annual milk production of Madagascar's undernourished zebu cows comes to 28.6 million liters, or about 5 liters per inhabitant.[99] Most of this comes from Tuléar province, but even there fewer than one-fourth of the cows are regularly milked. Members of the Bara, Antandroy, and Tsimehety tribes consume some cow's milk after it has curdled, but they consider it a tonic for young children and old people and not a drink suitable for healthy adults. Only near the main towns has a dairy industry been developed by local Indians, and its survival is precarious. Supplies are so scanty, irregular, and unhygienic that European residents and Occidentalized Malagasys prefer to buy imported condensed or powdered milk.

On the banknotes issued by the Republic of Madagascar the zebu's picture has the place of honor, but cattle certainly have not been a source of wealth to the Malagasys. The price paid for cattle in Madagascar is said to be one of the lowest in the world, partly because the market is poorly developed but more from lack of modern techniques in cattle-rearing. Despite the existence of sizable herds, numbering 7.6 million head, the 45 million hectares of potential pastureland could provide nourishment for twice this number. In 1960 animal husbandry supplied merely 6 per cent of the country's total revenues, and during the 1950 decade there was only a 10 per cent increase in the cash value of the island's animal products.[100] Obviously the incentives and guidance provided by the French administration failed to induce the people to forsake their sentimental and "contemplative" attitude toward cattle husbandry. Tsiranana has said that his government wants to double or even treble its output of animal products,[101] but it will take many years to accomplish the indispensable change in the Malagasys' outlook.

Pigs. Portuguese navigators are believed to have first brought pigs to

Madagascar, and these animals can be raised in all parts of the island. Only on the high plateaus, however, is there commercial hog-raising, which is a virtual monopoly of Betsileo and Merina herders. One cause of this geographical concentration is that the rearing of pigs and the eating of pork are *fady,* or taboo, for many of the coastal tribes. Among tribes with Arabic traditions, any contact with pigs is forbidden by the Muslim religion. To pagan tribes such as the Tanala, Antandroy, and some Betsimisaraka, the animals are *fady.*[102] No such inhibitions are felt by the peoples of the high plateaus, who have abundant feed for the pigs and numerous nearby consumers who eat fatty meat. Their regard for pigs as a source of meat and of cash income has caused some Merina and Betsileo herders to provide their animals with shelter at night and sometimes to fatten them for market, but otherwise they are reared in careless fashion.

In 1946, of Madagascar's 450,000 pigs, some 125,000 were slaughtered, of which 45,000 were used by packing plants, mainly for export to the Mascareignes. In 1949, when the pig count on the island had risen to about 504,000, there were predictions that pig-raising would soon become one of Madagascar's greatest sources of wealth.[103] The next year, however, the pig herds were attacked by the Teschen disease, and within three years they numbered no more than 265,000. The representative assembly, alarmed by this severe decline, voted the Animal Husbandry Service and the Pasteur Institute 33 million C.F.A. francs to produce vaccines against the disease. Systematic and successful inoculations by the Service's veterinarians—and even more, the high prices paid for pigs because they were in short supply— gave new hope to the Malagasy herders. The herds are being rapidly reconstituted (in 1960 they were estimated at 406,000), but they are less hardy than formerly. Nevertheless, in 1960 they were the source of 16,000 tons of meat and provided the budget of Tananarive province with approximately one-third of the total income it derived from animal husbandry.[104] Exports of live pigs and pork products rose from 4 tons in 1954 to 90 tons six years later, and were shipped principally by the Réunionais colonists at Sakay. Today less is expected from pig-raising than formerly, but it is once again important to the economy of the high plateaus, and under favorable circumstances it could develop considerably.

Sheep. Sheep have long been reared in Madagascar, the first European navigators who touched at the island having noted their presence there. In the early days, perhaps as many as 60,000 sheep lived on the high plateaus, where they supplied the population with meat, milk, and wool. As recently as 1946, Tananarive was by far the most important outlet for mutton, taking 11,000 of the 12,000 sheep slaughtered that year in the whole island. Now, however, the only important center of sheep-raising is in the Androy region of the extreme southwest.

From the Malagasy herders, sheep receive even less care than do the pigs and cattle with which they share pastures. Because they are held in much less esteem than cattle by the Malagasys, sheep are slaughtered more readily for food and also for sacrifices, although they are considered to have less value than cattle in the ancestral cult.[105] The fat-tailed sheep provides little meat and no wool, but the fat is used in the manufacture of a kind of hair-dressing. During the famines of 1920 and 1943 in the south, so many sheep were slaughtered for food that entire herds were wiped out. The sheep in that region, however, are extremely hardy and prolific, and by 1962 they once more numbered well over 120,000.

All the early attempts by *colons* to breed sheep for their wool were failures. In 1921 the administration established a sheep farm at Ambovombe, where it later successfully introduced Arles rams imported from France. During World War II, when such importations became impossible, Merino breeding stock was brought in from South Africa, but this experiment was not a success, and in 1949 the importation of Arles rams was resumed.[106]

Past experience seems to indicate that sheep-raising has no great future in Madagascar, even though Malagasys are eating more mutton than formerly. Sheep-rearing is limited in area not only by climatic conditions but also by the fact that sheep (like pigs) are taboo for some tribes. In the southwest, where the climate is suitable and sheep are not *fady* for the Antandroy, there is little pastureland. Inasmuch as sheep share the same pastures with cattle and pigs, it is thought that the maximum number that could be reared there without danger of overgrazing is 200,000.

Goats. The areas suited to goat-husbandry are more extensive than those for sheep, yet goats are found only on the west coast and especially in the extreme south of the island. For some years the total number has remained at around 200,000 to 300,000. The indigenous breed, introduced perhaps by the Arabs into Madagascar centuries ago, is used mainly for its milk, which is reputed to cure illness, and less for its meat, which is distasteful to some of the Malagasys of the high plateaus. This is one of the reasons why in the central region the goatherds are Indians, the great majority of whom are Muslims and thus forbidden to have any contact with pigs. In the south, goat meat and mutton are more widely consumed, especially during famines, in order to avoid slaughtering cattle. For certain tribes there, however, such as the Antanosy, goats are *fady* and are never used as sacrificial animals.[107]

On the eve of World War I, the Animal Husbandry Service introduced a few Angora goats into the Tuléar region, where they thrived and were crossbred with the indigenous goats. Southern breeders now prefer the crossbred animal to the indigenous one because of its greater resistance to disease and its more abundant meat, hair, and milk. Furthermore, the

Mahafaly population quickly learned to weave the mohair into rugs, cover-
lets, and *lamba,* or scarfs, and with official encouragement a weaving industry has grown up at Ampanihy. The future of goat-husbandry appears
to be unpromising except at Ampanihy, although local consumption of
goat meat rose from 500 tons in 1950 to 600 in 1960.[108]

Poultry. Practically all species of poultry—chickens, ducks, geese, and
guinea fowl—are found in abundance throughout Madagascar, totaling perhaps more than 50 million. Almost every Malagasy family keeps from ten
to 20 fowl, and the meat and eggs are an important source of protein. Poultry
receive no care or feeding, but roam the village streets picking up garbage,
rice husks, and even locusts. Occasionally cocks serve as sacrificial animals
in family ceremonies, and some Malagasys breed fighting cocks. Only near
the big cities are poultry grown for sale. Attempts to improve the indigenous
barnyard fowl by crossbreeding with imported stock have not been successful.

The Animal Husbandry Service

Madagascar's Animal Husbandry Service was founded in 1903 by the
farsighted Gallieni, but its activities have never been commensurate with
the importance of the island's livestock resources or their place in Malagasy
life. It has never been given the staff or funds needed to perform the multiple
and arduous tasks with which it is charged. These are protecting animals
against disease, crossbreeding native zebus, pigs, sheep, and goats with imported stock, improving pastureland by developing watering points and
fodder grass, inspecting abattoirs and markets, educating Malagasy herders,
and training Malagasy veterinarians. Other handicaps to its effectiveness
have been the lack of continuity in its policies, largely because of frequent
changes in its top echelons, and the indifference of Malagasys generally to
its work and to the veterinary profession.

On the other hand, some of the deficiencies of the service are the result
of its own failures and mistakes. Undoubtedly some of the errors committed
—for example, in regard to the timing of inoculations and the selecting of
animals for crossbreeding purposes—were inevitably associated with the
process of experimentation, but others should and could have been corrected
years ago. One of the more serious though remediable mistakes of the
service has been its overtheoretical approach and its aloofness from herders.
Too often its staff has remained isolated on pilot farms and in laboratories
and has made little effort to publicize and popularize the results of its
research. Probably the worst of its shortcomings has been the failure to
train more Malagasys to fill the higher posts in the service. As of 1960 there
was not a single Malagasy who held a state diploma in veterinary science

in all Madagascar, although one was then in training in France. Control of this service therefore has remained wholly in European hands, thus causing it to be a target for nationalist attacks.

Initially the Animal Husbandry Service was so small that its operations were wholly advisory and were confined to Imerina. Only gradually and through its immunization of cattle from certain diseases did it win the confidence of Merina herders, who still believe, however, that they are more qualified to give advice about rearing animals than they are in need of receiving it. World War I caused such a demand for Madagascar's beef that several preserved-meat plants were installed on the island. After the wartime demand had abated, the French realized that, if Malagasy beef were to hold its own in world markets, the quality must be improved and the output increased. More French veterinarians, therefore, were employed, and a beginning was made in training Malagasys to assist them, but a comprehensive program drawn up in 1925 was only partly carried out. By the time World War II began, the service had at its disposal seven main farms (the best of which was at Kianjasoa, 100 kilometers from Tananarive), three secondary farms, 21 stud farms, and, most important of all, a laboratory at Tananarive for research and the production of vaccines.

In the framework of the postwar effort to better Madagascar's economy, Governor Bargues founded a School for Veterinary Auxiliaries at Mahamasina in 1950. Candidates for admission had to possess a C.E.P., and each year 20 were admitted by competitive examination. Graduates who showed promise were named veterinary aides after they had gained some experience. By 1954, however, the French authorities felt that something more positive must be done, and quickly, to increase the effectiveness of the Animal Husbandry Service, which seemed unable to bring about improvements in Malagasy livestock either by persuasion or by coercion.

With the help of funds provided by F.I.D.E.S., an Ecole de Moniteurs et d'Assistants Vétérinaires was built at Ampandrianomby in 1956 to train Malagasy holders of a *brevet élémentaire* to replace European *controleurs* in the service. The prospect of becoming functionaries in the civil service attracted a fair number of Malagasy applicants. Reportedly, however, those admitted were disillusioned when they found that the curriculum at the new school was the same as at Mahamasina, and they also felt that the title of *auxiliaires* which they would receive lacked prestige. Their complaints were supported by the Malagasy Syndicat du Service Vétérinaire, whose leaders were apparently convinced that the island's European veterinaries were determined to keep a grip on the top posts in the service and were therefore opposing higher training for Malagasys.[109]

Since independence, the Animal Husbandry Service has been attacked occasionally by Malagasy assemblymen. They have disputed the service's claim to have checked cattle and pig diseases through inoculations with the vaccines manufactured at the Tananarive laboratory.* In addition, the deputies have blamed the veterinaries of the service for having developed cross-bred cattle (called *rana*) that either were more difficult to nourish and care for than the indigenous zebu or were aesthetically unsatisfactory to Malagasy herders because they lacked humps and beautiful horns.[110] Finally, they have reproached the service—and its director admitted the justice of this criticism—for not having been active enough in digging wells to water the herds in Madagascar's drought-ridden south.

In fact, it is the mediocre status of the Malagasy members of the service, and, even more, the pervasive feeling of impatience with the lack of progress in cattle husbandry, that lie behind the parliamentarians' exasperation. They believe that if conditions were made more attractive, Malagasy youths would quickly lose their prejudice against a veterinary career. More veterinarians are certainly needed, for at present there is only one agent of the service for every 35,000 animals.[111] Typically, the deputies' panacea is a thorough Malagasization of the cadres of the Animal Husbandry Service, which they seem convinced can be accomplished through the founding of a National Veterinary School.

FISHERIES

Considering that Madagascar has more than 5,000 kilometers of coastline, it is surprising that fish from the sea are much less important in the local food supply and as an item of trade than are freshwater fish. Yet the combined output does not meet the needs of Madagascar, which imports each year about 15 tons of tinned, frozen, and dried fish.

The importance of fish as a source of protein in the Malagasy diet is indicated by the evolution of the word *laoka,* which formerly meant "fish" but which has come to mean all foodstuffs other than rice.[112] Nevertheless, fishing as an industry has been stagnant for various reasons, foremost among them being the inadequacy of supply, the lack of esteem in which fishing as an occupation is held, and the primitive fishing boats and equipment. The best survey yet made of Madagascar's fish resources[113] indicates that the island's waters contain 92 species, none in abundance. The frequency of high winds on the east coast greatly limits the number of days in which it is possible for the Betsimisaraka fishermen to take their fragile dugouts and rudimentary tackle into deep waters. Climatic conditions are much more

---

* In 1959, the head of the service pointed out that this laboratory was also helpful to state revenues in that each year it earned some 300 million C.F.A. francs from the sale of vaccine to private purchasers.

propitious for fishing on the west coast, where the Vezo, professional Malagasy fishermen, live. This is the only tribe that engages in fishing as a regular and honorable occupation, for the other coastal peoples fish only when they themselves need food or cash to pay taxes or buy imported goods. Sea-fishing is carried on by so many individuals and so irregularly that it is impossible to obtain accurate data on the total catch. An estimate made in 1960 suggested that Tuléar produced 2,100 tons, Diégo-Suarez 420 tons, Majunga and Tamatave 350 tons each, and Fianarantsoa 280 tons.[114]

The Malagasys' indifference to fishing as an occupation also stems from the difficulties of marketing the catch. Almost all of it is sold fresh within a radius of 100 to 150 kilometers around the points where it is brought in, the remainder going to more distant markets in dried or smoked form. The lack of refrigeration and transport facilities has made it difficult and costly to ship fresh fish to the only large potential market—the towns of the high plateaus.[115] Much of the fish sent there by truck or plane arrives in poor condition, and the price is prohibitively high for Malagasy consumers. Fish bought for 45 C.F.A. francs a kilo at Tuléar costs 185 C.F.A. francs at Tananarive, where it is more expensive than meat (priced at about 112 C.F.A. francs a kilogram). Consequently the quantity of fresh sea fish sold in the capital declined from 12 tons a month in 1959 to only seven tons in 1961.

Any noticeable improvement in this situation depends not only on better transportation facilities but on scientific research. This latter need became obvious in the late 1940s, when several foreign companies gave up attempts to develop whale and tuna fishing off Madagascar's coast. Belatedly the government came to realize that sea-fishing could never become an industry unless greater knowledge of Madagascar's coastal waters and fish migrations were made available. Therefore, with funds supplied by F.I.D.E.S. and experts loaned by O.R.S.T.O.M. to its Malagasy branch, the Institut de Recherches Scientifiques (I.R.S.M.), an oceanographic station was installed at Nossi-Bé in 1953.[116] Years passed while the staff studied Madagascar's coastal waters and their fish, experimented with improved boats and tackle, worked on ways to stock and preserve the catch, and investigated the possibilities of a canned-fish industry. Malagasy nationalists became impatient at these time-consuming undertakings and the lack of perceptible improvements in the fishing industry. They urged that a more practical program be adopted and its execution entrusted to the Animal Husbandry Service.[117]

In 1962, finally, there was evidence that the efforts of the I.R.S.M. were bearing fruit. That year two Japanese companies, which had been operating in Madagascar's coastal waters, proposed to engage in tuna fishing on an industrial scale and also to promote a trade in the skins of crocodiles, which were to be reared at two centers, in Tamatave and Majunga. As always, a few Malagasy deputies expressed the fear that the foreign competition would hurt Malagasy producers, but they were reassured by the fact that the Japanese would operate in the framework of a local company of "mixed economy" and pledged themselves to train Malagasy technicians and fishermen. On September 23, 1963, therefore, an agreement was signed by the Japanese and the Malagasy government providing for joint formation of a Société Malgache de Pêche (SOMAPECHE).

Approximately 550,000 hectares of Madagascar's surface (barely 1 per cent) are covered by waterways, but they are so well distributed over the island that freshwater fish are available to all except the inhabitants of the most arid regions of the south. Nineteen lakes, the largest of which is Lake Alaotra, and the adjacent marshes have a combined surface of more than 200,000 hectares, and the east-coast lagoons (*pangalane* area) account for an additional 18,000 hectares where fishing can be carried on. Unfortunately the great majority of Malagasy men and boys much prefer farming and herding, and relegate the task of fishing to women and children. In fact, fishing is taboo (*fady*) for some tribes, and for this reason a fish-research station located at Bealanana in Tsimehety country had to be moved to Befandirana.[118]

Like sea-fishing, freshwater-fishing is done so irregularly and on such an individual basis that the catch is difficult to estimate. The only area for which statistics are available is Lake Alaotra, from which 3,000 to 3,200 tons of smoked and fresh fish are shipped each year by rail or truck to nearby markets. In 1960 it was calculated that the annual production of freshwater fish for the whole island totaled 20,000 to 25,000 tons.[119]

Freshwater-fishing has received more attention from the government and from enterprising individuals than sea-fishing, notably in the introduction of new species. Rainbow trout, black bass, carp, and, above all, tilapia have been brought in. To varying degrees the new species have thrived in the island's lakes, marshes, and rivers, and have been accepted by the local population. However, there has been some opposition to the black bass, because of their cannibalistic habits, and the tilapia, because they have damaged some rice fields.* With only moderate success the authorities have stressed the fact that tilapia damage rice only during inundations, and furthermore, that they provide a readily accessible source of protein needed by the hinterland Malagasys. Millions of tilapia, first developed at the Sisaony station in 1950, have been sent to the other 11 stations and hatcheries maintained by the Water and Forest Service. From these points they are

---

* One assemblyman, J. F. Jarison, went so far as to charge that the French had brought in tilapia in order to reduce the island's rice output. See minutes of the assembly, May 21, 1959.

distributed to Malagasy peasants, who are taught how to build ponds and care for the fish. As of 1960, there were 70,000 family ponds where tilapia were being grown, most of them in Fianarantsoa province.

FORESTRY

Madagascar's wooded area covers 16,700,000 hectares, or more than 28 per cent of its entire surface, but the trees growing on a quarter of that wooded area are so dispersed or so stunted that they can no longer be said to represent genuine forests. The tropical forests of the coastal zone and the lowland valleys produce the most valuable and useful trees, such as ebony, rosewood (*palissandre*), the raffia palm, and mangroves, as well as wild rubber vines. The valuable species become fewer and less accessible on the mountainous approaches to the high plateaus, which today are almost bare of trees. In all, Madagascar has perhaps 1,200 varieties of trees, none growing in compact stands, and as many as 100 species may be found on a single hectare.[120]

It is believed that at one time trees covered the whole island, but they probably began to disappear with the introduction of rice culture and the practice of *tavy*. On areas that were burned over and then abandoned after several years of producing crops, a secondary forest, called *savoka,* has grown up. By the early nineteenth century, deforestation was so far advanced that stands of trees then covered only about one-tenth of the island. The Merina monarchs, in an effort to prevent further destruction, placed the remaining forests under state control. This move was prompted in part by their concern for preserving the wooded area and in part by a theory that the forests afforded a measure of protection against possible foreign invasion.[121] In any case, the practice of *tavy* continued because the rulers lacked the means to enforce their regulations.

Soon after the conquest, the French took the first steps toward giving effective protection to Madagascar's forests by creating a Forestry Service and training Malagasys to staff it. At the same time, however, they indirectly furthered the devastation of the wooded land. Concessions totaling about 174,000 hectares, which contained some of the most valuable tree species, were granted to *colons* and companies whose operations contributed to the destruction of the tropical forest. In this process the government itself was not without sin, for it wastefully felled trees to construct the port towns of Majunga and Tamatave and to provide fuel for the island's railroads.[122]

By 1900, Gallieni had become conscious of the threat that French policy posed for Madagascar's forests. He then attempted to regulate more carefully the conceding and utilization of forest land, but by that time 72 such concessions had already been granted. The Forestry Service that he estab-

lished was staffed by only three or four Europeans and therefore could do
little more than serve in an advisory role. Because means to enforce legislation were still lacking, the stricter regulations issued in 1913 as well as the
initiating of a reforestation program were in effect empty gestures. No
further steps were taken until December 21, 1927, when a decree created
forest reserves in which no trees were to be felled and no forest produce
was to be gathered by Malagasys.[123] These reserves were placed under the
"scientific control" of the Paris Museum of Natural History, and their management was entrusted to a largely nonexistent Forestry Service. By the time
World War II began, the forest reserves theoretically covered 380,000 hectares, the largest of them (83,000 hectares) being situated in the region of
Morondava. Reforestation with eucalyptus trees was first undertaken near
the main centers, in order to provide the urban population with firewood,
improve the soil cover, and enrich and diversify the tree species.

In 1930, the French authorities took stock of the situation. They had come
to realize that too many regulations were not enforced and that there were
glaring omissions in the forest legislation. Moreover, by that year, a total
of more than 1 million hectares, including large wooded areas, had been
permanently ruined by wasteful cutting, and the remainder would require
at least 50 years of effort to reconstitute. Concessionaires and the government were not the only ravagers of forest land. The Malagasys participated
in the destruction by their continuing practice of *tavy* and the abusive collecting of forest produce for house-building and fuel. A comprehensive
"forestry code" was therefore drafted and was embodied in a decree of January 25, 1930.

By that decree, all forested land still in the public domain was made inalienable. Elsewhere the granting of concessions was limited to a maximum
period of 20 years in each case and was made subject to stricter controls.
Concessions of forested land smaller than 500 hectares could thenceforth
be granted only by the governor-general, those between 500 and 1,000 hectares by the governor-general-in-council, and those larger than 1,000 hectares
by the Minister of Colonies. On concessions already granted, an official permit would be necessary even to clear the ground. The traditional usage
rights of the Malagasys were recognized but beyond that they were limited
to the satisfying of personal and family needs. No brush fires were to be
permitted near the forested areas, and everywhere such fires could be set
only with the authorization of the local administrator. The Forestry Service
was to enforce these regulations, the infraction of which was to be severely
penalized.

During the 1930s the foregoing measures seemed to be effective, but the
situation got out of control after World War II began, with a marked re-

sumption of the practice of *tavy*. In one year more than 2,000 individuals and villages were sued in the courts for violating the forest regulations, and fines amounting to over 2.5 million francs were imposed. In 1941, therefore, the government took the Draconian measure of ordering the regrouping into compact villages of Malagasys living in the forest areas and of making them collectively responsible for fires started within the village limits. Nonetheless, many offenders continued to escape punishment because the Forestry Service lacked the staff to enforce the laws.

After the war, the administration continued to issue regulations designed to control felling and fires and to expand the area of forest reserves and the reforestation program—but with not much more success than before. The year 1957, which saw the *loi-cadre*'s entry into force and the coming to power of the P.S.D. government, marked a turning point in official forestry policy and its implementation. The policy of decentralization resulted in a transfer of competence and responsibility for forestry affairs from the central government to the provincial administrations. A Bureau for Soil Conservation, attached to the Forestry Service, was created, thus providing the organization needed to launch a large-scale offensive against what had become "Madagascar's national drama and its number-one rural scourge."[124] It remains to be seen whether an all-Malagasy government will be more effective than were the French in protecting, amplifying, and enriching its forest heritage.

Shortly after the end of World War II, the French administration began to realize more than ever before the dangers to Madagascar's future of the progressive erosion of the soil, which at the time was even farther advanced than in Negro Africa. To meet this threat the authorities undertook to map the forest zones, increase the area of reserves, intensify the reforestation program, and give an impetus to research through an increase in the number of forestry stations.

Practical difficulties as well as the opposition of the Malagasy peasantry have hindered the extension of the area described as classified forests. The delimitation of forest reserves was long delayed by the fact that considerable time was needed for systematic mapping of the wooded areas, a task that was not begun until the early 1950s. Then, too, more time was needed to create or enlarge Madagascar's five provincial and 25 secondary forest stations, and for their staffs to make an inventory of the forest flora, select species for the reforestation of different regions, and develop them in nurseries for distribution. Finally, whenever new zones were classified as reserves, there was covert resistance from farmers and herders and outcries were heard from Malagasy nationalists. The latter charged that the French were using that means to extend their grip on the Malagasys' land heritage, and the former complained that the reserves were monopolizing arable land needed to grow food crops for an expanding population.[125] Both groups protested against the "excessive zeal" shown by agents of the Forestry Service in imposing heavy fines on entire villages or individuals whom they accused of setting brush fires. The P.S.D. government, while admitting that some of these complaints were justified, nevertheless has continued to add to the forest reserves. As of 1960 there were 3,600,000 hectares so classified, and half a million more were slated to become reserves. Furthermore, an area comprising 18,200 hectares of forest land in Diégo-Suarez province was declared a national park.[126] In short, a government controlled by Malagasys has shown its determination to preserve the vestiges of the island's flora and fauna.

During the French administration the reforestation program suffered from errors in judgment and from the population's indifference to its objectives. Replanting with eucalyptus trees was soon abandoned because they exhausted the soil. Acacias and *filao* were the next species tried, and though the former enriched the soil and the latter were effective as windbreaks, the Malagasys complained that their wood—like that of the eucalyptus—was useless for building purposes. At present the favorite species used in replanting is pine; the wood is suited to construction and it may also provide the material needed for the paper and match industries which it is hoped will be created. Yet these changes in species used for replanting have not met with widespread popular cooperation. Many of the young trees distributed to villages for planting have died for lack of care, and sometimes money given to communal organizations for reforestation purposes was deflected to other uses.[127]

By 1951, the governor-general — in the hope of making the Malagasys aware of the problem and popularizing the replanting program — had launched what was called "La Semaine de l'Arbre." He and his principal aides set the example by personally planting trees, and this ritual has been perpetuated by the P.S.D. government, with the support of radio propaganda and inspired articles in the press. In this way several million trees are planted in Madagascar every year, but reportedly officials must exercise the strictest vigilance to prevent villagers from cutting down the saplings as soon as they are planted. Nevertheless, such success as the replanting program has had owes more to the zeal of individuals and collectivities than to the efforts of the Forestry Service. During the first postwar decade, no more than 12,000 hectares were reforested by the service with funds provided by F.I.D.E.S., whereas 150,000 hectares were replanted through the initiative of individuals and groups.[128]

After the disastrous floods of March 1959 had obviously accelerated the island's deforestation, Madagascar's assemblymen became more sympathetic to the government's reforestation program, and they even began to complain of slowness in carrying it out.[129] In principle the majority were persuaded that Madagascar's forest heritage must be safeguarded and enriched both by replanting and by prohibiting brush fires, but many assemblymen opposed fining peasants and herders who practiced *tavy*. The government agreed that, theoretically, it was better to educate than to punish offenders, but its spokesman admitted to being disillusioned by the failure to enlist peasant cooperation with the official program. In October 1962, the government proposed and the assembly accepted a law that made reforestation a "national duty." Thenceforth every male Malagasy between the ages of 17 and 60 was obligated to plant 100 saplings each year or pay a special tax.

Another program initiated by the French, which has been taken over and amplified by the P.S.D. government, is that of training Malagasys for posts in the Forestry Service. As early as 1897, Gallieni decreed that Malagasys should be given theoretical and practical training in forestry work at the Nanisana agricultural station. This venture proved to be so expensive, however, that it was soon abandoned. Later, several attempts were made to revive the project, but it was not until 1943 that an Ecole Forestière was established at Angavokely. To this school candidates who had attended preparatory classes in three regional schools were admitted by competitive examination. Its graduates, called supervisors or guards, were sent to serve successively in the island's five provincial stations.[130] Between 1944 and 1952 the school graduated only 123 Malagasys, but its attendance grew markedly in the years that followed. In May 1955 an Ecole Forestière Secondaire was founded at Ambatobe, which at the same time became the central station for forestry research. Candidates for admission were required to possess a *brevet élémentaire,* and graduates either served as agents of the Forestry Service or were sent to France for higher studies at the Forestry School of Nancy. By the time the P.S.D. government was installed in 1957, the Ambatobe school had graduated six agents, one Malagasy was studying for a degree in forestry engineering in France, and close to 40 per cent of the local Forestry Service's staff of 350 had been "Malagasized."[131]

As recently as 1946, most of Madagascar's lumber companies were still felling trees by hand, and they employed mainly Tanala, Betsimisaraka, and Betsileo tribesmen as woodcutters. They continued to use manual labor not only because it was relatively cheap but also because the mountainous nature of the terrain in which they operated made mechanization difficult. Moreover, only a few of the island's 31 sawmills were mechanized, and the annual output of sawn logs came to merely 9,000 cubic meters, or 15 per cent of the total wood production. Transportation accounted for a large part of the high production costs, because near the best stands there were no rivers deep enough to permit floating the logs out.

Despite these handicaps, the output of all types of wood grew steadily. Between 1930 and 1955, production rose from 20,000 cubic meters to 2,520,000. In 1955, 30 sawmills had been mechanized, but none of them turned out more than 2,000 cubic meters of sawn wood a year. At present Madagascar produces 15,000 cubic meters of cabinet woods, 200,000 cubic meters of building lumber, and 2 million cubic meters of firewood and charcoal.[132] Inasmuch as the island lacks other sources of fuel, it is understandable that 80 per cent of its wood production should be used for that purpose.

Since Madagascar became independent, foreigners have shown an interest in the island's forest resources that has given the Malagasys new hope that their wood may be an unsuspected source of wealth. The first to come, however, was an Italian mission in 1960 that issued a disappointing report on its findings. A Belgian group followed, and its members reported optimistically that Madagascar possessed at least 40 million cubic meters of commercially valuable wood. The first actual offer to cut trees and export lumber from Madagascar came from the Skeda company of South Africa, with which the P.S.D. government signed a provisional agreement in 1961. The agreement provided that the company was to have a seven-year monopoly of Madagascar's wood exports, in return for which it promised to build a large modern sawmill, give jobs and training to 1,000 Malagasys, and guarantee revenues to the island amounting to at least 80 million C.F.A. francs a year.

Considerable opposition to the agreement was manifested by Madagascar's assemblymen, who had been dazzled by the prospect of huge revenues from the island's forest produce. The members of the A.K.F.M., in particular, criticized the monopolistic nature of the Skeda agreement, and they predicted that it would be the opening wedge for a take-over of all the island's resources by foreign capitalists.[133] For reasons that have not been disclosed, the deal with the Skeda company fell through. In 1962 the P.S.D. leaders opened negotiations with a Dutch company, the Société Brunzeel, with which a very similar agreement was reached in January 1964.[134]

The government is fully as eager as its opponents to develop Madagascar's forest resources to the maximum, but its approach to the problem is more realistic. The P.S.D. leaders know that Madagascar does not now possess the skills and capital required to increase lumbering activity and exports, and must therefore enlist the cooperation of foreign companies. They also realize that abundant local resources are a prerequisite for their project to create paper and match industries, which therefore must await the maturing of the pine trees that have been and are being planted in the deforested areas. To all the Malagasy elite, the perspective recently opened up has shown for the first time the necessity of conserving and increasing the island's forest resources. It has been reported that the government is drafting a new "Forestry Code," which will penalize more severely than before those practicing *tavy* and will stimulate replanting.

Chapter twenty-one

INDUSTRY

Madagascar's industries labor under certain handicaps that are common to all underdeveloped countries—the lack of indigenous capital, of a skilled and stable labor force, and of managerial talent.[1] In addition, Madagascar has problems peculiar to it: a prolonged revolt after World War II, which frightened away some potential foreign investors, the dispersal of production and of internal markets, exceptionally high production costs, an insular situation remote from foreign markets and sources of supply, electric power that is meager and extremely expensive, and above all, very limited production. This last is the result of the great variety and small scale of the island's resources, particularly its minerals, and the temperament of the people, who are disinclined to put forth effort beyond what is indispensable for survival and for maintaining the cult of the dead. On the other hand, Madagascar has specific advantages, which to some extent offset its drawbacks. These include a political regime that is moderate in its economic policies and has maintained law and order since 1957, a fast-growing population with rising living standards, raw materials in great diversity, many of which could be produced in far greater quantity than at present, and remoteness from countries with competitive industries.

Industrialization in Madagascar is as yet in the early stages, and the majority of the island's industries (those concerned with sugar, meat, hides, sisal, and mineral ores) still process raw materials largely or altogether for export. The processing of coffee, vanilla, cloves, and perfume plants is so rudimentary that it cannot properly be called an industrial operation. Many of the so-called industries are actually craft enterprises, and they supply services—such as repairs—more than manufactured goods to the small mechanized sector of the economy. A minority of them (textiles, cigarettes, soap, beverages, shoes, and sacks) produce wholly or almost wholly for the domestic market, but most of the raw materials they use are imported. Yet the very existence of industries producing mainly for local consumers is, except for sack manufactures, a post–World War II phenomenon, and their number and output, with the exception of soap, are steadily growing, as is their use of indigenous primary products. Even so, all but a few of them supply less than half the needs of local consumers in their respective fields of activity.

As in French Negro Africa, the first industries established in Madagascar were those that processed raw materials, agricultural and mineral, almost entirely for the export market. The oldest and for many years the most important of these was the preserved-meat industry. Though meat production has fallen off since World War II, food industries as a group remain the most valuable sector of Madagascar's industrial complex. In 1960 it was estimated that 72 per cent of the island's total industrial output, valued at 3,790 million C.F.A. francs, came from industries producing foodstuffs, and about half of that value was accounted for by sugar. Aside from rice, only a small proportion of which is milled, all the traditional food industries, such as manioc starch and salt, have been comparatively stagnant. Textiles rank next after sugar, with 12 per cent, and manufactured tobacco products account for 8 per cent. The remainder of the industrial output comes from miscellaneous plants of only slight economic significance.

In Madagascar both the producing industries and the domestic markets which absorb their output are very dispersed, stocking facilities are inadequate, and transportation is so difficult and expensive as to make the provisioning of many regions of the island onerous and costly. Near the ports and at some points in the hinterland the prices of locally produced industrial goods are so high that they cannot compete with similar imported articles. Furthermore, the consumer goods that are in demand locally are so diverse —not to speak of the dispersal and low purchasing power of the Malagasy population—that it is not possible to mass-produce them and thus reduce prices. Only in the island's capital city is there a sizable concentration of consumers, so it is not surprising that Tananarive province accounts for 29 per cent of the total industrial production. The French naval base in the extreme north is another important consumer center, and it is in large part responsible for the fact that Diégo-Suarez holds second place (28 per cent) as an industrial producer among the provinces. In those of Majunga, Fiana-rantsoa, and Tuléar, however, markets are meager and scattered, and these provinces contribute, respectively, 18, 6.5, and 4.5 per cent of the island's entire industrial output.

Madagascar's government, like those of all the newly independent nations, is eager to industrialize the country, and plans to encourage industrialization have reflected an unusually realistic moderation. The French administration initiated the policy of aiding new local industries and of encouraging foreign investments by granting specific fiscal advantages. Official French support took the form of outright subsidies, price-support funds, and the partial or total exemption of certain industries from various types of taxation. Such aid was successfully dispensed either to launch a major export industry, such as SOSUMAV, or to save from bankruptcy an industry of purely local importance, as in the case of FITIM. The Malagasy government has taken over and considerably amplified this policy, mainly by promulgating an Investment Code on October 14, 1961 (which was revised on September 28, 1962). Under this code, the government is empowered to grant a wide range of advantages and concessions to new investors in undertakings that it believes will modernize and expand the island's economy. These privileges include total or partial exemption from export, import, and income taxes; protection for the output of the enterprise in the domestic market, either by means of tariff walls or by the imposition of quotas on competitive imports; and aid in recruiting local labor. The industries that it was initially decided to encourage by such means were mining, consumer goods, electric power, sugar, fisheries, hotel-building, and transportation.

Within six months of the code's promulgation, 30 companies had applied for concessions, and before a year had passed 1,700 million C.F.A. francs of new investments in local industrial enterprises had already created 2,000 jobs for Malagasy workers.[2] The success of the code encouraged the Malagasy government to push forward. In September 1962, it passed a "law of industrial readaptation," which emphasized the advantages that would be accorded to industries complying with the official economic-development plan, but which also contained an implicit threat that those companies refusing to go along might be forced out of business.[3] Since the adoption of the law, no such drastic action has been taken, but it is obvious that the government intends to guide and even partially control the island's industrial evolution. Its announced short-term policy is to replace by locally made articles as many as possible of the consumer goods that are now imported at the rate of some 30 billion Malagasy francs annually. Experts have encouraged the P.S.D. leaders to believe that this policy can be applied to one-third of the items that are currently imported. Its long-term policy aims to increase the value of existing industries, help in creating new ones, and expand the island's exports and make them competitive in world markets.

Crafts

It has become increasingly difficult to draw a distinction between Madagascar's crafts and its industries. Many so-called industries are largely of an artisan nature, and most industrial production in any case comes from small undertakings. Official reports add to this confusion by including in the craftsman category hairdressers and taxi drivers, who in most Western countries would be classified as skilled or professional workers.

Under the Merina monarchy, remarkable impetus was given to crafts-manship by Jean Laborde,* who trained Malagasys to make a wide range of articles—shoes, bricks, mats, pottery, and even cannon. In the nineteenth century, too, English Protestant missionaries trained converts to become carpenters and tinsmiths, and French Catholic nuns taught the Malagasy girls attending their schools how to embroider and make lace. To be sure, these Europeans often simply heightened skills that had been practiced in the island before their coming. Silk-weaving, for example, was encouraged by the Merina monarchs, and a curious type of paper was made by the Antaimoro, who had learned this art from Arab immigrants. Both those skills were already dying out by the time the French ocupied Madagascar.

Some weaving of silk and cotton is still done by many village women in their spare time, especially for making ceremonial garments and shrouds, but imported cloth has dealt this activity a severe blow. On the other hand, another traditional occupation—the weaving of reeds and raffia into cloth-ing, mats, hats, and baskets—has developed, owing in part to a small export trade in such items. Blacksmiths continue to forge iron into spades and knives as they have done for the past three centuries. Leather crafts have developed since the Malagasys, under European influence, gave up eating the skin along with the meat in the mid-nineteenth century. Artisans now either treat hides for export or make them into sandals, belts, and boxes for sale locally. Wood-carving for the ornamentation of tombs still flourishes in many parts of the island, and this craft has been extended to the manu-facture and carving of wooden furniture. Only in the central region, where the necessary raw materials are available, are bricks and pottery made for local use.

The French administration did little to encourage craftsmanship beyond giving a limited amount of training in a few state vocational schools and making some vain efforts to revive the silk industry. In 1956 it did create a special fund to provide loans to craftsmen for improving their equipment, but this fund—20 million C.F.A. francs—was too small to be of much help, and the craftsmen were too ignorant and too dispersed to profit greatly by it. Moreover, they lacked any organization through which their output might be exhibited and sold. The government of independent Madagascar has made a much greater effort to promote Malagasy crafts, not only because of its general desire to encourage all indigenous production but also because it aims to develop crafts into small industries. It is hoped that in this way Madagascar may soon be able to manufacture more of the items it now imports.

In 1961 the government took a sampling of the crafts existing in the

* See p. 7.

island's four main centers of craftsmanship—Ambositra, Ampanihy, Ambohimahasoa, and Ambalavao. From this survey it was concluded that there were some 3,000 persons who could be termed craftsmen, each of whom employed on the average one workman. The aggregate income of these 6,000-odd persons engaged in craft production was estimated at 1,365 million C.F.A. francs, and their contribution to the national revenues at 0.09 per cent. Nearly two-thirds of the craftsmen were occupied in making clothing, and one-third in weaving mats and in woodworking. Their main needs seemed to be more capital, better training, and a sales organization. At about the same time almost identical conclusions were reached by two French experts whom the Malagasy government had asked to make a study of the island's crafts and submit recommendations for their improvement. It was noted that at that time only one island-wide organization for craftsmen existed, the Association des Artisans Malgaches.

To learn the views of the artisans themselves regarding their needs and aspirations, the government called a meeting at Tananarive for November 21–23, 1961, to which craftsmen of the six provinces sent representatives. So unanimous were the recommendations of both the experts and the craftsmen that the government was able rapidly to draft a law under which the Centre Economique et Technique de l'Artisanat (C.E.T.A.) was founded in January 1962. This center's general objective was to develop all types of Malagasy crafts and to help craftsmen to form cooperative societies. The C.E.T.A. was a company of mixed economy, with a capital of 10 million C.F.A. francs provided by the national budget and the Crédit de Madagascar. As its first task, it was to study the needs of individual craftsmen, and then to lend money to the most needy and deserving, particularly to the makers of raffia mats (rabanes). The mat industry is one that the government is especially eager to develop for a wider domestic market as well as for export.

Madagascar's deputies have been fully in sympathy with the aims of the government program, but they have haggled over the requirement imposed by the authorities that craftsmen must have some professional training to qualify for a loan from C.E.T.A.[4] Some of them wanted Malagasy crafts to be given greater protection from foreign competition, and others urged that certain occupations be reserved exclusively to Malagasy nationals. At the government's insistence, however, such restrictive conditions were eliminated, and the official proposal was accepted.

Since January 1962, cooperative societies for craftsmen have increased in number and their situation generally has improved. Although the government has built a few Maisons de l'Artisanat, in which the best specimens of Malagasy crafts are exhibited and sold, the chief stumbling blocks to more effective action continue to be the dispersal of craftsmen and the high price of transporting their output to consumer centers. Even in the few towns that are visited by Madagascar's infrequent tourists, the Maisons de l'Artisanat provide no facilities for wrapping or shipping cumbersome articles.

Electric Power

Madagascar has no known petroleum resources and the only sizable coal deposits are believed to be economically not worth extracting.* It does, however, have many torrential rivers, particularly on the high plateaus, which could become substantial sources of hydroelectric power. Considering its hydroelectric potential and the fact that the public distribution of current on the island dates back to the early twentieth century, the consumption of electric current today in Madagascar is surprisingly small. Although consumption has greatly increased since World War II, rising from 26 million kilowatt hours in 1938 to 107 million in 1960, Madagascar lags behind French Negro Africa in this respect. Of total production in 1960, 61 million kilowatts came from public hydroelectric sources, 16 million from thermal plants using imported fuel, and 30 million from privately owned plants operated by various industrial enterprises for their own needs. The plants in public service had a total installed generating capacity of 46,000 kilowatts, and those belonging to private interests, 24,000 kilowatts.

Three main companies produce and distribute electric power. The smallest of these is Electricité de France Australe (E.D.F.A.), which operates thermal plants in Fort-Dauphin, Manakara, and Farafangana. The largest is Electricité et Eaux de Madagascar (E.E.M.), a private company originally financed by a group of capitalists in Lyon. Soon after receiving the concession to produce and distribute electric current (and water) in 1908, it built the island's first thermal plant at Mandroseza, a suburb of Tananarive. Thereafter its operations were steadily extended to include all the provincial capitals and Antsirabe.

After World War II, it became apparent that the E.E.M.'s current installations could not supply the growing needs of Tananarive, let alone meet the demand for power from many of the island's smaller towns. In 1948, therefore, the Minister of Overseas France asked Electricité de France to send a mission of experts to Madagascar to survey the island's hydroelectric resources, with a view to utilizing them not only for domestic and industrial needs but also for irrigation and to supply power to the east-coast railroad. Although the mission studied only about a fifth of the island's hydroelectric resources, giving its attention mainly to those it thought should be developed

* See pp. 410–11.

first, several years passed before it made a report.[5] In the meantime, Tana-narive's mounting demand for power urgently dictated that a solution to the problem be found, and the representative assembly in particular became im-patient for a more rapid increase in power supply than was being effected by the monopolistic E.E.M. Consequently a company of mixed economy, called the Société d'Energie de Madagascar (S.E.M.) was formed in 1953, with a capital of 200 million C.F.A. francs supplied jointly by the French govern-ment and the local administration, for rapid development of more of the island's hydroelectric resources. To provide the Tananarive region with an adequate supply of power, it built a dam at the waterfall of Mandraka, 70 kilometers from the capital, and then two other dams on tributaries of the Ikopa River. It also has constructed a dam on the Volobe River to supply Tamatave, as well as thermal plants for other coastal towns. Most of the current generated in the S.E.M.'s plants, however, is distributed by the E.E.M.

Between 1950 and 1960 the investments of French and Malagasy public funds in the island's electrical equipment totaled 4,450 million C.F.A. francs, of which the E.E.M. accounted for about 55 per cent, the S.E.M. 43 per cent, and the E.D.F.A. 2 per cent. Nevertheless, Madagascar's sources of electric energy at present are badly distributed and underutilized. Most of the island is underequipped in generating and distribution facilities because the aggre-gate demand is small and, above all, too widely dispersed. To distribute power generated on the high plateaus, which is already excessively costly in the central regions, to the coastal settlements would be prohibitively ex-pensive. Costs to consumers are not uniform throughout the island, but even where current is least expensive, the price is between 10 and 17 C.F.A. francs per kilowatt hour.[6] Although 60 per cent of the current consumed is for domestic use and 40 per cent for industrial purposes in Tananarive, three-fourths of the homes there have no electricity. Because of the high rates, only 9,000 kilowatts of the 12,000-kilowatt capacity of the plants in the Tana-narive region were utilized in 1960. It is hoped, however, that the capital's industrial expansion will provide enough consumers by 1970 to utilize its resources fully. At present the three companies claim that they cannot lower prices because there are too few consumers, whereas the people complain that they cannot buy current because it costs too much.

The P.S.D. government naturally is anxious to break this vicious circle, increase the supply of current throughout the island, and reduce Madagas-car's large and expensive imports of fuel. In October 1962 it granted a monopoly to the S.E.M. for all new operations to increase the production of hydroelectric current and to distribute it, both in urban and rural areas.[7] Some deputies regard this measure as inadequate and have urged the gov-ernment to nationalize the E.E.M., or at least to revise its agreement with that company so as to force down the cost of current in the areas where the E.E.M. is still the sole distributor of electric power.[8]

Mining

In relation to the value of Madagascar's total exports, mining plays a much smaller role now than it did in the early twentieth century.[9] Since that time, the island's agricultural exports have greatly increased, and, except for a few recently discovered ores, mineral shipments either have remained stationary or have actually declined. Madagascar possesses a great variety of minerals but none in abundance, and many of them are not worth the cost of extracting or shipping under present conditions.

Before the French occupation, such small-scale mining as was done in Madagascar was confined to the extraction of iron and gold in Imerina. Iron was first mined there in the sixteenth century but no gold was extracted until the early nineteenth century. Malagasys were allowed to mine iron freely for their own use, but gold-mining was *fady* and harsh penalties for violation were imposed by the Merina monarchs. The Merina government's growing need for gold in the late nineteenth century, however, led to a partial lifting of this ban in 1883. At first the output was reserved exclusively for the state treasury, but three years later the government began issuing gold-mining permits to foreigners because it was under great pressure to repay the loan it had contracted with the Comptoir National d'Escompte.* Many of these permits were never used, but others gave rise to considerable prospecting and some extraction.

Soon after the conquest Gallieni showed his determination that the French government should control all phases of mining on the island, though he recognized the validity of the rights granted under the Merina monarchy. A Mines and Geological Service was created and was assigned multiple tasks. It was made responsible for the application of mining legislation and for helping to promote private mining enterprises. Moreover, its competence included direct participation in production when private interests failed to prospect or to exploit deposits of economic value to the country. Legislation was progressively expanded to cover newly discovered deposits and to regulate in ever-greater detail the conditions under which prospecting and extraction permits, as well as concessions, were granted. Initially such laws dealt only with the mining of gold and precious stones, but later their scope was widened to include all other materials as well. The Malagasy government has carried this a step further by drawing up a code for petroleum mining, even though no oil has yet been found on the island.

Before World War I and even throughout the 1920s the French govern-

* See pp. 10 and 301.

ment showed little discrimination in granting mining concessions and in issuing permits for prospecting and extraction. By 1904, about 1,000 permits had been issued to 317 individuals and companies; in 1927 permit-holders numbered some 2,000, and upwards of 5,000 permits had been issued to them, Madagascar's deposits being so small and scattered that applicants were usually granted two or more permits. The world depression of the 1930s and then World War II automatically eliminated some of the excess, and by 1945 the number of permits had been reduced to 3,468, held by 350 individuals and companies. Although the French government was not able during the postwar years to bring order out of this confusion, it did greatly encourage the mining industry in its overseas dependencies, and in Madagascar it granted new mining rights on a more rational basis than before.

France's postwar mining policy was motivated more by economic considerations than by nationalistic ones, as in the past. In Madagascar, the primary aim was to promote the development of the country's mineral resources to the maximum, and for this purpose extraction permits were divided into two categories. Ordinary, or B-type, permits were issued for deposits that could be easily extracted and therefore did not require much capital and technical skill. A-type permits, on the other hand, were granted for long periods and large areas only to big companies or organizations able and pledged to invest considerable capital in their prospecting and mining operations. Furthermore, the French government directly promoted mining in Madagascar by offering financial and technical assistance, which was channeled through two new state organizations, the Bureau Minier and the C.C.O.M. Owing to the activity of the Bureau Minier, in particular, and its collaboration with the local mines service and big mining companies, a geological map of half of Madagascar was completed and important mineral deposits were discovered on the island.

When the first Malagasy government was installed in 1957, its leaders found that certain segments of the mining industry were making satisfactory progress, whereas others were either marking time or had retrogressed. They were predisposed to attribute the stagnation less to marketing conditions and the nature of Madagascar's mineral deposits than to the inactivity of many concessionaires. It is true that of the 451 concessions granted by the French administration prior to World War II, only 120 were then actually producing minerals. Of these, ten concessionaires were mining graphite, two rock crystal, ten mica, and 98 gold. One company was utilizing only one of the 33 permits it held, and another had not worked even one of the 23 concessions that had been granted to it 20 years before.[10]

The Malagasy elite is even more eager than were the French to develop Madagascar's mineral resources to the utmost, but its motives are not solely economic ones. Malagasy deputies are influenced more than is the P.S.D. government by nationalistic sentiments, and they are insistent that control of the mining industry be transferred at once to Malagasy hands. The government, for its part, is more aware of the financial and technical difficulties and of the losses to the island's revenues that would be caused by such a transfer. To be sure, during the first postwar decade mining contributed comparatively little to the budget, though its share is now increasing. In 1960 it provided 6.1 per cent of the total revenues, compared with 4.7 per cent in 1950, but its largest annual contribution has amounted to less than a billion C.F.A. francs. Most of the increase noted in the late 1950s and early 1960s came from the extraction of recently discovered ores. The production of graphite, mica, and rock crystal, which for years supplied almost all of Madagascar's mineral exports, is now virtually stationary, and the mining industry today employs no more than 6,610 persons, whereas a decade ago it had nearly twice that number.[11]

Despite the reports of geologists to the contrary, Malagasy nationalists are convinced that the inactive foreign concessionaires have deliberately adopted a dog-in-the-manger attitude, and are holding on tightly to land that contains rich mineral resources, which if worked could provide the island with great wealth. One enthusiastic deputy urged his fellow assemblymen to thank God and their ancestors that no big deposits had been found in Madagascar prior to independence because now they could be developed by and for the benefit of Malagasys.[12] The P.S.D. leaders are neither so optimistic nor so naïve as many of their compatriots, and thus far they have refused to consider nationalizing the mining industry. Although the government has increased taxes on mining concessions, largely for the purpose of recuperating those that have never been developed, it has been careful not to tax out of existence an industry that does not make large profits and is now in a precarious position.

In the field of mining legislation, the P.S.D. leaders have moved with their usual circumspection. After independence, the first mining law (September 4, 1960) did little to alter the existing situation, but the code relating to mining and petroleum promulgated October 1, 1962, did introduce important changes. Prospecting is now open to all, and B-type permits for extraction are issued only to Malagasy nationals, although the area for which they are granted has been reduced. On the other hand, the existing A-type agreements made with the big companies have not been tampered with. Because it realizes that the prospects of the mining industry on Madagascar are limited, the government has not encouraged Malagasys to become mining engineers. As of 1960 there were only five Malagasy scholarship-holders studying mining engineering and geology in France, and one full-fledged

Malagasy mining engineer working in the island. However, an agreement made with the United Nations in June 1963 envisaged the training of more Malagasys in such occupations. This agreement also included a grant of $1,800,000 from the U.N. Special Fund for prospecting operations in Madagascar, to which the Malagasy government has added $561,000 from local public funds.

Postwar mining in Madagascar has had a history of successive disillusionments. Huge sums running into billions of C.F.A. francs, which might more profitably have been spent on modernizing the island's agriculture, have been invested in prospecting for minerals that have not materialized or—with the exception of uranium and monazite—have proved to be uneconomic to extract, transport, and market. In all likelihood, Madagascar possesses no rich minerals in quantity, and this is an unpalatable truth that Malagasy nationalists as yet find hard to accept.

Gold. When the Merina government decided to permit the production of gold in the 1880s, it first encouraged and then forced villagers to prospect. Only after this proved to be unrewarding did it grant gold-mining concessions to foreigners. Because the government imposed onerous conditions for the mining and sale of the gold extracted, few peasants undertook prospecting. So Premier Rainilaiarivony, in ever-greater need of money, made gold-prospecting and extraction a *corvée.* Coercion was little more successful than persuasion, however, and under the Merina monarchs gold production never exceeded 100 kilograms a year.[13] More gold was produced from the areas conceded to foreigners, particularly from the enormous concession near Maevetanana granted in 1885 to a Frenchman named Suberbie. In six years he extracted 835 kilograms of gold from his concession, but labor difficulties caused him to abandon it in 1893.

Prospecting continued after the French occupation, first in the areas where gold was known to exist and then farther afield. In 1907 the discovery of particularly rich veins in the Andavakoera region, south of Diégo-Suarez, led to a veritable gold rush, in which Europeans as well as Malagasys participated. In consequence, a number of gold-mining companies were formed, of which the most substantial were the Société des Mines d'Or d'Andavakoera and the Société Franco-Malgache d'Entreprises. But the attempts to mine gold by industrial techniques failed, and after these companies had extracted ore from the most accessible deposits they stopped operations. Although gold is found in widely dispersed areas in Madagascar, it exists nowhere in large quantities.

Between 1897 and 1959, 51 tons of the metal were produced in Madagascar, most of it before World War I, when output averaged two tons a year. Production reached a peak in 1909, when 3.7 tons were extracted, mostly from the Andavokoera region.[14] From 1919 to 1945, annual production ranged between 200 and 500 kilograms, but it fell to about nine kilograms during some of the World War II years. After the war, France required its overseas territories to sell all their gold output at a fixed low price to the government. The result was that the known output declined steadily, falling to its lowest postwar point of 13 kilograms in 1959. Malagasy families continued to pan an unknown and presumably larger amount of gold, which was sold surreptitiously to Indian and Chinese traders.

After Madagascar became independent in 1960, the P.S.D. government began to encourage gold production. It wanted gold as backing for the Malagasy franc, and also to enable villagers, particularly in the west, to supplement their cash earnings from agricultural production. Panning gold is an occupation that is popular with the Malagasys because they can do it when and for as long or as short a time as they please. By liberally granting prospecting permits for gold, the government has in effect simply legalized a widespread illicit activity. Despite pressure from some assemblymen to permit the free sale of gold, the government still requires that the entire output be sold to it at a fixed price.[15]

Semiprecious and industrial stones. Early European explorers were responsible for Madagascar's reputation as a land of precious stones, and a treatise on the island's mineralogy by Professor Alfred Lacroix of the Paris Museum of Natural History encouraged this belief.[16] So far as is now known, Madagascar has only a few stones suitable for jewelry, and an even more limited number for industrial purposes. Some of its semiprecious stones, such as zircons, amethysts, moonstones, and tourmalines, have been exported since World War II only in negligible quantities, with a maximum annual value of 6 million C.F.A. francs. Their prices are high compared with those of similar stones from other sources. At present only garnets, beryl, and rock crystal make any appreciable contribution to the country's revenues, and exports of these stones fluctuate with the wide variations in market price. On the whole, they have declined with the progressive exhaustion of easily mined deposits. This industry employs only about 1,000 persons.[17]

Garnets are found in the regions of Ampanihy and Ihosy, and their extraction for export began in 1934. Production has been irregular, peak periods having been 1935–38, 1949–52, and 1955–58. Since 1958 they have almost ceased to figure in the island's exports, but their extraction may increase if the world price for garnets rises.

The production of beryl for industrial purposes is a post–World War II phenomenon. Since it first appeared in the mining statistics for 1950, beryl production has had its ups and downs, hitting a low point of 150 tons in 1956.

Exports in 1961, however, rose to 673 tons, worth 60 million C.F.A. francs, as the result of a larger world demand and higher price. Half the industrial beryl that is being mined comes from five enterprises located in Tamatave province, though small quantities continue to be extracted in many other parts of the island. The total output is sold to the Pechiney company of France.[18]

Rock-crystal exports have ranged between 6 and 19 tons annually in recent years, but present prospects, like those for beryl, seem fairly bright. Rock crystal is increasingly used by the electronics industry, which takes 1,000 tons a year. Although Brazil is a far larger exporter, Malagasy rock crystal holds second rank in the American market. In Madagascar it is found throughout the island but is mined principally in the regions of Vohémar and Ambositra by two French companies (Compagnie Générale de Madagascar and Société du Quartz de Madagascar).

Graphite and mica. Until the late 1950s, these two minerals were the only ones extracted on a truly industrial scale in Madagascar, and together they accounted for 92 per cent by value of the island's total mineral exports. Both are used mainly by the electronics industry. The two world wars and the Korean war gave a strong impetus to the production of both graphite and mica, but each conflict was followed by a marked slackening in demand, the accumulation of stocks, and a sharp fall in price. For many years the principal buyers of both minerals were the United States, France, and Great Britain. Purchases by those countries dwindled in the mid-1950s, after American stockpiling of strategic materials ceased and Western industrialists began to turn more and more to synthetics and other substitutes for graphite and mica. At about the same time, West Germany and Japan became buyers, but despite their purchases the market remains essentially tight. Overproduction has caused a steady price decline, and in Madagascar this has resulted in the elimination of most small-scale enterprises and a reduction of the labor force employed in extracting the two minerals. Such mining operations as have survived have therefore been concentrated in the hands of a few companies that have mechanized their equipment and improved the quality of their output.

In many respects, the graphite industry in Madagascar has been more fortunate than that of mica, and it has consistently been more profitable. For years the island enjoyed a near-monopoly of the production of graphite flakes, which were indispensable for the manufacture of metallurgical crucibles. Madagascar's mica, on the other hand, has always encountered severe competition from larger producers. Graphite exports started earlier (1907), have maintained a steadier level (13,000 to 15,000 tons a year), and have been subjected to more official controls than those of mica. Although graphite was never aided by a support fund such as was set up for mica, the government standardized the quality of its exports beginning in the 1920s, established a price control in 1946, contracted for the delivery of specified annual amounts to the United States between 1950 and 1955, and in 1959 decided to grant new prospecting permits for graphite only to the established companies.

The price paid for Madagascar's graphite flakes fell from $200 a ton in 1952 to $120 in 1961, so that Madagascar's shipments of 15,000 tons in 1961 earned for their producers considerably less than the same amount of exports in 1952. Madagascar has graphite reserves spread along the east coast and over the high plateaus that could easily yield 20,000 tons a year. But there is little prospect that world demand for them will ever come up to the island's potential. Indeed, many enterprises that formerly mined graphite have failed. Because graphite under present market conditions cannot support high transport costs, only those concerns located near the shipping port of Tamatave continue to operate.

Madagascar possesses two types of mica—the white muscovite variety and the amber-colored phlogopite—which are used by the electronics industry. Muscovite mica, which is found in limited quantities on the high plateaus, was first mined during World War I to help meet the needs of the French air force. From 1914 to 1918, production did not exceed four tons a year, and since then no more than 400 tons altogether have been mined in Madagascar. Extraction of muscovite mica began to taper off in 1931, and ceased entirely after World War II. It was replaced by the mining of phlogopite mica, which fortunately is more abundant in Madagascar and in greater world demand. Phlogopite mica is found throughout the south, from Ihosy to Fort-Dauphin, where at the peak of its production 90 enterprises provided employment for some 5,000 workers.[19]

From 1946 to 1951 Madagascar easily disposed of an annual output of phlogopite mica amounting to about 800 tons a year, mainly to the United States, France, and Great Britain. It never contributed, however, more than 3 per cent to the world output of this mineral, the market for which has been dominated by India, a country that produces 20 times more than Madagascar. Beginning in 1952, Madagascar encountered difficulty in selling this type of mica because American demand fell off, partly because of the irregularity and lack of homogeneity in output. Most of the phlogopite production then came from a multitude of small and insufficiently capitalized enterprises using rudimentary equipment. Production costs were generally very high but varied greatly from one enterprise to another. This variation, as well as the dispersal of the enterprises, complicated the task of distributing aid to them from the Fonds du Soutien du Mica created for this purpose by the government in 1953. Exports that year fell to 270 tons, and the combination of overproduction and low prices resulted in general abandonment of poorer deposits and elimination of the weakest enterprises. After West Germany and Japan began to buy phlogopite mica from Madagascar in 1956, the situation improved. By 1960 the island was producing 1,010 tons, of which 91 per cent came from seven major companies working 15 mines by modern methods. Although the situation of the mica industry is now far better than it was a decade ago, its market is still so small that the outlook cannot be regarded as promising.

Miscellaneous ores. Madagascar has a remarkably wide range of miscellaneous minerals, but most of them are not worth extracting, either because the deposits are small and the quality mediocre, or because they are inaccessible. Bauxite, lead, and manganese are found in many places, but prospecting has shown the quantities to be insignificant. The copper deposits at Vohibory have long been studied by the mines service—one French company even spent 1.5 million C.F.A. francs in prospecting there—but their quality did not justify extracting them. Iron deposits are widespread, and for many years Malagasy blacksmiths have been using about 12 tons of iron a year to make utensils and implements. Deposits long known to exist at Ambatoloana and Bekisopa contained reserves of around 90 million tons of mediocre-to-poor-quality ores. In the late 1950s a new deposit was found near Moramanga, which may contain a higher grade of iron.[20]

More promising than the above-mentioned minerals are Madagascar's nickel and chromium deposits, which have interested Ugine, one of France's biggest mining companies. In 1955 Ugine obtained an A-type permit to prospect for chromium in an area totaling 5,600 square kilometers in Tamatave province, and there it discovered two chromium deposits. The one at Ranomena has ore of indifferent quality, but its location—37 kilometers from the port of Tamatave—seemed to justify extraction. In 1961, Madagascar shipped from Ranomena its first chromium exports, and they are expected soon to average from 15,000 to 20,000 tons a year. The second deposit found by Ugine has richer ore but is so inaccessibly located in Tsaratana district as to necessitate the construction of a costly road before extraction can begin. As for nickel, the Valozoro deposits near Ambositra were studied in great detail and at considerable expense by Ugine's experts in the mid-1950s. They found that Valozoro has about 70,000 tons of nickel, but extraction would be worth while only if an abundant supply of cheap electric current were available. Plans to harness the waterfalls of Fetihite were drawn up by Ugine in collaboration with the Société d'Energie de Madagascar, and the whole project was submitted to the assembly for approval. After long discussion,[21] the assemblymen approved the project, but subsequently conditions in the nickel market deteriorated. In May 1960 Ugine informed the Malagasy government that it had decided against working the Valozoro deposits under existing market conditions.

Radioactive minerals. For some years after World War I, small uranium deposits in the region of Antsirabe were mined for radium, but the large production from Katanga's far-richer deposits brought activities in Madagascar to a halt in 1927. In the light of the new uses for uranium discovered during World War II, the newly created French Atomic Energy Commission (C.E.A.) established a mission in Madagascar in 1946; it worked the Antsirabe deposits until they were practically exhausted in 1951. Then prospecting led to the discovery two years later of a new area, 80 by 20 kilometers, in the south near Bahara, which contained thorianite with a much higher uranium content. Production from this zone came to 210 tons in 1955 and rose to 511 tons in 1960; the ore either was mined directly by the C.E.A. or was sold to it by concessionary companies. By 1960 the richer deposits were being exhausted, and, in any case, interest was flagging because thorianite was being used less and less for the production of atomic energy.

Fortunately for Madagascar, the C.E.A. in 1954 discovered in the black sands of the southern beaches much more important deposits of excellent-quality monazite, the main ore of thorium. Jointly with the Pechiney company, the C.E.A.—which holds a monopoly on the purchase of all radioactive minerals in Madagascar—formed the Société de Traitement des Sables du Sud de Madagascar (SOTRASSUM). This brought a new processing industry in 1958 to the Fort-Dauphin region, from which 122 tons of monazite were produced the following year and 427 tons in 1960.[22] SOTRASSUM anticipates an eventual annual production of 1,200 tons of monazite and 20,000 tons of infinitely less valuable ilmenite. Although SOTRASSUM's production is still in the early stages, monazite is already Madagascar's ranking mineral export in terms of value and is one of the few bright spots in an otherwise unpromising industry.

Fuel. Beginning in 1909, various individuals and companies of English, French, and South African origin began prospecting for petroleum in Madagascar and studying the country's many outcrops of bituminous sandstone. In 1928 the colonial authorities decided to put a stop to such activities because all the experts were then agreed that it would be uneconomic to attempt to develop such bituminous resources as had been discovered. Nevertheless, four years later, prospecting operations were resumed by a newly formed company, the Syndicat d'Etudes et Recherches des Pétroles (S.E.R.P.). It drilled in various places around Tuléar which the colony's geologists indicated were promising, but with no success.[23]

After World II the search continued, being conducted this time by a new state organization, the Société des Pétroles de Madagascar (S.P.M.). Stockholders were the powerful Société des Recherches Minières et Pétrolières, the Compagnie Française des Pétroles, and the Bureau Minier; they also included former members of the S.E.R.P. and the government-general of Madagascar. At the outset, the S.P.M. employed 500 Malagasy laborers and a staff of 27 European technicians, which was later increased to 100. It concentrated its prospecting and drilling in the sedimentary basin of Morondava, but with no better luck than its predecessor at Tuléar. After some hesitation the Madagascar assembly in 1957 granted long-term fiscal concessions to the S.P.M. on condition that they would be cancelled if and when it struck oil. By 1959 the S.P.M. had spent far larger sums than those required by its agreement with the local government, and had drilled 40 holes to depths ranging from 1,500 to 4,000 meters. In the course of its operations it had found many traces of petroleum but no real deposit other than a sizable one of bituminous sandstone at Bemolang near Morafenobe.

The hope of finding petroleum on the island is dimming, but the government wants drilling to continue. Its leaders now seem resigned to the probability that Madagascar has no rich petroleum resources, but they would be content if the S.P.M. were to find at least enough for Madagascar to be freed from having to import petroleum products, which in recent years have amounted to about 120,000 tons annually. Prospecting and drilling are continuing, because the S.P.M., too, is reluctant to abandon the search for petroleum, on which some 20 billion C.F.A. francs were spent during the 50 years from 1909 to 1959.[24]

Madagascar's only known source of fuel is the coal deposits located in the southwest near the Sakoa River, a tributary of the Onilahy. Reserves are estimated at some 75 million tons lying 100 meters below the ground and 700 million at 600 meters down. These deposits are located 150 kilometers from the coast, hence the transport problems involved in exporting coal mined there are not insuperable, but the quality is mediocre and the coal is not cokable. More important, there are no prospective foreign markets for Sakoa's coal. Experts believe that extraction would be profitable only if a minimum of 500,000 tons a year were produced. Madagascar's maximum needs and those of nearby Réunion amount at present to only 100,000 tons a year, so that more distant markets would have to be found for the balance of 400,000 tons. Aside from other considerations, the cost of transporting Sakoa's coal to Europe would be prohibitive, and Durban provides enough coal to supply the needs of South Africa and adjacent markets in East Africa.

As long ago as 1919, Sakoa's deposits were studied in detail. Mining problems there have given rise to prolonged debates in French parliamentary bodies[25] and have been analyzed and discussed by experts of the Bureau Minier, F.I.D.E.S., Madagascar's mines service, and various French and foreign mining companies. Successive estimates of the cost of extracting and transporting Sakoa's coal either for local use (a project called "la Petite Sakoa") or for export ("la Grande Sakoa") have been made, beginning during World War II and continuing to the present day. An estimate published in 1962 put the cost of extraction, building a road to the coast, and equipping a loading port at Saoalala at about 15 billion C.F.A. francs.[26]

The Malagasy elite is extremely skeptical of the adverse French reports regarding the economic value of Sakoa's coal, and the government of independent Madagascar has reopened the question with vigor. At President Tsiranana's request, fresh studies of Sakoa's potential output and markets have been undertaken by the Société des Forges et Ateliers de Comentry-Oissel and by the Charbonnages de France. Although their reports have not yet been published, it is believed that they have placed the whole question in the context of a large-scale chemical industry to be located in the Tuléar region and fueled by Sakoa's coal.

Food Industries

Sugar. Sugar manufacture is not only Madagascar's most important food industry but the premier industry of the whole island in concentration of operations, money earned, and number of workers employed.

Four large sugar mills produce almost all of Madagascar's output, and of these SOSUMAV—which began to function in 1953—is unquestionably outstanding.* SOSUMAV is responsible for half the total production, and is the sole manufacturer of refined sugar. Aside from SOSUMAV, which sells sugar throughout the island, each of the other major mills has a clearly defined domestic market. The Sucreries Marseillaises at Namakia supplies the needs of the southwest coast and the western part of the high plateaus. The Sucreries de la Côte Est at Brickaville performs the same service for the east coast and the eastern section of the high plateaus. And the Compagnie Agricole et Sucrière de Nossi-Bé provisions the ports of the northwest. Their combined production has now obviated Madagascar's need to import sugar, except for around 150 tons a year of white lump sugar, a form not yet put out by the local mills.

Since 1960, the total output of these four mills has approximated 85,000 tons a year, and annual exports have totaled close to 40,000 tons, valued at more than a billion C.F.A. francs. After World War II, the domestic consumption of sugar rose by 10 per cent a year until the late 1950s, when it leveled off at approximately 35,000 tons annually. (Much of the unexported sugar is used to distill rum for local use and export.) Malagasys who

* See p. 360.

used to chew raw cane now clearly prefer sugar, and they certainly would buy more if the price were lower.* The number of Malagasys employed by the mills has risen from 2,000 in 1949 to an annual average of 8,400, with as many as 10,000 at the height of the season. In 1960, wages totaled 882 million C.F.A. francs.[27]

SOSUMAV is largely responsible for the importance of Madagascar's sugar industry. Curiously enough, the hostility shown toward SOSUMAV at the beginning, as well as the role then assigned to it by the public powers, has undergone a striking change. Even Malagasy nationalists, usually so antagonistic to large foreign enterprises, now concede that SOSUMAV has proved beneficial to the country. At the outset, the considerable support given to this private undertaking by the French government, which included not only important fiscal concessions but a large quota for its exports in the high-priced French market, was based on a concept of the French Union that has now become obsolete. As a concrete manifestation of French Union solidarity, SOSUMAV was to buy a large part of its cane supplies from Réunion, and a considerable share of its output was to be shipped to French Negro Africa, where the demand for sugar was growing. In 1956 Madagascar ceased to import cane from Réunion, and at about the same time the growing consumption of sugar in Madagascar reduced the surplus available for export. Soon the privileged position that Madagascar's exports have enjoyed in the markets of the franc zone will disappear, after the agreement with the European Economic Community comes fully into force. Probably the future of the sugar industry must depend on the Malagasys themselves, as well as on the Indian Ocean and Middle Eastern markets. If this industry were to work to capacity, however, the local price of sugar could be considerably reduced.

Rice-milling. The situation of Madagascar's rice-milling industry is a paradoxical one, for which there is no simple explanation. Here is an industry for which the raw materials are abundant and increasing, and yet it now works far below capacity.

Between 1950 and 1960 the number of mills grew from 40 to 77, and their combined output of milled rice rose from 59,500 tons to 160,000.[28] Although Malagasy farmers are bringing more of their paddy to the mills, 79 per cent of the crop is still husked by hand. In other words, only some 260,000 tons of a total paddy production of 1,300,000 tons are milled.[29]

Inasmuch as many of the rice mills function only seasonally, it is difficult to estimate their individual output (perhaps 2,000 tons per unit) or the number of workers they jointly employ (approximately 2,400). They are scattered throughout the island, the greatest concentration being near the main

* See p. 361.

consumer center of Tananarive and in the principal producing region of Lake Alaotra. Although those two regions are certainly overequipped with mills, this is not true of the rest of the island.

Experts are at a loss to know how to instill new life into this industry. Most of the mills are small and poorly equipped, fail to utilize their by-products, and do not pay their way. One of their main handicaps is the difficulty and cost of obtaining supplies, for their maximum radius for collecting paddy is only 100 to 150 kilometers. In view of the fact that rice is the basic food of all Malagasys and that paddy is grown almost everywhere on the island, a geographical overconcentration of mills seems inadvisable. However, if the transport system and stocking were radically improved, it might be possible and certainly would be more economic to eliminate many of the smaller and poorly equipped mills and to concentrate the processing of paddy in a few large modern mills.

Meat-processing. The oldest of all Madagascar's industries—which at one time was the most important—is that producing preserved and frozen meat. In 1890, during the last years of the Merina monarchy, a French company built a sizable plant to preserve beef at Diégo-Suarez, but it soon closed because of insufficient demand. More successful was the Compagnie Générale Frigorifique, in which British capital was invested, and which began operations at Boanamary near Majunga in 1910. The needs of the French army for meat during World War I led to the establishment in Madagascar of other companies that prepared, sold, and exported beef and pork.* These companies were the Société Industrielle et Commerciale de l'Emyrne (S.I.C.E.) at Tananarive, the Société des Conserves Alimentaires de la Montagne d'Ambre (S.C.A.M.A.) at Diégo-Suarez and Tuléar, the Etablissements Rouchy-Laborde at Ambohimahasoa, and—most important of all —the Société Anonyme Rochefortaise des Produits Alimentaires (S.A.R.-P.A.) at Tamatave, Fianarantsoa, and Antsirabe.

These companies enjoyed good business during the interwar period, and in 1937—an exceptionally favorable year—their combined exports came to 8,000 tons of frozen beef, 237 tons of salt beef, and 4,000 tons of tinned beef and pork. World War II, like its predecessor, created an increased demand, first from the French armed forces and then from those of the Allies. As Madagascar's meat exports continued to find ready markets in the early postwar years, the eight meat factories modernized their equipment and built refrigeration facilities at the main shipping ports. The plants of the Compagnie Générale Frigorifique and the Société Rochefortaise turned out both frozen and preserved meat, whereas those of the other companies produced only tinned meat. Together they employed 8,000 to 10,000 men.

---

* Malagasy tinned beef was so unpopular with the *poilus* that they called it *"singe."*

In 1949 Madagascar's exports of tinned beef (7,366 tons) and pork products (5,041 tons) still held an honorable place in the island's foreign trade. They declined suddenly, however, in 1950 and, after a brief revival the next year, fell off even more sharply in 1954–55. Since then they have never returned to prewar levels, and in 1962 Madagascar exported only 3,227 tons of preserved beef and 73 tons of tinned pork products.[30] That year only six plants producing preserved meat were still operating. Three of these were managed by the S.A.R.P.A., which also shared in the management of two others through a subsidiary, the Société d'Exploitation des Viandes de Madagascar (SEVIMA).

It seems paradoxical that Madagascar, where meat-animal resources are enormous and the price of livestock is exceptionally low, should not be able even to maintain, much less expand, its long-established meat industry. To be sure, production costs are high, mainly because none of the plants works to capacity, and the only assured local market for their output is the naval base at Diégo-Suarez. But the main problem facing the plants has been the postwar decline in the animal supplies, both quantitatively and qualitatively.* Another important reason is the monopolistic practices of the surviving meat companies, especially the S.A.R.P.A., which maintains a sales policy of high prices and large profit.[31]

Manioc. Manioc in Madagascar is processed mainly for export in the form of starch and tapioca. The number of plants processing manioc—almost all of which are located northeast of Tananarive—declined from ten in 1953 to eight in 1961, and the size of the labor force shrank during the same period from 3,100 to 1,500 workers.[32] Tapioca production and exports have been holding their own, but those of starch have been declining steadily. Even in the first postwar years, when production was twice what it is now, its plants worked far below capacity to produce only some 26,000 tons a year. The outlook for this industry is considered unpromising unless it can turn out better-quality and lower-priced products.

Vegetable oils and soap. Some 20 mills in Madagascar prepare copra and crush various oleaginous products,† such as peanuts, aleurites, and castor beans, to produce edible and industrial oils. Some of these oils are exported, but most are used locally, in part for the manufacture of soap. Eleven of the mills have soap-making factories annexed to them. Most of the island's oil mills are located on the west coast, in Majunga and Tuléar provinces. In 1961 all the mills together turned out 2,104 tons of oil and 1,567 tons of soap. In recent years their oil production has remained fairly steady or even increased slightly, but their output of soap has declined markedly.

* See p. 375.
† See pp. 357–59.

Despite the existence in Madagascar of potentially large supplies of raw materials, the output of oil mills and soap factories is far from satisfying the domestic demand. In fact, about as much oil is imported as is processed locally, and Madagascar's soap output, as mentioned above, is declining, while imports of soap are increasing. Various explanations of this phenomenon have been offered, including the high production costs of all local oils, and of copra in particular, the dispersal and rudimentary equipment of the oil mills, and their failure to specialize in any one type of oil and to turn out a standardized product. The soap factories are especially handicapped because they import two-thirds of the raw materials they use, with the result that locally made soap is more expensive (and less attractively presented) than the imported.

Beer and soft drinks. Since 1949 the S.A.R.P.A. has operated a brewery at Antsirabe, which was modernized in 1957 at a cost of 88 million C.F.A. francs, and it also bottles table water drawn from the local springs. Soft drinks and ice are manufactured in all the main centers, but only five plants produce them on an industrial scale.

The output of local beer is growing, and in 1961 it amounted to 12,519 hectoliters as compared with 9,531 hectoliters in 1960. Nevertheless, production as yet covers only about one-fourth of a local demand that has been steadily growing. A Coca-Cola plant, which is the most important producer of soft drinks, was built at Tananarive in 1954. The total soft-drink output amounted in 1961 to 60,000 hectoliters, meeting a little over 90 per cent of local consumer demand. The brewery employs 180 workers, and the soft-drinks industry 170.[33]

This industry suffers from the usual handicaps of high transport charges and the dispersal of production and markets. These affect soft-drink sales more than those of beer, partly because of the impossibility of retrieving any sizable proportion of the containers. Locally made beer suffers from a prejudice on the part of affluent consumers in favor of imported brands, and the Antsirabe brewery has made little effort to offset this by pushing the sale of its product in cafés and restaurants. At present the Antsirabe plant works to only a third of capacity, and the soft-drinks manufacturers could double their current output. To promote both the beer and soft-drinks industries the government in 1961 imposed an import quota on competitive products and raised the sales tax on them.

Salt. Of Madagascar's two salt works, those at Diégo-Suarez are far more extensive and better equipped than the ones at Morombe. Two companies, the Salines de Djibouti and the Salines du Midi, have concessions in the northern province that cover 230 hectares. Only about 25 hectares are worked, by a labor force of some 120 men. During the 1950s, the amount of salt produced at Diégo-Suarez doubled, largely because of improvements in the equipment and a rising local demand for salt, and production now approaches 20,000 tons a year. Of that amount some 1,500 tons are exported annually to Réunion and 630 tons to the Comoro Islands, and the balance is sold in Madagascar.

Malagasy salt consumption has been growing since World War II, but even now it amounts to no more than about four kilograms per person a year.[34] Malagasys do not cook their rice with salt, but they like salt beef and pork. Europeans use fine table salt imported from Europe, to an annual total of five to six tons. The purchase and distribution of edible salt in the island are monopolized by three companies, but salt for industrial use is sold directly to consumers and serves mainly in the treatment of hides. The demand for edible salt has been increasing with the rise in Malagasy living standards. Also, the Animal Husbandry Service has been propagandizing the use of salt in cattle food. Production of salt in Madagascar could easily be expanded to meet a larger domestic demand, and the island's salt might possibly find a new export market in South Africa.

Miscellaneous Industries

Tobacco. Of the 11 plants manufacturing pipe and chewing tobacco and cigarettes, by far the most important is that of the Société Anonyme des Cigarettes Melia de Madagascar (SACIMEM). That company produces 22 different brands and employs 250 of the industry's total of 900 workers.

In recent years the production of pipe tobacco has steadily declined, whereas that of chewing tobacco has risen, from 500 tons in 1950 to 1,097 in 1960; in the latter year Madagascar's cigarette output reached a record total of 547 tons. SACIMEM's Melia brand now meets 71 per cent of the total demand for cigarettes made with black tobacco (17.8 million packs a year compared with 7.1 million imported), and since 1958 it has also been exporting 7 million packs a year to Réunion. Of the 657 tons of leaf tobacco used by this industry in 1960, only 61 tons were locally grown. To reduce the importation of leaves, the government is trying to grow in Madagascar some of the varieties of tobacco that are now imported.

Textiles and clothing. As of 1961, there were 17 such enterprises in Madagascar, employing a total of 1,728 laborers.[35] The majority of these concerns were formed during the 1950–60 decade and they are expanding their operations rapidly. Some already have considerable importance to the communities in which they work, but only three are significant for the whole island's economy.

In the first category are the mohair-weaving factory at Ampanihy and three enterprises at Tananarive, of which two make ready-made clothes for men and one manufactures knit goods. The mohair plant, which weaves rugs and hangings, is run by a cooperative society whose membership comprises angora goatherders and local craftsmen, and it has been so successful in encouraging goat husbandry that it cannot now absorb all the wool that is locally sheared. The knitwear company (TRICOMAD) makes 700,000 pieces a year and employs about 100 workers. The two ready-to-wear clothing factories turn out annually some 300,000 items and together employ about 200 persons.

The three major weaving enterprises jointly employ 1,300 workers—almost all the wage earners in this category of industry, or 4.3 per cent of all those employed in industrial establishments. SOCOFRAM (Société Cotonnière Franco-Malgache) uses only imported cotton; SIFOR (Société Industrielle de Fort-Dauphin) works only locally grown sisal; and FITIM (Société de Filature et de Tissage de Madagascar) utilizes both local *paka* and imported jute. All the raw materials these plants now use could be grown in sufficient quantity on the island. Of the three, only SIFOR exports—up to about half its total production—while the other two produce wholly for the domestic market.

FITIM is the only one of these three enterprises that antedates World War II. It was founded in 1930 at Majunga to spin and weave fibers into sacks, and its equipment was thoroughly modernized in the late 1940s.* Its capital has been successively raised to a total of 168 million C.F.A. francs, of which 60 million were added in the three years after Madagascar became independent. Irregularity in the amount and deliveries of its *paka* supplies, as well as competition from cheaper imported sacks, would have put this company out of business in 1953 had it not been for government assistance. In return for this aid, FITIM has had to accept the prices set each year by the administration both for its sacks and for its payments to *paka* producers. Two-thirds of the raw materials now used by FITIM are locally grown and one-third is imported, and its production has now been stabilized at around 3,000 tons of sacks annually.[36] Its output is sold to the industries processing tobacco, manioc, rice, and above all sugar, and it now supplies nearly all the needs of Madagascar and the Comoro Islands in sacks. If its present labor force of approximately 550 men were doubled and worked in two shifts, it could double its output.

In early 1952, SOCOFRAM was founded by a group of French industrialists, who brought to it the war-damage funds they had been granted, as well as the experience they had gained in cotton weaving in Indochina. At a cost of 245 million C.F.A. francs they built a weaving plant at Antsirabe, which began operating in July 1953. Because SOCOFRAM's production

---

* See pp. 363–64.

of cotton cloth has reduced Madagascar's sizable textile imports, and because it provides employment for 600 to 700 Malagasys, the government has for some years exempted its output from payment of the sales tax. In 1961, SOCOFRAM imported approximately 3,000 tons of cotton thread and produced 1,208 tons of ecru cotton cloth, which met about 60 per cent of Madagascar's needs, but only 62 per cent of the Antsirabe plant's capacity was utilized for that output. An appreciable increase in production is expected to follow completion of a spinning plant, which is to be annexed to the weaving factory and which will use the cotton fiber produced in the Mangoky valley.

Sisal is decorticated in eight plants located in southern Madagascar, but only SIFOR makes it into cord, string, and rugs. Although SIFOR uses no more than 15 per cent of the island's total sisal production, it draws its raw materials exclusively from the nearby Mandrare plantations; hence its production is closely linked to the fortunes of the sisal growers there. SIFOR was founded at Fort-Dauphin in 1952 with an initial capital of 90 million C.F.A. francs. Its equipment is modern but limited, its personnel small and almost wholly Malagasy; its main expense is the cost of fuel, which it must import to power its plant. In 1961 SIFOR exported to France and Réunion half its total output of some 800 tons.

Leather. Judging by the number of cattle slaughtered each year in Madagascar, 10,000 tons or more of rawhides should be produced there annually. Exports in recent years have ranged between 5,000 and 7,000 tons of hides, and 1,500-odd tons are taken by the local leather industry. Thus several thousand tons of hides are never used, chiefly because they are too badly damaged or too poorly prepared. In fact, in 1960 the country imported 2,435 tons of rawhides and 376 tons of finished leather products, worth altogether some 50 million C.F.A. francs.

Madagascar has a considerable but unknown number of artisans who make leather products. The two largest industrial firms that process hides are the Tanneries de Madagascar and the Etablissements Ottino, both located at Tananarive. Together they treat 1,200 tons of local hides a year and employ about 500 workers to manufacture straps, handbags, and shoes. The principal shoe manufacturer, however, is the Czech firm of Bata, which turns out 200,000 pairs a year and has a labor force of 150 men. Of the leather used by Bata, 15 per cent is of local origin, the rest being imported. Obviously neither Madagascar's resources in hides nor its manufacturing capacity is fully utilized.

Chemicals and pharmaceuticals. No real chemical industry exists in Madagascar, but there are a number of plants that have specialized in processing or partially using basic chemical products. Two factories annually make about 1,000 hectoliters of *eau de Javel,* and at Antsirabe carbonic gas is produced for the soft-drinks industry of that city. The principal output, however, is that of the Société d'Oxygène et d'Acetylène de Madagascar, an offshoot of the big French company Air Liquide. At three factories located in Tananarive, Diégo-Suarez, and Ampandrandava, it employed altogether 70 persons in 1962 and produced 230,000 cubic meters of oxygen and 56,000 of acetylene. Distributing agents in the main centers sell to about 1,000 customers, and it covers all the island's current needs in those commodities.

A company called FARMAD (Laboratoires Pharmaceutiques de Madagascar) was formed in February 1961 with a capital of 62.2 million C.F.A. francs, which was supplied in about equal parts by Malagasy and French investors. It has built a modern plant at Ivato, 15 kilometers from Tananarive, and employs about 50 persons for the manufacture of various drugs and vitamin pills.

One of the island's most recent industries is that of plastics. A factory built 12 kilometers northeast of the capital by the Compagnie Malgache de Produits Métallurgiques et Plastiques (COMEPLAST) began operation in April 1963. Its capital of 37.2 million C.F.A. francs was provided by four Metropolitan French companies, and at present it employs about 30 workers.

Metal containers. In 1953 the Société Malgache d'Emballages Métalliques was founded by the Metropolitan French firm of J. J. Carnaud to manufacture tin boxes and containers at Tamatave for Madagascar's wine and meat industries and also for petroleum imports. Subsequently two other similar companies began operations, one at Tananarive and the other at Diégo-Suarez. In the late 1950s this industry employed close to 1,200 persons, but from 1956 on, production leveled off because the meat industry declined and, more important, because gasoline was no longer sold in tins.

Motor vehicles. In 1962, two big French manufacturers of automobiles, Renault and Citroën, opened assembly plants at Tananarive, which now employ about 100 workers each. They use almost wholly imported parts, and produce passenger cars, small trucks, and station wagons. Renault has been turning out four cars a day and Citroën nearly twice that number.

Building and public works. When Madagascar became independent, the island had 226 building and public-works enterprises, which together employed one-fourth of all the country's wage earners. From this one might conclude that it is the most important sector of Madagascar's industry, but closer study shows a different picture. The great majority of these so-called building enterprises, notably those manufacturing bricks and tiles, are small-scale, widely dispersed businesses. Furthermore, because they are tied closely to the investment of public funds in construction, their activity is spasmodic and they suffer from a big turnover in labor. An inquiry carried out in 1960 showed that their equipment and the laborers they employed were utilized on the average to no more than half their capacity.[37] Eleven of the most important building and public-works enterprises employed 4,500 laborers throughout most of that year, but the remaining 215 averaged only 33 workers each.

So dispersed and unstable an industry inevitably is afflicted by high transport costs and labor deficiencies. In the production of cement, the one segment of the whole industry which seemingly should have flourished, the history of the Amboanio plant is instructive. Despite the existence of suitable raw materials in quantity and a rising demand for its output, this long-established factory has had a checkered and generally poor record.

During the 1920s private French interests built a factory at Amboanio in Majunga province, near large calcareous deposits and a main shipping port. Throughout the 1930s it produced in the neighborhood of 20,000 tons a year of good-quality cement, but during the war its owners went bankrupt. An Indian cloth merchant then bought the plant for less than a million francs as a speculative investment, which proved to be successful. For a high price he sold the plant to the public-works department, which was short of cement because of wartime shipping conditions. Its production was only fitful, however, and a few years after the war it closed down.

The impetus given to building by FIDES' investments in Madagascar increased the island's needs for cement to 100,000 to 120,000 tons a year during the early 1950s. Various plans were made to resume production at the Amboanio plant so that it could satisfy at least part of the increasing demand for cement. One such plan involved the investment at Amboanio of the war-damage funds granted to the Haiphong cement company of Indochina, and the use of Sakoa's coal to fuel the plant. Nothing came of this project, however, nor of the government-general's efforts to raise a loan from the C.C.O.M. to carry out the repairs and modernization needed if the Amboanio plant was to resume operation. In 1953, therefore, the government-general, with the reluctant consent of the representative assembly, invested in it nearly 200 million C.F.A. francs of the island's revenues. When this sum proved to be inadequate, a vain attempt was made to persuade French industrialists to supply funds as well as to run the plant. Finally, in 1956, the Compagnie des Ciments Belges de Gaurain-Ramecroix agreed to invest 220 million C.F.A. francs in the Amboanio plant and also to operate it. Together the Belgians and the government-general formed a Compagnie des Ciments Malgaches, in which the former were majority stockholders and the latter acquired stock valued at 44 million C.F.A. francs. The province of Majunga added 4 million from its own funds to build an access road from the coast to Amboanio, and later took over the government-general's stock in the company. Since that time the plant has been enlarged and modernized, but in 1961 it produced only 20,964 tons, or about the same amount as 30 years before.

The long delay in getting the Amboanio plant back into production caused the formation of two other cement-manufacturing companies. In 1959 it was reported that a company called Madagascar-Ciments proposed to build a plant at Tamatave, which would use imported raw materials and fuel to supply 70,000 tons of cement annually to builders on the east coast and the high plateaus. Then in 1961 it was announced that plans were being drawn up by French engineers formerly associated with the Haiphong plant to build a factory near Moramanga, which had the advantage of being on a railroad line and near abundant supplies of raw materials. The Compagnie des Ciments de Moramanga was hailed as the island's first large-scale industrial enterprise to be financed mainly by Malagasy capital and to be staffed mostly by Malagasys. Production at Moramanga was expected to reach 30,000 tons a year and was to begin in July 1962. Since then, there have been no further reports on either the Tamatave or the Moramanga company.

The government of independent Madagascar has every reason to encourage the local production of cement. In recent years cement imports have accounted for 25 per cent by volume of all Madagascar's imports and have been responsible for one-tenth of its annual trade deficits.

Electrical goods. Altogether about ten enterprises assemble, repair, and sell electrical equipment. However, their activity consists more of providing services to nearby industries and to the local administration than of manufacturing. One plant makes 5,000 storage batteries a year, but its output has not increased since 1958 and its capacity is far from being fully utilized, although there is a demand for 17,000 to 20,000 batteries a year. A new and promising development is the manufacture of transistor radios, which has received a strong impetus from the government's promotion of "Opération Transistor."* Since the end of 1961, the Société Electronique has employed about 30 persons to produce two models of receiving sets, which are being turned out at the rate of 600 a month.

Oil-refining. As the result of a series of agreements made in 1962–63 with the five main petroleum-distributing companies established in Madagascar—Shell, Esso, Caltex, Desmarais Frères, and the S.P.M.—a refinery is to be built at Tamatave. By 1968 it is expected to produce between 350,000 and 550,000 tons of petroleum products a year.

---

* See p. 241.

Chapter twenty-two

TRADE

For many years, Madagascar remained untouched by foreign commerce, largely because of geographic isolation and self-sufficiency in food and clothing.[1] Domestic trade, because of difficulties of internal communication and the perishable nature of much of the island's produce, was long confined to the exchange of dried fish, salt, and wood. Barter was the sole form of trade until the eighteenth century, when silver piasters from a number of countries were introduced by foreign merchants. Smaller denominations were obtained by cutting these piasters into pieces, but this led to so much fraud and counterfeiting that King Andrianampoinimerina tried to establish a reliable system of weights and measures. Despite the severe penalties for violation of the regulations, widespread fraud continued and the monetary system remained hopelessly complicated. Only in some places on the high plateaus did genuine markets develop.

Foreign Trade through World War II

In the nineteenth century, the Merina upper classes—who had been in contact with foreign missionaries and traders and a few of whom had sent their children to school in Europe—began to accept certain Western ways of living. They brought in at great expense and with little discrimination European clothing, furniture, and alcoholic beverages. Inevitably this affected adversely the output of local craftsmen, especially weavers, because at least half of all imports then consisted of cotton cloth. During the last years of the Merina monarchy, two-thirds of Madagascar's trade was represented by imports brought in by English, American, French, and German firms in foreign ships to the ports of Majunga, Mananjary, and Tamatave. Exports were collected at a larger number of ports—Mananjary (wax, rubber, and rice), Majunga (hides, rubber, and raffia), Nossi-Bé (vanilla and sugar), Vohémar (live cattle), and Fort-Dauphin (rubber). Beginning in 1885 the Comptoir National d'Escompte supervised the collection of customs duties, and its reports indicated that the value of Madagascar's trade in the last years of the century varied between 3 and 10 million francs annually. Smuggling, however, especially of imported goods, was so common that the island's foreign trade was probably much larger than those figures suggest.

The three French governors who ruled Madagascar from the time of the conquest to the outbreak of World War I tried to promote foreign trade, or, more, specifically, France's share in it. Gallieni, here as elsewhere, laid down the policy which his successors took over and amplified. His aim was generally to expand exports and imports, but above all to make Madagascar a secure market for French goods. He succeeded in doing this by erecting high tariff walls, which virtually eliminated France's competitors, especially Great Britain. As H. Deschamps aptly puts it,[2] Gallieni's conquest of Madagascar did not bring about the victory of French Catholicism over English Protestantism, but it did make the Roubaix-Tourcoing mills victorious over those of Manchester. France's share in Madagascar's imports rose during the pre–World War I period from 41 per cent to 85 per cent, and Madagascar's exports to France followed the same trend, although more slowly.

The arrival in Madagascar of many Europeans, the establishing there of big French import-export firms, and the extending of loans by France to the island resulted in a rapid development of public works and generally stimulated the economy. In addition, the maintenance of law and order throughout Madagascar, the expansion of the means of communication, the replacement of heterogeneous silver pieces by French coins, and the introduction of the French system of weights and measures, all created conditions more propitious for trade than in the past. From 1896 to 1913 imports rose from 14 to 46 million gold francs in value. In order of importance, these were cotton cloth, cement, petroleum products, metals, and foodstuffs. During the same span of years, exports—which for the first time exceeded imports in 1909—grew in value and volume from 3 million francs and 13,000 tons to 56 million and 125,000 tons. Gold was the most valuable single export, and toward the end of that period it was joined on the export list by another ore, graphite. To the existing exports, such as rubber, raffia, cattle, wax, and rice, were added on the eve of World War I agricultural products, such as manioc and cape peas. The appearance among the island's exports of a few manufactured items—mats, hats, and manioc starch—marked a departure from the past. Otherwise, Madagascar was a typical French colony of the period: an exporter of raw materials and an importer of such industrial goods as France cared to ship there. Because French merchandise was higher-priced than that of its competitors, the cost of living rose rapidly. Toward the end of Gallieni's incumbency he came to regret that he had made Madagascar a commercial *chasse gardée* for his compatriots.

Although the overall growth in Madagascar's foreign trade during the period under consideration was striking, it might well have been far larger had France not insisted on virtually monopolizing the island's markets. In 1903, three large local firms went bankrupt, and many smaller ones soon followed. Then came a depression that lasted four years, for which local businessmen blamed heavy taxation, the rising cost of living, and the construction of the east-coast railroad, which had taken thousands of Malagasys out of agricultural production. A major cause, which they rarely mentioned, however, was the overstocking of high-priced imported goods by Asian and Malagasy merchants, to whom the fiercely competitive French firms had granted almost unlimited credit.[3] When these merchants were not able to dispose of their stocks easily, they became panicky and either disappeared or sold their goods at ridiculously low prices. Governor Augagneur tried to prevent alien merchants from underselling the French firms by taxing them more heavily, but with little success. Pessimism about Madagascar's trading potential, which next became widespread, was as artificial as the boom that had preceded it. This delayed the island's economic recovery until 1916, when imports once again returned to the 1901 level.

World War I resulted in a considerable increase in Madagascar's exports, and its momentum carried over into the first postwar years. In 1924 the island's shipments reached a record volume of 302,000 tons, including 79,000 tons of rice, and were valued at 646 million francs. Olivier was governor during a period of unprecedented prosperity for Madagascar, and with his encouragement many new enterprises were established. Among the island's exports during this period, plantation crops became more important than uncultivated produce, aside from raffia and wax, which held their own. Olivier initiated the standardization of some of Madagascar's exports in order to assure greater homogeneity and better quality, and he also persuaded the Paris government to lend the island enough money to carry out a large public-works program.

From 1929 to 1933, Madagascar's exports declined in quantity from 200,000 to 179,000 tons and in value from 439 to 347 million francs, and its imports from 172,000 to 142,000 tons and from 807 to 309 million francs. A number of the firms that had been founded after World War I went out of business,* and the Chinese—ever a barometer of trade—began to leave the island. During that same span of years, the note circulation declined by one-third and the budget was cut by one-sixth, but the local effects of the world depression were cushioned by two favorable factors. One was the continuation of the public-works program, without which there would have been a sharper drop in local purchasing power and the level of imports, and the other was

---

* In 1930 there were 225 bankruptcies, and in 1931 and 1932 about 150 in each year.

France's agreement to pay premiums for some of Madagascar's exports of manioc, sisal, and coffee.

These premiums, along with the loans granted by the newly founded Crédit Agricole, saved many planters from ruin; they also helped the "rich" crops of vanilla, cloves, and, above all, coffee to forge ahead during the late 1930s. Although the government gave almost no aid to miners and industrialists during the depression, shipments of processed raw materials such as tinned meat and mineral ores also made progress during the second interwar decade. By 1933 the trade balance had again become favorable, and five years later, when the island's total foreign trade amounted to 230,000 tons, valued at 1,433 million francs, the value of Madagascar's exports exceeded that of its imports by 215 million francs. In part, this surplus was due to the decline in imports of building materials that followed completion of the public-works program, but the concurrent doubling of cotton-cloth imports reflected a general rise in Malagasy purchasing power. France continued to dominate Madagascar's foreign trade. Throughout the interwar period, it supplied from 73 to 82 per cent of the island's total imports and took from 75 to 85 per cent of Madagascar's exports. Of these exports, 15 to 20 per cent were re-exported, and perhaps as much as one-third of the island's total shipments were sold ultimately in non-franc markets.

World War II wrought striking but transient changes in the amount and orientation of Madagascar's foreign trade. During the early months of the war, shipping shortages reduced the island's exports and imports, but they were much more severely curtailed after France's defeat in June 1940 and the closing of the Suez Canal the next month. When Madagascar's government declared its loyalty to the Vichy regime, the British began to blockade the island, and in 1942 they occupied it. Exports that year fell sharply to 28,000 tons, and shortages resulting from the lack of imports began to be felt acutely. After the island was handed over to the Free French in January 1943, the new authorities tried by persuasion and by force to bring about an increase in production to meet some needs of the Allies, particularly in foodstuffs, sisal, and mica. Trading was resumed, but on a limited scale because shipping was still scarce and many of Madagascar's products were bulky and not in great demand. Between 1943 and 1946 Madagascar's exports did rise from 72,000 to 132,000 tons, but the latter figure did not come to even half the tonnage that had been exported in 1924. The British Empire and, to a lesser degree, the United States became Madagascar's chief provisioners and customers, but they could take only a portion of its accumulated stocks and supply only small amounts of imported goods.

To prevent hoarding and to restrain inflation and black-market operations, the government assumed wide powers by a decree of April 4, 1943, and instituted controls over prices, profits, and supplies. Malagasy farmers had to sell their paddy to the Office du Riz, merchants were required to declare their stocks, the exportation of some produce was forbidden altogether, and that of other items—as well as their internal transport—was made subject to official authorization. Imported goods, in very short supply, were divided among the established trading firms and merchants by the government, which also regulated the prices at which they might be sold. Inevitably procedures were slow and cumbersome, and the time of many administrators was almost wholly taken up by the paperwork that was involved.

In the first postwar years not only were these controls maintained but new ones were added, as a result of which France resumed its dominant position in Madagascar's trade by 1947. That year France supplied 67 per cent of the island's imports (but their total tonnage was far below the prewar level) and took 85 per cent of its exports, mainly accumulated stocks. Labor troubles in 1946 and then the revolt in 1947 kept exports at about 137,000 tons for each of those years, reversing the trade balance, which had been favorable to the island since 1933. Moreover, the French Office des Changes returned to Madagascar only a small percentage of the foreign currency that its exports had earned, and the French Groupements Nationaux d'Achat monopolized the purchase of Madagascar's main exports, for which those organizations paid far less than world prices.

Madagascar's producers, merchants, and consumers all complained bitterly about this policy of *dirigisme,* and gradually most of the controls were removed. Yet in 1949, when freedom of trade had been almost wholly restored on the island, the value of exports amounted to 7,370 million C.F.A. francs, whereas imports were valued at 11,789 million. In the next few years Madagascar's exports remained at virtually the same level while its imports rose sharply, thus not only perpetuating but increasing its annual trade deficits. The favorable trade balances of the years between 1933 and 1947 could be ascribed to the fact that the amount of goods imported was small and the growth in exports was steady. After the war the domestic consumption of imported items increased sharply, whereas the rise in the volume of exports did not assume the same proportions.

The Post–World War II Years[4]

The most striking characteristics of Madagascar's exports are their diversity and the ever-increasing importance of agricultural products. Among these agricultural products, however, changes have been taking place. Coffee, for example, although still the island's most important single export, has been losing ground, whereas sugar shipments have been markedly rising. Mineral ores occupy a modest but stable position (about 3.5 per cent of the total value), exports of animal origin have been declining (16 per cent in 1962), and industrial products are almost totally absent. Except for vanilla, cloves, raffia, cape peas, and perhaps mica, Madagascar's exports play only a very minor role in world trade.

Since World War II, over 90 per cent of Madagascar's exports have consisted of products of agricultural origin, an increasing proportion of these being processed or semiprocessed. Because the value of exports has been augmented and the bulk decreased by processing, and because of the changes in the composition of such exports, the tonnage of shipments and the money they earn have often been at variance. Exports during the interwar period consisted mainly of "poor" and cumbersome crops such as corn, manioc, and rice, whereas since 1946 the "rich" and less bulky crops such as coffee, sugar, tobacco, vanilla, cloves, and pepper have come to the fore. This evolution accounts in part for the failure of Madagascar's exports to show any marked quantitative growth since World War II, for tonnages did not even return to the prewar level until 1958.

The volume of Madagascar's total shipments has also been influenced by climate and price (including the effects of successive devaluations of the franc). Before World War II, the price factor predominated to such an extent that periods of world depression or prosperity were accurately and immediately reflected in the size of Madagascar's exports. Thus the peak years for exports were 1924 and 1938, whereas the low points occurred in 1921–22 and 1929–33. After World War II the price factor, though still important, was mitigated by new economic policies which to some extent insulated the island against world price fluctuations for its produce. Nevertheless, climatic conditions were not appreciably offset by improvements in farming techniques and irrigation, so that they continued to play almost as influential a role as before in production. Years in which climatic conditions were adverse (1954, 1957, and, above all, 1959) were those in which Madagascar's agricultural exports either declined or remained stationary. In those years also, shipments of goods of animal origin and of minerals became relatively more important.

The instituting of price-support funds, notably for coffee, vanilla, and cloves, represented a departure from established policy, as did the favored treatment that France accorded certain of Madagascar's exports. To the island's shipments of sugar, coffee, pepper, tobacco, and *vary lava* rice, France allotted generous annual quotas in its own market, and guarantied to pay prices between 33 and 100 per cent higher than those prevailing in world markets. The fact that Madagascar had to seek outlets in lower-priced markets for what it produced of those commodities over and above the French-guarantied quotas limited the incentive to increase production. Another development that served as a brake on exports was the imposition of ever-higher export duties to provide revenue for the budget (and also to finance the price-support funds). Although the duties on different commodities varied, they averaged nearly 10 per cent ad valorem in 1960 as compared with 7.4 per cent in 1950, and this added to Madagascar's already high production costs and to the difficulties of selling its produce outside the protected franc zone.

Because of the great diversity of Madagascar's production, inevitably the years in which prices are high for some of its exports are often those in which prices are low for others. For example, from 1951 to 1954, and again from 1958 to 1960, world prices were favorable for cloves, manioc, tapioca, corn, and crocodile skins, but unfavorable for ordinary rice and peanuts. A curious anomaly has resulted, however, from the official price supports and favored treatment given the principal exports, as well as from their continued dependence upon climatic conditions. The years in which world prices for its exports have generally declined, as was the case between 1954 and 1957, have often coincided with those in which the total volume of Madagascar's exports has risen. Only twice since World War II, in 1952 and in 1958, have quantitative increases in Madagascar's shipments taken place in years in which their value was also higher.

During the 1950-60 decade, Madagascar's exports were oriented to a great extent to France and the franc zone, where 15 of its commodities benefited by some form of protection or support. Yet, in terms of value, Madagascar's exports to those protected markets declined steadily, from 86 per cent in 1950 to 73 per cent ten years later. During that period France could no longer absorb or afford to subsidize the growing output of its overseas dependencies, and so it began to offer premiums to encourage African and Malagasy producers to seek markets outside the franc zone. Madagascar's sales outside the franc zone during the 1950-60 decade grew rapidly, from 14.2 per cent of the total to 27 per cent. They concerned mainly eight products, of which world production is small and Madagascar's contribution relatively large—vanilla, raffia, essential oils, cape peas, graphite, mica, and mats. Even though coffee is in surplus world production, Madagascar sells ever-increasing amounts to the United States. Because of the rise in dollar-zone purchases of Madagascar's coffee, cloves, and vanilla, the trade balance with that zone has now become favorable to the island. Madagascar's shipments to the sterling zone—notably cape peas and sugar to East Africa—are stable, but they amount to no more than 3 to 5 per cent of the total annual value of its exports. The Common Market countries other than France have slightly stepped up their purchases, but as yet they take only

6 per cent of the island's shipments in terms of value—West Germany alone accounting for half. Madagascar's live cattle are shipped exclusively to the Mascareignes.

Since independence, Madagascar has been trying to increase and improve its exports and also to expand its foreign markets, but as yet with little success. The year 1961 was a poor one for the island's production, although two new export commodities—bananas and chromium—were added to the traditional ones. In 1962, however, exports rose by 21 per cent in tonnage (300,000 tons), but declined in value (23,285 million C.F.A. francs) by 7 per cent compared with 1961. Volume was generally maintained in 1963, but there was a further decrease in the amount of money earned by exports. In February of that year the government set up an Office Malgache d'Exportation, among whose tasks was that of finding new buyers for Madagascar's exports. Trade missions were sent as far afield as Japan and also to the communist countries of eastern Europe. Yet France continued to take about 55 per cent of Madagascar's total exports, and the decline in franc-zone purchases was due almost wholly to smaller demand from Algeria. The Common Market countries, notably Holland and Italy, bought a little more than they ever had before. The dollar zone continued to rank second in importance, increasing its purchases from 15.5 per cent of the total in 1962 to 17.1 per cent in 1963. Owing to a shrinkage in the export of cloves to Malaya and of livestock to Mauritius, exports to the sterling zone lost ground. In 1963 all of Madagascar's traditional clients, with a few exceptions, bought less than they had the preceding year, but they maintained approximately the same share in this trade as before.

As to the individual commodities exported, shipments of three items—coffee (48,000 tons), rice (nearly 16,000 tons of *vary lava* and 11,000 tons of ordinary rice), and vanilla (292 tons)—declined in value compared with 1962 by 3.5 billion Malagasy francs. This decline was partly offset by larger exports of sugar (65,776 tons worth 2,179 million Malagasy francs), sisal (22,822 tons for 1,810 million), bananas (10,818 tons for 200 million), tobacco (3,941 tons for 969 million) and preserved meat (1,969 tons, or 400 tons more than in 1962). Mineral exports reached 33,495 tons worth 814 million, but they were lower than in 1962 by 6,505 tons and 130 million. Such variations in individual exports and in their relative and absolute value have long been conspicuous in Madagascar's foreign trade, but it has now become crucial both to increase production for export and to find new markets.

Of the many crops cultivated in Madagascar for export, all but sugar, coffee, and rice appear to be stagnating or even declining in output, and its major exports will lose their privileged position in the French market when the European Economic Community agreements come fully into force.

Madagascar's associate membership in that Community, according to the terms of its agreement renewed in October 1962, requires it to forgo the protection it has enjoyed in the franc zone and to adapt its exports progressively to meet more competitive conditions. In trying to do so, Madagascar must face the fact that there is overproduction in the world of most of its exports, and that its own output is small, costly, and dependent upon hazardous climatic conditions. Although these handicaps also afflict other tropical countries, Madagascar must compete with rivals exporting better-quality and cheaper produce and located nearer the centers of demand. Furthermore, the efforts being made by officials and technicians to improve Madagascar's exports, both quantitatively and qualitatively, encounter the obstacle of Malagasy apathy. It is the island's weakness as well as its strength that Madagascar is self-sufficient in the essentials of life, and that it depends on foreign trade only insofar as its people want to raise their living standards.

During the interwar period, Madagascar imported annually an average of 123,000 to 166,000 tons of merchandise, reaching a peak of 172,000 tons in 1929. This total was not subsequently exceeded until 1948, when the island's imports—largely as a result of application of the Plan—amounted to 264,000 tons. Beginning in that year, there was a fairly regular increase in their volume until 1957, when they suddenly soared to the record total of 468,476 tons. During the next six years they declined irregularly, but in 1963 they rose almost to the 1957 level, with 444,799 tons. In both 1957 and 1963 the value of imports also attained record heights (29,500 million C.F.A. francs and 31,400 million, respectively), but increases in tonnages have not always corresponded with a rise in value, which has been consistently greater than that of volume. In 1959, for example, the value of imports rose appreciably, although total tonnage fell sharply.

The island's imports, like its exports, naturally have been affected by the successive devaluations of the franc, but they have been influenced even more by other factors. Mainly responsible for the spectacular rise in the value of Madagascar's imports has been the high and ever-increasing cost of French manufactured goods, which have long constituted the bulk of its purchases. Another influence is represented by the disparities and fluctuations in the Malagasys' purchasing power. The income of producers is directly related to the sale of their exports—which have been slow to increase in volume and value and which vary from one year to another—and they tend to spend their money on staple consumer goods. The wage-earning class, on the other hand (which numerically is much smaller), has seen its income grow by leaps and bounds since World War II, and its members are more inclined to buy semiluxury items. A new element has been introduced recently into the trade picture by the government of independent Madagascar—the policy of curtailing the importation of such commodities as compete with existing local output or with those which, it is hoped, can soon be produced on the island.

In the course of the past 15 years the share of the franc zone, particularly that of France, in Madagascar's imports has been declining, but it is still of prime importance. In 1949 Madagascar bought more than 82 per cent of its supplies in the franc zone, and in 1963, 74 per cent. Imports from that zone enter Madagascar without special permits or the payment of customs duties, whereas imports from other countries require a specific authorization and are subject to quotas as well as to entry duties. Imports from France's Common Market partners, which fall into a special category, have been growing markedly, especially those from West Germany. They now represent well over 7 per cent of Madagascar's total imports in terms of value. As for the dollar zone, imports from that source declined from over 7 per cent during the first postwar years and leveled off in the early 1960s to 3 to 3.5 per cent. Similarly, commodities purchased from the sterling bloc during the same span of time decreased from some 7 per cent to between 3 and 5 per cent annually. Despite Madagascar's isolation, it trades little with its neighbors in English-speaking East and South Africa, but it does buy 90 per cent of its petroleum requirements from Middle Eastern countries. In conformity with the current official policy to reduce imports, it is expected that Madagascar will buy less in the franc zone and more in cheaper markets.

Normally, but not invariably, a correlation exists between the value of Madagascar's imports and the sale of its exports. Application of the French Plan for Modernization and Equipment to Madagascar in the late 1940s and early 1950s caused a rise in imports unrelated to any comparable growth in Malagasy purchasing power, although this increase did coincide with a period in which Madagascar's exports were selling well. Between 1949 and 1953, the value of imports rose rapidly, to reach 23,400 million C.F.A. francs in the latter year. After falling in 1954 and 1955, they increased again in 1957 —also a record year for the island's export trade. But still further expansion in 1959 was a direct result of the franc's devaluation, and in 1963 imports reached a record figure of 31.4 billion Malagasy francs, although exports had declined in value compared with the preceding year, when imports cost 30 billion and the government had initiated a policy of curtailing certain imports.

The strong upward trend in the value of Madagascar's imports, with only a few temporary setbacks, has of course not affected all categories of imported goods equally. However, the largest and steadiest increases have been noted in the case of consumer goods, which generally have accounted for 60 per cent of the total in terms of value. Between 1950 and 1960, the importation of such goods increased by 45 per cent. In 1963, textile imports alone accounted for 11,560 tons (and 4.5 billion Malagasy francs), and foodstuffs for 16 per cent of the total value. A hopeful sign that year, it should also be noted, was the increase in importation of equipment goods, which had been declining during the 1950–60 decade, to about 17 per cent of the total compared with 24 per cent in 1949. Completion of the public-works program undertaken by the Plan accounted in large part for declines in the import of machinery and such building materials as cement. The rise in consumer-goods imports was mainly due to the doubling of wages between 1950 and 1960 and not to increased purchasing by the peasantry, whose incomes over that period showed a gain of only 1.3 per cent.

The P.S.D. authorities are understandably concerned by the growing imbalance between urban and rural revenues and between imports and exports. They are now encouraging the local manufacture of commodities heretofore imported, such as the textiles produced by the Antsirabe factory. Before they can impose strict import quotas, however, there must be an appreciable increase in the island's production of consumer goods. In the meantime, they are trying to enhance rural purchasing power by stressing the need for increasing exports. In a very tentative way they are also trying to assure a more remunerative and stable income for the producer by exerting more control over the organization of trade.

Internal Trade

The lack of precise and reliable data concerning Malagasy purchasing power poses almost insuperable obstacles to the study of Madagascar's internal trade. Certainly the rapid growth of imports since World War II indicates an overall rise in the Malagasy's purchasing power, but obviously it is very unevenly distributed and varies not only from one year to another but also according to the season and the region.

The overwhelming majority of Malagasys live from the produce of agriculture and animal husbandry, whether as producers or as wage-earners. A Malagasy bourgeoisie exists but is confined very largely to the Merina, and it is composed almost wholly of civil servants and landowners who have only partially adopted European ways of living in regard to clothing, housing, and food. There is no more than a handful of Malagasy businessmen—perhaps 30 industrialists and 100 merchants—who operate on a large scale,[5] and virtually all the indigenous bourgeoisie live in Tananarive. Few Malagasys can buy imported goods, and for all except government employees their cash income depends on the sale abroad of the output of the rural economy. Consequently any decrease in the earnings from Madagascar's exports is reflected immediately in smaller purchases in the internal market.

Such reliable documentation as is available in regard to living costs and incomes concerns wage-earners, many of whom are urban. For town-dwellers the cost of living has risen sharply since World War II, having increased by as much as 34 per cent between 1950 and 1960. Taking the year 1950 as 100, the living-costs index in Tananarive rose to 291 and in Tuléar to 317 by 1960,[6] as a result of ever-higher rents, charges for public utilities, and prices of food and clothing. The main cause has been the steadily increasing cost of commodities imported from France, but local taxes have also had a part in forcing up retail prices for imported goods. The revenues derived from import duties, the economic-development tax, and the sales tax together brought in to the island's treasury 7,293 million C.F.A. francs in 1960. Although rates vary with the individual commodity, being high on textiles and luxury goods (27 to 30 per cent in 1960), and very high on alcoholic beverages (110 per cent), they are relatively low on imported food-stuffs (12 to 15 per cent), semifinished products, and equipment materials. Generally speaking, the rates of such taxes have been raised over the past 15 years, but it is principally increases in the volume and price of imports that have made them such large revenue-earners.

The great majority of Malagasys are peasants and herders who buy few imported goods and do not have most of the expenses incurred by town-dwellers. Moreover, they consume perhaps as much as 80 per cent of what they produce. According to Professor Gendarme,[7] the only serious study thus far of rural Malagasy "auto-consumption" was made by two French experts in 1955. They estimated that the average Malagasy rural household consumed what it produced to an annual value (at that time) of around 85,000 C.F.A. francs. More detailed studies have been made of rural family incomes, but they concern only certain regions of the high plateaus.[8] None of these analyses can serve as bases for generalizations because, obviously, marked variations exist between regions and years. An inescapable conclusion, however, is that the cash income of Malagasys as a whole is very low, even for an underdeveloped country, but it must be viewed in the context of Madagascar's self-sufficiency in foods and of the few and simple wants of its inhabitants.

In 1960 an attempt was made to estimate income from rural production in each of the island's six provinces, but this estimate admittedly did not take into account the sums earned from crafts or seasonal labor, or the pensions granted to military veterans. Nevertheless, the analysis shown in the tabulation below remains the most enlightening study thus far.[9]

Income from Rural Production

Province	Income (*Millions of* C.F.A. *francs*)	Rural Population	Revenue per Inhabitant
Diégo-Suarez	5,643	341,900	16,500
Majunga	6,555	597,700	10,900
Tamatave	7,996	786,600	10,200
Tuléar	6,909	770,700	8,900
Tananarive	8,434	964,200	8,700
Fianarantsoa	11,043	1,313,700	8,400
	46,580	4,774,800	9,800

Revenues Derived from Exported Rural Produce
(*Millions of C.F.A. francs*)

Category	Production	Exports	Percentage Exported
Crops	33,530	8,240	24.5
Woods	2,840	5	—
Animals, animal products . . .	9,440	475	5
Fish	770	—	—
	46,580	8,720	19

Trading Companies and Traders

Madagascar's trading economy resembles that of French-speaking Negro Africa in that it is almost wholly in the hands of foreigners. Malagasys have never had a taste for commerce, and only in the central region do they operate small rural stores and collect produce for sale to middlemen or the big companies. Foreign trade is dominated by a few French import-export firms, which are often controlled by large Metropolitan banks and businesses and which operate locally through Asian retail traders and middlemen. Since World War II, some of the more prosperous Asian merchants have started trading companies of their own, and many new enterprises have been founded. But almost as many firms go bankrupt or disappear each year, either because they are inadequately capitalized or because they cannot cope with local economic conditions. The Big Three—the Compagnie Marseillaise de Madagascar, the Société Industrielle et Commerciale de l'Emyrne, and the Compagnie Lyonnaise de Madagascar—not only are the oldest export-import firms on the island but have grown and have made handsome profits despite world wars and depressions and the transfer of sovereignty from French to Malagasy hands.

Marseille bankers and traders were the first in this field, and they still control two of the three big companies. They began trading with Madagascar under the Merina monarchs, multiplied their activities after the French conquest, and now have a controlling interest or hold shares in the major economic enterprises throughout the island. No longer is Marseille the world center for distribution of vanilla, as it was before World War II, but it is still the main shipping port for Madagascar and handles the sale of many Malagasy products.

It was a Marseillais, Léon Besson, who pioneered French big business in Madagascar. In 1894 he founded a trading post at Zanzibar, which became the point of departure for his operations in Madagascar, where he established his headquarters after Gallieni had conquered the island. In 1898 he founded the Compagnie Marseillaise, modestly capitalized at 600,000 francs. After World War I, he entered new fields, and in 1920 he created the Compagnie Agricole et Industrielle de Madagascar. Nine years later, in collaboration with another Marseille firm, the Raffineries St. Louis, he established the Sucreries Marseillaises de Namakia. Other companies that he created or helped to form were the Société Madagascar–Automobile, the Société Rizime, and SOSUMAV.

Besson's example was followed by another Marseille company, the Société Industrielle et Commerciale de l'Emyrne (S.I.C.E.), which was founded in 1911 with a capital of 700,000 francs. It has worked in close association with the Société d'Alimentation de Provence, but in 1949 it transferred its headquarters from Marseille to Tananarive. Like Besson's Compagnie Marseillaise, the S.I.C.E. has given birth to subsidiaries in a wide range of activities and has prospered mightily. However, it has never achieved quite the scope of the Compagnie Marseillaise, which has increased its capital many times and, since independence, has admitted to making annual profits of nearly 2 billion new francs.

The third of the big French import-export firms, the Compagnie Lyonnaise de Madagascar, has had much the same history. It was founded in 1897, has regularly increased its capital, and in 1963 announced profits for that year amounting to nearly 152 million new francs. It is directly engaged in graphite mining and tobacco culture, and has formed or participated in forming the Compagnie Agricole et Sucrière de Nossi-Bé, the Société des Futs Métalliques, and SOSUMAV.

These three companies have been sharply criticized by liberal Frenchmen and Malagasy nationalists for their grip on the island's economy, the subterfuges to which they have resorted to escape taxation and disguise their real earnings, and above all their failure to reinvest locally any appreciable proportion of their large profits.[10] Their sole policy, it is alleged, is to make money for the banks that have loaned them funds and have thereby come to control their operations—notably the Banque de Paris et des Pays Bas and the Banque de l'Indochine. Another Metropolitan financial concern that has evoked similar opprobrium is the Société Financière et Coloniale of Paris, which has subsidiaries throughout the former French empire. In Madagascar it controls the Société Malgache de Culture and the Société des Gemmes de Madagascar, and it also holds shares in the Salines de Diégo-Suarez and the Charbonnages de Sakoa.

There is no doubt that the close connection between Metropolitan financial circles, the European navigation companies, and the most important local trading firms has resulted in monopolies and has contributed to the high cost of living and of production in Madagascar. On the other hand, these companies have provided many Malagasys with jobs, taken risks, and pioneered many enterprises, persevering successfully in areas where others often have failed. Malagasy nationalists periodically demand that these foreign firms be nationalized, but the P.S.D. leaders feel that this would be premature and probably also actually harmful at this stage in the island's economic evolution. They realize that as yet there are no nationals who have the capital, managerial talent, experience, and international contacts required to supplant the big foreign firms.[11] For the time being, the best that the Malagasy government can do is to encourage the development of competitive cooperative societies and try to exert some control over the foreign firms, particularly in regard to their local organizations and the agents through which they operate, as well as the reinvestment locally of more of their profits.

Despite appearances to the contrary, there is a basic lack of organization and specialization in Madagascar's retail and semiwholesale trade. The big French companies have depots for stocking merchandise in the main ports, and they are represented there and in each district headquarters by one or more agents, who collect the produce that the big firms export and distribute the merchandise imported. These agents and their subagents are compartmentalized by ethnic origin, geographic location, and areas of trade in which they deal. About 125,000 Malagasys collect produce, mainly rice, on the high plateaus, where they also own small retail general stores. On the east coast the Chinese collect from planters the rich crops of coffee, cloves, and the like for sale to the large export firms, and monopolize the retail food trade. On the west coast, the Indians control the purchase of cape peas, and also the sale of cloth and jewelry to the Malagasys. Both the Chinese and the Indians keep a grip on Malagasy producers by advancing them merchandise or lending them money at usurious rates during the farming season against a share in the forthcoming harvest. In the capital city, the 440-odd Greek residents monopolize the semiwholesale trade in foodstuffs, but recently they have been losing ground to Chinese competitors.

Whereas the nature of the wholesale trade remains almost unchanged, the structure of the retail and semiwholesale trade has been undergoing profound modifications. This transformation, which began after World War II, has been gaining momentum in recent years. In the late 1940s, the shortage of imported goods and the ready sale to France of Madagascar's accumulated stocks offered new opportunities to traders to make profits at the expense of the gullible and defenseless Malagasy producers and customers. Early in 1946, the French Groupements Nationaux d'Achat (to which Madagascar's major exports were perforce sold until 1949) calculated that middlemen on the island were then getting from one-half to two-thirds as much as the Malagasy producers were receiving for their output.[12] Such large and easy profits inevitably encouraged more Asians to become middlemen, which further diminished the returns to the Malagasys. Not only did more middlemen mean larger cuts, but they developed new ways of falsifying weights on the produce they bought and of short-changing the Malagasy peasants, whom they also successfully tempted to buy more merchandise than they needed or could afford to purchase.[13]

After World War II, the Indians—who were the largest, fastest-growing, and most permanently established group of alien traders—moved into new fields of economic activity. Some of the wealthiest started commercial enterprises on their own account, and in some west-coast towns they became serious competitors of the big European firms. At the same time they also began to acquire real estate by taking over land in payment of loans made to the easily indebted Malagasys. The Chinese community also increased its activities—but in other ways. Until 1939 the Chinese normally were transients in Madagascar, leaving with their earnings in old age or in times of economic depression. Since World War II, and especially since the communists took over mainland China in 1949, the Chinese have come to regard Madagascar as their home and to organize strong associations and schools there on a permanent basis. Because of their greater adaptability and sociability, and also because they are less inclined to acquire land, they have won the confidence of the Malagasys far more than have the Indians, though their practices are no less harmful and unscrupulous.

Although the Indian and Chinese middlemen have been performing undeniably useful functions, which neither Europeans nor Malagasys have been willing or able to undertake, the administration has felt it necessary to take steps to control their number and operations. It was largely to put a stop to Asian hoarding, speculation, and black-market activities that the French administration in 1943–44 instituted a stricter standardization of exports, the obligatory declaration of stocks, a limitation on profits, and the imposition of official prices on merchandise locally sold. But these regulations were not enforced, mainly because the big import-export firms refused to cooperate. French businessmen in Madagascar have always resented any official interference in their freedom to trade, and they refused to heed the government's pleas to control their agents more strictly and to see that they complied with the law and respected ethical business practices.[14] Although the reliability of many of the new middlemen was uncertain, the companies readily granted them credit, and not until a series of bankruptcies and sudden defections occurred did the big firms realize the disadvantages to themselves of the anarchy that prevailed in trading conditions. Not before 1957, however, were the authorities able to win widespread support for some measures of control. These had the aim of eliminating superfluous and unscrupulous middlemen by requiring all collectors of produce to hold permits issued by the *chef de province* where they operated and to submit the produce they offered for sale to official inspection.

There is no doubt that the P.S.D. government is anxious to control if not eliminate the Asian middlemen, but there is no one to replace them. Malagasys have not yet acquired the taste or experience for trading, and current conditions in the domestic market are not such as to attract them. The clientele not only is small and scattered but varies markedly as to tastes in merchandise and purchasing power. It takes patience, which only Asians seem to possess to such a degree, to permit customers to handle every item in the store, and then to take their time to buy perhaps one cigarette or a lump of sugar. Rural retail traders, if they are to make any profit at all, must stock small quantities of an endless variety of goods, ranging from foodstuffs to toys and clothing. Only in the large towns, where customers are numerous and relatively prosperous, has it been possible to attain any specialization in the merchandise offered for sale.

It is obviously very difficult for the government to formulate policies for a country like Madagascar today, whose economy does not form an integrated whole. Foreign trading dominates the domestic markets; because of the mutual isolation of producing regions, it is difficult and expensive to send surpluses from one area to another; and there are wide variations in prices and purchasing power both geographically and seasonally. If the authorities curtail luxury imports, they may alienate the well-to-do, and if they give priority to equipment materials at the expense of consumer goods, they risk displeasing the masses.

As yet the P.S.D. government has apparently made no firm decision, and it seems disinclined to adopt any radical policies. Its leaders realize that to nationalize trade, as Guinea has so largely done, would probably end in failure and also keep out potential foreign investors. The present trend is toward the establishing of companies of mixed economy, in which the government would hold a majority of the shares, and these companies would compete with carefully licensed private merchants. By this means and by setting quotas for production and imports, superfluous middlemen might be eliminated and the overequipped sectors of the economy reduced. The clearest statement of the government's policy was contained in remarks made by President Tsiranana in April 1962. He described that policy as one of "intelligent autarky"—that is, Madagascar would buy abroad only what it could not itself produce.[15]

Tariff

In 1928 Madagascar became what was then called an "assimilated colony" of France in regard to its tariff regime. This meant that goods entering the island, with some exceptions, paid the same duties that they would have paid had they been imported into France, and that French merchandise entered Madagascar free of duty.

Because of the difficulties of provisioning Madagascar during World War II, the tariff regime was suspended, and it was not re-established until January 1, 1961. During that long interval, however, all imports—no matter what their origin—were subject to fiscal duties, and once inside the country their sale was also taxed. Madagascar's exports were likewise made subject to fiscal duties, which varied with the item exported and also with the country to which they were destined. Some exports to France were subject to French customs duties, whereas others entered duty-free.

After Madagascar became independent in mid-1960, the P.S.D. government used the special powers it then held to re-establish a tariff regime modeled after that of France. The customs duties, as applied beginning January 1, 1961, varied according to the origin or the destination of the merchandise. Under the new regulations, goods from the franc zone and countries of the European Economic Community entered Madagascar free of duty, with the result that only about one-tenth of all the island's imports were affected by the new tariff regime. The last-mentioned imports were subject to one or another of three types of duties—maximum, minimum, and intermediate. For exports, on the other hand, only one rate of customs duties was to be imposed. All imported goods, however, continued to bear fiscal duties and a sales tax, though the rates for both were somewhat lower than they had been before, averaging about 6 per cent ad valorem.

Inasmuch as the duties and taxes on imported merchandise have constituted almost half of Madagascar's total revenues, the authorities have naturally been cautious about tampering with them. In 1963–64, however, the P.S.D. government indicated its intention gradually to alter the primarily fiscal character of such taxation and, as the country becomes industrialized, to use tariff as a means of affording greater protection to locally manufactured goods. A significant step in that direction was taken in May 1962, when the duties on textiles imported into Madagascar were raised to prevent dumping from Far Eastern countries and thus protect the cloth output of the Antsirabe factory.

Chambers of Commerce

Even before Gallieni had completely pacified Madagascar, he created on November 7, 1896, a French Chamber of Commerce and Industry in each provincial capital. It was specifically charged with advising him on the best methods of encouraging white colonists to settle on the island. In February 1902 he set up similar bodies in all the administrative circumscriptions where there was any considerable trade or industry. At about the same time he founded a Chamber of Agriculture at Tamatave.

Gallieni's successors came to feel that these organizations functioned poorly because too many of their members belonged to more than one chamber and because the chambers often gave the governors contradictory advice. After World War I they were merged into a single body in each administrative region, to which the name Chambre de Commerce, d'Industrie et d'Agriculture was given, and they were granted subsidies as semipublic institutions. The duties assigned them now included representing the interests of their membership to the administration, supplying the government with advice on economic questions, and undertaking surveys of the economy either on their own initiative or at the request of the public powers. To enhance their usefulness and also to give them more income, the chambers were authorized to build and manage warehouses, give technical training courses to Malagasys, set up labor exchanges, and even create insurance companies. In 1924 their influence was greatly augmented when each chamber was empowered to elect—subject to the governor-general's approval—a representative to the newly established Economic and Financial Delegations.

After World War II, friction developed between some of the chambers and the government, and in 1948 the most influential members of the chambers of Tananarive and Majunga resigned in protest against the official policy of price controls and division of imported merchandise. At the same time rivalry became acute between the chambers themselves. Those in the coastal regions resented particularly the dominant role played by the Tananarive chamber, because its recommendations were the ones most often adopted by the government. All the chambers' members, however, agreed that they could be more effective vis-à-vis the government if they presented a united front,[16] so in 1949 the existing 12 chambers proposed forming a federation. The next year the government accepted this proposal in the hope of ironing out the difficulties that had developed between the chambers and of coordinating their economic views for the island as a whole.

For some years the federation functioned smoothly, but as Madagascar moved nearer to self-government the Malagasy nationalists became increasingly resentful of the domination of the chambers by European businessmen. The labor unions, in particular, demanded separate chambers of agriculture so that the voice of the Malagasy peasant could make itself heard. In July 1957 the government agreed to abolish the election system whereby European and Malagasy members voted separately for their own officers.[17] And though it did not accept the proposal to establish separate chambers of agriculture, it did create specialized agricultural sections within each chamber. This compromise did not wholly placate the Malagasy assemblymen, and they also became increasingly insistent that a larger place should be given to the small-scale Malagasy traders in the commercial sections of the chambers.[18] After 1961, however, when Malagasys replaced Europeans as presidents of the chambers, the nationalists became much less critical than before.

Most of the chambers' revenues are derived from their own economic activities, but they still receive a small subsidy from the national budget, which in 1961 approximated 20 million C.F.A. francs. That year the combined revenues of Madagascar's 12 chambers and the federation of chambers came to 355 million C.F.A. francs, more than two-thirds of which was accounted for by the chambers of Tananarive, Fianarantsoa, Tamatave, and Majunga.[19]

Chapter twenty-three

LABOR

Forced and Free Labor

In traditional Malagasy society, there was a clear-cut division of tasks between men and women, which was reinforced by taboos *(fady)*. Women husked rice, prepared meals, tended the poultry, replanted paddy, wove mats and baskets, and took care of the children. An old Malagasy saying warned, "If a man cares for the children, his body will be weakened; if he weaves mats or baskets, he will die at an early age; if he fetches water, the pitcher will break; and if he sweeps the house, he will be pursued by evil spirits."[1]

Many words in the Malagasy language distinguish lazy from industrious persons. The early Merina monarchs stressed the dignity of labor and often urged their subjects to work for the good of the community. At the same time, however, the economy of the realm was based primarily on slave and *corvée* labor. To be sure, such labor was in lieu of taxation and was the means by which public works were carried out, but it was not always put to productive use. Initially King Andrianampoinimerina decreed that each freeman owed his sovereign four days of unpaid labor a week, but his successors increased this already excessive liability to more and longer days.[2] High-ranking officials received no salaries, hence they tended to use the *corvée* for their own and not for the public benefit, and in most cases no control was exercised over such actions. At any time and for an indefinite period, peasants could be taken from their fields to build a residence or carry burdens, and the services of some artisans were even requisitioned for life.[3] The inevitable result was that those who possessed skills took pains to disguise them, and this hampered development of the economy. Abuses of the *corvée* were at the root of many revolts in the provinces during the early and middle nineteenth century.

Because this system made the condition of freemen hard, slaves (who were not subject to the *corvée*) often refused to be freed. Some condemned criminals were reduced to slavery, and the children of a slave mother were born slaves, but the great source of the *andevo* (slave) caste in Imerina was prisoners of war. As the Merina monarchs extended their conquests, they acquired more and more slaves, so that between the accession to the throne of Ranavalona I and that of Radama II, the number of slaves probably quintupled. Laws were passed, mainly under the influence of English missionaries, that ameliorated the condition of slaves. Radama I abolished the slave trade among the Malagasys, but the well-to-do upper classes then bought cheaper slaves from Africa. The code of 1881 permitted masters to punish but not to kill their slaves, and it forbade owners to separate children from their slave parents. Queen Ranavalona II proclaimed the freedom of slaves, but their emancipation was not carried out. In the last years of the Merina monarchy, there were perhaps 500,000 slaves altogether, of whom about half were in Imerina. Palace slaves were the best-treated, whereas those in rural areas suffered the worst hardships.[4] At the time of the French conquest, agricultural production on the high plateaus had come to depend very largely on slave labor.

On June 20, 1896, the French Parliament abolished slavery in Madagascar, and the day after the proclamation had been made public, Gallieni arrived at Tananarive. Some of the freed slaves soon drifted to the towns, but the great majority remained on the land where they had been. To stabilize them there, the French administration arranged labor contracts between them and their former masters, but their status soon degenerated to that of sharecroppers.

Elsewhere the French took over the Merina system and grouped the freed slaves into units of 100, 500, and 1,000,[5] each group being placed under a chief of the same ethnic origin. But this did not check the vagabondage and theft by freed slaves, which grew apace, especially in the urban centers. To cope with this problem, Gallieni decreed on October 1, 1896, that all Malagasy males between the ages of 16 and 60 who could not produce proof of employment would be subject to prestation (forced) labor on public works and roads.[6] After 50 days they were released, but they were encouraged to remain as "volunteers" at fixed wages. Soon the 50 days were reduced to 30, and the option of a money payment in lieu of labor was introduced. Then Gallieni exempted entirely from prestation labor those who accepted employment in private enterprises, in order to help the settlers who were having difficulty in finding workers for their plantations. This led to such abuses, however, that in 1901 he abolished prestation labor altogether and replaced it by a fairly heavy direct tax. The principle involved was called "regeneration through work," but its very practical aim was to force Malagasy men to earn at least enough money to pay the tax.

Gallieni resorted to coercion again reluctantly, and only after his efforts to develop a free labor market had failed. The central and regional labor offices that he had set up to serve as intermediaries between planters and workers failed to attract enough indigenous labor. The Malagasys had few wants, and they especially disliked working regular hours for others. The official missions sent by the local administration to the Far East in 1899 to recruit Oriental workers gave such unsatisfactory results that the French authorities never again tried to solve the island's labor problems in this way, although Comorian and Yemenese labor was brought into Madagascar after World War II. The policy of Gallieni's successor, Augagneur, reflected the growing discouragement of planters and officials alike with voluntary Malagasy labor as a means of developing the island's economy. He abolished the labor bureaus and reintroduced the element of constraint. Prestation labor was re-established in 1907 on the basis of ten days a month. At about the same time Augagneur instituted labor arbitration councils, and in 1910 a tax of 3 francs was imposed so as to provide free medical treatment to the Malagasys.

World War I reinforced the trend toward forced labor. Nearly 50,000 Malagasys were sent to France and many of them never returned. Labor shortages on the island became acute, especially in view of France's pressure to produce increased shipments of Madagascar's foodstuffs for its army. After the war, more white settlers came to the island, thereby increasing the demand for labor, which was in even shorter supply than before. The Economic Conference called by Governor Garbit in January 1919 discussed the labor problem, and one consequence of its recommendations was a sharp increase in taxation. Among other new fiscal measures, the poll tax was abruptly raised from 15 to 25 francs in November of that year. But the authorities were no longer content with using such indirect means to force the Malagasys to work for wages, and they also increased to 180 days a year the prestation labor owed by Malagasy men to the government. Nevertheless, they also moved in 1920 to protect employees as well as employers by enacting new labor laws, whose motivation was explained in an official circular:[7] "The acute character of the labor crisis is due to the instability of the Malagasy. Neither laws nor wages can make him keep his promises. Employers, however, also have some responsibility for this state of affairs, for some of them tend to recruit more workers than they actually need." In 1922, Garbit set up both a Department and an Advisory Council for Native Affairs, on each of which Malagasys were well represented.

After the depression of the early 1920s, prices for Madagascar's agricultural exports boomed, and this encouraged some Malagasys who had been working on European-owned plantations to begin raising export crops of their own. Wages had doubled but prices had quintupled, and a few months' effort brought to a Malagasy planter more money than he could have earned by wage labor during a whole year. Instead of raising wages further to meet this competition, the European planters turned to the administration for help, and in some instances they persuaded a district officer to requisition enough workers to harvest their crops. In the extreme south, professional recruiters for the first time induced Antaisaka and Antandroy to accept contracts for work on east-coast plantations.

Governor Olivier, Garbit's successor, realized that more was needed than temporary half-measures, and he appointed a commission composed of French settlers, officials, and traders as well as Malagasy Notables to undertake an exhaustive survey of the island's labor potential and needs. The results of their survey were incorporated in a law that he submitted for approval to the newly formed Economic and Financial Delegations. On September 22, 1925, its provisions were embodied in a decree called by its author Madagascar's Charter of Labor.[8]

By these provisions, the labor offices created by Gallieni were revived, the procedure of the arbitration councils was revised, and the loopholes that had appeared in the 1920 labor legislation were closed. To stop the proliferation of fictitious labor contracts, which had been used as a means of avoiding prestation labor, all contracts thenceforth had to be approved by an administrator, and violations were made punishable by fines and imprisonment. With the aim of safeguarding the welfare of Malagasy workers, the decree included strict regulations in regard to minimum wages and hours, medical care, clothing, housing, and repatriation of migrant laborers. To ensure impartiality in the application of labor laws, specialized officials were to replace the district officers who had been acting as labor inspectors. By this legislation, Malagasys who agreed to work for European planters were given special advantages and guaranties, and the employers also received legal protection against defection by workers.

Governor Olivier maintained in his book that this law marked the first direct legal intervention by local government in Madagascar in the field of labor recruitment.[9] Certainly it testified to the administration's desire to develop Madagascar's economy by means of voluntary Malagasy labor and to protect laborers against exploitation. At the same time it aimed to provide employers with greater facilities for recruiting workers and to protect them against an unreliable and unstable labor force. From the viewpoint of legislation, this decree marked a great advance over previous laws, but unfortunately it was ineffective, owing partly to failure to apply the law and partly to the almost concurrent birth of another brainchild of Governor Olivier—the Service de la Main-d'Oeuvre des Travaux d'Intérêt Général (S.M.O.T.I.G.).

Execution of the vast program of public works initiated by Governor Olivier was dependent upon the availability of a large and plentiful labor force, which simply could not be recruited by voluntary means. Believing that the overriding need to develop Madagascar's economy justified recourse to a barely disguised form of forced labor, Olivier hit upon the idea of utilizing Malagasy military recruits. Inasmuch as a large proportion of the Malagasy youths liable to three years of military duty were never actually called up to serve in the armed forces, Olivier decided to channel them into what was called a pioneer corps. Its members lived in camps with their families, were subject to military discipline, and received the same food, clothing, and medical care as army recruits. With this labor force the government was able to build roads, canals, ports, and, above all, the railroad from Fianarantsoa to Manakara, which probably would never otherwise have been constructed.

When the S.M.O.T.I.G. was sharply atacked in the French Parliament and the International Labor Organization as being deleterious to human dignity and liberty, Olivier ardently defended it on the grounds that it was being used for a "high moral purpose." He refuted the statement made at Geneva that in 1928 S.M.O.T.I.G. had been responsible for a million "victims" in Madagascar, asserting that there had been exactly 7,957 S.M.O.-T.I.G. pioneers that year and that deaths among them had numbered only 68.[10] From 1927 to 1930, when Olivier was succeeded by Governor Cayla, about 20,000 Malagasys had served in S.M.O.T.I.G., but in no one year did their number exceed 10,000, or about 8 per cent of all able-bodied Malagasys between the ages of 19 and 55.

In 1930, the French government reached an agreement with the I.L.O. to the effect that it would gradually abolish the S.M.O.T.I.G., and meanwhile would use it exclusively for works of public interest. During the world depression, many of the men, especially from the south, who were released from the S.M.O.T.I.G. decided to remain in the corps, since they were paid double the wages being offered by private employers. This infuriated some European members of the Delegations, who felt that the government was reprehensible in refusing to supply them with laborers and even luring away from them such few voluntary workers as were available.[11] This criticism, combined with that of the French liberals, who opposed forced labor on principle and claimed that it was being used in Madagascar by private individuals, spelled the end of the S.M.O.T.I.G. It was abolished in 1936, when the French government was taken over by the Popular Front, which also for the first time authorized the organizing of Malagasy trade unions. Throughout the remaining years of the decade, less than 10 per cent of the population of working age were wage-earners, and the great mass of Malagasys remained underemployed and resumed their contemplative living habits.

World War II disrupted the labor market in Madagascar. Soldiers and workers were sent to France, though not in such numbers as during the 1914–18 war. The lack of shipping for exports and imports removed most of the incentives for wage-earning, and this was reflected in a large-scale abandonment of plantations, including those devoted to raising food crops.[12] In 1942 the armed resistance of the local administration to the British occupation included destruction of many means of communication. Their subsequent repair by the Free French government necessitated a large number of laborers. At the same time, the government's pledge to provision the Allied forces created heavy demands for farm workers. When the authorities' appeals to the Malagasys to increase production went unheeded, the use of force was increasingly resorted to.

On April 3, 1943, the governor-general issued an order that every worker, whether under contract or not, must possess a working card. On May 1, the number of days for prestation labor was doubled. Workers employed in enterprises necessary for national defense or to produce local provisions were made liable to employment anywhere on the island, and the penalties for those who abandoned their work without official authorization were stiffened. These regulations opened the door to grave abuses. Private employers whose production was unrelated to the war effort were able with little difficulty to requisition workers. Since that time, the Malagasys have reacted strongly against any measures that imply a return to forced labor.

By mid-1943 so many villages had been deserted, nomadism had so increased, and food production had so declined that even the *colons* proposed an end to labor requisitioning. Although the Brazzaville Conference of early 1944 did not take a firm stand against forced labor as such, its recommendations echoed a growing conviction in Madagascar that the existing regulations must be eased. That year the government eliminated requisitioning for all enterprises not vital to the war effort, reduced the penalties for vagrancy, and raised wages to meet the rising cost of living. Governor de St. Mart, while solemnly proclaiming that he had raised labor to the "rank of a sacred duty" for the Malagasys, also admonished French settlers to show more understanding of their responsibilities toward their workers by improving living conditions.[13] The Labor Inspectorate began to draft new labor legislation, which among other things was to include "norms of production," that is, the optimum number of workers required by each enterprise, based on the type of crops it produced.* In 1945, the government announced that it would restore voluntary labor and would facilitate re-cruiting of workers by establishing employment bureaus and organizing transport for wage-earners.

In the midst of this purely local effort to solve Madagascar's chronic labor problems, the law passed by the French Constituent Assembly on April 11, 1946, abolishing all forms of forced labor fell like a bomb. Em-ployers were frightened and bewildered, although they expressed confi-dence that the law would soon be repealed.[14] This law, combined with the rapidly rising cost of living and the shortage of incentive goods, such as textiles, caused wholesale desertions by Malagasy workers. The situation was quickly exploited by Malagasy nationalists and French left-wing agi-tators, who organized politically oriented strikes in public as well as private enterprises. In June 1946, such strikes paralyzed loading operations in 20 of Madagascar's 22 ports, and to keep the ports and public services in opera-tion the government had recourse to army and penal labor. However, it did not requisition labor to tend and harvest crops.[15] Governor de Coppet called a conference at Tananarive June 21–26, 1946, to which he invited employer and employee representatives, as well as officials and assemblymen. This conference recommended increasing wages, creating an advisory labor committee, facilitating the migration of southern workers, importing more consumer goods for the working class, and propagandizing to popularize labor.

Within a month, the minimum wage was raised from 8-to-10 to 15-to-35 C.F.A. francs according to cost-of-living zones, tripartite advisory commit-tees were set up in each provincial capital and at Tananarive under the chairmanship of Labor Inspectors, and the transportation of Antaisaka and Antandroy tribesmen to regions particularly short of labor was orga-nized. To only a small degree, however, did these measures ease the situa-tion, because it was not within the power of the local authorities to remedy the basic difficulties. These were the indifference of the Malagasys to work-ing for wages, especially when consumer goods continued to be in short supply, and the determination of the C.G.T. labor leaders to link the work-ers' grievances to the nationalists' demands for independence. The revolt that broke out in 1947, and its repression, so retarded development of the trade-union movement in Madagascar that for years thereafter the regula-

* The basic principal of this proposal, according to its author, Jean Manicacci, was that each Malagasy male between the ages of 18 and 50 should work 200 days a year, either for himself or for an employer. Regional and crop differences were, however, to be taken into account, as well as ways in which labor shortages and surpluses between one region and another could be eliminated.

tion of labor problems was left almost entirely in the hands of the government and of employer groups.

Between 1947 and 1953, when the Overseas Labor Code began to be applied to Madagascar, minimum wages were increased several times, consumer goods were in normal supply although very expensive, and employers increasingly mechanized their operations, thus diminishing the need for workers. During that period, if the labor situation was no longer acute, it could hardly be called satisfactory. Members of the mission sent by the French Union Assembly late in 1948 reported on the labor situation as follows:[16]

For lack of a labor code, working conditions are subject to uncoordinated and inappropriate regulations. Wage-earners find themselves under the control of the *patronat* because, under present circumstances and for complex reasons, the unions cannot fully play their part. For equal work, wages differ, depending upon whether the wage-earner is Malagasy or European, and this injustice is felt keenly by the Malagasy workers. Furthermore, sanitary conditions in enterprises are not always satisfactory, nor are the safeguards against work accidents adequate.... Child labor is widely utilized for work that is often hard and unhealthy, and this situation should be brought under strict control.... We must stress the insufficiency of the labor inspectorate, although the work of individual labor inspectors is most praiseworthy.

Labor Legislation

Before World War II, Madagascar was one of the French colonies having the largest number of labor laws, but it lacked the machinery to enforce them. The Overseas Labor Code coordinated these laws and filled the gaps in existing legislation, but for lack of qualified magistrates and labor inspectors, law enforcement continued to be deficient. Replacement of labor arbitration councils in each district by labor courts only in the provincial capitals marked a retrogression, but progress was made when the code embodied measures instituting a 40-hour working week, paid vacations, and the like.

Madagascar's European parliamentarians at Paris, especially those in the French Union Assembly, fought passage of the 1942 code at every step, whereas the equally conservative Malagasy deputy, Jonah Ranaivo, told the National Assembly that the code would be the finest Christmas present that France could give to the island.[17] The main argument used by French opponents of the code was that any legislation drafted for the whole French Union would be inappropriate for an island with the particular labor problems of Madagascar. Contrary to their forebodings, however, application of the code in Madagascar was not accompanied by strikes and turbulence as it was in French West Africa, but took place in "calm and tranquillity."[18] This was largely due to Governor Bargues's policy of applying provisions of the code only partially and gradually.

Wages and prices were frozen for nearly four years, beginning in December 1953; unions were slow to organize effective action; a family-allowance fund did not operate before April 1, 1956; and the first collective agreement between employers and employees was not signed until January 1958. As the result of laws passed by the French government, which were extended to Madagascar, Malagasy civil servants fared better than did workers in the private sector. Differences of opinion on whether private insurance companies or the Family Allowance Fund should handle compensation for work accidents held up legislation in that domain, and it was not until November 13, 1959, that a decree required all private employers to insure their employees and servants and penalized those failing to do so.

Nevertheless, there were only two instances—in 1954 and 1957—when wage-earners organized protests against the government's failure to apply the new legislation strictly. Indeed, the 1952 code proved sufficiently satisfactory for the government of independent Madagascar to take over and amplify its provisions in the code it promulgated on October 1, 1960. The 1960 code was certainly more comprehensive than its predecessor in guaranties and safeguards for workers, and it embodied notably the Malagasy constitution's pronouncements in regard to labor. The 1959 constitution asserted that "labor is a right and a duty for each person, a sacred obligation for all who are not prevented from working by age or infirmity." The right to strike was affirmed, provided the goal was better working and living conditions and not political objectives. Despite nationalist pressures, neither the constitution nor the 1960 code guarantied the worker's freedom to choose his own union or excluded foreigners from practicing specific occupations.

Organized Labor

Among the Malagasys, some types of work have been organized traditionally on a collective basis for the benefit of the community as a whole. Villagers apparently have always helped each other in preparing the ground for rice-planting, in house-building, and in constructing and maintaining dams. This mutual aid was regarded with special approval by the Merina monarchs, who also encouraged the formation of craft organizations. During the reigns of Radama I and Ranavalona I, about 44 guilds were formed, each with its own set of regulations. In 1885 the strongest was that of the blacksmiths, which had 4,167 members, and there were others grouping porters (1,200 members), stonecutters (786), and carpenters (463).[19] After the French conquest these guilds gradually disappeared.

It was not until the interwar period that labor unions in the Western sense of the term were formed, and the first of these was organized by Frenchmen among their compatriots. In view of the economic stringency of the depression of the early 1930s, some socialist minor civil servants asked the French government for permission to organize a union to defend their interests. To this plea the Minister of Colonies replied, in a letter of August 13, 1934, that he would take the matter under consideration, but nothing further was heard from Paris until the Popular Front government came to power. Meantime, the French functionaries had organized an "illicit" union, and their Malagasy colleagues had followed suit. Although on March 13, 1937, Metropolitan legislation in regard to unionization was extended to Madagascar, its effectiveness there was hampered by the proviso that all union members must possess an official certificate attesting to their ability to read and write French. The following year, however, the French communist *centrale,* the C.G.T., which had just formed the first genuine labor union on the island, managed to have this requirement abrogated.

Largely as the result of Joseph Ravoahangy's leadership, the C.G.T. unions in Madagascar tried to combine French and Malagasys—peasants as well as workers—in their membership. This policy was resisted, however, by most of the French members, so that by 1939 only three of the C.G.T. unions had succeeded in putting it into effect, and not all of them maintained close relations with the C.G.T. headquarters in France.[20] Moreover, the communists' initiative had caused the Catholic mission to organize its own unions, which in 1938 were brought together in a Union des Syndicats Chrétiens de Madagascar. Thus, despite a relatively early start the labor movement on the island was from the outset compartmentalized. On the eve of World War II, there were separate unions for Malagasy and French civil servants and for Catholic workers, as well as some autonomous unions. Only the C.G.T. unions—and these to a very limited extent—could claim mixed membership.

During the early years of World War II the labor movement languished under an administration that took its orders from authoritarian Vichy, but the situation changed after the Free French acquired control of the island in 1943. Because of the hardships of the last war years, the Malagasys had genuine and specific grievances, and this made them more receptive than before to the propaganda of left-wing leaders. By the end of 1943, contact was established between the local C.G.T. leadership and the C.G.T. delegates at Algiers. Talks between them there focused on the question of setting up in Madagascar a single C.G.T. Union des Syndicats.[21] The Malagasys had difficulties in convincing their French comrades of the need for an integrated union, but finally a compromise was reached whereby there was to be both a French and a Malagasy secretary-general for a united movement. Pierre Boiteau and Joseph Ravoahangy were elected to the posts, and the Union des Syndicats de Madagascar was born—but the C.G.T.'s troubles did not end there.

Some of its French members in Madagascar refused to cooperate in implementing the C.G.T.'s policy of actively opposing the government in regard to requisitions of rice and labor, yet the Union des Syndicats took credit for the abolition of the Office du Riz and of forced labor in 1946. It also actively supported the M.D.R.M. and led the strikes of September 1946 which forced the government to improve working conditions. Although to some extent the success of those strikes was due to the collaboration of the Catholic and autonomous unions, the Union des Syndicats was credited with the victory, and its membership allegedly grew to 12,000 that year.

Nevertheless, the Union's lack of strong indigenous leadership was admittedly a grave weakness during that period. For this deficiency its French secretary-general blamed the administration, which was said to have arrested C.G.T. militants and to have succeeded in infiltrating the Union with its own "straw men," both French and Malagasy.[22] Another qualified and more impartial French observer, however, was inclined to hold the Malagasy "psychology of dependence" as primarily responsible. According to Mannoni,[23] the Malagasys chose as heads of their unions paternalistic Notables, who not only were incapable of defending the interests of members but unabashedly used the whole movement to further their own welfare. Other basic weaknesses were the rivalry between unions and the failure of all of them to enlist any appreciable segment of the rural population as members. In any case, organized labor as a whole was gravely weakened by the revolt and its repression, and it did not begin to recover strength until 1952.

The Overseas Labor Code passed by the French Parliament that year assigned an important role to trade unions. Consequently the local administration for the first time began to encourage union activity—but only by moderate labor leaders. The C.G.T., for its part, was in no position to stage a comeback. From 1947 on, the Metropolitan *centrale*—from which the Madagascar Union des Syndicats had drawn much of its strength—had steadily lost political influence in France. Specifically, it was unable to persuade the National Assembly to grant an amnesty to the M.D.R.M. deputies. In Madagascar the congress that the Union des Syndicats held at Tananarive in November 1949 was attended by only 60 delegates from all of the island's regions and was reportedly a dismal failure.[24] As a result, it was the Catholic unions which, with the backing of the administration and of the Catholic mission, forged ahead. In October 1952, the secretary-general of the Metropolitan Confédération Française des Travailleurs Chrétiens (C.F.T.C.) came to Madagascar to strengthen and unite the C.F.T.C.'s local branches around a program that avoided political issues and stressed the need for improvements in working conditions and for higher wages. By late 1954 the C.F.T.C. in Madagascar had built up a total of 31 unions with 34,761 members, whereas the C.G.T. had only 11 unions with 3,220 members, and the autonomous unions numbered 24 but had fewer than 5,000 members.[25] In fact, only about 17 per cent of the wage-earning population then belonged to any union at all, and nearly half of them were concentrated in Tananarive province. For all their apparent superiority over local competitors, the C.F.T.C. unions made little headway in promoting the well-being of their members.

In Madagascar the whole labor movement suffered from the dispersal of enterprises, their control by foreigners, the lack of industrial concentration, and the instability and nonchalance of the Malagasy laborers. Furthermore, both worker and employer organizations were handicapped by a spirit of individualism, caution, and mutual distrust. In Madagascar the *patronat* had been slow to organize, and it did so only in reaction to the postwar government's economic policies. On May 16, 1946, a federation of employer unions was formed, which called itself the Union des Syndicats d'Intérêt Economique (later renamed the Union des Syndicats Patronaux de Madagascar), and it claimed to represent all elements of economic enterprise on the island. Its members bewailed the high cost, inefficiency, and laziness of Malagasy workers, whose strikes they described as "refusals to work."[26] But its main censure was reserved for the administration's weakness vis-à-vis labor and its policy of *dirigisme*. The island's economy, they asserted, would disintegrate if the official controls were not removed.

Economic freedom was very largely restored in 1949, but three years later the enactment of the Overseas Labor Code once more aroused the employer unions, which by the end of 1954 had increased their number to 42 and their membership to 893. This renewed activity by the *patronat*'s organization heightened the distrust of all employers on the part of the workers' unions. Their distrust included the administration, which was the single largest employer of labor in Madagascar. In 1955, the C.F.T.C. unions formed a Confédération Chrétienne des Syndicats Malgaches (C.C.S.M.), and at a congress in Tananarive strongly urged the government to apply the Overseas Labor Code fully and to inaugurate a system of family allowances for all wage-earners.

For its part, the government was becoming worried by the lack of Malagasy leadership for the labor movement and by the inability of the existing unions to enlist agricultural workers in their membership. It was noted that among the labor leaders who came to assure Governor Soucadaux on May Day 1955 of their cooperation with his program to reduce living costs, all but one were Frenchmen, the exception being Richard Raberanto, head of the Federation of Malagasy Functionaries. To give agricultural workers an organization and the means for expressing their aspirations and grievances, the government sponsored a Congrès des Syndicats Agricoles at Tananarive on July 15–16, 1955, but nothing has since been heard of its activities. Obviously the labor movement in Madagascar was even weaker than that of French West Africa, which, in 1953, had forced the government there to accede to most of its demands. Madagascar had yet to develop unions that would be both useful and valid representatives of Malagasy workers.

In 1957, the Malagasy unions followed the example of their Negro African colleagues and broke their ties with the Metropolitan *centrales,* which had given them birth, although they did so more gradually and less completely. By that year the strength of the socialist (Force Ouvrière) unions had declined to such a point that their existence was largely nominal. The C.G.T. unions, which were the best organized of all and were dominant among the workers of Diégo-Suarez and Tamatave, took the Malagasy name of Firaisana Sendikaly Malagasy (FISEMA). Although nominally they severed their affiliation with the Metropolitan C.G.T., they nevertheless benefited from the popularity that that *centrale* was winning through its increasingly successful campaign for amnestying all political prisoners of the 1947 revolt. Of all the local labor federations, the C.C.M.S. remained numerically the strongest, and though it broke away from the parent organization in France, it retained very close ties with the local Catholic mission. That mission exerted its influence to keep the C.C.M.S. generally an apolitical organization, and in particular to win over to it members of the FISEMA. Its main efforts were directed toward improving working and living conditions for its members, particularly in regard to wages and the development of cooperative societies.

A prime weakness of organized labor in Madagascar has been the unions' conspicuous failure to sponsor strikes that attained their objectives. Labor disputes there have been rare, and most of them have been easily settled by the labor inspectors. In 1925 the dockers at Tamatave struck for two hours "in protest against the penalizing of a comrade."[27] The next year workers in a Ste. Marie perfume distillery won a small pay raise by stopping work for a day or two. Ten years later the first work stoppage that might be called a genuine strike occurred at the factory of the Société de l'Emyrne, but it was not until 1946 that strikes became frequent and effective.

One almost insuperable obstacle that the unions have encountered in organizing strikes has been the absence of a real proletariat in Madagascar. The great majority of wage-earners are unskilled peasants who work for pay no more than a few months of the year and then return to their villages. Only among the Tamatave dockers, the railroad *cheminots,* and above all the workers at the naval arsenal at Diégo-Suarez has there developed what can be called an *esprit ouvrier.* Usually Malagasy workers express dissatisfaction not by striking but by absenteeism. For example, those in forest enterprises and mines, where working conditions are the hardest, simply melt away into the jungle if they are dissatisfied, without formulating any grievances. More often than not they are displeased by the quality of the rice ration, and if this grievance is remedied, the disgruntled workers suddenly reappear and resume work. Application of the Overseas Labor Code to Madagascar multiplied the number of disputes referred to the Labor Inspectorate and labor courts and, increasingly, settled by those means. During the three years 1951–53, there were 30 short-lived and generally unsuccessful strikes.[28]

Because for many years the Diégo-Suarez arsenal had the greatest concentration of permanently employed Malagasy wage-earners and the largest percentage of French workers, it is the one place on the island where labor has been organized by professional leaders and where strikes are conducted along Western lines. Under the C.G.T. leadership the Malagasy workers there have agitated for better working conditions and, above all, for equality of pay with Metropolitan employees. For a time the C.G.T. leaders organized and controlled the Tamatave dockers, and in 1949 they effectively supported a big strike at the port of St. Denis, Réunion. But FISEMA's obvious links with international communism and local nationalist extremists have prevented it from gaining a larger membership and making common cause with the Catholic and autonomous unions. Only once (in November 1957) before Madagascar became independent did they jointly sponsor a strike, and its spectacular failure discouraged for some years further attempts to create inter-union solidarity.

In 1959, divergencies that arose over the question of whether all railroad workers should be incorporated into the civil service turned into a trial of strength between rival union federations. In general, the upper and middle echelons of railroad workers, who belonged to the Catholic and socialist unions, favored retention of their status under the *régie,* whereas the lower ranks, who preferred incorporation into the administration, were members of the autonomous unions and of the FISEMA.[29]

The struggle further widened the existing split in organized Malagasy labor. It also impelled Malagasy political parties—whose competitiveness was sharpened by the imminence of independence—to bid against each other for support from and control of the unions. It was logical that the FISEMA should come under the domination of the A.K.F.M., and its fortunes have since followed those of that party. Dues, which amount to no more than 50 C.F.A. francs a month for all the unions, count for little, but subsidies, which the labor federations receive from outside, are crucial to their operations. The P.S.D., being in power, naturally can offer more advantages to unions accepting its guiding hand than can other parties. Although the Catholic unions have generally remained aloof from political parties, the P.S.D. has gathered under its wing almost all the organized wage-earners who are not members of either the C.C.S.M. or the FISEMA. In 1960 it created a Confédération des Travailleurs de Madagascar et des Comores (C.T.M.C.). Although the C.T.M.C. is not yet so strong numerically as the C.C.S.M., it is growing more rapidly, as a result of the considerable support it receives from the P.S.D. and the International Confederation of Free Trade Unions, with which it is affiliated. The FISEMA, as might be expected, maintains ties with communist labor organizations, either directly or through the A.K.F.M. leaders; its secretary-general, Rémy Rakotobe, has attended C.G.T. congresses in France as well as the Casablanca meeting at which the All-African Trade Union Federation was founded.* As is shown by the following tabulation, the FISEMA was, as of 1960–61, the weakest of the three Madagascar labor federations.

Federation	Number of Member Unions	Membership
C.C.S.M.	231	31,000
C.T.M.C.	132	15,000
FISEMA	106	9,400

The P.S.D. government wants to unite the Catholic unions with the C.T.M.C.; although it has not yet been able to do so, it has succeeded in weakening the FISEMA unions everywhere except in Diégo-Suarez. Organized labor, never powerful in Madagascar, is even less strong than formerly as the result of its subordination to political parties. Only a small

* Albertini, "Le Communisme à Madagascar." Reportedly Russian experts on Madagascar differ as to whether the FISEMA does or does not belong to the W.F.T.U. See *The Mizan Newsletter*, April 1963.

proportion of Malagasy wage-earners—who totaled 175,352 as of January 1, 1962—belong to any union at all. A survey made at the end of 1960, summarized in the tabulation below, indicated that no more than 72,000 of them were unionized, and of these some 40,000 lived in the island's six main towns. In Fianarantsoa province the comparatively large number of organized workers reflected the strength of the Catholic mission in the provincial capital and the concentration of laborers at Mananjary port.

Province	Total of Organized Workers	Organized Workers in Provincial Capital
Tananarive	29,000	22,000
Diégo-Suarez	14,000	3,400
Majunga	4,500	3,800
Tamatave	3,300	2,800
Fianarantsoa	20,000	8,000
Tuléar	800	400

Like its French predecessor, the Malagasy government is having difficulty in finding responsible and authentic spokesmen for labor. In 1961 it opened a Université Syndicale at Tananarive and an Institut de Formation Syndicale at Fianarantsoa. At both places selected workers are being trained with a view to transforming them into qualified labor leaders. Such a transformation, however, may be delayed, because it is contingent upon the existence of a genuine working class, which Madagascar does not have at present.

Wages, Family Allowances, and Prices

For some years after World War II, the wage and price policies of the local administration followed those of France. They were based on the belief that by freezing wages and prices the cost of living could be prevented from spiraling. In Madagascar, the public powers have always determined the minimum wage (*salaire minimum interprofessionnel garanti,* or S.M.I.G.) after consultation with the labor advisory councils. At the government's request, the councils reported on the cost of items of prime necessity for the average Malagasy family in their respective regions. On the basis of these data the island was divided into ten wage zones, the highest wages being paid in the towns and the lowest in the most self-sufficient rural areas. The agricultural wage-earner was allotted the lowest wage, which was not unjust in the case of the few thousand contract workers who received facilities for housing, free medical care, and food and cloth rations. For the great majority of farm hands, however, the disparity between rural and urban wages gave an incentive to move to the towns, where more amenities and job opportunities were available, even though living costs were higher.

By 1949 it had become evident that in view of the steadily rising cost of living the government could not hold the wage line much longer. The average wage then was 30 C.F.A. francs a day, and the purchasing power of wage-earners was said to be only half of what it had been in 1939. By 1949, rice cost 20 to 29 C.F.A. francs a kilogram, cotton cloth from 70 to 125 C.F.A. francs a meter, and taxes took a month's wages from the unskilled worker.[30] To be sure, some employers paid far more than the S.M.I.G., for the shortage of labor had led to intense competition. But as a group the *patronat* stood firm against any overall wage increase, claiming that it would fatally increase production costs, which were already high. They also felt, and with some reason, that higher wages would not necessarily overcome the Malagasys' innate reluctance to hire out their services. Nevertheless, on March 1, 1949, the government did raise the minimum wage for men by 11 per cent and for women by 13 per cent. This small increase, however, did not offset the far more rapidly rising cost of living.

On April 1, 1950, Governor Bargues raised the salaries of civil servants, and because the administration was the largest single employer of labor, this had immediate repercussions on the private sector. As the clamor for wage increases from that quarter grew and employers remained adamant, the authorities made a study of the relationship between labor and production costs. Jean Manicacci, the chief labor inspector, reported that there had indeed been a general but small rise in the percentage of labor costs to total production costs in relation to 1937, when it had constituted 49 per cent, but he added that it differed markedly from one enterprise to another depending upon the amount of labor required.[31] He estimated that in 1950 labor accounted for 26 per cent of the production costs for vanilla, 50 per cent for building enterprises, 55 per cent for rice, 57 per cent for sisal and sugar, 70 per cent for ylang-ylang, and 74 per cent for copra. Regardless of these divergencies and because Madagascar's exports were selling well in the early 1950s, the minimum wage was raised in February 1952. This was also the year in which the French Parliament at long last passed the Overseas Labor Code. It was ostensibly to obviate any "unfortunate repercussions" from application of that code to Madagascar that Governor Bargues froze both prices and wages on December 10, 1953. No further increase in the minimum wage took place until November 1957.

During the four-year-long wage-price freeze, the focal point of interest in Madagascar's labor problems shifted to the question of family allowances for wage-earners as laid down under the new code. Theoretically the issue had been settled, so far as civil servants were concerned, by passage of the Lamine Gueye law of June 1950, but six years later only 17,825 beneficiaries in Madagascar had received a total of 495 million Metro. francs, whereas

the number of eligible children was estimated at 25,000.[32] A family-allowance fund for the other wage-earners was not set up until April 1, 1956,
and not until January 1, 1957, was it extended to include the children of
agricultural workers and domestic servants. Moreover, the initial monthly
rate of 100 C.F.A. francs per child was so patently inadequate that it was
doubled within a few weeks. In November 1957 it was raised to 300 C.F.A
francs and in April 1958 to 400, but even then only about 35,000 children
of the 80,000 or more believed to qualify for this allowance were actually
receiving it.[33] In large part this was due to the inability of many wage-
earners to produce the proofs required, given the almost total absence of
birth-registration facilities and the complicated formalities involved. In
January 1959, when the operations of the family-allowance fund had badly
bogged down, its director was dismissed and the procedures simplified.
Thus far, the P.S.D. government has held out against pressure to increase
the monthly rate to 600 C.F.A. francs, on the ground that Madagascar's
finances simply cannot afford it. A reason less frequently voiced is that the
family allowance, small as it is, has certainly stimulated Madagascar's gal-
loping birthrate.

When Governor Soucadaux raised the family-allowance rate for the
second time, in November 1957, he also announced a reduction in the number of wage zones from ten to eight and a rise in minimum wages of 15
to 40 per cent. On November 7 he told the representative assembly that he
had taken this step reluctantly because it was not justified by any marked
improvement in the economy. He also pointed out that it would cause
wages to rise faster than the cost of living and also disproportionately to the
income of Malagasy peasants, who formed the great majority of the population. Theoretically this measure should have pleased the labor unions,
but instead it triggered the biggest strike that Madagascar had yet experienced. The FISEMA, C.C.S.M., and autonomous unions formed a committee, which asserted that the proposed wage increases amounted in fact
to less than 14 per cent for the highest category of wage-earners and less than
1 per cent for rural workers, and they demanded a far larger overall wage
increase.

The political overtones of this strike were mainly responsible for its lack
of success. The Malagasy assemblymen were irked by the government's
unilateral albeit legal action, for the law required that they should be consulted not on minimum-wage increases but only on the rate of family allowances.[34] The unions, for their part, were angered by the government's
refusal to apply the conciliation procedures laid down by the code, on the
ground that this strike was illegal since it was directed against the executive power and not against employers. (This contention was upheld by the
Labor Court in March 1958.) The strongest unions—those of the civil ser-

vants—did not join the strike movement, less than 10 per cent of the workers in the private sector at Tananarive struck, and the strike order was ignored in Tamatave and Tuléar. Only in Diégo-Suarez, where labor was well organized and the C.G.T. and Catholic unions worked closely together, was the strike effective, and there it involved 1,600 workers.[35] Victorious in its trial of strength with organized labor, the government could afford to be lenient. It persuaded employers to take back the strikers without penalizing them, and in December 1958 it again raised minimum wages.

Inevitably the government of independent Madagascar has been subjected to even greater pressures than its French predecessor to abolish wage zones and to increase minimum wages substantially. In 1961 the P.S.D. leaders promised to re-examine these questions, and they appointed a Conseil National du Travail, composed of deputies and of representatives of employers and employees, to determine what effect such measures would have on the economy of the island's various regions. Somewhat surprisingly, the new council agreed with employers that under existing economic conditions any rise in the wage scale would be inadvisable. However, on December 1, 1963, the wage zones were reduced from eight to five, and the rates for both minimum wages and family allowances were raised, though not to the extent demanded by the unions. In the highest-paid zone, agricultural workers were allotted 25 C.F.A. francs an hour and nonagricultural workers 29 C.F.A. francs (Diégo-Suarez and Tananarive). The new figures for the lowest-paid zone (districts of Tuléar and Majunga) were 19 and 16 C.F.A. francs, respectively.

On the average, wages in 1960 were two to four times higher than they had been in 1950, aggregating 21,836 million C.F.A. francs for both the public and private sectors. Although government action in recent years has resulted in a lessening of the gap between the highest- and lowest-paid categories of wage-earners, the disparity between wage-earners' and peasants' revenues has been dangerously widened.

Number and Occupations of Wage-Earners

So many of Madagascar's wage-earners are seasonal workers that statistics on the total number differ considerably and are generally misleading. One authority states that the number increased from 120,000 in 1939 to 243,000 in 1957.[36] The latter figure is appreciably larger than the 204,924 given by the Labor Inspectorate for 1960, and much larger than the 175,352 cited by an authoritative Paris publication for January 1, 1962.[37] On the basis of the largest of the foregoing estimates, which doubtless included a considerable proportion of seasonal workers, Malagasy wage-earners constitute less than 5 per cent of the population (which totals roughly 5.5 million) and less than 10 per cent of all Malagasys of working age (estimated at more than 2.5 million).

Not only do wage-earners form an unusually small proportion of the total population, but all sources agree that their number is declining, both absolutely and relatively. This is particularly true of the unskilled category, but it also applies to some skilled and semiskilled workers. The establishment of the railroad *régie* in 1951 and dieselizing the lines had brought about a 25 per cent reduction, within four years, of the number of railroad employees.* A reorganization of the Tamatave dockers caused a reduction in permanent wage-earners among them from 700 in 1957 to 600 in 1962. The most conspicuous decreases have occurred since 1955–56, and they are especially marked in the agricultural domain, where the number of wage-earners fell from 75,721 in 1950 to 44,745 ten years later.[38] Much of this decline is attributed to the retrogression of big plantation enterprises, which employ unskilled farm hands on a permanent basis, and their replacement by family enterprises and sharecroppers. It is possible, however, that seasonal employment on small agricultural holdings has been increasing, though to what extent the Labor Inspectorate does not know because such labor is rarely declared to the authorities.

The number of women wage-earners, other than those employed in the public services, has never been large and has likewise been shrinking. It fell from some 41,000 in 1950 to 30,000 in 1960, and in the latter year about a fourth were engaged in agriculture and fishing. In mining, the decrease is more striking, the number of miners having declined from 12,590 to 6,612 between 1950 and 1960. The manufacturing industries, building, and public works all employ fewer workers than they did during the 1950s, when the French Plan was being carried out in Madagascar. Since then, the number and scope of such enterprises have declined, and increasing mechanization, higher wages, and, above all, the island's economic stagnation have contributed to reducing the wage-earning component.

The small size, dispersal, and foreign ownership of many enterprises have been a cause of the weakness of organized labor and of some resentment on the part of Malagasy nationalists. In 1960 it was estimated that Madagascar had 536 Malagasy employers of wage-earners, compared with 1,791 French, 795 Indian, and 419 Chinese.[39] Furthermore, three-fourths of the foremen were Frenchmen. As of January 1, 1961, there were only 11 enterprises that employed more than 1,000 workers, and of these six were owned or managed by Frenchmen and one by a Chinese. In addition, there were

* In 1938, there were 4,875 railroad employees and in 1955 there were 2,559. See *Chroniques d'Outre-Mer*, January 1957.

20 employing from 500 to 1,000 persons, 49 with 250 to 500, 125 with 100 to 250, 604 with 20 to 100, and about 3,000 employing only one to 20 workers.

Malagasy nationalists seem to resent the employment of French technicians by the government, even though they are paid by France, more than they do the predominance of Frenchmen among the country's entrepreneurs. This probably derives from the prestige of government service among the Malagasys, as well as their indifference to money-making enterprises. Among the Malagasy workers, it is national pride rather than the drive to earn large sums *per se* that has led to strikes aimed at attaining parity with Metropolitan wage-earners. Periodically the Malagasys employed at the French navy arsenal at Diégo-Suarez have agitated for equal pay with French employees, and Malagasy bank clerks struck in 1962 for equality of treatment with the banks' European employees. Yemenese have been eliminated as dockers at Tamatave port so as to provide more jobs for Malagasys, but no similar step has been taken against them elsewhere. Yet, surprisingly, the far more numerous Comorian workers have not been discriminated against on the west coast, where they are concentrated. This spirit of tolerance is not likely to last, and its existence thus far may be ascribed to the fact that the unemployed mostly consist of unskilled urban youths, particularly from Tananarive.

Nearly 22 per cent of all Malagasy wage-earners in the private sector, as indicated in the table on distribution of wage-earners, are employed in agriculture and fishing. The second-largest category (15.6 per cent) is that of domestic servants, whose employment depends upon the size and permanence of the European residential community. Next come the 12.8 per cent in trade and banking, and far below them are those employed in transportation and manufacturing (8.6 per cent and 7.1 per cent, respectively). Industrial activities, even if public works and mining are included, occupy barely one-fourth of the wage-earning contingent, and the only two provinces that have a sizable work force in this category are Tananarive (14,000) and Diégo-Suarez (7,000). The number of clerical and white-collar employees, including those in government service, is high compared with that of skilled manual workers. As might be expected, the largest single category of workers in the private sector is made up of unskilled laborers. In 1960, the number of persons employed in the private sector totaled 157,243, and in the public sector, 47,681.

Unemployment and Civil Service

The rapid growth of Madagascar's population coincided with a shrinkage in the demand for labor, thus transforming the basic labor problem from

Distribution of Wage-Earners, by Occupation and Type of Employment, 1960–61

Occupation	No. of Wage-Earners and % of Total Working Force	Categories of Wage-Earners, by % in Each Occupation			
		Professional and Skilled	Un-skilled	Clerical	Cadres
Agriculture and fishing . . .	44,746 (21.8)	9.9	86.6	2.5	1.0
Forests and sawmilling . . .	1,465 (0.7)	—	—	—	—
Mining	6,612 (3.2)	21.3	71.0	5.5	2.2
Manufacturing	17,718 (8.6)	34.5	54.3	8.3	2.9
Electricity, water supply, Health Service	1,975 (1.0)	38.2	40.5	17.5	3.8
Building and public works .	9,512 (4.7)	36.8	54.7	5.7	2.8
Transportation	14,700 (7.1)	40.5	42.8	13.2	3.5
Trade and banking	26,325 (12.8)	9.7	33.6	50.2	6.5
Liberal professions	2,120 (1.0)	—	—	—	—
Administration and public services	47,681 (23.4)	26.3	27.9	30.6	15.2
Domestic service	32,070 (15.6)	—	—	—	—

Sources: Malagasy Republic, *Economie Malgache: Evolution 1950–1960*, pp. 53–54; *Marchés Tropicaux*, July 20, 1963.

shortage to surplus. This became noticeable for the first time in the mid-1950s, and it is now a cause of great concern to the Malagasy authorities. In a country where the vast majority of wage-earners are both seasonal and unskilled, unemployment is difficult to define. There are thought to be perhaps 10,000 formerly employed Malagasys out of work, and they are concentrated almost exclusively in the main towns. Only in Tananarive does an employment bureau exist, and each year it has an increasing number of applicants, most of whom have never been employed; for these, jobs are getting harder to find. Various solutions to this problem have been proposed, including a reorientation of the school system so as to place more stress on technical skills. Malagasy deputies have proposed a tax moratorium, because wage-earners are now required to hold working permits, which they cannot obtain if they have failed to pay their taxes. But instead of solving the unemployment problem, a tax moratorium probably would simply bring out more job applicants who have been hiding in the city slums.

Increasingly the P.S.D. leaders have emphasized the need to add to job openings by increasing agricultural and other exports. They have assumed the attitude that because plenty of arable land is still available there is no such thing as genuine unemployment—only willful idleness. In 1960 the government offered to settle any applicants on plots of improved land and to provide a modest capital to tide them over the first year of farming. In

1961, the tone of Tsiranana's speeches on urban unemployment and rural underemployment became more forceful, and he pointed out that idlers were usually behind public disturbances.[40] The following year he spoke of the need to create new wants so that people would work harder in order to buy shoes, household utensils, and radios.[41] In October 1962, he announced that all able-bodied men not only would have to hold working cards but would be required to cultivate at least one hectare of rice or corn. Young men, he said, must be put to work, and he would soon submit to the Parliament a bill introducing civic service in conjunction with the obligation to perform military service.[42]

Even before Madagascar became independent, the P.S.D. leaders had hinted that they would institute civic service, but it was not actually put into practice until the spring of 1963, and then only experimentally and on a very small scale. There were several valid reasons for their caution and procrastination. On his visits to French-speaking Negro Africa, Tsiranana had seen for himself the miscarriage of the "human investment" programs there. He also knew that in its current financial straits Madagascar could not afford to undertake a large-scale operation and especially one whose success was dubious. An even more cogent reason for prudence was the Malagasys' resistance—based on memories of the S.M.O.T.I.G. and wartime coercion—to any move that might be construed as a revival of forced labor.

When President Tsiranana proposed that students should supply the leadership for the civic-service program, they reacted strongly. Their stand was upheld by the opposition press,[43] which claimed that students were the elite of the land and should not be diverted from their studies. Since most students were Merina, it was obvious, they charged, that the côtier government was trying to victimize the youth of the high plateaus. Their contention was that labor for public works should come from the ranks of unemployed urban youths. To all this, Tsiranana replied tartly that, far from persecuting the Merina, he was offering the young men a chance to prove their patriotism and to become the leaders of the nation. Civic service, he continued, was not simply a means of carrying out public works cheaply, as had been the case with the S.M.O.T.I.G.; its aim was also to combat illiteracy and to raise community living standards.

To avoid prohibitive expenditures as well as the risk of a conspicuous failure, the program is to be spread over a four-year period and to involve no more than 1,000 youths. In April 1963, Tsiranana inaugurated the Ecole des Cadres du Service Civique, whose 50 or more students are being given training in a trade, a course in civics, and physical education. The first graduates are to carry out community-development projects in Tuléar, Tananarive, and Majunga provinces.

NOTES

NOTES

Complete authors' names, titles, and publication data for works cited in short form are given in the Bibliography.

Chapter one

1. In large part, the basic material for this chapter has been derived from secondary sources, in particular the works of G. S. Chapus, H. Deschamps, G. Ferrand, G. J. H. Julien, and R. Kent.
2. Deschamps, *Madagascar*, p. 70.
3. A. Grandidier, *Ethnographie de Madagascar*.

Chapter two

1. Hatzfeld, pp. 39–40.
2. See Brunet, *L'Oeuvre de la France à Madagascar*.
3. Martin, p. 66.
4. *Ibid.*, p. 71.
5. For a description of this League from the communist viewpoint, see Boiteau, *Contribution à l'Histoire de la Nation Malgache*, p. 321.
6. Hyet, p. 140.
7. Boiteau, *Contribution*, p. 325.
8. Deschamps, *Histoire de Madagascar*, p. 263.
9. Martin, p. 228.
10. *Ibid.*, p. 158.
11. Boudry, *Jean-Joseph Rabearivelo et la Mort*, p. 23.

Chapter three

1. Deschamps, *Histoire de Madagascar*, p. 264.
2. Annet, *Aux Heures Troublées de l'Afrique Française, 1939–1943*.
3. *Ibid.*, p. 236.
4. Decary, "Madagascar," p. 50; Boiteau, *Contribution*, p. 340.
5. Free French Information Service bulletin, New York, April 1942.
6. Minutes of the French National Assembly, May 6, 1947.
7. Croft-Cooke, p. 238.   8. Rosenthal, p. 103.
9. Croft-Cooke, p. 240.   10. Decary, "Madagascar," p. 192.
11. Guernier, I, 203.
12. *Délégations Economiques et Financières, Procès-Verbaux*, session of Nov. 13, 1944.
13. R. W. Rabemananjara, *Madagascar, Histoire de la Nation Malgache*, p. 173.
14. Boudry, "Le Problème Malgache."

15. Boiteau, *Contribution*, p. 352. Duveau's estimate of 93,000 seems nearer the mark. See National Assembly debates, May 8, 1947.

16. R. W. Rabemananjara, *Madagascar, Histoire de la Nation Malgache*, p. 189.

17. *L'Epoque*, Sept. 22, 1946.

18. R. W. Rabemananjara, *Madagascar sous la Rénovation Malgache*, p. 163.

19. *Ibid.*, p. 65; Boiteau, *Contribution*, p. 366.

20. Boudry, "Le Problème Malgache."

Chapter four

1. See Kent, *From Madagascar to the Malagasy Republic*, pp. 109 *et seq.*, and Stibbe, p. 19.

2. National Assembly debates, June 6, 1952.

3. See article by M. Liotard, president of the Ligue des Intérêts Franco-Malgaches, in *L'Avenir de Madagascar*, Sept. 5, 1947.

4. R. W. Rabemananjara, *Madagascar sous la Rénovation Malgache*, p. 43.

5. R. W. Rabemananjara, *Madagascar, Histoire de la Nation Malgache*, p. 160.

6. Boiteau, *Contribution*, p. 371; National Assembly debates, May 9, 1947.

7. National Assembly debates, April 29, 1947.

8. Marius Moutet's speech in the National Assembly, May 9, 1947.

9. *Marchés Coloniaux*, April 26, 1947. For the settlers' viewpoint, see Casseville; also *L'Avenir de Madagascar*, April 18, 1947; *France-Madagascar*, April 28 and Sept. 6, 1947, and Jan. 2, 1948; and *Tana-Journal*, April 16, 1947.

10. Boiteau, *Contribution*, p. 372, and Raseta's speech in the National Assembly, May 6, 1947. It is interesting that, 16 years after the Madagascar revolt, Soviet Africanists were repeating this line. See *The Mizan Newsletter*, April 1963.

11. R. W. Rabemananjara, *Madagascar sous la Rénovation Malgache*, p. 146.

12. National Assembly debates, May 9, 1947.

13. *Ibid.*, May 8, 1947.

14. *Ibid.*, May 6, 8, and 9, June 6, and Aug. 1, 1947; Conseil de la République debates, June 17, July 18 and 24, and Aug. 7, 1947.

15. Mannoni, *Psychologie de la Colonisation*.

16. See R. Lombardo's speech in the French Union Assembly on May 25, 1949.

17. National Assembly debates, Jan. 12, Nov. 13, and Dec. 29, 1951.

18. *Ibid.*, Feb. 26, 1953, and June 17, 1954.

Chapter five

1. *Marchés Coloniaux*, March 14, 1949.

2. French Union Assembly debates, March 30, 1950.

3. *Ibid.*, May 24, 25, and 31, 1949.   4. *Ibid.*, Dec. 1 and 8, 1949.

5. *Marchés Coloniaux*, July 23, 1949.   6. *Ibid.*, Aug. 6, 1949.

7. French Union Assembly debates, April 10, 1951.

8. National Assembly debates, April 24, 1951.

9. For details of this election, see *Marchés Coloniaux*, April 5, 1952.

10. See Bargues's speeches to the Representative Assembly, Aug. 31, 1951, and April 19, 1952.

11. See assembly minutes for May 9, 1952; Sept. 27, 1953; and April 2, 1954.

12. National Assembly debates, April 18, 1956.

13. Hatzfeld, *Madagascar*, p. 119.

14. For a detailed account of this election, see *Marchés Tropicaux*, April 6, 1957.

Chapter six

1. See Albertini, "Le Communisme à Madagascar en 1960."
2. *Lumière*, Feb. 26, 1960.   3. *Le Monde*, Dec. 4, 1957.
4. *Ibid.*, Feb. 16–17, 1958.   5. *Marchés Tropicaux*, April 12, 1958.
6. See debates of March 29 and 31 and April 1, 1958.
7. *Marchés Tropicaux*, May 3, 1958.   8. Minutes of the assembly, May 6, 1958.
9. *Le Monde*, July 19, 1958.   10. *Ibid.*, June 24 and July 23, 1958.
11. *Marchés Tropicaux*, Sept. 27, 1958.   12. *L'Express*, Aug. 21, 1958.
13. *New York Times*, Aug. 22, 1958.
14. *Marchés Tropicaux*, June 7 and Oct. 4, 1958.
15. *Ibid.*, Sept. 20, 1958.

Chapter seven

1. Minutes of the Provisional Assembly, session of October 1958.
2. *Marchés Tropicaux*, Oct. 18, 1958.
3. *Lumière*, March 25, 1960.
4. Interview with Richard Andrianamanjato, Nov. 14, 1962.
5. *New York Times*, July 17, 1959.
6. Interview with André Resampa, Nov. 12, 1962.
7. *Lumière*, March 11, 1960.
8. *Le Monde*, Aug. 11, 1959.

Chapter eight

1. *Le Monde*, Jan. 7, 1960.
2. *Ibid.*, Feb. 18, 1960.
3. *Marchés Tropicaux*, March 12, 1960.
4. Interview with Maurice Merleau-Ponty, *L'Express*, Aug. 21, 1958.
5. *Marchés Tropicaux*, May 14, 1960.
6. *Ibid.*, July 11, 1959.
7. *Ibid.*, April 30, 1960.
8. National Assembly debates, June 9, 1960; Conseil de la République debates, June 16, 1960.
9. *Marchés Tropicaux*, July 30, 1960.
10. *Ibid.*, Aug. 13, 1960.

Chapter nine

1. *Marchés Tropicaux*, Oct. 20, 1960.
2. Minutes of the legislative assembly, May 9, 1961.
3. *Ibid.*, June 30, 1961.   4. *Ibid.*, July 7, 1961.
5. *Ibid.*, Oct. 6, 1961.   6. *Marchés Tropicaux*, May 13, 1961.
7. *Ibid.*, Jan. 28, 1961.
8. Interview with André Blanchet, *Nice-Matin*, May 23, 1961.
9. *Le Monde*, Oct. 22–23, 1961.
10. Interview with André Blanchet, *Nice-Matin*, May 23, 1961.
11. This was the source for a summary of the program that appeared in *Afrique Nouvelle*, Dec. 13, 1961.
12. *Marchés Tropicaux*, Jan. 27, 1962.

13. *Afrique Nouvelle,* March 7, 1962.

14. *Marchés Tropicaux,* Feb. 16, 1963.

15. See Albertini's articles in *Est et Ouest,* April 16–30, 1957; April 1–15, 1960; Nov. 1–15, 1960; and Nov. 1–15, 1961.

16. See accounts of recent P.S.D. congresses in *Marchés Tropicaux,* Sept. 1, 1962; Sept. 3, 1963; and May 2, 1964.

17. *Ibid.,* Aug. 17, 1963.

18. *Ibid.,* March 2, 1963.

19. Philippe Decraene, writing in *Le Monde,* May 21, 1964.

Chapter ten

1. F. Rambaud, "Structure Administrative," in E. Guernier, ed., *Madagascar et Ré-union,* I.

2. Priestley, p. 315.

3. Deschamps, *Histoire de Madagascar,* p. 205.

4. Condominas, pp. 99 *et seq.*

5. *Ibid.,* p. 134.

6. Speech to the representative assembly, Aug. 12, 1950.

7. See minutes of the representative assembly, March 12 and 24 and Sept. 26, 1953.

8. See Gaudemet, "La Provincialisation de Madagascar," and Luchaire, "Les Institutions Politiques et Administratives des Territoires d'Outre-Mer après la Loi-Cadre."

9. Minutes of the representative assembly, March 29, 1958.

10. Le Brun-Keris, "Madagascar à l'Heure de la Loi-Cadre."

11. Mounier, "Le Caractère des Institutions de la République Malgache."

12. Comte, "Les Communes Malgaches," p. 32.

13. *Ibid.,* p. 58.

14. *Ibid.,* p. 59.

15. Debousset, *L'Organisation Municipale à Madagascar.*

16. French Union Assembly debates, Dec. 14, 1951, and March 3, 1953.

17. Bargues's speech to the representative assembly, March 14, 1953.

18. National Assembly debates, July 5, 1955.

19. *Ibid.,* Oct. 25, 1955.

20. Comte, "Les Communes Malgaches," p. 53.

21. *Le Monde,* May 22, 1964.

Chapter eleven

1. Fénard, p. 233.

2. Speech to the Mixed Franco-Malagasy Commission, Nov. 27, 1944.

3. National Assembly debates, Jan. 27, 1950; French Union Assembly debates, July 5, 1951.

4. French Union Assembly debates, March 13, 1953.

5. See minutes of the representative assembly, Aug. 30, 1950; April 6, 1951; and Oct. 29, 1953.

6. See French Union Assembly debates, May 24, 1951, and Feb. 17, 1953; also National Assembly debates, Dec. 16, 1954.

7. Speech to the representative assembly, Aug. 31, 1951.

8. See minutes of the representative assembly, Oct. 29, 1953; April 1, 1954; and April 27, 1955.

9. *Ibid.,* Dec. 20, 1957.

10. *Ibid.,* June 28, July 5, and Nov. 28, 1957; March 29 and April 12, 1958.

11. *Marchés Tropicaux,* Nov. 23 and Dec. 28, 1957; minutes of the representative assembly, May 7, 1958.

12. *Marchés Tropicaux,* Feb. 29, 1964.

13. Minutes of the representative assembly, Oct. 2, 1961.

14. *Ibid.,* Nov. 24 and Dec. 5, 1959.

15. *Marchés Tropicaux,* Jan. 21, 1961.

16. Speech to the representative assembly, Oct. 6, 1959.

17. Minutes of the representative assembly, Jan. 18 and 19, 1960.

18. *Ibid.,* Nov. 29, 1960; July 6, 1961.

19. Priestley, p. 317.

20. Olivier, p. 250.

21. French Union Assembly debates, May 25, 1949.

22. Comte, "Les Communes Malgaches," p. 33.

23. See Mangin, "L'Organisation Judiciaire des Etats d'Afrique et de Madagascar."

24. French Union Assembly debates, Jan. 12, 1954.

25. Minutes of the representative assembly, Jan. 19 and Nov. 29, 1960, and May 18, 1961. See also Guth, "L'Institut d'Etudes Judiciaires Malgaches."

26. Minutes of the representative assembly, June 1, 1959; minutes of the senate, Dec. 3, 1959.

27. Guth, "Aspects Humains et Juridiques du Délit d'Usure à Madagascar," p. 704.

28. Minutes of the representative assembly, Dec. 21, 1957; April 9, 1958; Feb. 19 and Oct. 23, 1959.

Chapter twelve

1. Decary, "Madagascar et Dépendances," p. 75.

2. French Union Assembly debates, March 9, 1954.

3. "Perspectives Stratégiques et Réalisations Economiques."

4. *Le Monde,* June 26–27, 1960.

5. *Ibid.,* Aug. 20, 1958.

6. *Marchés Tropicaux,* May 9, 1964.

7. P. Decraene, writing in *Le Monde,* May 22, 1964.

8. National Assembly debates, May 9, 1947; French Union Assembly debates, March 18, 1949.

9. French Union Assembly debates, May 1, 1949.

10. *Ibid.,* May 25, 1949.

11. Minutes of the representative assembly, June 29, 1961.

12. *Le Monde,* Feb. 18, 1965.

13. *Ibid.,* May 22, 1964.

14. See Orlova, and *Mizan Newsletter,* April 1963.

15. Bartoli, "L'Opération Communauté à Madagascar."

16. Jumeaux, "Essai d'Analyse du Nationalisme Malgache."

17. *Nice-Matin,* May 21, 1961.

18. *Le Monde,* Jan. 19, 1963; *Marchés Tropicaux,* March 2 and June 1, 1963.

19. *Marchés Tropicaux,* May 11, 1963.
20. Tsiranana's speech to the Parliament, Oct. 6, 1964.
21. Interview with President Tsiranana, *Le Monde,* Jan. 24, 1964.
22. *Le Monde,* Oct. 27, 1960.
23. *Le Monde Diplomatique,* Nov. 1961.
24. Paris radio broadcast, March 23, 1961.
25. *West Africa,* July 25, 1964.
26. Agence France Presse dispatch, Addis Ababa, May 26, 1963.
27. *Marchés Tropicaux,* Aug. 1, 1964.

Chapter thirteen

1. Paulian, p. 55.
2. Ruud, p. 300.
3. P. and R. Gosset, p. 239.
4. Andrianamanjato, *Le Tsiny et le Tody dans la Pensée Malgache.*
5. See comments on works by Ferrand and others in Kent, *From Madagascar to the Malagasy Republic,* pp. 160–61.
6. Delval, "L'Islam à Madagascar," and Letourneau, "Aperçu sur les Musulmans des Territoires de la Communauté dans l'Océan Indien."
7. Pasteur G. Mondain, "L'Oeuvre des Missions Chrétiennes," in Guernier, II, 228–30.
8. Hardyman, *Madagascar on the Move,* p. 115.
9. Sibree, p. 288.
10. Deschamps, *Histoire de Madagascar,* p. 256.
11. Hyet, p. 144.
12. Bekker, "Cheminements vers l'Unité Ecclésiastique à Madagascar."
13. N. Rakotomalala, "Problèmes des Mouvements de Jeunesse Face à l'Evolution de Madagascar."
14. Malagasy Republic, *Economie Malgache: Evolution 1950–1960.*
15. Fournier, p. 183.
16. N. Rakotomalala, "Problèmes des Mouvements de Jeunesse Face à l'Evolution de Madagascar."
17. Dronne, "La Situation à Madagascar."
18. Boudry, *Jean-Joseph Rabearivelo et la Mort,* p. 32.
19. *La Croix,* Oct. 5, 1951.
20. *Le Monde,* Jan. 26, 1954.
21. Jumeaux, "Essai d'Analyse du Nationalisme Malgache."
22. See assembly minutes for April 27, April 28, and May 28, 1959.

Chapter fourteen

1. Deschamps, *Histoire de Madagascar,* p. 220.
2. Dandouau and Chapus, p. 282.
3. *Ibid.,* p. 280; also Mannoni, "L'Enseignement," p. 222.
4. French Union Assembly debates, April 10, 1951.
5. *Afrique* (Paris), January 1962; *Marchés Tropicaux,* Sept. 22, 1962.
6. Malagasy Republic, *Economie Malgache,* p. 9.
7. Minutes of the assembly, Nov. 5, 1957.
8. *Ibid.,* May 8, 1958.

9. For a debate by Malagasys on the merits and lacks of their own language, see *ibid.,* July 8, 1957.

10. French Union Assembly debates, Feb. 19, 1957.

11. Minutes of the assembly, April 16, 1958.

12. *Marchés Coloniaux,* Jan. 28, 1950.

13. French Union Assembly debates, Feb. 22, 1951.

14. Minutes of the assembly, Oct. 27, 1954.

15. Deschamps, *Histoire de Madagascar,* p. 309.

16. Minutes of the assembly, June 20, 1961.

17. *Ibid.,* May 8, 1958.

18. *L'Afrique d'Expression Française et Madagascar,* No. 409, p. 138.

19. Minutes of the representative assembly, April 16, 1958.

20. *Ibid.,* April 16 and 17, 1958, and Feb. 11 and 19, 1959.

21. French Union Assembly debates, May 20, 1949.

22. Hatzfeld, *Madagascar,* p. 58.

23. *Marchés Coloniaux,* July 31, 1954; *Chroniques d'Outre-Mer,* Aug.–Sept. 1954.

24. J. Auber, "L'Ecole Technique de Madagascar," *Revue de Madagascar,* 2me trimestre 1960, p. 49.

25. Malagasy Republic, *Economie Malgache,* p. 47; *L'Afrique d'Expression Française et Madagascar,* p. 138.

26. Minutes of the assembly, April 9, 1958.

27. *Ibid.,* Sept. 4, 1959.

28. French Union Assembly debates, Nov. 8, 1949, and Feb. 17, 1950.

29. *Le Monde,* March 1, 1964.

30. Malagasy Republic, *Economie Malgache,* p. 48.

31. N. Rakotomalala, "Problèmes des Mouvements de Jeunesse Face à l'Evolution de Madagascar."

32. Ancian, "Madagascar à la Recherche du Temps Perdu."

33. Kent, "Malagasy Republic," p. 264.   34. *Marchés Coloniaux,* July 22, 1950.

35. Minutes of the assembly, July 8, 1957.   36. *Ibid.,* Dec. 21, 1957.

37. *Ibid.,* Jan. 19, 1960.   38. *Ibid.,* Dec. 21, 1957.

39. *Marchés Tropicaux,* Oct. 29, 1960.   40. *Ibid.,* Aug. 24, 1963.

41. M. Daumet, "La Bibliothèque Nationale," *Revue de Madagascar,* 3me trimestre 1961.

42. Decary, "Madagascar et Dépendances," p. 93.

43. For a description of these and similar works, see Thiout, p. 65.

Chapter fifteen

1. Dandouau and Chapus, p. 286.

2. G. Dieux, "L'Imprimerie Officielle de Madagascar," *Revue de Madagascar,* 4me trimestre 1958.

3. For a survey of the literature, see H. Randzavola, "La Littérature Malgache," in Guernier, II, 219–24.

4. *Marchés Tropicaux,* Aug. 18, 1962.

5. *Lumière,* Feb. 10, 1961.

6. See Poisson, "Petite Histoire de la Presse à Madagascar."

7. Boudry, "J'ai Temoigné au Procès de Madagascar."

8. Thiout, p. 128.

9. *Marchés Tropicaux,* Sept. 5, 1964.

10. Madagascar, Gouvernement-général, *Plan de Développement Economique et Social, 1938–39,* p. 77.

11. French Union Assembly debates, Nov. 9, 1951.

12. Minutes of the assembly, Dec. 10, 1956.

13. Minutes of the permanent commission of the assembly, Feb. 28, 1958.

14. Kent, "Malagasy Republic," pp. 264–65.

15. Minutes of the assembly, July 7, 1961.

16. *Afrique,* March 1962.

Chapter sixteen

1. Gallieni, *Neuf Ans à Madagascar,* p. 272.

2. See Madagascar, *Délégations Economiques et Financières,* minutes for the session of Oct. 20, 1938.

3. An abridged version of the Rotival plan, entitled "Essai de Planification de Madagascar," was published at Tananarive in 1952. For a criticism of this plan, see Gendarme, p. 140.

4. Speech to the representative assembly, April 1, 1954.

5. See Dumont, *Evolution des Campagnes Malgaches* and "Les Principales Conditions d'un Rapide Développement de l'Agriculture Malgache."

6. *Marchés Tropicaux,* May 23, 1964.

Chapter seventeen

1. The writers are indebted for much of the information in this section to Hubert Deschamps's *Les Migrations Intérieures à Madagascar.*

2. Gendarme, p. 84.

3. See Roberts, Vol. 2, pp. 416 *et seq.*

4. Louis Chevalier, *Madagascar: Populations et Ressources.*

5. *Marchés Tropicaux,* Dec. 29, 1962.

6. French Union Assembly debates, June 26, 1956.

7. See minutes of the assembly, Dec. 7, 1960, for a debate on the status of *métis.*

8. See "Madagascar et la Grèce," *Revue de Madagascar,* 4me trimestre 1960.

9. Delval, "L'Islam à Madagascar."

10. *Ibid.*

11. *Chroniques d'Outre-Mer,* November 1957.

12. Deschamps, *Les Migrations Intérieures à Madagascar,* p. 145.

13. See Constituent Assembly debates, Sept. 10, 1946; National Assembly debates, March 18, 1958.

14. Minutes of the assembly, Dec. 21, 1957.

15. *Marchés Tropicaux,* Jan. 6, 1962.

16. Ratsima, "Les Congrégations Chinoises de Madagascar."

17. For much of the information in this section the writers are indebted to the manuscript by Delval, "L'Islam à Madagascar."

18. Hatzfeld, *Madagascar,* p. 48.

19. P. Launois, *Madagascar, Hier et Aujourd'hui* (Paris, 1947), p. 212.

20. Gayet, "Immigrations Asiatiques à Madagascar."
21. P. Guy, "La Nationalité des Descendants d'Asiatiques Nés à Madagascar," *Revue Juridique et Politique de l'Union Française,* January-March 1958.
22. Gayet, "Immigrations Asiatiques à Madagascar."
23. Quoted in French Union Assembly debates, March 7 and May 5, 1955.
24. For details regarding urban conditions in various Madagascar towns, see French Union Assembly debates, July 7, 1949; Decary, "Madagascar," p. 95; L. Wagemans, *Tananarive: La Banlieue Bouge* (Toulouse, 1951), p. 67 *et seq.*; Chapus, "Tuléar, Ville des Dunes"; Decary, "Fort-Dauphin"; G. de Bournat, "L'Habitat à Madagascar," *Marchés Coloniaux,* Nov. 21, 1953; "Fianarantsoa," *Marchés Coloniaux,* Oct. 29, 1955; and articles on housing and urbanization in *Marchés Coloniaux,* Nov. 5, 1955, and Feb. 18, 1956, and in *Marchés Tropicaux,* Nov. 9, 1957, and July 19 and 26, 1958.
25. See *Marchés Tropicaux,* Nov. 9, 1957.
26. See assembly debates for Jan. 29, 1959, and Jan. 20, 1960.

Chapter eighteen

1. Deschamps, *Histoire de Madagascar,* p. 277.
2. Roberts, Vol. 2, p. 414.
3. Deschamps, *Histoire de Madagascar,* p. 259.
4. Minutes of the assembly, Feb. 16, 1959.
5. Gendarme, p. 97.
6. *Marchés Tropicaux,* Nov. 9, 1957.
7. Minutes of the assembly, Jan. 30, 1957, and Nov. 29, 1960.
8. Malagasy Republic, *Economie Malgache,* p. 199.
9. Hapgood, *Madagascar.* Institute of Current World Affairs, New York, May 3, 1963.
10. Guernier, II, 133–35.
11. Minutes of the assembly, May 5, 1958.
12. Malagasy Republic, *Economie Malgache,* p. 197.
13. *Marchés Coloniaux,* May 18, 1946.
14. *Ibid.,* Feb. 7, March 7, and April 11, 1953.
15. Gendarme, p. 92.

Chapter nineteen

1. Malagasy Republic, *Economie Malgache,* p. 267.
2. *Marchés Coloniaux,* Jan. 29, 1949.
3. The French Union Assembly, on July 31, 1948, and May 20, 1949; the National Assembly, on Nov. 29 and Dec. 1, 1949; and the Conseil de la République, on Feb. 16, 1950.
4. Guernier, II, 118–19.
5. Malagasy Republic, *Economie Malgache,* p. 273.
6. *Marchés Coloniaux,* April 30, 1950.
7. *Marchés Tropicaux,* Nov. 9, 1957.
8. Minutes of the assembly, Dec. 4, 1957, and March 31, 1958.
9. Faure, "Introduction à l'Etude de la Concentration Monopoliste à Madagascar."
10. *L'Afrique d'Expression Française et Madagascar,* No. 409, March 1964, p. 134.
11. Gendarme, p. 58.

12. *Chroniques d'Outre-Mer,* April 1957.

13. A. Perodeau, "Les Investissements et le Problème de l'Expansion Economique," *Cahiers de l'Institut de Science Economique Appliquée,* Cahier No. 17, Série F (Paris, 1962), pp. 131–56.

14. E. S. Munger, *After the Rebellion* (pamphlet, Institute of Current World Affairs, New York), Jan. 20, 1953.

15. *La Vie Française,* Feb. 14, 1958.   16. *Marchés Coloniaux,* Dec. 29, 1956.

17. *Marchés Tropicaux,* Nov. 11, 1961.   18. *Ibid.,* Feb. 22, 1964.

19. Deschamps, *Histoire de Madagascar,* p. 208.

20. Priestley, p. 312.

21. Deschamps, *Histoire de Madagascar,* p. 251.

22. Quoted by Angammarre, p. 214.

23. H. Leroux, "Le Régime Fiscal des Entreprises," *Marchés Coloniaux,* April 17, 1954.

24. *Marchés Coloniaux,* Oct. 20, 1956.

25. Minutes of the assembly, Dec. 19, 1957, and April 9, 1958.

26. *Ibid.,* June 9, 1959.

27. Minutes of the national assembly, Nov. 3, 1962.

28. *Marchés Tropicaux,* Feb. 1, 1964.

Chapter twenty

1. Malagasy Republic, *Economie Malgache,* p. 82.

2. Published in the *Bulletin de Madagascar,* April, June, and July, 1957.

3. *Ibid.,* May 1958.

4. Malagasy Republic, *Economie Malgache,* p. 10.

5. *Ibid.,* p. 107.

6. See Humblot, "Le Problème des Concessions et les Problèmes Agraires de l'Afrique Tropicale et de Madagascar."

7. See appendixes to preliminary report by Dumont, "Les Principales Conditions d'un Rapide Développement de l'Agriculture Malgache."

8. Deschamps, *Histoire de Madagascar,* p. 210.

9. Murdock, p. 219.

10. Deschamps, *Histoire de Madagascar,* p. 210.

11. Roberts, II, 407.

12. Decary, "Madagascar et Dépendances," p. 146.

13. Deschamps, *Histoire de Madagascar,* p. 276.

14. Tardon, "Le Colonat Européen à Madagascar."

15. For analyses of this project and comments concerning it, see Chevalier; French Union Assembly debates, Nov. 13, 1953, Dec. 30, 1954, and Nov. 24, 1955; National Assembly debates, Dec. 16 and 17, 1954; and territorial assembly minutes, April 17, 1954.

16. See Dumont, *Evolution des Campagnes Malgaches,* p. 120, and "Les Principales Conditions d'un Rapide Développement de l'Agriculture Malgache," pp. 47–64; also *Marchés Tropicaux,* Sept. 29, 1962.

17. Malagasy Republic, *Economie Malgache,* p. 107. For further details, see Gendarme, p. 129.

18. See minutes of the assembly, Nov. 22, 1957, April 27, 1958, and April 29, 1959.

19. See assembly debates of Dec. 9, 1960, and June 30, 1961.

20. Le Thomas, in Guernier, I, 263–74.

21. See Humblot; also see speech by Bargues to the assembly, Sept. 18, 1952.

22. Minutes of the territorial assembly, April 28–29, 1958.

23. C. Frappa, "La Protection des Cultures," in Guernier, I, 353.

24. Minutes of the assembly, May 7, 1958.

25. *Ibid.,* April 14, 1958.

26. Malagasy Republic, *Economie Malgache,* p. 109.

27. Minutes of the assembly, Nov. 26, 1957.

28. C. Frappa, "La Protection des Cultures," in Guernier, I, 355.

29. *Marchés Coloniaux,* April 17, 1954, and Sept. 24, 1955.

30. Priestley, p. 326.

31. Minutes of the assembly, April 13, 1950.

32. French Union Assembly debates, June 5, 1956.

33. *Ibid.* See also *Bulletin de Madagascar,* Sept. 1, 1950.

34. Malagasy Republic, *Economie Malgache,* p. 48.

35. Chauffour, "Grains et Féculents," in Guernier, I, 285–89.

36. Gendarme, p. 16.

37. *Marchés Tropicaux,* Nov. 15, 1958.

38. *Ibid.,* Jan. 19, 1963.

39. *Ibid.,* Nov. 15, 1958.

40. See speech by Randretsa Rasafy, a Merina lawyer, in the French Union Assembly, Nov. 3, 1950.

41. Malagasy Republic, *Economie Malgache,* p. 82.

42. L. Dussel, "Produits Malgaches," *Bulletin de Madagascar,* June 1962.

43. *Marchés Tropicaux,* Nov. 9, 1957.

44. *Ibid.,* July 28, 1962.

45. Malagasy Republic, *Economie Malgache,* p. 89.

46. *Marchés Tropicaux,* June 1, 1963.

47. Gendarme, p. 42.

48. L. Dussel, "Produits Malgaches," *Bulletin de Madagascar,* June 1962.

49. Malagasy Republic, *Economie Malgache,* p. 89.

50. *Marchés Tropicaux,* Sept. 15, 1962.

51. *Ibid.,* Nov. 25, 1961; March 24, 1962.

52. Malagasy Republic, *Economie Malgache,* p. 101.

53. *Marchés Coloniaux,* June 26, 1954.

54. Minutes of the assembly, Dec. 7, 1960.

55. Chauffour, "Plantes Oléagineuses," in Guernier, I, 335.

56. Malagasy Republic, *Economie Malgache,* p. 82.

57. *Marchés Coloniaux,* Sept. 25 and Oct. 9, 1954.

58. Minutes of the assembly, April 14, 1958.

59. Malagasy Republic, *Economie Malgache,* p. 82.

60. Chauffour, "Les Plantes Saccharifères," in Guernier, I, 328.

61. French Union Assembly debates, June 2, 1949.

62. *Marchés Tropicaux,* Aug. 1, 1964.

63. *Marchés Coloniaux,* Dec. 21, 1951, and Jan. 19, 1957.

64. Minutes of the assembly, July 3, 1957, and May 12, 1958.

65. *Ibid.,* Nov. 6, 1959, and June 21, 1961.

66. Chauffour, "Plantes Textiles et Tabac," in Guernier, I, 339; *Marchés Coloniaux,* July 28, 1951.

67. Minutes of the assembly, Jan. 30, 1959.

68. *Bulletin de Madagascar,* January 1962.
69. Minutes of the assembly, Nov. 30, 1959, and of the Senate, Nov. 28, 1959.
70. Malagasy Republic, *Economie Malgache,* p. 103.
71. *Ibid.,* p. 104.
72. Minutes of the assembly, June 20, 1961.
73. See Thiout, p. 141.
74. For an amusing description of the vanilla trade at Antalaha, see Stratton, pp. 1–67.
75. Malagasy Republic, *Economie Malgache,* p. 95.
76. *Bulletin de Madagascar,* January 1962.
77. *New York Times,* Nov. 9, 1959.
78. *Marchés Tropicaux,* May 23, 1964.
79. Minutes of the assembly, April 29, 1958.
80. Malagasy Republic, *Economie Malgache,* p. 97.
81. *Marchés Tropicaux,* Dec. 21, 1957.
82. *Ibid.,* Sept. 8, 1962.
83. *Ibid.,* Oct. 3, 1964.
84. Tourneur, "Epices et Aromates," in Guernier, I, 310–21.
85. Malagasy Republic, *Economie Malgache,* pp. 82–97.
86. *Ibid.,* p. 100.
87. Ciolina and Tourneur, in Guernier, I, 299–309.
88. See speech by Governor Bargues to the assembly, Aug. 16, 1950.
89. *Marchés Coloniaux,* Aug. 30, 1952.
90. *Marchés Tropicaux,* Nov. 9, 1957.
91. Malagasy Republic, *Economie Malgache,* p. 123.
92. Decary, *Moeurs et Coutumes des Malgaches,* p. 120.
93. Deschamps, *Madagascar,* p. 111.
94. *Marchés Coloniaux,* March 11, 1950, and April 17, 1954.
95. French Union Assembly debates, Feb. 20, 1958.
96. Madagascar Senate debates, Dec. 4, 1959.
97. Malagasy Republic, *Economie Malgache,* p. 10.
98. *Marchés Tropicaux,* June 1, 1963.
99. *Ibid.,* July 22, 1961.
100. Malagasy Republic, *Economie Malgache,* p. 10.
101. *Marchés Tropicaux,* April 28, 1962.
102. Decary, *Moeurs et Coutumes des Malgaches,* p. 129.
103. *Marchés Coloniaux,* Dec. 10, 1949.
104. Malagasy Republic, *Economie Malgache,* p. 123.
105. Decary, *Moeurs et Coutumes des Malgaches,* p. 129.
106. *Marchés Coloniaux,* Sept. 12, 1953.
107. Decary, *Moeurs et Coutumes des Malgaches,* p. 129.
108. Malagasy Republic, *Economie Malgache,* p. 123.
109. Minutes of the assembly, June 23, 1962.
110. *Ibid.,* Jan. 19, 1960.
111. Malagasy Republic, *Economie Malgache,* p. 123.
112. Deschamps, *Madagascar,* p. 99.
113. Petit, *L'Industrie des Pêches à Madagascar.*
114. Malagasy Republic, *Economie Malgache,* p. 129.
115. *Marchés Coloniaux,* April 17, 1954.

116. *Ibid.,* Nov. 19, 1955.
117. Minutes of the assembly, April 30, 1958.
118. *Ibid.,* Oct. 27, 1954.
119. Malagasy Republic, *Economie Malgache,* p. 130.
120. *Ibid.,* p. 135.
121. Deschamps, *Histoire de Madagascar,* p. 210.
122. Priestley, p. 322.
123. Mouranches, in Guernier, II, 27–34.
124. *La République Malgache* (La Documentation Française, Paris: Notes et Etudes Documentaires, No. 2737), Dec. 23, 1960, p. 24.
125. Minutes of the assembly, April 5, 1951.
126. Malagasy Republic, *Economie Malgache,* p. 133.
127. Minutes of the assembly, April 29, 1958.
128. *La République Malgache,* p. 24.
129. Minutes of the assembly, Jan. 19, 1960.
130. *Marchés Coloniaux,* April 17, 1954.
131. Minutes of the assembly, April 29, 1958.
132. Uhart, "Le Problème Forestier à Madagascar."
133. Minutes of the assembly, Sept. 26, 1961.
134. *Marchés Tropicaux,* Jan. 25, 1964.

Chapter twenty-one

1. In this chapter, most of the statistical data relating to the post-independence period were obtained from Malagasy Republic, *Economie Malgache,* pp. 141, 143, 157–68, and *Europe-France-Outre-Mer,* No. 399, 1963.
2. *Marchés Tropicaux,* April 14 and Sept. 22, 1962.
3. *Ibid.,* Sept. 6, 1962.
4. Minutes of the assembly, June 8, 1962.
5. Apertet, "L'Aménagement Hydro-électrique Mandraka-Tsiazompaniry à Madagascar."
6. *Marchés Tropicaux,* July 9, 1960.
7. *Ibid.,* Oct. 6, 1962.
8. *Ibid.,* June 27, 1964.
9. For the historical information in this section, the writers are indebted to E. Devred's article "Les Mines," Guernier, II, 63–85.
10. Speech of the Minister of Production to the assembly, Dec. 11, 1957.
11. Malagasy Republic, *Economie Malgache,* p. 137.
12. Minutes of the assembly, Jan. 20, 1960.
13. Deschamps, *Histoire de Madagascar,* p. 211.
14. *Marchés Tropicaux,* Aug. 27, 1960.
15. Minutes of the assembly, Jan. 20, 1960.
16. Lacroix, *Minéralogie de Madagascar.*
17. Malagasy Republic, *Economie Malgache,* p. 141.
18. *Marchés Tropicaux,* April 7, 1956; March 31 and Aug. 27, 1962.
19. Malagasy Republic, *Economie Malgache,* p. 140; *Marchés Coloniaux,* Nov. 21, 1953.
20. Malagasy Republic, *Economie Malgache,* p. 143.

21. Minutes of the assembly, April 10 and May 6, 1958.
22. Malagasy Republic, *Economie Malgache*, p. 141.
23. *Marchés Coloniaux,* April 22, 1950; Aug. 30, 1952; and Aug. 4, 1956.
24. Gendarme, p. 23.
25. French Union Assembly debates, May 25, 1949; Jan. 26, 1950; and Feb. 26, 1954. French National Assembly debates, Jan. 26 and March 2, 1950.
26. *Marchés Tropicaux,* Jan. 5, 1963.
27. Malagasy Republic, *Economie Malgache*, p. 162.
28. *Ibid.,* p. 161.
29. *Europe-France-Outre-Mer,* No. 399, 1963.
30. *Marchés Tropicaux,* June 1, 1963.
31. Dumont, *Evolution des Campagnes Malgaches*, p. 127.
32. *Marchés Coloniaux,* June 6, 1953, and *Europe-France-Outre-Mer,* No. 399, 1963.
33. See *Europe-France-Outre-Mer,* No. 399, 1963, and Malagasy Republic, *Economie Malgache*, p. 164.
34. *Marchés Tropicaux,* June 3, 1961.
35. Malagasy Republic, *Economie Malgache*, p. 164.
36. *Bulletin de Madagascar,* January 1962.
37. Malagasy Republic, *Economie Malgache*, p. 168.

Chapter twenty-two

1. For much of the data concerning Madagascar's foreign trade during the period prior to World War II, the writers are indebted to Castel, Guernier, II, 101–14; Deschamps, *Madagascar,* pp. 122–25; and Deschamps, *Histoire de Madagascar,* p. 287.
2. Deschamps, *Madagascar,* p. 125.
3. Prunières, pp. 6–47.
4. Data in this section have been derived to a considerable extent from Malagasy Republic, *Economie Malgache,* pp. 209–43, and from the surveys of Madagascar's foreign trade published in *Marchés Coloniaux* and its successor, *Marchés Tropicaux,* on Oct. 4, 1947; July 31, 1948; Oct. 1, 1949; July 22, 1950; March 31, June 9, and June 23, 1951; Sept. 6, 1952; June 6 and Nov. 7, 1953; Sept. 25, 1954; April 16 and Aug. 27, 1955; Feb. 18 and Dec. 22, 1956; Nov. 9, 1957; Oct. 25, 1958; Feb. 7, 1959; May 14, 1960; March 4 and Aug. 19, 1961; March 24 and May 26, 1962; June 1 and July 20, 1963; and May 9, 1964.
5. Deschamps, *Histoire de Madagascar,* p. 301.
6. Malagasy Republic, *Economie Malgache*, p. 237.
7. Gendarme, p. 64.
8. Ancian, *Budget et Niveau de Vie des Cultivateurs Betsileo,* and "Budgets Familiaux dans l'Imerina et Fianarantsoa," *Bulletin de Madagascar,* April, June, and July 1957 and May 1958.
9. Malagasy Republic, *Economie Malgache,* p. 70.
10. Boiteau, *Contribution à l'Histoire de la Nation Malgache*, p. 233, and Faure, *Introduction à l'Etude de la Concentration Monopoliste à Madagascar.*
11. A. Blanchet, article in *Nice-Matin,* May 23, 1961.
12. Minutes of the French Constituent Assembly, March 21, 1946.
13. See Chevalier, p. 162.
14. See Guernier, II, 101–14; *Marchés Coloniaux,* Jan. 31 and March 20, 1948; A. Soucadaux's speech to the representative assembly, April 16, 1955.

15. *Marchés Tropicaux,* April 28, 1962.
16. French Union Assembly debates, Dec. 27, 1949.
17. *Marchés Tropicaux,* Nov. 2 and Dec. 7, 1957.
18. Minutes of the assembly, Jan. 30, 1959.
19. Malagasy Republic, *Economie Malgache,* p. 265.

Chapter twenty-three

1. Decary, *Moeurs et Coutumes des Malgaches,* p. 39.
2. Condominas, p. 86.
3. Deschamps, *Histoire de Madagascar,* p. 209.
4. *Ibid.,* p. 223.
5. Condominas, p. 92.
6. Kent, *From Madagascar to the Malagasy Republic,* p. 63.
7. Quoted by J. Manicacci, "Le Problème de la Main-d'Oeuvre à Madagascar," Guernier, I, 253.
8. Olivier, p. 86. 9. *Ibid.,* p. 91.
10. Priestley, p. 329. 11. Martin, p. 199.
12. *Madagascar dans la Guerre, Janvier 1943–Décembre 1944* (Tananarive, 1944), pp. 86–96.
13. Speech to the Mixed Franco-Malagasy Commission, Nov. 27, 1944.
14. Coppet, "Le Problème de la Main-d'Oeuvre à Madagascar et ses Nouveaux Aspects."
15. *Marchés Coloniaux,* Aug. 3 and 10, 1946.
16. French Union Assembly debates, Feb. 9, 1949.
17. See French Union Assembly debates, Feb. 17 and May 29 and 31, 1949, and National Assembly debates, Nov. 22, 1952.
18. Governor Bargues's speech to the representative assembly, Jan. 1, 1954.
19. Decary, "La Notion du Travail chez les Malgaches."
20. Boiteau, *Contribution à l'Histoire de la Nation Malgache,* p. 315.
21. *Ibid.,* pp. 352–58. 22. *Ibid.,* p. 354.
23. Mannoni, p. 69. 24. *Marchés Coloniaux,* Dec. 31, 1949.
25. *Ibid.,* Sept. 11, 1954. 26. *Ibid.,* June 1 and July 26, 1946.
27. Boiteau, *Contribution à l'Histoire de la Nation Malgache,* p. 269.
28. See *Bulletin de Madagascar,* August 1954.
29. Minutes of the assembly, April 29 and Nov. 25, 1959.
30. French Union Assembly debates, May 20, 1949.
31. *Marchés Coloniaux,* March 17, 1951.
32. Minutes of the representative assembly, July 6, 1957, and of the French National Assembly, Sept. 7, 1957.
33. Minutes of the representative assembly, May 9, 1958.
34. *Ibid.,* Nov. 28, 1957.
35. *Marchés Tropicaux,* Dec. 14, 1957.
36. Deschamps, *Histoire de Madagascar,* p. 303.
37. *L'Afrique d'Expression Française,* No. 409, March 1964.
38. Malagasy Republic, *Economie Malgache,* p. 53.
39. *Marchés Tropicaux,* Jan. 21, 1961.
40. *Ibid.,* Feb. 10, 1961. 41. *Ibid.,* April 28, 1962.
42. *Ibid.,* Oct. 13, 1962. 43. *Ibid.,* Jan. 14, 1961.

GLOSSARY OF MALAGASY TERMS

aloalo	Carved-wood tomb decoration of the Mahafaly tribe
andevo	Slave, lowest Merina caste
andriana	Noble, highest Merina caste
angady	Long-handled agricultural implement resembling a spade
antsy	Knife
baibo (or *baiboho*)	Term used by the Sakalava tribe, denoting fertile land made up of alluvial deposits left by river floods
fady	Taboo
fahavalo	Bandits; the term applied to rebels in the late-nineteenth-century uprising against the French occupation forces
famadihana	Ceremony of washing and reclothing the dead (*retournement des morts*)
fanjakana	The government or administration
filanzane	Chair on poles, carried by porters; a sort of palanquin, used in the old days by the aristocracy and by Europeans
fokonolona	Village community having a common ancestor
hova	Merina freeman
kabary	"Vocal expression"; discourses by Merina rulers or officials; also meetings where discourses were held
lamba	Long scarf; a distinctive part of the dress of peoples of the high plateaus
madinika	Governor under the Merina monarchy
mpiadidy	Village headman
pangalanes	Rocky outcrops in waterways
rabanes	Mats woven of raffia
ray amandreny	Council of village elders
rova	Fortress, palace
sikidy	Method of divining the future and determining the best course of action; of Arab origin, by way of the Comoro Islands
tanety	Sloping hillside

tavy	Practice of fertilizing land by burning vegetation
tody	Sense of security resulting from overcoming many difficulties
tsiny	Censure, reproach, retribution
vadintany	Category of officials of the Merina government
vary lava	High-quality variety of rice
vazaha	Europeans in general and the French in particular
vazimba	Early inhabitants of Madagascar, probably immigrants from the east coast of Africa; in Merina legend the term also denotes spirits of the bush and traditional masters of the land
zoma	Central market at Tananarive

BIBLIOGRAPHY

L'Afrique d'Expression Française et Madagascar (special numbers of *Europe-France-Outre-Mer*), No. 399, 1963; No. 409, 1964.

Albertini, G. "Le Communisme à Madagascar," *Est et Ouest,* April 16–30, 1957.

——— "Le Communisme à Madagascar en 1960," *Est et Ouest,* April 1–15, 1960.

——— "Les Communistes et les Elections à Madagascar," *Est et Ouest,* Nov. 1–15, 1960.

——— "Bilan d'Activité du P. C. Malgache," *Est et Ouest,* Nov. 1–15, 1961.

Alfano, V. P. "La Modernisation des Chemins de Fer Malgaches," *Marchés Coloniaux,* Nov. 17, 1951.

Allain, C. "Les Chambres de Commerce, d'Industrie, et d'Agriculture," in Guernier, II, 120.

Ancian, G. "Budget et Niveau de Vie des Cultivateurs Betsileo" (typescript). C.H.E.A.M., Paris, 1954.

——— "Madagascar à la Recherche du Temps Perdu," *Revue Militaire d'Information,* April 1957.

Andrianamanjato, R. *Le Tsiny et le Tody dans la Pensée Malgache.* Paris, 1957.

Andrianaranhinjaka, L. X. "Les Partis Politiques Malgaches," *Lumière,* Feb. 19 and 26, March 4, 11, 18, and 25, 1960.

——— "La Presse Malgache," *Lumière,* Feb. 10, 17, and 24, and March 3, 1961.

Angammarre, R. "Budget et Impôts," in Guernier, I, 212.

Annet, A. L. *Aux Heures Troublées de l'Afrique Française, 1939–1943.* Paris, 1952.

Apertet, J. "L'Aménagement Hydro-électrique Mandraka-Tsiazompaniry à Madagascar," *Encyclopédie Mensuelle d'Outre-Mer,* May 1956.

Arbousset, F. *Le Fokon'olona à Madagascar.* Paris, 1950.

Aspects Actuels et Perspectives de l'Economie de Madagascar. Institut de Science Economique Appliquée (Paris), Cahiers Série F, 1962.

Augagneur, V. *Erreurs et Brutalités Coloniales.* Paris, 1927.

Aujoulat, L. P. *Discours Prononcé à l'Occasion de la Réception Solonelle de M. le Docteur L. P. Aujoulat à l'Assemblée Représentative de Madagascar.* Tananarive, May 1950.

Bailly, P. "Le Commerce Extérieur de Madagascar en 1956," *Bulletin de Madagascar,* May 1957.

Baron, R. "L'Immigration Karany ou Indo-Pakistanaise à Madagascar," *L'Afrique et l'Asie,* 4e trimestre, 1954.

Bartoli, F. "L'Opération Communauté à Madagascar," *Quatrième Internationale,* July 1961.

Bastian, G. "La Politique Economique de la République Malgache," *Chroniques d'Outre-Mer,* July–Sept. 1961.

Baumont, J.-C. "Le Diagnostic du Sous-Développement Malgache," *Croissance des Jeunes Nations,* Oct. 1963.

Beaudouard, G. "Mica," *Encyclopédie Mensuelle d'Outre-Mer,* Nov. 1953.

Bekker, R. "Cheminements vers l'Unité Ecclésiastique à Madagascar," *Monde non Chrétien,* July–Sept. 1949.

Bilbao, R. "L'Organisation Judiciaire de la République Malgache," *Recueil Penant,* Jan.–March 1961.

Blanc, P. "Les Réformes Malgaches," *Recueil Penant,* June–July–Aug. 1961.

Boiteau, P. *Contribution à l'Histoire de la Nation Malgache.* Paris, 1958.

——— "Où en est Madagascar?" *Démocratie Nouvelle,* Dec. 1961.

Bora, P. D. "La Justice à Madagascar" (typescript). E.N.F.O.M., 1958–59.

Boudou, A. *Les Jésuites à Madagascar au XIXe Siècle.* 2 vols. Paris, 1940.

Boudry, R. "Art et Artisanat Malgaches," in Guernier, II, 199.

——— *Jean-Joseph Rabearivelo et la Mort.* Paris, 1958.

——— "Le Problème Malgache," *Esprit,* Feb. 1948.

——— "J'ai Témoigné au Procès de Madagascar," *Esprit,* Jan. 1949.

Bouriquet, G. *Le Vanillier et la Vanille dans le Monde.* Paris, 1954.

Boussenot, G. "Le Drame Malgache," *Revue Politique et Parlementaire,* May 1947.

Brunet, L. *L'Oeuvre de la France à Madagascar; la Conquête—l'Organisation—le Général Gallieni.* Paris, 1903.

"Budgets Familiaux dans l'Imerina," *Bulletin de Madagascar,* May 1958. (A similar study for Fianarantsoa province appeared in issues of April, June, and July, 1957.)

Bugaud, J. "La Modernisation du Paysannat à Madagascar," *Chroniques d'Outre-Mer,* June 1954.

Bulletin (Académie Malgache, Tananarive), 1902—.

Bulletin de Madagascar (Tananarive), 1954—.

Carle, R. "La Langue Malgache et l'Enseignement," *Chroniques d'Outre-Mer,* April 1956.

Casseville, Gen. Henry de. *L'Ile Ensanglantée.* Paris, 1948.

Castel, R. "Commerce Extérieur," in Guernier, II, 101.

Chapus, G. S. *80 Ans d'Influence Européenne en Imerina.* Paris, 1925.

——— "Tuléar, Ville des Dunes," *Encyclopédie Mensuelle d'Outre-Mer,* April 1953.

Chapus, G. S., and A. Dandouau. *Manuel d'Histoire de Madagascar,* Paris, 1961.

Chapus, G. S., and G. Mondain. *Rainilaiarivony.* Paris, 1953.

Chauffour, P. "Grains et Féculents," "Les Plantes Saccharifères," "Plantes Oléagineuses," "Plantes Textiles et Tabac," and "La Production Fruitière," in Guernier, I, 285, 328, 335, 339, 347.

Chevalier, L. *Madagascar: Populations et Ressources.* Paris, 1952.

Ciolina, F. "Organisation Technique et Outillage," in Guernier, I, 359.

——— "La Mécanisation de l'Agriculture à Madagascar," *Marchés Coloniaux,* Sept. 30, 1950.

——— "Développement Economique de Diverses Zones de Madagascar dans le Cadre du Plan," *Chroniques d'Outre-Mer,* Aug.–Sept. 1954.

Ciolina, F., and M. Tourneur. "Café et Cacao," in Guernier, I, 299.

Clergue, J. P. "Action Rurale dans l'Extrême-Sud Malgache" (typescript), E.N.F.O.M., Feb. 1959.

Colin, P. *Aspects de l'Ame Malgache.* Paris, 1959.

Comte, J. "Situation Politique et Partis Politiques à Madagascar" (typescript). C.H.E.A.M., Dec. 1959.

―――― "Les Communes Malgaches" (typescript). C.H.E.A.M., Oct. 1962.

Condamy, C. A. L. *L'Insurrection dans le Sud de Madagascar (1904–1905).* Paris, 1914.

Condominas, G. *Fokon'olona et Collectivités Rurales en Imerina.* Paris, 1960.

Conti-Zhendre, P. "Mémoire sur les Communes Rurales dans la République Malgache" (typescript). C.H.E.A.M., April 1961.

Coppet, M. de. "Le Problème de la Main-d'Oeuvre à Madagascar et ses Nouveaux Aspects," *Revue Internationale de Travail,* March 1949.

Cotte, P. V. *Regardons Vivre une Tribu Malgache, les Betsimisaraka.* Paris, 1947.

"Les CRAM au Secours du Paysannat Malgache," *L'Economie,* Dec. 17, 1954.

Crespin, Cdt., and Capt. Rabotovao. "Notice à l'Usage des Officiers Appelés à Servir à Madagascar" (mimeo.). Centre Militaire d'Information et de Spécialisation pour l'Outre-Mer, Paris, Sept. 1961.

Croft-Cooke, R. *The Blood Red Island.* London, 1953.

Cros, L. *Madagascar pour Tous.* Paris, 1922.

Dama Ntsoha. *Histoire Politique et Réligieuse des Malgaches.* Tananarive, 1952.

Dandouau, A., and G. S. Chapus. *Histoire des Populations de Madagascar.* Paris, 1952.

Danel, B. C. "Les Evènements de Madagascar" (typescript). E.N.F.O.M., 1948–49.

Darsac, R. "Contradictions et Partis Malgaches," *Revue d'Action Populaire,* July–Aug. 1958.

Debousset, O. *L'Organisation Municipale à Madagascar.* Paris, 1942.

Decary, R. *L'Androy (extrême sud de Madagascar).* 2 vols. Paris, 1930–33.

―――― *Moeurs et Coutumes des Malgaches.* Paris, 1951.

―――― "Les Contacts de Civilisations et les Problèmes Fonciers à Madagascar," *Civilisations,* 1952.

―――― "Madagascar et Dépendances," in *La France de l'Océan Indien: Madagascar, les Comores, la Côte Française des Somalis, l'Inde Française.* Paris, 1952, pp. 7–225.

―――― "Fort-Dauphin," *Encyclopédie Mensuelle d'Outre-Mer,* June 1954.

―――― "Pays Sakalava," *Encyclopédie Mensuelle d'Outre-Mer,* October 1954.

―――― "Démographie," *Encyclopédie Mensuelle d'Outre-Mer,* November 1954.

―――― "La Notion du Travail chez les Malgaches," *Encyclopédie Mensuelle d'Outre-Mer,* July–Aug. 1956.

―――― "La Pisciculture à Madagascar," *Encyclopédie Mensuelle d'Outre-Mer,* January 1957.

―――― *L'Habitat à Madagascar.* Pau, 1958.

―――― *La Mort et les Coutumes Funéraires à Madagascar.* Paris, 1962.

Decraene, P. "Madagascar, République-Soeur," *Le Monde,* Aug. 11, 12, 13, 1959.

―――― "Madagascar, An VII de la République," *Le Monde,* May 20, 21, 22, 23, 1964.

Defos du Rau, J., "Le Sisal dans le Sud Malgache," *Les Cahiers d'Outre-Mer,* Jan.–March 1959.

Delélée-Desloges, J. G. *Madagascar et Dépendances.* Paris, 1931.

Delteil, P. *Le Fokon'olona et les Conventions de Fokon'olona.* Paris, 1931.

Delval, R. "L'Islam à Madagascar" (mimeo.). C.H.E.A.M., Dec. 1953.

Deschamps, H. J. *Les Antaisaka.* Tananarive, 1936.

―――― *Madagascar.* 2d ed. Paris, 1951.

―――― *Les Migrations Intérieures (Passées et Présentes) à Madagascar.* Paris, 1959.

―――― *Histoire de Madagascar.* Paris, 1960.

Deschamps, H. J., and P. Chauvet. *Gallieni, Pacificateur.* Paris, 1949.

Deschamps, H. J., and S. Vianès. *Les Malgaches du Sud-est: Antemoro, Antesaka, Antambahoaka* ... Paris, 1959.

Devic, J. *Tananarive; Essai sur Ses Origines, Son Développement, Son Etat Actuel.* Tananarive, 1952.

Devred, E. "Les Mines," in Guernier, II, 63.

Dronne, R. "La Situation à Madagascar," *Marchés Coloniaux,* July 22, 1950.

Dubois, H. *Monographie des Betsileo (Madagascar).* Paris, 1938.

—— "La Réligion Malgache," *Cahiers Charles de Foucauld.* Vol. 21, 1951.

Dubosc de Pesquidoux, Capt. R. "Essai de Comparaison entre les Races de Madagascar" (typescript). C.H.E.A.M., 1961.

Duignan, P. *Madagascar (the Malagasy Republic). A List of Materials in the African Collections of Stanford University and the Hoover Institution on War, Revolution and Peace.* Stanford, Calif., 1962.

Dumont, R. *Evolution des Campagnes Malgaches.* Tananarive, 1959.

—— "Les Principales Conditions d'un Rapide Développement de l'Agriculture Malgache" (mimeo.). Tananarive, Aug.–Sept. 1961.

Ellis, W. *History of Madagascar.* 2 vols. London, 1838.

Faublee, J. *La Cohésion des Sociétés Bara.* Paris, 1954.

—— *Les Esprits de la Vie à Madagascar.* Paris, 1954.

Faure, R. "Introduction à l'Etude de la Concentration Monopoliste à Madagascar" (typescript). E.N.F.O.M., 1946–47.

Fenard, G. *Les Indigènes Fonctionnaires à Madagascar.* Paris, 1939.

Ferrand, G. *Les Musulmans à Madagascar et aux Iles Comores.* 3 vols. Paris, 1891–1902.

—— "Madagascar," *Encyclopédie de l'Islam.* Vol. III. Paris, 1936.

Fertil, G. "Le Cabotage à Madagascar," *Bulletin de Madagascar,* June 1962.

Feuer, G. "Madagascar: Etat des Travaux," *Revue Française de Science Politique,* Dec. 1962.

Fontanière, J. de. "L'Evolution des Méthodes de Mise en Valeur au Cours des Deux Derniers Siècles," *Marchés Coloniaux,* April 17, 1954.

—— "La Situation de l'Industrie," *Marchés Tropicaux,* Nov. 9, 1957.

Fournier, C. *Dialogues à Madagascar.* Paris, 1961.

French Government. *Journal Officiel (Débats de l'Assemblée Nationale, Débats de l'Assemblée de l'Union Française,* and *Débats du Conseil de la République).*

—— Ambassade de France, Service de Presse et d'Information. *Madagascar: Birth of a New Republic. Ten Years of French Economic Assistance, 1949–1959.* New York, 1959.

—— Ambassade de France, Service de Presse et d'Information. *The Malagasy Republic—Hour of Independence.* New York, 1960.

—— La Documentation Française. *La Situation Economique et Sociale de Madagascar, Notes et Etudes Documentaires* No. 1799, Nov. 2, 1953.

—— La Documentation Française. *Les Investissements et les Problèmes de Développement dans l'Economie de la République Malgache, Notes et Etudes Documentaires* No. 2707, Oct. 13, 1960.

—— La Documentation Française. *La République Malgache, Notes et Etudes Documentaires* No. 2737, Dec. 23, 1960.

—— Haut Commissariat à Madagascar et Dépendances. *Plan Décennal d'Equipement Economique et Social, 1947–1950.* Tananarive, 1961.

—— Ministère de la France d'Outre-Mer. *Madagascar 1955. Journées d'Etudes Malgaches, Paris, 19–20 Février 1955.* Paris, 1955.

Frère, S. *Madagascar; Panorama de l'Androy.* Paris, 1958.

Galdi, P., and Mme. Rochefort. "Notes sur l'Historique de l'Enseignement à Madagascar," *Bulletin de Madagascar,* April, June, Aug., Dec. 1960.

Gallieni, J. S. *Madagascar de 1896 à 1905.* 2 vols. Tananarive, 1905.

—— *Neuf Ans à Madagascar.* Paris, 1908.

Garbit, H. *L'Effort de Madagascar Pendant la Guerre.* Paris, 1919.

Gaudemet, P. M. "La Provincialisation de Madagascar," *Revue Juridique et Politique de l'Union Française,* April–June, 1958.

Gaussin, P.-R. "L'Université de Madagascar," *Europe-France-Outre-Mer,* No. 405, Oct. 1963.

Gayet, G. "Immigrations Asiatiques à Madagascar," *Civilisations,* No. 5, 1955.

Gendarme, R. *L'Economie de Madagascar.* Paris, 1960.

Gendreau, Y. "Les Chemins de Fer," in Guernier, II, 136.

Gosset, P., and R. Gosset *L'Afrique, les Africains.* Vol. III. Paris, 1959.

Gourou, P. "Milieu Local et Colonisation Réunionaise sur les Plateaux de la Sakay," *Les Cahiers d'Outre-Mer,* Jan.–March, 1956.

Grandidier, A. *Ethnographie de Madagascar.* 5 vols. Paris, 1908–28.

Grandidier, G. *Bibliographie de Madagascar, 1904–1933.* Paris, 1935.

Guernier, E., ed. *Madagascar et Réunion.* 2 vols. Paris, 1947.

Guillermin, A. "Les Produits Forestiers," in Guernier, II, 34.

Guinaudeau, H. "L'Industrie," in Guernier, II, 86.

Guth, J.-M. "Aspects Humains et Juridiques du Délit d'Usure à Madagascar," *Recueil Penant,* 1952, p. 704.

—— "La Cour Criminelle à Madagascar," *Revue Juridique et Politique de l'Union Française,* Jan.–March, 1958.

—— "L'Institut d'Etudes Judiciaires Malgaches," *Revue de Madagascar,* 1er trimestre, 1961.

Hance, W. A. "Transportation in Madagascar," *Geographical Review,* 1958.

Hanotaux, G. *L'Affaire de Madagascar.* Paris, 1896.

Hapgood, D. "Madagascar." Institute of Current World Affairs report, New York, March 3, 1963.

Hardyman, J. T. "Madagascar Problems," *Contemporary Review,* Dec. 1947.

—— *Madagascar on the Move.* London, 1950.

—— "Madagascar Faces the Future," *Contemporary Review,* March 1959.

Hatzfeld, O. *Madagascar.* Paris, 1952.

—— "Evolution Actuelle de la Société Malgache," *Monde non Chrétien,* July–Sept. 1953.

Humblot, P. "Le Problème des Concessions et les Problèmes Agraires de l'Afrique Tropicale et de Madagascar," *Marchés Coloniaux,* Aug. 15, 1953.

Hyet, E. L. *Tragédie Malgache?* Paris, 1936.

Isnard, H. *Madagascar.* Paris, 1955.

—— "Nouvelle Orientation de la Modernisation du Paysannat Malgache," *Les Cahiers d'Outre-Mer,* Oct.–Dec. 1957.

Julien, G. J. H. *Institutions Politiques et Sociales de Madagascar.* 2 vols. Paris, 1908–9.

—— *Madagascar et ses Dépendances.* Paris, 1926.

Jumeaux, R. "Essai d'Analyse du Nationalisme Malgache," *L'Afrique et l'Asie,* No. 40, 4e semestre, 1957.

Keller, B. "Les Arabes du Yemen à Madagascar" (typescript). C.H.E.A.M., 1951.

Kent, R. K. *From Madagascar to the Malagasy Republic.* New York, 1962.

—— "Malagasy Republic," in H. Kitchen, ed., *The Educated African*. New York, 1962.

Kling, G. "Tamatave et le Canal des Pangalanes," *Encyclopédie Mensuelle d'Outre-Mer*, Feb. 1955.

—— "Sainte-Marie de Madagascar," *Encyclopédie Mensuelle d'Outre-Mer*, Doc. No. 39, July 1955.

—— "Le Betsileo," *Encyclopédie Mensuelle d'Outre-Mer*, Doc. No. 43, Nov. 1955.

Lacroix, A. *Minéralogie de Madagascar*. 3 vols. Paris, 1922.

Laugier, M. "Monographie de la Population de Diégo-Suarez" (typescript). C.H.E.-A.M., May 10, 1961.

Leblond, M. *La Grande Ile de Madagascar*. Paris, 1946.

Le Brun-Keris, G. "Madagascar à l'Heure de la Loi-Cadre," *Marchés Tropicaux*, Nov. 9, 1957.

Lechat, E. "Les Communications Intérieures et Extérieures," *Europe-France-Outre-Mer*, No. 405, October 1963.

Leduc, G. "L'Economie Malgache au Seuil de l'Indépendance," *Marchés Tropicaux*, July 9, 1960.

Lemoyne, R. "La Monnaie," Institut de Science Economique Appliquée (Paris), Cahiers Série F, No. 17, Jan. 1962.

Lessault, S. "Le Problème de l'Electricité et de l'Eau à Madagascar," *Communautés et Continents*, Oct.–Dec. 1960.

Le Thomas, G. "La Mutualité Agricole," in Guernier, I, 263.

Letourneau, R. "Aperçu sur les Musulmans des Territoires de la Communauté dans l'Océan Indien," *L'Afrique et l'Asie*, No. 49, 1er trimestre, 1960.

Linton, R. *The Tanala, a Hill Tribe of Madagascar*. Chicago, 1933.

Loisy, X., ed. *Madagascar, Etude Economique*. Paris, 1914.

Luchaire, F. "Les Institutions Politiques et Administratives des Territoires d'Outre-Mer Après la Loi-Cadre," *Revue Juridique et Politique de l'Union Française*, April–June 1958.

Lyautey, L. H. G. *Lettres du Sud de Madagascar, 1900–1902*. Paris, 1935.

Madagascar, special number of *Tropiques*, March–April 1953.

Madagascar, special numbers of Cahiers Charles de Foucauld, Vols. 20 (1950) and 21 (1951).

Madagascar, Comores, Réunion, Ile Maurice (Les Guides Bleus). Paris, 1955.

Madagascar et Réunion, ed. E. Guernier. 2 vols. Paris, 1947.

Madagascar, Etudes et Perspectives Economiques. Institut de Science Economique Appliquée (Paris), Cahiers Série F, No. 17, Jan. 1962.

Madagascar, Assemblée Representative. *Procès-Verbaux des Séances*, 1947–58.

—— Congrès des Assemblées Provinciales. *Procès-Verbaux*, session of Oct. 1958. Tananarive, 1959.

—— Délégation Parlementaire Malgache. *Madagascar Devant la France Constituante*. Paris, 1946.

—— Délégations Economiques et Financières. *Procès-Verbaux des Séances* (Tananarive, annually), 1925–39.

—— Gouvernement-Général. *Plan de Développement Economique et Social 1938–39*. Tananarive, 1939.

—— Gouvernement-Général. *Madagascar dans la Guerre, Janv. 1943–Déc. 1944*. Tananarive, 1944.

—— Secretariat Général. *Compte-Rendu Officiel des Travaux des Délégations Financières Provisoires, 1921–23*. Tananarive, 1922–24.

—— Service de Statistique Générale. *Bulletin Mensuel de Statistique*, Oct. 1955 to date.

Malagasy Republic. *Annuaire National*. Tananarive, 1962.

—— *Assemblée Nationale Constituante et Législative, Procès-Verbaux des Séances, 1958–60.*

—— *Assemblée Nationale de Madagascar, Procès-Verbaux des Séances*, 1960 to date.

—— *Code de la Nationalité Malgache*. Tananarive, 1960.

—— *Economie Malgache: Evolution 1950–1960*. Commissariat-Général au Plan, Tananarive, June 1962.

—— *Journal Officiel*, 1960 to date.

—— *Plan de Développement Economique et Social Juillet 1958–30 Juin 1959*. Tananarive, 1960.

—— *Recueil de Textes Relatifs à l'Organisation Judiciaire de Madagascar*. Tananarive, 1961.

—— "Rôle, Méthode et Organisation du Commissariat Général au Plan" (mimeo.). Tananarive, no date (c. 1961).

—— *Sénat, Procès-Verbaux*, 1959–60.

"The Malgache Republic," *Foreign Agriculture*, April 1960.

Mangin, G. "L'Organisation Judiciaire des Etats d'Afrique et de Madagascar," *Revue Juridique et Politique de la France d'Outre-Mer*, Jan.–March 1962.

Manicacci, J. "Le Problème de la Main-d'Oeuvre," in Guernier, I, 253.

—— "Le Problème des Salaires à Madagascar," *Marchés Coloniaux*, March 17 and 24, 1951.

—— *Madagascar: Guide Pratique de l'Immigrant*. Paris, 1951.

—— "L'Office de Placement de Tananarive," *Chroniques d'Outre-Mer*, April 1956.

Mannoni, O. "L'Enseignement," in Guernier, I, 221.

—— *Psychologie de la Colonisation*. Paris, 1950.

Le Marché Malgache. Special number of *Marchés Tropicaux*, July 20, 1963.

Mariani, P. F. "Le Régime des Terres," in Guernier, I, 247.

Martin, A. *Les Délégations Economiques et Financières de Madagascar*. Paris, 1938.

Martonne, E. de. "Essai d'Explication de la Révolte Malgache," *Marchés Coloniaux*, Aug. 14, 1948.

Mejan, F. *Le Vatican contre la France d'Outre-Mer*. Paris, 1957.

Mémoires. Académie Malgache, Tananarive, 1902—.

Mende, T. "Les Morts et les Zébus Paralysent Madagascar," *Jeune Afrique*, June 10, 1962.

—— "Les Passions Couvent à Madagascar," *Jeune Afrique*, June 17, 1962.

Michel, L. "Essai sur la Littérature Malgache," *Revue de Madagascar*, 3e trimestre, 1956.

—— "Les Gemmes Malgaches," *Encyclopédie Mensuelle d'Outre-Mer*, Oct. 1956.

—— *Moeurs et Coutumes Bara*. Tananarive, 1957.

Minelle, J. *L'Agriculture à Madagascar*. Paris, 1959.

Molet, L. *Le Bain Royal à Madagascar*. Tananarive, 1956.

Mondain, G. *Raketaka; Tableau de Moeurs Féminines Malgaches*, Paris, 1925.

—— *Un Siècle de Mission à Madagascar*. Paris, 1948.

Mounier, B. "Le Caractère des Institutions de la République Malgache," *Revue Juridique et Politique de l'Union Française*, July–Sept. 1960.

—— "Le Parlement de la République Malgache," *Revue Juridique et Politique de l'Union Française*, Oct.–Dec. 1960, Jan. 1961.

Mouranches, R. "Les Forêts," in Guernier, II, 23.

Muracciole, L. "Les Modifications de la Constitution Malgache," *Revue Juridique et Politique d'Outre-Mer,* July–Sept. 1962.

Murdock, G. P. *Africa: Its Peoples and Their Culture History.* New York, 1950.

Olivier, M. *Six Ans de Politique Sociale à Madagascar.* Paris, 1931.

Orlova, A. S. "Les Communautés Rurales à Madagascar à l'Epoque Féodale," in *Des Africanistes Russes Parlent de l'Afrique.* Paris, 1960.

Osborn, C. S. *Madagascar, Land of the Man-eating Tree.* New York, 1924.

Ottino, P. "Paysannerie Malgache et Développement," in Cahiers de l'Institut de Science Economique Appliquée, Série F, No. 17, 1962.

—— *Les Economies Paysannes Malgaches du Bas-Mangoky.* Paris, 1963.

Paulian, R. "Aperçu Ethnographique et Folklorique," in *Madagascar, Comores, Réunion, Ile Maurice* (Les Guides Bleus). Paris, 1955.

"Perspectives Stratégiques et Réalisations Economiques, *Encyclopédie Mensuelle d'Outre-Mer,* July 1953.

Petit, G. *L'Industrie des Pêches à Madagascar.* Paris, 1930.

"Les Plantes Aromatiques et les Huiles Essentielles d'Origine Coloniale," *Marchés Coloniaux,* May 31, 1947.

Platon, P. "Le Marché et les Industries Textiles à Madagascar," *Marchés Coloniaux,* July 2, 1955.

—— "Le Centre Océanographique de Nossi–Bé," *Revue de Madagascar,* 2e trimestre, 1956.

—— "Le Marché des Produits Alimentaires à Madagascar," *Marchés Coloniaux,* Nov. 24, 1956.

Poisson, H. "La Pêche," in Guernier, II, 55.

—— "Petite Histoire de la Presse à Madagascar," *Revue de Madagascar,* 3e trimestre, 1955.

Priestley, H. I. *France Overseas: A Study of Modern Imperialism.* New York, 1938.

Prunières, A. *Madagascar et la Crise.* Paris, 1935.

Puybaudet, J. de. "Madagascar à l'Heure de Développement, *Economie et Humanisme,* Sept.–Oct. 1960.

Rabemananjara, J. *Témoignage Malgache et Colonialisme.* Paris, 1956.

—— "Les Fondements Culturels du Nationalisme Malgache," *Présence Africaine,* Feb.–March 1958.

—— *Nationalisme et Problèmes Malgaches.* Paris, 1958.

Rabemananjara, R. W. *Madagascar, Histoire de la Nation Malgache.* Paris, 1952.

—— *Madagascar sous la Rénovation Malgache.* Paris, 1953.

Rabenoro, C. "Les Objectifs et les Moyens du Premier Plan Quinquennal," *Europe-France-Outre-Mer,* No. 405, Oct. 1963.

Rabesahala, E., "Evolution de l'Art Malgache et Culture Française," *Encyclopédie Mensuelle d'Outre-Mer,* Dec. 1955.

Rakotomalala, L. "Le Crédit à Madagascar," *Marchés Tropicaux,* Nov. 9, 1957.

Rakotomalala, N. "Problèmes des Mouvements de Jeunesse Face à l'Evolution de Madagascar." Ms, E.N.F.O.M. collection. Paris, 1958–59.

Ralaimihoatra, G. "Psychologie de l'Enfant Malgache," *Revue de Madagascar,* 1er trimestre, 1958.

Ramandraivonona, D. *Le Malgache: sa Langue, sa Réligion.* Paris, 1959.

Ramangasoavina, A. "Le Sénat et les Récentes Modifications Apportées à la Constitution de la République Malgache," *Revue Juridique et Politique d'Outre-Mer,* Jan.–March 1963.

Ranaivo, C. "Les Expériences de Fokonolona à Madagascar," *Monde non Chrétien,* April–June 1949.
Randrianarisoa, P. *Madagascar, Croyances et Coutumes Malgaches.* Caen, 1958.
Randzavola, H. "La Littérature Malgache," in Guernier, II, 219.
Rason, R. "Etude Raisonnée et Folklorique de la Musique Malgache," *Cahiers Charles de Foucauld,* Vol. 21, 1951.
Ratsima, J. "Les Congrégations Chinoises de Madagascar," *Revue de Madagascar,* 3ᵉ trimestre, 1960.
Ratsiraka, E. "Question de Races dans le Problème de l'Indépendance de Madagascar" (typescript). E.N.F.O.M., 1958–59.
Ravony, J. "Les Problèmes Malgaches à l'Ordre du Jour," *Lumière,* Dec. 22, 1961.
La République Malgache à Cinq Ans, special number of *Europe-France-Outre-Mer,* No. 405, Oct. 1963.
Revue de Madagascar (Tananarive), quarterly, 1933 to date.
Robequain, C. *Madagascar et les Bases Dispersées de l'Union Française.* Paris, 1958.
Roberts, S. H. *History of French Colonial Policy (1870–1925).* London, 1929, Vol. 2, p. 375.
Rosenthal, E. *Japan's Bid for Africa; Including the Story of the Madagascar Campaign.* Johannesburg, 1944.
Rossin, M. "L'Agriculture Malgache et le Soutien des Productions," *Marchés Tropicaux,* Nov. 9, 1957.
Rusillon, H. *Un Petit Continent, Madagascar.* Paris, 1933.
Ruud, J. *Taboo, a Study of Malagasy Customs and Beliefs.* Oslo, 1960.
Saint-Chamant, J. de. "A Madagascar, Le Président Tsiranana et la Situation Politique," *Revue des Deux Mondes,* Nov. 15, 1959.
——— "Madagascar, Etat Pilote de l'Océan Indien," *Le Monde Diplomatique,* July 1960.
——— "Madagascar, An I," *Revue des Deux Mondes,* Dec. 1, 1960.
Saron, G. "Les Halls d'Information à Madagascar," *Revue de Madagascar,* 4ᵉ trimestre, 1956.
Sarraut, A. *La Mise en Valeur des Colonies Françaises.* Paris, 1923.
Sartre, Mgr. V. "Les Missions Catholiques à Madagascar," *Cahiers Charles de Foucauld.* Vol. 21, 1951.
Sauvy, A. "La République de Madagascar; Population, Economie et Perspectives de Développement," *Population,* July–Sept. 1962.
Sibree, J. *Fifty Years in Madagascar; Personal Experiences of Mission Life and Work.* London, 1924.
Silberman, L. "France and Madagascar," *The Listener* (London), Oct. 9, 1958.
Smadja, E. "Promotion du Travailleur Malgache au Rang des Travailleurs de l'Ere Moderne" (typescript). C.H.E.A.M., 1960.
Soucadaux, A. "La Situation de la Grande Ile en 1955," *Revue de Madagascar,* 4ᵉ trimestre, 1955.
——— *Discours.* Tananarive, 1956.
——— "Economie de Madagascar," *Revue de Madagascar,* 2ᵉ trimestre, 1956.
Souchet, R. "La Radiodiffusion de Madagascar," *Revue de Madagascar,* 1ᵉ trimestre, 1960.
"Soviet Writing on Madagascar," *The Mizan Newsletter,* April 1963.
Stephane, R. "Le Procès de Tananarive," *Les Temps Modernes,* Oct. 1948.
Stibbe, P. *Justice pour les Malgaches.* Paris, 1954.
Stratton, A. *The Great Red Island.* New York, 1964.

Tardon, R. "Le Colonat Européen à Madagascar," *Marchés Coloniaux,* April 17, 1954.
——— "Cette Terre est pour les Malgaches," *France-Outre-Mer,* Dec. 1955.
Taton, R. "Interview de M. Philibert Tsiranana, Président de la République Malgache," *Europe-France-Outre-Mer,* No. 405, Oct. 1963.
Thebault, E.-P.: *Traité de Droit Civil Malgache.* 3 vols. Paris, 1951.
——— *Les Lois et Coutumes Malgaches, Code des 305 Articles.* Tananarive, 1960.
Thenault, J. "Le Port de Tamatave," *Marchés Coloniaux,* May 18, 25, 1946.
Thierry, S. *Madagascar* (Collection Petite Planète). Paris, 1961.
Thiout, M. *Madagascar et l'Ame Malgache,* Paris, 1961.
Tourneur, M. "Epices et Aromates" and "Plantes à Parfum," in Guernier, I, 310, 322.
Traizet, P. "Le Service Géographique de Madagascar," *Revue de Madagascar,* 1er trimestre 1959.
"Transports," *Afrique,* Oct. 1962.
Tsiranana, P. *Discours,* Tananarive, Oct. 1959.
Uhart, E. "Le Problème Forestier à Madagascar," Institut de Science Economique Appliquée (Paris), Cahiers Série F, No. 17, Jan. 1962.
Urbain-Faublée, M. *L'Art Malgache,* Paris, 1963.
You, A. "Les Principes de l'Enseignement Indigène à Madagascar," *L'Afrique Française,* 1930, supplement, p. 539.
——— *Madagascar, Colonie Française 1896–1930.* Paris, 1931.
Zafimahova, J. A., and M. R. Ridoux. "L'Industrie Minière Malgache," *Bulletin de Madagascar,* Dec. 1961.

INDEX

Académie Malgache, 19, 221, 226f

Africa, *see* East Africa; English-speaking Negro Africa; French Negro Africa; North Africa; *and individual countries*

African immigrants, 259, 265

Agricultural Service, 340–46 *passim,* 350, 354f, 373; experimental stations, 343–45, 349, 365f, 371

Agriculture, 246, 253, 323–75, 432, 461ff; productivity, 15, 323, 334; techniques, 259, 264, 325–29 *passim,* 333f, 341, 427; credit, 305, 337–39, 340; equipment, 325f, 332, 340f. *See also* Animal husbandry; Crops

Aid, foreign, 175–81 *passim,* 254–55, 307–8, 309, 319; French, 99f, 109, 175ff, 251, 306–7, 316–21 *passim*; as political issue, 107, 114, 127, 130f; U.S., 172–79 *passim,* 307–8, 309

Air service, 29, 281, 285, 291–93; Air Madagascar, 292–93

A.K.F.M., 87f, 103–38 *passim,* 155–56, 166, 200, 456; internal development of, 104–7, 131–34; economic views, 107, 114, 252–53, 254, 392; foreign policy, 114, 127, 174, 176, 180

Alien minorities, 259, 265–77, 281f. *See also various nationalities by name*

Amnesty: of 1921, 22; after 1947 revolt, 57, 66–69, 77–82 *passim,* 88–95 *passim,* 102–9 *passim,* 113–18 *passim,* 131, 454

Ancestors: cult of, 14, 55, 63, 187–89, 252, 324f, 329, 381; common, 139, 142, 149, 187. *See also* Cult of the dead; *Fokonolona*; Tombs, family

Andrianamanjato, Rev. Richard, 105f, 112, 121, 127–38 *passim,* 155f, 176, 189, 200, 254

Andrianampoinimerina, King, 4–5, 8, 139, 329, 422, 442

Andriantsitohaina, Daniel, 292

Animal husbandry, 280ff, 324, 340, 375–84. *See also* Cattle; Goats; Hides industry; Meat; Pigs; Poultry; Sheep

Animal Husbandry Service, 375, 380–85 *passim,* 416

Annet, Gov. Armand, 35, 37f

Annexation law of 1896, 14–17 *passim,* 141, 267, 330; abrogation, 42, 47, 82, 94, 99, 101

Antaifasy tribe, 265, 281

Antaimoro tribe, 4, 190, 258, 264, 278f, 397

Antaisaka tribe, 92, 258, 263, 278–81 *passim,* 445, 448

Antandroy tribe, 103, 258, 263, 279f, 445, 448; customs, 134, 329, 379ff; backwardness, 206n, 214, 263

Antankarana tribe, 265, 279

Antanosy tribe, 258, 264, 381

Arabs: influence of, 3–4, 190, 380f, 397; foreign relations with, 180, 183; immigrants, 259, 264f. *See also* Yemenese immigrants

Aridy, Celestin, 120, 134

Arnault, Jacques, 72

Asian immigrants, 172, 261, 265–66, 367, 444; as middlemen, 245, 260, 424, 434, 437. *See also* China, immigrants from, *and* Indian immigrants

Assembly, legislative, 120–21, 125–26, 127, 136, 147f, 167

Assembly, representative, 51f, 58, 76–79 *passim,* 84, 93–97 *passim,* 102, 111, 144–48 *passim,* 154, 160f, 216, 314

Augagneur, Gov. Victor, 20–21, 153, 197, 311, 424, 444; and schools, 20, 194, 205

050489